M000105528

Inside Microsoft Dynamics® AX 2009

Lars Dragheim Olsen, Michael Fruegaard Pontoppidan, Hans Jørgen Skovgaard, Tomasz Kaminski, Deepak Kumar, Mey Meenakshisundaram, Michael Merz, Karl Tolgu, Kirill Val

PUBLISHED BY
Microsoft Press
A Division of Microsoft Corporation
One Microsoft Way
Redmond, Washington 98052-6399

Library of Congress Control Number: 2009927101

Printed and bound in the United States of America.

1 2 3 4 5 6 7 8 9 QWT 4 3 2 1 0 9

Distributed in Canada by H.B. Fenn and Company Ltd.

A CIP catalogue record for this book is available from the British Library.

Microsoft Press books are available through booksellers and distributors worldwide. For further information about international editions, contact your local Microsoft Corporation office or contact Microsoft Press International directly at fax (425) 936-7329. Visit our Web site at www.microsoft.com/mspress. Send comments to mspinput@microsoft.com.

Acquisitions Editor: Ben Ryan
Developmental Editor: Maria Gargiulo
Project Editor: Valerie Woolley
Editorial Production: Macmillan Publishing Solutions
Technical Reviewer: Arijit Basu; Technical Review services provided by Content Master, a member of CM Group, Ltd.
Cover: Tom Draper Design

Body Part No. X15-77861

Contents at a Glance

Table of Contents

Part IV Appendices

Foreword

In the course of our engagement with numerous partners and customers, we have learned how much developers enjoy working with Microsoft Dynamics AX. We love building ever-more-powerful versions of Dynamics AX that help our customers increase their competitiveness; our partners love our product's powerful set of development tools, which allow them to build affordable and flexible enterprise resource planning (ERP) systems whose quality and adaptability are second to none. Some of the examples in this book, such as creating and exposing custom data sets to external applications through a Web service, can be performed in 10 minutes or less. The very same examples would take at least a week to complete in other ERP systems.

This is the second edition of this book. We received very positive feedback on the first edition, *Inside Microsoft Dynamics AX 4.0*, from people who used the book for a variety of purposes: from ramping up new teams and using the information in it to build presentations, to giving copies to customers, prospects, and colleagues. Our aspiration for this new edition is to incorporate the feedback we received on the original book and to cover the technologies added to Dynamics AX 2009, such as ASP.NET for Enterprise Portal, new Workflow functionality, Role Centers with advanced business intelligence, and the new Batch framework.

We believe that this book, which aims to provide developers with solid information on advanced concepts, can make your entry into the powerful toolset for building business applications a much smoother and more digestible learning experience. We hope that this book is received as an insightful resource for many people working with Dynamics AX 2009.

I want to thank the coauthors for using their evenings and weekends to contribute to this book.

I wish you success with your implementation and customization of Microsoft Dynamics AX 2009.

Hans J. Skovgaard
Product Unit Manager
Microsoft Corporation

Acknowledgments

We want to thank all the people who assisted us in making this book become a reality. The list of people is long—if we inadvertently missed anyone, we apologize. A special thanks goes to the following people on the Microsoft Dynamics AX product team:

- Heidi Boeh, who pitched this book to Microsoft Press and then worked to pull together great content from 24 contributors (from 10 countries of origin), across three development centers.
- Hal Howard and Hans Jørgen Skovgaard, who sponsored the project.
- Michael Fruergaard Pontoppidan, one of the principle authors of this book. Michael's dedication and broad and deep product knowledge brought excellence to this book that it would not have otherwise achieved.
- The people on the product team who provided reviews, comments, and editorial assistance, and otherwise moved small mountains to make this book happen:

  Wade Baird
  Arijit Basu
  Sue Brandt
  Ben Buresh
  Hua Chu
  Christian Heide Damm
  Hitesh Dani
  Julie Deutz
  Krishnan Duraisamy
  Ahmad El Husseini
  Arthur Greef
  Jan Jakobsen
  Peter Jerkewitz
  Andrew Jewsbury
  Brian King
  Steve Kubis
  Arif Kureshy
  Stuart Macrae
  Donna Marshall
  Scott McDonald
  Gene Milener
  Becky Newell
  Adrian Orth
  Marko Perisic
  Jen Pfau
  Gustavo Plancarte
  Pepijn Richter
  David Robinson
  Finnur Saemundsson
  Karen Scipi
  Dianne Siebold
  Stella Sorensen
  Gandhi Swaminathan
  Piotr Szymanski
  Tracy Taylor
  Bill Thompson
  Shyla Thompson
  Van Vanslette
  Peter Villadsen

- The early reviewers from the Dynamics AX Partner Advisory Board, who provided us with the crucial partner perspective.

We also want to thank the people at Microsoft Press who helped support us throughout the book writing and publishing process:

- Ben Ryan, who championed the book project at Microsoft Press.
- Maria Gargiulo, who provided valuable feedback during the developmental editing cycle.
- Valerie Woolley, who was our outstanding, efficient, and always calming project editor. Val, we can't thank you enough.
- Arijit Basu, the technical reviewer, who asked the countless questions that made this book better than it would have been otherwise. Arijit, you rock.
- Sally Stickney, who provided the final editing passes on this book. Her questions were insightful and precise, and her feedback was excellent. She went above and beyond the call of duty to bring excellence to this project.

The Microsoft Dynamics AX author team

Introduction

We understand if you're a bit skeptical when we tell you that you are about to fall for a piece of software. We want you to know up front that our intention is to show you all the wonderful and amazing benefits that Microsoft Dynamics AX 2009 has to offer your business.

Here are some reactions from our partners and customers who have been involved in the early adoption.

> The release of Microsoft Dynamics AX 2009 shows a tremendous development effort on Microsoft's side not only for those already familiar with the product but for newcomers too. This is the best release yet.
>
> *Jesper R. Hansen, Partner, thy:innovation*

> The completeness of the . . . release of Microsoft Dynamics AX 2009 will help existing and new customers reduce the cost of additional customization and therefore reduce the total implementation cost.
>
> *Sven Sieverink, Business Consultant, Dynamics Software*

> The out-of-the-box Role Centers in Microsoft Dynamics AX 2009 add value from day one for all employees in our organization. Our users see enormous value with the visuals, the ability to easily design cues, and the year-to-year comparison.
>
> *John Elmer, Vice President of Information Systems, Rodgers and Hammerstein*

> The Business Intelligence possibilities and integrated workflow offer my team powerful tools to do the job themselves.
>
> *Greg Brock, Director Information Systems, Techmer PM*

Who Is This Book For?

This book delves into the technology and tools in Dynamics AX 2009. New and experienced developers are the intended target audience, and consultants will also benefit from reading this book. The intention is not to give guidance on application functionality but rather to offer as much technical information between the two covers as possible. It is also beyond the scope of this book to include details about installation, upgrade, deployment, and sizing of production environments. Refer to the extensive installation and implementation documentation supplied with the product for more information on these topics.

To get full value from this book, you should have knowledge of common object-oriented concepts from languages such as C++, C#, and Java. Knowledge of Structured Query Language (SQL) is also an advantage. SQL statements are used to perform relational database tasks such as data updates and data retrieval.

Note If you don't have the Dynamics AX license that provides developer rights, you won't be able to perform most of the actions in this book. A virtual PC version of Dynamics AX 2009, with developer rights, is available for partners to download at *https://mbs.microsoft.com/partnersource/deployment/methodology/vpc/vpcimageax2009.htm*.

The History of Microsoft Dynamics AX

Historically, Dynamics AX envelops more than 25 years of experience in business application innovation and developer productivity. Microsoft acquired Dynamics AX in 2002; the success of the product has spurred an increasing commitment of research and development resources, which allow Dynamics AX to continuously grow and strengthen its offering.

The development team that created Dynamics AX 2009 consists of three large teams, two of which are based in the United States (Fargo, North Dakota, and Redmond, Washington) and one based in Denmark (Copenhagen). The Fargo team focuses on finance and human resources (HR), the Redmond team concentrates on Microsoft Project and CRM, and Copenhagen team delivers Supply Chain Management (SCM). In addition, a framework team, distributed over the three sites, develops infrastructure components. Finally, a worldwide distributed team localizes the Dynamics AX features to meet national regulations or local differences in business practices, allowing the product to ship in 24 main languages in 38 countries.

To clarify a few aspects of the origins of Dynamics AX, the authors contacted people who participated in the early stages of the Dynamics AX development cycle. The first question we asked was, How was the idea of using X++ as the programming language for Dynamics AX conceived?

> We had been working with an upgraded version of XAL for a while called OO XAL back in 1996/1997. At some point in time, we stopped and reviewed our approach and looked at other new languages like Java. After working one long night, I decided that our approach had to change to align with the latest trends in programming languages, and we started with X++.
>
> *Erik Damgaard, cofounder of Damgaard Data*

Of course, there were several perspectives among the developers on this breakthrough event.

> One morning when we came to work, nothing was working. Later in the morning, we realized that we had changed programming languages! But we did not have any tools, so for months we were programming in Notepad without compiler or editor support.
>
> *Anonymous developer (but among the authors of this book!)*

Many hypotheses exist regarding the origin of the original product name, Axapta. Axapta was a constructed name, and the only requirement was that the letter *X* be included, to mark the association with the predecessor XAL. The *X* association carries over in the name Dynamics AX.

Organization of This Book

Part I , "A Tour of the Development Environment," is mainly for people new to Dynamics AX. It describes the application architecture from the perspective of development, deployment, and administration. The chapters in Part I also provide a tour of the internal Dynamics AX development environment to help new developers familiarize themselves with designers, tools, the X++ programming language, and the object-oriented application framework that they will use to implement their customizations, extensions, and integrations.

Parts II ("Core Development Concepts") and III ("Under the Hood") are largely devoted to illustrating how developers use the Dynamics AX application framework. Through code samples written for a fictitious bicycle sales and distribution company, Part II describes how to customize and extend Dynamics AX. The examples show how the fictitious company customizes, extends, and integrates the application to support its online make-to-order sales, distribution, and service operations.

Reading Guide

If you are an experienced Dynamics AX developer, you might want to skip the tour of the development environment after reading Chapter 1, "Architectural Overview," and move straight to Part II or Part III, which consist of chapters that can be read in random order. Or use the book as a reference for subjects that you are especially interested in.

Differences from Inside Microsoft Dynamics AX 4.0

This book is an update to the book *Inside Microsoft Dynamics AX 4.0.* Along with changes made to existing chapters, we added several new chapters, on workflow, Role Centers, the Batch framework, reporting, and code upgrade. We have significantly expanded the performance chapter, and the Enterprise Portal chapter now describes the new ASP.NET tooling.

We greatly extended the chapter "XML Document Integration" in the first edition, renaming it as "The Application Integration Framework" (Chapter 17).

We removed the chapters on advanced MorphX forms and system classes because these were least referenced by readers. You can find extensive documentation on MorphX forms and system classes in the Dynamics AX 2009 software development kit (SDK), which is on MSDN. And the previous version of this book is still a good source of information because some of the technologies haven't changed much. We also removed the chapter on upgrade and data migration and replaced that content with a significantly enhanced series of chapters on the version upgrade process, found in the bonus eBook, which can be found on this book's companion Web site: *http://www.microsoft.com/learning/en/us/books/13345*. Finally, the chapter on unit testing has been merged into the chapter on the MorphX tools (Chapter 3).

Product Documentation

In addition to this book, you can read thousands of topic pages of product documentation on application and system issues in the online Help. Extensive documentation on installation and implementation is available in the Microsoft Dynamics AX 2009 SDK and the Microsoft Dynamics AX Implementation Guide, both supplied with the product. You can also find the product documentation on MSDN. And if you have an installation of Dynamics AX 2009, you have access to the following topic areas on the Help menu: Administrator Help, Developer Help, and User Help.

Product Web Site

The user portal for Dynamics AX encompasses product and purchase information as well as guidelines for using the product and links to online newsgroups and user communities.

For more information, visit the site *http://www.microsoft.com/dynamics/ax*.

Naming

With the latest version of the application, the name of the product changed to Microsoft Dynamics AX 2009. The previous product versions were named Microsoft Axapta and Microsoft Dynamics AX 4.0. For easier reading, this book refers to the 2009 version of the product as Dynamics AX 2009 or just Dynamics AX and refers specifically to earlier versions where appropriate.

Code

All relevant code examples are available for download. For details on the companion Web site, see the "Code Samples" section later in this introduction. You might need to modify some of the code samples to execute them. The necessary changes are described either in the .xpo files themselves or in the readme file associated with the code samples on the companion Web site.

Glossary

Like all software, Dynamics AX involves the use of many abbreviations, acronyms, and technical expressions. Much of this information is available in a glossary that you will find at the back of the book. For a larger list of terms and abbreviations, refer to the glossary provided with the product documentation.

Special Legend

To distinguish between SQL and X++ statements, this book uses the common practice for SQL keywords, which is to display them in all capital letters. The following code shows an example of this in connection with nested transactions, where a transaction is started in X++ and later sent to a SQL server.

```
boolean b = true;  ;  ttsbegin; // Transaction is not initiated here
update_recordset custTable      setting creditMax = 0; // set implicit transactions on
if ( b == true )          ttscommit; // COMMIT TRANSACTION  else
    ttsabort; // ROLLBACK TRANSACTION
```

System Requirements

You need the following hardware and software to build and run all the code samples for this book:

- Microsoft Dynamics AX 2009: .NET Business Connector, Microsoft Dynamics AX 2009 Rich Client, Application Object Server (AOS; up and running)
- Windows Vista Business Edition, Ultimate Edition, or Enterprise Edition, Service Pack 1 or Windows XP Professional Edition, Service Pack 2/3 (for Microsoft Dynamics AX 2009 Rich Client)
- Windows Server 2003 with Service Pack 2 or Windows Server 2008 (AOS Server)
- Microsoft SQL Server 2008 or Microsoft SQL Server 2005, Service Pack 2, Service Pack 3, or Oracle Database 10*g* R2
- Windows SharePoint Services 3.0 with Service Pack 1 or Microsoft Office SharePoint Server 2007, Enterprise Edition Service Pack 1 (to run Enterprise Portal or Role Centers)
- Microsoft SQL Server 2008 Reporting Services or Microsoft SQL Server 2005 Reporting Services with SQL Server Service Pack 2/3 (to run SQL Reporting Services)

- Microsoft Visual Studio 2008
- Microsoft .NET Framework 3.5
- Intel Pentium/Celeron family or compatible Pentium III Xeon or higher processor minimum; 1.1 gigahertz (GHz) or higher recommended
- 1 gigabyte (GB) RAM or more recommended
- Video: at least 1024 × 768 high color 16-bit
- DVD-ROM drive
- Microsoft mouse or compatible pointing device

Because the requirements typically evolve with service packs that support new versions of underlying technologies, we recommend that you check for the latest updated system requirements at *http://www.microsoft.com/dynamics/ax/using/2009systemrequirements.mspx*.

Release Software

This book was reviewed and tested against the RTM version of Dynamics AX 2009. Any changes or corrections to this book will be added to a Microsoft Knowledge Base article. For details, see the "Support for This Book" section in this introduction.

Technology Updates

As technologies related to this book are updated, links to additional information will be added to the Microsoft Press Technology Updates Web site. Visit this site periodically for updates on Microsoft Visual Studio 2005 and other technologies: *http://www.microsoft.com/mspress/updates*.

Code Samples

All code samples discussed in this book can be downloaded from the book's companion content page at the following address: *http://www.microsoft.com/learning/en/us/books/13345.aspx*.

Bonus Content

On the companion Web site you'll find an eBook that contains several bonus chapters. Chapter 1, "Introduction to Upgrade," Chapter 2, "Code Upgrade" (also Chapter 18 of this book), Chapter 3, "Data Upgrade," and Chapter 4 "Upgrade Additional Topics."

The upgrade information you find in this eBook gives you a solid overview of the Dynamics AX 2009 upgrade process, tells you about the tools that are available to walk you through the upgrade process, and gives you some tips and best practice guidelines; it does not give you detailed procedures—simply because version upgrade is such a large topic. A wealth of procedural and other information on the upgrade process is available with the Dynamics AX product; we have included a list of those resources at the end of this introduction. You can download the eBook from *http://www.microsoft.com/learning/en/us/books/13345.aspx*.

Find Additional Content Online

As new or updated material becomes available that complements your book, it will be posted online on the Microsoft Press Online Developer Tools Web site. The type of material you might find includes updates to book content, articles, links to companion content, errata, sample chapters, and more. This Web is available at *www.microsoft.com/learning/books/online/developer*, and is updated periodically.

Support for This Book

Every effort has been made to ensure the accuracy of this book and the companion content. As corrections or changes are collected, they will be added to a Microsoft Knowledge Base article. To view the list of known corrections for this book, visit the following article:

http://support.microsoft.com/kb

Microsoft Press provides support for books and companion content at the following Web site:

http://www.microsoft.com/learning/support/books

Questions and Comments

If you have comments, questions, or ideas regarding the book or the companion content, or questions that are not answered by visiting the sites mentioned earlier, please send them to Microsoft Press via e-mail:

mspinput@microsoft.com

You may also send your questions via postal mail to

Microsoft Press
Attn: *Inside Microsoft Dynamics AX 2009* Project Editor
One Microsoft Way
Redmond, WA 98052-6399

Please note that Microsoft software product support is not offered through these addresses.

Part I

A Tour of the Development Environment

In this part:

Chapter 1

Architectural Overview

In this chapter:

The objectives of this chapter are to:

- Introduce the architecture of Microsoft Dynamics AX 2009.
- Describe how Dynamics AX applications are developed through application modeling and program specification.
- Provide an overview of the application model layering system.
- Provide an overview of the application framework.
- Explain the design of Enterprise Portal and the Reporting Framework.
- Provide an overview of the operations environment.

Introduction

The architecture of Dynamics AX comprises client and server components that scale to support many concurrent users who integrate with external applications and interoperate with many Microsoft products and technologies. This architecture includes a layered application model and the X++ programming language; it is supported by the MorphX development environment and executed by the Dynamics AX runtime environment.

The Dynamics AX architecture also provides an application framework that takes care of some of the technology requirements for business applications, allowing developers to focus on meeting enterprise resource planning (ERP) domain requirements for rich client, Web client, and integration applications.

This chapter gives a developer's-eye overview of the Dynamics AX architecture, starting with a description of the Dynamics AX application development and runtime configurations, followed by a description of the components of the Dynamics AX architecture, and concluding with an overview of the operations environment.

Before diving into the specifics of the architecture, let's look at how the architectural design enables developer productivity.

Design Philosophy and Benefits

The architecture of Dynamics AX has been designed to make it easy to build, customize, and extend Dynamics AX ERP applications. One of the design goals of the architecture is to enable application developers to focus on business domain requirements by reducing and simplifying the technological aspects of a developer's job. This design philosophy is enabled by a software design methodology, called model-driven development, that is based on developing a model for an application rather than writing actual code.

For example, the design of the Dynamics AX architecture can help you spend your time meeting financial, production, and logistics domain requirements rather than meeting user interface, client/server, and database access technology requirements. Dynamics AX makes this possible by satisfying technology requirements for the following set of typical application developer tasks:

- Create a database schema and bind it to forms and reports, allowing users to enter and view data.
- Navigate users between forms and reports while ensuring that role-based security is enforced.
- Exchange data and calculated data with external applications.

Modeling Scenario

The following scenario illustrates how productive developers can be when they use tools that support a model-based architecture.

Suppose you need to implement a feature to edit and batch print account number and account name data. MorphX, the Dynamics AX integrated development environment (IDE), allows quick definition of the required application model using nothing more than mouse clicks.

First you define a database table in MorphX with two fields, one that stores account numbers and one that stores account names. Dynamics AX automatically creates the physical tables in the Microsoft SQL Server or the Oracle database.

Then you define a rich client form containing a grid control. The data in the grid control is bound to the fields in the previously defined table. The appearance of the form automatically honors the size of the fields, the user's preferred language, security access, and so on.

Rich client forms have a built-in reporting feature that can send the form data to a screen preview, a printer, a file, the print archive, or an e-mail account. The rich client reporting feature also has built-in batching capability. These built-in features and supporting tools allow you to fulfill the domain requirements of your particular scenario without having to spend time on the technology requirements.

Application Development and Runtime Configurations

The Dynamics AX development and runtime environments support three logical configurations, as illustrated in Figure 1-1:

- Rich client application
- Web client application
- Integration client application

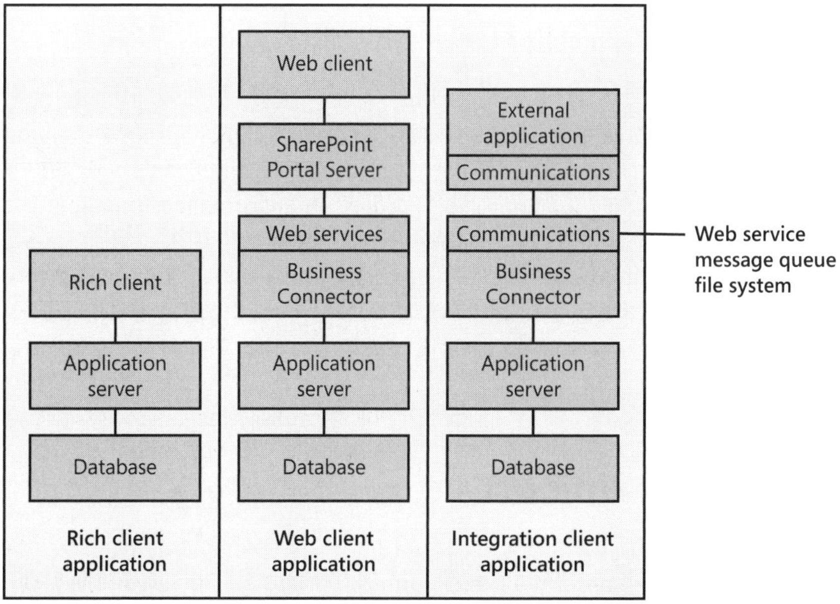

FIGURE 1-1 Dynamics AX application configurations

Rich Client Application

The rich client is the primary client for Dynamics AX. It is a regular Windows application with a user interface consisting of menus, toolbars, forms, and so on.

You can develop a rich client application configuration using only the MorphX development environment. The rich client application is hosted by the Dynamics AX runtime environment. Rich clients communicate with the Application Object Server (AOS) using the Microsoft remote procedure call (RPC) communication technology.

Web Client Application

The Web client is a client for Dynamics AX that runs inside a Web browser. It supports many of the same capabilities as the rich client does.

You develop a Web client application configuration by using the MorphX development environment, Microsoft Visual Studio 2008, and the Windows SharePoint Services framework. A Web client application is hosted by the Dynamics AX runtime, the ASP.NET runtime, and the Windows SharePoint Services runtime environments. SharePoint and ASP.NET components communicate via the Dynamics AX .NET Business Connector. For more information on the Dynamics AX Enterprise Portal, see Chapter 7, "The Enterprise Portal," and for more on .NET Business Connector, see Chapter 10, ".NET Business Connector."

Integration Client Application

An integration client application brings Dynamics AX functionality into external applications, such as Microsoft Office Excel and Microsoft Office Outlook. An integration client application configuration is mostly developed using Visual Studio or other tools with .NET support or Windows Communication Foundation (WCF) support. Integration client applications are hosted by the Microsoft Dynamics AX runtime environment. ASP.NET Web services and IIS are required for hosting Web services. The external application communicates with the Dynamics AX runtime via the Dynamics AX Application Integration Framework (AIF) server or .NET Business Connector. For more on the AIF, see Chapter 17, "The Application Integration Framework."

Architecture of Dynamics AX

As a developer of Dynamics AX applications, your primary focus should be on modeling application elements to meet business requirements, relying on the rest of the architecture to meet technical requirements. Before looking at application modeling, explained in the following section, take some time to review the stack diagram in Figure 1-2, which illustrates the key functional areas of the Dynamics AX architecture.

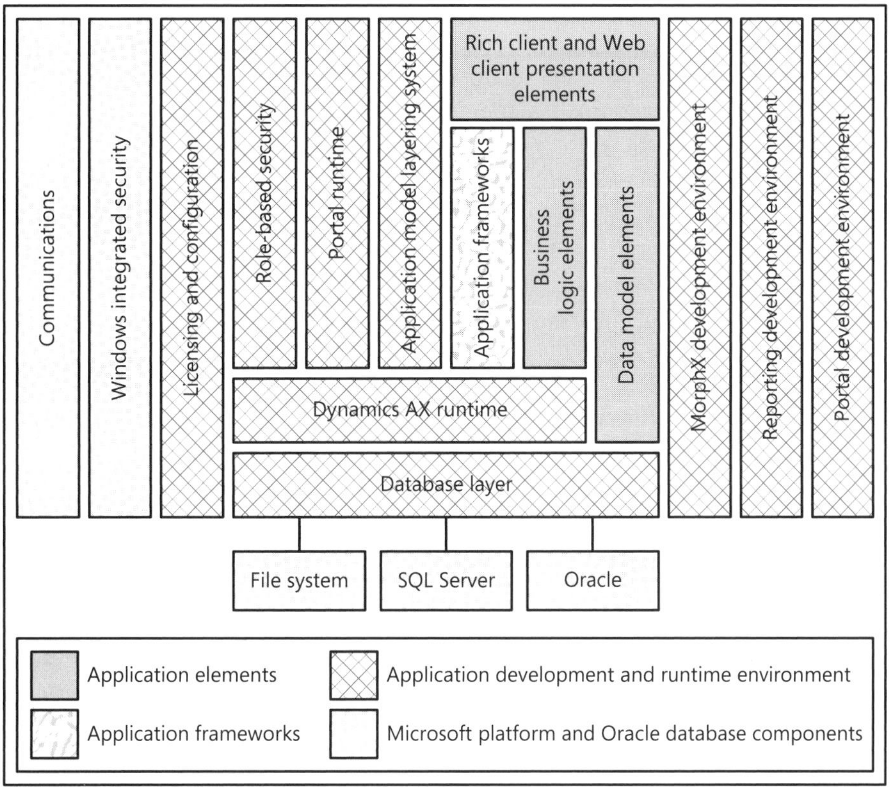

FIGURE 1-2 Architecture of Dynamics AX

The following sections explore key elements of this diagram and tell you where you can find more information about each.

Development Environments

The Dynamics AX development environments are MorphX and Visual Studio. MorphX is described in Chapter 2, "The MorphX Development Environment." Visual Studio, primarily used for developing Enterprise Portal and reports, is covered in Chapter 7 and Chapter 11, "Reporting in Dynamics AX." These environments provide a set of application modeling and programming tools for developing and extending Dynamics AX applications. Chapter 3, "The MorphX Tools," provides more information about the individual tools.

Application Modeling

Application modeling is a method of declaratively specifying the structure and behavior of an application that is faster, less error-prone, and more precise than imperative programming. Specifying that data is mandatory for a field in a database record, for example, is fairly easy in the Dynamics AX application model because the Dynamics AX runtime environment ensures that the condition is true in all parts of the application that manipulate data in the table. This obsoletes the programming effort that would otherwise be required to maintain data integrity throughout the application.

The Dynamics AX application model also supports defining workflows. The defined workflows describe states and available actions for types of business documents. For example, a developer could model a Purchase Order Approval workflow that maps the tasks required to approve a purchase order. The workflows are honored by the Dynamics AX runtime environment, and the Windows Workflow Foundation engine is used for processing and configuring the workflows. Workflows are discussed in more depth in Chapter 9, "Workflow in Dynamics AX."

Logic Elements and Data Elements

Because application modeling typically isn't flexible enough to meet all business requirements, the Dynamics AX business logic is specified by the X++ programming language. X++ is an object-oriented language, much like C# and Java, that supports inheritance, encapsulation, and polymorphism. The language also includes syntax for writing database statements, much like those found in the SQL database manipulation language.

The following X++ code snippet uses the X++ SQL syntax. The language combines the simplicity of data lookup from SQL with the expressive power of object-oriented programming. You can invoke a method call directly on an object retrieved from the database.

```
while select customer
    where customer.zipcode == campaignZipCode
{
    customer.sendEmail(campaignId);
}
```

For more details on the X++ programming language, refer to Chapter 4, "The X++ Programming Language."

The model elements and X++ source code that comprise an object's definition are called application elements, and they are managed with the Application Object Tree (AOT) development tool. The AOT is a user control in the MorphX environment that manages a dictionary of application elements.

> **Note** The name *Application Object Tree* is something of a misnomer. Application objects are instantiated only by the Dynamics AX runtime environment, and their definitions are developed with the help of the AOT. The tree also contains resources and references in addition to application object definitions. This book uses the abbreviation AOT to refer to the *tree* control, but it describes the nodes in the tree as mapping to application elements contained in a dictionary.

Application Frameworks

While developing your application, you can leverage a range of built-in application frameworks that provide typical technology requirements such as batching, number sequence generation, and error logging. The application frameworks in Dynamics AX are described in greater depth later in this chapter.

Runtime Environments

The Dynamics AX runtime environment and the Dynamics AX Enterprise Portal runtime environment execute the ERP application defined by the application model elements. The Dynamics AX runtime environment has model-driven features that are required for the support of user interaction with ERP database applications. For example, if you specify that a column model element on a user interface grid control requires mandatory data entry, the Dynamics AX runtime environment ensures that users enter data in that particular column.

The Dynamics AX runtime environment also has client and server features that are required to support the three-tier operations environment. For example, by automatically marshalling parameters, return values, and object references across the tiers, the Dynamics AX runtime environment ensures that all X++ business logic marked to run on the server tier will execute on the AOS. As a developer, you still need to pay attention to these aspects because they can impact performance. For more details, see Chapter 12, "Performance."

Communications

Dynamics AX leverage many different standard communication protocols, including RPCs, HTTP, and SOAP, to invoke Web services.

As an application developer in Dynamics AX, you don't have to understand the implementation details of these protocols, but you must pay close attention to the performance aspects when invoking logic on remote tiers. You need to keep in mind network properties such as bandwidth and latency to ensure the resulting application is responsive.

Model Layering

A cardinal requirement of an ERP system is that it be able to meet the customer's needs. If you're in the business of building general solutions that many customers license and install, you need a way for individual customers to customize your solution.

The application model layering system supports fine-grained partner and customer customizations and extensions. The MorphX development environment manages the application elements that exist in multiple layers of the model, and the runtime environment assembles the application elements from different layers so that application object instances can be created with customized and extended structure and behavior. The application model layering system is described in greater depth later in this chapter.

Licensing, Configuration, and Security

Any ERP application has technical requirements for licensing, configuration, and security. In Dynamics AX, the developer can control the behavior of these aspects directly in the application model. Licensing, configuration, and role-based security are enforced at run time—for example, the only enabled user interface components the user sees are those that he or she has access to. For more information see Chapter 13, "Configuration and Security."

User and external application interactions are authenticated by the Windows integrated security system before any application features can be accessed. After authentication, the Active Directory service is used to associate a Windows user with a Dynamics AX user. Dynamics AX provides a security framework for authorizing Dynamics AX user and user group access to menu items and database data.

Database Layer

The Dynamics AX database layer supports both SQL Server and Oracle database systems. The database layer enables developers to focus on modeling the tables and fields required for various business scenarios without being concerned about SQL Server or Oracle specifics. For example, you can use the same X++ logic to query data regardless of which physical database engine the data is persisted in. Refer to Chapter 14, "The Database Layer," for more details.

The Windows XP, Windows Vista, and Windows Server operating systems provide the technology that components use to communicate with the Dynamics AX runtime environment.

Application Model Layering System

Application model layering is the architectural principle in Dynamics AX that allows granular customizations and extensions to model element definitions and hence the structure and behavior of applications. When a version of Dynamics AX is released that is not specific to any country/region, all model elements that define the application reside in the lowest layer of an element layering stack. The Dynamics AX runtime environment, however, uses more than these element definitions when it instantiates application objects—it assembles an element definition from model elements at all levels of the element layering stack. Elements defined at higher levels of the element layering stack override elements defined at lower levels of the stack. The object that the runtime environment eventually instantiates is thus an instance of a dynamic type definition composed of model elements at multiple layers of the element layering stack.

Figure 1-3 illustrates the components in the application model layering system. Model elements are stored in a separate file on each layer whenever they are saved from MorphX. Element definitions are read from these files and dynamically composed by the Dynamics AX runtime environment. Object instances are created on either the server or the client, based on the model element definition. The client can be the MorphX development environment, the rich client, or the .NET Business Connector client.

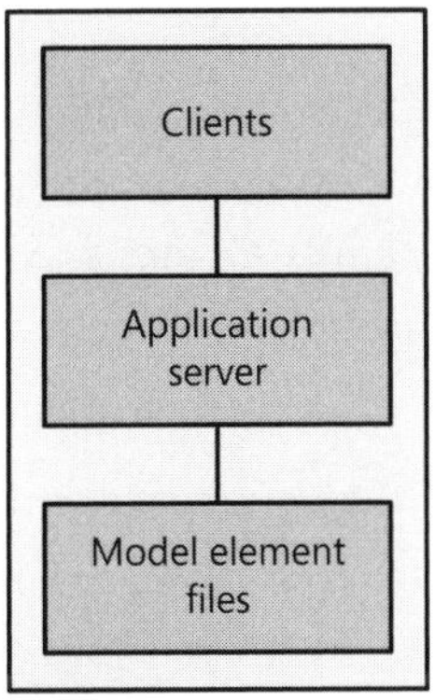

FIGURE 1-3 Components of the application model layering system

Figure 1-4 shows the element layers in the application model layering system.

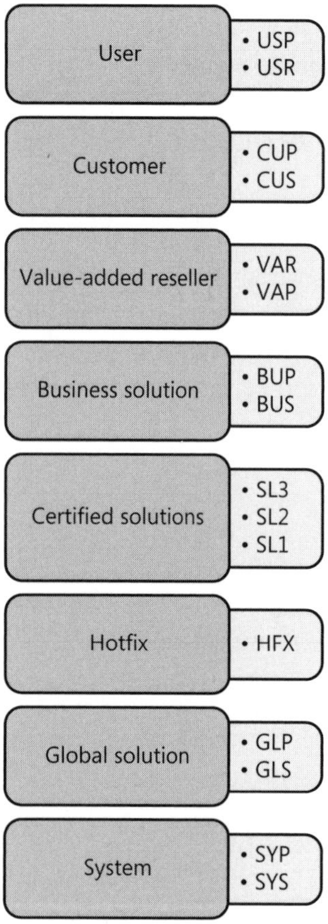

FIGURE 1-4 Element layers in the application model layering system

Table 1-1 contains a description of each element layer, including ID ranges.

TABLE 1-1 Layer Descriptions

Layer	Description	ID Range
USP USR	**User** Individual companies or companies within an enterprise can use this layer to customize unique customer installations.	50001–60000
CUP CUS	**Customer** Companies and business partners can modify their installations and add company-specific modifications to this layer. This layer is included to support the need for in-house development without jeopardizing modifications made by business partners.	40001–50000

Layer	Description	ID Range
VAP VAR	**Value-added reseller** Business partners use this layer, which has no business restrictions, to add any development done for their customers.	30001–40000
BUP BUS	**Business solution** Business partners develop and distribute vertical and horizontal solutions to other partners and customers.	20001–30000
SL3 SL2 SL1	**Certified solutions** Partners certified under the Microsoft Dynamics Industry Solution program distribute their solutions in the SL layers.	1–20000
HFX	**Hotfix** The Dynamics AX Sustained Engineering team delivers critical hotfixes using the HFX layer.	1–20000
GLP GLS	**Global solutions** The Dynamics AX Global Development and Localization team provides a set of GLS layers that contain country/region-specific functionality.	1–20000
SYP SYS	**System** This is the lowest model element layer and the location of the standard Dynamics AX application. Only Microsoft has access to the element definitions at this layer.	1–20000

Working with the Layers

As you see in Figure 1-4, the lowest layer is the system layer, and the highest is the user layer. You use the client configuration utility to specify the layer at which you want to customize and extend the Dynamics AX application. When the MorphX environment is launched, it adds or modifies elements at this layer, the working layer, of the model layering system. It cannot, however, modify or delete a model element defined at a higher model layer.

> **Note** The Dynamics AX runtime environment always composes model elements starting with the user layer, regardless of the layer in which you are working.

When you modify a model element at a layer lower than the working layer, the element is copied to the working model element layer. A class header or method element, for example, is copied to the working layer when it is modified. A table header, field, field group, index, or method element is copied to the working layer when modified. An entire form or report element is copied if any of its members are modified. For example, if you add a button to a form, the entire form is copied to the current layer. If you delete the model element from the working layer, the model element at a lower layer is used instead. In this way, you can undo modifications and easily return to the original model element definitions. You can also compare objects from two different layers by using the MorphX Compare tool.

As shown in Figure 1-4 all model element layers (except HFX and SL1 through SL3) have an associated patch layer. Patch layers handle patches, minor updates, service packs, and hotfixes. Logically, a patch layer is placed directly above the layer that it is patching. A patch layer's name contains the first two characters of the element layer's name and then the letter *P*. For example, the first three patch layers are named SYP, GLP, and BUP. As a best practice, you should move the content of the patch layer into the main layer with each release of the application.

The solution layers (SL1, SL2, and SL3) are new in Dynamics AX 2009. They are intended for Microsoft certified solutions. Any of these solutions can be installed in the SL1, SL2, SL3, BUS, or BUP layer. Prior to installation, rename the layer file to match the desired layer. These solution layers enable customers to use up to five certified solutions simultaneously.

Model Element IDs

Most model elements have a unique identifier (ID) that is represented as an unsigned 16-bit integer. To avoid conflict, each layer has a range of available IDs, as listed in Table 1-1. The lower four layers share one ID range. Microsoft avoids ID conflicts in these layers by using version control and the Team Server. For more information on version control and the Team Server, see Chapter 3.

You should never change model element IDs. When an element is deprecated, the IDs can be reused. The IDs must not be altered because they are used as business data and in element definitions. In business data, IDs are typically used to model polymorphic relationships. In element definitions, they are used as references between elements and to relate class and table members across layers. Changing an element ID after it is deployed to an operations environment would result in data inconsistency and require model element ID scrubbing. Because either of these situations is highly undesirable, you must ensure that you use the appropriate layer when deploying application customizations and extensions to operations environments.

A model element can be moved between layers and retain its ID. This procedure can be used to free up a layer, but it puts limitations on the freed layer because IDs are still used, even if they are in another layer. This procedure can be applied if both layers can be fully controlled. For example, Microsoft successfully moved all model elements from the Axapta 3.0 GLS layer to the Dynamics AX 4.0 SYS layer. Keeping the element IDs from the GLS layer provides consistency for business data and element definitions, but it prevents Microsoft from reusing the IDs of the moved model elements in future GLS layers.

> **Note** Two features make ID management easier. The Team Server, which is a model element ID generator for version control, ensures that unique IDs are allocated across multiple developer application installations. Also, best practice rules detect whether a model element ID value has changed, providing an early warning that can help you solve potential problems before the application is deployed to an operations environment.

Application Frameworks

The Dynamics AX application framework is a set of model elements that provide most of the technology requirements for ERP applications. You can utilize these frameworks when you design the business process requirements so that you can focus on meeting the domain requirements rather than focus on the underlying technology. These frameworks also provide a consistent user experience across existing and new features. Presenting all the Dynamics AX application frameworks in this book would be impossible, so only the most commonly used frameworks are described in this section.

RunBase Framework

The RunBase application framework runs or batches an operation. An operation is a unit of work, such as the posting of a sales order or calculation of a master schedule. The RunBase framework uses the Dialog framework to prompt a user for data input. It uses the SysLastValue framework to persist usage data and the Operation Progress framework to show operation progress.

Batch Framework

The Batch application framework creates batch entries in the Dynamics AX batch queue. These entries execute at time intervals specified by a user interacting with a dialog box provided by the framework. The RunBaseBatch framework extends the RunBase framework, and X++ classes that extend this framework can have their operations enlisted in the batch queue. For more information about the Batch framework, see Chapter 16, "The Batch Framework."

Dialog Framework

The Dialog application framework creates a dynamic dialog box that is not defined in the AOT. You can customize the dialog box by setting the caption and adding fields, field groups, menu items, text, and images. You typically use the Dialog framework to create dialog boxes when data input is required from the user.

Operation Progress Framework

The Operation Progress application framework displays a dialog box that shows the progress of a processing task. You can customize the framework by setting the total number of steps in the operation and the dialog box caption and animation type. You control the progress by increme0nting the progress value in derived classes.

> **Best Practices** include setting the total step count only if it is known (or if it can be accessed rapidly), partitioning the process task into as many steps as possible, and ensuring that steps have similar durations. If you use multiple progress bars, the first bar should show overall progress. The framework automatically calculates the time remaining for an operation.

Number Sequence Framework

The Number Sequence application framework creates a new sequential number for uniquely identifying business transaction records in database tables. You can specify whether the numbers are continuous or gaps are allowed in the generated sequences. You can also specify the number format by using a format string.

SysLastValue Framework

The SysLastValue application framework stores and retrieves user settings or usage data values that persist between processes. You use this framework to save, retrieve, and delete containers of usage data.

Application Integration Framework

The Application Integration Framework (AIF) sends business transactions to external applications and responds to requests from external applications. This framework comprises XML document classes, message queue management, Web services, and data mapping features. For details on how to use this framework to build integration applications, see Chapter 17.

Wizard Framework

The Wizard application framework helps users configure application features. You can use the Wizard wizard to generate a set of default classes that extend the Wizard framework. (See Chapter 6, "Extending Dynamics AX," for more information about the Wizard wizard.) The resulting wizard provides start and finish pages and a user-defined number of empty pages in between. You customize the generated classes by populating the wizard pages with controls and controlling the page flow.

Infolog Framework

You use the Infolog application framework when business transaction status logging is required. The information log form control displays the logged message. The Infolog framework is also the default exception handler, so it catches any exception not caught by application code. You can extend this framework to provide customized logging features.

Enterprise Portal and Web Parts

The Dynamics AX Enterprise Portal enables customers, vendors, business partners, and employees to access relevant business information directly and conduct business transactions with Dynamics AX through personalized, role-based Web portals called Role Centers.

Enterprise Portal is built on Windows SharePoint Services; it combines the content and collaboration functionality of an unstructured SharePoint site with the structured business data in Dynamics AX. It also serves as the platform for front-end application integration and business processes.

Enterprise Portal is a complete SharePoint site. It comes with a site definition that includes hundreds of standard Web pages and content and collaboration elements.

Enterprise Portal Web parts are the front-end user interface elements that connect to Dynamics AX through .NET Business Connector, and they render the HTML generated by the ASP.NET Web user controls. Web parts are used in the Enterprise Portal Web part pages together with other Windows SharePoint Services Web parts. These pages, along with page templates and Windows SharePoint Services elements, are packaged as a SharePoint site definition. All the content and collaboration functionality comes from Windows SharePoint Services, and Enterprise Portal Web parts expose the business data from Dynamics AX.

You author Web pages by using page designer tools in Windows SharePoint Services. The pages define the layout and host the Web parts and their properties. You author Web User Controls by using Visual Studio tools, and you then add them to the AOT. The Web User Controls define the user interface for interacting with the business data. They connect to Dynamics AX via .NET Business Connector and Enterprise Portal framework. The Windows SharePoint Services Web parts connect to the Windows SharePoint Services database for content and collaboration functionality. The page definition from Windows SharePoint Services Web pages is imported into the AOT so that those pages are automatically created when the site is created.

The Web elements in the AOT can be categorized into three groups:

- Content definition elements, including data sets, Web controls, and Web content. These elements define the data source, the business logic, the user interface, and security.

- Navigation definition elements, including the Web menu, Web menu items, and Web modules.
- Files and definitions used to deploy Enterprise Portal sites and components to the Web server.

Enterprise Portal Web elements are placed under the Web nodes in the AOT, as you can see in Figure 1-5.

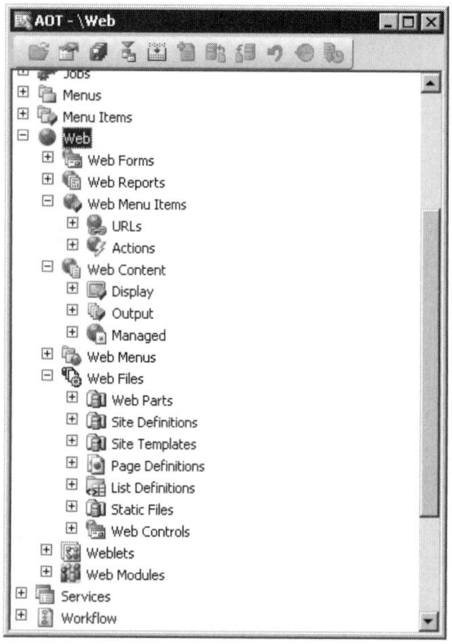

FIGURE 1-5 Web elements in the AOT

When a user browses to the URL, the Web part connects to the Web framework through .NET Business Connector and gets the Web content. The Web content security key setting is checked and, depending on the user's permission, the Web user control generates the HTML to be rendered by the Web part.

Enterprise Portal uses Integrated Windows authentication for authorization, and it leverages Dynamics AX user groups and security models for the business data and uses SharePoint site groups for the content and collaboration data. Web content, Web menu items, and Weblets are secured with Dynamics AX security keys. Users are granted permission to these objects based on their Dynamics AX user groups. Windows SharePoint Services document libraries and lists are secured with SharePoint site groups. Users are granted permission to these objects based on their site groups.

Enterprise Portal provides a common integrated search across the business data contained in Dynamics AX and Windows SharePoint Services. The Dynamics AX Data Crawler indexes application data, and Windows SharePoint Services indexes the document libraries and lists. Enterprise Portal search uses both indexes to provide a combined search result.

Reporting Framework

The production reporting framework for Dynamics AX uses a model-based reporting framework build on top of Visual Studio 2008. It enables developers, partners, and independent software vendors (ISVs) to build Microsoft SQL Server Reporting Services reports using metadata available from Dynamics AX. You can use the Reporting Framework to build reports that source data from multiple data sources, such as Dynamics AX for Online Transaction Processing (OLTP) data, Microsoft SQL Server Analysis Services for aggregated analytical data, and other third-party databases.

Reports built using the Dynamics AX Reporting Framework are deployed to a Reporting Services report server, which provides the run-time engine. Users can access these reports from a variety of locations, including the Dynamics AX rich client, Role Centers, Enterprise Portal, and Report Manager in Reporting Services.

Dynamics AX ships with hundreds of reports built on the Dynamics AX Reporting Framework. Some of these reports source data from the Dynamics AX transactional system via .NET Business Connector. Other reports source analytical data from the Dynamics AX OLAP database built on top of Analysis Services. In addition to these reports, Dynamics AX ships a number of style and layout templates that you can use to define the look and feel of your reports.

You can author new reports or customize existing ones using the Dynamics AX Reporting Extensions built on top of Visual Studio. The Dynamics AX reports library project in Visual Studio lets you define the different facets of your reports, such as types of reports, data sources, style templates, layout templates, and images in a model-based development environment similar to the AOT. You can build reports that connect to Dynamics AX data using queries defined in the AOT or via managed business logic that can connect to Dynamics AX via .NET Business Connector. Once built, these reports can be integrated into the Dynamics AX application via Menu Items in the AOT. The menu items can be started from Menus in the rich client or Dynamics Report Server Report Web parts in Role Centers and Enterprise Portal.

When a user tries to access a report from a Dynamics AX rich client, a report viewer form opens. This form issues a request to the Reporting Services report server to render the report for the current company in the user's current language. The report server then connects to Dynamics AX via .NET Business Connector to fetch data. Once the data is retrieved from Dynamics AX (and potentially other data sources), the Reporting Services report server renders the report and returns it to the client, which then displays the report to the user.

The Reporting Services report server uses Windows integrated security for authorization. It uses the Dynamics AX security model for securing business data from the Dynamics AX database and Reporting Services roles for securing content on the Report Manager. Menu items are secured using Dynamics AX security keys. Users are granted access to these objects based on their membership in Dynamics AX user groups.

Operations Environment

Dynamics AX is a three-tiered client/server application that is typically deployed in operations environments configured to meet the needs of customers.

The Dynamics AX Application Object Server (AOS) can be hosted on one machine, but it can also scale out to many machines when more concurrent user sessions or dedicated batch servers are required. The server can also access one database or a scaled-out database cluster if the database becomes a processing bottleneck. For more information on performance in Dynamics AX, see Chapter 12.

Dynamics AX rich clients communicate with the AOS by using Microsoft RPC technology. For example, an Excel component hosted on a rich client form communicates directly with Analysis Services via Web services. A SQL Server reporting client communicates directly with Reporting Services via Web services. The application database servers update the Analysis Services databases, and Reporting Services reads data from the application databases. Dedicating one or more batch servers for batch processing jobs is common. For more information on reporting with Dynamics AX, see Chapter 11.

The Dynamics AX Enterprise Portal is typically hosted on its own machine or on many scaled-out machines that also host IIS, Microsoft Office SharePoint Portal Server, and Windows SharePoint Services. Enterprise Portal communicates with Dynamics AX via .NET Business Connector, which communicates with the application servers by using RPC technology. For more information on Enterprise Portal, see Chapter 7.

Dynamics AX uses the Application Integration Framework (AIF) to interoperate with Microsoft BizTalk Server, Microsoft Message Queuing (MSMQ), and the file system. The AIF also hosts Web services that respond to requests for data from external applications. Dynamics AX can also interoperate with Component Object Model (COM) components and Microsoft .NET components via the COM and Microsoft common language runtime (CLR) interoperability technologies. For more information on AIF, see Chapter 17.

Dynamics AX uses the Windows Workflow Foundation for processing and configuring workflows. The Windows Workflow Foundation Server is typically hosted on its own machine, one that also hosts IIS. Dynamics AX communicates with the Windows Workflow Foundation Server via .NET Business Connector. For more information on .NET Business Connector, see Chapter 10.

Microsoft Office clients can interoperate directly with the AOS via .NET Business Connector, and Dynamics AX application servers can interoperate natively with Microsoft Exchange Server.

Chapter 2

The MorphX Development Environment

In this chapter:

The objectives of this chapter are to:

- Introduce MorphX, the Microsoft Dynamics AX 2009 integrated development environment (IDE).
- Show how the MorphX IDE is used throughout a typical product cycle model.
- Describe the application model elements and their relationships.

Introduction

Dynamics AX has two development environments: Microsoft Visual Studio, used primarily for developing Enterprise Portal and reports, and MorphX, the main Dynamics AX IDE and the focus of this chapter. For more information about Enterprise Portal, see Chapter 7, "Enterprise Portal," and for more on reports, see Chapter 11, "Reporting in Dynamics AX."

MorphX is a model-based, object-oriented development environment. Developers use X++—the MorphX programming language—and the MorphX toolset to develop, customize, and extend Microsoft Dynamics AX applications. You can find more information about X++ in Chapter 4, "The X++ Programming Language."

This chapter provides an overview of the MorphX IDE. First, in the context of a product cycle model, we introduce the MorphX tools you use when building a Microsoft Dynamics AX application. The tools are described in more detail in Chapter 3, "The MorphX Tools." Then we cover the key elements in the application model of the Application Object Tree (AOT).

Developing with MorphX

Like most IDEs, MorphX includes, among other tools, a source code editor, a compiler, a version control system, and a debugger.

In this section, you'll see how these tools map to a typical product cycle model, shown in Figure 2-1. Again, refer to Chapter 3 for more in-depth information about the MorphX tools.

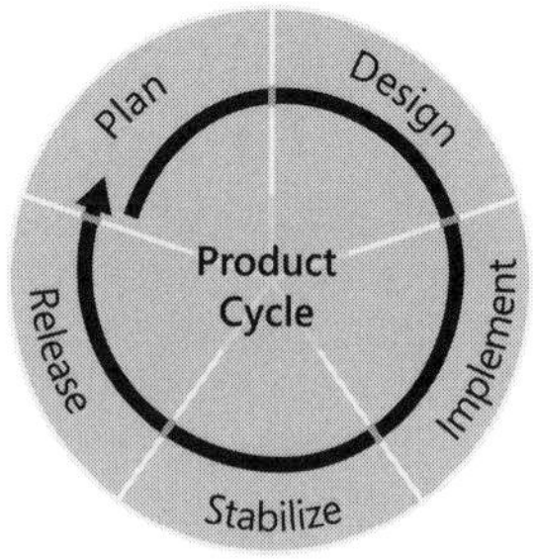

FIGURE 2-1 A product cycle model

You can follow the model shown in Figure 2-1 strictly, use variations, or manage your projects less formally. Whatever style of project management you choose for running your projects, you need to consider what should happen in each of these five phases: planning, designing, implementing, stabilizing, and releasing.

Most software projects start with a planning phase. In this phase, product planners decide on the market segment, establish the vision for the product, and allocate resources.

In the design phase, design documents are created, design reviews are conducted, prototypes are implemented, and requirements are documented. In the next phase, implementation, code is written, tested, and shipped. When implementation is complete, the stabilization phase begins. Here the focus is to validate the product quality: Are all requirements met? Does the product work as intended? Does the product meet performance goals?

When the product stability is satisfactory, the product can be released. The release phase includes packaging, marketing, and maintenance, which might involve releasing error corrections and service packs.

The product cycle starts over with the next version of the product.

> **Note** It is beyond the scope of this book to discuss how to run software projects optimally. For more information about how to best manage software projects, see Steve McConnell's book *Rapid Development* (Microsoft Press, 1996).

Planning Phase

Unlike many development environments, in the Dynamics AX IDE, you never start from scratch. Even in your first Dynamics AX project, when you might have a lot of learning to do, practices to formulate, and partnerships to form, you have a code base to start with.

In the planning phase of a Dynamics AX project, application designers and developers investigate the existing functionality and plan how to integrate with this functionality at a high level. Typically, this takes place at the user interface level.

Best Practices It's a good idea to do this kind of investigation in demo mode. Dynamics AX automatically enters demo mode when you skip the License Information step in the Installation checklist. The main benefit of investigating in demo mode is that all product functionality is available; if a license file is loaded, only the functionality purchased for that particular license is available. When all functionality is available, you can more effectively plan how to integrate with existing functionality—and avoid implementing redundant functionality.

Keep in mind that when you work in demo mode, the number of users, allowed active instances of Application Object Server (AOS), and companies is limited. In demo mode, the MorphX IDE isn't available, the date-handling algorithm is limited, and dates after a certain threshold date can't be used.

Design Phase

As we said earlier, in the design phase of the product cycle, prototypes are implemented, design documents are created, design reviews are conducted, and requirements are documented.

As you develop your designs and prototypes, the first Dynamics AX tool you're likely to use is the Application Object Tree (AOT). Accessible through the Dynamics AX user interface by pressing Ctrl+D or by clicking the toolbar icon, the AOT is typically the starting place for all development in Dynamics AX. It is the repository for all the elements that together constitute the existing business application.

The next tools you encounter are the property sheet and the X++ code editor. Most nodes in the AOT have a set of properties that you can inspect and modify by using the property sheet. Method nodes contain X++ source code. You use the X++ code editor to view and modify the code.

With these tools, you can, for example, see the structure of forms (by using the AOT), the properties specified on each control (by using the property sheet), and the event handlers' implementation (by using the X++ code editor). You use these tools throughout the remaining phases of the product cycle.

If you use the Version Control tool, you benefit from all elements being read-only. In read-only mode, you can investigate without the risk of changing the existing code. If you're working on the first version of your project, you can also use the layering technology to provide the same safeguard.

The tools mentioned so far reveal implementation details at the element level. Three additional tools show how elements relate to each other at a higher level: the Cross-reference tool, the Find tool, and the Reverse Engineering tool.

The Cross-reference tool shows you where any specific element is used. In the design phase, you can use this tool to determine where table fields are displayed, initialized, read, modified, and so on. The Find tool allows you to search any element in the AOT. In the design phase, you typically search the entire AOT. The Reverse Engineering tool raises the abstraction level. With this tool, you can generate Microsoft Visio Unified Modeling Language (UML) models and Entity Relationship Diagrams (ERDs). If you find yourself struggling to understand the object hierarchies or the data models, looking at a UML diagram can be useful.

During the design phase, you should also consider your approach to testing. Designing for testing from the beginning makes your life easier later in the product cycle, and it typically results in a better design. See Chapter 3 for information on implementing unit tests by using MorphX.

Implementation Phase

When your design documents and functional specifications are complete and you're ready to start developing, you should consider setting up the Version Control tool. Version control allows you to keep track of all changes, which is particularly useful when you are working in large teams. You can also specify criteria for code quality. Code that doesn't conform to the code quality you specify is rejected in the version control check-in process, so you can be sure that code that doesn't meet the quality standard isn't allowed into your project.

In your first implementation, you should use the Development Project to group related elements. Without it, working efficiently in the AOT can be difficult because of the many elements it contains. A project provides a view into the AOT, allowing you to focus on the elements you're working with. Using a development project also allows you to define what you want to see and the structure in which you see it.

After you've written your source code with the X++ code editor, you must compile it. The compiler generates the bytecode from your X++ source code and presents any syntax errors. The compiler also triggers the Best Practices tool, which validates your implementation of X++ code and element definitions according to development guidelines, allowing you to automatically detect coding errors and warnings.

You can also use the Visual Form Designer and the Visual Report Designer to construct your forms and reports. If you're developing a multilingual feature, you can use the Label Editor to create localizable text resources.

You might want to refer to code examples during the implementation phase. The Find tool and the Cross-reference tool can help you identify examples for API usage. The Cross-reference tool is also helpful if you need to refactor your code.

If your code doesn't produce the results you expect or it has errors, you can use the Dynamics AX Debugger to track the problem. The debugger starts automatically when execution hits a breakpoint. You might also need to see the data that your feature is using. You can use the Table Browser tool to look at this data.

Stabilization Phase

When you've completed your implementation, you should find and correct any problems in your code—without introducing new problems. You can use the debugger to find problems in your code. If a problem mandates a change of method profiles (return values or parameters), you should use the Cross-reference tool to perform an impact analysis of your changes before you make them. If you use the Version Control tool to track changes, you can use the Compare tool to highlight differences in each revision of an element.

Release Phase

When upgrading your customers from one version of an application to the next, say, from an earlier version of Dynamics AX or from one version of your functionality to the next, you need to ensure that no code conflicts exist. To detect any conflicting changes to elements, you can use the Detect Code Upgrade Conflicts option, which is available from the Upgrade checklist or the Microsoft Dynamics AX drop-down menu in the client: Tools\Development Tools\Code Upgrade. To resolve conflicts, the Compare tool is unmatched. It allows you to compare versions of elements, and, based on the results, upgrade elements. See Chapter 18, "Code Upgrade," for more information about finding and resolving conflicts.

Application Model Elements

You build an application with MorphX using modeling. The building blocks available for modeling are commonly known as *application model elements*. In this section, we introduce the different kinds of application model elements and their relationships, describe the tools necessary for working with application model elements, and explain the sequence in which to apply the tools. For a more thorough explanation of the application model elements, refer to the Microsoft Dynamics AX SDK on MSDN.

The application model dictionary in the AOT organizes the application model elements. For example, rich client forms are grouped under Forms, rich client reports are grouped under Reports, and Web client forms and reports are collected under a Reported Libraries group.

Tip To better understand the application model element structure as you read, start Dynamics AX 2009 and open the AOT.

Operational and Programming Model Elements

Operational model elements are used to model how the application should behave according to security, configuration, and licensing in an operational environment. For example, certain functionality is available only if it is enabled system-wide and the user is authorized to use it. Programming model elements provide ways to reference library code, definitions, and resources. They also allow you to write small X++ scripts to experiment with the X++ language capabilities.

Here are the operational model elements:

- License codes
- Configuration keys
- Security keys

These model elements change the operational characteristics of the Dynamics AX development and runtime environments.

These are the types of programming model elements:

- **Reference elements** Elements whose properties identify the Microsoft .NET assemblies referenced in X++ statements
- **Resource elements** Named file resources loaded into the memory
- **Macro elements** Libraries of X++ string replacement procedures
- **Job elements** X++ programs primarily used for testing and debugging an executable from within the development environment

Figure 2-2 illustrates the operational and programming element categories in the AOT.

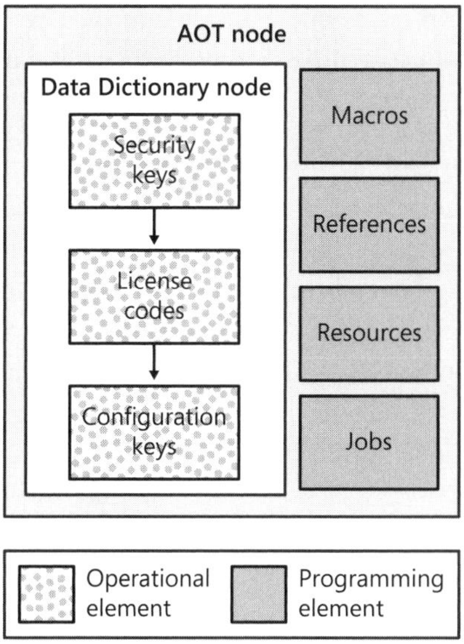

FIGURE 2-2 Operational and programming model elements

Operational Model Elements

You use the AOT and the property sheet to declaratively group related application features by associating configuration keys with menu item elements and data elements. This enables the application administrator to enable and disable application features. The MorphX IDE synchronizes table and view elements with the database schema only if they are associated with an active configuration key or if they have no configuration key. For details, see the section "Database Model Elements" later in this chapter and the section "Database Synchronization" in Chapter 14, "The Database Layer." The Dynamics AX runtime environment renders presentation controls only for menu items that are associated with an active configuration key or that have no configuration key. You can enable and disable application logic by using X++ to test for the state of a configuration key.

Dynamics AX includes all the application modules developed by Microsoft. These modules are locked with license codes that must be unlocked with license keys. You can also configure an unlocked module by using configuration keys. Dynamics AX administrators manually enable and disable configuration keys by using the check boxes in the system configuration dialog box at Administration\Setup\System\Configuration. You can manually activate configuration keys associated with license code elements only if there is a valid license key for the corresponding license code element.

Security keys are part of the Dynamics AX security framework. When a user identified by a Windows principal logs on to a Dynamics AX application, he or she is authenticated with the Windows platform security infrastructure and then associated with a Dynamics AX application user group that denotes the application user's role. An application user role determines which user interface actions a user is authorized to perform and which data the user is authorized to view and modify.

Security keys are associated with menu item elements and data elements so that related elements can be grouped together into a security group. Access permissions that are assigned to a security key apply to all elements that are members of the associated security group. Access permissions can also be assigned to individual elements in a security group. The security grouping provided by security keys is used to display a tree of security keys and application elements when they are displayed in the User Group Permissions dialog box. This makes it easier for the application administrator to navigate the thousands of menu item elements and data elements that need to be assigned user group permissions.

Programming Model Elements

The following list describes the programming model elements:

- **Reference elements** Reference elements hold references to .NET assemblies for the .NET common language runtime (CLR) types to be incorporated natively into X++ source code. The X++ editor reads type data from the referenced assemblies so that IntelliSense is available for CLR namespaces, types, and type members. The MorphX compiler uses the CLR type definitions in the referenced assembly for type and member syntax validation, and the Dynamics AX runtime uses the reference elements to locate and load the referenced assembly.
- **Resource elements** Resource elements hold references to file resources that are read from the file system and stored in memory. Image and animation files used when developing Web client applications are referenced as resources. The name of the file that contains the resource also references the resource when it is stored in the database.
- **Macro elements** Macro elements are libraries of X++ syntax replacement procedures included in the X++ source code. You should use macro libraries to provide readable names for constants. See Chapter 4 for an example of a macro procedure and an example that shows how to include a macro library in X++ source code.
- **Job elements** Job elements are X++ source code statements that are easily executed by selecting the Command\Go menu item or by pressing F5 on the keyboard while using MorphX. Job elements offer a convenient method of experimenting with features of the X++ language when they are used to write sample code. See Chapter 4 for an example of X++ code statements written in a job model element. You shouldn't use job elements for writing application code. In fact, the Dynamics AX enterprise resource planning (ERP) application model contains no job element when it is released to customers and development partners.

Value Type, Database, and Data Association Model Elements

Figure 2-3 illustrates the value type, database, and data association element categories that are located in the *Data Dictionary* node in the AOT. Configuration key elements can be associated with base enumeration and extended data type elements as well as with table, view, and map elements. Table, view, and map application elements can also be associated with security key elements.

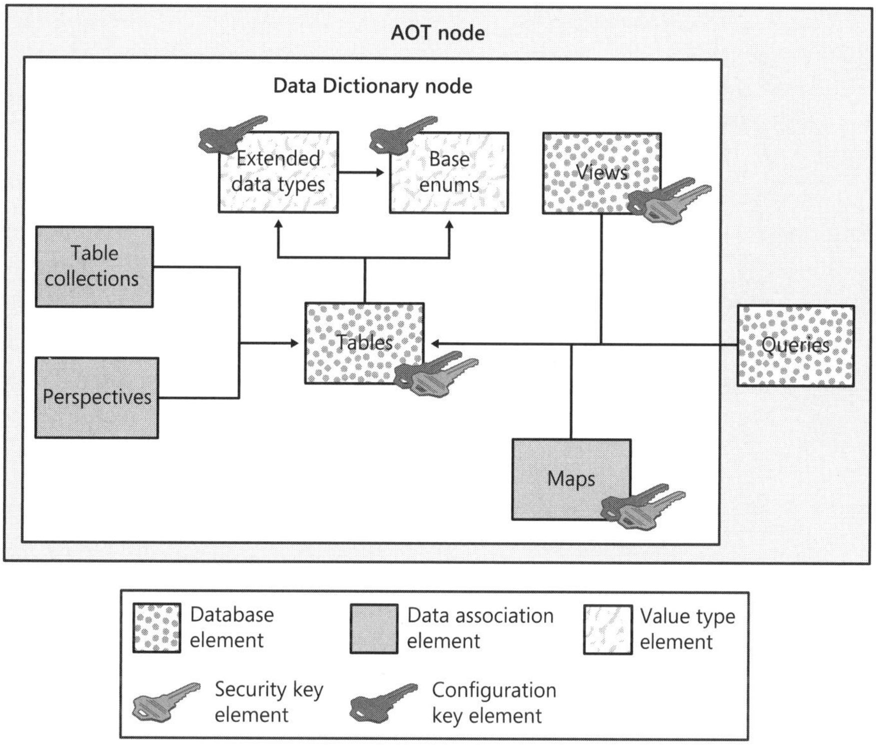

FIGURE 2-3 Value type, database, and data association model elements

Value Type Model Elements

A *base enumeration element* (sometimes shortened to *enum*) defines a name for a group of symbolic constants that are used in X++ code statements. For example, an enumeration with the name *WeekDay* can be defined to name the group of symbolic constants that includes *Monday, Tuesday, Wednesday, Thursday, Friday, Saturday,* and *Sunday.*

An *extended data type element* can extend a base enumeration by providing a new name for a group of symbolic constants that includes the base enumeration elements. An extended data type element can also extend the *string, boolean, int, real, date, time, UtcDateTime, int64, guid,* and *container* types. An extended data type definition can also comprise a set of application parameters that define how the Dynamics AX runtime renders user interface controls. For example, an extended data type representing an account number extends a *string* value type, restricts its length to 10 characters, and sets its user interface label to "Account number."

Extended data types also support inheritance. For example, an extended data type that defines an account number can be specialized by other extended data types defining customer and vendor account numbers. The specialized extended data type inherits properties, such as string length, label, and help text. You can override some of the properties on the specialized extended data type. You constrain the possible values of an extended data type and define a database table association by adding a relationship from the extended data type to a table field element. The Dynamics AX runtime automatically ensures that the values of the extended data type are consistent with this relationship. The runtime also uses the defined relationship to navigate between rich client and Web client main table forms when a user selects the Go To The Main Table Form menu item. This menu item appears when a user right-clicks a form data grid column that is mapped to a table element field whose type is an extended data type with a defined relationship.

Database Model Elements

Database model elements are database table and view definitions that correspond to database server entities and relationships as well as query elements that define database query statements. The MorphX IDE synchronizes table and view element definitions with database schema definitions. This feature allows Dynamics AX to use either Microsoft SQL Server or Oracle database server as an application database. MorphX synchronizes only those database elements that have configuration keys enabled and corresponding valid license keys.

Database element keys and indexes are used to create database entity keys and indexes, but data element interrelationships are not used to create integrity relationships in a database. Instead, they validate data entries to automatically join and select database data as a user navigates between forms, and they join data sources associated with a form. For example, a user sees confirmations only for the selected sales orders when navigating from a sales order form to a sales order confirmation form. Moreover, MorphX automatically converts between X++ programming value types such as *string*, *enum*, and *boolean* and their corresponding database data types, such as *nvarchar* and *int*. For example, an X++ string defined to have a maximum length of 10 characters is stored as a database *nvarchar* data type defined to have a maximum length of 10 characters.

A table element can also define table field groups, menu item references, table relationships, delete actions, and methods that are used by the Dynamics AX runtime when it renders data entry presentation controls and ensures the referential integrity of the database. The X++ editor also uses these elements to support developers with IntelliSense when they write X++

statements that create, read, update, and delete data in the database. You can also use the AOT to associate table elements with data source elements on forms, reports, queries, and views.

View elements define database table view entities and are synchronized with the application database. View elements can include a query that filters data in a table or data joined from multiple tables. View element definitions also include table field mappings and methods. Views are read-only and primarily provide an efficient method for reading data. View elements can be associated with form and report data sources and are instantiated in X++ variable declarations.

Query elements define a database query structure that can be executed from X++ statements, particularly X++ statements used in classes that derive from the *RunBase* class. You add tables to query element data sources and specify how they should be joined. You also specify how data is returned from the query, such as by using sort order and range specifications.

> **Note** You don't have to use the query element as form and report data sources because these data sources have a similar built-in query specification capability.

Data Association Model Elements

Map elements don't define database entities, so they're not synchronized with the database. They actually define X++ programming elements that wrap table objects at run time. Map elements associate common fields and methods for tables that are not in third-normal form. For example, the *CustTable* and *VendTable* table elements in the Dynamics AX application model are mapped to the *AddressMap* map element so that developers can use one *AddressMap* object to access common address fields and methods. The MorphX compiler validates that table variables assigned to map variables are defined as valid element mappings.

> **Note** Maps provide a useful common interface to data entities and prevent the need to duplicate methods on denormalized tables, but you should use maps only when normalization isn't an option.

Table collection elements define groups of tables that can be shared by two or more Dynamics AX companies that share virtual company accounts. The application administrator creates a virtual company and then adds table collections to it. The administrator also adds the virtual company accounts to an actual Dynamics AX company's accounts. The Dynamics AX runtime uses the virtual company data area identifier instead of the actual company data area identifier when it inserts or reads data in the tables in the table collection.

Caution The tables placed in a table collection shouldn't have foreign key relationships with tables outside the table collection unless specific extensions are written to maintain the relational integrity of the database.

Perspective elements define views on the Dynamics AX database model by grouping related tables. Perspectives are used to design and generate ad hoc reports in Microsoft SQL Server Reporting Services.

Class Model Elements

Class elements define the structure and behavior of business logic types that work on ERP reference data and business transaction data. These elements comprise object-oriented type definitions that instantiate business objects at run time. You define type declaration headers and methods by using the X++ programming language. You associate rich client and Web client menu item elements in the AOT with class element methods by using the property sheet in MorphX. This allows the Dynamics AX runtime to instantiate corresponding business logic objects when users select action, display, or output menu item controls on a user interface.

The Dynamics AX runtime also invokes business object methods when they overload event handlers on tables, forms, and reports. Class elements are also defined for application integration scenarios that aren't driven by a user interface. Chapter 17, "The Application Integration Framework," describes how these elements are associated with XML document elements that read from and write to the file system, Microsoft Message Queuing (MSMQ), and Web services.

Presentation Model Elements

The two types of presentation elements include rich client model elements and Web client model elements. The rich client element categories, Forms and Reports, are located under the AOT root node, and the Web client element categories, Web Forms and Web Reports, are under the Web node. Presentation elements are form, report, menu, or menu item definitions for either a Windows client application, called a rich client application, or a Windows SharePoint Services client application, called a Web client application. Both types of clients have a control layout feature called IntelliMorph. IntelliMorph automatically lays out presentation controls based on model element property and security settings. Presentation controls are automatically supplied with database and calculated data when their data source elements are associated with database or temporary table fields.

Rich Client Model Elements

Figure 2-4 illustrates the rich client elements and their relationships. Configuration key and security key elements can be associated with menu and menu item elements. This association prevents users from executing application code that doesn't have a license key or an active configuration key.

Table elements can also be associated with menu item elements. Each table element definition includes an optional display menu item element reference that, by convention, launches a form presentation control that renders the data from the database table in a grid control. The Dynamics AX runtime also automatically adds a Go To The Main Table Form menu item to a drop-down menu that appears when a user right-clicks a grid cell whose associated table column has a foreign key relationship with another table. The Dynamics AX runtime uses the referenced table's menu item element to launch the form that renders the data from the foreign key table.

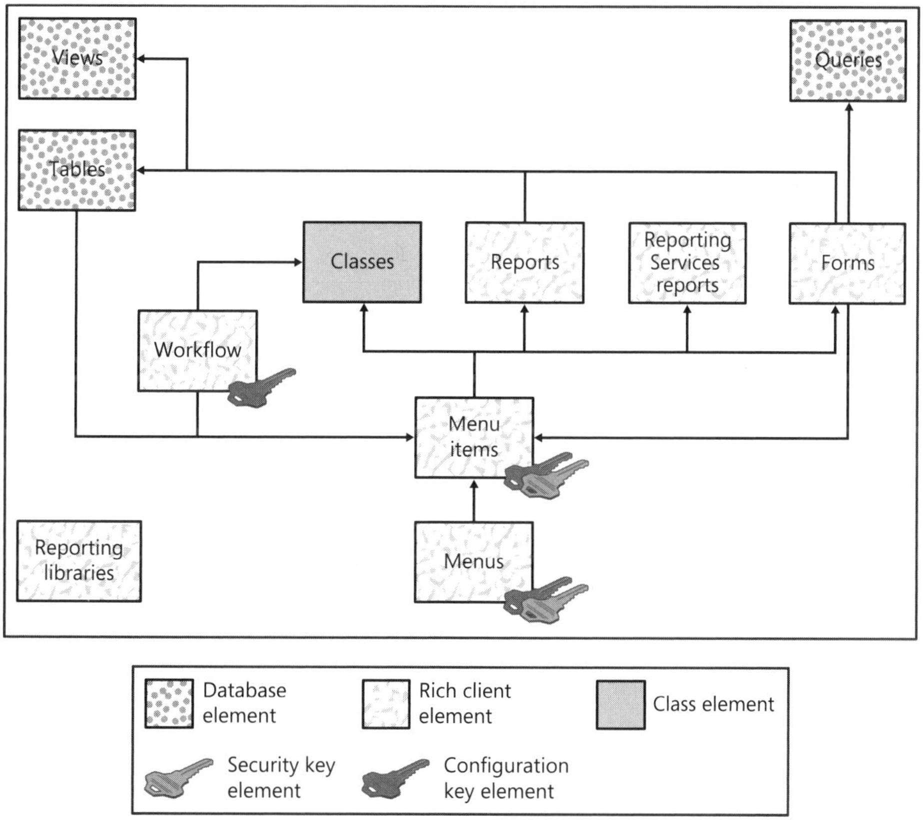

FIGURE 2-4 Rich client model elements

Menu elements define logical menu item groupings. Menu definitions can include submenu elements and other menu elements. The menu element named MainMenu defines the menu entries for the Dynamics AX navigation pane. As a new feature in Dynamics AX 2009, menus can also work as a hyperlink. This is modeled by specifying a menu item.

Menu item elements define hyperlinks labeled for display, action, and output that the Dynamics AX runtime uses to instantiate and execute reports, Reporting Services reports, business logic objects (defined by using class elements), and forms. When rendering forms and reports, the Dynamics AX runtime ignores menu items that are disabled by configuration keys, security keys, or role-based access permissions.

Form elements define a presentation control with which users insert, update, and read database data. A form definition includes a data source and a design element that defines the controls that must be rendered on the form as well as their data source mappings. A form is launched when a user clicks a display menu item control, such as a button. Data sources on a form can be table, view, or query elements.

Report elements define a presentation control that renders database and calculated data in a page layout format. A report can be sent to the screen, a printer, a printer archive, an e-mail account, or the file system. A report definition includes a data source and a design element that define the output-only controls that must be rendered on the report as well as their data source mappings. A report is launched when a user clicks an output menu item control, such as a button.

Report libraries are a logical grouping of Reporting Services reports, data sources, style templates, layout templates, and images. Each report library represents a single Dynamics AX Reports Library project. You can edit an existing report library or create a new one using Microsoft Visual Studio 2008 if you have the Dynamics AX Reporting Tools component installed. Reporting Services reports that are part of a report library in the AOT can be associated with menu items. For more information on reporting with Dynamics AX, see Chapter 11, "Reporting in Dynamics AX."

Workflow elements define workflow documents and event handlers by using class elements. Workflow elements define the workflow tasks, such as approve and reject, by associating the tasks with menu items. When a form is workflow enabled, it automatically renders controls supporting the user in performing the tasks in the workflow.

Web Client Model Elements

Figure 2-5 illustrates the Web client model elements used to define Enterprise Portal. You can associate configuration key and security key elements with Web menu items and Web content elements to ensure that code without license keys are an active configuration key that can't be executed.

Web menu elements define logical Web menu item groupings. Web menu definitions can include submenu application elements and other Web menu application elements. Web menu items are rendered as hyperlinks on Web pages.

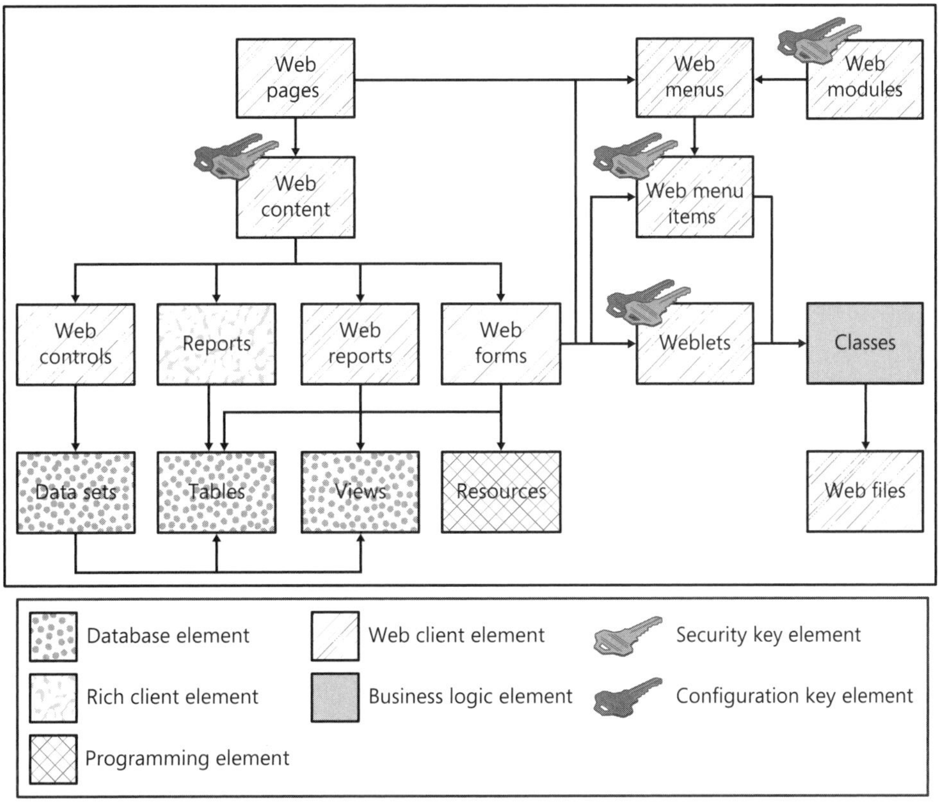

FIGURE 2-5 Web client model elements used by Enterprise Portal

Web menu item elements define hyperlinks containing URLs and class labels that the Dynamics AX runtime environment uses to navigate between Web pages and to generate Web pages, respectively. Web module elements define the site structure. The Web modules are created as subsites under one parent home site in Windows SharePoint Services.

Web file elements define file references to components required by Windows SharePoint Services. These components include site definitions, templates, and Web part installation files. The MorphX IDE saves these files to a specified Web server at deployment time.

Data set elements define the data sources used by the Web user controls. They offer a rich programming model in the AOT for defining data access, validation, calculation, and so on. The data set elements also expose business data to Web user controls through standard ASP.NET data binding via the *AxDataSource* control.

Web control elements store the Web user control's markup and code-behind files. You can create Web user controls in Visual Studio 2008 and add them directly to the AOT by using the Dynamics AX Visual Studio add-in. Web user controls define the user interface for interacting with business data.

Data sets, Web controls, and report libraries are the elements used by the newly architected, ASP.NET-based Enterprise Portal framework. (The Enterprise Portal framework has been rewritten for Dynamics AX 2009. For more information on Enterprise Portal, see Chapter 7.) These elements replace the X++-based Enterprise Portal framework (supported in deprecated mode in Dynamics AX 2009), which uses Weblet, Web form, and Web report elements.

Weblet elements define references to class application elements that extend the Weblet class definition. Weblet objects return HTML documents whose format is governed by input parameters.

Web form elements define Web presentation controls with which users insert, update, and read database data. A Web form definition includes a data source and a design element that defines the controls that must be rendered on the Web form, as well as their data source mappings. A Web form is generated when a Web page hosting the Web form is generated.

Web report elements define Web presentation controls that render database and calculated data in a Web format. A report definition includes a data source and a design element that define the output-only controls that must be rendered on the report, as well as their data source mappings. A Web report is generated when a Web page hosting the Web form is generated.

Web content elements define managed, display, and output elements that reference Web user control, Web form, Web report, and (rich) report elements for their content.

Web page elements define the composition of an HTML document element that comprises Web content elements and Web menu elements.

Chapter 3

The MorphX Tools

In this chapter:

The objectives of this chapter are to:

- Provide an overview of the tools used when developing a Microsoft Dynamics AX 2009 enterprise resource planning (ERP) application with MorphX.
- Share tips and tricks on how to use the MorphX tools efficiently.
- Demonstrate how to personalize and extend the MorphX tools.

Introduction

Dynamics AX includes a set of tools, the MorphX development tools, that allow developers to build and modify Dynamics AX business applications. Each feature of a business application uses the application model elements described in Chapter 2, "The MorphX Development Environment." The MorphX tools enable developers to create, view, modify, and delete the application model elements, which contain metadata, structure (ordering and hierarchies of elements), properties (key and value pairs), and X++ code. For example, a table element includes the name of the table, the properties set for the table, the fields, the indices, the relations, the methods, and so on.

This chapter describes the most commonly used tools and offers some tips and tricks for working with them. You can find additional information and an overview of other MorphX tools in the MorphX Development Tools section of the Microsoft Dynamics AX software development kit (SDK) 2009 on MSDN.

> **Tip** To enable the development mode of Dynamics AX 2009, press Ctrl+Shift+D. Ctrl+Shift+D is a toggle key that also returns you to content mode.

Table 3-1 lists the MorphX tools that are discussed in this chapter.

TABLE 3-1 MorphX Tools

Tool	Use This Tool To:
Application Object Tree (AOT)	Start development activities. The AOT is the main entry point for all development activities. It is the repository for all elements that together comprise the business application. You can use the AOT to invoke the other tools and to browse and create elements.
Project Designer	Group related elements into projects.
Property sheet	Inspect and modify properties of elements. The property sheet shows key and value pairs.
X++ Code Editor	Inspect and write X++ source code.
Label Editor	Create and inspect localizable strings.
Visual Form Designer and the Visual Report Designer	Design forms and reports in a What You See Is What You Get (WYSIWYG) fashion.
Compiler	Compile X++ code into an executable format.
Best Practices tool	Automatically detect defects in both your code and your elements.
Debugger	Find bugs in your X++ code.
Reverse Engineering tool	Generate Microsoft Office Visio Unified Modeling Language (UML) and Entity Relationship Diagrams (ERDs) from elements.
Table Browser tool	View the contents of a table directly from the table element.
Find tool	Search for code or metadata patterns in the AOT.
Compare tool	See a line-by-line comparison of two versions of the same element.
Cross-reference tool	Determine where an element is used.
Version Control tool	Track all changes to elements and see a full revision log.
Unit Test tool	Build automated tests that can exercise your code and detect regressions.

You can access these development tools from the following places:

- The Development Tools submenu on the Tools menu. From the Microsoft Dynamics AX drop-down menu, point to Tools, and then point to Development Tools.
- The context menu on elements in the AOT.

> **Note** The Microsoft Dynamics AX SDK contains valuable developer documentation and is updated frequently. Find it in the Microsoft Dynamics AX Developer Center on *msdn.microsoft.com*.

You can personalize the behavior of many MorphX tools by clicking Options on the Tools menu. Figure 3-1 shows the Options dialog box.

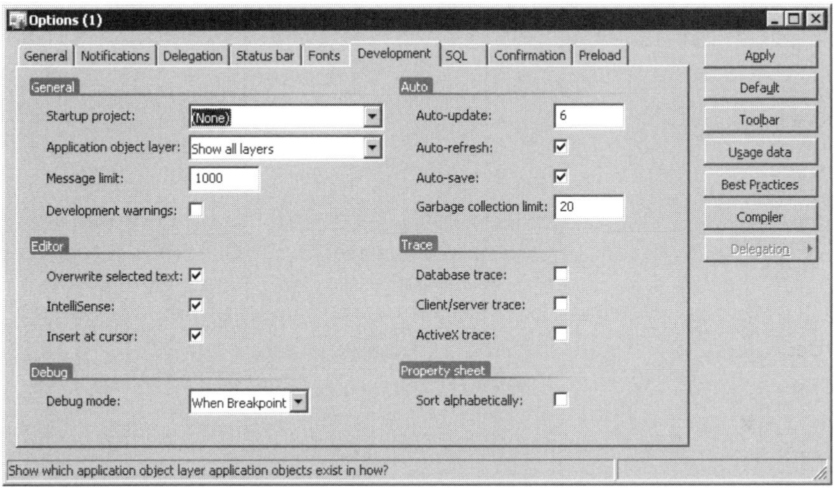

FIGURE 3-1 Options dialog box, in which development options are specified

Application Object Tree

The AOT is the main entry point to MorphX and is the repository explorer for all metadata. You can open the AOT by clicking the AOT icon on the toolbar or by pressing Ctrl+D. The AOT icon looks like this:

Navigating the AOT

As the name implies, the AOT is a tree view. The root of the AOT contains the element categories, such as Classes, Tables, and Forms. Some elements are grouped into subcategories to provide a better structure. For example, Tables, Maps, Views, and Extended Data Types reside under Data Dictionary, and all Web-related elements are found under Web. Figure 3-2 shows the AOT.

You can navigate the AOT by using the arrow keys on the keyboard. Pressing the Right arrow key expands a node if it has any children.

Elements are ordered alphabetically. Because thousands of elements exist, understanding the naming conventions and adhering to them is important to effectively using the AOT.

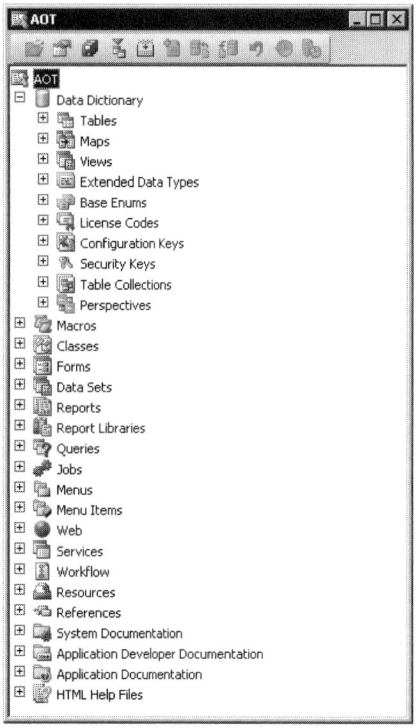

FIGURE 3-2 Application Object Tree

All element names in the AOT follow this structure:

<Business area name> + <Business area description> + <Action performed or type of content>

In this naming convention, similar elements are placed next to each other. The business area name is also often referred to as the *prefix*. Prefixes are commonly used to indicate the team responsible for an element.

Table 3-2 contains a list of the most common prefixes and their descriptions.

TABLE 3-2 Common Prefixes

Prefix	Description
Ax	Dynamics AX typed data source
Axd	Dynamics AX business document
BOM	Bill of material
COS	Cost accounting
Cust	Customer
HRM	Human resources management
Invent	Inventory management
JMG	Shop floor control
KM	Knowledge management
Ledger	General ledger
PBA	Product builder
Prod	Production
Proj	Project
Purch	Purchase
Req	Requirements
Sales	Sales
SMA	Service management
SMM	Sales and marketing management
Sys	Application frameworks and development tools
Tax	Tax engine
Vend	Vendor
Web	Web framework
WMS	Warehouse management

Tip When creating new elements, make sure to follow the recommended naming conventions. Any future development and maintenance will be much easier.

The Project Designer, described in detail later in this chapter, provides an alternative view of the information organized by the AOT.

Creating New Elements in the AOT

You can create new elements in the AOT by right-clicking the element category node and selecting New <*Element Name*>, as shown in Figure 3-3.

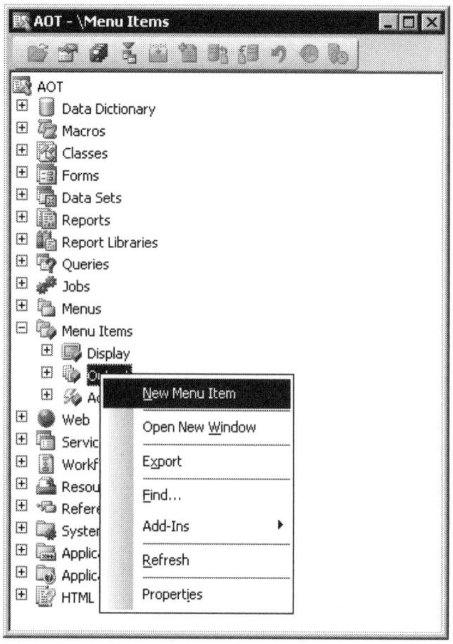

FIGURE 3-3 Creating a new element in the AOT

Objects are given automatically generated names when they are created. However, you should replace the default names with new names in accordance with the naming conventions.

Modifying Elements in the AOT

Each node in the AOT has a set of properties and either subnodes or X++ code. You can use the property sheet (shown in Figure 3-9) to inspect or modify properties, and you can use the X++ code editor (shown in Figure 3-11) to inspect or modify X++ code.

The order of the subnodes can play a role in the semantics of the element. For example, the tabs on a form display in the order in which they are listed in the AOT. You can change the order of nodes by selecting a node and pressing the Alt key while pressing the Up or Down arrow key.

A red vertical line next to an element name marks it as modified and unsaved, or *dirty*, as shown in Figure 3-4.

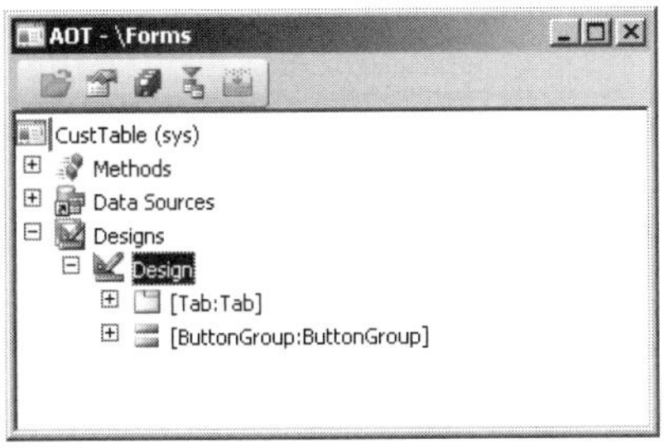

FIGURE 3-4 A dirty element in the AOT, indicated by a vertical line next to *CustTable (sys)*

A dirty element is saved in the following situations:

- The element is executed.
- The developer explicitly invokes the Save or Save All action.
- Autosave takes place. You specify the frequency of autosave in the Options dialog box accessible from the Tools menu.

Refreshing Elements in the AOT

If several developers modify elements simultaneously in the same installation of Dynamics AX, each developer's local elements could become out of sync with the latest version. To ensure that the local versions of remotely changed elements are updated, an autorefresh thread runs in the background. This autorefresh functionality eventually updates all changes, but you might want to explicitly force a refresh. You do this by right-clicking the element you want to restore and then selecting Restore. This action refreshes both the on-disk and the in-memory versions of the element. The following is a less elegant way of ensuring that the latest elements are used:

1. Close the Dynamics AX client to clear in-memory elements.
2. Close the Dynamics Server service on the Application Object Server (AOS) to clear in-memory elements.
3. Delete the application object cache files (*.auc) from the Local Application Data folder (located in Documents and Settings\<*User*>\Local Settings\Application Data) to remove the on-disk elements.

> **Note** Before Dynamics AX 4.0, the application object cache was stored in .aoc files. To support Unicode, the file extension was changed to .auc in Dynamics AX 4.0.

Element Actions in the AOT

Each node in the AOT contains a set of available actions. You can access these actions from the context menu, which you can open by right-clicking the node in question.

Here are two facts to remember about actions:

- The actions available depend on the type of node you select.
- You can select multiple nodes and perform actions simultaneously on all the nodes selected.

A frequently used action is Open New Window, which is available for all nodes. It opens a new AOT window with the current nodes as the root. We used this action to create the screen capture of the *CustTable* element shown in Figure 3-4. Once you open a new AOT window, you can drag elements into the nodes, saving time and effort when you're developing an application.

You can extend the list of available actions on the context menu. You can create custom actions for any element in the AOT by using the features provided by MorphX. In fact, all actions listed on the Add-Ins submenu are implemented in MorphX by using X++ and the MorphX tools.

You can enlist a class as a new add-in by following this procedure:

1. Create a new menu item and give it a meaningful name, a label, and Help text.
2. Set the menu item's *Object Type* property to Class.
3. Set the menu item's *Object* property to the name of the class to be invoked by the add-in.
4. Drag the menu item to the *SysContextMenu* menu.
5. If you want the action available only for certain nodes, you need to modify the *verifyItem* method on the *SysContextMenu* class.

Element Layers in the AOT

When you modify an element from a lower layer, a copy of the element is placed in the current layer. All elements in the current layer appear in bold type (as shown in Figure 3-5), which makes it easy to recognize changes. For a description of the layer technology, see the section "Application Model Layering System" in Chapter 1, "Architectural Overview."

FIGURE 3-5 An element in the AOT that exists in several layers

You can use the Application Object Layer setting in the Options dialog box to personalize the layer information shown in the AOT. Figure 3-5 shows a class with the option set to All Layers. As you can see, each method is suffixed with information about the layers in which it is defined, such as *sys*, *var*, and *usr*. If an element exists in several layers, you can right-click it and select Layers to access its versions from lower layers. We highly recommend the All Layers setting during code upgrade because it provides a visual representation of the layer dimension directly in the AOT.

> **Note** If you modify an element that exists in a higher layer than your current layer, all modifications are redirected to the upper layer where the element is defined.

Project Designer

For a fully customizable overview of the elements, you can use projects. In a *project*, elements can be grouped and structured according to the developer's preference. The Project Designer is a powerful alternative to the AOT because you can collect all the elements needed for a feature in one project.

Creating a New Project

You open the Project Designer by clicking the Project button on the toolbar. Figure 3-6 shows the Project Designer and its Private and Shared projects.

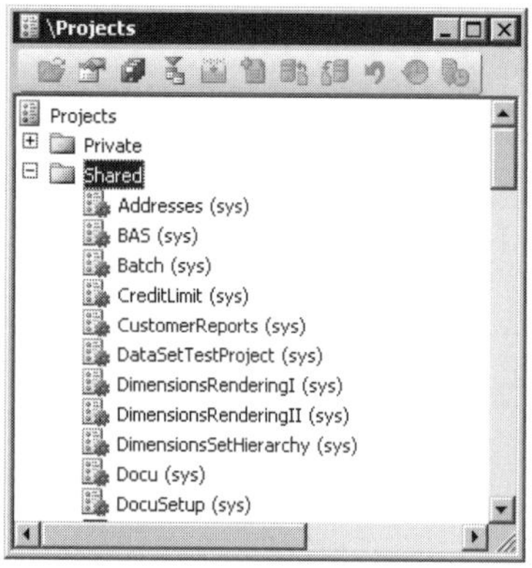

FIGURE 3-6 Project Designer, showing available private and shared projects

Except for its structure, the Project Designer behaves exactly like the AOT. Every element in a project is also present in the AOT.

When you create a new project, you must decide whether it should be private or shared among all developers. You can't set access requirements on shared projects. You can make a shared project private (and a private project shared) by dragging it from the shared category into the private category.

> **Note** Central features of Dynamics AX 2009 are captured in shared projects to provide an overview of all the elements in a feature. No private projects are included with the application.

You can specify a startup project in the Options dialog box. If specified, the chosen project automatically opens when Dynamics AX is started.

Automatically Generated Projects

Projects can be automatically generated in several ways—from using group masks to customizing special project types—to make working with them easier. We discuss the various ways to automatically generate projects in the sections that follow.

Group Masks

Groups are folders in a project. When you create a group, you can have its contents be automatically generated by setting the *ProjectGroupType* property (All is an option) and a regular expression as the *GroupMask* property. The contents of the group are created automatically and kept up to date as elements are created, deleted, and renamed. Using group masks ensures that your project is always current, even when elements are created directly in the AOT.

Figure 3-7 shows the *ProjectGroupType* property set to Tables and the *GroupMask* property set to <xRef on a project group. All table names starting with *xRef* (the prefix for the Cross-reference tool) will be included in the project group.

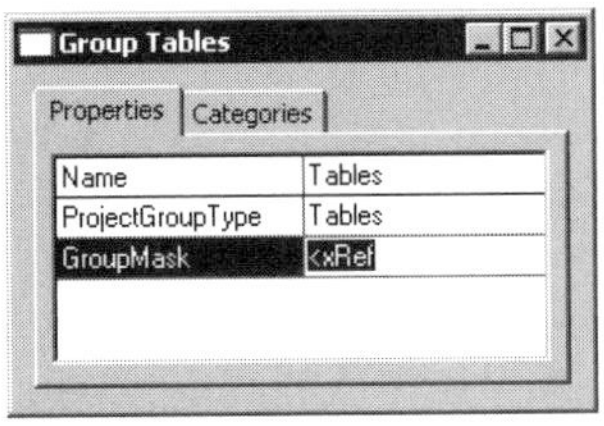

FIGURE 3-7 Property sheet specifying settings for *ProjectGroupType* and *GroupMask*

Figure 3-8 shows the resulting project when the settings from Figure 3-7 are used.

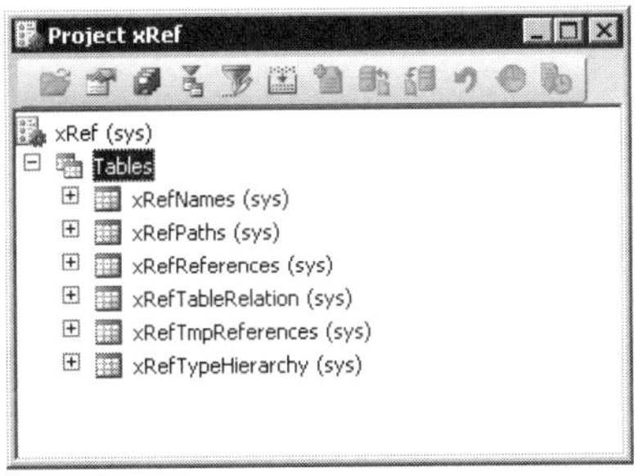

FIGURE 3-8 Project created by using group masks

Filters

You can also generate a project based on a filter. Because all elements in the AOT persist in a database format, you can use a query to filter elements and have the results presented in a project. You create a project filter by clicking the Filter button on the project's toolbar. Depending on the complexity of the query, a project can be generated instantly or might take several minutes.

Filters allow you to create projects containing the following kinds of elements:

- Elements created or modified within the last month
- Elements created or modified by a named user
- Elements from a particular layer

Development Tools

Several development tools, such as the Wizard wizard, produce projects containing elements the wizard creates. The result of running the Wizard wizard is a new project that includes a form, a class, and a menu item—all the elements comprising the newly created wizard.

You can also use several other wizards, such as the Report Wizard and the Class Wizard, to create projects. You can access these wizards from the Microsoft Dynamics AX drop-down menu by clicking Tools\Development Tools\Wizards.

Layer Comparison

You can compare all the elements in one layer with the elements in another layer, called the reference layer. If an element exists in both layers, and the definitions of the element are different or the element doesn't exist in the reference layer, the element will be added to the resulting project. You can compare layers by clicking Tools\Development Tools\Code Upgrade from the Microsoft Dynamics AX drop-down menu.

Upgrade Projects

When you upgrade from one version of Dynamics AX to another or install a new service pack, you need to deal with any new elements that are introduced and existing elements that have been modified. These changes might conflict with customizations you've implemented in a higher layer.

The Create Upgrade Project feature makes a three-way comparison to establish whether an element has any upgrade conflicts. It compares the original version with both the customized version and the updated version. If a conflict is detected, the element is added to the project.

The resulting project provides a list of elements to update based on upgrade conflicts between versions. You can use the Compare tool, described later in this chapter, to see the conflicts in each element. Together, these features provide a cost-effective toolbox to use when upgrading. For more information about upgrading code, see Chapter 18, "Code Upgrade."

You can create upgrade projects by clicking Tools\Development Tools\Code Upgrade\Detect Code Upgrade conflicts from the Microsoft Dynamics AX drop-down menu.

Project Types

When you create a new project, you can specify a project type. So far in this chapter, we've limited our discussion to standard projects. Two specialized project types are also provided in Dynamics AX:

- **Test project** Project used to group a set of classes for unit testing
- **Help Book project** Project used for the table of contents in the online Help system

You can create a custom specialized project by creating a new class that extends the *ProjectNode* class. Specialized projects allow you to control the structure, icons, and actions available to the project.

Property Sheet

Properties are an important part of the metadata system. Each property is a key and value pair. The property sheet allows you to inspect and modify properties of elements.

Open the property sheet by pressing Alt+Enter or by clicking the Properties button. The property sheet automatically updates itself to show properties for any element selected in the AOT. You don't have to manually open the property sheet for each element; you can simply leave it open and browse the elements. Figure 3-9 shows the property sheet for a *TaxSpec* class. The two columns are the key and value pairs for each property.

Tip Pressing Esc in the property sheet sets the focus back to your origin.

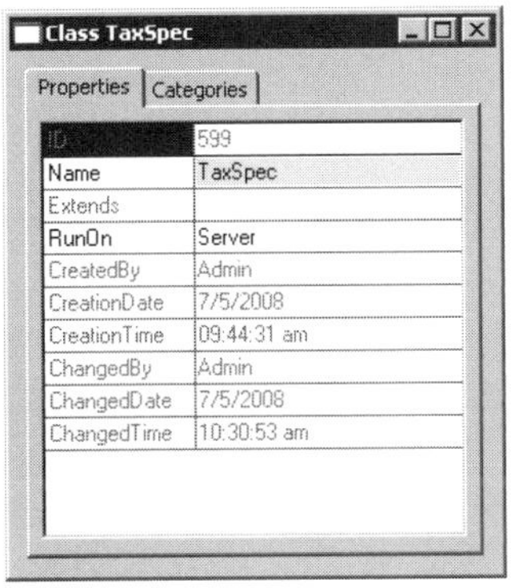

FIGURE 3-9 Property sheet for an element in the AOT

Figure 3-10 shows the Categories tab for the class shown in Figure 3-9. Here, related properties are categorized. For elements with many properties, this view can make it easier to find the right property.

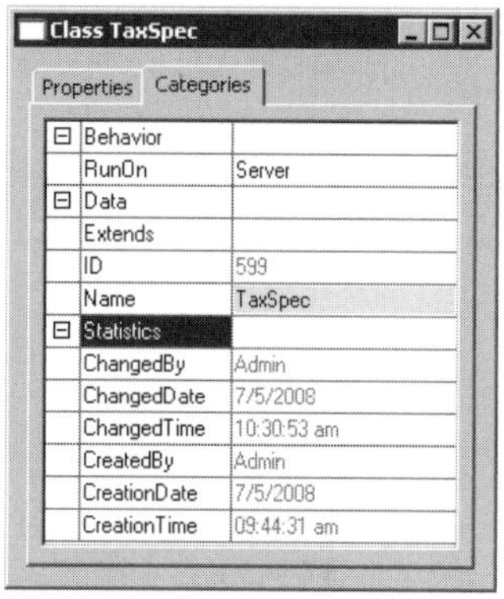

FIGURE 3-10 Categories tab on the property sheet for an element in the AOT

Read-only properties appear in gray. Just like files in the file system, elements contain information about who created them and when they were modified. The Microsoft build process ensures that all elements that ship from Microsoft have the same time and user stamp.

The default sort order places related properties near each other. Categories were introduced in an earlier version of Dynamics AX to make finding properties easier, but you can also sort properties alphabetically by setting a parameter in the Options dialog box. (Thanks to Erik Damgaard, founder of Damgaard Data, the default sorting order is retained in the current version for developers familiar with the original layout of properties.)

You can dock the property sheet on either side of the screen by right-clicking the title bar. Docking ensures that the property sheet is never hidden behind another tool.

X++ Code Editor

You write all X++ code with the X++ code editor. You open the editor by selecting a node in the AOT and pressing Enter. The editor contains two panes. The left pane shows the methods available, and the right pane shows the X++ code for the selected method, as shown in Figure 3-11.

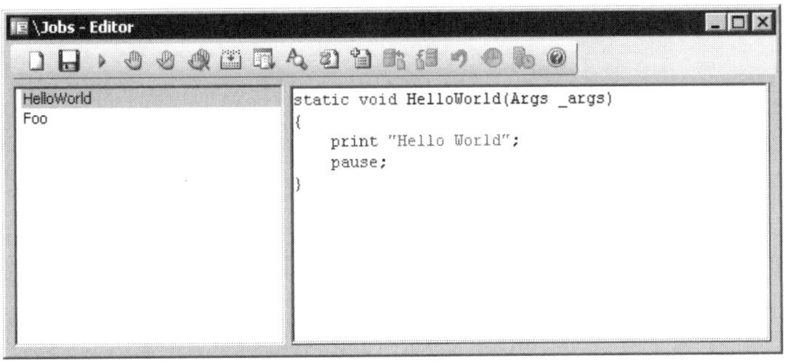

FIGURE 3-11 X++ code editor

The X++ code editor is a basic text editor that supports color coding and IntelliSense.

Shortcut Keys

Navigation and editing in the X++ code editor use standard shortcuts, as described in Table 3-3.

TABLE 3-3 X++ Code Editor Shortcut Keys

Action	Shortcut	Description
Show Help window	F1	Opens context-sensitive Help for the type or method currently selected in the editor.
Go to next error message	F4	Opens the editor and positions the cursor at the next compilation error, based on the contents of the compiler output window.
Execute current element	F5	Starts the current form, report, or class.
Compile	F7	Compiles the current method.
Toggle a breakpoint	F9	Sets or removes a breakpoint.
List enumerations	F11	Provides a drop-down list of all enumerations available in the system.
List reserved words	Shift+F2	Provides a drop-down list of all reserved words in X++.
List built-in functions	Shift+F4	Provides a drop-down list of all built-in functions available in X++.
Run an editor script	Alt+R	Lists all available editor scripts and lets you select one to execute (such as Send to mail recipient).
Open the Label Editor	Ctrl+Alt+Spacebar	Opens the Label Editor and searches for the selected text.

Action	Shortcut	Description
Show parameter information or IntelliSense list members	Ctrl+Spacebar	Shows parameter information as a ScreenTip or shows members in a drop-down list.
Go to implementation (drill down in code)	Ctrl+Shift+Spacebar	Goes to the implementation of the selected method. Highly useful for fast navigation.
Go to the next method	Ctrl+Tab	Sets focus on the next method in the editor.
Go to the previous method	Ctrl+Shift+Tab	Sets focus on the previous method in the editor.
Enable block selection	Alt+O	Enables block selection, instead of the default line selection.

Editor Scripts

The X++ code editor contains a set of editor scripts that you can invoke by clicking the Script button on the X++ Code Editor toolbar or by pressing Alt+R. Editor scripts provide functionality such as the following:

- Send to mail recipient.
- Send to file.
- Comment or uncomment code.
- Check out element, if version control is enabled.
- Generate code for standard code patterns.
- Open the AOT for the element that owns the method.

> **Note** Code generation allows you to create, in a matter of minutes, a new class with the right constructor method and the right encapsulation of member variables by using *parm* methods. *Parm* methods (*parm* is short for "parameter") are used as simple property getters/setters on classes. Naturally, code generation is carried out in accordance with X++ best practices.

The list of editor scripts is extendable. You can create your own scripts by adding new methods to the *EditorScripts* class.

Label Editor

The term *label* in Dynamics AX simply refers to a localizable text resource. Text resources are used throughout the product as messages to the user, form control labels, column headers, Help text in the status bar, captions on forms, and text on Web forms, to name just a few places. Labels are localizable, meaning that they can be translated into most languages. Because the space requirement for displaying text resources typically depends on the language, you might fear that the actual user interface must be manually localized as well. However, with IntelliMorph technology, the user interface is dynamically rendered and honors any space requirements imposed by localization.

The technology behind the label system is simple. All text resources are kept in a Unicode-based label file that must have a three-letter identifier. The label file is located in the application folder (Program Files\Microsoft Dynamics AX\50\Application\Appl\Standard) and follows this naming convention:

Ax<Label file identifier><Locale>.ALD

The following are two examples, the first showing U.S. English and the second a Danish label file:

Axsysen-us.ALD

Axtstda.ALD

Each text resource in the label file has a 32-bit integer label ID, label text, and an optional label description. The structure of the label file is very simple:

@*<Label file identifier><Label ID> <Label text>*

[*Label description*]

Figure 3-12 shows an example of a label file.

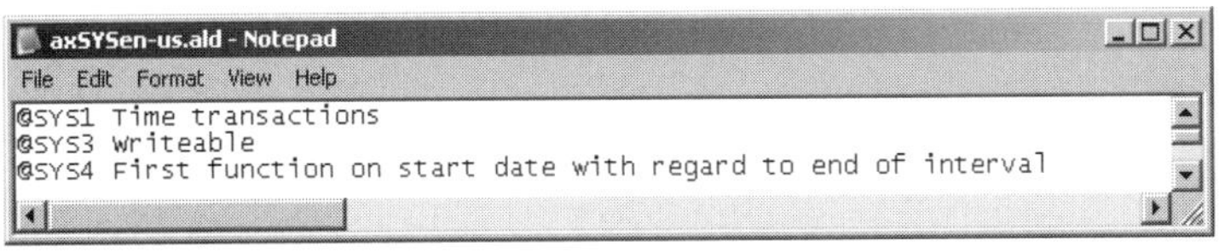

FIGURE 3-12 Label file opened in Microsoft Notepad showing a few labels from the en-us label file

This simple structure allows for localization outside Dynamics AX using third-party tools.

After the localized label files are in place, the user can choose a language in the Options dialog box. When the language is changed, the user must close and restart the Dynamics AX client.

You can create new label files by using the Label File Wizard, which you access from the Microsoft Dynamics AX drop-down menu by clicking Tools\Development Tools\Wizards\Label File Wizard. The wizard guides you through the steps for adding a new label file or a new language to an existing label file. After you run the wizard, the label file is ready to use.

> **Note** You can use any combination of three letters when naming a label file, and you can use any label file from any layer. A common misunderstanding is that the label file identifier must be the same as the layer in which it is used. This misunderstanding is caused by the Microsoft label file identifiers. Dynamics AX ships with a SYS layer and a label file named SYS; service packs contain a SYP layer and a label file named SYP. This naming standard was chosen because it is simple, easy to remember, and easy to understand. Dynamics AX doesn't impose any limitations on the label file name.

The following are tips for working with label files:

- When naming a label file, choose a three-letter ID that has a high chance of being unique, such as your company's initials. Don't choose the name of the layer, such as VAR or USR. Eventually, you'll likely merge two separately developed features into the same installation, a task that will be more difficult if the label files collide.
- Feel free to reference labels in the Microsoft-provided label files, but avoid making changes to labels in these label files, because they are updated with each new version of Dynamics AX.

Creating a New Label

You use the Label Editor to create new labels. You can start it using any of the following procedures:

- Clicking Tools\Development Tools\Label\Label Editor from the Microsoft Dynamics AX drop-down menu
- Clicking the Lookup Label/Text button on the X++ code editor toolbar
- Clicking the Lookup button on text properties in the property sheet

The Label Editor (shown in Figure 3-13) allows you to find existing labels. Reusing a label is often preferable to creating a new one. You can create a new label by pressing Ctrl+N or by clicking the New button.

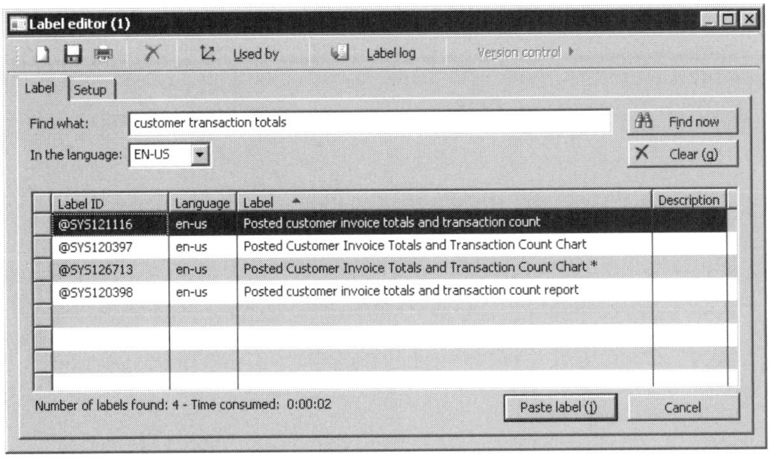

FIGURE 3-13 Label Editor

In addition to allowing you to find and create new labels, the Label Editor can also show where a label is used. It also logs any changes to each label.

The following are tips to consider when creating and reusing labels:

- When reusing a label, make sure that the label meaning is what you intend it to be in all languages. Some words are homonyms, meaning words that have many meanings, and they naturally translate into many different words in other languages. For example, the English word *can* is both a verb and a noun. The description column describes the intended meaning of the label.
- When creating new labels, make sure to use complete sentences or other stand-alone words or phrases in each label. Don't construct complete sentences by concatenating labels with one or few words, because the order of words in a sentence differs from one language to another.

Referencing Labels from X++

In the MorphX design environment, labels are referenced in the format @*<LabelFileIdentifier>* *<LabelID>*. If you don't want a label reference to automatically convert to the label text, you can use the *literalStr* function. When a placeholder is needed to display the value of a variable, you can use the *strFmt* function and a string containing %*n*, where *n*> = 1. Placeholders can also be used within labels. The following code shows a few examples.

```
// prints: Time transactions
print "@SYS1";

// prints: @SYS1
print literalStr("@SYS1");

// prints: Microsoft Dynamics is a Microsoft brand
print strFmt("%1 is a %2 brand", "Microsoft Dynamics", "Microsoft");
```

The following are some best practices to consider when referencing labels from X++:

- You should always create user interface text by using a label. When referencing labels from X++ code, use double quotation marks.
- You should never create system text such as file names by using a label. When referencing system text from X++ code, use single quotation marks. You can place system text in macros to make it reusable.

Using single and double quotation marks to differentiate between system text and user interface text allows the Best Practices tool to find and report any hard-coded user interface text. The Best Practices tool is described in depth later in this chapter.

Visual Form Designer and Visual Report Designer

MorphX has two visual designers, one for forms and one for reports, that allow you to drag controls onto the design surface in WYSIWYG fashion. IntelliMorph determines the actual position of the controls, so you can't place them precisely.

You can override these layout restrictions by changing property values, such as Top, Left, Height, and Width, from Auto to a fixed value, allowing the visual designers to lay out the controls. However, doing so interferes with the automated layout attempted by IntelliMorph, which means that there is no guarantee that your forms and reports will display well when translated, configured, secured, and personalized.

It is a best practice to let IntelliMorph control all the layout. (More detailed information about IntelliMorph is in Chapter 13, "Configuration and Security.") Most forms and reports that ship with Dynamics AX are designed by using the AOT. When the visual designer is opened, a tree structure of the design is displayed, making it fairly simple to add new controls to the design. You can either drag fields or field groups from the data source to the design or right-click the design and choose New Control.

> **Note** IntelliMorph and MorphX treat form and report designs as hierarchical structures. A control can be next to another control or inside a group control. This arrangement makes a lot of sense for business applications. If you require controls to be on top of one another, you must use absolute pixel positions. The order of the controls in the AOT mandates the z-order—that is, the order in which controls are virtually stacked in the display.

You can use a Report Wizard, accessed from the Microsoft Dynamics AX drop-down menu at Tools\Development Tools\Wizards, to help you create reports. The wizard guides you through the process step by step, allowing you to specify data sources, sorting, grouping, layout, and other settings before producing a report in the AOT. You can read more about developing reports in Chapter 11, "Reporting in Dynamics AX."

Visual Form Designer

The designers can be helpful tools for learning how the IntelliMorph layout scheme works. If you have the Visual Form Designer open when you start designing a form, you immediately see what the form will look like, even when it is modified in the AOT. In fact, after creating a few forms, you'll probably feel so confident of the power of IntelliMorph and the effectiveness of designing forms in the AOT that you'll only rarely use the Visual Form Designer.

You open the Visual Form Designer by right-clicking a form's design in the AOT and selecting Edit. The designer is shown in design mode in Figure 3-14. Next to the form is a toolbar with all the available controls, which can be dragged onto the form's surface. You can also see the property sheet showing the selected control's properties.

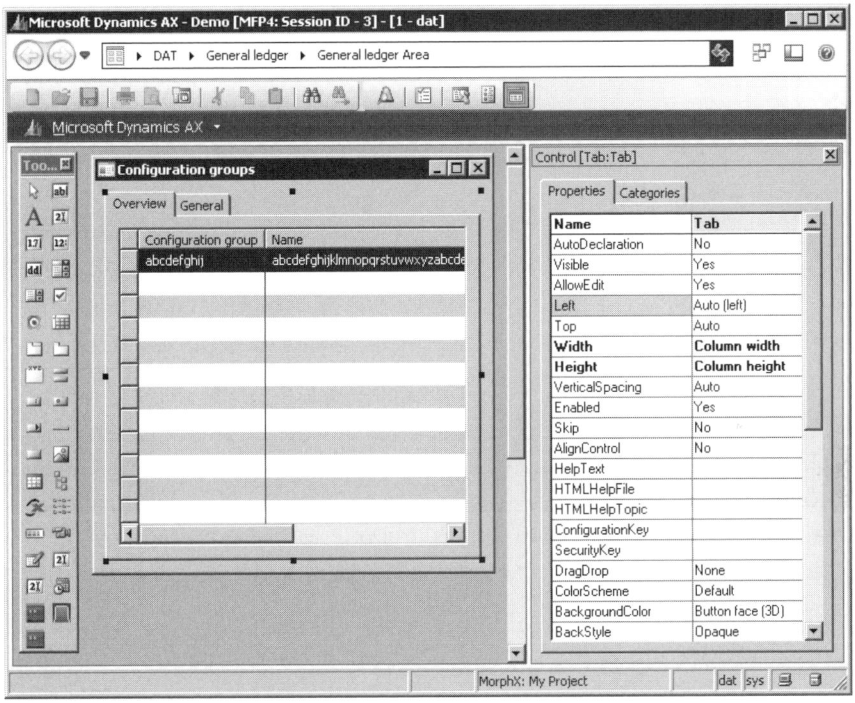

FIGURE 3-14 Visual Form Designer

One interesting form that overrides IntelliMorph is the form *tutorial_Form_freeform*. Figure 3-15 shows how a scanned bitmap of a payment form is used as a background image for the form, and the controls positioned where data entry is needed.

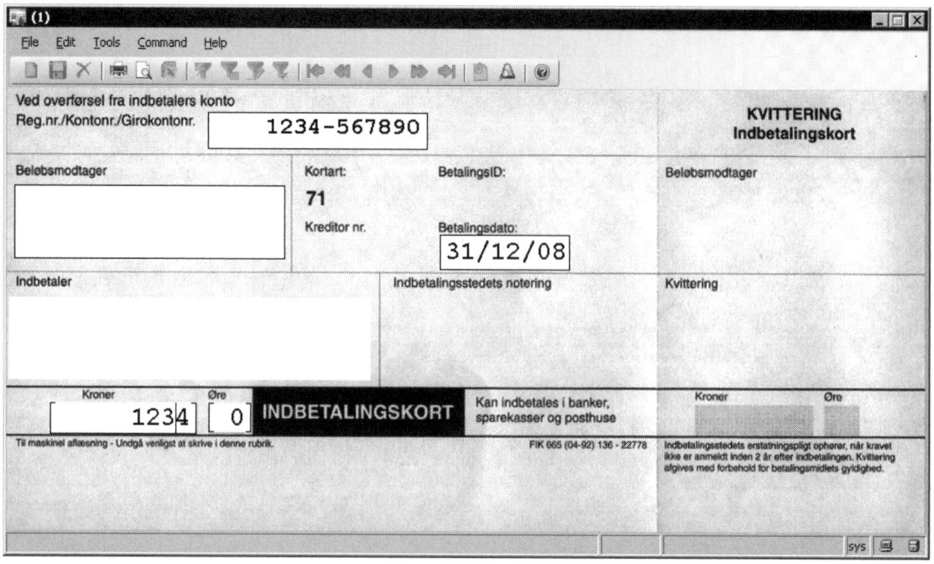

FIGURE 3-15 Nonstandard form that uses a bitmap background

Visual Report Designer

The majority of MorphX reports fall into two categories—internal and external. Requirements for reports used internally in a company are often more relaxed than requirements for external reports. External reports are often part of the company's face to the outside world. An invoice report is a classic example of an external report.

Leveraging the features of IntelliMorph, internal reports typically follow an autodesign that allows the consumer of the report to add and remove columns from the report and control its orientation, font, and font size.

External reports typically use a generated design, which effectively overrides IntelliMorph. So for external reports, the Visual Report Designer is clearly preferable. Often, external reports are printed on preprinted paper containing, for example, the company's letterhead, so the ability to easily control the exact position of each control is essential.

You create a generated design from an autodesign by right-clicking a design node of a report in the AOT and selecting Generate Design. You can open the Visual Report Designer by right-clicking a generated design and selecting Edit. As shown in Figure 3-16, each control can be moved freely, and new controls can be added.

Notice the zoom setting in the lower-right corner of Figure 3-16. This setting allows you to get a close-up view of the report and, with a steady hand, position each control exactly where you want it.

The rendering subsystem of the report engine can print only generated designs because it requires all controls to have fixed positions. If a report has only an autodesign, the report engine generates a design in memory before printing.

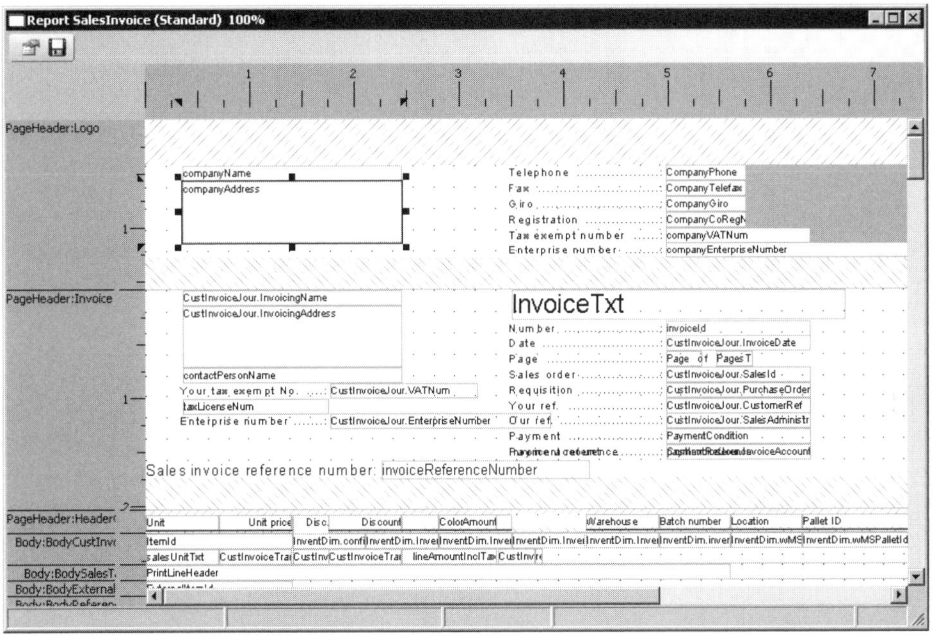

FIGURE 3-16 Visual Report Designer

Code Compiler

Whenever you make a change to X++ code, you must recompile, just as you would in any other development language. You start the recompile by pressing F7 in the X++ code editor. Your code also recompiles whenever you close the editor or save a dirty element.

The compiler also produces a list of the following information:

- **Compiler errors** These prevent code from compiling and should be fixed as soon as possible.
- **Compiler warnings** These typically indicate that something is wrong in the implementation. See Table 3-4, later in this section, for a list of compiler warnings. Compiler warnings can and should be addressed. Check-in attempts with compiler warnings are rejected.
- **Tasks (also known as to-dos)** The compiler picks up single-line comments that start with TODO. These comments can be useful during development for adding reminders, but you should use them only in cases in which implementation can't be completed.

For example, you might use a to-do comment when you're waiting for a check-in from another developer. You should avoid using to-do comments just to postpone work. For a developer, there is nothing worse than debugging an issue at a customer site and finding a to-do comment indicating that the issue was already known but overlooked.

> **Note** Unlike other languages, X++ requires that you compile only code you've modified. This is because the intermediate language the compiler produces is persisted along with the X++ code and metadata. Of course, your changes can require other methods consuming your code to be changed and recompiled if, for example, you rename a method or modify its parameters. If the consumers are not recompiled, a run-time error is thrown when they are invoked. This means that you can execute your business application even when compile errors exist, as long as you don't use the code that can't compile. You should always compile the entire AOT when you consider your changes complete, and you should fix any compilation errors found.

- **Best practice deviations** The Best Practices tool carries out more complex validations. See the section "Best Practices Tool" later in this chapter for more information.

The Compiler Output dialog box provides access to everything reported during compilation, as shown in Figure 3-17. Each category of findings has a dedicated tab: Status, Errors And Warnings, Best Practices, and Tasks. Each tab contains the same information for each issue that the compiler detects—a description of the issue and its location. For example, the Status tab shows a count of the detected issues.

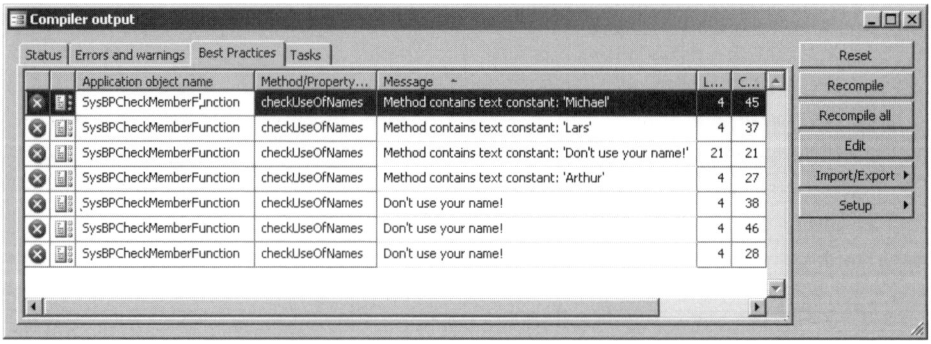

FIGURE 3-17 Compiler Output dialog box

You can export compile results. This capability is useful if you want to share the list of issues with team members. The exported file is an HTML file that can be viewed in Microsoft Internet Explorer or re-imported into the Compiler Output dialog box in another Dynamics AX session.

In the Compiler Output dialog box, click Setup and then click Compiler to define the types of issues that the compiler should report. Compiler warnings are grouped into four levels, as shown in Table 3-4.

TABLE 3-4 Compiler Warnings

Warning Message	Level
Break statement found outside legal context	1
The new method of a derived class does not call super()	1
The new method of a derived class may not call super()	1
Function never returns a value	1
Not all paths return a value	1
Assignment/comparison loses precision	1
Unreachable code	2
Empty compound statement	3
Class names should start with an uppercase letter	4
Member names should start with a lowercase letter	4

Dynamics AX SDK

Constructing quality software has become a daunting task in the 21st century. Many new competencies are expected of the developer, and mastering them fully and at all times is nearly impossible. Today you must write code conforming to many technical requirements, including security, localization, internationalization, customization, performance, accessibility, reliability, scalability, compatibility, supportability, interoperability, and so on. The list seems to grow with each software revision, and keeping up with all of these competencies is increasingly difficult.

Microsoft Dynamics AX 2009 includes a software development kit (SDK) that explains how to satisfy these requirements when you use MorphX. You can access the SDK from the application Help menu under Developer Help. We highly recommend that you read the Developer Help section—it's not just for novices but also for experienced developers, who will find that the content has been extensively revised for Dynamics AX 2009. The SDK is frequently refreshed with new content, so you might want to check it often on MSDN.

Among other critical information, the Developer Help section of the SDK includes an important discussion on conforming to best practices in Dynamics AX. The motivation for conforming to best practices should be obvious to anyone. Constructing code that follows proven standards and patterns can't guarantee a project's success, but it certainly minimizes the risk of failure. To ensure your project's success, you should learn, conform to, and advocate best practices within your group.

The following are a few benefits of following best practices:

- You avoid less-than-obvious pitfalls. Following best practices helps you avoid many obstacles, even those that surface only in border scenarios that would otherwise be difficult and time consuming to detect and test. Using best practices allows you to leverage the combined experiences of Dynamics AX expert developers.

- The learning curve is flattened. When you perform similar tasks in a standard way, you are more comfortable in an unknown area of the application. Consequently, adding new resources to a project is more cost efficient, and downstream consumers of the code are able to make changes more readily.
- You are making a long-term investment. Code that conforms to standards is less likely to require rework during an upgrade process, whether you're upgrading to Dynamics AX 2009, installing service packs, or upgrading to future releases.
- You are more likely to ship on time. Most of the problems you face when implementing a solution in Dynamics AX have been solved at least once before. Choosing a proven solution results in faster implementation and less regression. You can find solutions to known problems in both the Developer Help section of the SDK and the code base.

Best Practices Tool

A powerful supplement to the best practices discussion in the SDK is the Best Practices tool. This tool is the MorphX version of a static code analysis tool, similar to FxCop for the Microsoft .NET Framework and PREfix and PREfast for C and C++. The Best Practices tool is embedded in the compiler, and the results are located on the Best Practices tab of the Compiler Output dialog box.

The purpose of static code analysis is to automatically detect defects in the code. The longer a defect exists, the more costly it becomes to fix—a bug found in the design phase is much cheaper to correct than a bug in shipped code running at several customer sites. The Best Practices tool allows any developer to run an analysis of his or her code and application model to ensure that it conforms to a set of predefined rules. Developers can run analysis during development, and they should always do so before implementations are tested.

The Best Practices tool displays deviations from the best practice rules, as shown in Figure 3-17. Double-clicking a line on the Best Practices tab opens the X++ code editor on the violating line of code.

Understanding Rules

The Best Practices tool includes about 350 rules, a small subset of the best practices mentioned in the SDK. You can define the best practice rules that you want to run in the Best Practice Parameters dialog box: from the Microsoft Dynamics AX drop-down menu, click Tools\Options and then the Best Practices button.

> **Note** You must set the compiler error level to 4 if you want best practice rule violations to be reported. To turn off the Best Practices tool, click Tools\Options\Compiler, and then set the diagnostic level to less than 4.

The best practice rules are divided into categories. By default, all categories are turned on, as shown in Figure 3-18.

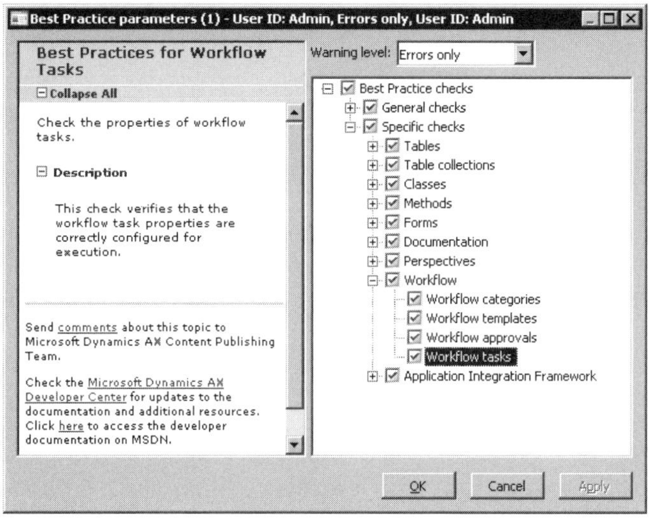

FIGURE 3-18 Best Practice Parameters dialog box

The best practice rules are divided into three levels of severity:

- **Errors** The majority of the rules focus on errors. Any check-in attempt with a best practice error is rejected. You must take all errors seriously and fix them as soon as possible.
- **Warnings** Follow a 95/5 rule for warnings. This means that you should treat 95 percent of all warnings as errors; the remaining 5 percent constitute exceptions to the rule. You should provide valid explanations in the design document for all warnings you choose to ignore.
- **Information** In some situations, your implementation might have a side effect that isn't obvious to you or the user (e.g., if you're assigning a value to a variable but you never use the variable again). These are typically reported as information messages.

Suppressing Errors and Warnings

The Best Practices tool allows you to suppress errors and warnings. A suppressed best practice deviation is reported as information. This gives you a way to identify the deviation as reviewed and accepted. To identify a suppressed error or warning, place a line containing the following text just before the deviation.

```
//BP Deviation Documented
```

Only a small subset of the best practice rules can be suppressed. Use the following guidelines for selecting which rules to suppress:

- Where exceptions exist that are impossible to detect automatically, you should examine each error to ensure the correct implementation. Dangerous APIs are often responsible for such exceptions. A dangerous API is an API that can compromise a system's security when used incorrectly. If a dangerous API is used, a suppressible error is reported. You are allowed to use some so-called dangerous APIs when you take certain precautions, such as using code access security. You can suppress the error after you apply the appropriate mitigations.
- About 5 percent of all warnings are false positives and can be suppressed. Note that only warnings caused by actual code can be suppressed, not warnings caused by metadata.

After you set up the best practices, the compiler automatically runs the best practices check whenever an element is compiled. The results are displayed on the Best Practices tab in the Compiler Output dialog box.

Adding Custom Rules

The X++ Best Practices tool allows you to create your own set of rules. The classes used to check for rules are named *SysBPCheck<ElementKind>*. You call the *init*, *check*, and *dispose* methods once for each node in the AOT for the element being compiled.

One of the most interesting classes is *SysBPCheckMemberFunction*, which is called for each piece of X++ code whether it is a class method, form method, macro, or other method. For example, if developers don't want to include their names in the source code, you can implement a best practice check by creating the following method on the *SysBPCheckMemberFunction* class.

```
protected void checkUseOfNames()
{
    #Define.MyErrorCode(50000)
    container devNames = ["Arthur", "Lars", "Michael"];
    int i;
    int j;
    int pos;
    str line;
    int lineLen;

    for (i=scanner.lines(); i; i--)
    {
        line = scanner.sourceLine(i);
        lineLen = strlen(line);
        for (j=conlen(devNames); j; j--)
        {
```

```
                pos = strscan(line, conpeek(devNames, j), 1, lineLen);
                if (pos)
                {
                    sysBPCheck.addError(#MyErrorCode, i, pos,
                        "Don't use your name!");
                }
            }
        }
    }
```

To enlist the rule, make sure to call the preceding method from the *check* method. Compiling this sample code results in the best practice errors shown in Table 3-5.

TABLE 3-5 Best Practice Errors in *checkUseOfNames*

Message	Line	Column
Method contains text constant: 'Arthur'	4	27
Don't use your name!	4	28
Method contains text constant: 'Lars'	4	37
Don't use your name!	4	38
Method contains text constant: 'Michael'	4	45
Don't use your name!	4	46
Method contains text constant: 'Don't use your name!'	20	59

In a real-world implementation, names of developers would probably be read from a file. Make sure to cache the names to prevent the compiler from going to the disk to read the names for each method being compiled.

Debugger

Like most development environments, MorphX features a debugger. The debugger is a stand-alone application, not part of the Dynamics AX shell like the rest of the tools mentioned in this chapter. As a stand-alone application, the debugger allows you to debug X++ in any of the Dynamics AX components in the following list:

- Microsoft Dynamics AX client
- Application Object Server (AOS)
- Enterprise Portal
- Business Connector

Using the Debugger

For the debugger to start, a breakpoint must be hit during execution of X++ code. You set breakpoints by using the X++ code editor in the Microsoft Dynamics AX client. The debugger starts automatically when any component hits a breakpoint.

You must enable debugging for each component as follows:

- In the Microsoft Dynamics AX client, click the Microsoft Dynamics AX drop-down menu, point to Tools and then Options. On the Development tab, select When Breakpoint in the Debug Mode list.
- For the AOS, open the Microsoft Dynamics AX Server Configuration utility under Start\Administrative Tools. Create a new configuration (if necessary), and select the check box labeled Enable Breakpoints To Debug X++ Code Running On This Server.
- For Batch jobs, open the Microsoft Dynamics AX Server Configuration utility under Start\Administrative Tools. Create a new configuration (if necessary), and select the check box labeled Enable Global Breakpoints To Debug X++ Code Running In Batch Jobs.
- For Enterprise Portal and Business Connector, open the Microsoft Dynamics AX Configuration utility under Start\Administrative Tools. Select one of two check boxes on the Developer tab: Enable User Breakpoints For Debugging Code Running In The Business Connector or Enable Global Breakpoints For Debugging Code Running In The Business Connector Or Client. The latter is useful for debugging incoming Web requests.

> **Caution** We recommend that you do not enable any of the debugging capabilities in a live environment. If you do, execution will stop when it hits a breakpoint, and users will experience a hanging client.

The debugger allows you to set and remove breakpoints by pressing F9. You can set a breakpoint on any line you want. If you set a breakpoint on a line without an X++ statement, however, the breakpoint will be triggered on the next X++ statement in the method. A breakpoint on the last brace will never be hit.

You can enable or disable a breakpoint by pressing Ctrl+F9. For a list of all breakpoints, press Shift+F9.

Breakpoints are persistent in the *SysBreakpoints* database table. Each developer has his or her own set of breakpoints. This means that your breakpoints are not cleared when you close Dynamics AX and that other Dynamics AX components can access them and break where you want them to.

Debugger Interface

The main window in the debugger initially shows the point in the code where a breakpoint was hit. You can control execution one step at a time while variables and other aspects are inspected. Figure 3-19 shows the debugger opened to a breakpoint with all the windows enabled.

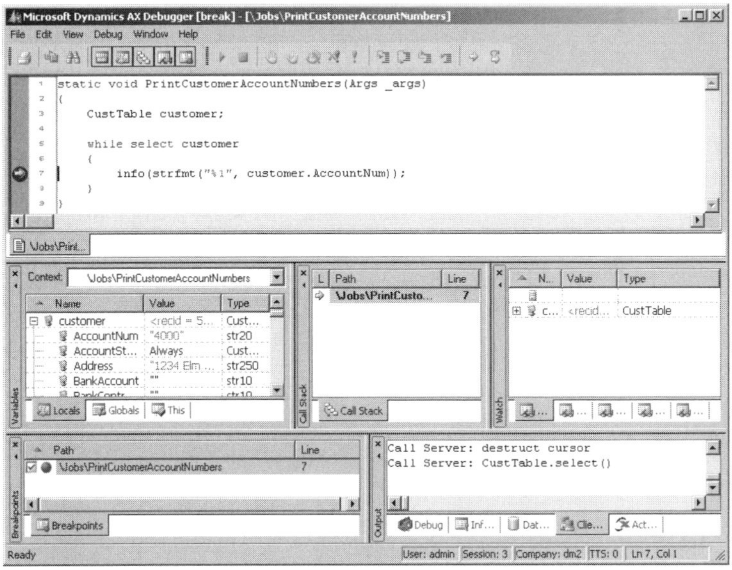

FIGURE 3-19 Debugger with all windows enabled

In the following subsections, we briefly describe the debugger's various windows and some of its other features.

Main Window

The main debugger window shows the current X++ code. Each variable has a ScreenTip that reveals its value. You can drag the next-statement pointer in the left margin. This pointer is particularly useful if the execution path isn't what you expected or if you want to repeat a step.

Variables Window

In this window, local, global, and member variables are shown. Local variables are variables in scope at the current execution point. Global variables are the global classes that are always instantiated: *Appl*, *Infolog*, *ClassFactory*, and *VersionControl*. Member variables make sense only on classes, and they show the class member variables.

The Variables window shows the name, value, and type of each variable. If a variable is changed during execution stepping, it is marked in red. Each variable is shown associated with a client or server icon. You can modify the value of a variable by double-clicking the value.

> **Tip** As a developer, you might want to provide more information in the value field than what is provided by default. For a class, the defaults are *New* and *Null*. You can change the defaults by overriding the *toString* method. If your class doesn't explicitly extend *object* (the base class of all classes), you must add a new method named *toString*, returning *str* and taking no parameters, to implement this functionality.

Call Stack Window

The Call Stack window shows the code path followed to arrive at a particular execution point. Clicking a line in the Call Stack window opens the code in the Code window and updates the local Variables window. A client or server icon indicates the tier on which the code is executed.

Watch Window

In the Watch window, you can inspect variables without the scope limitations of the Variables window. You can drag a variable here from the Code window or the Variables window.

The Watch window shows the name, value, and type of the variables. Five different Watch windows are available. You can use these to group the variables you're watching in the way that you prefer.

Breakpoints Window

The Breakpoints window lists all your breakpoints. You can delete, enable, and disable the breakpoints via this window.

Output Window

The Output window shows the traces that are enabled and the output sent to the Infolog application framework, which we introduced in Chapter 1. The Output window includes the following pages:

- **Debug** You can instrument your X++ code to trace to this page by using the *printDebug* static method on the *Debug* class.
- **Infolog** This page contains messages in the queue for the Infolog.
- **Database, Client/Server, and ActiveX Trace** Any traces enabled on the Development tab in the Options dialog box appear on these pages.

Status Bar

The status bar at the bottom of the debugger offers the following important context information:

- **Current user** The ID of the user who is logged on to the system. This information is especially useful when you are debugging incoming Web requests.
- **Current session** The ID of the session on the AOS.
- **Current company accounts** The ID of the current company accounts.
- **Transaction level** The current transaction level. When reaching zero, the transaction is committed.

Debugger Shortcut Keys

Table 3-6 lists the most important shortcut keys available in the debugger.

TABLE 3-6 Debugger Shortcut Keys

Action	Shortcut	Description
Run	F5	Continue execution
Stop debugging	Shift+F5	Break execution
Step over	F10	Step over next statement
Run to cursor	Ctrl+F10	Continue execution but break at the cursor's position
Step into	F11	Step into next statement
Step out	Shift+F11	Step out of method
Toggle breakpoint	Shift+F9	Insert or remove breakpoint
Variables window	Ctrl+Alt+V	Open or close Variables window
Call Stack window	Ctrl+Alt+C	Open or close Call Stack window
Watch window	Ctrl+Alt+W	Open or close Watch window
Breakpoints window	Ctrl+Alt+B	Open or close Breakpoints window
Output window	Ctrl+Alt+O	Open or close Output window

Visio Reverse Engineering Tool

Dynamics AX allows you to generate Visio models from existing metadata. Considering the amount of metadata available in Dynamics AX 2009 (more than 30,000 elements and more than 7 million lines of text when exported), it's practically impossible to get a clear view of how the elements relate to each other just by using the AOT. The Visio Reverse Engineering tool is a great aid when you need to visualize metadata.

Note You must have Office Visio 2003 or later installed to use the Visio Reverse Engineering tool.

The Reverse Engineering tool can generate a Unified Modeling Language (UML) data model, a UML object model, or an entity relationship data model, including all elements from a private or shared project. To open the tool, right-click a project or a perspective, point to Add-Ins, and then click Reverse Engineer. You can also open the tool by selecting Reverse Engineer from the Development Tools menu. In the dialog box shown in Figure 3-20, you must specify a file name and model type.

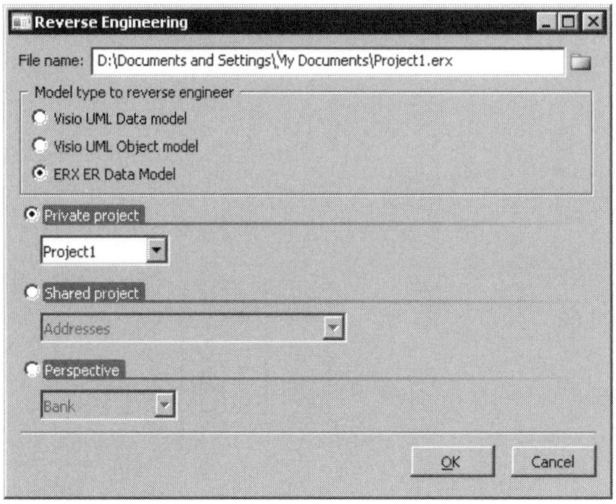

FIGURE 3-20 Visio Reverse Engineering dialog box

When you click OK, the tool uses the metadata for all elements in the project to generate a Visio document that opens automatically in Visio. You can drag elements from the Visio Model Explorer onto the drawing surface, which is initially blank. Any relationship between two elements is automatically shown.

UML Data Model

When generating a UML data model, the Reverse Engineering tool looks for tables in the project. The UML model contains a class for each table and view in the project and its attributes and associations. Figure 3-21 shows a class diagram with the *CustTable* (Customers), *InventTable* (Inventory Items), *SalesTable* (Sales Order Header), and *SalesLine* (Sales Order Line) tables. To simplify the diagram, some attributes have been removed.

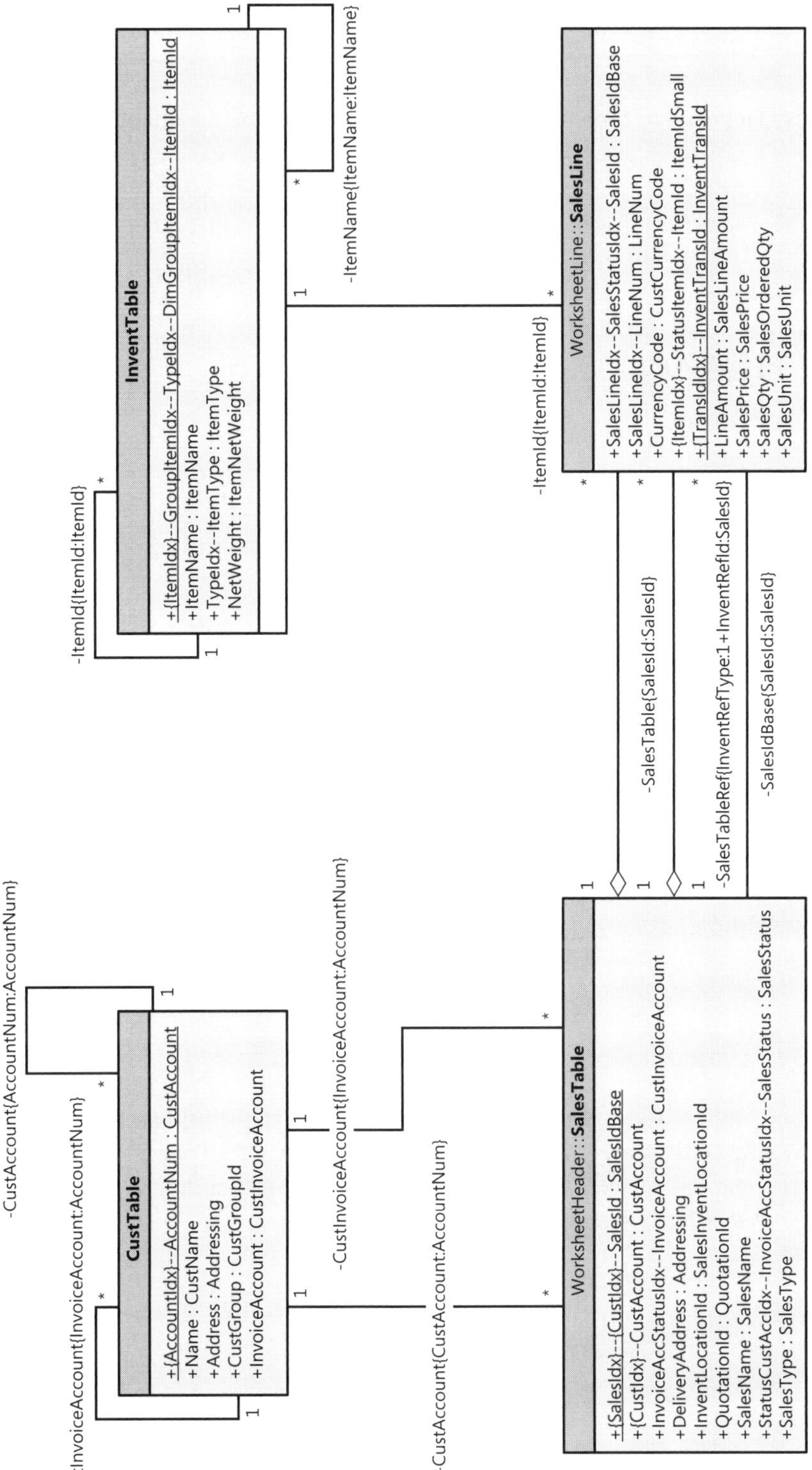

FIGURE 3-21 UML data model diagram

The UML model also contains referenced tables and all extended data types, base enumerations, and X++ data types. You can include these items in your diagrams without having to run the Reverse Engineering tool again.

Fields in Dynamics AX are generated as UML attributes. All attributes are marked as public because of the nature of fields in Dynamics AX. Each attribute also shows the type. The primary key field is underlined. If a field is a part of one or more indexes, the names of the indexes are prefixed to the field name; if the index is unique, the index name is noted in brackets.

Relationships in Dynamics AX are generated as UML associations. The aggregation property of the association is set based on two conditions in metadata:

- If the relationship is validating (the validate property is set to Yes), the aggregation property is set to shared. This is also known as UML aggregation, visualized by a white diamond.
- If a cascading delete action exists between the two tables, a composite association is added to the model. A cascading delete action ties the life span of two or more tables and is visualized by a black diamond.

The end name on associations is the name of the Dynamics AX relationship, and the names and types of all fields in the relationship appear in brackets.

UML Object Model

When generating an object model, the Reverse Engineering tool looks for Dynamics AX classes, tables, and interfaces in the project. The UML model contains a class for each Dynamics AX table and class in the project and an interface for each Dynamics AX interface. The UML model also contains attributes and operations, including return types, parameters, and the types of the parameters. Figure 3-22 shows an object model of the most important *RunBase* and *Batch* classes and interfaces in Dynamics AX. To simplify the view, some attributes and operations have been removed, and operation parameters are suppressed.

The UML model also contains referenced tables, classes and tables, and all extended data types, base enumerations, and X++ data types. You can include these elements in your diagrams without having to run the Reverse Engineering tool again.

Fields and member variables in Dynamics AX are generated as UML attributes. All fields are generated as public attributes, whereas member variables are generated as protected attributes. Each attribute also shows the type. Methods are generated as UML operations, including return type, parameters, and the types of the parameters.

The Reverse Engineering tool also picks up any generalizations (classes extending other classes), realizations (classes implementing interfaces), and associations (classes using each other). The associations are limited to references in member variables.

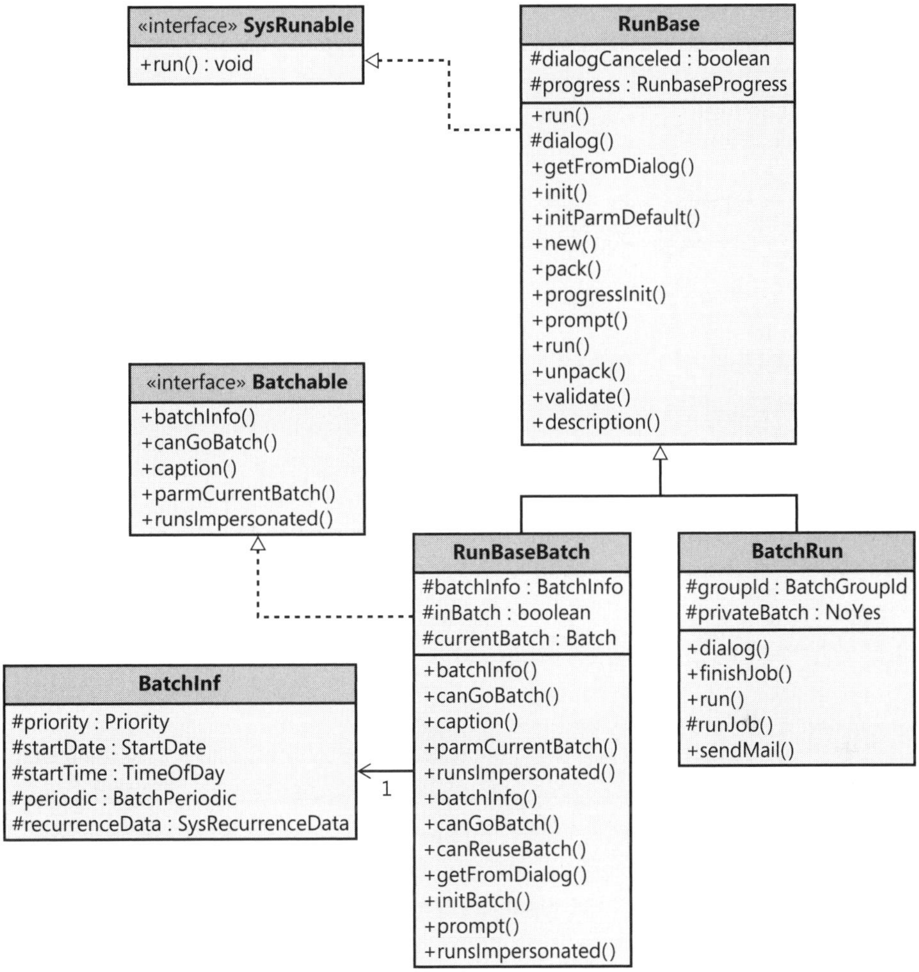

FIGURE 3-22 UML object model diagram

Note To get the names of operation parameters, you must reverse engineer in debug mode. The names are read from metadata only and placed into the stack when in debug mode. You can enable debug mode on the Development tab in the Options dialog box by selecting When Breakpoint in the Debug Mode list.

Entity Relationship Data Model

When generating an entity relationship data model, the Reverse Engineering tool looks for tables and views in the project. The entity relationship model contains an entity type for each AOT table in the project and attributes for each table's fields. Figure 3-23 shows an Entity Relationship Diagram (ERD) with the *CustTable* (Customers), *InventTable* (Inventory Items), *SalesTable* (Sales Order Header), and *SalesLine* (Sales Order Line) tables. To simplify the diagram, some attributes have been removed.

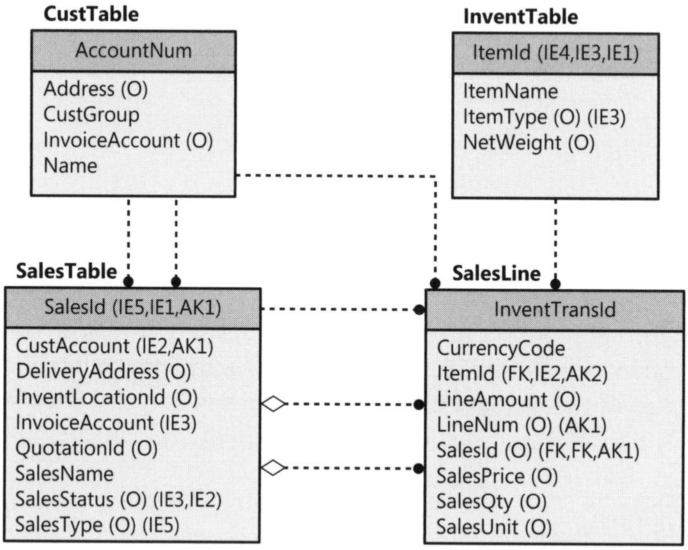

FIGURE 3-23 ERD using IDEF1X notation

Fields in Dynamics AX are generated as entity relationship columns. Columns can be foreign key (FK), alternate key (AK), inversion entry (IE), and optional (O). A foreign key column is used to identify a record in another table, an alternate key uniquely identifies a record in the current table, an inversion entry identifies zero or more records in the current table (these are typical of the fields in nonunique indexes), and optional columns don't require a value.

Relationships in Dynamics AX are generated as entity relationships. The *EntityRelationshipRole* property of the relationship in Dynamics AX is used as the foreign key role name of the relation in the entity relationship data model.

> **Note** The Reverse Engineering tool produces an ERX file. To work with the generated file in Visio, you must start Visio, create a new Database Model Diagram and select Database, and point to Import and then Import Erwin ERX file. Afterward you can drag relevant tables from the Tables And Views pane (available from the Database menu) to the diagram canvas.

Table Browser Tool

This small, helpful tool can be used in numerous scenarios. The Table Browser tool lets you see the records in a table without requiring you to build any user interface. This tool is useful when you're debugging, validating data models, and modifying or cleaning up data, to name just a few uses.

You can access the Table Browser tool from the Add-Ins submenu in the AOT on:

- Tables
- Tables listed as data sources in forms, reports, Web forms, and Web reports
- System tables listed in the AOT under System Documentation\Tables

> **Note** The Table Browser tool is implemented in X++. You can find it in the AOT under the name *SysTableBrowser*. It is a good example of how to bind the data source to a table at run time.

Figure 3-24 shows the Table Browser tool started from the *CustTable* table. In addition to the querying, sorting, and filtering capabilities provided by the grid control, the Table Browser tool allows you to type an SQL SELECT statement directly into the form using X++ *SELECT* statement syntax and see a visual display of the result set. This tool is a great way to try out complex SELECT statements. It fully supports grouping, sorting, aggregation, and field lists.

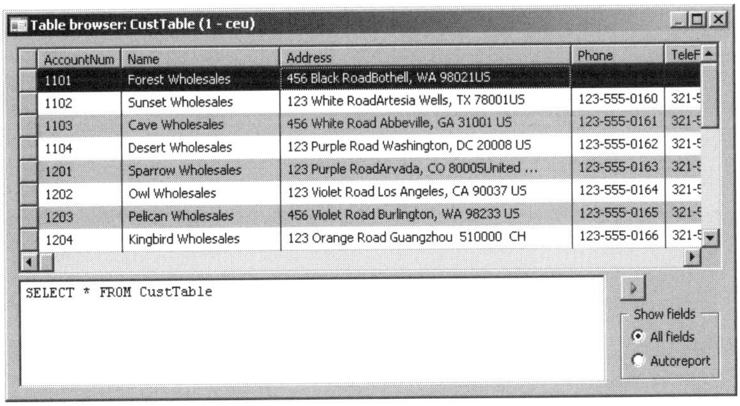

FIGURE 3-24 Table Browser tool, showing *CustTable* from demo data

The Table Browser tool also allows you to choose to see only the fields from the auto-report field group. These fields are printed in a report when the user clicks Print in a form with this table as a data source. Typically, these fields hold the most interesting information. This option can make it easier to find the values you're looking for in tables with many fields.

Note The Table Browser tool is just a normal form that uses IntelliMorph. It can't display fields for which the *visible* property is set to No or fields that the current user doesn't have access to.

Find Tool

Search is everything! The size of Dynamics AX applications calls for a powerful and effective search tool.

Tip You can use the Find tool to search for an example of how to use an API. Real examples can complement the examples found in the documentation.

You can start the Find tool, shown in Figure 3-25, from any node in the AOT by pressing Ctrl+F or by clicking Find on the context menu. The Find tool supports multiple selections in the AOT.

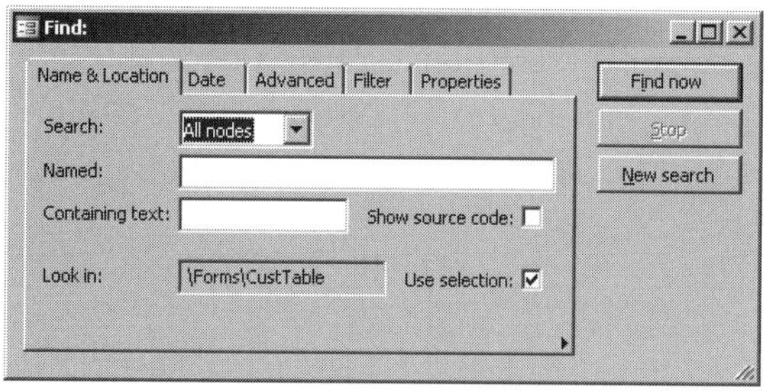

FIGURE 3-25 Find tool

The Name & Location tab defines what you're searching for and where to look:

- In Search, the menu options are Methods and All Nodes. When you choose All Nodes, the Properties tab appears.
- The Named text box limits the search to nodes with the name you specify.
- The Containing Text box specifies the text to look for in the method expressed as a regular expression.
- When you select the Show Source Code check box, results include a snippet of source code containing the match, making it easier to browse the results.
- By default, the Find tool searches the node (and its subnodes) selected in the AOT. If you change focus in the AOT while the Find tool is open, the Look In value is updated. This is quite useful if you want to search several nodes using the same criterion. You can disable this behavior by clearing the Use Selection check box.

In the Date tab, you specify additional ranges for your search, such as Modified Date and Modified By.

On the Advanced tab, you can specify more-advanced settings for your search, such as the layer to search, the size range of elements, the type of element, and the tier on which the element is set to run.

The Filter tab, shown in Figure 3-26, allows you to write a more complex query by using X++ and type libraries. The code written in the Source text box is the body of a method with the following profile.

```
boolean FilterMethod(str _treeNodeName,
                     str _treeNodeSource,
                     XRefPath _path,
                     ClassRunMode _runMode)
```

The example in Figure 3-26 uses the class *SysScannerClass* to find any occurrence of the *TTSAbort* X++ keyword. The scanner is primarily used to pass tokens into the parser during compilation. Here, however, it detects the use of a particular keyword. This tool is more accurate (though slower) than using a regular expression, because X++ comments don't produce tokens.

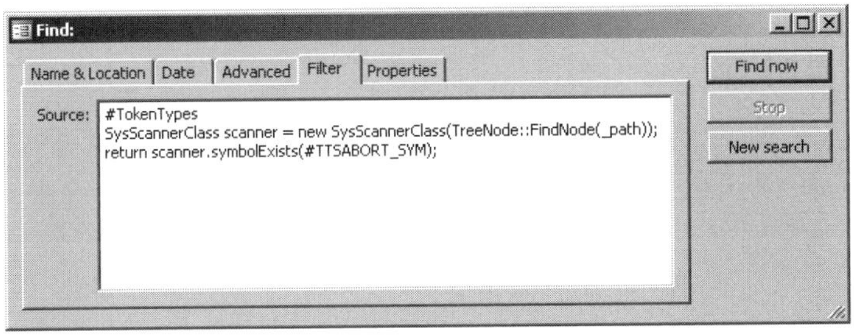

FIGURE 3-26 Filtering in the Find tool

The Properties tab appears when All Nodes is selected in the Search menu. You can specify a search range for any property. Leaving the range blank for a property is a powerful setting when you want to inspect properties: it matches all nodes, and the property value is added as a column in the results, as shown in Figure 3-27. The search begins when you click Find Now. The results appear at the bottom of the dialog box as they are found.

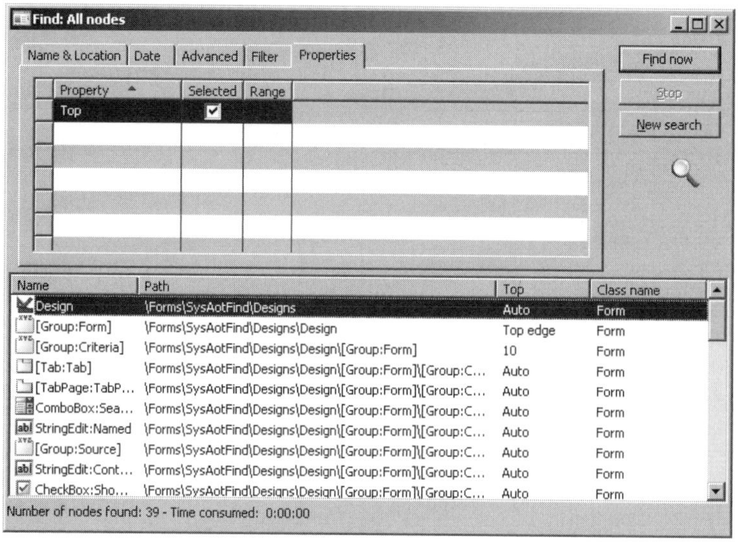

FIGURE 3-27 Search results in the Find tool

Double-clicking any line in the result set opens the X++ code editor with focus on the matched code example. When you right-click the lines in the result set, a context menu containing the Add-Ins menu opens.

Compare Tool

Several versions of the same element typically exist. These versions might emanate from various layers or revisions in version control, or they could be modified versions that exist in memory. Dynamics AX has a built-in Compare tool that highlights any differences between two versions of an element.

The comparison shows changes to elements, which can be modified in three ways:

- A metadata property can be changed.
- X++ code can be changed.
- The order of subnodes can be changed, such as the order of tabs on a form.

Starting the Compare Tool

You open the Compare tool by right-clicking an element and then clicking Compare on the Add-Ins submenu. A dialog box allows you to select the versions of the element you want to compare, as shown in Figure 3-28.

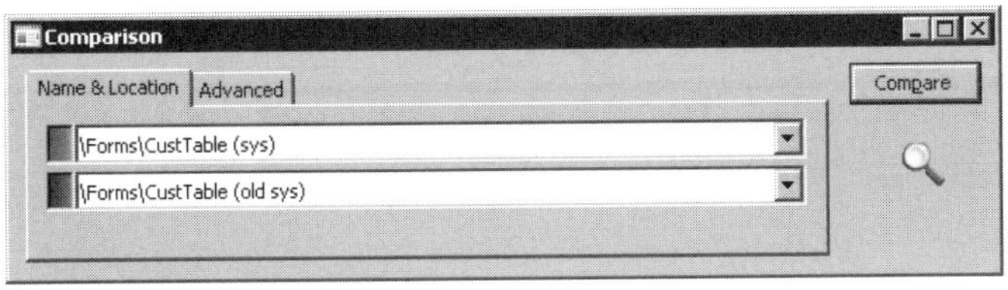

FIGURE 3-28 Comparison dialog box

The versions to choose from come from many sources. The following is a list of all possible types of versions:

- **Standard layered version types** These include sys, syp, gls, glp, hfx, sl1, sl2, sl3, bus, bup, var, vap, cus, cup, usr, usp.
- **Old layered version types (old sys, old syp, and so on)** If .aod files are present in the Old Application folder (located in Program Files\Microsoft Dynamics AX\50\Application\Appl\Standard\Old), elements from the files are available here. This allows you to compare an older version of an element with its latest version. See Chapter 1 for more information on layers. In Chapter 1, Figure 1-3 illustrates the components in the application model layering system.
- **Version control revisions (Version 1, Version 2, and so on)** You can retrieve any revision of an element from the version control system individually and use it for comparison. The version control system is explained later in this chapter.
- **Best practice washed version (Washed)** A few simple best practice issues can be resolved automatically by a best practice "wash." Selecting the washed version shows you how your implementation differs from best practices. To get the full benefit of this, select the Case Sensitive check box on the Advanced tab.
- **Export/import file (XPO)** Before you import elements, you can compare them with existing elements (which they overwrite during import). You can use the Compare tool during the import process (Command\Import) by selecting the Show Details check box in the Import dialog box and right-clicking any elements that appear in bold. Objects in bold already exist in the application; objects not in bold do not.
- **Upgraded version (Upgraded)** MorphX can automatically create a proposal for how a class should be upgraded. The requirement for upgrading a class arises during a version upgrade. The Create Upgrade Project step in the Upgrade Checklist automatically detects customized classes that conflict with new versions of the class. A class is conflicting when you've changed the original version of the class, and the publisher of the class has also changed the original version. MorphX constructs the proposal by merging your changes and the publisher's changes to the class. MorphX requires access to all three versions of the class—the original version in the Old Application folder, a version with your changes in the current layer in the Old Application folder, and a version with the publisher's changes in the same layer as the original. The installation program

ensures that the right versions are available in the right places during an upgrade. The conflict resolution is shown in Figure 3-29.

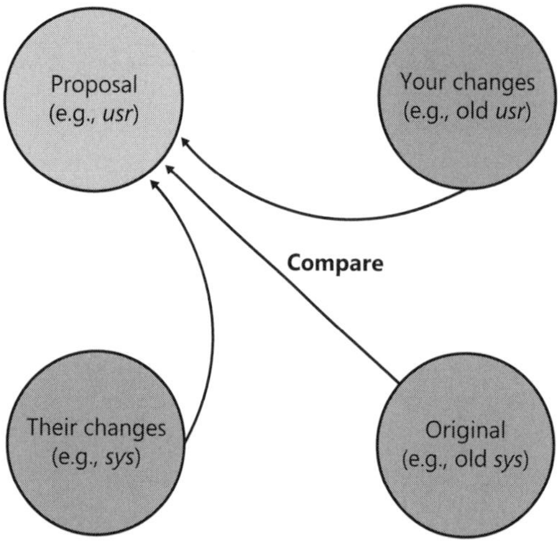

FIGURE 3-29 How the upgraded version proposal is created

> **Note** You can also compare two different elements. To do this, select two elements in the AOT, right-click, point to Add-Ins, and then click Compare.

Figure 3-30 shows the Advanced tab, on which you can specify comparison options.

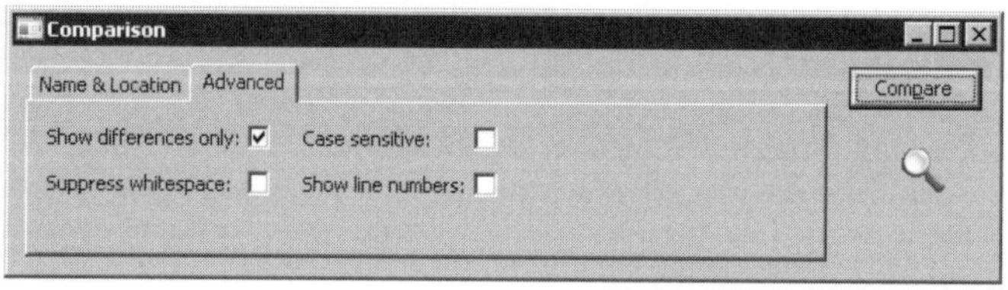

FIGURE 3-30 Comparison options on the Advanced tab

The comparison options shown in Figure 3-30 are described in the following list:

- **Show Differences Only** All equal nodes are suppressed from the view, making it easier to find the changed nodes. This option is selected by default.
- **Suppress Whitespace** White space, such as spaces and tabs, is suppressed into a single space when comparing. The Compare tool can ignore the amount of white space, just as the compiler does. This option is selected by default.
- **Case Sensitive** Because X++ is not case-sensitive, the Compare tool is also not case-sensitive by default. In certain scenarios, case sensitivity is required and must be

enabled, such as when you're using the best practice wash feature mentioned earlier in this section. The Case Sensitive option is not selected by default.

- **Show Line Numbers** The Compare tool can add line numbers to all displayed X++ code. This option is not selected by default but can be useful during an upgrade of large chunks of code.

Using the Compare Tool

After you choose elements and set parameters, you can start the comparison by clicking Compare. Results are displayed in a three-pane dialog box, as shown in Figure 3-31. The top pane is the element selection, the left pane is a tree structure resembling the AOT, and the right pane shows details of the tree selection.

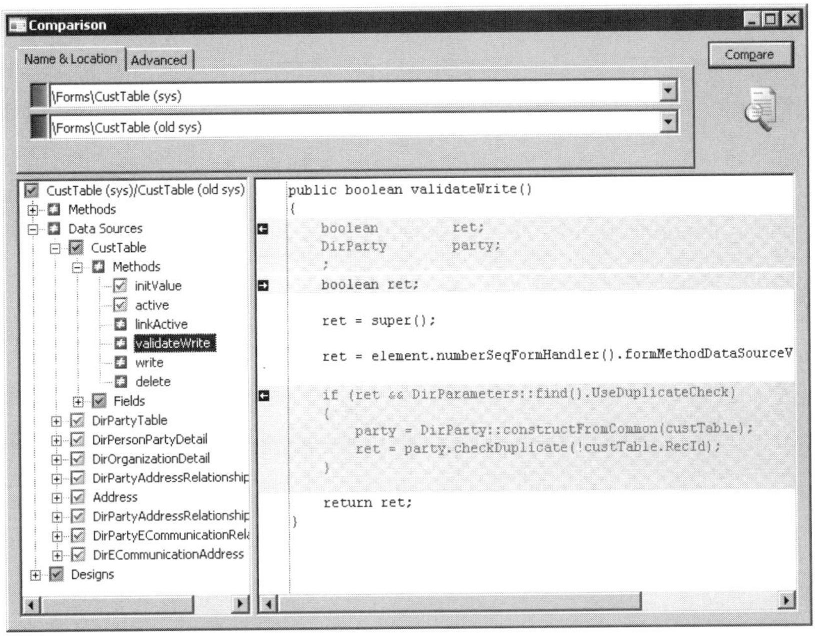

FIGURE 3-31 Comparison results

The icons in the tree structure indicate how each node has changed. A red or blue check mark indicates that the node exists only in a red or blue element. Red corresponds to the *sys* layer, and blue corresponds to the old sys layer. A gray check mark indicates that the nodes are identical but one or more subnodes are different. A not-equal-to symbol (≠) on a red and blue background indicates that the nodes are different in the two versions.

> **Note** Each node in the tree view has a context menu that provides access to the Add-Ins submenu and the Open New Window option. The Open New Window option provides an AOT view on any element, including old layer elements.

Details of the differences are shown in the right pane. Color coding is also used in this pane to highlight differences. If an element is editable, small action icons appear. These icons allow you to make changes to source, metadata, and nodes, which can save you time when performing an upgrade. A right or left arrow removes or adds the difference, and a bent arrow moves the difference to another position. These arrows always come in pairs, so you can see where the difference is moved to and from. An element is editable if it is from the current layer and checked out if a version control system is used.

Compare APIs

Although Dynamics AX uses the comparison functionality for development purposes only, the general comparison functionality can be used more widely. The available APIs allow you to compare and present differences in the tree structure or text representation of any type of entity.

The *Tutorial_CompareContextProvider* class shows how simple it is to compare business data by using these APIs and presents it by using the Compare tool. The tutorial consists of two parts:

- ***Tutorial_Comparable*** This class implements the *SysComparable* interface. Basically, it creates a text representation of a customer.
- ***Tutorial_CompareContextProvider*** This class implements the *SysCompareContext-Provider* interface. It provides the context for comparison. For example, it lists a *tutorial_Comparable* class for each customer, sets the default comparison options, and handles context menus.

Figure 3-32 shows a comparison of two customers, the result of running the tutorial.

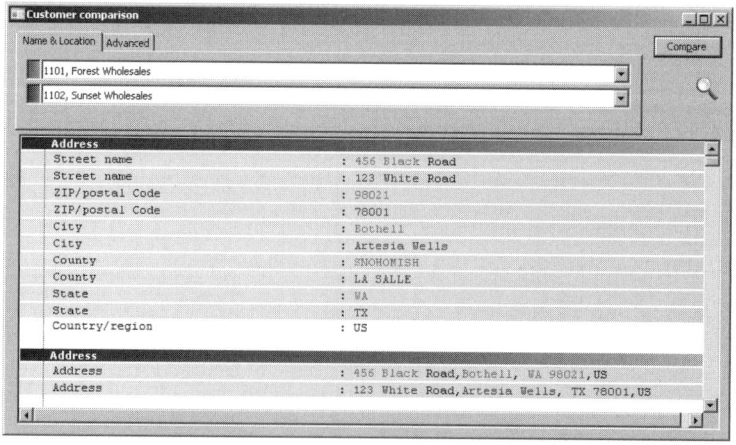

FIGURE 3-32 Result of comparing two customers using the Compare API

You can also use the line-by-line comparison functionality directly in X++. The static *run* method on the *SysCompareText* class, shown in the following code, takes two strings as parameters and returns a container that highlights differences in the two strings. You can also use a set of optional parameters to control the comparison.

```
public static container run(str _t1,
                            str _t2,
                            boolean _caseSensitive      = false,
                            boolean _suppressWhiteSpace = true,
                            boolean _lineNumbers        = false,
                            boolean _singleLine        = false,
                            boolean _alternateLines    = false)
```

Refer to the Microsoft Dynamics AX 2009 SDK for documentation of the classes.

Cross-Reference Tool

The concept of cross-references in Dynamics AX is simple. If an element uses another element, the reference is recorded. Cross-references allow you to determine which elements a particular element uses as well as which elements other elements are using. Dynamics AX provides the Cross-reference tool to access and manage cross-reference information.

You must update the Cross-reference tool regularly to ensure accuracy. The update typically takes several hours. The footprint in your database is about 1 gigabyte for the standard application.

You can update the Cross-reference tool by going to the Microsoft Dynamics AX drop-down menu and then pointing to Tools\Development Tools\Cross-reference\Periodic\Update. Updating the Cross-reference tool also compiles the entire AOT because the compiler emits cross-reference information.

Tip Keeping the Cross-reference tool up to date is important if you want to rely on its information. If you work in a shared development environment, you share cross-reference information with your team members. Updating the Cross-reference tool nightly is a good approach for a shared environment. If you work in a local development environment, you can keep the Cross-reference tool up to date by enabling cross-referencing when compiling. This option does slow down the compilation, however. Another option is to manually update cross-references for the elements in a project. You can do so by right-clicking the project, pointing to Add-Ins, pointing to Cross-reference, and then clicking Update.

In addition to the main cross-reference information, two smaller cross-reference subsystems exist:

- **Data model** This cross-reference subsystem stores information about relationships between tables. It is primarily used by the query form and the Reverse Engineering tool.
- **Type hierarchy** This cross-reference subsystem stores information about class and data type inheritance. It is used only in the Application Hierarchy Tree. The Application Hierarchy Tree is available from the Microsoft Dynamics AX drop-down menu, at Tools\Development Tools\Application Hierarchy Tree.

Further discussion of these tools is beyond the scope of this book. Refer to the Microsoft Dynamics AX 2009 SDK for more information on these subsystems and the tools that rely on them.

The cross-reference information the Cross-reference tool collects is quite complete. The following list shows the kinds of elements it cross-references. (Cross-reference information for elements followed by an asterisk is new in Dynamics AX 2009.) You can find the following list of cross-referenced elements and their values by opening the AOT, expanding the System Documentation node, and clicking Enums and then xRefKind.

BasicType
Class
ClassInstanceMethod
ClassStaticMethod
ClrType
ClrTypeMethod
ConfigurationKey
Dataset*
Enum
Enumerator
ExtendedType
Form*
Job*
Label
LicenseCode
Map
MapField
MapInstanceMethod
MapStaticMethod
Menu*
MenuItemAction
MenuItemDisplay
MenuItemOutput
Predefined (system functions)
Query*
Report*
SecurityKey
Table
TableField
TableIndex
TableInstanceMethod
TableStaticMethod
WebActionItem
WebDisplayContentItem
WebForm*
WebManagedContentItem*
WebMenu*
WebModule*
WebOutputContentItem
WebReport*
WebUrlItem

When the Cross-reference tool is updated, it scans all metadata and X++ code for references to elements of the kinds listed here.

> **Tip** It's a good idea to use intrinsic functions when referring to elements in X++ code. An intrinsic function can evaluate to either an element name or an ID. The intrinsic functions are named <*ElementKind*>Str or <*ElementKind*>Num, respectively. Using intrinsic functions provides two benefits: you have compile-time verification that the element you reference actually exists, and the reference is picked up by the Cross-reference tool. Also, there is no run-time overhead. An example follows.

```
// Prints ID of MyClass, such as 50001
print classNum(myClass);

// Prints "MyClass"
print classStr(myClass);

// No compile check or cross-reference
print "MyClass";
```

> See Chapter 15, "Reflection," for more information about intrinsic functions.

The primary function of the Cross-reference tool is to determine where a particular element is being used. Here are a couple of scenarios:

- You want to find usage examples. If the product documentation doesn't help, you can use the Cross-reference tool to find real implementation examples.
- You need to perform an impact analysis. If you're changing an element, you need to know which other elements are affected by your change.

To access usage information, right-click any element in the AOT, point to Add-Ins, point to Cross-reference, and then click Used By. If the option isn't available, either the element isn't used or that cross-reference hasn't been updated.

Figure 3-33 shows where the *prompt* method is used on the *RunBaseBatch* class.

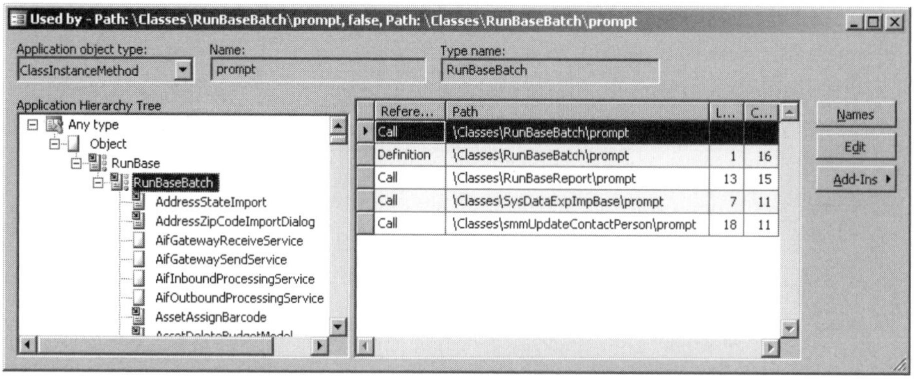

FIGURE 3-33 Cross-reference tool, showing where *RunBaseBatch.prompt* is used

When you view cross-references for a class method, the Application Hierarchy Tree is visible, allowing you to see whether the same method is used on a parent or subclass. For types that don't support inheritance, such as tables, table methods, and table fields, the Application Hierarchy Tree is hidden.

Version Control

The Version Control tool is a feature in MorphX that makes it possible to use a version control system, such as Microsoft Visual SourceSafe or Microsoft Visual Studio Team Foundation Server, to keep track of changes to elements in the AOT. The tool is accessible from several places: from the Microsoft Dynamics AX drop-down menu at Tools\Development Tools\Version Control, from toolbars in the AOT and X++ code editor, and from the context menu on elements in the AOT.

Using a version control system offers several benefits:

- **Revision history of all elements** All changes are captured along with a description of the change, making it possible to consult change history and retrieve old versions of an element.
- **Code quality enforcement** The implementation of version control in Dynamics AX enables a fully configurable quality bar for all check-ins. With the quality bar, all changes are verified according to coding practices. If the change doesn't meet the criteria, it is rejected. Microsoft uses the quality bar for all check-ins, which has helped raise the quality of X++ code to an unprecedented level. Microsoft developers cannot check in code with compiler errors, compile warnings, or best practice errors. In the final stages of development, tasks in code (to-dos) are also prohibited.

- **Isolated development** Each developer can have a local installation and make all modifications locally. When modifications are ready, they can be checked in and made available to consumers of the build. So a developer can rewrite fundamental areas of the system without causing any instability issues for others. Developers are also unaffected by any downtime of a centralized development server.

Even though using a version control system when developing is optional, we strongly recommend you consider one for any development project. Dynamics AX 2009 supports three version control systems: Visual SourceSafe 6.0 and Team Foundation Server, which are designed for large development projects, and MorphX VCS. MorphX VCS is designed for smaller development projects that previously couldn't justify the additional overhead that using a version control system server adds to the entire process. Table 3-7 shows a side-by-side comparison of the version control system options.

TABLE 3-7 Overview of Version Control Systems

	Classic MorphX (No Version Control)	MorphX VCS	Visual SourceSafe	Team Foundation Server
Application Object Servers required	1	1	1 per developer	1 per developer
Database servers required	1	1	1 per developer	1 per developer
Team server required	No	Optional	Yes	Yes
Build process required	No	No	Yes	Yes
Master file	AOD	AOD	XPOs	XPOs
Isolated development	No	No	Yes	Yes
Multiple check-out	N/A	No	Configurable	Configurable
Change description	No	Yes	Yes	Yes
Change history	No	Yes	Yes	Yes
Change list support (atomic check-in of a set of files)	N/A	No	No	Yes
Code quality enforcement	No	Configurable	Configurable	Configurable

The elements persisted in the version control server are file representations of the elements in the AOT. The file format used is the standard Dynamics AX export format (.xpo). Each .xpo file contains only one element.

There are no additional infrastructure requirements when you use MorphX VCS, which makes it a perfect fit for partners running many parallel projects. In such setups, each developer often works simultaneously on several projects, toggling between projects and returning to past projects. In these situations, the benefits of having change history are enormous. With just a few clicks, you can enable MorphX VCS to persist the changes in the business database. Although MorphX VCS provides many of the same capabilities as a version control server, it does have some limitations. For example, MorphX VCS does not provide any tools for maintenance, such as backup, archiving, or labeling.

In contrast, Visual SourceSafe and Team Foundation Server are designed for large projects in which many developers work together on the same project for an extended period of time (e.g., an independent software vendor building a vertical solution).

Figure 3-34 shows a typical deployment using Visual SourceSafe or Team Foundation Server, in which each developer locally hosts the AOS and the database. Each developer also needs a copy of all .xpo files. When a developer communicates with the version control server, the .xpo files are transmitted. A unique ID is required when the developer creates a new element or label. A Team Server, available as a Microsoft .NET Web service, is required to ensure uniqueness of IDs across all the local developers' environments. The Team Server is a component available with Dynamics AX.

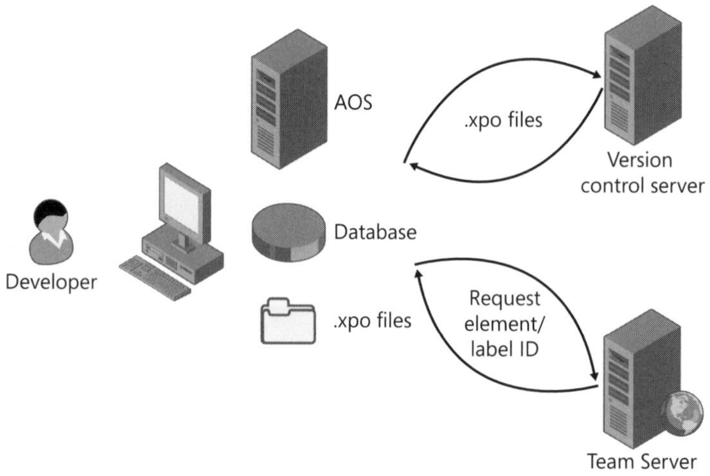

FIGURE 3-34 Typical deployment using version control

Element Life Cycle

Figure 3-35 shows the element life cycle in a version control system. When the element is in a state marked with green, it can be edited; otherwise it is read-only.

You can create a new element in two ways:

- Create a completely new element.

- Customize an existing element, resulting in an overlayered version of the element. Because elements are stored per layer in the version control system, customizing an element effectively creates a new element.

After you create an element, you must add it to the version control system. First give it a proper name in accordance with naming conventions, and then click Add To Version Control on the context menu. After you create the element, you must check it in.

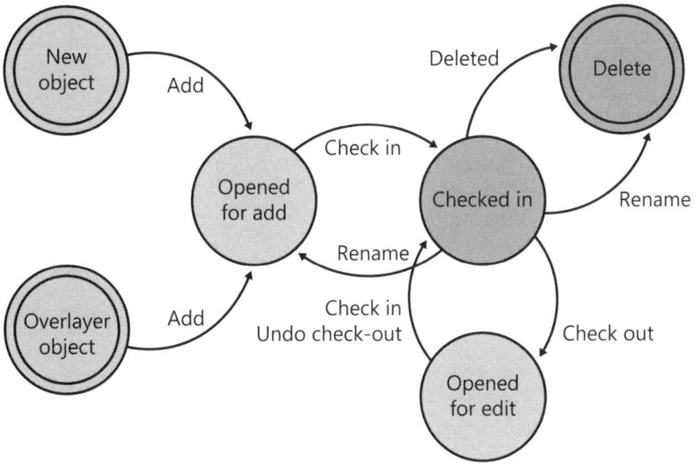

FIGURE 3-35 Element life cycle

An element that is checked in can be renamed. Renaming an element deletes the element with the old name and adds an element with the new name.

Check-Out

To modify an element, you must check it out. Checking out an element locks it so that others can't modify it while you're working.

By clicking Tools\Development Tools\Version Control\Pending Objects from the Microsoft Dynamics AX drop-down menu, you can see which elements you currently have checked out. The elements you've checked out (or that you've created and not yet checked in), appear in blue, rather than black, in the AOT.

Undo Check-Out

If you decide that you don't want to modify an element that you checked out, you can undo the check-out. This releases your lock on the element and imports the server version of the element to undo your changes.

Check-In

When you have finalized your modifications, you must check in the elements for them to be part of the next build. When you click Check-In on the context menu, the dialog box shown in Figure 3-36 appears, displaying all the elements that you currently have checked out. The Check In dialog box shows all open elements by default; you can remove any elements not required in the check-in from the list by pressing Alt+F9.

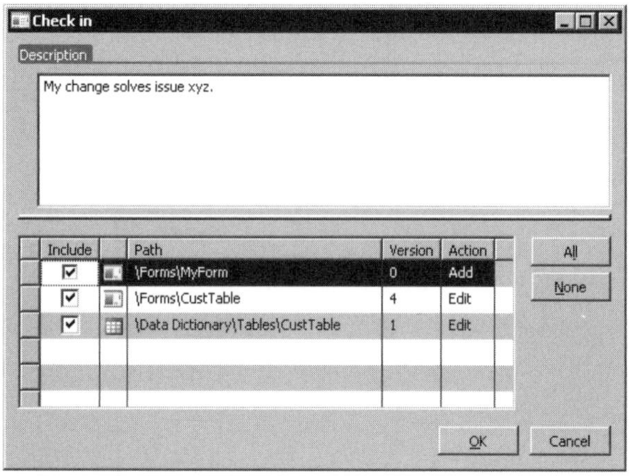

FIGURE 3-36 Check In dialog box

We recommend the following procedure for checking in your work:

1. Perform synchronization to update all elements in your environment to the latest version.
2. Verify that everything is still working as intended. Compilation is not enough!
3. Check in the elements.

Quality Checks

Before the version control system accepts a check-in, it might subject the elements to quality checks. You define what is accepted in a check-in when you set up the version control system. The following checks are supported:

- Compiler errors
- Compiler warnings
- Compiler tasks
- Best practice errors

When a check is enabled, it is carried out when you do a check-in. If the check fails, the check-in stops. You must address the issue and restart the check-in.

Updating Source Code Casing

You can set the Source Code Titlecase Update tool, available on the Add-Ins submenu, to automatically execute before elements are checked in to ensure uniform casing in variable and parameter declarations and references. You can specify this parameter when setting up the version control system by selecting the Run Title Case Update check box.

Creating New Elements

When using version control, you create new elements just as you normally would in the MorphX environment without a version control system. These elements are not part of your check-in until you click Add To Version Control on the context menu.

You can also create all element types except those listed in System Settings (from the Microsoft Dynamics AX drop-down menu: Tools\Development Tools\Version Control\Setup\System Settings). By default, jobs and private projects are not accepted.

New elements should follow Dynamics AX naming conventions. The best practice naming conventions are enforced by default, so you can't check in elements with names such as *aaaElement*, *Del_Element*, *element1*, or *element2*. (The only *Del* elements allowed are those required for version upgrade purposes.) You can change naming requirements in System Settings.

Renaming Elements

An element must be in the checked-in state to be renamed. Because all references in .xpo files are strictly name based (not ID based), all references to renamed elements must be updated. For example, when you rename a table field, you must also update any form or report that uses that field. Most references in metadata in the AOT are ID based, thus not affected when an element is renamed; in most cases, it is enough to simply check out the form or report and include it in the check-in to update the .xpo file. You can leverage the cross-reference functionality to identify references. References in X++ code are name based. You can use the compiler to find affected references.

An element's revision history is kept intact when elements are renamed. No tracking information in the version control system is lost because of a rename.

Deleting Elements

You delete an element as you normally would in Dynamics AX. The delete operation must be checked in before the deletion is visible to other users of the version control system. You can see pending deletions in the Pending Objects dialog box.

Labels

Working with labels is very similar to working with elements. To change, delete, or add a label, you must check out the label file containing the label. You can check out the label file from the Label Editor dialog box.

The main difference between checking out elements and checking out label files is that simultaneous check-outs are allowed for label files. This means that others can change labels while you have a label file checked out.

When you check in a label file, your changes are automatically merged into the latest version of the file. If you modify or delete a label that another person has also modified or deleted, your changes are lost. Lost changes are shown in the Infolog.

The ID server guarantees that label IDs are unique; adding labels won't generate conflicts.

Get Latest

If someone else has checked in a new version of an element, the Get Latest option on the context menu allows you to get the version of the element that was most recently checked in. This option isn't available when you have the element checked out yourself.

Get Latest is not applicable to MorphX VCS.

Synchronization

Synchronization allows you to get the latest version of all elements. This step is required before you can check in any elements. You can initiate synchronization from the Microsoft Dynamics AX drop-down menu: Tools\Development Tools\Version Control\Periodic\Synchronize.

Synchronization is divided into three operations that happen automatically in the following sequence:

1. Copy the latest files from the version control server to the local disk.
2. Import the files into the AOT.
3. Compile the imported files.

You should use synchronization to make sure your system is up to date. Synchronization won't affect any new elements that you have created or any elements that you have checked out.

Figure 3-37 shows the Synchronization dialog box.

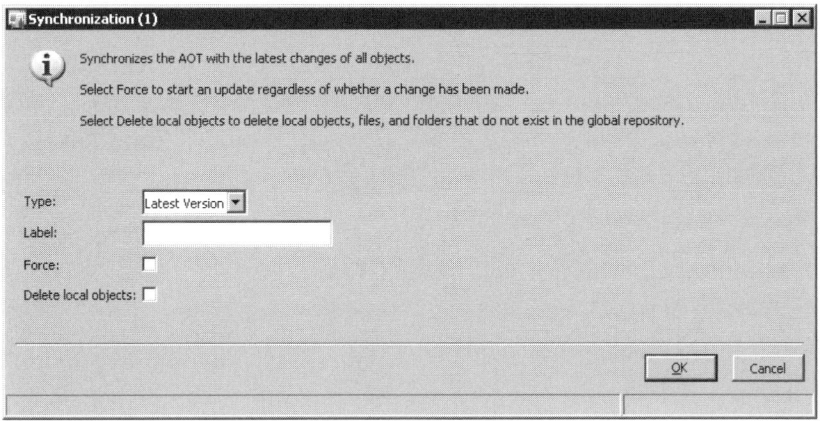

FIGURE 3-37 Synchronization dialog box

Selecting the Force check box gets the latest version of all files, whether or not they have changed, and then imports every file.

When using Visual SourceSafe, you can also synchronize to a label defined in Visual SourceSafe. This way you can easily synchronize to a specific build or version number.

Synchronization is not applicable to MorphX VCS.

Synchronization Log

How you keep track of versions on the client depends on the version control system being used. Visual SourceSafe requires that Dynamics AX keep track of itself. When you synchronize the latest version, it is copied to the local repository folder from the version control system. Each file must be imported into Dynamics AX to be reflected in the AOT. To minimize the risk of partial synchronization, a log entry is created for each file. When all files are copied locally, the log is processed, and the files are automatically imported into Dynamics AX.

When synchronization fails, the import operation is usually the cause of any problems. Synchronization failure leaves your system in a partially synchronized state. To complete the synchronization, you must restart Dynamics AX and restart the import. You use the synchronization log to restart the import, and you access it from the Microsoft Dynamics AX drop-down menu at Tools\Development Tools\Version Control\Inquiries\Synchronization Log.

The Synchronization Log dialog box, shown in Figure 3-38, displays each batch of files, and you can restart the import by clicking Process. If the Processed check box is not selected, the import has failed and should be restarted.

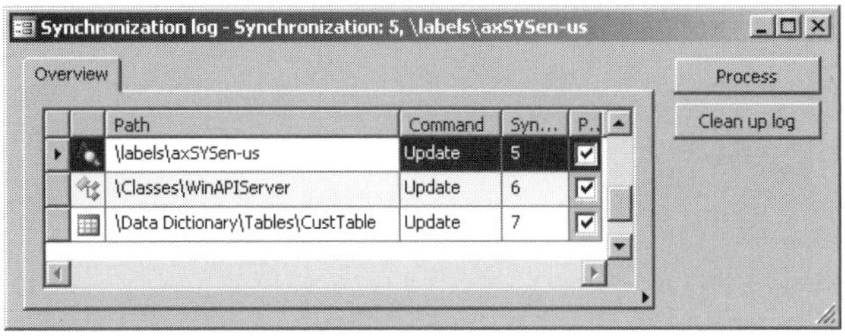

FIGURE 3-38 Synchronization Log dialog box

The Synchronization Log is not available in MorphX VCS.

Show History

One of the biggest advantages of version control is the ability to track changes to elements. Selecting History on an element's context menu displays a list of all changes to an element, as shown in Figure 3-39.

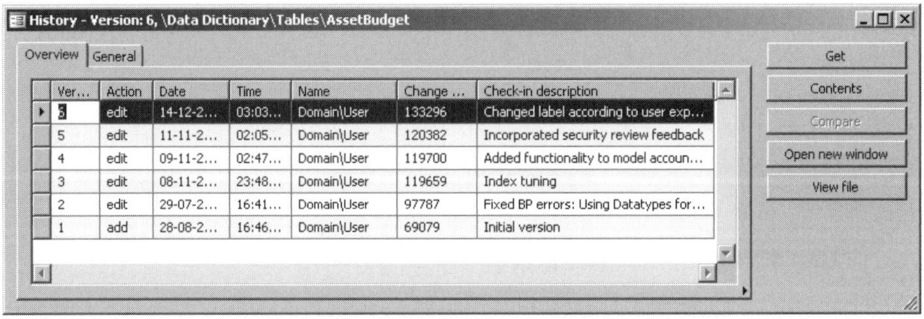

FIGURE 3-39 Revision history of an element

This dialog box shows the version number, the action performed, the time the action was performed, and who performed the action. You can also see the change number and the change description.

A set of buttons in the revision history dialog box allows further investigation of each version. Clicking Contents opens a form that shows other elements included in the same change. Clicking Compare opens the Compare dialog box, which allows you to do a line-by-line comparison of two versions of the element. The Open New Window button opens an AOT window that shows the selected version of the element, which is useful for investigating properties because it allows you to use the standard MorphX toolbox. Clicking View File opens the .xpo file for the selected version in Notepad.

Revision Comparison

Comparison is the key to harvesting the benefits of a version control system. You can start a comparison from several places, including the Compare option on the Add-Ins submenu. Figure 3-40 shows the Comparison dialog box where two revisions of the form *CustTable* are selected.

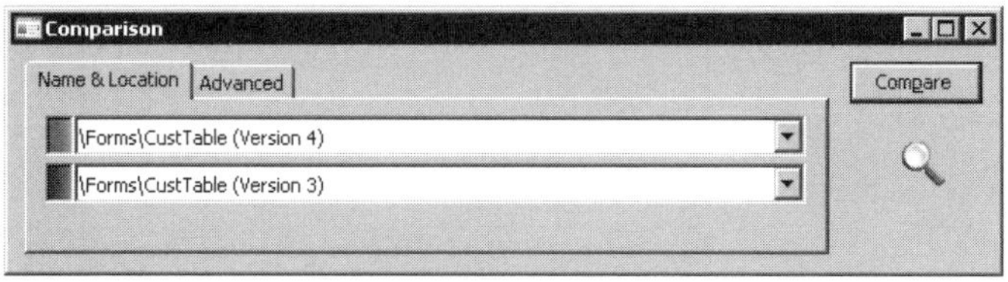

FIGURE 3-40 Comparing element revisions from version control

The Compare dialog box contains a list of all checked-in versions, in addition to the layer element versions, when a version control system is used.

Pending Elements

When you're working on a project, it's easy to lose track of which elements you've opened for editing. The Pending Objects dialog box, shown in Figure 3-41, lists the elements that are currently checked out in the version control system. Notice the column containing the action performed on the element. Deleted elements are available only in this dialog box; they are no longer shown in the AOT.

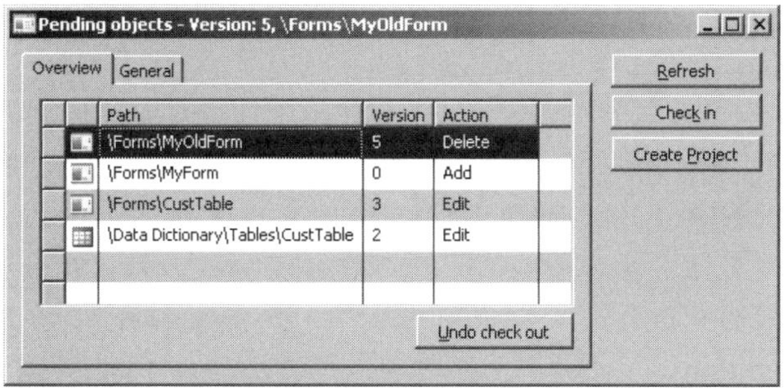

FIGURE 3-41 Pending elements

You can access the Pending Objects dialog box from the Microsoft Dynamics AX drop-down menu: Tools\Development Tools\Version Control\Pending Objects.

Build

Because the version control system contains .xpo files, and not an .aod file, a build process is required to generate an .aod file from the .xpo files. The following procedure is a high-level overview of the build process.

1. Use the CombineXPOs command-line utility to create one .xpo file by combining all .xpo files. The purpose of this step is to make the .xpo file consumable by Dynamics AX. Dynamics AX requires all referenced elements to be present in the .xpo file or to already exist in the AOT to maintain the references during import.
2. Import the new .xpo file by using the command-line parameter -AOTIMPORTFILE=<*FileName*.xpo> to Ax32.exe. This step imports the .xpo file and compiles everything. After it is complete, the new .aod file is ready.

You must follow these steps for each layer you build. The steps are described in more detail in the Microsoft Dynamics AX 2009 SDK.

The build process doesn't apply to MorphX VCS.

Integration with Other Version Control Systems

The implementation of the version control system in Dynamics AX is fully pluggable. This means that any version control system can be integrated with Dynamics AX.

Integrating with another version control system requires a new class implementing the *SysVersionControlFileBasedBackEnd* interface. It is the implementation's responsibility to provide the communication with the version control system server being used.

Unit Test Tool

A *unit test* is a piece of code that exercises another piece of code and ascertains that it behaves correctly. The developer who implements the unit to be tested typically writes the unit test. Thought leaders in this area recommend writing unit tests as early as possible, even before writing a single line of the unit's code. This principle is called *test-driven development.* (You can read more about test-driven development on MSDN and more about unit testing in the Unit Test Framework section of the Microsoft Dynamics AX 2009 SDK.)

Writing unit tests early forces you to consider how your code will be consumed; this in turn makes your APIs easier to use and understand, and it results in constructs that are more likely to be robust and long lasting. With this technique, you must have at least one unit test for each requirement; a failing unit test indicates an unfulfilled requirement. Development efforts should be targeted at making the failing unit test succeed—no more, no less.

To reap the full benefits of unit testing, you should execute test cases regularly, preferably each time code is changed. The Unit Test framework in Dynamics AX supports you regardless of your approach to writing unit tests. For example, the unit test capabilities are fully embedded in MorphX, and you can easily toggle between writing test cases and writing business logic.

If you're managing an implementation project for Dynamics AX, you should advocate testing and support your team members in any way required. At first glance, unit testing might seem like more work, but the investment is well worth the effort. If you're a team member on a project that doesn't do unit testing, you should convince your manager of its benefits. Plenty of recent literature describes the benefits in great detail.

When implementing unit tests, you write a test class, also referred to as a *test case*. Each test case has several test methods that exercise the object being tested in a particular way. As you build your library of test cases, you'll find that you need to organize them into groups. You can group test cases into test suites. The simplest way to do this is to use test projects, which are simply special kinds of AOT projects.

Test Cases

To implement a unit test case, you must create a new class that extends the *SysTestCase* class, which is part of the Unit Test framework. You should give the class the same name as the class it is testing, suffixed with *Test*. This is illustrated in the following example, where a unit test for the *Stack* class is declared.

```
class StackTest extends SysTestCase
{
}
```

If you were to run the unit test at this point, you would find that zero tests were run and zero tests failed.

This default naming convention tells the Unit Test framework which test class to collect code coverage data for. If the default test class name doesn't suit your needs, you can override the *testsElementName* method. You can also override the *testsElementType* method to set the kind of element for which the framework collects code coverage data.

To create a useful test, you must add one or more test methods to the class. All test method names must start with *test*. The test methods must return void and take no parameters. In the following code, a test method is added to the *StackTest* class.

```
void testPushPop()
{
    //Create an instance of the class to test.
    Stack stack = new Stack();
    ;
    //Push 123 to the top of the stack.
    stack.push([123]);
    //Pop the value from the stack and assert that it is 123.
    this.assertEquals([123], stack.pop());
}
```

Within each test method, you should exercise the object you test and confirm that it behaves correctly. Running the unit test at this point tells you that one test was run and zero tests failed.

Your testing needs should be met by the assertion methods available on *SysTestCase* (which extends *SysTestAssert*), as shown in Table 3-8.

TABLE 3-8 Assertion Methods on the *SysTestCase* Class

Method	Parameters	Action
assertEquals	(*anyType, anyType*)	Asserts that two values are equal. When the argument is of type *object*, the *equal* method is called to compare them.
assertFalse	*(boolean)*	Asserts that the value is false.
assertNotEqual	*(anyType, anyType)*	Asserts that two values are different.
assertNotNull	*(object)*	Asserts that the value is not null.
assertNotSame	*(object, object)*	Asserts that the objects referenced are not the same.
assertNull	*(object)*	Asserts that the value is null.
assertRealEquals	*(real, real [, real delta])*	Asserts that real values differ no more than the delta.
assertSame	*(object, object)*	Asserts that the objects referenced are the same.
assertTrue	*(boolean)*	Asserts that the value is true.

If an assertion fails, the test method fails. You can configure the framework to stop at first failure or continue with the next test method in the Unit Test Parameters dialog box: from the Microsoft Dynamics AX drop-down menu, point to Tools\ Development Tools\Unit Test\ Parameters. The following code adds a new failing test method.

```
//Test the qty method, which returns the quantity of values on the stack.
void testQty()
{
    //Create an instance of the class to test.
    Stack stack = new Stack();
    ;
    //Push 123 to the top of the stack.
    stack.push([123]);
    //Pop the value from the stack and assert that it is 0.
    this.assertEquals(0, stack.qty());
}
```

Running the unit test at this point shows that two tests were executed and one failed. The failing test appears in the Infolog. Clicking Edit opens the X++ code editor on the assert call that failed.

You might have noticed code redundancy in the test methods shown so far. In many cases, initialization code is required before the test method can run. Instead of duplicating this code in all test methods, you can refactor it into the *setUp* method. If teardown logic is required, you can place it in the *tearDown* method. When the framework runs a test method, it instantiates a new test case class, which is followed by calls to *setUp* and test methods, and finally a call to the *tearDown* method. This prevents in-memory data from one test method from affecting another test method. Test suites, which are covered in the next section, provide ways to isolate data persisted in the database between test cases and methods. The following code uses the *setUp* method to refactor the sample code.

```
class StackTest extends SysTestCase
{
    Stack stack;

    public void setUp()
    {;
        super();
        //Create an instance of the class to test.
        stack = new Stack();
    }
    void testPushPop()
    {;
        stack.push([123]);
        this.assertEquals([123], stack.pop());
    }
    ...
}
```

The Unit Test framework also supports testing of exceptions. If a method is expected to throw an exception, you can instruct the framework to expect an exception to be thrown. If you expect an exception and none is thrown, the framework reports the test case as failed. You inform the framework that an exception is expected by calling *parmExceptionExpected([boolean, str])*. You can specify an exception text that must exactly match the text thrown with the exception, or the test case will fail. You shouldn't write more asserts after the method call expected to throw an exception because execution should never get that far. The following code adds a test method that expects an exception message to be thrown.

```
void testFailingPop()
{;
    //Assert that an exception is expected.
    this.parmExceptionExpected(true, "Stack is empty!");

    //Call the method expected to throw an exception.
    stack.pop();
}
```

The sample test case now has three test methods. By following these steps, you can run the test case from MorphX:

1. Right-click the method, point to Add-Ins, and then click Run Tests.
2. Type the name in the Test toolbar, and then click Run.
3. Start the Dynamics AX client with the following command line:

```
StartupCmd=RunTestProject_<Name of test case class>
```

If you wanted to run the test case programmatically, you could use a test runner class. To do this, you would typically place the following logic in your test class's *main* method, which is invoked when you press F5 in the X++ code editor.

```
static void main(args _args)
{
    SysTestRunner runner = new SysTestRunner(classStr(StackTest));
    SysTestListenerXML listener =
        new SysTestListenerXML(@"c:\tmp\StackTest.xml");
    ;
    runner.getResult().addListener(listener);
    runner.run();
}
```

Notice that you also register a listener. If you didn't register a listener, you wouldn't know the result of the test. Listeners are described in the section "Test Listeners" later in this chapter.

Test Suites

Test suites serve two purposes:

- **Collection of test cases and test suites** A test suite can contain any number of test cases and other test suites. This arrangement means that you can group test cases in a hierarchy.
- **Test case isolation** Each test case could have different needs for isolation, depending on what data it changes. In fact, each method within the test case could have a need for isolation.

Dynamics AX includes the following five test suites that provide different levels of isolation:

- ***SysTestSuite*** This test suite is the default. It provides no isolation. You can override the *setUp* and *tearDown* methods, if necessary. Note that these methods are not the same as the *setUp* and *tearDown* methods on the test case.
- ***SysTestSuiteCompanyIsolateClass*** This test suite constructs an empty company account for the entire test class and runs each test method in the company account. After all test methods have been executed, the company account is deleted.
- ***SysTestSuiteCompanyIsolateMethod*** This test suite constructs an empty company account for each test method and runs the test method in the company account. After the test methods have been executed, the company account is deleted. This test suite provides the highest isolation level. It does, however, have a noticeable effect on performance.
- ***SysTestSuiteTTS*** This test suite wraps each test method in a transaction. After the test method has been completed, the transaction is aborted. This provides a fast alternative to the company isolation suites, but it has a couple of limitations:
  - Exceptions can't be handled. Exceptions thrown inside a transaction abort the transaction automatically and can't be caught inside the transaction.
  - Test cases that require data to be committed can't use this test suite.
- ***SysTestSuiteCompIsolateClassWithTts*** This test suite provides a combination of *SysTestSuiteCompanyIsolateClass* and *SysTestSuiteTTS*.

For each test case, you can override the *createSuite* method to select the appropriate suite for your test case. The following code shows how to use the company isolation test suite in the *StackTest* class.

```
public SysTestSuite createSuite()
{;
    return new SysTestSuiteCompanyIsolateClass(this);
}
```

We recommend that you use test projects to group your test cases into suites. You can, however, create your own class extending from *SysTestSuite* and programmatically add test cases and other test suites to it. You can run each test suite in one of the following ways:

- Type the name in the Test toolbar, and then click Run.
- Start the Dynamics AX client with the following command line:

```
StartupCmd=RunTestProject_<Name of test suite class>
```

- Implement a static *main* method similar to the one shown in the test case example.

The following code shows the entire *StackTest* test case. Notice the refactoring and the changes in *testQty* to make the test case succeed.

```
class StackTest extends SysTestCase
{
    Stack stack;

    public SysTestSuite createSuite()
    {;
        return new SysTestSuiteCompanyIsolateClass(this);
    }
    public void setUp()
    {;
        super();
        stack = new Stack();
    }
    void testPushPop()
    {;
        stack.push([123]);
        this.assertEquals([123], stack.pop());
    }
    void testQty()
    {;
        stack.push([100]);
        this.assertEquals(1, stack.qty());
        stack.push([200]);
        this.assertEquals(2, stack.qty());
        stack.clear();
        this.assertEquals(0, stack.qty());
    }
    void testFailingPop()
    {;
        //Assert that an exception is expected.
        this.parmExceptionExpected(true, "Stack is empty!");

        //Call the method expected to throw an exception.
        stack.pop();
    }
    static void main(args _args)
    {
        //This method illustrates how to run a test case programmatically.
```

```
        SysTestRunner runner = new SysTestRunner(classStr(StackTest));
        SysTestListenerXML listener =
           new SysTestListenerXML(@"c:\tmp\StackTest.xml");
        ;
        runner.getResult().addListener(listener);
        runner.run();
    }
}
```

Test Projects

The easiest way to group test cases is to use a test project. You can create a test project with the Project Designer in MorphX. The test project can contain groups of test case classes and references to other test projects. You create a new test project by selecting the project type Test Project when creating either a shared or private project. A test project can also contain references to other test projects, which allows the project to scale across many development teams. You create a reference by right-clicking the project root node and selecting New Reference To Test Project.

Figure 3-42 shows a test project that includes a group of common tests containing the test case example and references to two other test projects.

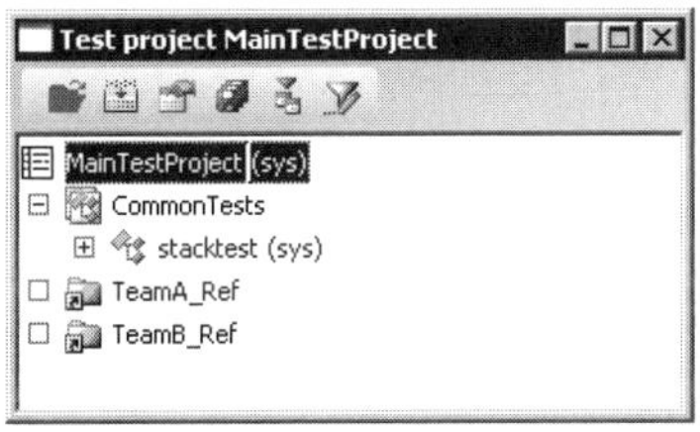

FIGURE 3-42 Test project containing references and a test case

Each test project has its own settings that are persisted with the project definition. This allows you to specify test project settings that follow the project, even through import and export, redeployment, and so on.

You can run a test project in several ways:

- Right-click it, and then click Run.
- Type the name in the Test toolbar, and then click Run.
- Start the Dynamics AX client with the following command line:

```
StartupCmd=RunTestProject_<Name of test project>
```

- Use the version control functionality during check-in. Check-in stops if the test fails. You specify the project to run during check-in: from the Microsoft Dynamics AX drop-down menu, point to Tools\Development Tools\Version Control\Setup\System Settings.

The Test Toolbar

When you're working with unit testing, you should open the Test toolbar. You access the Test toolbar, shown in Figure 3-43, from the Microsoft Dynamics AX drop-down menu: Tools\Development Tools\Unit Test\Show Toolbar.

FIGURE 3-43 Test toolbar

You can type the name of the test case, test suite, or test project you want to run, click Run to execute it, and then, to get information about the result, click Details to open the Test Jobs window. The Test Jobs window shows you the following information collected during the test execution:

- The status of each test case
- Environmental information
- Timing (when the test started and stopped, the duration of the test, and so on)
- Code coverage, when enabled
- Information sent to the Infolog during the test case execution

> **Note** The database listener collects the information displayed in the Test Jobs window. This listener is automatically registered when you run a test via the toolbar.

Code Coverage

The Unit Test framework can collect code coverage information during execution, including a percentage value that indicates how thoroughly you have tested the unit. It also allows you to focus your implementation of the test cases on the parts not covered by other test cases. In addition, the Test Jobs window offers a line-by-line view of the code lines visited. You can enable code coverage in the Unit Test Parameters dialog box: from the Microsoft Dynamics AX drop-down menu, point to Tools\Development Tools\Unit Test\Parameters. However, because much more data is collected, enabling code coverage when executing unit tests dramatically affects performance during execution. Figure 3-44 shows an example of the code coverage recorded by the *testFailingPop* method from the preceding test case example.

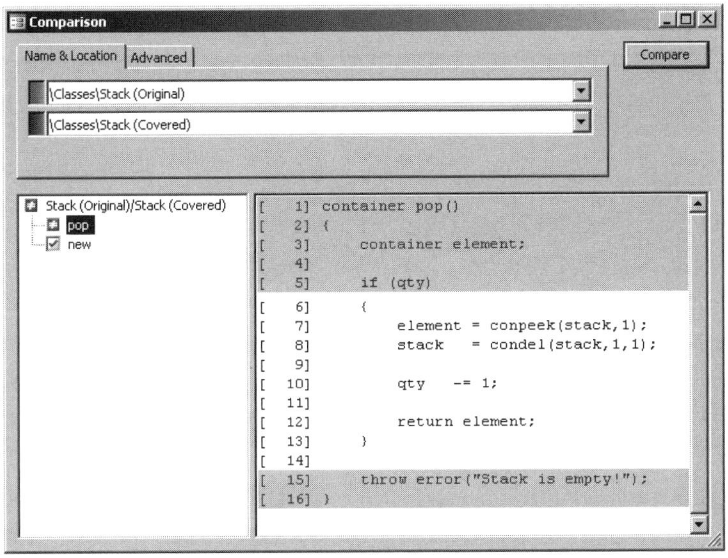

FIGURE 3-44 Visualization of code coverage

The lines highlighted in gray (lines 1 through 5 and 15 through 16) are the lines visited during execution. The lines not shaded (lines 6 through 14) haven't been visited.

Test Listeners

The value of running a test case is dramatically increased if good reporting options exist. When running a test case or a suite of tests, you can enable one or more listeners. Each listener produces its unique output. Dynamics AX includes many listeners, allowing output to text files, XML files, the database, the Infolog, the Message window, the Print window, and the Progress bar. You can enable test listeners in the Unit Test Parameters dialog box.

Here is the XML generated by the XML listener when you run the *StackTest* unit test.

```
<?xml version="1.0" encoding="utf-8" standalone="yes"?>
<!-- Created by SysTestListenerXML -->
<test-results date="08-07-2008" time="10:51:34" success="false">
  <test-suite name="stacktest" time="52" success="true" coverage="61.54">
    <results>
      <test-case name="stacktest.testFailingPop" time="31" success="true"
coverage="23.08" />
      <test-case name="stacktest.
testPushPop" time="0" success="true" coverage="50.00" />
      <test-case name="stacktest.testQty" time="21" success="true" coverage="30.77" />
    </results>
  </test-suite>
</test-results>
```

> **Note** Listeners that generate a file write the file to the application log directory. The only way to change the file name and location is to manually register a listener, which we demonstrated in the *StackTest* code on pages 102 to 103.

If you must create a new listener to output to a type of media not supported by default, you can do so by following these steps:

1. Create your own listener class implementing the *SysTestListener* interface. Alternatively, you can inherit from one of the existing test listeners. The methods on your class are invoked when events such as the start and end of test suites and test cases occur and when test cases fail. A *SysTestListenerData* object is passed to each method. The object contains information about the test case or suite, coverage data, and much more. By extracting the information, you can generate output to suit your needs.
2. Modify the base enumeration *SysTestListeners*. You must add an entry that has the same name as your listener class and a label of your choice. This causes the listener to appear in the test parameters form.

Object Model

So far in this chapter we've described the classes in the Unit Test framework and explained how they interact. Figure 3-45 shows this information as a UML object model.

The *SysTestCase* class implements quite a few interfaces. In fact, the Unit Test framework can use any class that implements the *SysTestable* interface as a test case. You can implement the other interfaces if you want more control. It's far easier, however, to create test case classes that extend the *SysTestCase* base class. (For simplicity, Figure 3-45 doesn't show the *SysTestSuite* derived classes or the *SysTestListener* derived classes.)

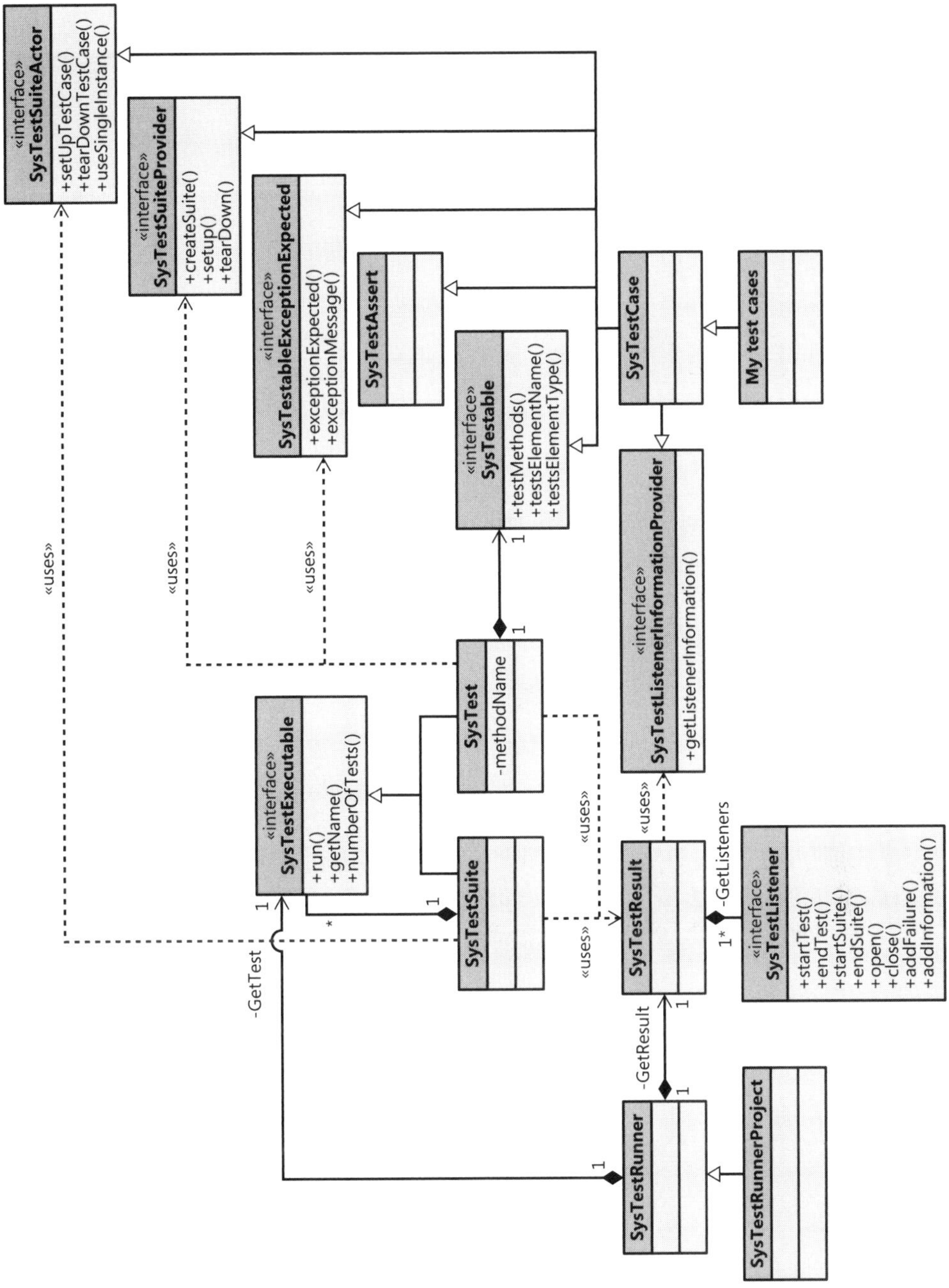

FIGURE 3-45 UML diagram of the Unit Test framework

Chapter 4

The X++ Programming Language

In this chapter:

The objectives of this chapter are to:

- Provide an introduction to the X++ programming language.
- Introduce job model elements, which are useful for executing X++ samples.
- Describe the Microsoft Dynamics AX 2009 runtime type system that supports value types, reference types, and type hierarchies.
- Explain the syntax of X++ and provide examples of variable declarations, expressions, statements, macros, and comments.
- Describe the syntax of class and interface definitions.
- Explain Dynamics AX code access security.
- Describe design and implementation patterns.

Introduction

X++ is an object-oriented, application-aware, and data-aware programming language. The language is object oriented because it supports object abstractions, abstraction hierarchies, polymorphism, and encapsulation. It is application aware because it includes keywords such as *client*, *server*, *changecompany*, and *display* that are useful for writing client/server enterprise resource planning (ERP) applications. And it is data aware because it includes keywords such as *firstFast*, *forceSelectOrder*, and *forUpdate*, as well as a database query syntax, that are useful for programming database applications.

You use the Dynamics AX designers and tools to edit the structure of application types. You specify the behavior of application types by writing X++ source code using the X++ editor. The

X++ compiler compiles this source code into bytecode intermediate format. Model data, X++ source code, and intermediate bytecode are stored in .aod files. The Dynamics AX runtime dynamically composes object types by loading overridden bytecode from the highest level definition in the model layering stack. (For more information about the layering technology, see Chapter 1, "Architectural Overview.") Objects are instantiated from these dynamic types.

This chapter describes the Dynamics AX runtime type system and the features of the X++ language that are essential to writing ERP applications. It will also help you avoid common programming pitfalls that stem from implementing X++. For an in-depth discussion of the type system and the X++ language, refer to the Microsoft Dynamics AX 2009 SDK, available on MSDN.

Jobs

Jobs are model elements that you create by using the Application Object Tree (AOT). The following X++ code example provides an example of a job model element that prints the "Hello World" string to an automatically generated window. The *pause* statement stops program execution and waits for user input from a dialog box.

```
static void myJob(Args _args)
{
    print "Hello World";
    pause;
}
```

Jobs are globally defined functions that execute in the rich client runtime environment. Jobs are frequently used to test a piece of business logic because they are easily executed from within the MorphX integrated development environment (IDE), by either pressing F5 or selecting Go on the command menu. You shouldn't use jobs as a core part of your application's core design. The examples provided in this chapter can be run as jobs.

The Type System

The Dynamics AX runtime manages the storage of value type data on the call stack and reference type objects on the memory heap. The *call stack* is the memory structure that holds data about the active methods called during program execution. The *memory heap* is the memory area that allocates storage for objects that are destroyed automatically by the Dynamics AX runtime.

Value Types

Value types include the built-in primitive types, extended data types, enumeration types, and built-in collection types:

- The primitive types are *boolean, int, int64, real, date, utcdatetime, timeofday, str,* and *guid.*
- The extended data types are specialized primitive types and specialized base enumerations. User-defined extended data types are dynamically composed from application model layers.
- The enumeration types are base enumerations and extended data types. User-defined enumeration types are dynamically composed from application model layers. Dynamics AX runtime enumeration types are exposed in the system API.
- The collection types are the built-in array and container types.

By default, variables declared as value types are assigned their zero value by the Dynamics AX runtime. These variables can't be set to null. Variable values are copied when variables are used to invoke methods and when they are used in assignment statements. Therefore, two value type variables can't reference the same value.

Reference Types

Reference types include the record types, class types, and interface types:

- The record types are *table*, *map*, and *view*. User-defined record types are dynamically composed from application model layers. Dynamics AX runtime record types are exposed in the system API.

> **Note** Although they are not visible in the AOT, all record types implement the methods that are members of the system *xRecord* type, a Dynamics AX runtime class type.

- User-defined class types are dynamically composed from application model layers and Dynamics AX runtime class types exposed in the system API.
- Interface types are type specifications and can't be instantiated in the Dynamics AX runtime. Class types can, however, implement interfaces.

Variables declared as reference types contain references to objects that the Dynamics AX runtime instantiates from dynamically composed types defined in the application model layering system and from types exposed in the system API. The Dynamics AX runtime also performs memory deallocation (garbage collection) for these objects when there are no longer any references to them. Reference variables declared as record types reference objects that the Dynamics AX runtime instantiates automatically. Class type objects are programmatically instantiated using the *new* operator. Copies of object references are passed as reference parameters in method calls and are assigned to reference variables, so two variables could reference the same object.

More Info Not all nodes in the AOT name a type declaration. Some class declarations are merely *syntactic sugar*—convenient, human-readable expressions. For example, the class header definition for all rich client forms declares a *FormRun* class type, the class header definition for all rich client reports declares a *ReportRun* class type, and the class header definition for a Web client form declares a *WebFormRun* class type. *FormRun*, *ReportRun*, and *WebFormRun* are also, however, class types in the system API. Allowing their declarations is syntactic sugar because it is technically impossible to have two types with the same name in the Dynamics AX class type hierarchy.

Type Hierarchies

The X++ language supports the definition of type hierarchies that specify generalization and specialization relationships between class types. For example, a check payment method is a type of payment method. A type hierarchy allows code reuse. Reusable code is defined on base types defined higher in a type hierarchy as they are inherited, or reused, by derived types defined lower in a type hierarchy.

Tip You can use the Application Hierarchy Tree tool in MorphX to visualize and browse the hierarchy of any type.

This section introduces the base types provided by the Dynamics AX runtime and describes how they are extended in type hierarchies.

Caution The Dynamics AX type system is known as a weak type system because X++ accepts certain type assignments that are clearly erroneous and lead to run-time errors. Be aware of the caveats outlined in the following sections, and try to avoid weak type constructs when writing X++ code.

The *anytype* Type

The Dynamics AX type system doesn't have a strict type hierarchy with a concrete base type for all types. The *anytype* type therefore imitates a base type for all types. Variables of the *anytype* type behave like value types when they are assigned a value type variable and like reference types when they are assigned a reference type variable. You can us the *SysAnyType* class to explicitly box all types, including value types, and make them behave like reference types.

The *anytype* type, shown in the following code sample, is syntactic sugar that allows methods to accept any type as a parameter or allows a method to return different types.

```
static str queryRange(anytype _from, anytype _to)
{
    return SysQuery::range(_from,_to);
}
```

You can declare variables by using *anytype*. However, the underlying data type of an *anytype* variable is set to match the first assignment, and you can't change its type afterward, as shown here.

```
anytype a = 1;
print strfmt("%1 = %2", typeof(a), a); //Integer = 1
a = "text";
print strfmt("%1 = %2", typeof(a), a); //Integer = 0
```

The *common* Type

The *common* type is the base type of all record types. Like the *anytype* type, record types are context-dependent types whose variables can be used as though they reference single records or a record cursor that can iterate over a set of database records.

Using the *common* type allows you to cast one record type to another (possibly incompatible) record type, as shown in this example.

```
//customer = vendor; //Compile error
common = customer;
vendor = common;     //Accepted
```

Table maps defined in the AOT are a more type-safe method of capturing commonalities between record types, and you should use them to prevent incompatible record assignments. A table map defines fields and methods that safely operate on one or more record types.

The compiler doesn't validate method calls on the *common* type. For example, the compiler accepts the following method invocation even though the method doesn't exist.

```
common.nonExistingMethod();
```

For this reason, you should use reflection to confirm that the method on the *common* type exists before you invoke it, as shown in this example:

```
if (tableHasMethod(new DictTable(common.tableId), identifierStr(existingMethod)))
{
    common.existingMethod();
}
```

The *object* Type

The built-in *object* type is a weak reference type whose variables reference objects that are instances of class or interface types in the Dynamics AX class hierarchy.

The type system allows programmers to implicitly cast base type objects to derived type objects and to cast derived type objects to base type objects, as shown here.

```
baseClass = derivedClass;
derivedClass = baseClass;
```

The *object* type allows you to use the assignment operator and cast one class type to another, incompatible class type, as shown in the following code. The probable result of this action, however, is a run-time exception when your code encounters an object of an unexpected type.

```
//textIO = binaryIO; //Compile error
Object = textIO;
binaryIO = object;    //Accepted
```

Use the *SysDictClass* class instead of the assignment operator to prevent these incompatible type casts. *SysDictClass* provides the *is* method to safely cast derived types of base types and the *as* method to safely cast base types to derived types.

Keep in mind that the compiler doesn't validate method calls on the *object* type. The compiler accepts the following method invocation even though the method doesn't exist.

```
object.nonExistingMethod();
```

Extended Data Types

You use the AOT to create extended data types that model concrete data values and data hierarchies. For example, the *Name* extended data type is a string, and the *CustName* and *VendName* extended data types extend the *Name* data type.

The X++ language supports extended data types but doesn't offer any type checking according to the hierarchy of extended data types. X++ treats any extended data type as its primitive type; therefore, code such as the following is allowed.

```
CustName customerName;
FileName fileName = customerName;
```

When used properly, extended data types improve the readability of X++ code; it's easier to understand the intended use of a *CustName* data type than a *string* data type, even if they are both used to declare string variables.

Extended data types are more than just type definitions to make X++ code more readable. On each extended data type, you can also specify how the system displays values of this type to users. Further, you can specify a relationship between the extended data type and a table field. The relationship serves two primary purposes. First, it ensures a foreign key relationship is automatically created for any table field using the extended data type. Second, it enables the form's rendering engine to automatically build lookup forms for form controls using the extended data type, even when they are not bound to a data source. On string-based extended data types, you can specify the maximum string size of the type. The database layer uses the string size to define the underlying columns for fields using the extended data type. Having the string size defined in only one place makes it easy to change.

Syntax

The X++ language belongs to the "curly brace" family of programming languages (those that use curly braces to delimit syntax blocks), such as C, C++, C#, and Java. If you're familiar with any of these languages, you won't have a problem reading and understanding the X++ syntax.

Unlike many programming languages, X++ is not case-sensitive. However, using camel casing (camelCasing) for variable names and Pascal casing (PascalCasing) for type names is considered a best practice. (More best practices for writing X++ code are available in the Microsoft Dynamics AX 2009 SDK.) You can use the Source Code Titlecase Update tool (accessed from the Add-Ins submenu in the AOT) to automatically apply casing in X++ code to match the best practice recommendation.

CLR types, which are case-sensitive, are one important exception to the casing guidelines. We explain how to use CLR types in the section "CLR Interoperability" later in this chapter.

Variable Declarations

You must place variable declarations at the beginning of methods. Table 4-1 provides examples of value type and reference type variable declarations, as well as example variable initializations. Parameter declaration examples are provided in the "Classes and Interfaces" section later in this chapter.

TABLE 4-1 X++ Variable Declaration Examples

Type	Examples
anytype	`anytype type = null;` `anytype type = 1;`
record types	`common record = null;` `CustTable custTable = null;`

object types	`object obj = null;`
	`MyClass myClass = new MyClass();`
	`System.Text.StringBuilder sb = new System.Text.StringBuilder();`

boolean	`boolean b = true;`
int	`int i = -5;` `int h = 0xAB;`

int64	`int64 i = -5;`
	`int64 h = 0xAB;`
	`int64 u = 0xA0000000u;`

real	`real r1 = 3.14;` `real r2 = 1.0e3;`
date	`date d = 31\12\2008;`
utcdatetime	`utcdatetime dt = 2008-12-31T23:59:59;`
timeofday	`timeofday time = 43200;`

str	`str s1 = "a string";`
	`str s2 = 'a string';`
	`str 40 s40 = "string 40";`

guid	`guid g = newguid();`
container	`container c1 = ["a string", 123];` `container c2 = connull();`
base enumeration types	`NoYes theAnswer = NoYes::Yes;`
extended data types	`Name name = "name";`

Declaring variables with the same name as their type is a common practice. At first glance, this approach might seem confusing. Consider this class and its getter/setter method to its field.

```
Class Person
{
    Name name;

    public Name Name(Name _name = name)
    {
        ;
        name = _name;
        return name;
    }
}
```

Because X++ is not case-sensitive, the word *name* is used in eight places in the preceding code. Three refer to the extended data type, four refer to the field, and one refers to the method ("*_name*" is used twice). To improve readability, you could rename the variable to something more specific, such as *personName*. However, using a more specific variable name implies that a more specific type should be used (and created if it doesn't already exist). Changing both the type name and the variable name to *PersonName* wouldn't improve readability. The benefit of this practice is that if you know the name of a variable, you also know its type.

Because X++ allows you to define variables with the same name as their type, variable names can become ambiguous. The X++ compiler expects methods to start with variable declarations. To denote a variable with an ambiguous name and not a type, you must add a hanging semicolon, as shown in the preceding example, to signify the end of variable declarations. Including the hanging semicolon is considered a best practice because it allows your code to easily accommodate new types. Variable names could become ambiguous when new extended data types are created, causing compilation errors.

Expressions

X++ expressions are sequences of operators, operands, values, and variables that yield a result. Table 4-2 summarizes the types of expressions allowed in X++ and includes examples of their use.

TABLE 4-2 X++ Expression Examples

Category	Examples

Object creation operators	new MyClass() //X++ object creation
	new System.DateTime() //CLR object wrapper and
	//CLR object creation
	new System.Int32[100]() //CLR array creation

Values and variables	"string" myVariable

Access operators	this //Instance member access
	element //Form member access
	<datasource>_ds //Form data source access
	x.y //Instance member access
	E::e //Enum access
	a[x] //Array access
	[v1, v2] = c //Container access
	Table.Field //Table field access
	Table.(FieldId) //Table field access
	(select statement).Field //Select result access
	System.Type //CLR namespace type access
	System.DayOfWeek::Monday //CLR enum access

Category	Examples

Method invocations	`super() //Base member invocation`
	`MyClass::m() //Static member invocation`
	`myObject.m() //Instance member invocation`
	`this.m() //This instance member invocation`
	`myTable.MyMap::m(); //Map instance member invocation`
	`f() //Built-in function call`

Arithmetic operators	`x = y + z // Addition`
	`x = y - z // Subtraction`
	`x = y * z // Multiplication`
	`x = y / z // Division`
	`x = y div z // Integer division`
	`x = y mod z // Integer division remainder`

Shift operators	`x = y << z // Shift left` `x = y >> z // Shift right`

Relational operators	`x < y // Less than`
	`x > y // Greater than`
	`x <= y // Less than or equal`
	`x >= y // Greater than or equal`
	`x == y // Equal`
	`x != y // Not equal`
	`select t where t.f like "a*" // Select using wildcards`

Logical operators	`if (!obj) // Logical NOT`
	`if (a && b) // Logical AND`
	`if (a || b) // Logical OR`

Bitwise operators	`x = y & z // Bitwise AND`
	`x = y | z // Bitwise OR`
	`x = y ^ z // Bitwise exclusive OR (XOR)`
	`x = ~z // Bitwise complement`

Conditional operators	`x ? y : z`
String concatenation	`"Hello" + "World"`
Parentheses	`(x)`

Statements

X++ statements specify object state and object behavior. Table 4-3 provides examples of X++ language statements that are commonly found in many programming languages. In-depth descriptions of each statement are beyond the scope of this book.

TABLE 4-3 X++ Statement Examples

Statement	Example

assignment statement

```
int i = 42;
;
i = 1;
i++;
++i;
i--;
--i;
i += 1;
i -= 1;
```

compound statement

```
int i;
{
    i = 3;
    i++;
}
```

print statement

```
int i = 42;
;
print i;
print "Hello World";
print 5.2;
pause;
```

if statement

```
boolean b = true;
int i = 42;
;
if ( b == true )
{
    i++;
}
else
{
    i--;
}
```

break statement

```
int i;
;
for ( i = 0; i < 100; i++ )
{
    if ( i > 50 )
    {
        break;
    }
}
```

continue statement

```
int i;
int j = 0;
;
for( i = 0; i < 100; i++ )
{
    if ( i < 50 )
    {
        continue;
    }
    j++;
}
```

Statement	Example

while statement	`int i = 4;`
	`;`
	`while ( i <= 100 )`
	`{`
	`    i++;`
	`}`

do while statement	`int i = 4;`
	`;`
	`do`
	`{`
	`    i++;`
	`}`
	`while ( i <= 100 );`

for statement	`int i;`
	`;`
	`for ( i = 0; i < 42; i++ )`
	`{`
	`    print i;`
	`    pause;`
	`}`

switch statement	`str s = "test";`
	`;`
	`switch ( s )`
	`{`
	`    case "test" :`
	`        print s;`
	`        break;`
	`    default :`
	`        print "fail";`
	`}`
	`pause;`

pause statement	`print "Hello World";` `pause;`

window statement	`window 100, 10 at 100,10;`
	`print "Hello World";`
	`pause;`

breakpoint statement	`breakpoint; //Causes the debugger to be invoked`

return statement	`int foo()`
	`{`
	`    return 42;`
	`}`

throw statement	`throw error("Error text");`

Statement	Example

try statement	try
	{
	    throw error("Force exception");
	}
	catch(exception::Error)
	{
	    print "Error";
	    pause;
	}
	catch
	{
	    print "Another exception";
	    pause;
	}

retry statement	try
	{
	    throw error("Force exception");
	}
	catch(exception::Error)
	{
	    retry;
	}

.NET CLR interoperability statement	System.Text.StringBuilder sb;
	sb = new System.Text.StringBuilder();
	sb.Append("Hello World");
	print sb.ToString();
	pause;

local function	static void myJob(Args _args)
	{
	    str myLocalFunction()
	    {
	        return "Hello World";
	    }
	    ;
	    print myLocalFunction();
	    pause;
	}

system function	guid g = newguid();
	;
	print abs(-1);

flush statement	MyTable myTable; ; flush myTable;

Statement	Example

changecompany statement	`MyTable myTable;`
	`;`
	`while select myTable`
	`{`
	`    print myTable.myField;`
	`}`
	`changecompany("ZZZ")`
	`{`
	`   while select myTable`
	`   {`
	`       print myTable.myField;`
	`   }`
	`}`
	`pause;`

Data-Aware Statements

The X++ language has built-in support for querying and manipulating database data. The syntax for database statements is similar to Structured Query Language (SQL), and this section assumes that you're familiar with SQL. The following code shows how a *select* statement is used to return only the first selected record from the MyTable database table and how the data in the record's *myField* field is printed.

```
static void myJob(Args _args)
{
    MyTable myTable;
    ;
    select firstOnly * from myTable where myTable.myField1=='value';
    print myTable.myField2;
    pause;
}
```

The "* from" part of the *select* statement in the example is optional. You can replace the asterisk (*) character with a comma-separated field list, such as *myField2, myField3*. You must define all fields, however, on the selection table model element, and only one selection table is allowed immediately after the *from* keyword. The *where* expression in the *select* statement can comprise any number of logical and relational operators. The *firstOnly* keyword is optional and can be replaced by one or more of the optional keywords. Table 4-4 describes all the possible keywords. For more information on database-related keywords see Chapter 14, "The Database Layer."

TABLE 4-4 Keyword Options for *select* Statements

Keyword	Description
Firstfast	Fetches the first selected record faster than the remaining selected records.
Firstonly *Firstonly1*	Returns only the first selected record.
Firstonly10	Returns only the first 10 selected records. Supported only on the Oracle database platform.
Firstonly100	Returns only the first 100 selected records. Supported only on the Oracle database platform.
Firstonly1000	Returns only the first 1000 selected records. Supported only on the Oracle database platform.
Forupdate	Selects records for updating.
Nofetch	Specifies that the Dynamics AX runtime should not execute the statement immediately because the records are required only by some other operation.
Forceplaceholders	Forces the Dynamics AX runtime to generate a query with placeholder field constraints. For example, the query generated for the preceding code example looks like this: *select * from myTable where myField1=?.* Database query plans are reused when this option is specified. This is the default option for *select* statements that don't join table records. This keyword can't be used with the *forceliterals* keyword.
Forceliterals	Forces the Dynamics AX runtime to generate a query with the specified field constraints. For example, the query generated for the preceding code example looks like this: *select * from myTable where myField1='value'*. Database query plans aren't reused when this option is specified. This keyword can't be used with the *forceplaceholders* keyword.
Forceselectorder	Forces the Microsoft SQL Server query processor to access tables in the order in which they are specified in the query. (The Oracle query processor ignores this keyword.)
Forcenestedloop	Forces the SQL Server query processor to use a nested-loop algorithm for table join operations. Other join algorithms, such as hash-join and merge-join, are therefore not considered by the query processor.
Reverse	Returns records in reverse of the *select* order.
Crosscompany	Forces the Dynamics AX runtime to generate a query without automatically adding the *where* clause in the *dataAreaId* field. This keyword can be used to select records from all or from a set of specified company accounts. For example, the query `while select crosscompany:companies myTable { }` selects all records in the *myTable* table from the company accounts specified in the *companies* container.

Keyword	Description
optimisticlock	Overrides the table's *OccEnabled* property and forces the optimistic locking scheme. This keyword can't be used with the *pessimisticlock* and *repeatableread* keywords.
Pessimisticlock	Overrides the table's *OccEnabled* property and forces the pessimistic locking scheme. This keyword can't be used with the *optimisticlock* and *repeatableread* keywords.
Repeatableread	Locks all records read within a transaction. This keyword can be used to ensure consistent data is fetched by identical queries for the duration of the transaction, at the cost of blocking other updates of those records. Phantom reads can still occur if another process inserts records that match the range of the query. This keyword can't be used with the *optimisticlock* and *pessimisticlock* keywords.

The following code example demonstrates how a table index clause is used to suggest the index that a database server should use when querying tables. The Dynamics AX runtime appends an *order by* clause and the *index* fields to the first *select* statement's database query. Records are thus ordered by the index. The Dynamics AX runtime can insert a query hint into the second *select* statement's database query, if the hint is reasonable to use.

```
static void myJob(Args _args)
{
    MyTable1 myTable1;
    MyTable2 myTable2;
    ;
    while select myTable1
        index myIndex1
    {
        print myTable1.myField2;
    }

    while select myTable2
        index hint myIndex2
    {
        print myTable2.myField2;
    }
    pause;
}
```

The following code example demonstrates how the results from a *select* query can be ordered and grouped. The first *select* statement specifies that the resulting records must be sorted in ascending order based on *myField1* values and then descending order based on *myField2* values. The second *select* statement specifies that the resulting records must be grouped by *myField1* values and sorted in descending order.

```
static void myJob(Args _args)
{
    MyTable myTable;
    ;
    while select myTable
        order by Field1 asc, Field2 desc
    {
        print myTable.myField;
    }
    while select myTable
        group by Field1 desc
    {
        print myTable.Field1;
    }
    pause;
}
```

The following code demonstrates use of the *avg* and *count* aggregate functions in *select* statements. The first *select* statement averages the values in the *myField* column and assigns the result to the *myField* field. The second *select* statement counts the number of records the selection returns and assigns the result to the *myField* field.

```
static void myJob(Args _args)
{
     MyTable myTable;
     ;
     select avg(myField) from myTable;
     print myTable.myField;

     select count(myField) from myTable;
     print myTable.myField;
     pause;
}
```

Caution The compiler doesn't verify that aggregate function parameter types are numeric, so the result the function returns could be assigned to a field of type *string*. The compiler also performs rounding if, for example, the *average* function calculates a value of 1.5 and the type of *myField* is an integer.

Table 4-5 describes the aggregate functions supported in X++ *select* statements.

TABLE 4-5 Aggregate Functions in X++ *select* Statements

Function	Description
avg	Returns the average of the non-null field values in the records the selection returns.
count	Returns the number of non-null field values in the records the selection returns.
sum	Returns the sum of the non-null field values in the records the selection returns.
minof	Returns the minimum of the non-null field values in the records the selection returns.
maxof	Returns the maximum of the non-null field values in the records the selection returns.

The following code example demonstrates how tables are joined with *join* conditions. The first *select* statement joins two tables by using an equality *join* condition between fields in the tables. The second *select* statement joins three tables to illustrate how you can nest *join* conditions and use an *exists* operator as an existence test with a *join* condition. The second *select* statement also demonstrates how you can use a *group by* sort in *join* conditions. In fact, the *join* condition can comprise multiple nested *join* conditions because the syntax of the *join* condition is the same as the body of a *select* statement.

```
static void myJob(Args _args)
{
     MyTable1 myTable1;
     MyTable2 myTable2;
     MyTable3 myTable3;
     ;
     select myField from myTable1
        join myTable2
           where myTable1.myField1=myTable2.myField1;
     print myTable1.myField;

     select myField from myTable1
        join myTable2
          group by myTable2.myField1
          where myTable1.myField1=myTable2.myField1;
             exists join myTable3
                where myTable1.myField1=myTable3.mField2;
     print myTable1.myField;
     pause;
}
```

Table 4-6 describes the *exists* operator and the other *join* operators that can be used in place of the *exists* operator in the preceding example.

TABLE 4-6 Join Operators

Operator	Description
exists	Returns true if any records are in the result set after executing the *join* clause. Returns false otherwise.
notexists	Returns false if any records are in the result set after executing the *join* clause. Returns true otherwise.
outer	Returns the left outer join of the first and second tables.

The following example demonstrates use of the *while select* statement that increments the *myTable* variable's record cursor on each loop.

```
static void myJob(Args _args)
{
    MyTable myTable;
    ;
    while select myTable
    {
        Print myTable.myField;
    }
}
```

You must use the *ttsbegin*, *ttscommit*, and *ttsabort* transaction statements to modify records in tables and to insert records into tables. The *ttsbegin* statement marks the beginning of a database transaction block; *ttsbegin-ttscommit* transaction blocks can be nested. The *ttsbegin* statements increment the transaction level; the *ttscommit* statements decrement the transaction level. The outermost block decrements the transaction level to zero and commits all database inserts and updates performed since the first *ttsbegin* statement to the database. The *ttsabort* statement rolls back all the database inserts, updates, and deletions performed since the *ttsbegin* statement. Table 4-7 provides examples of these transaction statements for single records and operations and for set-based (multiple-record) operations.

The last example in Table 4-7 demonstrates the method *RowCount*, which is new in Dynamics AX 2009. Its purpose is to get the count of records that are affected by set-based operations, namely, *insert_recordset*, *update_recordset*, and *delete_from*.

RowCount facilitates application scenarios that use set-based update operations. If no records are impacted by an update operation, the method application performs an insert or a set-based insert. In such a scenario, the application checks *RowCount* to see whether the *update_recordset* statement impacted any rows. In the absence of *RowCount*, the application does another round-trip to the database to get the count of records impacted by the set-based update, an extra step that can degrade performance.

TABLE 4-7 Transaction Statement Examples

Statement Type	Example

ttsbegin
ttscommit
ttsabort
	`boolean b = true;`
	`;`
	`ttsbegin;`
	`if ( b == true )`
	`    ttscommit;`
	`else`
	`    ttsabort;`

select forupdate	`MyTable myTable;`
	`;`
	`ttsbegin;`
	`select forupdate myTable;`
	`myTable.myField = "new value";`
	`myTable.update();`
	`ttscommit;`

insert method	`MyTable myTable;`
	`;`
	`ttsbegin;`
	`myTable.id = "new id";`
	`myTable.myField = "new value";`
	`myTable.insert();`
	`ttscommit;`

update_recordset	`MyTable myTable;Int64 numberOfRecordsAffected;`
	`; ttsbegin;`
	
	`update_recordset myTable setting`
	`    myField1 = "value1",`
	`    myField2 = "value2"`
	`    where myTable.id == "001";`
	`numberOfRecordsAffected = myTable.RowCount();`
	`ttscommit;`

insert_recordset	`MyTable1 myTable1;`
	`MyTable2 myTable2;`
	`Int64 numberOfRecordsAffected;`
	`;`
	`ttsbegin;`
	`insert_recordset myTable2 ( myField1, myField2 )`
	`    select myField1, myField2 from myTable1;`
	`numberOfRecordsAffected = myTable.RowCount();`
	`ttscommit;`

delete_from	`MyTable myTable;`
	`Int64 numberOfRecordsAffected;`
	`;`
	`ttsbegin;`
	`delete_from myTable`
	`    where myTable.id == "001";`
	`numberOfRecordsAffected = myTable.RowCount();`
	`ttscommit;`

Exception Handling

It is a best practice to use the X++ exception handling framework instead of programmatically halting a transaction by using the *ttsabort* statement. An exception (other than the update conflict exception) thrown inside a transaction block halts execution of the block, and all the inserts and updates performed since the first *ttsbegin* statement are rolled back. Throwing an exception has the additional advantage of providing a way to recover object state and maintain database transaction consistency. Inside the *catch* block, you can use the *retry* statement to run the *try* block again. The following example demonstrates throwing an exception inside a database transaction block.

```
static void myJob(Args _args)
{
    MyTable myTable;
    boolean state = true;
    ;
    try
    {
        ttsbegin;
        state = false;
        update_recordset myTable setting
            myField = "value"
            where myTable.id == "001";
        if(state==false)
        {
            throw error("Error text");
        }
        ttscommit;
    }
    catch(Exception::Error)
    {
        state = true;
        retry;
    }
    catch
    {
        print "Unhandled Exception";
        pause;
    }
}
```

The *throw* statement throws an exception that causes the database transaction to halt and roll back. Code execution can't continue inside the scope of the transaction, so the runtime ignores *try* and *catch* statements when inside a transaction. This means that an exception thrown inside a transaction can be caught only outside the transaction, as shown here.

```
static void myJob(Args _args)
{
    try
    {
        ttsbegin;
        try
        {
            ...
            throw error("Error text");
        }
        catch  //Will never catch anything
        {
        }
        ttscommit;
    }
    catch
    {
        print "Got it";
        pause;
    }
}
```

Although a *throw* statement takes the exception enumeration as a parameter, using the *error* method to throw errors is the best choice. The *try* statement's catch list can contain more than one *catch* block. The first *catch* block in the preceding example catches error exceptions. The *retry* statement performs a jump to the first statement in the outer *try* block. The second *catch* block catches all exceptions not caught by *catch* blocks earlier in the *try* statement's catch list. Table 4-8 describes the Dynamics AX system *Exception* data type enumerations that can be used in *try-catch* statements.

TABLE 4-8 *Exception* Data Type Enumerations

Element	Description
Deadlock	Thrown when a database transaction has deadlocked.
*Error**	Thrown when an unrecoverable application error occurs. A *catch* block should assume that all database transactions in a transaction block have been halted and rolled back.
Internal	Thrown when an unrecoverable internal error occurs.
Break	Thrown when a user presses the Break key or Ctrl+C.
DDEerror	Thrown when an error occurs in the use of a Dynamic Data Exchange (DDE) system class.
Sequence	Thrown by the Dynamics AX kernel if a database error or database operation error occurs.
Numeric	Thrown when an unrecoverable error occurs in the *str2int*, *str2int64*, or *str2num* system function.

Element	Description
CLRError	Thrown when an unrecoverable error occurs in a CLR process.
CodeAccessSecurity	Thrown when an unrecoverable error occurs in the *demand* method of a *CodeAccessPermission* object.
UpdateConflict	Thrown when an update conflict error occurs in a transaction block using optimistic concurrency control. The *catch* block should use a *retry* statement to attempt to commit the halted transaction.
UpdateConflictNotRecovered	Thrown when an unrecoverable error occurs in a transaction block using optimistic concurrency control. The *catch* block shouldn't use a *retry* statement to attempt to commit the halted transaction.
DuplicateKeyException	Thrown when a duplicate key error occurs during an insert operation. The *catch* block should change the value of the primary keys and use a *retry* statement to attempt to commit the halted transaction.
DuplicateKeyExceptionNot-Recovered	Thrown when an unrecoverable duplicate key error occurs during an insert operation. The *catch* block shouldn't use a *retry* statement to attempt to commit the halted transaction.

* The *error* method is a static method of the global X++ class for which the X++ compiler allows an abbreviated syntax. The expression *Global::error("Error text")* is equivalent to the error expression in the code examples earlier in this section. Don't confuse these global X++ methods with Dynamics AX system API methods, such as *newguid*.

Dynamics AX 2009 introduces *DuplicateKeyException*. *UpdateConflictException* and now *DuplicateKeyException* are the only data exceptions that a Dynamics AX application can handle. Specifically, with *DuplicateKeyException*, the database transaction isn't rolled back and the application is given a chance to recover. *DuplicateKeyException* facilitates application scenarios (such as Master Planning) that perform batch processing and handles duplicate key exceptions without aborting the transaction in the midst of the resource-intensive processing operation.

The following example illustrates the usage of *DuplicateKeyException*.

```
static void DuplicateKeyExceptionExample(Args _args)
{
    MyTable myTable;

    ttsbegin;
    myTable.Name = 'Microsoft Dynamics AX';
    myTable.insert();
    ttscommit;

    ttsbegin;
    try
```

```
        {
            myTable.Name = 'Microsoft Dynamics AX';
            myTable.insert();
        }
        catch(Exception::DuplicateKeyException)
        {
            info(strfmt('Transaction level: %1', appl.ttsLevel()));
            info(strfmt('%1 already exists.', myTable.Name));
            info(strfmt('Continuing insertion of other records'));
        }
        ttscommit;
    }
```

In the preceding example, the *catch* block handles the duplicate key exception. Notice that the *ttslevel* (transaction level) is still 1, indicating that the transaction hasn't aborted and the application can continue processing other records.

Interoperability

The X++ language has statements that allow interoperability (interop) with .NET CLR assemblies and COM components. The Dynamics AX runtime achieves this interoperability by providing Dynamics AX object wrappers around external objects and by dispatching method calls from the Dynamics AX object to the wrapped object.

CLR Interoperability

You can write X++ statements for CLR interoperability using one of two methods: strong typing or weak typing. We recommend that you use strong typing because it is type-safe and less error-prone than weak typing, and it results in code that is easier to read. The MorphX IDE also provides IntelliSense as you type.

The examples in this section assume that you have added the .NET *System.Xml* assembly to the AOT references node. (See Chapter 2, "The MorphX Development Environment," for a description of programming model elements.) The programs are somewhat verbose because the compiler supports only one method call per statement and because CLR types must be identified by their fully qualified name. For example, the expression *System.Xml.XmlDocument* is the fully qualified type name for the .NET Framework XML document type.

Caution X++ is case-sensitive when referring to CLR types!

The following example demonstrates strongly typed CLR interoperability with implicit type conversions from Dynamics AX strings to CLR strings in the string assignment statements and shows how CLR exceptions are caught in X++.

```
static void myJob(Args _args)
{
   System.Xml.XmlDocument doc = new System.Xml.XmlDocument();
   System.Xml.XmlElement rootElement;
   System.Xml.XmlElement headElement;
   System.Xml.XmlElement docElement;
   System.String xml;
   System.String docStr = "Document";
   System.String headStr = "Head";
   System.Exception ex;
   str errorMessage;
   ;
   try
   {
       rootElement = doc.CreateElement(docStr);
       doc.AppendChild(rootElement);
       headElement = doc.CreateElement(headStr);
       docElement = doc.get_DocumentElement();
       docElement.AppendChild(headElement);
       xml = doc.get_OuterXml();
       print ClrInterop::getAnyTypeForObject(xml);
       pause;
   }
   catch(Exception::CLRError)
   {
       ex = ClrInterop::getLastException();
       if( ex )
       {
           errorMessage = ex.get_Message();
           info( errorMessage );
       }
   }
}
```

The following example illustrates how static CLR methods are invoked by using the X++ static method accessor ::.

```
static void myJob(Args _args)
{
    System.Guid g = System.Guid::NewGuid();
}
```

Dynamics AX 2009 supports CLR arrays. The following example illustrates this new capability.

```
static void myJob(Args _args)
{
    System.Int32 [] myArray = new System.Int32[100]();
    ;
    myArray.SetValue(1000, 0);
    print myArray.GetValue(0);
}
```

Another new capability in Dynamics AX 2009 is the support for passing parameters by reference to CLR methods. Changes the called method makes to the parameter also change the caller variable's value. When non object type variables are passed by reference, they are wrapped temporarily in an object. This operation is often termed *boxing* and is illustrated in the following example.

```
static void myJob(Args _args)
{
    int myVar = 5;
    ;
    MyNamespace.MyMath::Increment(byref myVar);
    print myVar;   // prints 6
}
```

The called method could be implemented in C# like this.

```
// Notice: This example is C# code
static public void Increment(ref int value)
{
    value++;
}
```

Note Passing parameters by reference is supported only for CLR methods, not for X++ methods.

The second method of writing X++ statements for CLR uses weak typing. In the following example, CLR types that perform the same steps as in the first CLR interoperability example are shown. In this case, however, all references are validated at run time, and all type conversions are explicit.

```
static void myJob(Args _args)
{
    ClrObject doc = new ClrObject("System.Xml.XmlDocument");
    ClrObject docStr;
    ClrObject rootElement;
    ClrObject headElement;
    ClrObject docElement;
    ClrObject xml;
    ;
    docStr = ClrInterop::getObjectForAnyType("Document");
    rootElement = doc.CreateElement(docStr);
    doc.AppendChild(rootElement);
    headElement = doc.CreateElement("Head");
    docElement = doc.get_DocumentElement();
    docElement.AppendChild(headElement);
    xml = doc.get_OuterXml();
    print ClrInterop::getAnyTypeForObject(xml);
    pause;
}
```

The first statement in the preceding example demonstrates the use of a static method to convert between X++ primitive types and CLR objects. The *print* statement shows the reverse, converting CLR value types to X++ primitive types. Table 4-9 lists the value type conversions that Dynamics AX supports.

TABLE 4-9 Type Conversions Supported in Dynamics AX

CLR Type	Dynamics AX Type
Byte, SByte, Int16, UInt16, Int32	*Int*
Byte, SByte, Int16, UInt16, Int32, Uint32, Int64	*Int64*
DateTime	*Utcdatetime*
Double, Single	*Real*
Guid	*Guid*
String	*Str*
Dynamics AX Type	**CLR Type**
int	*Int32, Int64*
int64	*Int64*
utcdatetime	*DateTime*
real	*Single, Double*
guid	*Guid*
str	*String*

The preceding code example also demonstrates the X++ method syntax used to access CLR object properties, such as *get_DocumentElement*. The CLR supports several operators that are not supported in X++. Table 4-10 lists the supported CLR operators and the alternative method syntax.

TABLE 4-10 CLR Operators and Methods

CLR Operators	CLR Methods
Property operators	*get_<property>, set_<property>*
Index operators	*get_Item, set_Item*
Math operators	*op_<operation>(arguments)*

The following features of CLR can't be used with X++:

- Public fields (can be accessed by using CLR reflection classes)
- Events and delegates
- Generics
- Inner types
- The *Container* composite type
- Namespace declarations

COM Interoperability

The following code example demonstrates COM interoperability with the XML document type in the Microsoft XML Core Services (MSXML) 6.0 COM component. The example assumes that you've installed MSXML. The MSXML document is first instantiated and wrapped in a Dynamics AX COM object wrapper. A COM variant wrapper is created for a COM string. The direction of the variant is into the COM component. The root element and head element variables are declared as COM objects. The example shows how to fill a string variant with an X++ string and then use the variant as an argument to a COM method, *loadXml*. The statement that creates the head element demonstrates how the Dynamics AX runtime automatically converts Dynamics AX primitive objects into COM variants.

```
static void Job2(Args _args)
{
    COM doc = new COM("Msxml2.DomDocument.6.0");
    COMVariant rootXml = new COMVariant(COMVariantInOut::In,COMVariantType::VT_BSTR);
    COM rootElement;
    COM headElement;
    ;
```

```
    rootXml.bStr("<Root></Root>");
    doc.loadXml(rootXml);
    rootElement = doc.documentElement();
    headElement = doc.createElement("Head");
    rootElement.appendChild(headElement);
    print doc.xml();
    pause;
}
```

Macros

The macro capabilities in X++ enable you to define and use constants and perform conditional compilation. Macros are unstructured because they are not defined in the X++ syntax. Macros are handled before the source code is compiled. You can add macros anywhere you write source code: in methods and in class declarations.

Table 4-11 shows the supported macro directives.

TABLE 4-11 Macro Directives

Directive	Description
#define *#globaldefine*	Defines a macro with a value. `#define.MyMacro(SomeValue)` Defines the macro *MyMacro* with the value *SomeValue*.

#macro
…
#endmacro
 	
#localmacro
…
#endmacro
	Defines a macro with a value spanning multiple lines.
	
	`#macro.MyMacro`
	`   print "foo";`
	`   print "bar";`
	`#endmacro`
	
	Defines the macro *MyMacro* with a multiple-line value.

#macrolib	Includes a macro library. As a shorthand form of this directive, you can omit *macrolib*.
	
	`#macrolib.MyMacroLibrary`
	`#MyMacroLibrary`
	
	Both include the macro library *MyMacroLibrary*, which is defined under the Macros node in the AOT.

Directive	Description

#MyMacro	Replaces a macro with its value.
	`#define.MyMacro("Hello World")`
	`print #MyMacro;`
	Defines the macro *MyMacro* and prints its value. In this example, "Hello World" would be printed.

#definc *#defdec*	Increments and decrements the value of a macro; typically used when the value is an integer. `#defdec.MyIntMacro` Decrements the value of the macro *MyIntMacro*.
#undef	Removes the definition of a macro. `#undef.MyMacro` Removes the definition of the macro *MyMacro*.

#if
...
#endif
	Conditional compile. If the macro referenced by the *#if* directive is defined or has a specific value, the following text is included in the compilation.
	`#if.MyMacro`
	`print "MyMacro is defined";`
	`#endif`
	If *MyMacro* is defined, the *print* statement is included as part of the source code.
	`#if.MyMacro(SomeValue)`
	`print "MyMacro is defined and has value: SomeValue";`
	`#endif`
	If *MyMacro* has *SomeValue*, the *print* statement is included as part of the source code.

#ifnot
...
#endif
	Conditional compile. If the macro referenced by the *#ifnot* directive isn't defined or doesn't have a specific value, the following text is included in the compilation.
	`#ifnot.MyMacro`
	`print "MyMacro is not defined";`
	`#endif`
	If *MyMacro* is not defined, the *print* statement is included as part of the source code.
	`#ifnot.MyMacro(SomeValue)`
	`print "MyMacro does not have value: SomeValue; or it is not defined";`
	`#endif`
	If *MyMacro* is not defined, or does not have *SomeValue*, the *print* statement is included as part of the source code.

The following example shows a macro definition and reference.

```
void myMethod()
{
    #define.HelloWorld("Hello World")
;
    print #HelloWorld;
    pause;
}
```

As we noted in Table 4-11, a macro library is created under the Macros node in the AOT. The library is included in a class declaration header or class method, as shown in the following example.

```
class myClass
{
    #MyMacroLibrary1
}
public void myMethod()
{
    #MyMacroLibrary2
    ;
    #MacroFromMyMacroLibrary1
    #MacroFromMyMacroLibrary2
}
```

A macro can also use parameters. The compiler inserts the parameters at the positions of the placeholders. The following example shows a local macro using parameters.

```
void myMethod()
{
    #localmacro.add
        %1 + %2
    #endmacro

    print #add(1, 2);
    print #add("Hello", "World");
    pause;
}
```

When a macro library is included or a macro is defined in the class declaration of a class, the macro can be used in the class and in all classes derived from the class. A subclass can redefine the macro.

Comments

X++ allows single-line and multiple-line comments. Single-line comments start with *//* and end at the end of the line. Multiple-line comments start with */** and ended with **/*. You can't nest multiple-line comments.

You can add reminders to yourself in comments that the compiler picks up and presents to you as tasks in its output window. To set up these tasks, start a single-line comment with the word *TODO* (all uppercase). Be aware that tasks occurring inside multiple-line comments are treated as commented out, so the compiler doesn't pick them up.

Here is a code example with comments reminding the developer to add a new procedure while commenting out an existing procedure.

```
public void myMethod()
{
    //Declare variables
    int value;

//TODO Validate if calculation is really required
/*
    //Perform calculation
    value = this.calc();
*/
    ...
}
```

XML Documentation

You can document XML methods and classes directly in X++ by writing */// (triple slash)* followed by structured documentation in XML format. The XML documentation must be above the actual code.

The contents of XML are strict and must align with the code. The Best Practices tool contains a set of rules that can validate the XML documentation. The supported tags are shown in Table 4-12.

TABLE 4-12 XML Tags Supported for XML Documentation

Tag	Description
<summary>	Describes a method or a class.
<param>	Describes the parameters of a method.
<returns>	Describes the return value of a method.

Tag	Description
<remarks>	Adds information that supplements the information provided in the *<summary>* tag.
<exception>	Documents exceptions that are thrown by a method.
<permission>	Describes the permission needed to access methods using *CodeAccessSecurity.demand.*
<seealso>	Lists references to related and relevant documentation.

You can extract the written XML documentation for an AOT project by using the Add-Ins menu option Extract XML Documentation. One XML file containing all the documentation written for the elements inside the project is produced. You can also use this XML file to publish the documentation.

Here is a code example in which XML documentation has been written for a static method on the *Global* class.

```
/// <summary>
/// Converts an X++ utcdatetime value to a .NET System.DateTime object.
/// </summary>
/// <param name="_utcDateTime">
/// The X++ utcdatetime to convert.
/// </param>
/// <returns>
/// A .NET System.DateTime object.
/// </returns>
static client server anytype utcDateTime2SystemDateTime(utcdatetime _utcDateTime)
{
    ;
    return CLRInterop::getObjectForAnyType(_utcDateTime);
}
```

Classes and Interfaces

You define types and their structure in the AOT, not in the X++ language. Other programming languages that support type declarations do so within code, but Dynamics AX supports an object layering feature that accepts X++ source code customizations to type declaration parts that comprise variable declarations and method declarations. Each part of a type declaration is managed as a separate compilation unit, and model data is used to manage, persist, and reconstitute dynamic types whose parts can comprise compilation units from many object layers.

You use X++ to define logic, including method profiles (return value, method name, and parameter type and name). The X++ editor allows you to add new methods to the AOT, so you can continue to use the X++ editor while constructing types.

You use X++ class declarations to declare protected instance variable fields that are members of application logic and framework reference types. You can't declare private or public variable fields. You can declare classes abstract if they are incomplete type specifications that can't be instantiated. You can also declare them final if they are complete specifications that can't be further specialized. The following code provides an example of an abstract class declaration header.

```
abstract class MyClass
{
}
```

You can also structure classes into single-inheritance generalization or specialization hierarchies in which derived classes inherit and override members of base classes. The following code shows an example of a derived class declaration header that specifies that *MyDerivedClass* extends the abstract base class *MyClass*. It also specifies that *MyDerivedClass* is final and can't be further specialized by another class. Because X++ doesn't support multiple inheritance, derived classes can extend only one base class.

```
final class MyDerivedClass extends MyClass
{
}
```

X++ also supports interface type specifications that specify method signatures but don't define their implementation. Classes can implement more than one interface, but the class and its derived classes should together provide definitions for the methods declared in all the interfaces. If it fails to provide the method definitions, the class itself is marked as abstract. The following code provides an example of an interface declaration header and a class declaration header that implements the interface.

```
interface MyInterface
{
    void myMethod();
}
class MyClass implements MyInterface
{
    void myMethod()
    {
    }
}
```

Fields

A field is a class member that represents a variable and its type. Fields are declared in class declaration headers; each class and interface has a definition part with the name *classDeclaration* in the AOT. Fields are accessible only to code statements that are part of the class declaration or derived class declarations. Assignment statements are not allowed in class declaration headers. The following example demonstrates how variables are initialized with assignment statements in a *new* method.

```
class MyClass
{
    str s;
    int i;
    MyClass1 myClass1;

    public void new()
    {
        i = 0;
        myClass1 = new MyClass1();
    }
}
```

Methods

A method on a class is a member that uses statements to define the behavior of an object. An interface method is a member that declares an expected behavior of an object. The following code provides an example of a method declaration on an interface and an implementation of the method on a class that implements the interface.

```
interface MyInterface
{
    public str myMethod()
    {
    }
}
class myClass implements MyInterface
{
    public str myMethod();
    {
        return "Hello World";
     }
}
```

Methods are defined with public, private, or protected access modifiers. Methods are publicly accessible by default. Additional method modifiers supported by X++ are provided in Table 4-13.

TABLE 4-13 Method Modifiers Supported by X++

Modifier	Description
static	Static methods are accessed via class declarations. Fields can't be accessed from within a static method.
final	Final methods can't be overridden by methods with the same name in derived classes.
abstract	Abstract methods have no implementation. Derived classes must provide definitions for abstract methods.
server	Server methods can execute only on an Application Object Server. The *server* modifier is allowed only on static methods.
client	Client methods can execute only on a MorphX client. The *client* modifiers are allowed only on static methods.
display	Display methods are invoked each time a form or report is redrawn. The *display* modifier is allowed only on table, form, form data, report, and report design methods.
edit	The *edit* method is invoked each time a form is redrawn or a user provides input through a form control. The *edit* modifier is allowed only on table, form, and form data source methods.

Method parameters can have default values that are used when parameters are omitted from method invocations. The following code sample prints "Hello World" when *myMethod* is invoked with no parameters.

```
public void myMethod(str s = "Hello World")
{
    print s;
    pause;
}

public static void main(Args _args);
{
    myMethod();
}
```

A constructor is a special instance method that is invoked to initialize an object when the *new* operator is executed by the Dynamics AX runtime. You can't call constructors directly from X++ code. The following sample provides an example of a class declaration header and an instance constructor method that takes one parameter as an argument.

```
class myClass
{
    int i;

    public void new(int _i)
    {
        i = _i;
    }
}
```

Code Access Security

Code access security (CAS) is a mechanism designed to protect systems from dangerous APIs that are invoked by untrusted code. CAS has nothing to do with user authentication or authorization; it is a mechanism allowing two pieces of code to communicate in an uncompromisable manner.

> **Caution** X++ developers are responsible for writing code that conforms to Trustworthy Computing guidelines. You can find those guidelines in the white paper "Writing Secure X++ Code," available from the Microsoft Dynamics AX Web site (*http://microsoft.com/dynamics/ax/using/productdocumentation/technicalarticles*).

In the Dynamics AX implementation of CAS, trusted code is defined as code from the AOT running on the Application Object Server (AOS). The first part of the definition ensures that the code is written by a trusted X++ developer. Developer privileges are the highest level of privileges in Dynamics AX and should be granted only to trusted personnel. The second part of the definition ensures the code the trusted developer has written hasn't been tampered with. If the code executes outside the AOS—on a client, for example—it can't be trusted because of the possibility that it was altered on the client side before execution. Untrusted code also includes code that is executed via the *runBuf* and *evalBuf* methods. These methods are typically used to execute code generated at run time based on user input.

CAS enables a secure handshake between an API and its consumer. Only consumers who provide the right handshake can invoke the API. Any other invocation raises an exception.

The secure handshake is established through the *CodeAccessPermission* class or one of its specializations. The consumer must request permission to call the API, which is done by calling *CodeAccessPermission.assert*. The API verifies that the consumer has the right permissions by calling *CodeAccessPermission.demand*. The *demand* method searches the call stack for a matching assertion. If untrusted code exists on the call stack before the matching assert, an exception is raised. This process is illustrated in Figure 4-1.

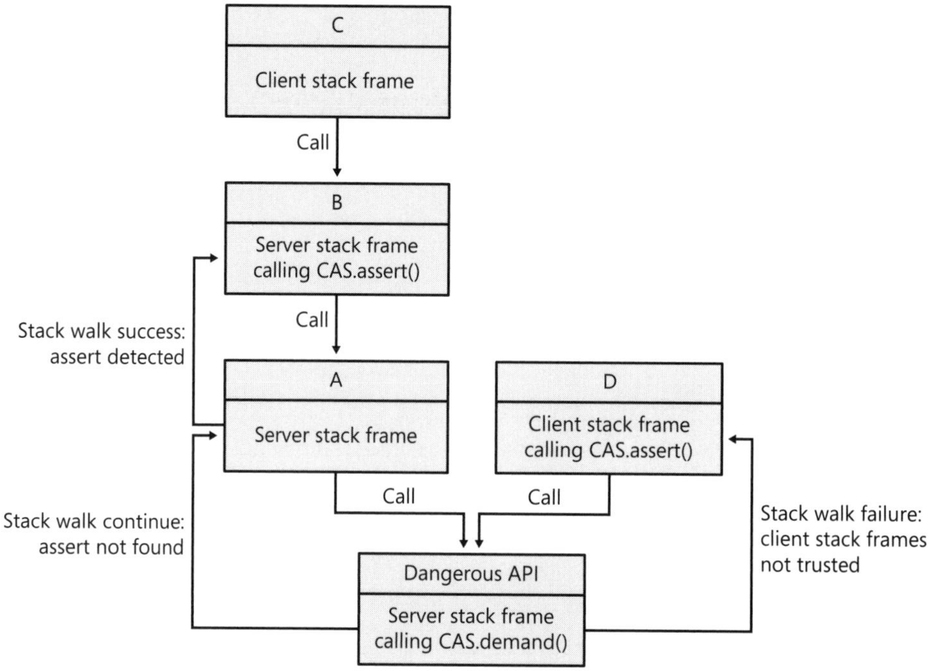

FIGURE 4-1 Code access security stack frame walk

Here is an example of a dangerous API protected by CAS and a consumer providing the right permissions to invoke the API.

```
class WinApiServer
{
    // Delete any given file on the server
    public server static boolean deleteFile(Filename _fileName)
    {
        FileIOPermission    fileIOPerm;
        ;
        // Check file I/O permission
        fileIOPerm = new FileIOPermission(_fileName, 'w');
        fileIOPerm.demand();

        // Delete the file
        System.IO.File::Delete(_filename);
    }
}

class Consumer
{
    // Delete the temporary file on the server
    public server static void deleteTmpFile()
```

```
    {
        FileIOPermission    fileIOPerm;
        FileName            filename = @"c:\tmp\file.tmp";
        ;
        // Request file I/O permission
        fileIOPerm = new FileIOPermission(filename, 'w');
        fileIOPerm.assert();

        // Use CAS protected API to delete the file
        WinApiServer::deleteFile(filename);
    }
}
```

WinAPIServer::deleteFile is considered a dangerous API because it exposes the .NET API *System.IO.File::Delete(string fileName)*. Exposing this API on the server is dangerous because it allows the user to remotely delete any file on the server, possibly bringing the server down. In the example, *WinApiServer::deleteFile* demands that the caller has asserted that the input filename is valid. The demand prevents use of the API from the client tier and from any code not stored in the AOT.

Caution When using *assert*, make sure that you don't create a new API that is just as dangerous as the one CAS has secured. When you call *assert*, you are asserting that your code doesn't expose the same vulnerability that required the protection of CAS. For example, had the *deleteTmpFile* method in the foregoing example taken the filename as a parameter, it could have been used to bypass the CAS protection of *WinApi::deleteFile* and delete any file on the server.

Design and Implementation Patterns

So far in this chapter, we've described the individual elements of X++. You've seen that statements are grouped into methods, and methods into classes, tables, and other model element types. These structures enable you to inspect X++ code on higher levels of abstractions. The following example shows how an assignment operation can be encapsulated into a method to raise the level of abstraction.

```
control.show();
```

is on a higher level of abstraction than

```
flags = flags | 0x0004;
```

Patterns enable developers to communicate their solutions more effectively and to reuse proven solutions to common problems. Using patterns offers readers of the source code the benefit of quickly understanding the purpose of a particular implementation. You should always bear in mind that even as a code author you spend more time reading source code than writing it.

Implementations of patterns are typically recognizable by the names used for classes, methods, parameters, and variables. Arguably, naming these elements so that they effectively convey the intention of the code is the developer's most difficult task. A lot of the information in the existing literature on design patterns pertains to object-oriented languages, and you can benefit from exploring that information to find patterns and techniques you can apply when you're writing X++ code. Design patterns express relationships or interactions between several classes or objects. They don't prescribe a specific implementation, but they do offer a template solution for a typical design problem. In contrast, implementation patterns are implementation specific and can have a scope that spans only a single statement.

This section highlights some of the most frequently used patterns specific to X++. More descriptions are available in the Microsoft Dynamics AX SDK on MSDN.

Class-Level Patterns

These patterns apply to classes in X++.

Parameter Methods

To set and get a class field from outside the class, you should implement a parameter method. The parameter method should have the same name as the field and be prefixed with *parm*. Parameter methods come in two flavors: *get-only* and *get/set*.

```
public class Employee
{
    EmployeeName name;

    public EmployeeName parmName(EmployeeName _name = name)
    {
        name = _name;
        return name;
    }
}
```

Constructor Encapsulation

The purpose of the constructor encapsulation pattern is to enable *Liskov's class substitution principle*. In other words, constructor encapsulation lets you replace an existing class with a customized class without using the layering system. Just as in the layering system, this pattern enables changing the logic in a class without having to update any references to the class. Be careful to avoid overlayering because it often causes upgrade conflicts. For more information on upgrading code, see Chapter 18, "Code Upgrade."

Classes that have a static *construct* method are following the constructor encapsulation pattern. The *construct* method should instantiate the class and immediately return the instance. The *construct* method must be static and shouldn't take any parameters.

When parameters are required, you should implement the static *new* methods. These methods call the *construct* method to instantiate the class and then call the parameter methods to set the parameters; in this case, the *construct* method should be private.

```
public class Employee
{
    ...
    protected void new()
    {
    }

    protected static Employee construct()
    {
        return new Employee();
    }

    public static Employee newName(EmployeeName name)
    {
        Employee employee = Employee::construct();
        ;
        employee.parmName(name);
        return employee;
    }
}
```

Serialization with the *pack* and *unpack* Methods

Many classes require the ability to serialize and deserialize themselves. Serialization is an operation that extracts an object's state into value-type data; deserialization creates an instance from that data.

X++ classes implementing the *Packable* interface support serialization. The *Packable* interface contains two methods: *pack* and *unpack*. The *pack* method returns a container with the object's state; the *Unpack* method takes a container as a parameter and sets the object's state accordingly. You should include a versioning number as the first entry in the container to make the code resilient to old packed data stored in the database when the implementation changes.

```
public class Employee implements SysPackable
{
    EmployeeName name;
    #define.currentVersion(1)
    #localmacro.CurrentList
        name
    #endmacro
    ...

    public container pack()
    {
        return [#currentVersion, #currentList);
    }

    public boolean unpack(container packedClass)
    {
        Version version = runbase::getVersion(packedClass);

        switch (version)
        {
            case #CurrentVersion:
                [version, #CurrentList] = packedClass;
                break;
            default:   //The version number is unsupported
                return false;
        }
        return true;
    }
}
```

Observers and Listeners

The Observer/Listener design pattern is used in many languages. It is particularly useful in X++ because X++ doesn't support an event concept. This pattern enables a class to subscribe to an event and to be invoked when the event occurs. Classes and interfaces that have "Observer" or "Listener" as part of their names are implementations of the Observer/Listener pattern.

Here is an implementation of the Observer pattern. In this example, an *Observer* class is assumed to exist and have a public *invoke* method.

```
List observers = new List(Types::Class);

public void registerObserver(object observer)
{
    observers.addEnd(observer);
}
```

```
private void invokeObservers()
{
    ListEnumerator listEnum = observers.getEnumerator();
    Object observer;

    while (listEnum.moveNext())
    {
        observer = listEnum.current();
        //Call invoke() on all observers
        observer.invoke();
    }
}
```

Table-Level Patterns

The patterns described in this section—the *Find* and *Exists* methods, polymorphic associations (Table/Group/All), and Generic Record References—apply to tables.

Find and *Exists* Methods

Each table must have the two static methods *Find* and *Exists*. They both take the table's primary keys as parameters and return the matching record or a Boolean value, respectively. Besides the primary keys, the *Find* method also takes a *Boolean* parameter that specifies whether the record should be selected for update.

For the *CustTable* table, these methods have the following profiles.

```
static CustTable find(CustAccount accountNum, boolean _forUpdate = false)
static boolean exist(CustAccount accountNum)
```

Polymorphic Associations

The Table/Group/All pattern is used to model a polymorphic association to either a specific record in another table, a collection of records in another table, or all records in another table. For example, a record could be associated with a specific item, all items in an item group, or all items.

You implemented the Table/Group/All pattern by creating two fields and two relations on the table. By convention, the first field's name has the suffix *Code*, as in *ItemCode*. This field is modeled using the enum *TableGroupAll*. The second field's name usually has the suffix *Relation*, for example, *ItemRelation*. This field is modeled using the extended data type that is the primary key in the foreign tables. The two relations are both of the type *Fixed* field relation. The first relation specifies that when the *Code* field equals 0 (*TableGroupAll::Table*), the *Relation* field equals the primary key in the foreign master data table. The second relation specifies that when the *Code* field equals 1 (*TableGroupAll::Group*), the *Relation* field equals the primary key in the foreign grouping table.

Figure 4-2 shows an example.

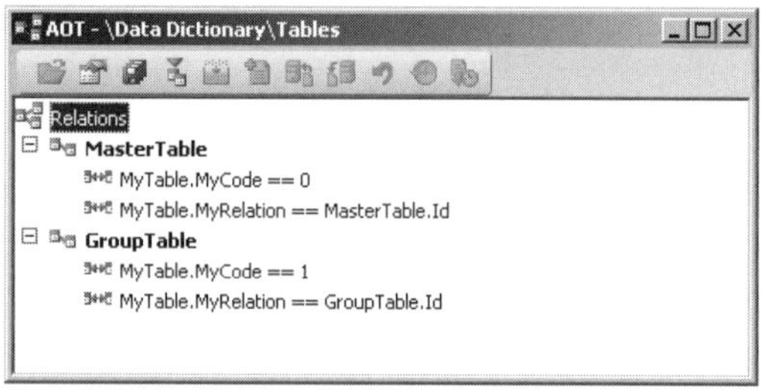

FIGURE 4-2 A polymorphic association

Generic Record Reference

The Generic Record Reference pattern is a variation of the Table/Group/All pattern. It is used to model an association to a foreign table. It comes in three flavors: (a) an association to any record in one specific table, (b) an association to any record in a fixed set of specific tables, and (c) an association to any record in any table.

All three flavors of this pattern are implemented by creating a field using the *RefRecId* extended data type.

To model an association to any record in one specific table (flavor a), a relation is created from the *RefRecId* field to the foreign table's *RecId* field, as illustrated in Figure 4-3.

FIGURE 4-3 An association to one specific table

For flavors b and c, an additional field is required. This field is created using the *RefTableId* extended data type. To model an association to any record in a fixed set of specific tables (flavor b), a relation is created for each specific foreign table from the *RefTableId* field to the foreign table's *TableId* field, and from the *RefRecId* field to the foreign table's *RecId* field, like shown in Figure 4-4.

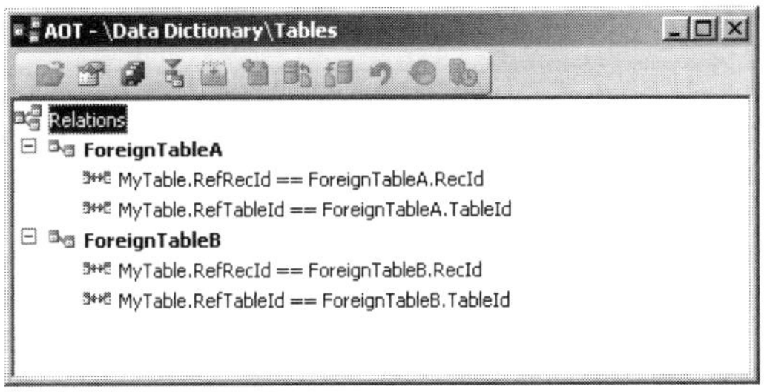

FIGURE 4-4 A association to any record in a fixed set of tables

To model an association to any record in any table (flavor c), a relation is created from the *RefTableId* field to the generic table *Common TableId* field and from the *RefRecId* field to *Common RecId* field, as shown in Figure 4-5.

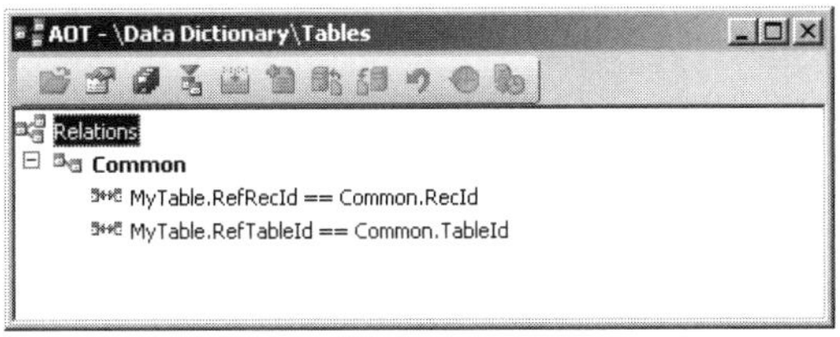

FIGURE 4-5 An association to any record in any table

Part II

Core Development Concepts

In this part:

Chapter 5

Customizing Dynamics AX

In this chapter:

The objectives of this chapter are to:

- Describe how to customize Microsoft Dynamics AX 2009 inventory tables and classes to implement new inventory dimensions.
- Explain how to customize forms in Dynamics AX.
- Describe how to customize reports in Dynamics AX.
- Explain how to customize the number sequence classes in Dynamics AX to implement a new number sequence.

Introduction

Dynamics AX allows you to customize an application by changing or adding metadata or modifying the application's source code. The unique layering feature ensures that you can always return to the point at which you began to make modifications or restore the original metadata and X++ code.

The next section of this chapter describes how to customize Dynamics AX to include a set of new inventory dimensions by customizing a set of tables and classes. The new dimensions automatically appear in forms and reports without requiring you to change the original code or metadata of any of these elements.

The chapter also describes form and report customizations. The sales order form is modified to include a product image, and the sales invoice report is modified to include promotional text.

The last section of the chapter explains how to customize the number sequence classes to enable the use of a new number sequence, which is useful for creating invoice numbers, voucher numbers, and so on.

Table and Class Customization

By default, Dynamics AX 2009 comes with nine default inventory dimensions. (The user can define additional inventory dimensions.) Dimensions describe the characteristics of items or item lots. Item dimensions might include characteristics such as configuration, model, and size. Item lots might have storage dimensions, such as site, warehouse, location, or pallet, or they might be identified by a serial number and batch number. The site dimension is new in Dynamics AX 2009.

The following customization scenario describes how to customize tables and classes used by the inventory dimension feature to implement two new item dimensions that describe a specific bicycle configuration: frame size and wheel size. This description isn't an exhaustive list of elements that you must change; instead, it offers guidelines for finding the elements necessary to customize the full implementation of a new inventory dimension.

Creating New Dimension Types

When implementing new inventory dimensions, your first task is to create extended data types for each of the dimensions. Doing so provides the following benefits:

- To apply the inventory dimensions to multiple tables, you define the type just once and then apply it to each table.
- The *Label* property, the *HelpText* property, and a few constraints can be defined on the data type, ensuring consistent behavior and appearance of fields of the same type.
- If the type is declared as a parameter or a return type for a method, you can declare variables of the type in X++ code to optimize IntelliSense responsiveness and to improve the readability of the code.

This scenario defines a table in which a field of the specific type is part of the primary key. You can define the relationship to this table on the extended data type and subsequently instruct the application runtime to provide lookups and Go To The Main Table Form support.

In this example, you enter the Data Dictionary in the Application Object Tree (AOT) and create a *BikeFrameSize* extended data type and a *BikeWheelSize* extended data type. Table 5-1 lists the property settings that deviate from the default settings.

TABLE 5-1 ***BikeFrameSize* and *BikeWheelSize* Property Settings**

Property	*BikeFrameSize*	*BikeWheelSize*
Type	Real	Real
Label	Frame size	Wheel size
HelpText	Frame size in inches	Wheel size in inches
AllowNegative	No	No
ShowZero	No	No
NoOfDecimals	0	0

Figure 5-1 shows the property sheet for the *BikeFrameSize* extended data type, accessible by clicking Properties on the context menu for the type.

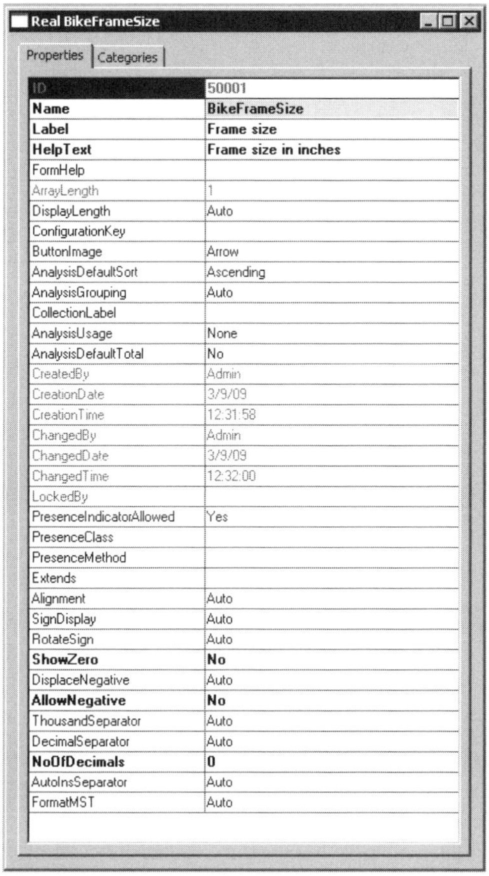

FIGURE 5-1 Property sheet for the *BikeFrameSize* extended data type

> **Best Practices** Creating labels for text in the *Label* and *HelpText* properties is, of course, a best practice, but the text in this example is written as a literal (as opposed to referencing a label) to improve readability.

Next, create two tables, named *BikeFrameSizeTable* and *BikeWheelSizeTable*, in which the frame and wheel sizes for each item can be stored. In addition to the specific inventory dimension types, the tables also contain an *ItemId* field and a *Name* field. The *ItemId* and dimension in each table constitute the table's primary index.

Table 5-2 lists the *BikeFrameSizeTable* property settings that deviate from the default settings. (The property settings for *BikeWheelSizeTable* are identical except for the *BikeWheelSize* field and its extended property type.)

TABLE 5-2 Field Property Settings

Property	*ItemId*	*BikeFrameSize*	*Name*
Type	*String*	Real	String
ExtendedDataType	*ItemId*	*BikeFrameSize*	Name
Mandatory	Yes	Yes	No (default)
AllowEdit	No	No	Yes (default)

Create a unique index on both tables. For *BikeFrameSizeTable*, name the index *FrameIdx* and make it contain the *ItemId* field and the *BikeFrameSize* field. For *BikeWheelSizeTable*, name the index *WheelIdx* and make it contain the *ItemId* field and the *BikeWheelSize* field. Declare the indexes as the *PrimaryIndex* on the respective tables. In the AOT, the fields and the indexes appear as shown in Figure 5-2.

FIGURE 5-2 *BikeFrameSizeTable* definition

In addition to the fields and index shown in Figure 5-2, you should also set properties in the tables for caching, form references, and so on, and the table should contain field groups and methods for checking the validity of the fields. However, it is beyond the scope of this chapter to describe these enhancements. The Microsoft Dynamics AX 2009 software development kit (SDK) contains guidelines and best practices for creating tables.

After you define the tables, you should update the extended data types to reflect their relationship to the individual tables, as shown in Figure 5-3.

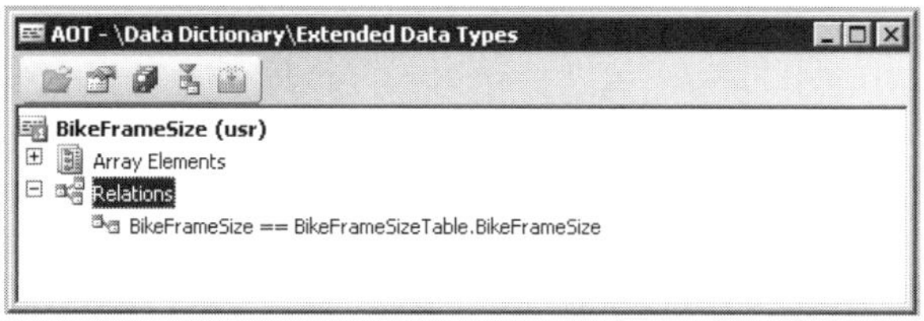

FIGURE 5-3 Extended data type relations of *BikeFrameSize*

This relationship instructs the Dynamics AX runtime to provide lookup and Go To The Main Table Form functionality when fields of these types appear on forms. The application runtime uses the related table as the data source for the lookup form and also to find the main table form from the *FormRef* property on the table. You must therefore create forms for the *BikeFrameSizeTable* and *BikeWheelSizeTable* tables and menu items to open the forms. These menu items are added to the *FormRef* properties on the corresponding tables. You could design the forms to mirror the form shown in Figure 5-4. See the Microsoft Dynamics AX 2009 SDK for general information on designing forms.

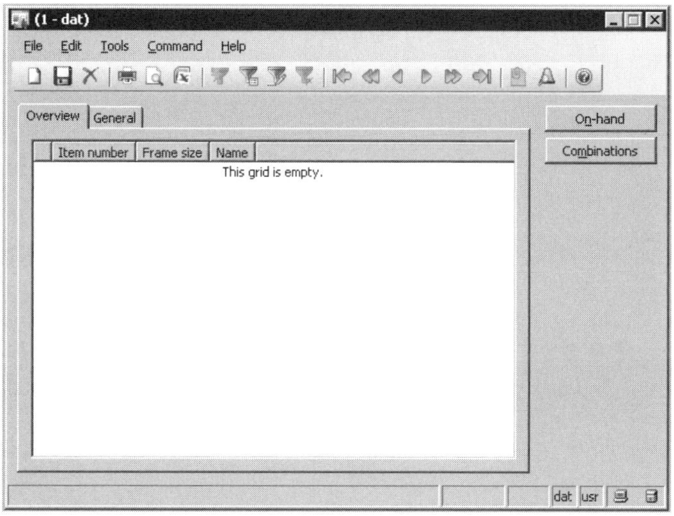

FIGURE 5-4 Frame Sizes form

Adding New Dimensions to a Table

To store transactions with the new inventory dimensions, the dimensions must be added to the *InventDim* table. You do this by creating two new fields, *BikeFrameSize* and *BikeWheelSize*, of the corresponding type on the *InventDim* table. You should also add these fields to the unique *DimIdx* index because any combination of inventory dimensions can exist only once in the *InventDim* table.

The display of inventory dimensions in almost any form in the Dynamics AX application is based on field groups and where the content of the field group in the form is built at run time. The forms runtime in Dynamics AX builds the group from the list of fields in the associated field group defined on the *InventDim* table. Therefore, by adding the new fields to the *InventoryDimensions* field group on the *InventDim* table, you make the two new fields available in almost any form that displays inventory dimensions. Position the fields in the field group based on where you want them to appear relative to the other dimensions, as shown in Figure 5-5.

Figure 5-5 shows *usr* flags on the *AutoReport* and *ItemDimensions* field groups, indicating that the custom fields have been added to these groups as well. The *AutoReport* group is modified so that it prints the new dimensions if you create an auto report by clicking Print on a form; the *ItemDimensions* group is modified because the new dimensions are considered to be item dimensions.

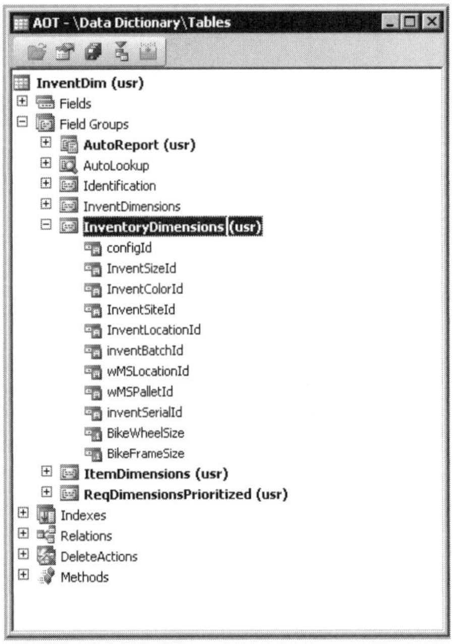

FIGURE 5-5 *InventDim* table with customized *InventoryDimensions* field group

Although the inventory dimensions are now available in any form because of the interpretation of the field groups by the Dynamics AX forms runtime, the fields still aren't visible or editable because they aren't enabled in any inventory dimension group. Moreover, the two new inventory dimensions automatically appear in the Dimension Groups form because the inventory dimension feature also interprets the *InventoryDimensions* field group on the *InventDim* table to find all the currently available inventory dimensions. To make the form work with the new dimensions, you merely state whether the new dimensions are item dimensions. You do this by adding the new dimensions to the *isFieldItemDim* method on the *InventDim* table, as shown in the following X++ code. The added lines are shown in bold.

```
static public boolean isFieldIdItemDim(fieldId dimFieldId)
{
    ;
    #InventDimDevelop

    switch (dimFieldId)
    {
        case (fieldnum(InventDim,ConfigId))         :
        case (fieldnum(InventDim,InventSizeId))     :
        case (fieldnum(InventDim,InventColorId))    :
        case (fieldnum(InventDim,BikeFrameSize))    : // Frame size added
        case (fieldnum(InventDim,BikeWheelSize))    : // Wheel size added
            return true;

        case (fieldnum(InventDim,InventSiteId))     :
        case (fieldnum(InventDim,InventLocationId)) :
        case (fieldnum(InventDim,InventBatchId))    :
        case (fieldnum(InventDim,wMSLocationId))    :
        case (fieldnum(InventDim,wMSPalletId))      :
        case (fieldnum(InventDim,InventSerialId))   :
            return false;
    }

    throw error("@SYS70108");
}
```

The new dimensions will be available for setup in the Dimension Groups form, which is reached through the navigation pane under Inventory Management\Setup\Dimensions\Dimension Groups. The dimensions are located in the Item Dimensions grid, as shown in Figure 5-6.

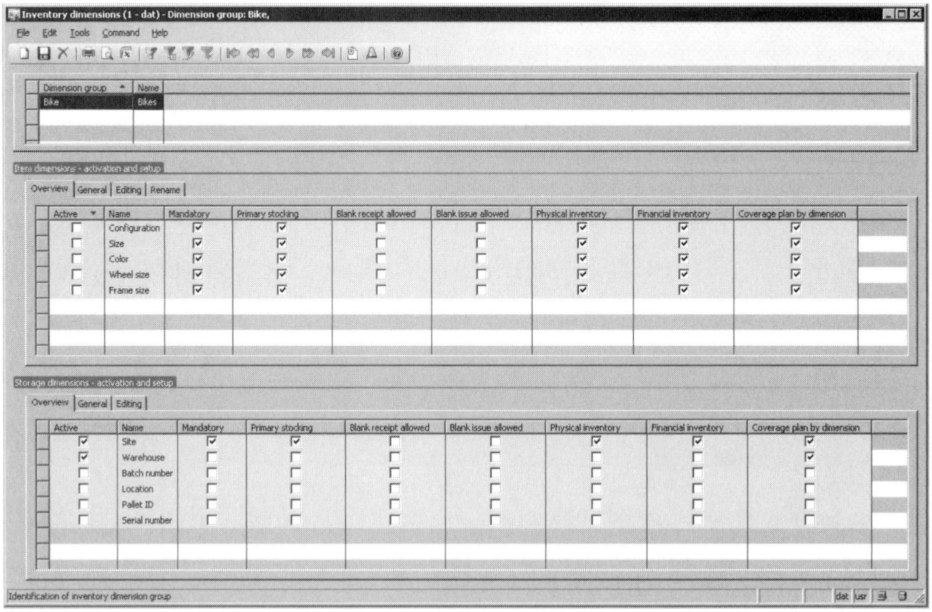

FIGURE 5-6 Dimension Groups form with new item dimensions

> **Important** You need to restart the Application Object Server (AOS) after adding fields to the *InventoryDimensions* field group because the list of fields in the group is cached in memory on both the client and the server tiers.

Enabling New Dimensions in Forms

You can enable new dimensions by setting up dimension groups, but you won't see them yet in the forms. The inventory dimension feature uses a temporary table named *InventDimParm* to carry certain information, such as whether a dimension has the following attributes:

- Is enabled
- Is an item dimension
- Is a primary stocking dimension
- Is visible
- Serves as a filter-by term
- Serves as a group-by term
- Serves as an order-by term

The dimension groups are enabled and controlled by reflecting each inventory dimension as a boolean flag field on the *InventDimParm* table and then matching the corresponding fields in the X++ code. For example, when a dimension group is queried to determine which dimensions are active, an *InventDimParm* record is returned where the corresponding flag field is set to true for the active dimensions. The remaining flags are set to false. You must therefore add a frame-size flag and a wheel-size flag to the *InventDimParm* table, as shown in Table 5-3.

TABLE 5-3 *BikeFrameSizeFlag* and *BikeWheelSizeFlag* Property Settings

Property	*BikeFrameSizeFlag*	*BikeWheelSizeFlag*
Type	enum	enum
Label	Frame size	Wheel size
HelpText	View by frame size	View by wheel size
ExtendedDataType	*NoYesId*	*NoYesId*
Enum	*NoYes*	*NoYes*

You should also add the new fields to the *FixedView* and *View* field groups defined on the *InventDimParm* table, because they are used in forms from which it is possible to specify whether a dimension should be visible.

When you add fields to the table and field groups, you must map the new fields on the *InventDim* table to the corresponding fields on the *InventDimParm* table in the X++ code. To do this, you modify the *dim2DimParm* method on the *InventDim* table, as shown in the following X++ code. The added mappings of *BikeFrameSize* and *BikeWheelSize* appear in bold.

```
static public fieldId dim2dimParm(fieldId dimField)
{
    ;
    #InventDimDevelop

    switch (dimField)
    {
        case (fieldnum(InventDim,ConfigId))         :
            return fieldnum(InventDimParm,ConfigIdFlag);
        case (fieldnum(InventDim,InventSizeId))     :
            return fieldnum(InventDimParm,InventSizeIdFlag);
        case (fieldnum(InventDim,InventColorId))    :
            return fieldnum(InventDimParm,InventColorIdFlag);
        case (fieldnum(InventDim,InventSiteId))     :
            return fieldnum(InventDimParm,InventSiteIdFlag);
        case (fieldnum(InventDim,InventLocationId)) :
            return fieldnum(InventDimParm,InventLocationIdFlag);
        case (fieldnum(InventDim,InventBatchId))    :
            return fieldnum(InventDimParm,InventBatchIdFlag);
        case (fieldnum(InventDim,wMSLocationId))    :
            return fieldnum(InventDimParm,WMSLocationIdFlag);
        case (fieldnum(InventDim,wMSPalletId))      :
            return fieldnum(InventDimParm,WMSPalletIdFlag);
        case (fieldnum(InventDim,InventSerialId))   :
```

```
            return fieldnum(InventDimParm,InventSerialIdFlag);
        case (fieldnum(InventDim,BikeFrameSize))     : // Add mapping
            return fieldnum(InventDimParm,BikeFrameSizeFlag);
        case (fieldnum(InventDim,BikeWheelSize))     : // Add mapping
            return fieldnum(InventDimParm,BikeWheelSizeFlag);
    }

    throw error(strfmt("@SYS54431",funcname()));
}
```

You must make the same modification to the *dimParm2Dim* method on the same table to map *InventDimParm* fields to *InventDim* fields.

Customizing Other Tables

The customizations made so far allow the new dimensions to be enabled on dimension groups and presented in forms. However, you should also consider customizing the following tables by adding inventory dimensions to them:

- *BOMTmpUsedItem2ProducedItem*
- *InventCostTmpTransBreakdown*
- *InventDimCombination*
- *InventSumDateTrans*
- *InventSumDeltaDim*
- *PBADefault*
- *PBATreeInventDim*
- *PriceDiscTmpPrintout*
- *InterCompanyInventDim*

Whether and how you should customize these tables depends on the functionality you're implementing. Be sure to examine how the inventory dimensions are implemented and used for each of the tables before you begin customizing.

Adding Dimensions to Queries

Because of the generic implementation of the inventory dimension concept using the *InventDim* and *InventDim Parm* tables, a substantial number of queries written in X++ use just a few patterns to select, join, and filter the inventory dimensions. So that you don't have to repeatedly copy and paste the same X++ code, these patterns exist as macros that you can apply in your code. To modify these queries, you simply customize the macros and then recompile the entire application to update the X++ code with the new dimensions.

You should customize the following macros:

- *InventDimExistsJoin*
- *InventDimGroupAllFields*
- *InventDimJoin*
- *InventDimSelect*

The bold text in the following X++ code shows the changes that you must make to the *InventDimExistsJoin* macro to enable the two new dimensions for all exists joins written as statements involving the *InventDim* table.

```
/* %1 InventDimId           */
/* %2 InventDim             */
/* %3 InventDimCriteria     */
/* %4 InventDimParm         */
/* %5 Index hint            */

exists join tableId from %2
    where
   (%2.InventDimId       == %1) &&
   (%2.ConfigId          == %3.ConfigId          || ! %4.ConfigIdFlag)         &&
   (%2.InventSizeId      == %3.InventSizeId      || ! %4.InventSizeIdFlag)     &&
   (%2.InventColorId     == %3.InventColorId     || ! %4.InventColorIdFlag)    &&
   (%2.BikeFrameSize     == %3.BikeFrameSize     || ! %4.BikeFrameSizeFlag)    &&
   (%2.BikeWheelSize     == %3.BikeWheelSize     || ! %4.BikeWheelSizeFlag)    &&
   (%2.InventSiteId      == %3.InventSiteId      || ! %4.InventSiteIdFlag)     &&
   (%2.InventLocationId == %3.InventLocationId || ! %4.InventLocationIdFlag) &&
   (%2.InventBatchId     == %3.InventBatchId     || ! %4.InventBatchIdFlag)    &&
   (%2.WMSLocationId     == %3.WMSLocationId     || ! %4.WMSLocationIdFlag)    &&
   (%2.WMSPalletId       == %3.WMSPalletId       || ! %4.WMSPalletIdFlag)      &&
   (%2.InventSerialId    == %3.InventSerialId    || ! %4.InventSerialIdFlag)

#InventDimDevelop
```

The three remaining macros are just as easy to modify. Just remember to recompile the entire application after you make your changes.

Adding Lookup, Validation, and Defaulting X++ Code

In addition to macro customizations and the customizations to the previously mentioned methods on the *InventDim* table, you must implement and customize lookup, validation, and defaulting methods. These include methods such as the *InventDim::findDim* lookup method, the *InventDim.validateWriteItemDim* validation method, and the *InventDim.initFromInventDimCombination* defaulting method. The necessary changes in the *InventDim::findDim* lookup method for the new inventory dimensions are shown in bold in the following X++ code.

```
server static public InventDim findDim(InventDim _inventDim,
                                       boolean   _forupdate = false)
{
    InventDim   inventDim;
    ;
    if (_forupdate)
        inventDim.selectForUpdate(_forupdate);

    select firstonly inventDim
        where inventDim.ConfigId           == _inventDim.ConfigId
           && inventDim.InventSizeId       == _inventDim.InventSizeId
           && inventDim.InventColorId      == _inventDim.InventColorId
           && inventDim.BikeFrameSize      == _inventDim.BikeFrameSize
           && inventDim.BikeWheelSize      == _inventDim.BikeWheelSize
           && inventDim.InventSiteId       == _inventDim.InventSiteId
           && inventDim.InventLocationId == _inventDim.InventLocationId
           && inventDim.InventBatchId      == _inventDim.InventBatchId
           && inventDim.wmsLocationId      == _inventDim.wmsLocationId
           && inventDim.wmsPalletId        == _inventDim.wmsPalletId
           && inventDim.InventSerialId     == _inventDim.InventSerialId;

    #inventDimDevelop

    return inventDim;
}
```

Notice the use of the *inventDimDevelop* macro in the preceding method. This macro contains only the following comment:

```
/* used to locate code with direct dimension references */
```

Performing a global search for use of the *inventDimDevelop* macro should be sufficient to find all the X++ code that you must consider when implementing a new dimension. This search returns all the methods that require further investigation. Figure 5-7 shows results of a search for the use of the macro on all tables.

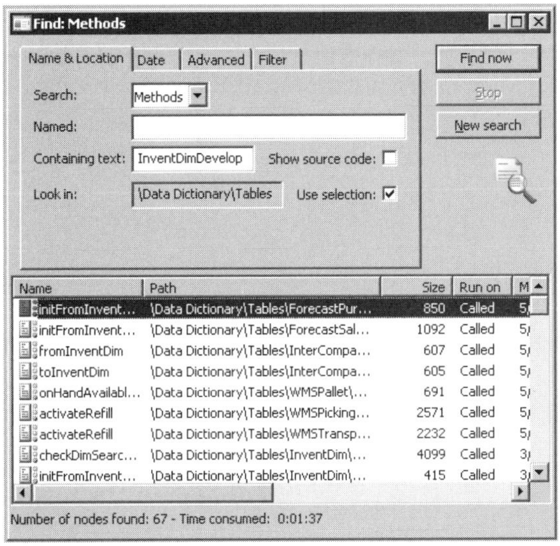

FIGURE 5-7 Search results for the *inventDimDevelop* macro

Best Practices Inserting the *inventDimDevelop* macro in X++ code when it makes a direct reference to an inventory dimension is considered a best practice. Doing so makes implementing new dimensions easier.

Most of the methods you find when searching for the macro are lookup, validation, and defaulting methods, but you also see methods that aren't in these categories. Such methods include those that modify the *Query* object, such as the *InventDim::queryAddHintFromCaller* method, and methods that describe dimensions, such as *InventDimParm.isFlagSelective*. You should also review these methods when investigating the X++ code.

Tip Although the inventory dimension feature is implemented with the *inventDimDevelop* macro to direct developers to the methods they need to change, you might encounter methods with no macro included or tables, forms, or reports for which the inventory dimensions are not used generically. We therefore advise you to use the cross-reference system on an existing dimension that has the same behavior as the new dimension to determine its use and review it appropriately. You should also investigate whether the new dimension is or should be available in the same element.

Form Customization

Like most of the elements in the AOT, forms can be customized to include additional information and actions, such as fields and buttons, and to fulfill user requirements. The design and behavior of a form are provided by a combination of the form and the tables that are bound to the form.

> **Best Practices** Even though you can implement all necessary customizations by modifying just the form, we don't recommend this approach. As a best practice, you should implement application customizations at the lowest level possible, preferably through changes to a table or a class rather than through changing specific forms.

The best way to implement forms is to keep most of the business logic and design decisions in tables and classes, focusing only on the positioning of fields and menu items when designing the form. This approach has several advantages:

- X++ code in forms is executed on the client tier only; X++ code in table methods can be executed on the server tier to optimize performance.
- Customizations made to a form are restricted to that form; customizations made to a table or a class apply to all forms that use that table or class as a source of data. This results in a consistent user experience wherever the table is used.
- When a form is customized, the entire form is copied to the current layer; customizations to tables and classes are more granular. When fields, field groups, and methods are customized, a copy of the specific element is in the current layer only. This makes upgrading to service packs and new versions easier.
- X++ customizations to the validate, default, and database trigger methods on forms, such as create, validateWrite, and write, affect only the records that are modified through the user interface. If records are modified somewhere other than that form, then that customized form's X++ code doesn't execute.

The following actions be customized only on the form, not by customizing a table:

- Enable and disable fields and other user interface elements (*Enabled* = Yes/No)
- Show and hide fields and other user interface elements (*Visible* = Yes/No)

However, you should consider having a table or a class method determine the business logic on the form. An example of this is shown in the following lines of X++ code from the InventTable form, in which a method on the table determines whether a field can be edited.

```
void setItemDimEnabled()
{
    boolean     configActive    = inventTable.configActive();
```

```
    ...
    inventTable_ds.object(
            fieldnum(InventTable,StandardConfigId)).allowEdit(configActive);
    inventTable_ds.object(
            fieldnum(InventTable, StandardConfigId)).skip(!configActive);
    ...
}
```

By moving these decision-making methods to a table or class, you make them available to other forms.

Learning Form Fundamentals

The rich client user interface in Dynamics AX is made up of forms that are declared in metadata and often contain associated code. Ideally, you should customize these forms as changes to metadata and make any changes at the lowest level (i.e., table level rather than form level) possible to ensure the greatest amount of metadata and code reuse.

The most visible change from Dynamics AX 4.0 to Dynamics AX 2009 is the change from a predominantly *multiple-document interface* (MDI) to a predominantly *single-document interface* (SDI). Forms with a *WindowType* property value of *Standard* (the default) are now SDI forms, and the *WindowType* values of *ListPage* and *ContentPage* have been added to fill the Workspace content area to provide a navigation experience similar to that in Microsoft Office Outlook. The different *WindowType* values share the same object model, metadata, and method overrides, so form customization skills are applicable across all forms.

Customizing with Metadata

Metadata customization is preferred over code customization because metadata changes (also called deltas) are easier to merge than code changes.

When customizing forms, you should be aware of the important properties, the metadata associations, and the metadata inheritance that is being used to fully define the form and its contents.

Metadata associations You edit the metadata in Dynamics AX by using the AOT. The base definitions for forms contained within the *AOT\Forms* node is composed of a hierarchy of metadata that is located in other nodes in the AOT. To fully understand a form, you should investigate the metadata associations it makes. For example, a form uses tables that are declared in the *AOT\Data Dictionary\Tables* node, security keys that are declared in the *AOT\Data Dictionary\Security Keys* node, menu items that are declared in the *AOT\Menu Items* node, queries that are declared in the *AOT\Queries* node, and classes that are declared in the *AOT\Classes* node.

Metadata inheritance You need to be aware of the inheritance within the metadata used by forms. For example, tables use Base Enums, Extended Data Types, and Configuration Key. A simple example of inheritance is that the *Image* properties on a *MenuItemButton* are inherited from the associated *MenuItem* if they aren't explicitly specified on that *MenuItemButton*. Table 5-4 shows important examples of pieces of metadata that are inherited from associated metadata.

Inheritance also occurs within forms. Controls that are contained within other controls receive certain metadata property behaviors from their parents unless different property values are specified, including HTMLHelpFile, HTMLHelpTopic, Security Key, Configuration Key, Enabled, and the various Font properties.

TABLE 5-4 Examples of Metadata Inheritance

Type of Metadata	Sources
Labels and HelpText	MenuItem→MenuItemButton Control Base Enum→Extended Data Type→Table Field→Form DataSource Field→Form Control (The *Base Enum Help* property is the equivalent of the *HelpText* property found in the other types.)
Relations	Extended Data Type→Table
Security keys	Table Field→Table→Form Control MenuItem→MenuItemButton Control Form→Form Control
Configuration keys	Base Enum→Extended Data Type→Table Field→Form DataSource Field→Form Control
Image properties (e.g., *NormalImage*)	MenuItem→MenuItemButton Control

Menu definitions Dynamics AX 2009 has a number of new navigation capabilities in the form of area pages and the address bar to complement the existing navigation pane (sometimes referred to as the "WunderBar"). In terms of metadata, the area pages and address bar are mostly just additional methods of exposing the existing menu metadata defined in the *AOT\Menus* and *AOT\Menu Items* nodes. The modules are defined in AOT\Menus\MainMenu, and you can follow the menu structure from that starting point. For example, the *Accounts Receivable* module is represented by the AOT\Menus\MainMenu\Cust MenuReference and is defined as AOT\Menus\Cust.

The menu metadata for list pages and content pages has some small changes. A primary list page is implemented as a submenu with *IsDisplayedInContentArea=Yes*, *MenuItemType=Display*, and *MenuItemName* populated. A secondary list page, a list page that adds ranges to a primary list page, is implemented as a menu item under the submenu of its primary list page. The list pages and content pages are navigation places, so all their menu item and submenu references are set to *IsDisplayedInContentArea=Yes* so that they appear in the Places group in the area pages and the Places section in the navigation pane. The other menu items in the root of each module's menu definition are displayed in the Common Forms group in the area pages and in the root of the Forms section in the navigation pane.

Important metadata properties Many properties are available to developers, but some are more important than others. Table 5-5 describes the most important form design properties, and Table 5-6 describes the most important form data source properties.

TABLE 5-5 Important Form *Design* Metadata Properties

Property	Explanation
Caption	The caption text shown in the title bar of a standard form or in the Filter Pane of a list page.
TitleDataSource	The data source information displayed in a standard form's caption text and used to provide filter information in the caption text of a list page.
WindowType	*Standard* - (Default) A standard SDI form that opens as a separate window with a separate entry in the Windows taskbar. *ContentPage* - A form that fills the Workspace content area. *ListPage* - A special style of ContentPageused to display records in a simple way that provides quick access to filtering capabilities and actions. It requires at least an Action Pane and a Grid. *Workspace* - A form that opens as an MDI window within the workspace. Workspace forms should be developer-specific forms. *Popup* - A form that opens as a subform to its parent. Popup forms don't have a separate entry in the Windows taskbar and can't be layered with other windows.
AllowFormCompanyChange	Specifies whether the form allows company changes when used as a child form with a cross-company dynalink. No - (Default) Form closes if parent form changes its company scope. Yes - Form dynamically changes company scope as needed.
HTMLHelpFile	Specifies the path to the Help topic file.
HTMLHelpTopic	Specifies the topic to use from the referenced Help file.

TABLE 5-6 Important Form *DataSource* Metadata Properties

Property	Explanation
Name	Named reference for the data source. A best practice is to use the same name as the table name.
Table	Specifies the table used as the data source.
CrossCompanyAutoQuery	*No* - (Default) Data source gets data from the current company. *Yes* - Data source gets data from all companies (e.g., retrieves customers from all companies).

Property	Explanation
JoinSource	Specifies the data source to link or join to as part of the query. For example, in the SalesTable form, SalesLine is linked to SalesTable. Data sources joined together are represented in a single query whereas links are represented as a separate query.
LinkType	Specifies the link or join type used between this data source and the data source specified in the *JoinSource* property. Joins are required when two data sources are displayed in the same grid. Joined data sources are represented in a single query whereas a linked data source is represented in a separate query. **Links** *Delayed* - (Default) A pause is inserted before linked child data sources are updated, enabling faster navigation in the parent data source because the records from the child data sources are not updated immediately. For example, the user could be scrolling past several orders without immediately seeing each order line. *Active* - The child data source is updated immediately when a new record in the parent data source is selected. Continuous updates consume lots of resources. *Passive* - Linked child data sources are not updated automatically. The link is established by the kernel, but the application developer must trigger the query to occur when desired by calling "ExecuteQuery" on the linked data source. **Joins** *InnerJoin* - Selects records from the main table that have matching records in the joined table, and vice versa. There is one record for each match. Records without related records in the other data source are eliminated from the result. *OuterJoin* - Selects records from the main table whether or not they have matching records in the joined table. An outer join doesn't require each record in the two joined tables to have a matching record. *ExistJoin* - Selects a record from the main table for each matching record in the joined table. *NotExistJoin* - Selects records from the main table that don't have a match in the joined table.
InsertIfEmpty	*Yes* - (Default) A record is automatically created for the user if none is present. *No* - The user needs to manually create the first record. This setting is often used when a special record creation process or interface is used.

Image metadata Dynamics AX 2009 makes greater use of images and icons throughout the application to provide the user with additional visual cues. Icons are used extensively in list pages to help users identify specific actions. The metadata properties used to associate images and icons with buttons, menus (menu items), and other controls depends on their location. Table 5-7 describes the metadata properties used for the three common image locations.

TABLE 5-7 Image Metadata

Image Location	Explanation
Embedded	Embedded image resources are associated with buttons, menus, and other controls using the *NormalResource* and *DisabledResource* properties. These resources are compiled into the kernel and therefore you can't add to the embedded resources list. The full list of embedded resources can be seen in the Embedded Resources form (Tools\Development Tools\Embedded Resources).
File	File image resources are associated with buttons, menus, and other controls using the *NormalImage* and *DisabledImage* properties. File image resources should be on the local computer wherever possible for performance reasons, but can be on a file share if needed.
AOT	AOT image resources cannot be utilized simply through metadata. AOT resources can be utilized only by adding code that copies the AOT resource into a temp folder and sets the *NormalImage* property at run time. The following code should be added into a dependable form method override (such as the *Init* method after the super call) for execution at run time: `SomeButton.normalImage(SysResource::getImagePath("<AOT Resource Name>"));`

Customizing with Code

You should customize forms with code only as a last resort. Customizing with metadata is much more upgrade friendly since metadata change conflicts are straight forward to resolve whereas code change conflicts need deeper investigation that sometimes involves creating a new merged method that attempts to replicate the behavior from the two original methods.

When you start to customize Dynamics AX, the following ideas may provide good starting points for investigation:

- Leverage examples in the base Dynamics AX 2009 codebase by using the *Find* command on the *Forms* node in the AOT (Ctrl+F).
- Refer to the system documentation entries (AOT\System Documentation) for information about system classes, tables, functions, enumerations, and other system elements that have been implemented in the AX kernel.
- When investigating the form method call hierarchy for a suitable location to place customization code, add a debug breakpoint in the *Form Init* method and step through the execution of method overrides. Note that control events (e.g., clicked) do not trigger debugging breakpoints. An explicit breakpoint (i.e., "*breakpoint;*") keyword is needed in the X++ code.

To enable simpler code maintenance, the following rules should be followed:

- Utilize the table and field functions of *FieldNum* (e.g., *fieldnum(SalesTable, SalesId)*) and *TableNum* (e.g., *tablenum(SalesTable)*) when working with form data sources.
- Avoid hard coding strings by using *sys* labels (e.g., *throw error("@SYS88659");*) and functions like *FieldStr* (e.g., *fieldstr(SalesTable, SalesId)*) and *TableStr* (e.g., *tablestr(SalesTable)*).
- Use as few method overrides as possible. Each additional method override has a chance of causing merge issues during future upgrades, patch applications, or code integrations.

When X++ code is executed in the scope of a form, there are some form-specific global variables created in X++ to help developers access important objects related to the form. These global variables are described in Table 5-8.

TABLE 5-8 Form-Specific Global X++ Variables

Variable	Use and Example

Element	Variable that provides easy access to the *FormRun* object in scope. Commonly used to call methods or change the design.
	`element.args().record().TableId == tablenum(SalesTable)`
	`name = element.design().addControl(FormControlType::String, "X");`

DataSourceName (e.g., *SalesTable*)	Variable that provides easy access to the *current/active record/cursor* in each data source. Commonly used to call methods or *get/set* properties on the current record. `if (SalesTable.type().canHaveCreditCard())`
DataSourceName_DS (e.g., *SalesTable_DS*)	Variable that provides easy access to each data source. Commonly used to call methods or *get/set* properties on the data source. `SalesTable_DS.research();`

DataSourceName_Q (e.g., *SalesTable_Q*)	Variable that provides easy access to each data source's *Query* object. Commonly used to access the data source query to add ranges prior to query execution/run. Equivalent to *SalesTable_DS.query*.
	`rangeSalesLineProjId    = salesLine1_q.dataSourceTable-(tablenum(SalesLine)).addRange(fieldnum(SalesLine, ProjId));`
	`rangeSalesLineProjId.value(ProjTable.ProjId);`

Variable	Use and Example
DataSourceName_QR (e.g., *SalesTable_QR*)	Variable that provides easy access to each data source *QueryRun* object that contains a copy of the query that was most recently executed. The query inside the *QueryRun* object is copied during the *FormDataSource ExecuteQuery* method. Commonly used to access the query that was executed so that query ranges can be inspected. Equivalent to *SalesTable_DS.queryRun*. `SalesTableQueryBuildDataSource = SalesTable_QR.query().dataSourceTable(tablenum(SalesTable));`
ControlName (e.g., *SalesTable_SalesId*)	Variable created for each control set as *AutoDeclaration=Yes*. Commonly used to access controls not bound to a data source field, such as the fields used to implement custom filters. `backorderDate.dateValue(systemdateget());`

Form method overrides allow developers to influence the form life cycle and how the form responds to some user-initiated events. The most important form method overrides are described in Table 5-9. The two most overridden form methods are *Init* and *Run*.

TABLE 5-9 Form Method Override Explanations

Method	Explanation
Init	Called when the form is initialized. Prior to the call to *super*, much of the form (*FormRun*) is not initialized, including the controls and the query. Commonly overridden to access the form at the earliest stage possible.
Run	Called when the form is initialized. Prior to the call to *super*, the form is initialized but isn't visible to the user. Commonly overridden to make changes to form controls, layout, and cursor focus.
Close	Called when the form is being closed. Commonly overridden to release resources and save user settings and selections.
CloseOk	Called when the form is being closed via the *Ok* command/task, such as when the user clicks a *CommandButton* with a *Command* property of *Ok*. Commonly overridden on dialog forms to perform the action the user has initiated.
CloseCancel	Called when the form is being closed via the *Cancel* command/task, such as when the user clicks a *CommandButton* with a *Command* property of *Cancel*. Commonly overridden on dialog forms to clean up after the user indicates that an action should be cancelled.
CanClose	Called when the form is being closed. Commonly overridden to ensure that data is in a good state before the form is closed. Returning *false* aborts the close action and keeps the form open.

Form data source and form data source field method overrides allow developers to influence how the form reads and writes its data and allows developers to respond to user-initiated data-related events. The most important form data source method overrides are described in

Table 5-10. The five most overridden form data source methods are *Init*, *Active*, *ExecuteQuery*, *Write*, and *LinkActive*.

TABLE 5-10 Form Data Source Method Override Explanations

Method	Explanation
Active	Called when the active/current record changes, such as when the user clicks a different record. Commonly overridden to enable and disable buttons based on whether or not they are applicable to the current record.
Create	Called when a record is being created, such as when the user presses Ctrl+N. Commonly overridden to change the user interface in response to a record creation.
Delete	Called when a record is being deleted, such as when the user presses Alt+F9. Commonly overridden to change the user interface in response to a record creation.
ExecuteQuery	Called when the data source's query is executed, such as when the form is run (from the *super* of the form's *Run* method) or when the user refreshes the form by pressing F5. Commonly overridden to implement the behavior of a custom filter added to the form.
Init	Called when the data source is initialized during the *super* of the form's *Init* method. Commonly overridden to add or remove query ranges or change dynalinks.
InitValue	Called when a record is being created. Record values set in this method count as original values rather than changes. Commonly overridden to set the default values of a new record.
LeaveRecord	Called when the user is moving focus from one data source join hierarchy to another, which can happen when the user moves between controls. Commonly overridden to coordinate between data sources, but developers are encouraged to use the *ValidateWrite* and *Write* methods where possible. *ValidateWrite* and *Write* are called immediately after *LeaveRecord*.
LinkActive	Called when the active method in a dynalinked parent form is called. Commonly overridden to change the user interface to correspond to a different parent record (*element.args().record()*).
MarkChanged	Called when the marked set of records changes, such as when the user multi-selects a set of records. Commonly overridden to enable/disable buttons that work on a multi-selected (marked) set of records.
ValidateDelete	Called when the user attempts to delete a record. Commonly overridden to provide form-specific deletion event validation. Return *false* to abort the delete. Use the *ValidateDelete* table method to provide record deletion validation across all forms.
ValidateWrite	Called when the record is being saved, such as when the user presses the Close or Save buttons or clicks a field from another data source. Commonly overridden to provide form-specific write/save event validation. Return *false* to abort the write. Use the *ValidateWrite* table method to provide record write/save validation across all forms.
Write	Called when the record is being saved after validation has succeeded. Commonly overridden to perform additional form-specific write/save event logic such as updating the user interface. Use the *Write* table method to respond to the record write/save event across all forms.

Three commonly used form data source field method overrides are described in Table 5-11. The most overridden form data source field method is the *Modified* method.

TABLE 5-11 Form Data Source Field Method Override Explanations

Method	Explanation
Modified	Called when the value of a field changes. Commonly overridden to make a corresponding change to the user interface or to change other field values.
Lookup	Called when the Lookup button of the field is clicked. Commonly overridden to build a custom lookup form. Use the *EDT.FormHelp* property to provide lookup capabilities to all forms.
Validate	Called when the value of a field changes. Commonly overridden to perform form-specific validation needed prior to saving or to validate. Return *false* to abort the change. Use the *ValidateField* table method to provide field validation across all forms.

Displaying an Image

The following example illustrates how to customize the sales order form to allow a user to upload and display an image of a custom order. In this example, a customer must be able to place an order for a bike through Enterprise Portal and upload a sketch of the bike at the same time. An example of a customer-supplied bike image is shown in Figure 5-8.

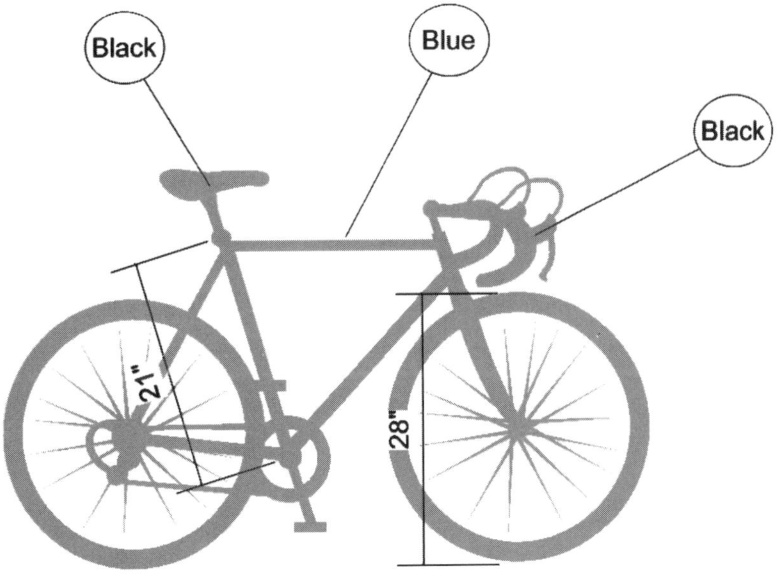

FIGURE 5-8 Uploaded bike image

This image must be stored in the database and attached to the sales order line. Sales order lines are stored in the *SalesLine* table. You could add a new field to the *SalesLine* table of the type container and store the image in this field, but this example uses the document management functionality in Dynamics AX. The image is therefore stored in the *DocuValue* table with a reference to a record in the *DocuRef* table from the image record in *DocuValue* to the *SalesLine* record. The relationship and multiplicity among the three tables is shown in Figure 5-9.

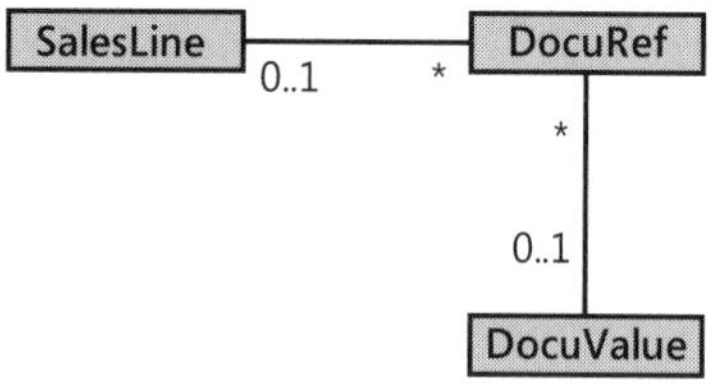

FIGURE 5-9 Relationship among the *SalesLine*, *DocuRef*, and *DocuValue* tables

In this example, a document type named Image stores the attached file in the disk folder. The Image document type is shown in Figure 5-10. The Document Type form is located in the navigation pane, Basic\Setup\Document Management\Document Types.

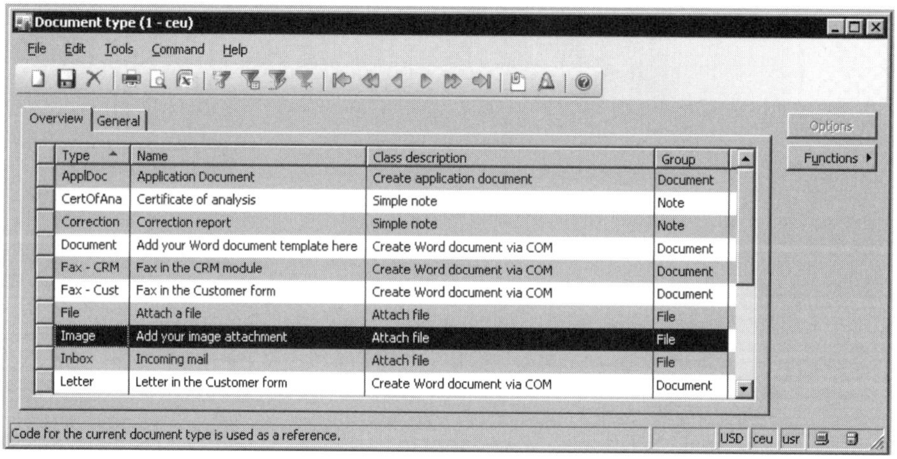

FIGURE 5-10 Image document type

Any uploaded image is therefore stored in the document management system; a user can view the image by either clicking the Document Handling icon on the status bar or choosing Document Handling on the Command menu. The user sees the dialog box shown in Figure 5-11, in which the image can be viewed, modified, or deleted, and additional notes or documents can be attached.

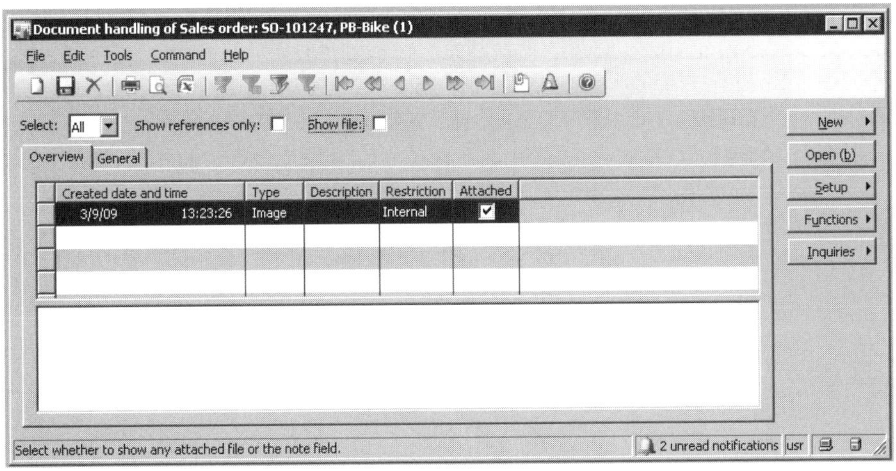

FIGURE 5-11 Storage of the uploaded bike image in the document management system

Displaying an Image on a Form

You can display the image directly by placing it on a separate Image tab on the sales order form. Figure 5-12 shows an order for a bike with a frame size of 21 inches and a wheel size of 28 inches. The user can click the Image tab to view the uploaded bike image and confirm that it matches the ordered item before confirming the sales order. The Sales Order form (AOT\Forms\SalesTable) is located in the navigation pane, Accounts Receivable\Sales Order.

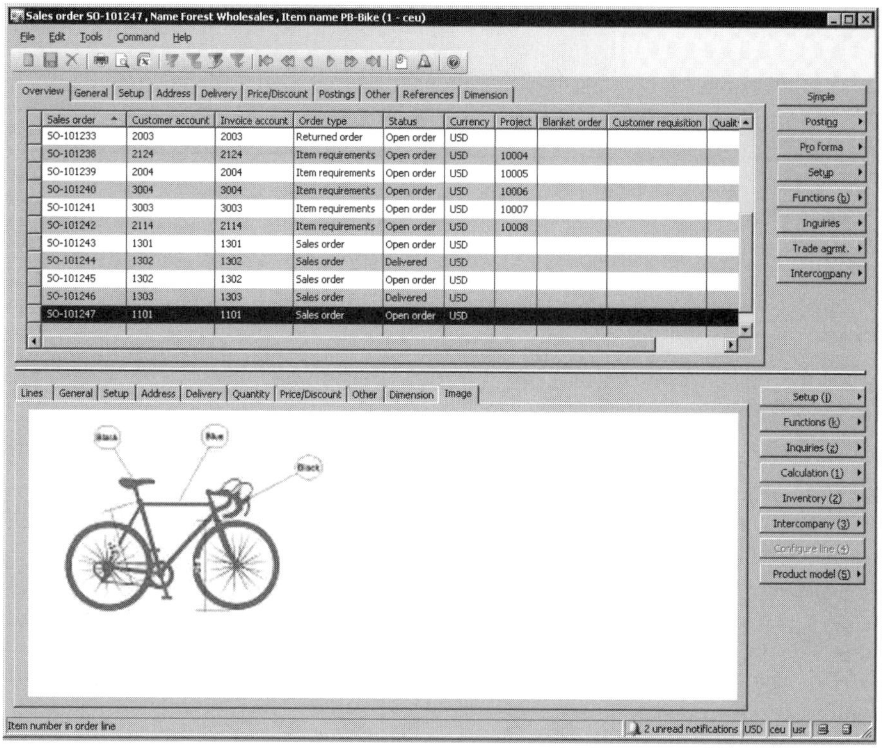

FIGURE 5-12 Uploaded bike image displayed on the Sales Order form Image tab

The following two example implementations describe how to use the document management tables as data sources in the form and how to create a separate method on the *SalesLine* table. These examples demonstrate customization of the *SalesTable* sales order form and the *SalesLine* table.

Displaying an Image by Using Joined Data Sources

One way to display the image is to apply the *DocuRef* and *DocuValue* tables as data sources for the *SalesTable* form. The following example creates a *DocuRef* data source based on the relationship among the *SalesLine*, *DocuRef*, and *DocuValue* tables shown in Figure 5-9. The *DocuRef* data source relates to the *DocuRef* table and is joined to the *SalesLine* data source. Additionally, a *DocuValue* data source is created to connect to the *DocuRef* data source. Table 5-12 shows additional properties of the data sources.

TABLE 5-12 *DocuRef* and *DocuValue* Property Settings

Property	*DocuRef*	*DocuValue*
Table	*DocuRef*	*DocuValue*
AllowEdit	No	No
AllowCreate	No	No
AllowDelete	No	No
JoinSource	*SalesLine*	*DocuRef*
LinkType	Active	Active

The properties *JoinSource* and *LinkType* allow the *DocuRef* and *DocuValue* records to be fetched when the user moves from one line to another. The remaining properties disable editing of the records.

You can attach multiple files, documents, and notes to a *SalesLine* record by using the document management feature, but the goal of this example is to display an image from a linked document named Image. You can limit the retrieved records from the *DocuRef* table by adding a range to the query used by the *DocuRef* data source. You do this by customizing the *Init* method on the *DocuRef* data source, as shown here.

```
public void init()
{
    super();

    docuRef_ds.query().dataSourceTable(
                       tableNum(DocuRef)).addRange(
                       fieldNum(DocuRef,TypeId)).value(queryValue('Image'));
}
```

This X++ code limits the query so that it retrieves only records from the *DocuRef* table in which the *TypeId* field is equal to the value *'Image'*.

> **Note** The use of a constant such as the word *Image* is not a best practice. The value must be retrieved from a configuration table so that the user can decide the naming. *'Image'* is hard coded in the preceding example only to improve the readability and limit the scope of the example.

The image is displayed by using a window control, which is placed in a tab control, as shown in Figure 5-13.

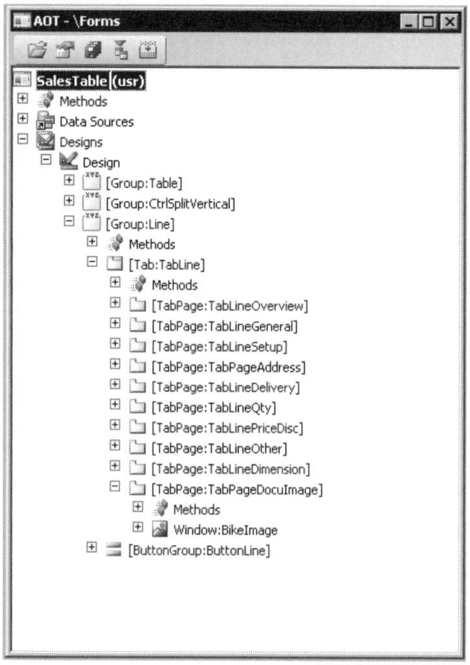

FIGURE 5-13 Tab and window controls in the SalesTable form

Although the image is stored in the *File* field on the *DocuValue* table, to display the image you can't simply link the field as a *DataField* value on the window control property sheet. The image must be parsed to the control by using a method on the control in X++ that uses the *FormWindowControl* object. The *AutoDeclaration* property on the *FormWindowControl* object is therefore set to Yes so that the forms designer automatically declares an object handle with the same name. This handle can be used in X++ and manipulated at run time because the form application runtime automatically ensures that it is a handle to the *FormWindowControl* object. The *Width* and *Height* properties are set to *Column width* and *Column height* so that the image takes up all the space on the tab.

The last step is to parse the retrieved image from the *DocuValue* table to the *BikeImage* *FormWindowControl* object. You can do this when a *DocuValue* record buffer is present. This record must contain an image that is stored in the database, and the X++ code should be placed in the active method on the *DocuValue* data source and look like the following.

```
public int active()
{
    Image   image;
    int     ret;
    ret = super();
    if (docuValue.File)
    {
```

```
            image = new Image();
            image.setData(docuValue.File);
            bikeImage.image(image);
        }
        else
        {
            bikeImage.imageResource(0);
        }
        return ret;
    }
```

This code determines whether a value exists in the *File* field and, if so, instantiates an image object and parses the *File* field value to the image object. This object is then parsed by using the *Image* method to the *FormWindowControl* object that displays the image. If the *File* field doesn't contain a value, the *imageResource* method on the *FormWindowControl* object is called with a value of 0 to clear the control of any previous content. The active method is executed only if a *DocuValue* record has been retrieved. However, if a user moves from an order line with an image to an order line without an image, the image isn't cleared because the active method isn't executed. If you add the following line to the active method on the *SalesLine* data source, the image is cleared when a new order line becomes active and before the *DocuRef* and *DocuValue* records are retrieved.

```
docuBikeImage.imageResource(0);
```

The customizations described in this section make it possible to display the image on the Image tab. This solution has one downside, however. Whenever a user moves from one order line to another or a line is created or saved, calls are made from the client to the server, and lookups are made in the database for the *DocuRef* and *DocuValue* data sources. You can see this by turning on the client/server or SQL trace option in the Options dialog box, which you access from the Tools menu. The next section addresses this issue and offers a solution—decreasing the number of client/server calls and lookups in the database.

Displaying an Image When Activating the Image Tab

The following example implements a solution similar to the previous example, but it results in calls to the server and the database only when the image is actually displayed.

The *TabPage* control must be added to the *SalesTable* form and contain a *FormWindowControl* with property settings similar to those in the preceding example. The *DocuRef* and *DocuValue* tables are not, however, added as data sources for the form. Instead, this example retrieves the image—the only element shown on the Image tab—from the database only when the user chooses to display the content of the Image tab. You configure this by adding the following X++ code to the *pageActivated* method on the *TabPage* control.

```
public void pageActivated()
{
    Image           image;
    DocuValueFile   docuValueFile;
    ;
    docuValueFile = salesLine.bikeImage();
    if (docuValueFile)
    {
        image = new Image();
        image.setData(docuValueFile);
        bikeImage.image(image);
    }
    else
    {
        bikeImage.imageResource(0);
    }

    super();
}
```

This code is very similar to the code added to the *DocuValue* active method, but in this case the value is retrieved from a *bikeImage* method on the *SalesLine* table. The *bikeImage* method is a new method created on the *SalesLine* table with the following content.

```
server public DocuValueFile bikeImage()
{
    DocuRef     docuref;
    DocuValue   docuValue;
    ;
    select  firstonly tableid from docuRef
        where docuRef.RefCompanyId  == this.DataAreaId  &&
              docuRef.RefTableId    == this.TableId     &&
              docuRef.RefRecId      == this.RecId       &&
              docuRef.TypeId        == 'Image'
    join file from docuValue
        where docuValue.RecId   == docuRef.ValueRecId;

    return docuValue.File;
}
```

The select statement in the *bikeImage* method is a combination of the two lookups in the database produced by the runtime shown in the first sample implementation, which used data sources. However, the statements in this method are joined. The *bikeImage* method could simply be implemented in the *SalesTable* form, but implementing it on the *SalesLine* table allows it to be reused in other forms or reports and executed on the server tier, if required.

The advantage of this implementation method is that both database lookups and calls from the client to the server are reduced by half. And because calls are made only when the Image tab is activated, they aren't made when a user simply moves through the order lines without viewing the content of the Image tab. The disadvantage, however, is that the user can't personalize the form or move the display of the image to another tab because retrieval of the image is dependent on activation of the Image tab.

Report Customization

Reports, like forms, can be customized to include and exclude information, and you can modify their design and layout. As with forms, the design and layout of a report depend on settings on the table and on the report itself. The best practice is, once again, to keep as much of the business logic as possible with the table methods or metadata. The X++ code in reports must deal with the functionality for the specific report. All other X++ code must generally be implemented on the table to be reused by other areas in the application. Here are some of the advantages to such an approach:

- Customizations made to a report are isolated; customizations made to a table affect all reports using that table, resulting in a consistent user experience wherever the table is used.
- Customization of a report copies the entire report to the current layer; customizations made to tables are more granular because customization of fields, field groups, and methods results in a copy of the specific element to the current layer only. This makes upgrading to service packs and new versions easier.
- Methods in reports always execute on the tier where the report is generated; methods on tables can be targeted to execute on the server tier. Where a report is generated is controlled by the *RunOn* property on the menu item that starts the report. The property can be set to Client, Server, or Called From.

Creating Promotional Materials

The example in this section demonstrates how to customize the sales order invoice report named SalesInvoice (AOT\Reports\SalesInvoice). The invoice is customized to include promotions based on items listed on the invoice. The promotion appears below each item on the invoice associated with a promotion. Figure 5-14 shows an example of an invoice that displays a promotion for a water bottle.

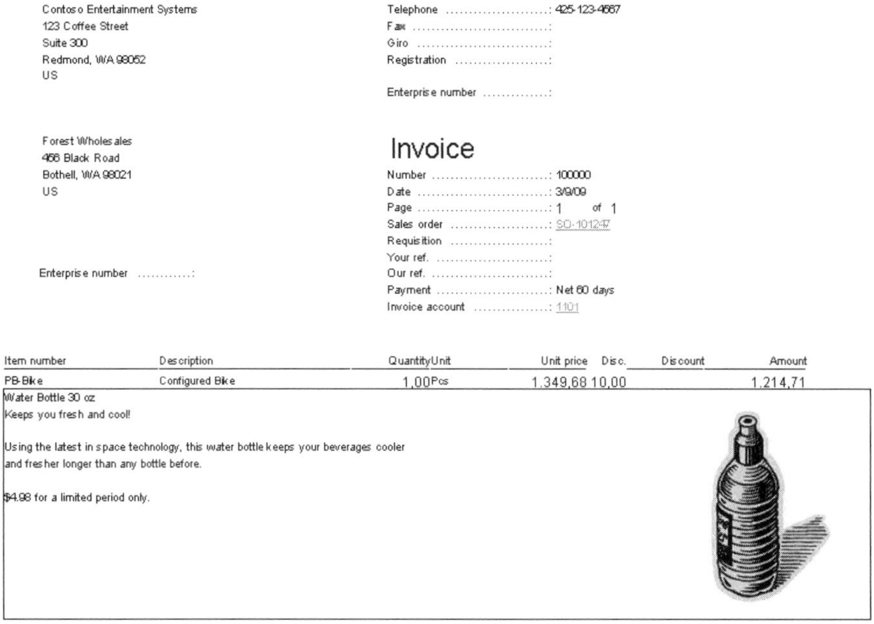

Contoso Entertainment Systems
123 Coffee Street
Suite 300
Redmond, WA 98052
US

Telephone ....: 425-123-4567
Fax ....:
Giro ....:
Registration ....:

Enterprise number ....:

Forest Wholesales
456 Black Road
Bothell, WA 98021
US

Enterprise number ....:

Invoice

Number ....: 100000
Date ....: 3/9/09
Page ....: 1 of 1
Sales order ....: SO-101247
Requisition ....:
Your ref. ....:
Our ref. ....:
Payment ....: Net 60 days
Invoice account ....: 1101

Item number	Description	Quantity	Unit	Unit price	Disc.	Discount	Amount
PB-Bike	Configured Bike	1,00	Pcs	1.349,68	10,00		1.214,71

Water Bottle 30 oz
Keeps you fresh and cool!

Using the latest in space technology, this water bottle keeps your beverages cooler and fresher longer than any bottle before.

$4.98 for a limited period only.

FIGURE 5-14 Promotion on an invoice

Like the forms example, this example uses the document management feature in Dynamics AX. You use document handling to store the text and image in the database. The information is attached to the item table as two different types of document information, named *PromoText* and *PromoImage*, for storing the text and image. Figure 5-15 shows the *PromoText* and *PromoImage* document types.

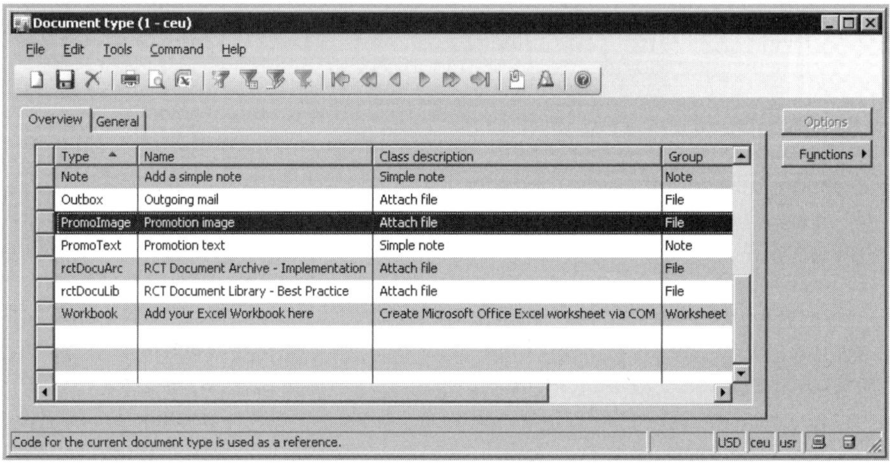

FIGURE 5-15 *PromoText* and *PromoImage* document types

Figure 5-16 shows the text and image attached to an item named PB-Bike.

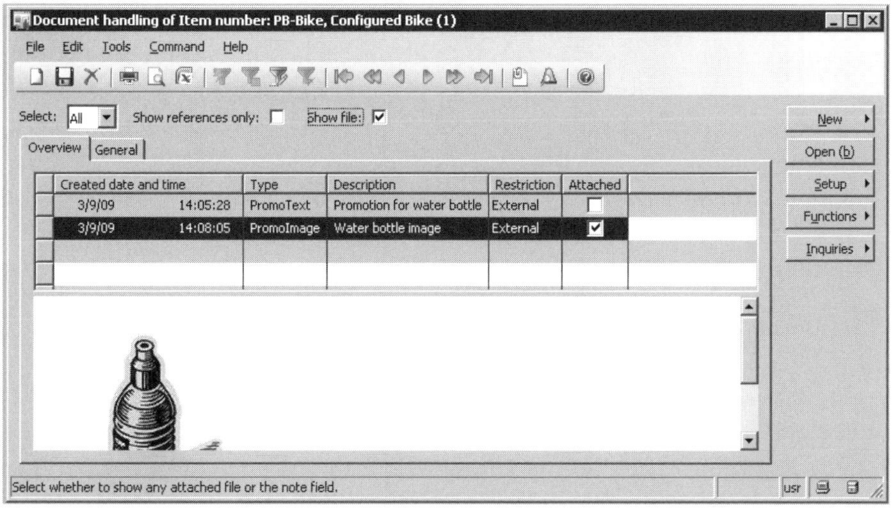

FIGURE 5-16 Text and image attached to an item

The X++ code used to display the promotion on the invoice looks up the item in the *InventTable* table and searches the document handling for documents of type *PromoText* and *PromoImage* to print on the invoice. If neither type is attached to the item, no promotion information prints.

Adding Promotional Materials to an Invoice Report

Before you customize the *SalesInvoice* report for this example, you must decide where in the design of the report to place the printing of the promotion. The printed information should be printed for each invoiced item, so you must place it under the *CustInvoiceTrans* section group because the *CustInvoiceTrans* table contains the invoiced items. The *CustInvoiceTrans* section group contains a reference body section that can print other pieces of reference information, such as from inventory dimensions or the packing slip lines posted when the invoiced item is shipped. The promotion resembles this kind of information in terms of when and how it is printed.

This example, therefore, creates a new section group within the reference body section below the existing three groups. The new section group must reference a table type so that it can be invoked when a record buffer of the same type is sent to the report by using the *element.send* method. The *DocuRef* table stores the promotion text, and the *DocuValue* table stores the promotion image with an association created in the *DocuRef* table.

Although the storage of the text and image results in the creation of *DocuRef* records, the choice of *DocuRef* as the reference table type for the new section group isn't an optimal solution. First, the information is stored as two records in the *DocuRef* table, but the text and image should be printed side by side for this example. The *element.send* method should be called only once, parsing in only a single record buffer. Also, two other section groups already use *DocuRef* as the table type, so using this type might result in the other section groups getting invoked as well when the promotion prints. You could prevent this by introducing a variable to control which section group to invoke, but then you would have to customize even more of the report, making it harder to upgrade the report when a new version or service pack is installed.

Both of the *DocuRef* records are, however, related to the same *InventTable* record, so you can use this table as the type for the section group, and an *InventTable* record buffer is sent to the report to print the promotion text and image. Figure 5-17 shows the new section group, named *InventTable*, and its positioning within the report.

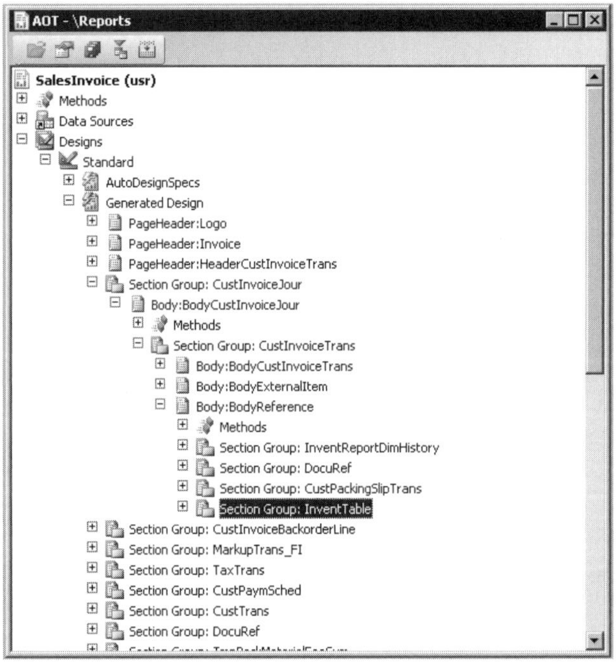

FIGURE 5-17 *InventTable* section group in the *SalesInvoice* report

Implementing Promotional Methods

When the promotion text and image print, an *InventTable* record buffer is sent to the report. For this reason, this example implements two methods to return the text and image by using an *InventTable* record buffer. The methods can be implemented directly in the report, but because the methods are not report specific—and therefore can be reused in other reports, or even forms—they are implemented as instance methods on *InventTable*. The following code shows the new methods. The *PromotionImage* method is implemented like the *BikeImage* method in the forms example discussed earlier. However, the *PromotionImage* method must look in only the *DocuRef* table to find the text.

```
display server public DocuValueFile PromotionImage()
{
    DocuRef      docuref;
    DocuValue    docuValue;
    ;
    select  firstonly tableid from docuRef
        where docuRef.RefCompanyId  == this.DataAreaId  &&
              docuRef.RefTableId    == this.TableId     &&
              docuRef.RefRecId      == this.RecId       &&
              docuRef.TypeId        == 'PromoImage'
    join file from docuValue
        where docuValue.RecId    == docuRef.ValueRecId;

    return docuValue.File;
}


display server public Notes PromotionText()
{
    DocuRef      docuref;
    ;
    select firstonly notes from docuRef
        where docuRef.RefCompanyId  == this.DataAreaId  &&
              docuRef.RefTableId    == this.TableId     &&
              docuRef.RefRecId      == this.RecId       &&
              docuRef.TypeId        == 'PromoText';

    return docuRef.Notes;
}
```

Both methods are implemented as display methods to allow them to bind directly to report controls and to print the information.

Binding Display Methods to Report Controls

The next step is to bind the methods to report controls. A new body section named *BodyInventTable* is created in the *InventTable* section group, and several of its properties are altered, as shown in Table 5-13.

TABLE 5-13 ***BodyInventTable* Property Settings**

Property	Settings
NoOfHeadingLines	0
LineAbove	Solid
LineBelow	Solid
LineLeft	Solid
LineRight	Solid

The *NoOfHeadingLines* property must be set to 0 because the text and image must not include any headings when printed. The *Line* property settings create a border around the promotion.

In the body section, a string control, named *PromotionText*, and a bitmap control, named *PromotionImage*, are added and bound to the two new *InventTable* methods. The properties shown in Table 5-14 are changed on the two controls.

TABLE 5-14 ***PromotionText* and *PromotionImage* Property Settings**

Property	*PromotionText*	*PromotionImage*
Left		Auto (right)
Width	70.00 char	2.0 inch
Height		2.0 inch
DynamicHeight	Yes	
ShowLabel	No	No
Table	*InventTable*	*InventTable*
DataMethod	*PromotionText*	*PromotionImage*

The *ShowLabel* properties are set to No because no headings should be printed. The *PromotionText* control is set to a fixed width of 70 characters with a dynamic height so that the text won't be truncated. The *PromotionImage* has a fixed size of 2 inches by 2 inches and is right-justified on the page.

The last step is to look up an *InventTable* record buffer based on the invoiced item and then send the buffer to the report. You do this with the following new method on the *BodyReference* body section.

```
void printInventTable()
{
    InventTable inventTable = custInvoiceTrans.inventTable();
    if (inventTable.RecId)
    {
         element.send(inventTable);
    }
}
```

The method uses the *InventTable* lookup method on the *CustInvoiceTrans* table, which returns a record buffer for the invoiced item, which the method subsequently sends to the report.

The preceding method should be called from the *executionSection* method on the same body section. The following method is therefore customized by including the call to the *printInventTable* method.

```
void  executeSection()
{;
    this.printCustPackingSlipTrans();
    this.printDimHistory();
    this.printInventTable();
}
```

The positioning of the body section, report control, and report methods is shown in Figure 5-18.

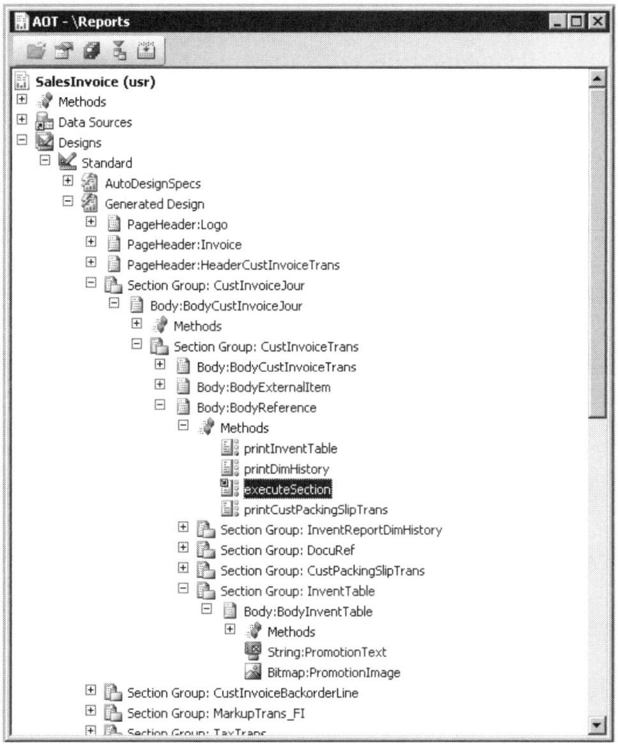

FIGURE 5-18 Position of the new sections, control, and methods in the *SalesInvoice* report

After the completion of all the customizations to the *SalesInvoice* report and the addition of new methods to *InventTable*, the report prints the promotion below each invoiced item on the report, as shown in Figure 5-14.

Preventing Printing of an Empty Body Section

The solution thus far has one flaw: it prints an empty *BodyInventTable* body section if there is no document reference for the *PromoText* and *PromoImage* document types, which causes an empty box to appear below each item on the invoice. You could easily fix this by altering the *printInventTable* method to include a check for text or images, as shown in the following change to the *printInventTable* method.

```
void printInventTable()
{
    InventTable inventTable = custInvoiceTrans.inventTable();
    if (inventTable.RecId &&
        (inventTable.PromotionText() || inventTable.PromotionImage()))
    {
         element.send(inventTable);
    }
}
```

This code ensures that the *InventTable* record buffer is sent to the report only if the *PromotionText* method or the *PromotionImage* method returns a value.

In terms of performance, this change isn't optimal because methods could be executed twice if a promotion were added to the *InventTable* record. This could result in as many as five round-trips to the database for each printed invoiced item: two from the *printInventTable* method, two when printing the values, and one when the report runtime determines the height of the *PromotionText* control.

A better solution is to cache the returned values from the *PromotionText* and *PromotionImage* methods when they are called in the *printInventTable* method and then use the cached values instead of retrieving them from the database when printing the *PromotionText* and *PromotionImage* controls.

The cache variables must be added to the *classDeclaration* of the report, so the following lines are inserted there.

```
    DocuValueFile           promotionImage;
     Notes                   promotionText;
```

The *printInventTable* method is modified to store the returned values from the *PromotionText* and *PromotionImage* methods on the *InventTable* record buffer in the newly created variables, as shown in the following copy of the method.

```
void printInventTable()
{
    InventTable inventTable = custInvoiceTrans.inventTable();
    ;
    promotionImage  = inventTable.PromotionImage();
    promotionText   = inventTable.PromotionText();

    if (inventTable.RecId &&
        (promotionText || promotionImage))
    {
        element.send(inventTable);
    }
}
```

In addition to these two new display methods, *PromotionText* and *PromotionImage* are created to return the values of the variables. The following code samples show these methods, implemented in the *BodyInventTable* body section.

```
display Notes PromotionText()
{
    return promotionText;
}
```

```
display DocuValueFile PromotionImage()
{
    return promotionImage;
}
```

With these two methods named similarly to the *InventTable* methods, you must remove only the value in the *Table* property on the *PromotionImage* and *PromotionText* report controls to enable the report to retrieve the value from the local report methods instead of the *InventTable* methods. You can even remove the display method modifiers from the two *InventTable* methods because they are no longer used as display methods.

When you print the report again, no empty *BodyInventTable* body sections appear, and the printing of this specific section is optimized. The report will never result in more than two round-trips to the database for each invoiced item. The only disadvantages are that return types of the methods on the *InventTable* and the equivalent methods on the report should be kept synchronized, and these return types should again be kept synchronized with the types of the cache variables. This synchronization wasn't necessary earlier in the example, before the values in the report were cached.

Number Sequence Customization

In Chapter 6, "Extending Dynamics AX," the sample X++ code shows that a service order feature must have a *number sequence* to generate a unique identification number. To achieve this, you must customize the number sequence class, setting up the relationship between a module and a number sequence reference, and also associating the number sequence reference with the extended data type in which you want to store a number from the sequence.

When you want to create a new number sequence, you must first create an extended data type. The ID of the type is used as the identifier for the number sequence reference, so it must be unique. Figure 5-19 shows a string data type named *BikeServiceOrderId*.

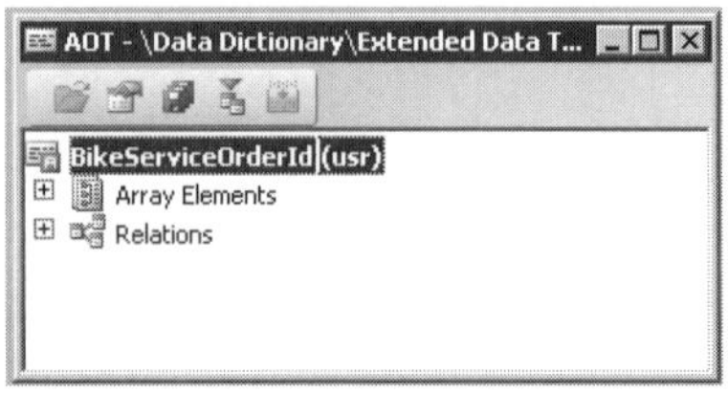

FIGURE 5-19 *BikeServiceOrderId* extended data type

The properties on the extended data type are set to create a type with a maximum length of 20 characters, as shown in Table 5-15.

TABLE 5-15 ***BikeServiceOrderId* Property Settings**

Property	Settings
Type	String
Label	Service order
HelpText	Service order ID
StringSize	20

To implement a number sequence reference for service orders and assign it a specific service order number sequence, you must make changes to a *NumberSeqReference* class. To implement the reference in the Accounts Receivable module, among other references used by the sales order functionality, you add the following lines of X++ code to the *loadModule* method on the *NumberSeqReference_SalesOrder* class.

```
numRef.DataTypeId           = typeId2ExtendedTypeId(
                              typeid(BikeServiceOrderId));
numRef.ReferenceHelp        = "Unique key for the service order table, "+
                              "used when identification of a service "+
                              "order is allocated automatically.";
numRef.WizardContinuous     = false;
```

```
    numRef.WizardManual          = NoYes::No;
    numRef.WizardAllowChangeDown = NoYes::No;
    numRef.WizardAllowChangeUp   = NoYes::No;
    numRef.SortField             = 100;
    this.create(numRef);
```

These are the only modifications necessary to set up a new number sequence reference. The reference is available in the Accounts Receivable parameter form, and a number sequence can be created automatically by using the Number Sequence Wizard. You start the Number Sequence Wizard by clicking the Wizard button in the Number Sequences form located in the navigation pane under Basic\Setup\Number Sequences\Number Sequences.

The *numRef* table buffer in the preceding example is of a *NumberSequenceReference* table type. This table contains several fields that can be set depending on the reference you want to create. These fields are described in Table 5-16.

TABLE 5-16 ***NumberSequenceReference* Field Explanations**

Field	Explanation
DataTypeId	The ID for the reference. Use the ID of the extended data type.
ConfigurationKeyId	The configuration key that must be enabled for the reference to display. The configuration key should be set only if it is different from the key associated with the extended data type.
ReferenceLabel	The number sequence reference label should be set only if it is different from the label on the extended data type.
ReferenceHelp	The number sequence reference user interface Help field should be set only if the Help text is different from text in the *HelpText* property on the extended data type.
DataTypeSameAsId	Indicates that the reference can use the number from another number sequence. To make this possible, set the ID for the reference to the listed number sequence. This setting is usually applied to voucher references that use the ID of the journal as the voucher number.
GroupEnabled	Indicates that the reference is enabled for use with number sequence groups. This setting should be specified only if the reference can be set up for each number sequence group.
SortField	The position of the reference in the list. Use a sufficiently high number to avoid conflict with other or future references within the same module.
WizardLowest	The default value for the Smallest field when creating the number sequence with the Number Sequence Wizard.
WizardHighest	The default value for the Largest field when creating the number sequence with the Number Sequence Wizard.
WizardManual	The default value for the Manual field when creating the number sequence with the Number Sequence Wizard.

Field	Explanation
WizardContinuous	The default value for the Continuous field when creating the number sequence with the Number Sequence Wizard.
WizardAllowChangeDown	The default value for the To A Lower Number field when creating the number sequence with the Number Sequence Wizard.
WizardAllowChangeUp	The default value for the To A Higher Number field when creating the number sequence with the Number Sequence Wizard.
WizardFetchAheadQty	The default value for the Quantity Of Numbers pre allocation field when creating the number sequence with the Number Sequence Wizard. This field also enables the pre allocation number sequence feature, but it can't be used in combination with a sequence marked Continuous.

Finally, the following method is implemented on the *SalesParameters* table. The method returns the new number sequence reference and should be used in the X++ code that requires numbers from the number sequence.

```
static client server NumberSequenceReference  numRefBikeServiceOrderId()
{
    return NumberSeqReference::findReference(
                          typeId2ExtendedTypeId(typeid(BikeServiceOrderId)));
}
```

Chapter 6

Extending Dynamics AX

In this chapter:

The objectives of this chapter are to:

- Explain how to create wizards with the same look and feel as the standard wizards in Microsoft Dynamics AX 2009.
- Demonstrate how to use the *RunBase* application framework to implement new business transaction jobs.

Introduction

A wizard is a special form of user assistance that automates a single task or a set of tasks. A wizard presents users with a series of pages to collect information necessary to complete a task. Wizards are especially useful for complex or infrequent tasks that the user might have difficulty learning or doing and for tedious, frequently performed tasks. The first part of this chapter shows how to build a simple wizard to create inventory items.

The second part of the chapter examines the *RunBase* framework. The *RunBase* framework supports business transaction jobs, such as exchange rate adjustment or inventory closing. The framework helps developers write new business transaction jobs by supplying all the programming infrastructure so that the developer can focus solely on the business logic. This chapter implements a sample *RunBase* class that sends bike-tuning service offers to customers via e-mail.

Wizard Framework Extension

The wizard framework supplies the programming infrastructure to create wizards with a consistent look and feel. When developing wizards, you should follow some simple guidelines to ensure that all the wizards you create have the same general style and are as helpful as possible to the user. For example, all wizards should clearly state their purpose on the first page and present a very limited set of choices and controls on every subsequent page. Figure 6-1 shows a sample first page.

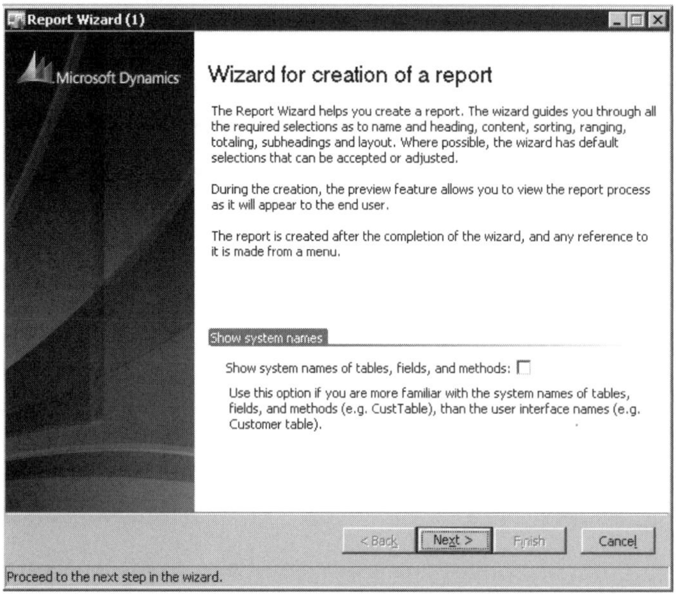

FIGURE 6-1 Sample first page, stating a clear purpose

You should provide enough instructions to users to make the concepts the wizard implements easy to understand. Consider using graphics as well as text, as shown in Figure 6-2, to explain complex concepts.

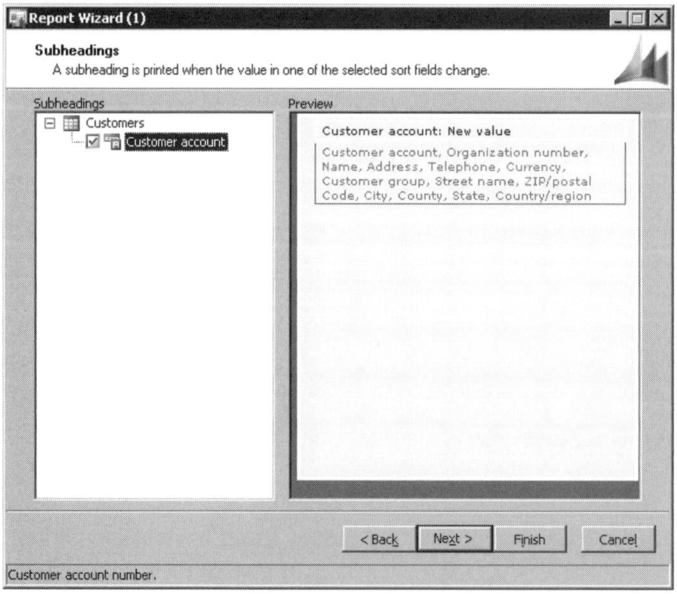

FIGURE 6-2 Wizard page that provides clear, complete instructions and visual guidance

The user should be able to finish the entire task within the wizard itself. Don't confuse users by redirecting them to other forms to complete the wizard. Include default values or settings (as shown in Figure 6-3) wherever possible. If you can, enable the Finish button as soon as the wizard has collected enough information to skip the rest of the wizard pages. Try to minimize the number of decisions the user must make.

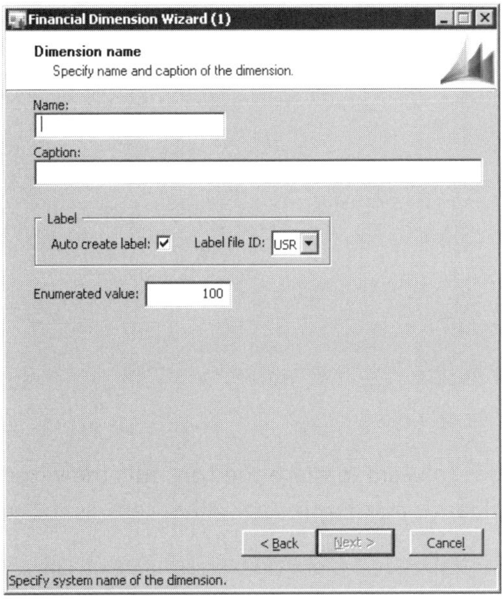

FIGURE 6-3 Wizard page showing default values for Auto Create Label, Label File ID, and Enumerated Value of user-defined dimension

Make sure the wizard clearly states the actions it will take and how the user should proceed when the wizard has been completed. You can present this information on the last page of the wizard as fixed text with a summary of the selected values and settings, as shown in Figure 6-4.

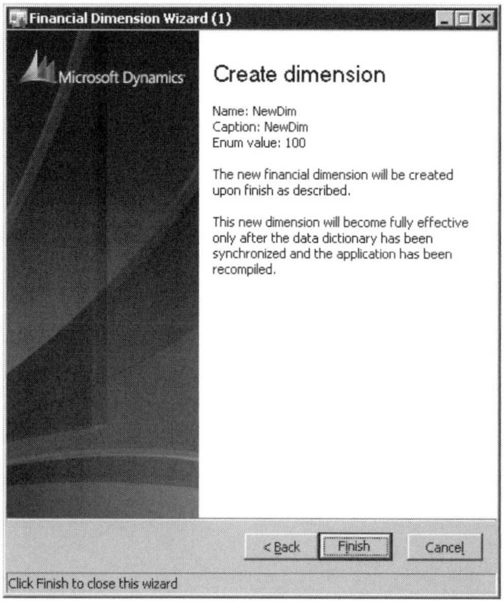

FIGURE 6-4 Final wizard page that explains what will happen when user clicks Finish

Creating a New Wizard

The Wizard Wizard is a special wizard in Dynamics AX that helps you create wizards that have the same look and feel as the standard wizards in Dynamics AX. You open the Wizard Wizard, shown in Figure 6-5, from the Dynamics AX menu bar: click Tools\Development Tools\Wizards\Wizard Wizard.

FIGURE 6-5 Wizard Wizard Welcome page

As shown in Figure 6-6, the wizard asks you to choose between two types of wizards: a standard wizard, for any kind of job, and a default data wizard, especially designed to help the user create basic default data in the system. This section demonstrates how to use the Wizard Wizard to create a standard wizard that is available from the navigation pane and the area page of Dynamics AX.

Note An area page contains menu items that link to frequently used forms for the selected module. Area pages are accessed from the navigation pane.

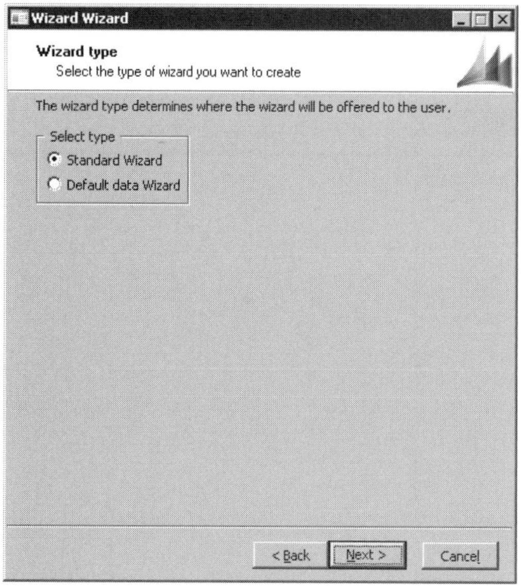

FIGURE 6-6 Wizard Type page

When you enter a name for your wizard on the next page (shown in Figure 6-7), you can see how the names of the elements that are created in the Application Object Tree (AOT) are suffixed with either *Wizard* or *DefaultDataWizard*, depending on the type of wizard.

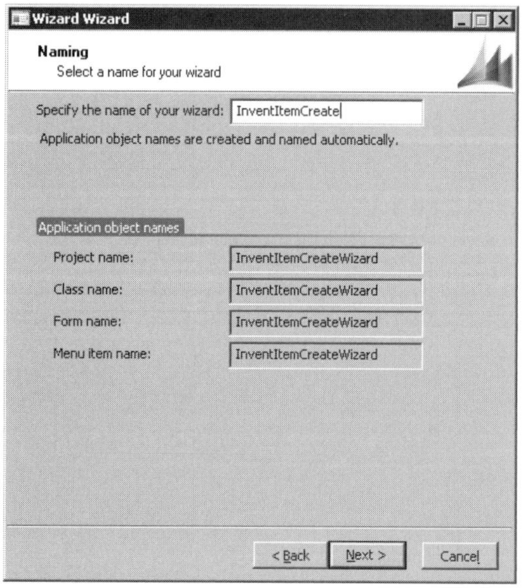

FIGURE 6-7 Naming page

In the last step before the summary page, Setup, you enter the number of steps you want in your wizard, as shown in Figure 6-8. This number includes the Welcome page and the Summary page. If you change your mind about the number of steps you want after completing the wizard, you can change the elements generated by the wizard in the AOT.

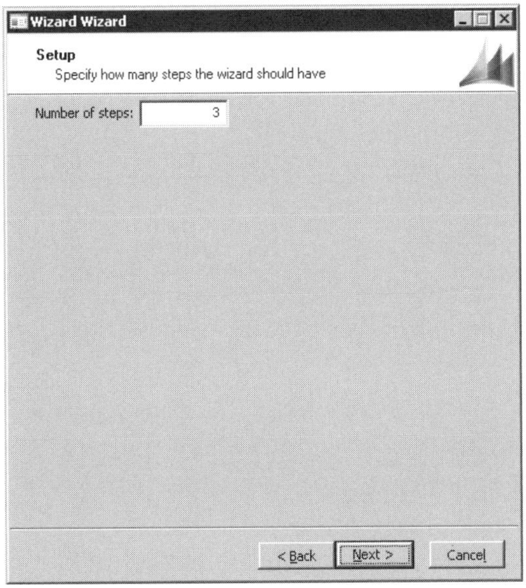

FIGURE 6-8 Setup page

Because this sample wizard doesn't include any complicated selections, the summary page, shown in Figure 6-9, is rather short.

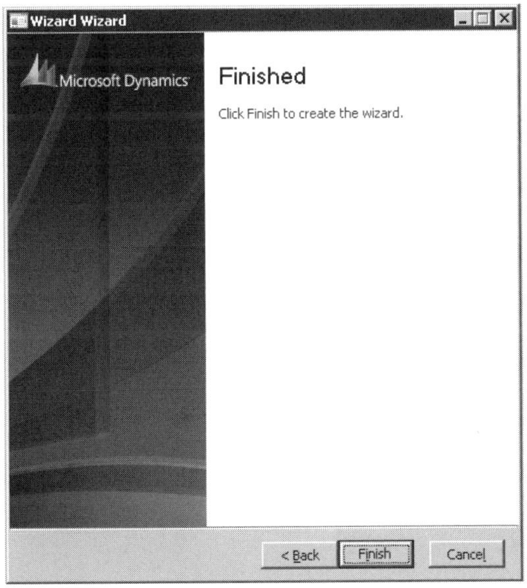

FIGURE 6-9 Summary page

The Wizard Wizard creates a private project, shown in Figure 6-10, that contains three new elements, described from top to bottom:

- A class for holding the business logic of the wizard and the logic for running the wizard in the framework. The class extends either *SysWizard* or *SysDefaultDataWizard*, depending on the type of wizard.
- A form with the user interface of the wizard.
- A display menu item to start the wizard. The menu item starts the class that starts the form.

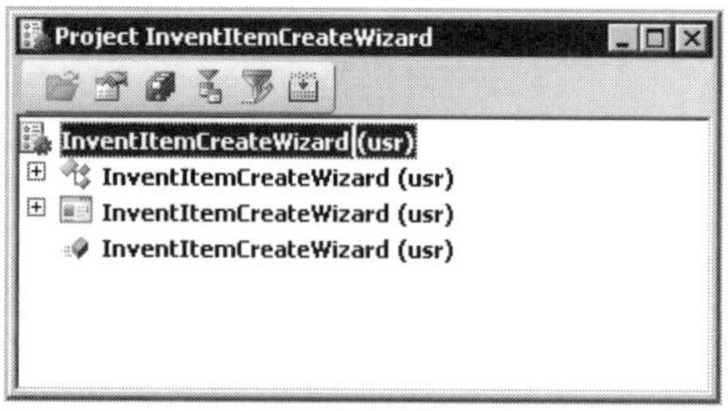

FIGURE 6-10 Elements of a new wizard collected in a private project

> **Note** The Wizard Wizard doesn't add the new elements to the version control system if version control is enabled. You must add them manually.

Creating Labels

After creating the basic frame for your new wizard, the next step is to add labels. To open the Label Editor, click Tools\Development Tools\Label\Label Editor. The Label Editor is shown in Figure 6-11.

The Label Editor creates labels in your default language. The Setup tab allows you to set the default language and displays the default label file in which new labels are stored. (If there is no default label file, you must create one with the Label File Wizard, located in Tools \Development Tools\Wizards\Label File Wizard, and then you must select it as the default on the Setup tab.) You can change these default settings. Read more about the Label Editor in Chapter 3, "The MorphX Tools."

Labels are identified with an ID consisting of the label file name and a counter. The label IDs displayed depend on any existing labels and your choice of label file. In Table 6-1, a default label file—USR—results in the label IDs @USR1, @USR2, @USR3, and so on.

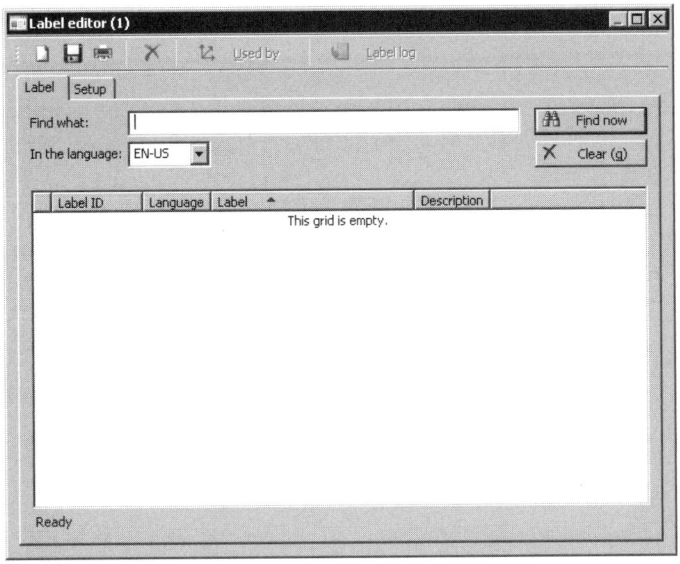

FIGURE 6-11 Label Editor

Press Ctrl+N to create the new labels shown in Table 6-1. The label ID is generated automatically when you provide text in the Label field; the Description field is optional.

TABLE 6-1 Label IDs and Labels

Label ID	Label
@USR1	Create inventory item wizard.
@USR2	This wizard helps you create a new inventory item.
@USR3	Item identification.
@USR4	Item number and description.
@USR5	Select proper group relationships for the item.
@USR6	Create inventory item.
@USR7	This is all the wizard needs to know to create the inventory item.
@USR8	Click Finish to create and save the item.

Take note of the label numbers you're given so that you can use them in your code if you have label numbers other than those listed in the table. You can also use the Label Editor to search for previously created labels based on their content.

Adding Content to the Wizard

Next you can add selection fields to the wizard you created and write the logic to create the inventory item. You edit the wizard form by using the AOT. In the AOT, scroll to the name of the wizard form you want to design and right-click it. Select Properties, and then set the *Caption* property of the form design to @USR1.

Right-click TabPage:Step1, select Properties, and then change the *Caption* property from "Step 1 Title" to @USR1. Add a *StaticText* control to TabPage:Step1 by right-clicking it and selecting New Control\Static Text. A *Text* property appears in the properties list; set it to @USR2.

On TabPage:Step2, change the *Caption* property from "Step 2 Title" to @USR3. Set the *HelpText* property to @USR4.

Now you can begin adding input fields. In this example, the user must be able to enter an item ID, item name, and item description. Start by investigating the types of item IDs. The table in which items are stored is called *InventTable*. Look up the item ID on the table, open the properties, and note that the extended data type of the field is *ItemId*. Using this extended data type directly in the wizard will cause a problem, because the extended data type has a relationship with *InventTable*; the drop-down list for the extended data type displays existing item IDs associated with the field. You must find the name of the parent of the extended data type for use in the new wizard.

Locate the extended data type in the AOT and examine the properties. You can see that the type extends the *ItemIdBase* extended data type; because this type doesn't have any database relationships, you can safely use it in the wizard. In other situations, if you can't find a suitable extended data type, you can either create one or change the *LookupButton* property of the form control to *Never*.

Right-click TabPage:Step2, point to New Control, and then click StringEdit. Open the properties of the new field and change the *Name* property to *ItemId*, change the *ExtendedDataType* property to *ItemIdBase*, and change the *AutoDeclaration* property to *Yes*. (Setting the *AutoDeclaration* property to *Yes* allows you to easily address the control by using X++ code later; the runtime automatically creates an object handle, which allows access to the control.)

Repeat this procedure to add a field for the *ItemName* of *InventTable*. The *ExtendedDataType* type should be *Name*. Remember to set the *AutoDeclaration* property to *Yes*.

Finally, add the inventory description field. Give it the name ItemDescription. The inventory item description field is in the *InventTxt* table, not in *InventTable* as in the previous case, so you must open *InventTxt* to determine the extended data type. As you can see from the *Txt* field on the table, the extended data type is *ItemFreeTxt*. Supply this type in the *ExtendedDataType* property. Again, remember to set the *AutoDeclaration* property to *Yes*.

On the third page of the wizard, the user should be able to link the item to the mandatory item group, inventory model group, and dimension group. To make this possible, open the properties list for TabPage:Step3 and change the *Caption* property from "Step 3 Title" to @SYS1177, reading "Groups," and change the *HelpText* property to @USR5. Using the procedure described earlier, add three fields to the page with the following extended data types: *ItemGroupId*, *InventModelGroupId*, and *InventDimGroupId*. Name the fields to match the extended data type name, and remember to set the *AutoDeclaration* property to *Yes*.

The fourth page of the wizard is dedicated to prices. For this example, you add a sales price field. Change the *Caption* property of the fourth tab from "Step 4 Title" to @SYS73780, reading "Pricing," and change the *HelpText* property to @SYS87796, reading "Set up sales prices." Add a *RealEdit* control with the extended data type *Price* to the tab. Change the *Name* property to *Price* and remember to set the *AutoDeclaration* property to *Yes*.

On the fifth and final page, you add a short summary that describes what the wizard does when the user clicks Finish. Change the *Caption* property of the tab from "Step 5 Title" to @USR6. Add a *StaticText* control to the tab. Change the *Name* property to *TxtFinish*, change the *AutoDeclaration* property to *Yes*, change the *Width* property to *Column Width*, change the *Height* property to *Column Height*, and remove the text value from the *Text* property. Because this summary text is composed of several sentences with more than one label, you need to write X++ code to set the text. You must add the code to the *setTexts* method on the form, as shown here.

```
void setTexts()
{
;

    txtFinish.text("@USR7" + '\n\n' +
                   "@USR8" + '\n'   +
                   "@SYS68351");
}
```

Next, you set up the navigation for the wizard. You need to implement three simple rules:

- The Next button must not be enabled on the Item Identification page if an item ID hasn't been entered.
- The Next button must not be enabled on the Groups page unless all three fields have a value.
- The Finish button must be enabled as soon as the Groups page is filled in. It isn't mandatory for the user to enter a price, so the user can safely skip that step.

Start in the class declaration of the *InventItemCreateWizard* class by defining macro variables so that you can address the tabs by name rather than by number, as shown in this example.

```
public class InventItemCreateWizard extends SysWizard
{
    #define.Welcome(1)
    #define.Id(2)
    #define.Groups(3)
    #define.Prices(4)
    #define.Finish(5)
}
```

To make the Finish button available before the last page, override the *hasFinishButton* method by right-clicking the InventItemCreateWizard class, clicking Override Method, and choosing hasFinishButton. Set the return value to *true*, as shown here.

```
boolean hasFinishButton()
{
;
    return true;
}
```

The *setupNavigation* method describes the initial navigation settings that apply when the wizard is opened. To override this method, use the following code.

```
void setupNavigation()
{
;
    nextEnabled[#Welcome]   = true;
    backEnabled[#Welcome]   = false;
    finishEnabled[#Welcome] = false;

    nextEnabled[#Id]        = false;
    backEnabled[#Id]        = true;
    finishEnabled[#Id]      = false;

    nextEnabled[#Groups]    = false;
    backEnabled[#Groups]    = true;
    finishEnabled[#Groups]  = false;

    nextEnabled[#Prices]    = true;
    backEnabled[#Prices]    = true;
    finishEnabled[#Prices]  = true;

    nextEnabled[#Finish]    = false;
    backEnabled[#Finish]    = true;
    finishEnabled[#Finish]  = true;
}
```

To enable the Next button when an item ID has been entered, find the *ItemId* control on the form and override the *textChange* method with the following code.

```
public void textChange()
{
;
    super();

    if (this.text())
    {
        if (!sysWizard.isNextEnabled())
        {
            sysWizard.nextEnabled(true, sysWizard.curTab(), false);
        }
    }
    else
    {
        if (sysWizard.isNextEnabled())
        {
            sysWizard.nextEnabled(false, sysWizard.curTab(), false);
        }
    }
}
```

On the Groups page, all three fields must be filled in before the Next button is enabled. Create a single method on the form, in the Methods section directly under the form name node, to control the values *Next* and *Finish*, as shown here.

```
void enableNextOnGroups()
{
;
    if (itemGroupId.text()          &&
        inventModelGroupId.text()   &&
        inventDimGroupId.text())
    {
        if (!sysWizard.isNextEnabled())
        {
            sysWizard.nextEnabled(true, sysWizard.curTab(), false);
        }

        if (!sysWizard.isFinishEnabled())
        {
            sysWizard.finishEnabled(true, sysWizard.curTab(), false);
        }
    }
    else
    {
        if (sysWizard.isNextEnabled())
        {
            sysWizard.nextEnabled(false, sysWizard.curTab(), false);
        }
```

```
        if (sysWizard.isFinishEnabled())
        {
            sysWizard.finishEnabled(false, sysWizard.curTab(), false);
        }
    }
}
```

Override the *textChange* method of each of the three controls on the Groups page as follows.

```
public void textChange()
{
;
    super();

    element.enableNextOnGroups();
}
```

Also override the *modified* method of each of the three controls as follows.

```
public boolean modified()
{
    boolean ret;
    ;
    ret = super();

    element.enableNextOnGroups();

    return ret;
}
```

Before you can write the business logic to create the inventory item, you must create methods on the form to return the selected values from the controls you've added, as shown in the following code.

```
public ItemId itemId()
{
;
    return itemId.text();
}

public ItemName itemName()
{
    ;
    return itemName.text();
}
```

```
public ItemFreeTxt itemDescription()
{
;
    return itemDescription.text();
}

public itemGroupId itemGroupId()
{
;
    return itemGroupId.text();
}

public InventModelGroupId inventModelGroupId()
{
;
    return inventModelGroupId.text();
}

public InventDimGroupId inventDimGroupId()
{
;
    return inventDimGroupId.text();
}

public Price price()
{
;
    return price.realValue();
}
```

You can now write the X++ code that uses the selections made in the wizard and creates the inventory item. You insert the following code in the *run* method of the *Wizard* class.

```
void run()
{
    InventTable         inventTable;
    InventTxt           inventTxt;
    InventTableModule   inventTableModule;
    InventItemLocation  inventItemLocation;
    ;

    ttsBegin;

    inventTable.initValue();
    inventTable.ItemId      = formRun.itemId();
    inventTable.ItemName    = formRun.itemName();
    inventTable.ItemGroupId = formRun.itemGroupId();
    inventTable.ModelGroupId= formRun.inventModelGroupId();
    inventTable.DimGroupId  = formRun.inventDimGroupId();
    inventTable.insert();
```

```
        inventTxt.initValue();
        inventTxt.ItemId          = formRun.itemId();
        inventTxt.LanguageId      = CompanyInfo::find().LanguageId;
        inventTxt.Txt             = formRun.itemDescription();
        inventTxt.insert();

        inventTableModule.initValue();
        inventTableModule.ItemId        = formRun.itemId();
        inventTableModule.ModuleType    = ModuleInventPurchSales::Invent;
        inventTableModule.insert();

        inventTableModule.ItemId        = formRun.itemId();
        inventTableModule.ModuleType    = ModuleInventPurchSales::Purch;
        inventTableModule.insert();

        inventTableModule.ItemId        = formRun.itemId();
        inventTableModule.ModuleType    = ModuleInventPurchSales::Sales;
        inventTableModule.Price         = formRun.price();
        inventTableModule.insert();

        inventItemLocation.initValue();
        inventItemLocation.ItemId       = formRun.itemId();
        inventItemLocation.InventDimId  = InventDim::inventDimIdBlank();
        inventItemLocation.insert();

        ttsCommit;
    }
```

You could include calls to *validateWrite* of the tables to ensure that the wizard uses the same validation rules that are used when a user creates a new item from the Item form. This ensures that the validations required to create an item are consistent, regardless of where you create a new item.

Adding the Wizard to the Navigation Pane and the Area Page

To make the wizard available from the area page and the navigation pane in Dynamics AX, you must add the menu item to the main menu in the AOT. First, you must associate the menu item with a configuration key and a security key.

Open properties for the menu item, and change the *ConfigurationKey* property to *LogisticsBasic*. The *SecurityKey* property must match the position of the menu item on the main menu or navigation pane, so set *SecurityKey* to *InventPeriodic*. Because the wizard adds data to the system, you must also change the *NeededAccessLevel* property to *Add*. Finally, change the *Label* property of the menu item to @USR1 and the *HelpText* property to @USR2.

Now you can add the menu item to the main menu. The main menu consists of several submenus; you add the wizard menu item to the Inventory Management submenu. In the AOT, expand Menus, right-click Invent, point to New, and then click Menu Item. Right-click the new menu item, and then select Properties. Make sure that *MenuItemType* is set to *Display*, and set *MenuItemName* to *InventItemCreateWizard*. Then drag the menu item to the Periodic folder. Save the menu, and then restart the Dynamics AX client to make the new menu item appear in the navigation pane and the area page. When the menu item is saved in the main menu, it is visible in the navigation pane and the area page, which are different views of the main menu.

> **Tip** You could also add the menu item to the menu by simply dragging it from the Menu Items node and dropping it on the *Invent* node in the AOT.

Creating a Default Data Wizard

Default data wizards are targeted especially for creating base data in the system. An example is the Unit Creation Wizard available from Basic\Setup\Units\Units\Functions\Unit Creation Wizard. A default data wizard has one step more than a standard wizard. In this additional step, you must choose from two types of default data wizards:

- Set up several groups of tables.
- Set up one group of tables.

If you select the first type of default data wizard, a grid on the second tab allows the user to select the areas in which to run the wizard. You typically use the second type of default data wizard for complex wizards that will operate on only a few tables. This kind of wizard is typically started from the main form for the table for which it creates data, and not from the menu.

> **Note** Dynamics AX includes a sample default data wizard named TutorialDefaultData Wizard.

RunBase Framework Extension

Use the *RunBase* framework throughout Dynamics AX whenever you must execute a business transaction job. Extending the *RunBase* framework allows you to implement business operations that don't have default support in the Dynamics AX application. The *RunBase* framework supplies many features, including dialog boxes, query windows, validation-before-execution windows, the progress bar, client/server optimization, pack-unpack with versioning, and optional scheduled batch execution at a given date and time.

Inheritance in the *RunBase* Framework

Classes that use the *RunBase* framework must inherit from either the *RunBase* class or the *RunBaseBatch* class. If the class extends *RunBaseBatch*, it can be enabled for scheduled execution in batch mode.

In a good inheritance model, each class has a public construction mechanism, unless the class is abstract. If the class doesn't have to be initialized, use a static construct method. Because X++ doesn't support method name overloading, you should use a static *new* method if the class must be initialized further upon instantiation. Static *new* methods have the following characteristics:

- They are public and static.
- Their names are prefixed with *new*.
- They are named logically or with the arguments that they take. Examples include *newInventTrans* and *newInventMovement*.
- They usually take nondefault parameters only.
- They always return a valid object of the class type, instantiated and initialized, or throw an error.

> **Note** A class can have several *new* methods with different parameter profiles. The *NumberSeq* class is an example of a class with multiple *new* methods.

The default constructor (the *new* method) should be protected to force users of the class to instantiate and initialize it with the static construct or *new* method. If *new* has some extra initialization logic that is always executed, you should place it in a separate *init* method.

> **Best Practice** To ease the task of writing customizations, a best practice is to add construction functionality for new subclasses (in higher layers) without mixing code with the construct method in the original layer.

Property Method Pattern

To allow other business operations to run your new business operation, you might want to run it without presenting any dialog boxes to the user. If you decide not to use dialog boxes, you need an alternative to them to set the values of the necessary member variables of your business operation class.

In Dynamics AX classes, member variables are always protected. In other words, they can't be accessed outside of the class; they can be accessed only from within objects of the class or its subclasses. To access member variables from outside the class, you must write accessor methods. The accessor methods can get, set, or both get and set member variable values. All accessor methods start with *parm*. In Dynamics AX, accessor methods are frequently referred to as *parm* methods.

Best Practice A Dynamics AX best practice is not to use separate get and set accessor methods. The accessor methods are combined into a single accessor method, handling both get and set, in a pattern called the *property method pattern*. Accessor methods should have the same name as the member variable that they access, prefixed with *parm*.

The following is an example of what a method implementing the property method pattern could look like.

```
public NoYesId parmCreateServiceOrders(NoYesId _createServiceOrders =
createServiceOrders)
{
;
    createServiceOrders = _createServiceOrders;

    return createServiceOrders;
}
```

If you want the method to work only as a *get* method, change it to something such as this.

```
public NoYesId parmCreateServiceOrders()
{
;
    return createServiceOrders;
}
```

And if you want the method to work only as a *set* method, change it to this.

```
public void parmCreateServiceOrders(NoYesId _createServiceOrders =
createServiceOrders)
{
;
    createServiceOrders = _createServiceOrders;
}
```

When member variables contain huge amounts of data (such as large containers or memo fields), the technique in the following example is recommended. This technique determines whether the parameter is changed. The disadvantage of using this technique in all cases is the overhead of an additional method call.

```
public container parmCode(container _code = conNull())
{
;
    if (!prmIsDefault(_code)
    {
        code = _code;
    }

    return code;
}
```

> **Tip** From the X++ editor window, you can access a template script to help you create *parm* methods. Right-click the editor window, point to Scripts, point to Template, point to Method, and then click Parm. A dialog box appears in which you must enter the variable type and name of the member variable that you want the *parm* method to give access to. You can also access the script by pressing Shift+F10 in the editor window and then selecting Scripts.

Pack-Unpack Pattern

When you want to save the state of an object with the option to reinstantiate the same object later, you must use the pack-unpack pattern. The *RunBase* framework requires that you implement this pattern to switch the class between client and server (for client/server optimization) and to present the user with a dialog box that states the choices made at the last execution of the class. If your class extends the *RunBaseBatch* class, you also need to use the pack-unpack pattern for scheduled execution in batch mode.

The pattern consists of a *pack* method and an *unpack* method. These methods are used by the *SysLastValue* framework, which stores and retrieves user settings or usage data values that persist between processes.

> **Note** A reinstantiated object is not the same object as the saved object. It is a copy of the object with the same values as the packed and unpacked member variables.

pack and *unpack* Methods

The *pack* method must be able to read the state of the object and return it in a container. Reading the state of the object involves reading the values of the variables needed to hydrate and dehydrate the object. Variables used at execution time that are declared as member variables don't have to be included in the *pack* method. The first entry in the container must be a version number that identifies the version of the saved structure. The following code is an example of the *pack* method.

```
container pack()
{
;
    return [#CurrentVersion, #CurrentList];
}
```

Macros must be defined in the class declaration. *CurrentList* is a macro defined in the *ClassDeclaration* holding a list of the member variables to pack. If the variables in the *CurrentList* macro are changed, the version number should also be changed to allow safe and versioned unpacking. The *unpack* method can support unpacking previous versions of the class, as shown in the following example.

```
class InventCostClosing extends RunBaseBatch
{
    #define.maxCommitCount(25)

    // Parameters

    TransDate                   transDate;
    InventAdjustmentSpec        specification;
    NoYes                       prodJournal;
    NoYes                       updateLedger;
    NoYes                       cancelRecalculation;
    NoYes                       runRecalculation;
    FreeTxt                     freeTxt;
    Integer                     maxIterations;
    CostAmount                  minTransferValue;
    InventAdjustmentType        adjustmentType;
    boolean                     collapseGroups;



    ...

    #DEFINE.CurrentVersion(4)
    #LOCALMACRO.CurrentList
        TransDate,
        Specification,
        ProdJournal,
        UpdateLedger,
        FreeTxt,
        MaxIterations,
        MinTransferValue,
        adjustmentType,
        cancelRecalculation,
        runRecalculation,
        collapseGroups
    #ENDMACRO

}
```

```
public boolean unpack(container packedClass)
{
    #LOCALMACRO.Version1List
        TransDate,
        Specification,
        ProdJournal,
        UpdateLedger,
        FreeTxt,
        MaxIterations,
        MinTransferValue,
        adjustmentType,
        del_minSettlePct,
        del_minSettleValue
    #ENDMACRO

    #LOCALMACRO.Version2List
        TransDate,
        Specification,
        ProdJournal,
        UpdateLedger,
        FreeTxt,
        MaxIterations,
        MinTransferValue,
        adjustmentType,
        del_minSettlePct,
        del_minSettleValue,
        cancelRecalculation,
        runRecalculation,
        collapseGroups
    #ENDMACRO

    Percent    del_minSettlePct;
    CostAmount del_minSettleValue;

    boolean         _ret;
    Integer         _version    = conpeek(packedClass,1);

    switch (_version)
    {
        case #CurrentVersion:
            [_version, #CurrentList] = packedClass;
            _ret = true;
            break;

        case 3:
            // List has not changed, just the prodJournal must now always be updated
            [_version, #CurrentList] = packedClass;
            prodJournal                = NoYes::Yes;
            updateLedger               = NoYes::Yes;
            _ret = true;
            break;
```

```
        case 2:
            [_version, #Version2List] = packedClass;
            prodJournal               = NoYes::Yes;
            updateLedger              = NoYes::Yes;
            _ret = true;
            break;

        case 1:
            [_version, #Version1List] = packedClass;
            cancelRecalculation       = NoYes::Yes;
            runRecalculation          = NoYes::No;
            _ret = true;
            break;

        default:
            _ret = false;
    }
    return _ret;
}
```

If any member variable isn't packable, the class can't be packed and reinstantiated to the same state. If any of the members are other classes, records, cursors, or temporary tables, they must also be made packable. Other classes that don't extend *RunBase* can implement the *pack* and *unpack* methods by implementing the *SysPackable* interface.

When the object is reinstantiated, it must be possible to call the *unpack* method, which reads the saved state and reapplies the values of the member variables. The *unpack* method can reapply the correct set of member variables according to the saved version number, as shown in this example.

```
public boolean unpack(container _packedClass)
{
    Version    version = conpeek(_packedClass, 1);
;
    switch (version)
    {
        case #CurrentVersion:
            [version, #CurrentList] = _packedClass;
            break;

        default:
            return false;
    }
    return true;
}
```

The *unpack* method returns a Boolean value that indicates whether the initialization succeeded.

As mentioned earlier in this section, the *pack* and *unpack* methods have three responsibilities:

- Switching a *RunBase*-derived class between client and server.
- Presenting the user with final choices made when the class was last executed.
- Scheduling the execution of the class in batch mode.

In some scenarios, it is useful to execute specific logic depending on the context in which the *pack* or *unpack* method is called. You can use the *isSwappingPrompt* method on *RunBase* to detect whether the *pack* or *unpack* method is called in the context of switching between client and server. The *isSwappingPrompt* method returns *true* when called in this context. You can use the *isInBatch* method on *RunBaseBatch* to detect whether the *unpack* method is called in the context of executing the class in batch mode.

Bike-Tuning Service Offers Example

In this section, you create an extension of the *RunBase* class to send bike-tuning service offers to customers via e-mail. Each bike-tuning offer could result in the creation of a service order transaction. To follow this example, you must have created an extended data type and a number sequence for bike-tuning service orders, as described in Chapter 5, "Customizing Dynamics AX."

> **Note** To send e-mail messages, you must first set up the e-mail parameters in Dynamics AX. You access the e-mail parameters from Administration\Setup\E-Mail Parameters. To run the example without sending e-mail messages, omit the bits that use the *SysMailer* class.

Creating the Labels

Start by creating the labels you need. Open the Label Editor from Tools\Development Tools\Label\Label Editor. The label numbers that appear in the Label Editor depend on your existing labels and choice of label file. This example refers to the labels as @USR9, @USR10, and @USR11. Press Ctrl+N to create the labels shown in Table 6-2.

TABLE 6-2 Bike-Tuning Label Numbers and Text

Label Number	Text
@USR9	Bike-tuning offers.
@USR10	Create bike-tuning offers.
@USR11	Send bike-tuning offers to existing customers via e-mail.

Keep in mind that you need to use label numbers in your code, so don't forget the ones you're given.

Creating the Table

To store information about the generated service orders, a simple table with only two fields must be created. If you're not confident in your ability to create new tables, the Microsoft Dynamics AX 2009 software-development kit (SDK) offers detailed information about creating tables.

The table must be created with the following properties.

Name	*BikeServiceOrderTable*
Label	@SYS79051 The label reads "Service Orders."

Add two fields to identify the service order and the customer. The fields must have the following properties.

Name	*CustAccount*
ExtendedDataType	*CustAccount*
Name	*BikeServiceOrderId*
ExtendedDataType	*BikeServiceOrderId*

Finally, add an index with the following properties to the table.

Name	*ServiceOrderIdx*
AllowDuplicates	No
DataField	*BikeServiceOrderId*

Creating the Class

Now you can begin to create the business transaction class itself. Create a new class that extends the *RunBase* class, as shown in this example.

```
public class BikeTuningOffers extends RunBase
{
}
```

Implement the two abstract *pack* and *unpack* methods of *RunBase*. For now, you'll make a very simple implementation to be able to compile the class. You'll make the final implementation with the correct class members later. Insert to-do comments in the code, as shown in the following example, so that compile log messages remind you to revisit the methods.

```
public container pack()
{
;
    //TODO Make the final implementation.
    return conNull();
}

public boolean unpack(container _packedClass)
{
;
    //TODO Make the final implementation.
    return true;
}
```

To enable the example for execution, you must implement the *run* method. Because it's too early to add the business operation, you implement an empty method, as shown here.

```
public void run()
{

}
```

Implementing the Class Description

You must implement a static method that returns a description of what the class does. This method sets the title of the dialog box and can also be used for different kinds of user interface presentations on the class. The description method must effectively be executed on the tier from which it is called, so define it as *client server*. Use one of the labels created earlier, as shown in this example.

```
client server static ClassDescription description()
{
;
    return "@USR9";
}
```

Implementing Constructors

Next, you create a custom static constructor as shown here.

```
public static BikeTuningOffers construct()
{
    BikeTuningOffers    bikeTuningOffers;
    ;

    bikeTuningOffers = new BikeTuningOffers();

    return bikeTuningOffers;
}
```

To force users of the class to use your constructor rather than the default constructor (*new*), make the default constructor protected. Right-click the class, point to Override Method, click N5ew, and change the method as shown here.

```
protected void new()
{
;
    super();
}
```

To enable your job to run from a menu item, you must create the static constructor that is called by the menu item that you'll eventually create. This is the method with the name *main*, and it should look like this.

```
public static void main(Args args)
{
    BikeTuningOffers    bikeTuningOffers;
    ;

    bikeTuningOffers = BikeTuningOffers::construct();

    if (bikeTuningOffers.prompt())
    {
        bikeTuningOffers.run();
    }
}
```

In the *main* method, you call the *prompt* method of the framework. This method opens the user dialog box. It returns *true* if the user clicks OK and the values entered are free of errors. The *run* method of the framework starts the actual job.

Implementing a User Dialog Box

The user dialog box should allow the user to choose whether to create service orders automatically for each bike-tuning offer sent to customers via e-mail. To make this option available, you must have two global member variables in the class declaration. One is the dialog box field object shown in the dialog box, and the other is a variable used to store the value entered in the dialog box field. The changed class declaration looks like this.

```
public class BikeTuningOffers extends RunBase
{
    DialogField dialogCreateServiceOrders;

    NoYesId     createServiceOrders;
}
```

The *RunBase* framework sets up the basic dialog box by using the dialog framework, so you must add your dialog box field to the dialog box by overriding the *dialog* method. The following code sample displays what the system gives you when you override the *dialog* method.

```
protected Object dialog(DialogRunBase dialog, boolean forceOnClient)
{
    Object ret;

    ret = super(dialog, forceOnClient);

    return ret;
}
```

Rewrite this code as shown here so that it is more readable and follows the general pattern for the method.

```
protected Object dialog()
{
    DialogRunBase   dialog;
    ;

    dialog = super();

    return dialog;
}
```

Now add your field to the dialog box, as shown in the following code. Dialog box fields are objects of the *DialogField* class.

```
protected Object dialog()
{
    DialogRunBase   dialog;
    ;

    dialog = super();

    dialogCreateServiceOrders = dialog.addField(typeId(NoYesId), "@SYS79091",
"@SYS79091");

    return dialog;
}
```

To use the values entered in the dialog box, you must retrieve them from the dialog box fields and store them in member variables. When the user clicks OK or Cancel, the framework calls the *getFromDialog* method to retrieve and save the values. Implement an override of this method as follows.

```
public boolean getFromDialog()
{
    boolean ret;
    ;
    ret = super();

    createServiceOrders = dialogCreateServiceOrders.value();

    return ret;
}
```

When the user clicks OK, the framework calls the *validate* method. Although further validation isn't necessary for this example, the following code shows how to implement an override that prevents the user from running the job without selecting the Create Service Orders check box.

```
public boolean validate()
{
    boolean ret;
    ;
    ret = super();

    if (ret && createServiceOrders == NoYes::No)
    {
        ret = checkFailed("You cannot run the job without creating service orders.");
    }

    return ret;
}
```

You can view the user dialog box, shown in Figure 6-12, by opening the class. Right-click the class in the AOT, and then click Open.

FIGURE 6-12 Create Bike-Tuning Offers dialog box

Implementing the *run* Method

You can now write the *sendOffers* method that contains your business operation as follows.

```
private void sendOffers()
{
    CustTable                custTable;
    BikeServiceOrderId       bikeServiceOrderId;
    BikeServiceOrderTable    bikeServiceOrderTable;
    SysMailer                sysMailer;
    ;

    sysMailer = new SysMailer();

    ttsBegin;

    while select custTable
    {
        if (createServiceOrders)
        {
            bikeServiceOrderId  =
NumberSeq::newGetNum(SalesParameters::numRefBikeServiceOrderId()).num();
            bikeServiceOrderTable.BikeServiceOrderId    = bikeServiceOrderId;
            bikeServiceOrderTable.CustAccount           = custTable.AccountNum;
            bikeServiceOrderTable.insert();
        }

        sysMailer.quickSend(CompanyInfo::find().Email,
                            custTable.Email,
                            "Tune your bike",
                            strFmt("Hi %1,\n\nIt's time to tune your
                            bike....", custTable.name));
    }

    ttsCommit;
}
```

To call the *sendOffers* method, you must add it to the *run* method, which, as you might remember, is called from the value *main* if the user clicks OK in the dialog box and the values pass validation. The *run* method follows a specific pattern, as shown here.

```
public void run()
{
    #OCCRetryCount
    ;
    if (! this.validate())
        throw error("");

    try
    {
        ttsbegin;

        // Place the code that carries out the actual business transaction here.

        ttscommit;
    }
    catch (Exception::Deadlock)
    {
        retry;
    }
    catch (Exception::UpdateConflict)
    {
        if (appl.ttsLevel() == 0)
        {
            if (xSession::currentRetryCount() >= #RetryNum)
            {
                throw Exception::UpdateConflictNotRecovered;
            }
            else
            {
                retry;
            }
        }
        else
        {
            throw Exception::UpdateConflict;
        }
    }
}
```

This pattern ensures that the transaction is carried out within the scope of a database transaction and that the execution can recover from a deadlock or update conflict in the database. The *run* method calls validation again because someone could call *run* without showing the dialog box. In *run*, an error is thrown to completely stop the execution if validation fails. (Using the class without showing the dialog box is discussed later in this section.) When you add the call to the *sendOffers* method that holds your business operation, the *run* method looks like this.

```
public void run()
{
    #OCCRetryCount
    ;
    if (! this.validate())
        throw error("");

    try
    {
        ttsbegin;

        this.sendOffers();

        ttscommit;
    }
    catch (Exception::Deadlock)
    {
        retry;
    }
    catch (Exception::UpdateConflict)
    {
        if (appl.ttsLevel() == 0)
        {
            if (xSession::currentRetryCount() >= #RetryNum)
            {
                throw Exception::UpdateConflictNotRecovered;
            }
            else
            {
                retry;
            }
        }
        else
        {
            throw Exception::UpdateConflict;
        }
    }
}
```

Implementing the *pack* and *unpack* Methods

Now is a good time to revisit the *pack* and *unpack* methods. Start in the class declaration by setting up the member variables you want to store. In this example, you store the *createServiceOrders* variable. State the version number of the current set of member variables. The version number allows you to add new member variables later and still retrieve the old settings from the last execution of the operation. Also, you can specify the version number to be treated as the first version of the member variable list in the #Version1 declaration. This allows you to treat another version as the first version, which you might choose to do if you simply want to ignore a range of older versions. The first version is typically version 1.

```
public class BikeTuningOffers extends RunBase
{
    DialogField dialogCreateServiceOrders;

    NoYesId     createServiceOrders;

    #define.CurrentVersion(1)
    #define.version1(1)
    #localmacro.CurrentList
        createServiceOrders
    #endmacro
}
```

When more variables are stored in the *#CurrentList* macro, separate each variable by a comma.

You must change the *pack* method to follow this specific pattern.

```
public container pack()
{
;
    return [#CurrentVersion, #CurrentList];
}
```

And you must change the *unpack* method to follow this pattern.

```
public boolean unpack(container _packedClass)
{
    Version version = runbase::getVersion(_packedClass);
    ;

    switch (version)
    {
        case #CurrentVersion:
            [version, #CurrentList] = _packedClass;
            break;

        default:
            return false;
    }

    return true;
}
```

You also need to make the following change to your implementation of the *dialog* method to show the old values in the dialog box fields.

```
protected Object dialog()
{
    DialogRunBase   dialog;
    ;

    dialog = super();

    dialogCreateServiceOrders = dialog.addFieldValue(typeId(NoYesId),
createServiceOrders, "@SYS79091", "@SYS79091");

    return dialog;
}
```

Notice that you call the *addFieldValue* method rather than the *addField* method. The *addFieldValue* method allows you to pass a default value to the dialog box field. The *RunBase* framework ensures that the variable is set to the value saved in the *SysLastValue* framework at this point in time.

Creating a Menu Item

To make the operation available from the area page and the navigation pane, you must create a menu item for the operation. The menu item must be attached to a configuration key and a security key.

To create a new configuration key, open the AOT and expand Data Dictionary, right-click Configuration Keys, and then select New Configuration Key. Right-click the new configuration key and select Properties to open the property sheet. Change the name to BikeTuningOffers, and add the label number @USR9 to the *Label* field. The label should read "Bike-tuning offers." If you want to make the configuration dependent on another configuration key, you should fill in the *ParentKey* property. For this example, make the configuration key dependent on the *Quotation* configuration key by entering *QuotationBasic* in the *ParentKey* property field.

You should choose the security key property for the menu item from the existing security keys. The chosen security key must match the position of the menu item on the area page or in the navigation pane. For example, if you want to put your menu item under Accounts Receivable\Periodic, the security key must be *CustPeriodic*.

With the configuration and security keys in place, you're ready to create the menu item. In the AOT, expand Menu Items, right-click Action, and then select New Menu Item. Right-click the new menu item, and then select Properties. Fill out the properties as described in the Table 6-3.

TABLE 6-3 Bike-Tuning Menu Item Properties

Property	Value	Explanation
Name	*BikeTuningOffers*	Name of the menu item as it appears in the AOT.
Label	@USR10	The label should read, "Create bike-tuning offers."
HelpText	@USR11	The label should read, "Send bike-tuning offers to existing customers via e-mail."
ObjectType	*Class*	Type of object opened by the menu item.
Object	*BikeTuningOffers*	Name of the object opened by the object.
RunOn	*Server*	Execute the job on the server tier.
ConfigurationKey	*BikeTuningOffers*	The new configuration key that you just created.
SecurityKey	*CustPeriodic*	The security key chosen according to the position of the menu item on the area page or in the navigation pane.

Tip You can drag the class node in the AOT onto the *Action* node under Menu Items to create a new menu item with the same name as the class and the *ObjectType* and *Object* properties already defined.

Now add the menu item to the Accounts Receivable submenu. In the AOT, expand Menus, right-click Cust, point to New, and then click Menu Item. Right-click the new menu item, and then select the Properties tab. Change *Name* to BikeTuningOffers. Change *MenuItemType* to Action, and *MenuItemName* to BikeTuningOffers. Finally, move the menu item to the Periodic folder of the menu. Save the menu, and then restart the Dynamics AX client to make the new menu item appear in the navigation pane and on the area page.

Adding Property Methods

Suppose you want to run the Bike-Tuning Offers business operation directly from another piece of code without presenting the user with a dialog box. To do so, you must implement property methods according to the property method pattern. This pattern allows you to set and get the properties that would otherwise be inaccessible because member variables in Dynamics AX are protected.

Start by writing a *parm* method for the property as follows.

```
public NoYesId parmCreateServiceOrders(NoYesId _createServiceOrders =
createServiceOrders)
{
    ;
    createServiceOrders = _createServiceOrders;

    return createServiceOrders;
}
```

This job demonstrates how you can run the operation without showing the dialog box.

```
static void createBikeTuningOffersJob(Args _args)
{
    BikeTuningOffers    bikeTuningOffers;
    ;

    bikeTuningOffers = BikeTuningOffers::construct();
    bikeTuningOffers.parmCreateServiceOrders(NoYes::Yes);

    bikeTuningOffers.run();
}
```

Adding Constructors

As mentioned earlier in this chapter, X++ doesn't support method name overloading, and you should avoid using default parameters on constructors. You must create individually named *new* methods with different parameter profiles instead.

In the preceding example, you created an instance of the class and set the necessary parameters. Imagine that there is one more parameter in your class that indicates a certain customer account number for creating bike offers. Add a new member variable to the class declaration, and then add the new parameter method, like this.

```
public class BikeTuningOffers extends RunBase
{
    DialogField dialogCreateServiceOrders;

    NoYesId     createServiceOrders;
    CustAccount custAccount;
```

```
    #define.CurrentVersion(1)
    #define.version1(1)
    #localmacro.CurrentList
        createServiceOrders
    #endmacro
}

public CustAccount parmCustAccount(CustAccount _custAccount = custAccount)
{
    ;
    custAccount = _custAccount;

    return custAccount;
}
```

Suppose that the customer record contains information about the option to create service orders with bike offers. For example, imagine that offers are not sent to the customer if the customer has been stopped for new transactions. Because you want to avoid using default parameters in the construct method, you must call both of these *parm* methods when you create an instance based on a customer record.

Running the business operation from a job with a specific customer would look like this.

```
server static void createBikeTuningOffersJobCustomer(Args _args)
{
    CustTable           custTable = CustTable::find('4001');
    BikeTuningOffers    bikeTuningOffers;
    ;

    bikeTuningOffers = BikeTuningOffers::construct();
    bikeTuningOffers.initParmDefault();
    bikeTuningOffers.parmCustAccount(custTable.accountNum);
    bikeTuningOffers.parmCreateServiceOrders(custTable.blocked == CustVendorBlocked::
No);

    bikeTuningOffers.run();
}
```

This code is a good candidate for the static *new* pattern, so implement a static *newCustTable* method on the *BikeTuningOffers* class to create an instance based on a customer record, as shown here.

```
server static public BikeTuningOffers newCustTable(CustTable  _custTable)
{
    BikeTuningOffers    bikeTuningOffers;
;

    bikeTuningOffers = BikeTuningOffers::construct();
    bikeTuningOffers.initParmDefault();
    bikeTuningOffers.parmCustAccount(_custTable.accountNum);
    bikeTuningOffers.parmCreateServiceOrders(_custTable.blocked == CustVendorBlocked::
No);

    return biketuningOffers;
}
```

Now change your job to a simpler version to be assured that the class gets properly instantiated and initialized.

```
server static void createBikeTuningOffersJobCustomer(Args _args)
{
    CustTable           custTable = CustTable::find('4001');
    BikeTuningOffers    bikeTuningOffers;
    ;

    bikeTuningOffers = BikeTuningOffers::newCustTable(custTable);

    bikeTuningOffers.run();
}
```

Adding a Query

Adding a query to the business operation class allows the user to select a range of targets to apply the operation to, such as sending bike-tuning offers to selected customers. To use the query, you must be able to create an instance of *QueryRun*. Start by adding *QueryRun* as a member variable, as shown here.

```
public class BikeTuningOffers extends RunBase
{
    DialogField dialogCreateServiceOrders;

    NoYesId     createServiceOrders;
    CustAccount custAccount; // This member won't be used with the query.
    QueryRun    queryRun;
```

```
    #define.CurrentVersion(2)
    #define.version1(1)
    #localmacro.CurrentList
        createServiceOrders
    #endmacro
}
```

To initialize the *QueryRun* object, override the *initParmDefault* method, as shown in the following code. This method is called by the *RunBase* framework if no saved object state is found by the *SysLastValue* framework via the *unpack* method.

```
public void initParmDefault()
{
    Query   query;
    ;

    super();

    query = new Query();
    query.addDataSource(tableNum(CustTable));

    queryRun = new QueryRun(query);
}
```

You must modify the *pack* method, as shown in the following example, so that you can save the state of the *QueryRun* object.

```
public container pack()
{
;
    return [#CurrentVersion, #CurrentList, queryRun.pack()];
}
```

Consequently, you must also modify the *unpack* method to reinstantiate the *QueryRun* object, as shown here.

```
public boolean unpack(container _packedClass)
{
    Version     version = runbase::getVersion(_packedClass);
    Container   packedQuery;
    ;
```

```
    switch (version)
    {
        case #CurrentVersion:
            [version, #CurrentList, packedQuery] = _packedClass;

            if (packedQuery)
               queryRun = new QueryRun(packedQuery);

            break;

        default:
            return false;
    }

    return true;
}
```

To make the *QueryRun* object available for presentation in the dialog box, override the *queryRun* method to return your *QueryRun* object, as shown in the following code.

```
public QueryRun queryRun()
{
;
    return queryRun;
}
```

To show the query in the dialog box, you must override the *showQueryValues* method to return the value *true*, as follows.

```
boolean showQueryValues()
{
;
    return true;
}
```

If you open the class now, you can see that the query is embedded in the dialog box, as shown in Figure 6-13.

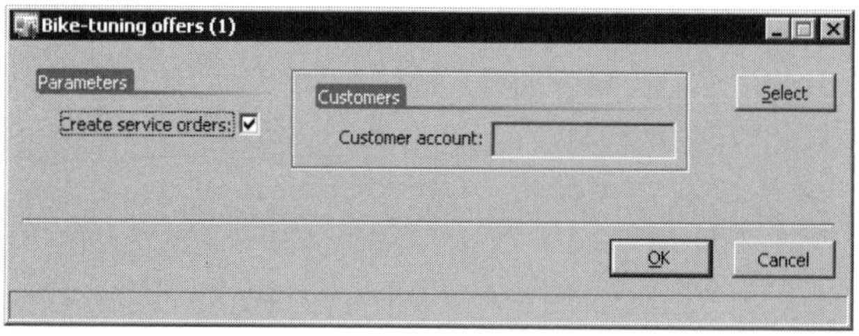

FIGURE 6-13 Create Bike-Tuning Offers dialog box with embedded query

Finally, you must change your business logic method, *sendOffers*, so that it uses the *QueryRun* object, as shown here.

```
private void sendOffers()
{
    CustTable               custTable;
    BikeServiceOrderId      bikeServiceOrderId;
    BikeServiceOrderTable   bikeServiceOrderTable;
    SysMailer               sysMailer;
    ;

    sysMailer = new SysMailer();

    ttsBegin;

    while (queryRun.next())
    {
        custTable = queryRun.get(tableNum(CustTable));

        if (createServiceOrders)
        {
            bikeServiceOrderId  = NumberSeq::newGetNum(SalesParameters::
numRefBikeServiceOrderId()).num();
            bikeServiceOrderTable.BikeServiceOrderId    = bikeServiceOrderId;
            bikeServiceOrderTable.CustAccount           = custTable.AccountNum;
            bikeServiceOrderTable.insert();
        }

        sysMailer.quickSend(CompanyInfo::find().Email,
                            custTable.Email,
                            "Tune your bike",
                            strFmt("Hi %1,\n\nIt's time to tune your bike....",
custTable.name));
    }

    ttsCommit;
}
```

Client/Server Considerations

Typically, you want to execute business operation jobs on the server tier because these jobs almost always involve several database transactions. However, you want the user dialog box to be executed on the client to minimize client/server calls from the server tier. Fortunately, the *RunBase* framework can help you run the dialog box on the client and the business operation on the server.

To run the business operation job on the server and push the dialog box to the client, you should be aware of two settings. On the menu item that calls the job, you must set the *RunOn* property to *Server*; on the class, you must set the *RunOn* property to *Called From*. Figure 6-14 shows where to set the *RunOn* property of a class.

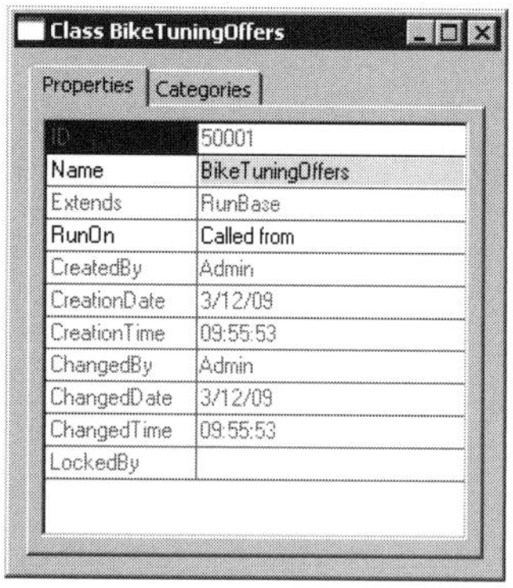

FIGURE 6-14 Execution tier of the class set to Called From

When the job is initiated, it starts on the server, and the *RunBase* framework packs the internal member variables and creates a new instance on the client, which then unpacks the internal member variables and runs the dialog box. When the user clicks OK in the dialog box, *RunBase* packs the internal member variables of the client instance and unpacks them again in the server instance.

Chapter 7

Enterprise Portal

In this chapter:

The objectives of this chapter are to:

- Introduce Enterprise Portal.
- Highlight new features in Microsoft Dynamics AX 2009 Enterprise Portal.
- Provide insight into the ASP.NET Enterprise Portal Web framework design and runtime components.
- Illustrate the integration of the Application Object Tree (AOT), Microsoft Visual Studio, and Windows SharePoint Services.
- Offer a detailed look at Enterprise Portal security.

This chapter explores the Enterprise Portal framework, from the concepts on which it is based to its inner workings. Both Dynamics AX developers and ASP.NET Web developers can customize Web applications or build new ones easily within Enterprise Portal. This chapter covers how the Enterprise Portal framework brings Dynamics AX development into the managed world of ASP.NET and Visual Studio, allowing developers to use Dynamics AX, AJAX, and ASP.NET to leverage the Dynamics AX data and business logic programming model and use ASP.NET to build rich Web presentations with great user interfaces, interaction, and responsiveness.

Introduction

Enterprise Portal is the Web platform for Dynamics AX 2009. Using the Enterprise Portal framework, developers can create new Web applications for Dynamics AX or customize existing ones. Enterprise Portal enables customers, vendors, business partners, and employees to directly access relevant business information and collaborate and conduct business transactions from anywhere through an easy-to-use Web user interface.

Enterprise Portal enables organizations to extend and expand the use of enterprise resource planning (ERP) software and reach out to customers, vendors, business partners, and employees and access business applications from anywhere. By allowing them to interact directly with the business system, Enterprise Portal improves customer satisfaction, reduces support and help desk calls, empowers employees to collaborate effectively and make informed decisions, and improves overall efficiency.

Users access Enterprise Portal through a Web browser remotely or from within a corporate intranet, depending on how Enterprise Portal is configured and deployed. Enterprise Portal contains a set of default Web pages and user roles that you can use as-is or modify to meet your customer's unique business needs. Enterprise Portal serves as the central place for users to access any data, structured or unstructured, such as transactional data, reports, charts, key performance indicators (KPIs), documents, and alerts. They can access and collaborate on this data from anywhere. Figure 7-1 shows the home page of an Enterprise Portal site.

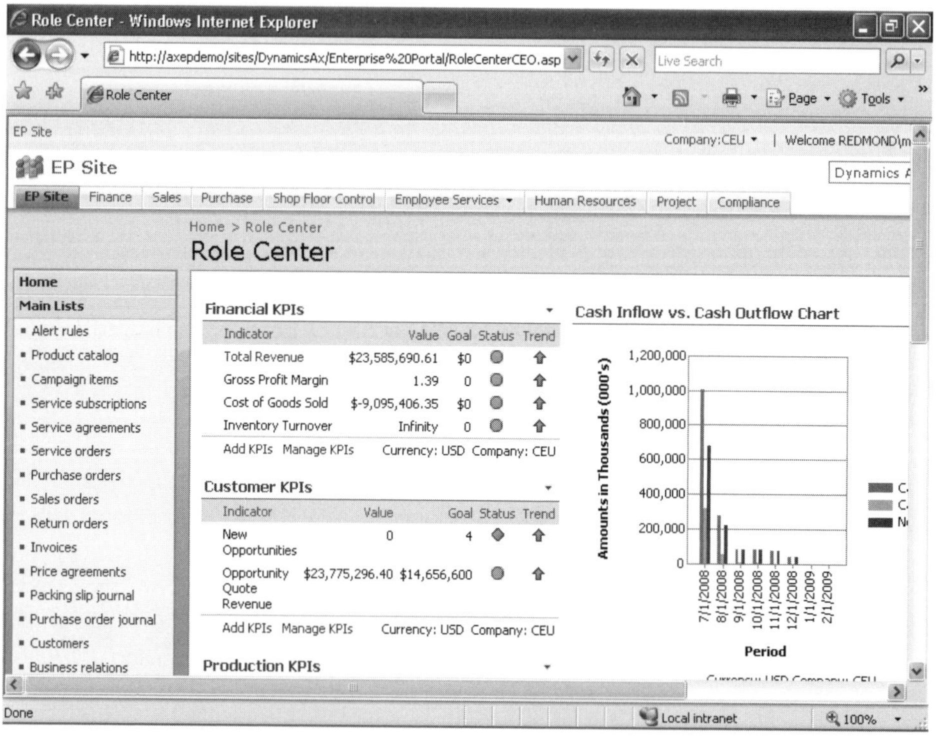

FIGURE 7-1 Example of an Enterprise Portal home page

Inside Enterprise Portal

Built on ASP.NET and Windows SharePoint Services products and technologies, Enterprise Portal combines all the rich content and collaboration functionality in Windows SharePoint Services with the structured business data in Dynamics AX. It also brings the power and flexibility of ASP.NET and Visual Studio to help you build responsive, modern Web applications. This section introduces the underlying technology components that make up Enterprise Portal. In the subsequent sections, we discuss each component in detail.

With the rich Dynamics AX programming model, Enterprise Portal defines data access and business logic in MorphX, similar to the desktop client. It exposes data and business logic through data binding, data and metadata APIs, and proxy classes to ASP.NET, and it uses ASP.NET to define the user interface. Enterprise Portal uses the Web Part page framework from Windows SharePoint Services to build Web pages that allow easy customization and personalization. Enterprise Portal also brings the best of Dynamics AX, ASP.NET, and Windows SharePoint Services together and unifies them in the Application Object Tree (AOT) for easy deployment.

Developers define the business logic and data access in MorphX and use Visual Studio to build Web User Controls and define the Web user interface elements. Within the Web User Control, they can use Enterprise Portal controls or any ASP.NET control and use data binding and the standard ASP.NET programming model to define the user interface logic, seamlessly leveraging the business logic defined in MorphX and accessing Dynamics AX metadata and business data.

Developers use Windows SharePoint Services to define Web pages. Enterprise Portal Web pages use Enterprise Portal Web parts and other Windows SharePoint Services or Microsoft Office SharePoint Server (MOSS) Web parts. The Enterprise Portal Web parts present information and expose functionality from Dynamics AX and are implemented with Windows SharePoint Services Web part technology. One such Web part is the Dynamics User Control Web part, which can host any ASP.NET Web User Control and connect to Dynamics AX through the Enterprise Portal framework and the .NET Business Connector. Windows SharePoint Services Web parts fulfill content and collaboration needs. Figure 7-2 shows the high-level components of Enterprise Portal.

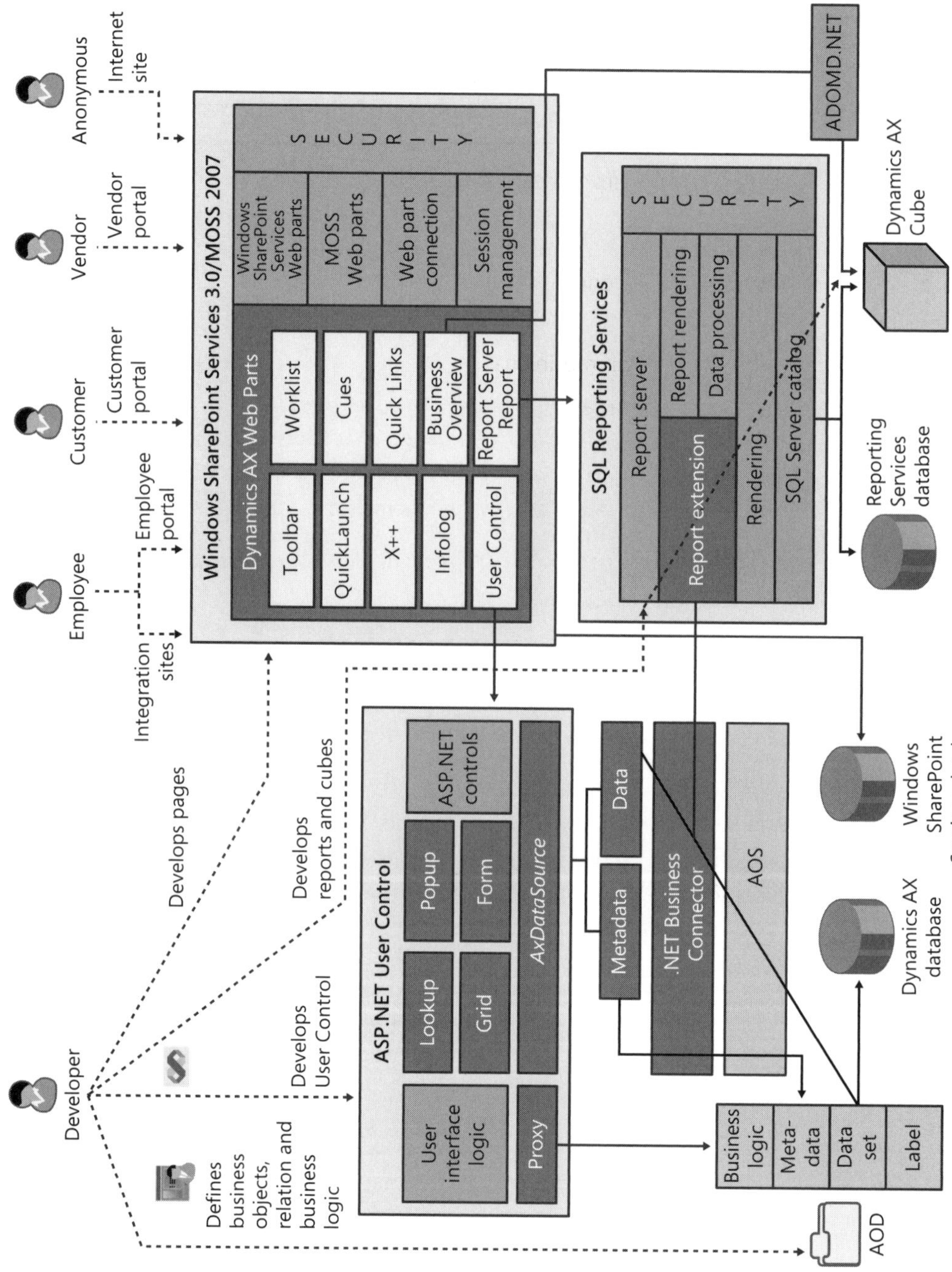

FIGURE 7-2 Enterprise Portal components

Page Processing

The first step in developing or customizing an application on Enterprise Portal is to understand the interactions between the user's browser on the client and Enterprise Portal on the server when the user accesses Enterprise Portal. The following sequence of interactions occurs when a user accesses Enterprise Portal:

1. The user opens the browser on his or her machine and navigates to Enterprise Portal.
2. The browser establishes a connection with the Internet Information Services (IIS) Web server.
3. Based on the authentication mode enabled, IIS authenticates the user.
4. After the user is authenticated, the Windows SharePoint Services Internet Server Application Programming Interface (ISAPI) filter intercepts the page request and checks the user's right to access the site.
5. After the user is authorized by Windows SharePoint Services, the Web page routes to a custom Microsoft ASP.NET page handler object of Windows SharePoint Services.

   Figure 7-3 shows a simplified version of the page request process.

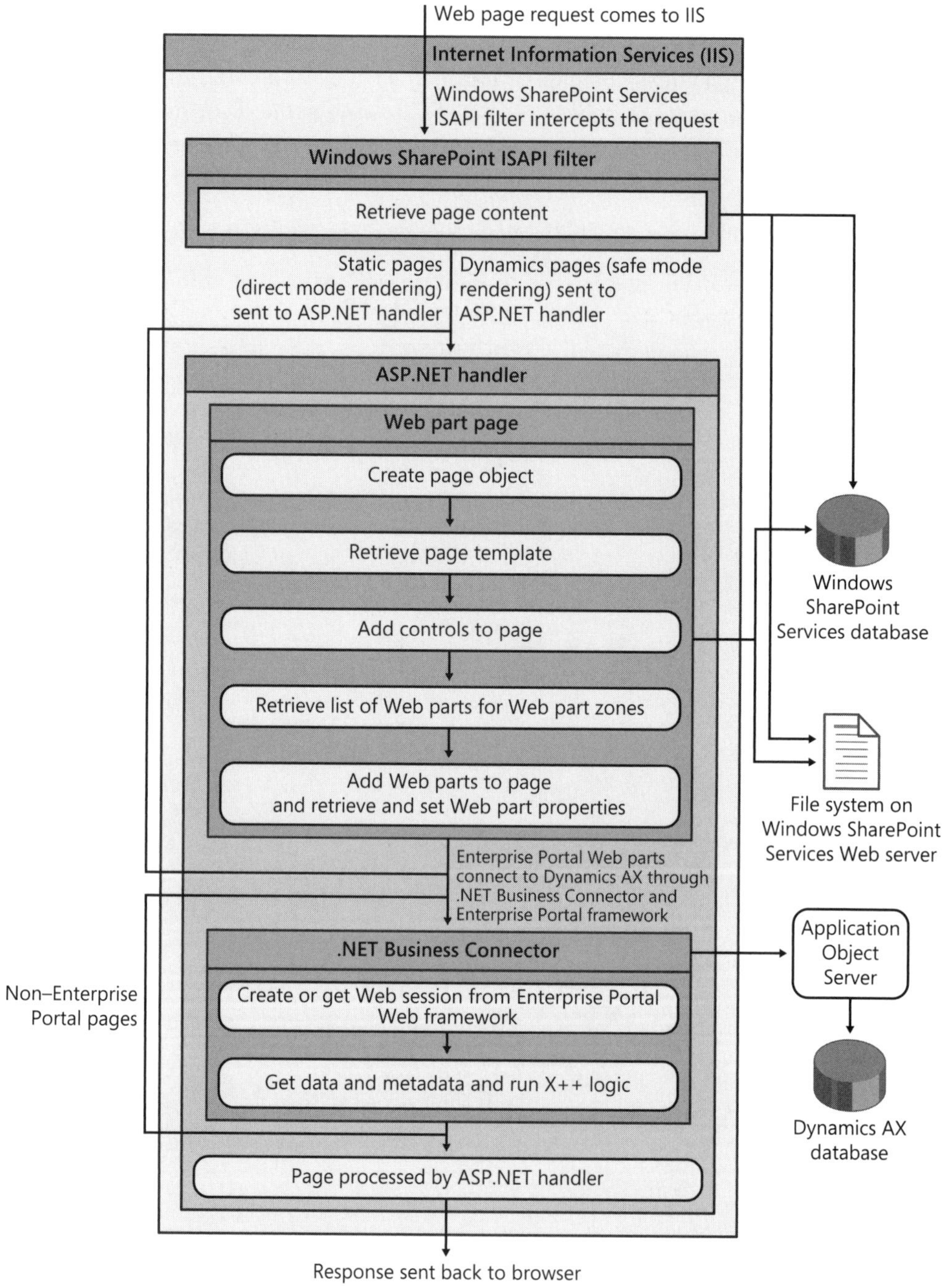

FIGURE 7-3 Page request flow in Enterprise Portal

6. The page handler pulls the Web part page data from the Windows SharePoint Services content database. This data contains information such as the page template ID, the Web parts used and their properties, and the page template stored on the file system on the Web server. Windows SharePoint Services then processes the page and creates and initializes the Web parts on the page with any properties and personalization data.
7. When initialing Enterprise Portal Web parts, Enterprise Portal initializes a Web session with the Enterprise Portal Web framework through the .NET Business Connector to the Application Object Server (AOS).
8. The Web framework checks for Dynamics AX authorization and then calls the appropriate Web handlers in the Web framework to process the Enterprise Portal objects that the Web part points to.
9. The Dynamics User Control Web part runs the Web User Control that it's pointing to. The Web User Control connects to Dynamics AX through .NET Business Connector and renders the HTML to the Web part.
10. The Web page assembles all the HTML returned by all the Web parts and renders the page to the user's browser.
11. The Enterprise Portal Web session ends.

As you can see in this sequence, the AOS processes all the business logic and data retrieval, ASP.NET processes the user interface elements, and Windows SharePoint Services handles the overall page layout and personalization.

New Features in Dynamics AX 2009 Enterprise Portal

Microsoft Dynamics AX 2009 EP provides many new features to empower developers to build and customize rich Web user interface that enables end users to find and access business information quickly and efficiently. Here is a list of high-level Enterprise Portal features introduced in Dynamics AX 2009.

- New Web framework for supporting ASP.NET-based Web user interface
- Visual Studio add-in for Web development and integration to the AOT
- ASP.NET controls for common user interface elements
- Use of AJAX for rich user interactions
- Web parts for common page elements
- AOT nodes for storing and securing components for the new Web framework
- A single site for all Dynamics AX companies similar to the client and the ability to switch companies through the company switcher

- Context-specific Help for Enterprise Portal
- Top and left navigation providers for integrating navigation elements in Windows SharePoint Services with business application navigation defined in the AOT
- Modules created as subsites for easy management
- Consistent navigation for Web modules in Quick Launch
- New applications: CRM in Sales Module, Expense Management, Purchase Requisition, Service Management, Compliance Center
- Role Centers in the client and in Enterprise Portal
- Migration of all out-of-the-box pages to the new ASP.NET framework
- Enterprise Portal deployment completely automated and integrated with Dynamics AX setup
- In-place upgrade from Windows SharePoint Services 3.0 and Microsoft Office SharePoint Server (MOSS) 2007 sites to Dynamics AX 2009 Enterprise Portal sites

Enterprise Portal Development Tools

You develop the data and business tier components of Enterprise Portal using MorphX, the integrated development environment (IDE) in Dynamics AX. You define navigation and site hierarchy in MorphX. You develop the presentation tier components in Visual Studio and design the Web page using Windows SharePoint Services. AOT serves as the single master of all metadata for Enterprise Portal. It stores all the controls and pages you developed using Visual Studio and Windows SharePoint Services, and other supporting files, definitions, and features, under the *Web* node.

MorphX

MorphX is used for developing and debugging data and business tier components, defining navigation elements, storing unified metadata and files, importing and deploying controls, storing page and list definitions, and generating proxies.

For Enterprise Portal data access purposes, the new programmable object Data Sets is added to the AOT. Data Sets in Enterprise Portal are equivalent to the Form data source for the Desktop form. You can create Data Sets with one or more joined data sources pointing to related tables in Dynamics AX. You can override or add new methods in data sets, data sources, and tables as well as define the data access logic.

You generally define the business logic in classes in the AOT. These classes are referenced either in the data set or through C# proxy classes in the presentation components in Enterprise Portal.

You can generate proxy classes either from Visual Studio or from MorphX (Tools\Development Tools\Web Development\Proxies). The tables and classes from which proxy files need to be generated are defined in AOT\Web\Web Files\Static Files\Proxies. Web-related components are stored under AOT\Web.

The Web User Controls for the presentation tier that you develop in Visual Studio are added to the AOT under AOT\Web\Web Files\Web Controls. These controls are referenced and secured by AOT\Web Content\Managed Nodes. The Visual Studio add-in for Dynamics AX lets you add the controls from Visual Studio to the AOT directly.

Static files that Enterprise Portal uses, such as style sheets, configuration files, and aspx files, are kept under AOT\Web Files\Static Files. Images and resources are kept at AOT\Resources.

The pages and lists you create in Windows SharePoint Services are exported to the AOT and stored under AOT\Web\Web Files\Page Definitions and AOT\Web\Web Files\List Definitions.

Enterprise Portal Web parts site definitions are kept under AOT\Web\Web Files\Web Parts and AOT\Web\Web Files\Site Definitions. The *Site Templates* node is for any customized Windows SharePoint Services templates.

For Web sites, consistent navigation is important for users to perform their tasks quickly and easily. Site navigation in Enterprise Portal consists of a global menu bar that is displayed at the top of the site, the module-level QuickLaunch navigation, which is on the left side, and toolbars that are inside the page.

Web modules define the site hierarchy and the top-level navigation. Web menus define the menu hierarchy used by the Dynamics QuickLaunch Web part or the toolbar. Web menu items that point to the page or class are used in Web menus.

Visual Studio

You develop and debug presentation-tier components in Visual Studio. The Visual Studio add-in for Enterprise Portal provides a project and control template for Web user interface development. You define all the user interface logic in Web User Controls using Enterprise Portal development tools, and you use the Enterprise Portal framework to access data and metadata for ASP.NET controls. The Visual Studio add-in also provides an easy way to add controls to the AOT, import controls or style sheets from the AOT, and generate proxies. It also provides a test page for previewing the user interface and debugging.

Windows SharePoint Services

You use Windows SharePoint Services to develop Web part pages or lists and to edit master pages, which contain the common elements for all the pages. You can use the Create or Edit Page tools of Windows SharePoint Services in the browser and use one or more Enterprise Portal or any Web parts and design your Web page. You can also use the Microsoft Office SharePoint Designer 2007 tool to create or edit Web part pages or master pages.

Developing Data Sets

Data Sets is a new AOT node in Dynamics AX 2009. It is used to define the data access logic. A *data set* is a collection of data usually presented in tabular form. The data set brings the familiar data and programming model known from Dynamics AX forms together with ASP.NET data binding. In addition, the data set offers an extensive X++ programming model for validating and manipulating the data when creating, reading, updating, or deleting in Enterprise Portal. The *AxDatasource* control in ASP.NET uses data sets to display and manipulate data from any ASP.NET control that supports data binding. A data set can contain one or more data sources that are joined together. The data sources could point to a table or a view in Dynamics AX. Data sources can be joined to display data from multiple tables as a single data source. To do this, you use inner or outer joins. To display parent-child data, you use active joins. To surface data from joined data sources or from parent-child data sets, you use dynamic data set views (*DataSetView*). With a view-based interface, tables are accessed through dynamic data set views rather than directly. You can access inner-joined or outer-joined tables through only one view, which has the same name as the primary data source's name. Two views are available with active-joined data sources: one with the same name as the parent data source, and another with the same name as the child data source. The child data source contains records related only to the current active record in the parent data source.

Each data set view could contain zero or more records, depending on the data. Each data set view also has a corresponding special view, which contains just the current, single active record. This view has the same name as the original view with *_Current* appended to the view name. Figure 7-4 shows the data set views inside a data set and the data binding.

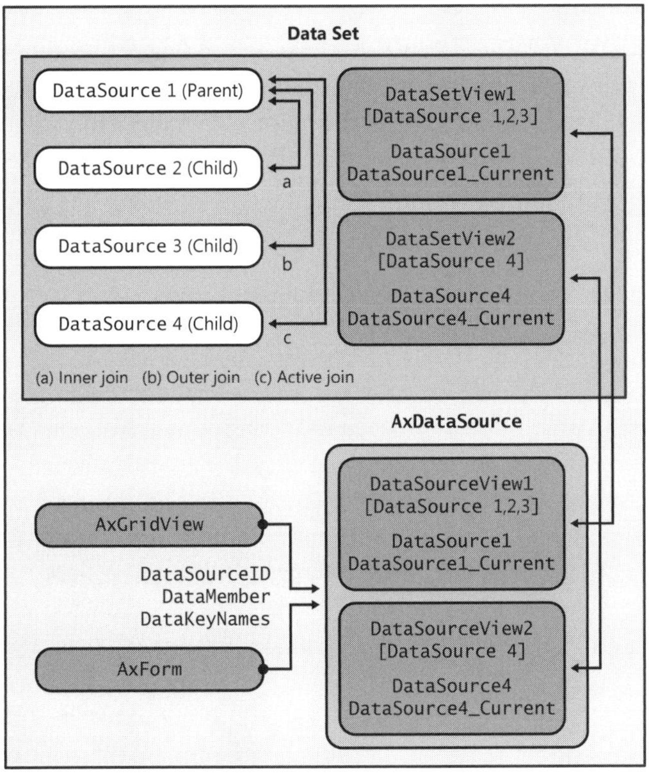

FIGURE 7-4 Data set views

Data sets offer an extensive and familiar X++ programming model for validating and manipulating data. Some of the methods you'll be using frequently include *init*, *run*, *pack*, and *unpack*.

- The *init* method is called when the data set is initialized. It is activated immediately after *new* and creates the run-time image of the data set. Typical uses of *init* include adding ranges to restrict the data, checking the arguments and parameters passed, and initializing and modifying variables and queries.
- The *run* method is called after the data set is initialized and opened, and immediately after *init*. Typical uses of *run* include conditionally making fields visible or hidden, changing the access level on fields, and modifying queries.
- The *pack* method is called after the data set is run. You generally use the *pack/unpack* pattern to save and store the state of an object, which you can later reinstantiate. A typical use of *pack* is to persist a variable used in the data set between postbacks.
- The *unpack* method is called if a data set was previously packed and then accessed. If a data set was previously packed, *init* and *run* aren't called. Instead, only *unpack* is executed.

Data sources within a data set also include a number of methods you can override. These methods are similar to those in the *FormDataSource* class on the Desktop. You can use them to initialize the default values and validate values and actions. For more information about these events, such as when they are executed and the common usage scenarios, refer to the "Methods on a Form Data Source" topic in the Microsoft Dynamics AX 2009 software development kit (SDK), on MSDN.

Developing Web User Interface Components

Enterprise Portal has a built-in set of ASP.NET controls you can use to access, display, and manipulate Dynamics AX data. It also includes APIs for programmatic access to data and metadata, a C# proxy class framework to access Dynamics AX business logic, and helper classes and a Visual Studio add-in for adding and importing files to and from the AOT. Figure 7-5 shows a sample Visual Studio project for Enterprise Portal development.

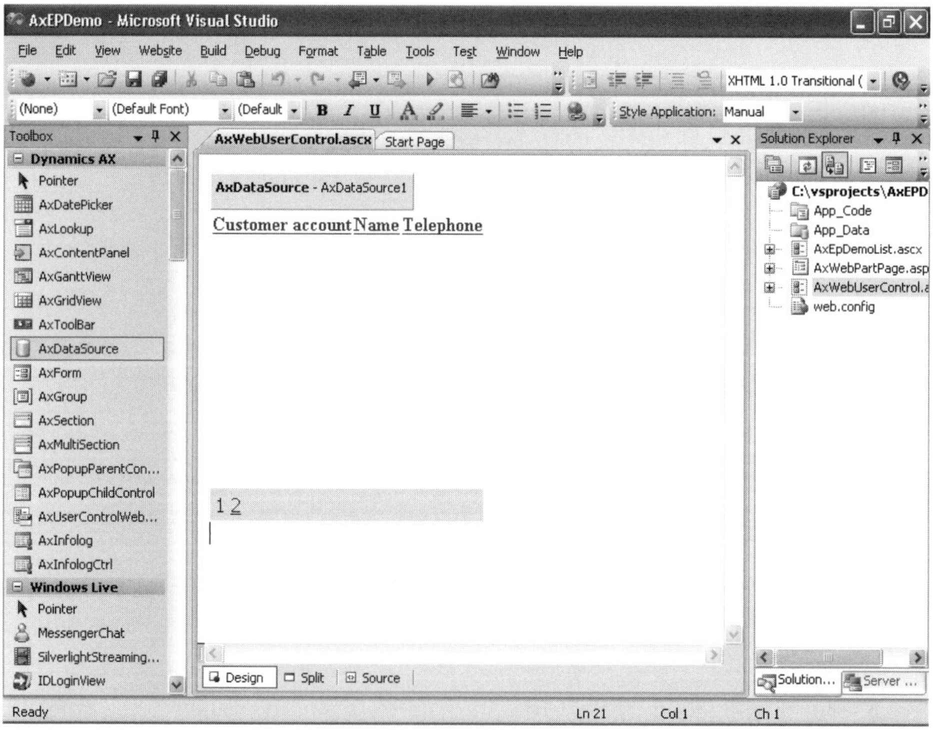

FIGURE 7-5 Enterprise Portal Visual Studio project

AxDataSource

Data sets you create in the AOT are exposed to ASP.NET through the *AxDataSource* control. *AxDataSource* abstracts the data store and the operations that can be performed on the data, from connecting to or reading/writing from the data store. You can associate ASP.NET data-bound user interface controls with *AxDataSource* through the *DataSourceID* property. Using this standard ASP.NET data binding, you can rapidly develop user interface logic without needing specific domain knowledge about how to connect to or access data from Dynamics AX. Because *AxDataSource* takes care of the data access from Dynamics AX, developers don't have to worry about data access and can focus on the business aspect.

The data source control is simply a container for one or more uniquely named views (*AxDataSourceView*). All the logic is encapsulated in this *DataSourceView*-derived class. *AxDataSourceView* implements all the functionality to read and write data. The data-bound control can identify the set of enabled capabilities and display the right set of user interface controls and enable or disable them. You use the *DataMember* property of a data-bound control to select a particular view. *AxDataSourceView* maps to the data set view. So for each dynamic data set view based on the number of data sources and the type of join, you get an equivalent number of *AxDataSourceView* in the *AxDataSource* control to which any data-bound control can bind.

The data source control also supports filtering records within and across other data source controls and data source views. When you set the active record on the data source view within a data source control, all the child data source views are also filtered based on the active record. You can filter across data source controls through Record Context. In Record Context, one data source control acts as the provider of the context, and zero or more data source controls act as consumers. One data source can act as both provider and consumer. When the active record changes on the provider data source control, the record context is passed to other consuming data source controls, and they apply that filter as well. You use the *Role* and *ProviderView* properties of *AxDataSource* for this purpose. One Web User Control can contain any number of *AxDataSource* controls. Only one of them can have the property *Role* set to *Provider*. Any number of them can be set to *Consumer*.

You can use the *DataSetViewRow* object to access the rows in a *DataSetView*. The *GetCurrent* method returns the current row.

```
DataSetViewRow row = this.AxDataSource1.GetDataSourceView("View1").DataSetView.
GetCurrent();
```

The *GetDataSet* method on *AxDataSourceControl* specifies the data set to bind. The *DataSetRun* property provides the run-time instance of the data set, and you can use

AxaptaObjectAdapter to call the methods. So to invoke methods defined in data sets from a Web User Control, you would use the following code.

```
this.AxDataSource1.GetDataSet().DataSetRun.AxaptaObjectAdapter.Call("method1");
```

AxGridView

The *AxGridView* control displays the values of a data source in a table format in which each column represents a field and each row represents a record. With *AxGridView*, you can select, sort, group, expand, filter, edit, and delete items. *AxGridView* extends the ASP.NET *GridView* control and lets you provide selection, grouping, expansion rows, filtering, context menus, and other enhanced capabilities within the Dynamics AX Enterprise Portal user interface.

AxGridView also includes built-in data modification capabilities. Using *AxGridView* with the declarative *AxDataSource*, you can easily configure and modify data without writing a single line of code. *AxGridView* also has many properties, methods, and events that you can easily customize with application-specific user interface logic.

You can find the full set of properties, methods, and events for *GridView* and *AxGridView* on MSDN. Listed here are some of the *AxGridView* properties you'll likely use most often:

- ***AllowDelete*** If enabled and if the user has delete permission on the selected record, *AxGridView* displays a Delete Selected Item button and allows the user to delete the row.
- ***AllowEdit*** If enabled and if the user has update permission on the selected record, *AxGridView* displays Save and Cancel buttons on the selected row and allows the user to edit and save or cancel edits. When a row is selected, it automatically goes into edit mode, and edit controls are displayed for all columns for the selected record where the *AllowEdit* property for the column is set to true.
- ***AllowGroupCollapse*** If grouping is enabled, this setting allows the user to collapse the grouping.
- ***AllowGrouping*** If set to true, and a group field is specified, the rows are displayed in groups and sorted by group field. Page size is maintained, so one group might span multiple pages.
- ***AllowSelection*** If set to true, the user can select a row.
- ***ContextMenuName*** If *ShowContextMenu* is enabled, *ContextMenuName* defines the name of the Web menu in the AOT to be used as a context menu when the user right-clicks the row.
- ***DisplayGroupFieldName*** Gets or sets a value that indicates whether the *GroupFieldName* is displayed in the group header text of a group view of a *GridView* control. The default is true.

- ***GroupField*** Data field that is used to group *GridView*. This property is used only when *AllowGrouping* is set to true.
- ***GroupFieldDisplayName*** Display name for the group field used in the display *<GroupFieldDisplayName>* : *<GroupFieldValue>*. If a name isn't specified, by default the label of the *GroupField* renders in group view. This property is used only when *AllowGrouping* is set to true.
- ***ShowContextMenu*** If set to true, displays the Web menu defined in the *ContextMenuName* property as the context menu when the user right-clicks the row.
- ***ShowFilter*** If set to true, displays the filter control in *AxGridView*.
- ***ExpansionColumnIndexesHidden*** A comma-separated list of integers, starting with 1, that represents which columns to hide from the expansion row.
- ***ExpansionTooltip*** The tooltip displayed on the expansion row link.
- ***ShowExpansion*** Specifies whether an expansion is available for each row in the grid. When set to true, the expansion row link is displayed for each row in the grid.

Figure 7-6 shows a sample list page with the filter control and context menu set.

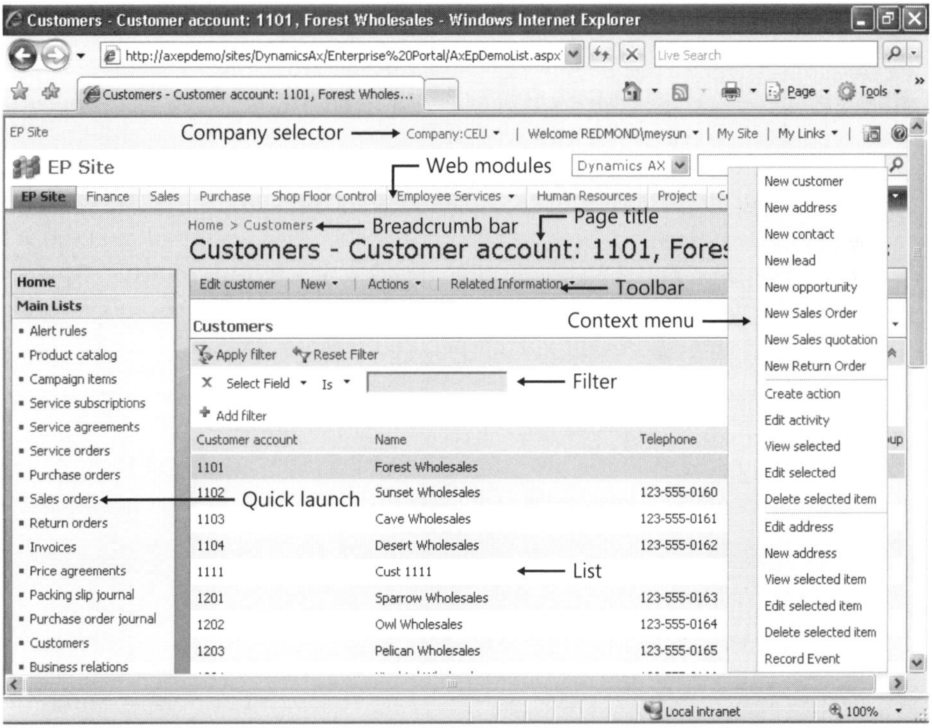

FIGURE 7-6 Enterprise Portal list page with filter control and context menu

ContextMenu

The *ContextMenu* object also allows you to add menu items and separators at run time. It provides methods to remove menu items and resolve client or Enterprise Portal URLs. You can access the *ContextMenu* object from *AxGridview.ContextMenu.*

ActionMenuItemClicked, *ActionMenuItemClicking*, and *SetMenuItemProperties* are three *ContextMenu* events.

SelectedIndexChanged, *DataBound*, and *Row** events are *AxGridView* events for which you commonly write code to specify actions to take when the selection is changed, to inspect and change styles when data is rendered, and to react when rows are modified, respectively.

AxFilterControl

If the *ShowFilter* property of *AxGridview* is set to true, *AxGridView* embeds *AxFilterControl. AxFilterControl* is displayed at the top of *AxGridView. AxFilterControl* reads the metadata from the *AxDataSourceControl* the *AxGridView* is binding to and displays controls dynamically to allow the user to filter the data source with any of its field that are not hidden or locked. You can access the filter control through the *AxGridView FilterControl* property and the filter XML through *Filter.*

The filter control sets the filter on *AxDataSetView* using *AxDataSourceView,* which is responsible for keeping the data in sync with the filter set by calling *SetAsChanged* and *ExecuteQuery* if data has changed. *AxDataSourceView* and *DataSetView* expose the *SystemFilter* and *UserFilter* properties and the *ResetUserFilter* method APIs for the filter control to set the filter programmatically.

For example, you can set the range in the data set in X++ as follows.

```
qbrBlocked = qbds.addRange(fieldnum(CustTable,Blocked));qbrBlocked.value(queryValue-
(CustVendorBlocked::No));qbrBlocked.status(RangeStatus::Hidden);
```

In the Web User Control, you can read the *SystemFilter* set on the data source.

```
this.AxDataSource1.GetDataSourceView(this.AxGridView1.DataMember).SystemFilter.ToXml()
```

or

```
this.AxDataSource1.GetDataSet().DataSetViews[this.AxGridView1.DataMember].
SystemFilter.ToXml();
```

returns

```
<?xml version="1.0" encoding="utf-16"?><filter xmlns:xsi="http://www.w3.org/2001/
XMLSchema-instance" xmlns:xsd="http://www.w3.org/2001/XMLSchema" name="CustTable">-
<condition attribute="Blocked" operator="eq" value="No" status="hidden" /></filter>
```

DataSourceView and *DataSetView* have the following methods, which allow you to read the different types of filters and reset them.

- *SystemFilter* gets the complete list of ranges on the query, including *open*, *hidden*, and *locked*, into the *conditionCollection* on the filter object.
- *UserFilter* gets only the open ranges on the *QueryRun* into the *conditionCollection* on the filter object.
- *ResetFilter* method clears the filter set on the *QueryRun* and thus resets to the filter (ranges) set programmatically.

Here is a code snippet to set the filter programmatically.

```
this.AxDataSource1.GetDataSourceView(this.AxGridView1.DataMember).SystemFilter.AddXml-
(@"<filter name='CustTable'><condition attribute='CustGroup' status='open' value='10'
operator='eq' /></filter>");
```

AxForm

AxForm displays a single record from a data source, where each data row represents a field in the record. The first column in the row often displays the name of the field, and the second column displays the value of the field for the record. The *AxForm* control allows you to view, create, and update a single record.

AxForm is a data-bound control with built-in data modification capabilities. When you use *AxForm* with the declarative *AxDataSource* control, you can easily configure it to display and modify data without needing to write any code. It also provides a rich set of properties, methods, and events you can customize with application-specific user interface logic.

The *DataSourceID*, *DataMember*, and *DataKeyNames* properties define the data-binding capabilities of the *AxForm* control. *AxForm* also provides properties to autogenerate action buttons, setting their text and the mode. You set the *UpdateOnPostback* property if you want the record cursor to be updated at post back so that other controls can read the change. *AxForm* also provides events for all the actions that can be taken on the form before and after that action is completed. You can write code in these events for user interface or application-specific logic before or after the action is completed.

The *AxForm* control is a container for a collection of controls. If your form contains many fields and requires visually grouping the related fields, allowing them to be expanded or collapsed, you use the *AxMultiSection* control inside the *AxForm* control. If your form is simple and has only a few fields, you can use the *AxGroup* control.

AxMultiSection

AxMultiSection allows you to define a collection of *AxSection* controls, where each *AxSection* control contains child controls. By default, all sections are in expanded mode and rendered vertically, one after the other. Users can keep any number of them in expanded or collapsed mode. You can also configure *AxMultiSection* so that only one section is expanded at any point. In this mode, expanding a second section causes the first one to collapse, keeping just one section active. Set the *ActiveMode* property to true to enable that behavior. You use the *ActiveSectionIndex* property to get or set the active section. The *AxMultiSection* component can contain only *AxSection* components.

AxSection

AxSection is a generic control container. Any control can be a child of *AxSection*. All *AxSection* controls are rendered vertically, one after the other. Each *AxSection* includes a header that contains the title of the section and an image button that allows the user to expand or collapse the section. *AxSection* provides properties to display or hide the header and border. You can also set a security key on *AxSection* so that it's visible only to users who have access to that security key in Dynamics AX. You can also write code when the section is expanded or collapsed through the events exposed by *AxSection*.

AxGroup

The *AxGroup* control contains the bound fields collection that displays the record information. You add *AxGroup* controls as descendents of *AxSection* controls. Typically, the immediate child of an *AxSection* control is a table control or an HTML table with *AxGroup* controls within the table cells. Figure 7-7 shows a sample task page in Enterprise Portal.

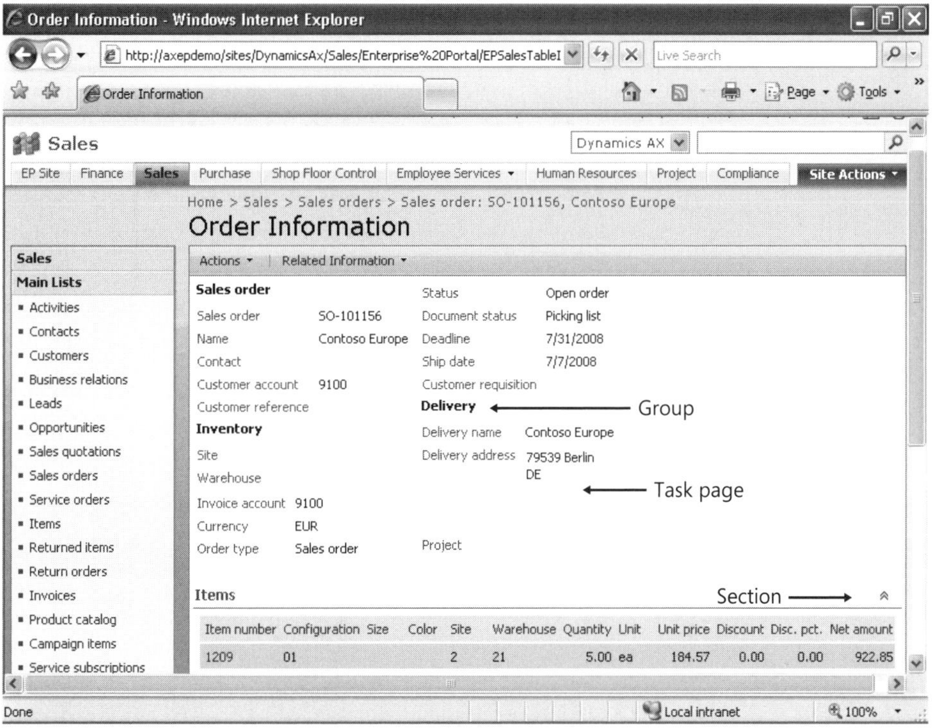

FIGURE 7-7 An Enterprise Portal task page with section and group controls

Following are some high-level control hierarchies for different form layouts.

Here is a form with a list of fields that are displayed one below the other.

```
<AxForm>
    <AxGroup><Fields>BoundFields or TemplateFields…</Fields> </AxGroup>
</AxForm>
```

This form has two expandable sections, with fields displayed one below the other.

```
<AxForm>
    <AxMultiSection>
        <AxSection>
              <AXGroup><Fields>BoundFields or TemplateFields…</Fields> </AxGroup>
        </AxSection>
        <AxSection>
              <AxGroup><Fields>BoundFields or TemplateFields…</Fields> </AxGroup>
              <AxGroup><Fields>BoundFields or TemplateFields…</Fields> </AxGroup>
        </AxSection>
    </AxMultiSection>
</AxForm>
```

The following form has two expandable sections, with fields displayed one below the other. In the second section, the groups are displayed in two columns.

```
<AxForm >
    <AXMultiSection>
        <AxSection>
            <AXGroup><Fields>BoundFields or TemplateFields…</Fields> </AXGroup>
        </AXSection>    <AxSection>
            <table>
                <tr><td>
                    <AXGroup><Fields>BoundFields or TemplateFields…</Fields> </AXGroup>
                </td><td>
                    <AXGroup><Fields>BoundFields or TemplateFields…</Fields> </AXGroup>
                </td></tr>
            </table>
        </AXSection>
    </AxMultiSection>
</AxForm>
```

Here is a wizard with two steps.

```
<AxForm>
    <asp:Wizard>
        <asp:WizardSteps>
            <asp:WizardStep>
                <AXGroup><Fields>BoundFields or TemplateFields…</Fields> </AXGroup>
            </asp:WizardStep>
           <asp:WizardStep>
                <AXGroup><Fields>BoundFields or TemplateFields…</Fields> </AXGroup>
            </asp:WizardStep>
        </asp:WizardSteps>
    </asp:Wizard>
</AxForm>
```

AxLookup

AxLookup is used in data entry pages to help the user pick a valid value for a field that references keys from other tables. In Enterprise Portal, lookups are metadata driven by default and are automatically enabled for fields based on the relationship defined in metadata in the AOT. An example is the customer group lookup on the customer creation page. The extended data type (EDT) and table relationship metadata in the AOT define a relationship between the customer table and the customer group table, so a lookup is rendered to pick a customer group on the customer group field when creating a customer record. You don't need to write any code to enable this behavior—it happens automatically.

In some application scenarios, however, the automatic behavior isn't sufficient, and you might be required to customize the lookup. The lookup infrastructure of Enterprise Portal is designed to offer flexibility and customization options in both X++ and in C# for developers to tailor the lookup user interface and the data retrieval logic to their needs.

In the AOT *Data Set* node, you can override the *dataSetLookup* method of the field in the data source to control the lookup behavior. For example, if you want to filter the values displayed for a zip code field based on what has been entered for a country, state, or county, you override *dataSetLookup*, as shown in the following code.

```
void dataSetLookup(SysDataSetLookup sysDataSetLookup)
{
    ;
    if (custTable.CountryRegionId)
sysDataSetLookup.parmQuery().dataSourceNo(1).addRange(
fieldnum(AddressZipCode,CountryRegionId)).value(queryValue(
custTable.CountryRegionId));
    if (custTable.State)
sysDataSetLookup.parmQuery().dataSourceNo(1).addRange(
fieldnum(AddressZipCode,State)).value(queryValue(custTable.State));
    if (custTable.County)
sysDataSetLookup.parmQuery().dataSourceNo(1).addRange(
fieldnum(AddressZipCode,County)).value(queryValue(custTable.County));
}
```

In the preceding example, *addRange* is used to restrict the value. For some scenarios, you might want to build the entire list dynamically. In that case, you can override the *dataSetLookup* method and build the entire query yourself.

```
...
...

Query               query;
List                _list;
_list = new List(Types::String);
query = new Query();
query.addDataSource(tablenum(ReturnReasonCode));
_list.addEnd(fieldstr(ReturnReasonCode,ReasonCodeId));
_list.addEnd(fieldstr(ReturnReasonCode,ReasonCodeGroupId));
_list.addEnd(fieldstr(ReturnReasonCode,Description));
sysDataSetLookup.parmLookupFields(_list);
sysDataSetLookup.parmQuery(query);
...
...
```

SysDataSetLookup in X++ provides many properties and methods to control the behavior of the lookup.

You can also customize the lookup in C# in the Web User Control by writing code in the *Lookup* event of bound fields or by using the *AxLookup* control for fields that don't have data binding. To use *AxLookup* to provide lookup values for any ASP.NET control that isn't data bound, you should set the *TargetControlID* property of the *AxLookup* to the ASP.NET control. You can base *AxLookup* on the EDT, the data set, the custom data set, or the custom User Control by specifying the *LookupType* property. You can also control what fields are displayed in the lookup and which one is a select field, either through the markup or through code. You can write code to override the *Lookup* event and control the lookup behavior, as shown in the following code.

```
protected void AxLookup1_Lookup(object sender, AxLookupEventArgs e)
    {
        AxLookup lookup = (AxLookup)sender;
        // Specify the lookup fields
        lookup.Fields.Add(AxBoundFieldFactory.Create(this.AxSession, lookup.
LookupDataSetViewMetadata.ViewFields["CustGroup"]));
        lookup.Fields.Add(AxBoundFieldFactory.Create(this.AxSession, lookup.
LookupDataSetViewMetadata.ViewFields["Name"]));
}
```

AxToolbar

The *AxToolbar* control provides an intuitive and consistent way to organize and display functions that the user performs frequently on your application's Web pages. Typically, toolbars are displayed at the top of the page or grid control. *AxToolbar* extends the Windows SharePoint Services toolbar controls. *AxToolbarMenu*, used within *AxToolbar*, is derived from *Microsoft.SharePoint.WebControls.Menu*. The *AxToolbar* control is used to render a toolbar button with a drop-down menu that is rendered when the menu is clicked via a callback. In other words, *AxToolbarMenu* lets you modify the menu item properties before the menu items are rendered.

AxToolbarButton, used within the *AxToolbar* control, is derived from *SPLinkButton*. It is used to render top-level buttons.

Depending on your application, you can use either the *AxToolbar* ASP.NET control or the Dynamics Toolbar Web part to display the toolbar menu items on top of the list, overview, or task page. Generally, you use the Dynamics Toolbar Web part to control the display of toolbar menu items. But if you have a task page that contains master/detail information, such as a Purchase Requisition header and line items, you should use the *AxToolbar* ASP.NET control inside your Web User Control above the detail *AxGridview* control to allow the user to add and manage the line items.

You can use *AxToolbar* bound to *AxDataSource* or as an unbound control. When the controls are bound, the menu item context is automatically based on the current item selected on the grid view. When the controls are unbound, you have to write code to manage the toolbar context.

You can point the toolbar to Web Menus in the AOT through the *WebMenuName* property. The AOT Web Menus allow you to define multilevel menu structure with the *SubMenu*, *MenuItem*, and *MenuItem* reference nodes. Each top-level submenu in a Web menu is rendered by the *AxToolbar* control using *AxToolbarMenu* as a drop-down menu. Each top-level menu item is rendered using *AxToolbarButton* as a link button. If you have a submenu within a submenu, the second and further levels are displayed as flyout menus.

SetMenuItemProperties, *ActionMenuItemClicking*, and *ActionMenuItemClicked* are *AxToolbar* control-specific events. You use *SetMenuItemProperties* to change the behavior of drop-down menus, such as showing or hiding menu items based on the currently selected record, setting or removing context, and so on. An example of changing the menu item context in the *SetMenuItemProperties* event is shown in the following code.

```
void Webpart_SetMenuItemProperties(object sender, SetMenuItemPropertiesEventArgs e)
    {
        // Do not pass the currently selected customer record context, since this menu
is for creating new (query string should be empty)
     if (e.MenuItem.MenuItemAOTName == "EPCustTableCreate")
            ((AxUrlMenuItem)e.MenuItem).MenuItemContext = null;
    }
```

If you have user interface logic defined in a Web User Control and want to call this function instead of the one defined in the AOT when a toolbar item is clicked, you use *ActionMenuItemClicking* and *ActionMenuItemClicked*. For example, you can prevent the menu item from executing the action defined in the AOT by using the *ActionMenuItemClicking* event and defining your own action in C# using the *ActionMenuItemClicked* event in the Web User Control, as shown here.

```
void webpart_ActionMenuItemClicking(object sender, ActionMenuItemClickingEventArgs e)
    {
        if (e.MenuItem.MenuItemAOTName.ToLower() == "EPCustTableDelete")
        {
            e.RunMenuItem = false;
        }
    }
```

```
void webpart_ActionMenuItemClicked(object sender, ActionMenuItemEventArgs e)
{
if (e.MenuItem.MenuItemAOTName.ToLower() == "EPCustTableDelete")
    {
            int selectedIndex = this.AxGridView1.SelectedIndex;
            if (selectedIndex != -1)
            {
                this.AxGridView1.DeleteRow(selectedIndex);
            }
    }
}
```

AxPopup

AxPopup controls are used to open a page in a pop-up browser window, to close a pop-up page, and to pass data from the pop-up page back to the parent page and trigger an *OnPopupClosed* server event on the parent. This functionality is encapsulated in two controls: *AxPopupParentControl* to use on the parent page and *AxPopupChildControl* to use on the pop-up page. Both controls derive from *AxPopupBaseControl*. These controls are AJAX compatible, so you can create them conditionally as part of a partial update. *AxPopupParentControl* allows a page, typically a Web part page, to open in a pop-up window. You can open a pop-up window from a client-side script by using the *GetOpenPopupEvent-Reference* method. The returned string is a JavaScript statement that can be assigned, for example, to a button's *onclick* attribute or to a toolbar menu item. The following code shows how a developer can open a pop-up window using client-side scripting by modifying the *OnClick* event.

```
protected void SetPopupWindowToMenuItem(SetMenuItemPropertiesEventArgs e)
{
    AxUrlMenuItem menuItem = new AxUrlMenuItem("EPCustTableCreate");
   //Calling the JavaScript function to set the properties of opening Web page on
clicking the menuitems.
      e.MenuItem.ClientOnClickScript = this.AxPopupParentControl1.GetOpenPopupEventR
eference(menuItem);
  }
```

You can also open a pop-up window from a server method by calling the *OpenPopup* method. Because pop-up blockers can block server-initiated pop-up windows, use *OpenPopup* only when absolutely necessary, for example, when only the server code can decide whether a pop-up window needs to be opened.

When placed on a pop-up page, *AxPopupChildControl* allows the page to close. You can close the pop-up page from a client-side script by using the *GetClosePopupEventReference* method, as shown in the following example.

```
this.BtnOk.Attributes.Add("onclick",
this.popupChild.GetClosePopupEventReference(true, true) + "; return false;");
```

You can close a pop-up window from the server event by using the *ClosePopup* method. Use the server method when additional processing is needed upon closing, such as performing an action or calculating values to be passed back to the parent page. There are two parameters to the *ClosePopup* and *OpenPopup* methods:

- The boolean *setFieldValues* parameter indicates whether data needs to be passed back to the parent page.
- The boolean *updateParent* parameter indicates whether the parent page needs to post back after the pop-up page is closed. If the value is true, *AxPopupChildControl* makes a call (via a client-side script) to the parent page to post back, with the *AxPopupParentControl* being the target. *AxPopupParentControl* then fires the *PopupClosed* server event, on which the parent page application code can get the values passed from the pop-up page and perform an action or simply update its state.

Data can be passed from the pop-up page back to the parent page using *AxPopupField* objects. You expose these objects via the *Fields* property of the *AxPopupBaseControl*, from which both *AxPopupParentControl* and *AxPopupChildControl* are derived.

AxPopupParentControl and *AxPopupChildControl* have fields with the same names. When the pop-up page closes, the value of each field of *AxPopupChildControl* is assigned (via a client-side script) to the corresponding field in *AxPopupParentControl*.

AxPopupField can optionally be associated with another control, such as *TextBox* or any other control, by assigning its *TargetId* property to the *ID* property of the target control. This is useful, for example, when the pop-up page has a *TextBox* control. To pass the user input to the parent page upon closing the pop-up page—and to do it entirely on the client to avoid a round-trip—you need to associate a field with the *TextBox* control. When *AxPopupField* isn't explicitly associated with a target control, it gets implicitly associated with a *HiddenField* control automatically created by *AxPopupParentControl* or *AxPopupChildControl*.

You can then set the value of the field on the server via the *SetFieldValue* method. Typically, you call *SetFieldValue* on *AxPopupChildControl*, and you can call it at any point of user interaction with the pop-up page, including the initial rendering or the closing of the page. The value of the field can be retrieved via the *GetFieldValue* method. Typically, it is called on *AxPopupParentControl* during the processing of the *PopupClosed* event. You can clear the values of nonassociated fields by calling the *ClearFieldValues* method.

You can also set or retrieve values of *AxPopupFields* on the client by manipulating the target control value. You can retrieve target control, whether explicitly or implicitly associated, by using the *TargetControl* property.

BoundField Controls

BoundField controls are used by data-bound controls (such as *AxGridView*, *AxGroup*, ASP.NET *GridView*, and *DetailsView*) to display the value of a field through data binding. They are displayed differently depending on the data-bound control in which they are used. For example, the *AxGridView* control displays a *BoundField* object as a column, whereas the *AxGroup* control displays it as a row.

The Enterprise Portal framework provides a number of enhanced *AxBoundField* controls that are derived from ASP.NET-bound field controls but integrated with the Dynamics AX metadata.

Table 7-1 describes the *AxBoundField* controls.

TABLE 7-1 *AxBoundField* Controls

Type	Purpose
AxBoundField	You use *AxBoundField* to display text values. The *DataSet*, *DataSetView*, and *DataField* properties define the source of the data.
AxHyperLinkBoundField	You use *AxHyperLinkBoundField* to display hyperlinks. You use the *MenuItem* property to point to a Web menu item in the AOT for generating the URL and the *DataSet*, *DataSetView*, and *DataField* properties to define the source of the data. If the Web menu name is stored within the record, you use *DataMenuItemField* instead of *MenuItem*.
AxBoundFieldGroup	You use *AxBoundFieldGroup* to display *FieldGroups* defined in the AOT. The *DataSet*, *DataSetView*, and *FieldGroup* properties define the source of the data.
Other *BoundFields*	You use *AxCheckBoxBoundField* to display a *boolean* field in a check box, *AxDropDownBoundField* to display a list of values in a drop-down menu, and *AxRadioButtonBoundField* to display a list of values as radio buttons. For all these properties, you use *DataSet*, *DataSetView*, and *DataField* to define the source of the data. For a radio button, you use *RepeatDirection* to define whether the radio button should be rendered horizontally or vertically.

Depending on the field type, *BoundFieldDesigner* automatically groups fields under the correct *BoundField* type. The *BoundField* type displays text that allows you to control the lookup behavior through the *LookupButtonDisplaySettings* property and the lookup event.

Web Parts

Web parts are pluggable and reusable Windows SharePoint Services components that generate HTML and provide the foundation for the modular presentation of data. Web parts are easily integrated to assemble a Web page and support customization and personalization.

Enterprise Portal comes with a standard set of Web parts, including the following, that expose the business data from Dynamics AX:

- **Dynamics User Control** Used for hosting any ASP.NET control. The Dynamics User Control Web part points to a Managed Web Content Item that secures the Web control. The Dynamics User Control Web part can serve as a provider, a consumer, or both when connected with other Web parts. The Web part role property defines the role and is used to pass or record context and refresh the control using AJAX without the entire page being refreshed.
- **Dynamics Infolog Web Part** Used for displaying Dynamics AX Infolog messages on the Web page. When you create a new Web part page, Enterprise Portal page templates automatically add the Infolog Web Part to the new Web part's header zone. Any error, warning, or information message Dynamics AX generates is automatically displayed by the Dynamics Infolog Web Part. If you need to display some information from your Web User Control in the Dynamics Infolog Web Part, you need to add the message to the C# proxy class for the X++ Infolog object.
- **Dynamics Page Title** Used for displaying the page title and the browser title. When you create a new Web part page, the Dynamics Page Title Web part is automatically added to the title bar zone. By default, the Dynamics Page Title Web part displays the title information specified in the *PageTitle* property of the *Page Definition* node in the AOT. If no page definition exists, the page name is displayed. You can override this default behavior and make this Web part get the title from any other Web part in the Web page by using a Web part connection. For example, if you're developing a list page and you want to display some record information, such as Customer Account and Name as the page title, you can connect the Dynamics User Control Web part that displays the grid to the Dynamics Page Title Web part. When you select a different record in the customer list, the page title and the browser title change to display the currently selected Customer Account and Name.
- **Dynamics QuickLaunch** Used for displaying navigation links on the left side of pages in Enterprise Portal. When you create a new Web part page, the Dynamics QuickLaunch Web part is automatically added to the Left Column zone if the template that you chose has this zone. The Dynamics QuickLaunch Web part displays the Web menu set in the *QuickLaunch* property of the Web module in the AOT for that page. All the pages in a given Web module (subsite) display the same left navigation.
- **Dynamics Left Navigation** Used to display page-specific navigation instead of module-specific navigation if necessary. You would then use the Dynamics Left Navigation Web part instead of the Dynamics QuickLaunch Web part.
- **Dynamics Toolbar** Used to display the toolbar at the page level. The Web menu property points to the *WebMenu* node in the AOT. The toolbar is generally connected to the Dynamics User Control Web part, which displays a grid or form for taking action.

You can write code in the Web User Control displayed by the Dynamics User Control Web part to control the toolbar behavior rendered by the Dynamics Toolbar Web part.

- **Dynamics Unified Worklist** Used to display workflow action, alert notification, and tasks, generally in the Role Center or on the Home page.
- **Dynamics Report Server Report** Used to display SQL Server Reporting Services for Dynamics AX.
- **Cues** Used to display information as a visual paper stack in Role Centers. See Chapter 8, "Role Centers," for in-depth coverage of cues.
- **Quick Links** Used to display shortcuts to frequently used menu items in Role Centers. Chapter 8 discusses Quick Links in depth.
- **Business Overview** Used to display KPIs and historical comparisons in Role Centers. Refer to Chapter 8 for details.

Figure 7-8 shows the Add Web Parts dialog box in Enterprise Portal.

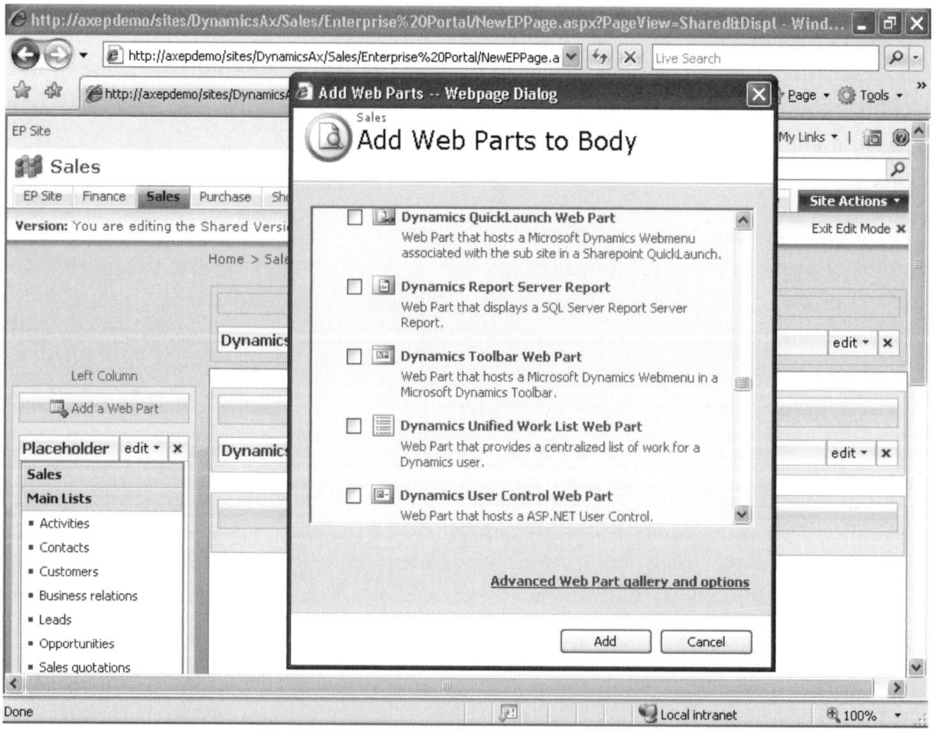

FIGURE 7-8 Add Web Parts dialog box in Enterprise Portal

Programming Enterprise Portal Controls

This section covers some of the common programming tasks involved in building and modifying Enterprise Portal controls and explains the technology behind them with code samples.

AJAX

ASP.NET AJAX allows the developer to create ASP.NET Web pages that can update data on the Web page without completely reloading the page. ASP.NET AJAX provides client-side and server-side components that use the *XMLHttpRequest* object along with JavaScript and DHTML to enable portions of the page to update asynchronously, again without reloading the entire page. With ASP.NET AJAX, you can develop Enterprise Portal Web pages, just as you would any regular ASP.NET page, and you can declaratively mark the components that need to be rendered asynchronously.

Using the *UpdatePanel* server control, you can enable sections of the Web page to be partially rerendered without an entire page postback. The Dynamics User Control Web part contains the *UpdatePanel* internally, and *ScriptLibrary* is included in the master page, so any control that you use in the Web User Control instantly leverages AJAX without you needing to write any explicit markup or code.

For example, if you add a text box and button, writing code for the button's click event on the server, without AJAX, when you click the button, the entire page refreshes. But when you load the same control through the Dynamics User Control Web part, it leverages AJAX and updates the text box without refreshing the entire page.

```
<asp:TextBox ID="TextBox1" runat="server"></asp:TextBox><asp:Button ID="Button1"
runat="server" onclick="Button1_Click" Text="Button" />
```

And in the code-behind, update the text box with the current time after 5 seconds.

```
protected void Button1_Click(object sender, EventArgs e)
    {
     System.Threading.Thread.Sleep(5000);
     TextBox1.Text = System.DateTime.Now.ToShortTimeString();
    }
```

If you want to override the AJAX behavior and force a full postback, you can use the *PostBackTrigger* control in your Web User Control, as shown here.

```
<%@ Register assembly="System.Web.Extensions, Version=3.5.0.0, Culture=neutral, PublicK
eyToken=31bf3856ad364e35" Namespace="System.Web.UI" TagPrefix="asp" %>
<asp:UpdatePanel ID="UpdatePanel1" runat="server">
    <ContentTemplate>
        <asp:TextBox ID="TextBox1" runat="server"></asp:TextBox>
        <asp:Button ID="Button1" runat="server" onclick="Button1_Click" Text="Button" />
    </ContentTemplate>
    <Triggers>
        <asp:PostBackTrigger ControlID="Button1" />
    </Triggers>
</asp:UpdatePanel>
```

Session

All the Web parts in a Web page share the same session in Dynamics AX. Once the page is served, the session is torn down. To optimize performance, you can control the time frame for tearing down the session through a web.config setting. For example, add the *Microsoft.Dynamics sectionGroup* to web.config as in the following code.

```
<sectionGroup name="Microsoft.Dynamics">
<section name="Session" type="System.Configuration.SingleTagSectionHandler, System,
Version=1.0.5000.0, Culture=neutral,PublicKeyToken=b77a5c561934e089" />
</sectionGroup>
```

Add the *<Microsoft.Dynamics>* element under *</system.web>* and then add the following text to the file.

```
<Microsoft.Dynamics>
    <Session Timeout="15" />
</Microsoft.Dynamics>
```

Many of the methods you use in the Enterprise Portal framework to add code to User Controls require access to the *Session* object. You need to pass the *Session* object when using proxy classes. You can access the *Session* object through the Web part hosting the User Control, as shown here.

```
        AxBaseWebPart webpart = AxBaseWebPart.GetWebpart(this);
        return webpart == null ? null : webpart.Session;
```

Context

Context is a data structure used to share data related to the current environment and user actions taking place with different parts of a Web application. Context lets you know what's happening in one control so you can react to it via another control or Web part, or pass that information to a new page. Generally, information about the current record the user is working on forms the context. For example, when the user selects a row in a grid view, other controls might need to get information about the newly selected row to react.

AxContext is an abstract class that encapsulates the concept of the context. *AxTableContext* and *AxViewContext* derive from and implement *AxContext*. *AxTableContext* is for table-based context, and *AxViewContext* is for data set view context. A view can contain more than one table, so it contains an *AxTableContext* object for each table in the view in the *TableContextList* collection. The RootTableContext property returns the *TableContext* of the root table in that data set view. *AxViewDataKey* uniquely identifies the *AxViewContext*, and it contains the *TableDataKeys* collection. *AxTableDataKey* uniquely identifies *AxTableContext*. An event is raised whenever the context changes. If the context is changed within the Web User Control, the *CurrentContextChanged* event is raised. If the context changes from other Web parts that are connected to it, the *ExternalContextChanged* event is raised.

You can write code in these events on the *AxBaseWebPart* from your Web User Control and use the *CurrentContextProviderView* or *ExternalContextProviderView* and *ExternalRecord* properties to get the record associated with the context. You can fire all these events programmatically from your application logic by calling *FireCurrentContextChanged* or *FireExternalContextChanged* so that all other connected controls could react to the change you made through your code.

Following is sample code to fire the *CurrentContextChanged* event.

```
void CurrentContextProviderView_ListChanged(object sender, System.ComponentModel.
ListChangedEventArgs e)
    {
/* The current row (which is the current context) has changed -
 update the consumer webparts.Fire the current context change event to refresh
 (re-execute the query) the consumer webparts
*/
AxBaseWebPart webpart = this.WebPart;
webpart.FireCurrentContextChanged();
    }
```

Sample code for getting the record from the connected Web part follows. First subscribe to the *ExternalContextChanged* event in the consumer Web User Control, as here.

```
protected void Page_Load(object sender, EventArgs e)
    {
   //Add Event handler for the ExternalContextChange event. Whenever selecting
//the grid of the provider Web part changes, this event gets fired.

        (AxBaseWebPart.GetWebpart(this)).ExternalContextChanged += new
EventHandler<Microsoft.Dynamics.Framework.Portal.UI.AxExternalContextChangedEventArgs>
(AxContextConsumer_ExternalContextChanged);
}
```

Then get the record passed through the external context, as shown here.

```
    void AxContextConsumer_ExternalContextChanged(object sender, Microsoft.Dynamics.
Framework.Portal.UI.AxExternalContextChangedEventArgs e)
    {
        //Get the AxTableContext from the ExternalContext passed through web part
connection and construct the record object
        //and get to the value of the fields
        IAxaptaRecordAdapter currentRecord = (AxBaseWebPart.GetWebpart(this)).
ExternalRecord;
        {
   if (currentRecord != null)
            {
   lblCustomer.Text = (string)currentRecord.GetField("Name");
            }
        }
    }
```

Data

The Enterprise Portal ASP.NET controls access and manipulate data through data binding to *AxDataSource*. You can also access the data through the APIs directly. The *Microsoft.Dynamics.Framework.Data.Ax* namespace contains several classes that work together to retrieve data.

For example, use the following code to get the current row from the *DataSetView*.

```
private DataSetViewRow CurrentRow
    {
        get
        {
            try
            {
                DataSetView dsv = this.ContactInfoDS.GetDataSet().DataSetViews[this.
ContactInfoGrid.DataMember];
                return (dsv == null) ? null : dsv.GetCurrent();
            }
            // CurrentRow on the dataset throws exception in empty data scenarios
            catch (System.Exception)
            {
                return null;
            }
        }
    }
```

To set the menu item with the current records context, use the following code.

```
…
…
DataSetViewRow currentContact = this.dsEPVendTableInfo.GetDataSourceView(gridConatcts.
DataMember).DataSetView.
GetCurrent();
     using (IAxaptaRecordAdapter contactPersonRecord = currentContact.GetRecord())
                {
   ((AxUrlMenuItem)e.MenuItem).MenuItemContext = AxTableContext.Create(AxTableDataKey.
Create(this.BaseWebpart.Session, contactPersonRecord, null));
                }
```

Metadata

The Enterprise Portal framework provides a rich set of APIs to access the metadata from the AOT in managed code. The *Microsoft.Dynamics.Framework.Metadata.Ax* namespace contains several classes that work together to retrieve metadata from the AOT. Enterprise Portal controls use the metadata for retrieving formatting, validation, security, and other information from the AOT and apply it on the Web user interface automatically. Developers can also use these APIs to retrieve the metadata in their user interface logic.

MetadataCache is the main entry point to accessing metadata and provides static methods. For example, to get the *EnumMetadata*, you use *MetadataCache.GetEnumMetadata*, as shown here.

```
/// <summary>
/// Loads the dropdown with the Enum values.
/// </summary>
private void LoadDropdownList()
    {
   EnumMetadata salesUpdateEnum = MetadataCache.GetEnumMetadata(this.AxSession,
EnumMetadata.EnumNum(this.AxSession, "SalesUpdate"));
        foreach (EnumEntryMetadata entry in salesUpdateEnum.EnumEntries)
        {
   ddlSelectionUpdate.Items.Add(new ListItem(entry.GetLabel(this.AxSession), entry.
Value.ToString()));
        }
    }
```

To get the label value for a table field, use the following code.

```
…
…
TableMetadata tableSalesQuotationBasketLine = MetadataCache.GetTableMetadata(
                            this.AxSession, "CustTable");
TableFieldMetadata fieldItemMetadata = tableSalesQuotationBasketLine.FindDataField-
("AccountNum");
String s = fieldItemMetadata.GetLabel(this.AxSession);
…
…
```

Figure 7-9 shows some key object access hierarchy for metadata. Not all APIs are included in this figure.

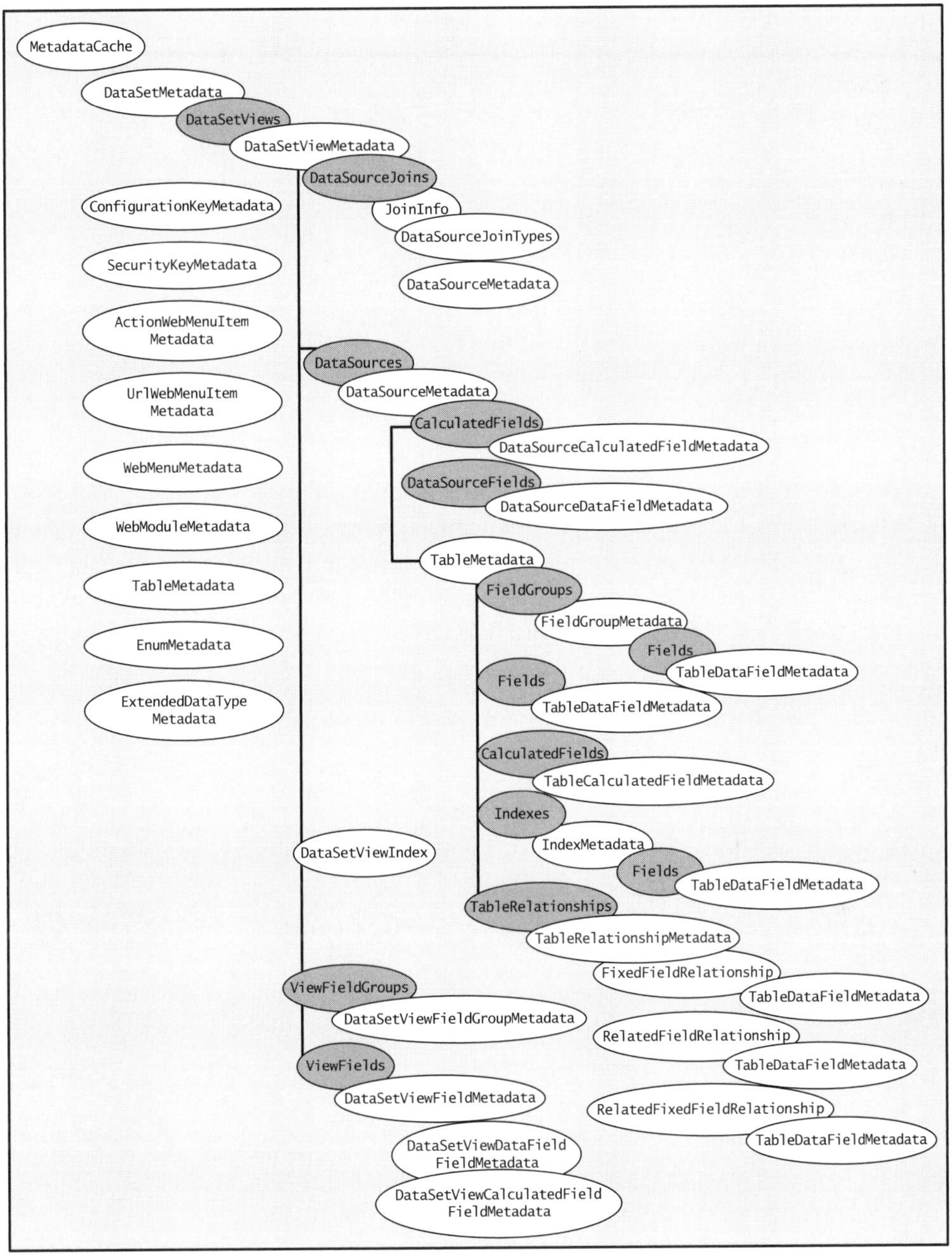

FIGURE 7-9 Metadata object hierarchy

Labels

Dynamics AX uses a localizable text resource file, the label file, to provide messages to the user and for user interface text, Help text in the status bar, captions, and so on. You can use labels to specify the user interface text in Web User Controls and for the AOT *Web* node element properties. You can add labels by setting the *Label* property in the AOT or by using X++ code.

When you use data-bound controls such as *AxGridView* or *AxForm* for the user interface, the bound fields automatically pick the label associated with the field in the AOT and render it in the user's language at run time.

If you want to show a label in your Web User Control for non-data-bound scenarios, use the *AxLabel* expression.

AxLabel is a standard ASP.NET expression that looks up the labels defined in the AOT and renders them in the user's language when the page is rendered. To add the *AxLabel* expression, you can use the expression editor available in the design view of the User Control by clicking the button that appears on the (*Expressions*) property. Alternatively, you can type the expression directly in the markup, like this.

```
<asp:Button runat="server" ID="ButtonChange" Text="<%$ AxLabel:@SYS70959 %>"
OnClick="ButtonChange_Click" />
```

You can also add labels through code using the *Labels* class, as shown here.

```
string s = Microsoft.Dynamics.Framework.Portal.UI.Labels.GetLabel("@SYS111587");
```

Enterprise Portal caches the labels for all 41 languages for better performance. So if you add or change a label in the AOT, you need to clear the cache on the Enterprise Portal site by using the Refresh AOD admin option.

Formatting

Dynamics AX is a truly global product, supporting multiple languages and used in many countries. Displaying data in the correct format for each localized version is a critical requirement for any global product. Through metadata, the Enterprise Portal framework recognizes the user's current locale and system settings and automatically displays data in the correct format in the data-bound controls.

If you're not using data-bound controls and want your unbound ASP.NET controls to be formatted just like Enterprise Portal controls, you can leverage the *AxValueFormatter* class in the Enterprise Portal framework. This class implements *ICustomFormatter* and the *IFormatProvider* interface and defines a method that supports custom, user-defined formatting of an object's value and provides a mechanism for retrieving an object to control formatting. For the various data types, specific *ValueFormatter* classes derived from *AxValueFormatter* are implemented: *AxStringValueFormatter, AxDateValueFormatter, AxDateTimeValueFormatter, AxTimeValueFormatter, AxRealValueFormatter, AxNumberValueFormatter, AxGuidValueFormatter,* and *AxEnumValueFormatter.*

You use *AxValueFormatterFactory* to create *AxValueFormatter* objects. You can create any of the preceding formatters, or you can create a formatter based on an EDT in Dynamics AX. The data type for the extended data is retrieved from the metadata object for the EDT, and the culture information comes from the context. The various rules for languages and countries, such as number formats, currency symbols, and sort orders, are aggregated into a number of standard cultures. The Enterprise Portal framework identifies the culture based on the user's language setting in Dynamics AX and makes this information available in the context. Formatter objects have a *Parse* method you can use to convert a string value back into the underlying data type. For example, the following code formats the data based on a given EDT.

```
private string ToEDTFormattedString(object data, string edtDataType)
    {
   ExtendedDataTypeMetadata edtType = MetadataCache.GetExtendedDataTypeMetadata(
            this.AxSession,
            ExtendedDataTypeMetadata.TypeNum(this.AxSession, edtDataType)
        );
        IAxContext context = AxContextHelper.FindIAxContext(this);
        AxValueFormatter valueFormatter = AxValueFormatterFactory.
CreateFormatter(this.AxSession, edtType, context.CultureInfo);
        return valueFormatter.FormatValue(data);
    }Validation
```

You use ASP.NET validator controls to validate user input on the server as well as (optionally) on the client (browser). The Enterprise Portal framework has ASP.NET validators specific to Dynamics AX: *AxBaseValidator* derives from *BaseValidator,* and *AxValueFormatValidator* derives from *AxBaseValidator.* Both are metadata driven and are used intrinsically by bound fields, but you can also use them in unbound scenarios.

ASP.NET validators are automatically validated when a postback that causes validation occurs. For example, an ASP.NET *Button* control causes validation on the client and the server when clicked. All validators registered on the page are validated. If any validator is found to be invalid, the page becomes invalid, and *Page.IsValid* returns false.

The importance of *Page.IsValid* is best highlighted with an example. Let's say you add an ASP.NET button in which some business logic is performed in *OnClick* before it is redirected. As mentioned, the button causes validation by default, so validators are executed before the *OnClick* event is fired. If you don't check whether the page is valid in your *OnClick*, you will be redirected even though a validation error that requires the user's attention occurs.

Enterprise Portal controls such as *AxForm* and *AxGridView* won't perform the requested action if validation fails and navigates away from the page. The Dynamics AX validator controls automatically write any validation errors to the Infolog.

> **Best Practices** When you're using ASP.NET controls directly rather than using Enterprise Portal controls, as a best practice, make sure the *Pages.IsValid* flag is checked before any actions, such as navigating away from the current page, are completed. You want to do this because, in case any errors occur, you want to keep the current page with Infolog displaying the errors for the users so that they will notice them and take corrective action.

Error Handling

In Enterprise Portal, .NET Business Connector (including proxies), the metadata, and the data layer all throw exceptions in case of error conditions. The Enterprise Portal ASP.NET controls automatically handle these exceptions, taking appropriate actions and displaying the errors in Infolog.

Exceptions in Enterprise Portal are divided into three categories. These exception categories are defined in the enumeration *AxExceptionCategory*:

- ***NonFatal*** The exception handling code should respond appropriately and allow the request to continue normally.
- ***AxFatal*** Indicates that an unrecoverable error has occurred in Enterprise Portal. Enterprise Portal content will not display. Content not related to Enterprise Portal should display as expected.
- ***SystemFatal*** Indicates that a serious error, such as out of memory, has occurred and the request must be aborted. Errors of this kind often cause an HTTP error code 500.

If your code directly calls methods in data or metadata layers from Enterprise Portal or with proxy class calling X++ methods, it must handle these exceptions. The following code shows how to use *AxControlExceptionHandler* in the *try-catch* statement to handle exceptions.

```
Try
{
    // Code that may encounter exceptions goes here.
}
catch (System.Exception ex)
{   AxExceptionCategory exceptionCategory;
    // Determine whether the exception can be handled.
    if (AxControlExceptionHandler.TryHandleException(this, ex, out exceptionCategory)
== false)
    {
        // The exception was fatal and cannot be handled. Rethrow it.
        throw;
    }
    if (exceptionCategory == AxExceptionCategory.NonFatal)
    {
   // Application code to properly respond to the exception goes here.
    }
}
```

AxControlExceptionHandler tries to handle Dynamics AX exceptions based on the three exception categories just mentioned. It returns true if the exception is *NonFatal*.

ViewState

The Web is stateless, which means that each request for a page is treated as a new request, and no information is shared. When loaded, each ASP.NET page goes through a regular page life cycle, from initialization and page load onward. When a user interacts with the page, causing the need for the server to process some control events, ASP.NET posts the values of the form to the same page for processing the event on the server. A new instance of the Web page class is created each time the page is requested from the server. When postback happens, ASP.NET uses the *ViewState* feature to preserve the state of the page and controls so that any changes made to the page during the round-trip are not lost. The Enterprise Portal framework leverages this feature, and Enterprise Portal ASP.NET controls automatically save their state to *ViewState*. The ASP.NET page reads the view state and reinstates the page and control state in its regular page life cycle. So you don't need to write any code to manage the state if you're using Enterprise Portal controls. But if you want to persist any values in memory variables, you can write code to add or remove items from *StateBag* in ASP.NET.

If you need to save the state of an X++ data set, you can use the pack and unpack design pattern to store the state, as shown here.

```
public int Counter
{
    get
     {
        Object counterObject = ViewState["Counter"];
        if (counterObject == null)
        {
            return 0;
        }
       return (int)counterObject;
     }
    set
     {
        ViewState["Counter"] = value;
    }
}
```

The Enterprise Portal framework uses the *EPStateStore* table in Dynamics AX to store the state of *AxDataSourceControl*. The states of all other controls are stored in the ASP.NET view state for added security. This storage is per user, and each user can read only his or her information. Writes and deletes are protected with AOS methods, and read is protected via code access permission.

Page Life Cycle

When an Enterprise Portal page runs, it goes through a life cycle in which it performs a series of steps and raises events at various states so developers can write code to control the behavior of the page and its controls, create dynamic controls, and write user interface logic. Understanding the sequence of the page processing and events helps you write the user interface logic at the appropriate level.

Proxy Classes

If you need to call X++ classes or table methods or enums in your Web User Control, the Enterprise Portal framework provides an easy way of creating managed wrappers for these X++ objects and using them in your Web User Control. A proxy file internally wraps the .NET Business Connector calls and provides a simple, easy-to-use, typed interface for C# applications. The proxies file under Web\Web Files\Static Files in the AOT contains information about all the X++ objects for which a proxy file needs to be generated. The proxy generation tool uses this file when the Enterprise Portal site is deployed. The proxy files are automatically created and deployed to the App_Code folder of the IIS Web site. Table 7-2 describes the various command line options for the proxy generator.

TABLE 7-2 Proxy Generator Command Line Options

Option	Purpose
/class	Specifies the name of a class to generate. The */method* option is used to further specify the composition of the generated class type.
/enum	Specifies the name of a base enumeration to generate.
/generate	Specifies the generate mode: optional values are *classes*, *enums*, and *tables*. If the */generate* option isn't specified or if no option value is specified, the */class*, */enum*, and */table* options determine what types are generated. If the *classes* value is specified, all AOT classes are generated. If the *enums* value is specified, all AOT base enumerations are generated. If the *tables* value is specified, all AOT tables are generated.
/method	Specifies the name of a method to generate. The class (or table) and method name must be specified as follows: *class.method.*
/methods+	Specifies that all methods will be generated, ignoring the methods specified by the */method* options.
/methods-	Default. Specifies that only the methods specified by the */method* options will be generated.
/namespace	Specifies the namespace for the generated proxies.
/references+	Specifies that all class references will be generated. A reference is a generated type that appears as a base class, or as a method return type or parameter type.
/references-	Default. Specifies that no class references will be generated.
/table	Specifies the name of a table to generate. The */method* option is used to further specify the composition of the generated class type.
/warn	Specifies the proxy generator warning level: 0 Off, 1 Error, 2 Warn, 3 Info, and 4 Verbose.

For example, to generate a proxy file for the *SampleProxy* class, add the following code to the *Web\Web Files\Static Files\Proxies* node in the AOT.

```
warn:2 /references+ /methods- /namespace:Microsoft.Dynamics.Portal.Application.Proxy

/class:SampleProxy
  /method:SampleProxy.sampleProxiesNoParameters
  /method:SampleProxy.sampleProxiesStaticMethod
```

The first line of the preceding code provides the generation options for the proxy file. The second line provides information about the X++ class for which the proxy file needs to be generated. When Enterprise Portal is deployed, a SampleProxy.cs is created; it contains two methods and is deployed to the App_Code folder of the IIS Web site.

From Visual Studio, you can right-click the App_Code folder in a Dynamics AX Web project and choose the Generate Proxies option. The Visual Studio add-in generates the proxy files defined in the Proxies file and adds them to the Visual Studio project.

To use the proxy from C# code in the Web User Controls, first add a *using* statement to the proxy namespace, like this.

```
using Microsoft.Dynamics.Portal.Application.Proxy;
```

Then you can access these X++ methods as if they were in C#. You can access some items in the proxy, such as enums, directly, without any additional code. Accessing methods from the proxy requires passing the *IAxaptaAdapter* object together with the method call. So you need to get the session and pass it to the constructor to create the C# proxy object, as shown here.

```
protected string NoParamProxyCall_Click(object sender, EventArgs e)
    {
        AxBaseWebPart webpart = AxBaseWebPart.GetWebpart(this);
        SampleProxy sampleProxy = null;
        sampleProxy = new SampleProxy(webpart.Session.AxaptaAdapter);
        string s = sampleProxy.sampleProxiesNoParameters();
        return s;
    }
```

Securing Web Elements

To securely expose Web User Controls through Web parts in Windows SharePoint Services, you must create a *Web* managed node pointing to the Web control in the AOT. You can assign security keys, along with other configuration keys, to the *Web* node. You can assign parameters (if the Web User Control uses them) to exhibit different behavior on different pages. Figure 7-10 shows the *SecurityKey* property of a *Web* node.

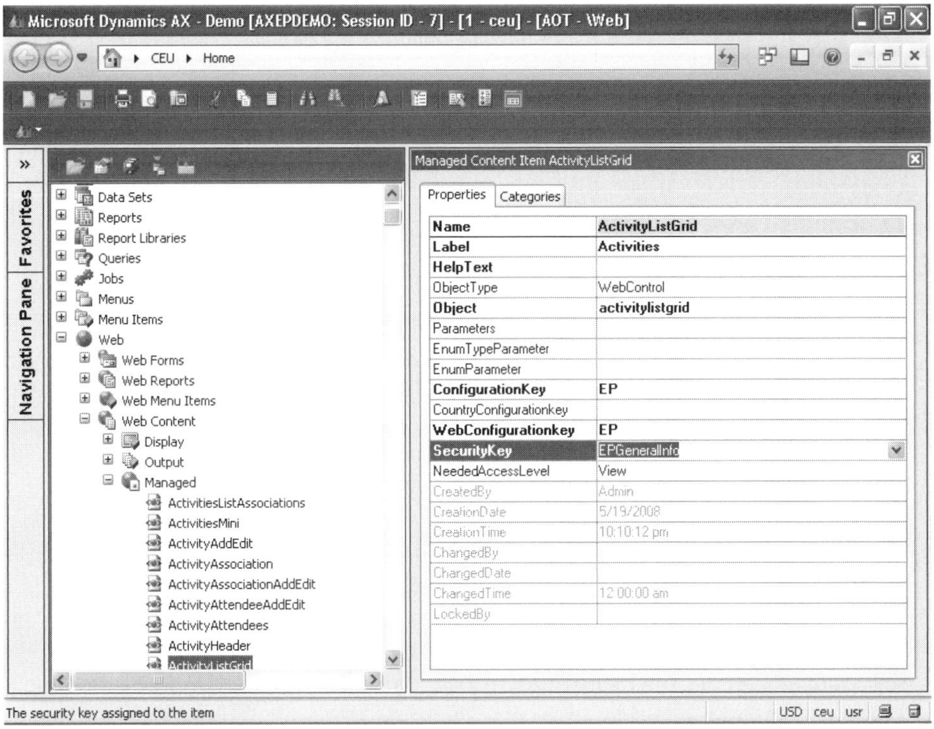

FIGURE 7-10 Assigning a security key to Web content

You can also secure both Web and non-Web applications in Dynamics AX at the data access level by using table-level, field-level, or record-level security settings. Using security keys is the primary way to set permission levels for groups in Dynamics AX. After you configure security keys to define the features the application should include, the keys are used to grant permissions to individual groups. These permissions regulate how group members are allowed to work with each object in a database. You can apply more granular control by creating your own groups, assigning appropriate permissions to those groups, and then adding users to the groups.

At logon, the security keys determine user access. Access depends on which user groups the user is in and on the user's company or domain. Because the access to an individual security key depends on its parent, the system automatically traverses the security key hierarchy and presents the correct access level to the user. You can set up access to Web menu items and Web content in the User Group Permissions dialog box (accessible from Administration\Setup\Security\User Group Permissions). You can use the Viewing list to apply a different view to the tree structure.

If a user doesn't have access to a Web menu item, that item doesn't appear on the user's Web menu. If the Web menu item is linked from other Web User Controls the user has access to, the item linked with the Web menu item appears as text rather than a link.

If the user doesn't have access to Web content on a Web page, the content isn't rendered on the page. The Web part properties also limit the items displayed in the drop-down list based on the user permissions for the underlying objects. Moreover, the types of operations that are allowed on these objects depend on the access level set for the objects on the groups to which the user belongs.

Developing the Navigation

Web modules are resources in the AOT that define the sites and subsites in Windows SharePoint Services that make up an Enterprise Portal installation. Web module resources also define the top-level navigation structure for Enterprise Portal.

Web menu items define the basic navigational element. They can point to either a URL or a class. Web menu items can be secured by security keys. You can use menu items in Web menus as navigational elements on a Web page, or you can use controls (e.g., buttons) in Web User Controls to provide links. Whether the links are shown or hidden is based on user permissions. Consider Web menu items the glue and the navigation mechanism throughout the Web site to help you create sites that are dynamic and versatile.

A Web menu defines the hierarchical navigational scheme and comprises Web menu items, submenu headings, and references to other Web menus. Web menus can be included on the Web page through the Dynamics Quick Launch, Dynamics Left Navigation, or Dynamics Toolbar Web part.

The Web framework uses the *WebLink* class to generate hyperlinks. This class has all the properties and methods the framework needs to pass information back and forth between the browser and the server. More important, it has a method that returns the URL for the link. *WebLink* also has several methods for passing record information.

Figure 7-11 shows the AOT nodes for Web menus, Web menu items, and Web modules.

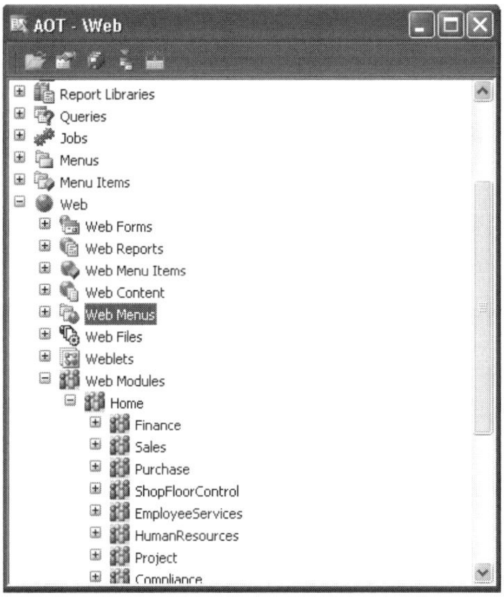

FIGURE 7-11 Web Menus and Web menu items

Windows SharePoint Services displays a *TopNavigation* bar by using a *SPNavigationProvider* registered in web.config. This bar is used on the master page as a *SiteMapDataSource* for the *QuickLaunch* and *TopNavigationMenus*, respectively. Office SharePoint Server overrides the Windows SharePoint Services *SPNavigationProvider* and uses *Microsoft.SharePoint.Publishing.Navigation.PortalSiteMapProvider* to display *TopNavigation* and *QuickLaunch*.

The Enterprise Portal site uses the Windows SharePoint Services navigation elements and object model for showing Dynamics AX navigation items from the AOT. To display Web menus from the AOT as the top and left navigation elements on the Windows SharePoint Services site, Enterprise Portal setup adds the navigation providers *DynamicsLeftNavProvider* and *DynamicsTopNavProvider*, which are new in Dynamics AX 2009. For MOSS, *DynamicsMOSSTopNavProvider* is added instead of *AxTopNavProvider*. Both navigation providers override the default *TopNavigationDataSource* and *QuickLaunchDataSource* (for Windows SharePoint Services) and the default *PortalSiteMapDataSource* (for MOSS).

Web Files

You can customize Windows SharePoint Services sites by using site definitions or custom templates built on existing site definitions. The site definitions encompass multiple files located on the file system on each Web server. These files define the structure and schema for the site. You can create new site definitions by copying the existing site definition files and modifying them to meet the needs of the new sites. You create custom templates by using the user interface to customize existing sites and storing them as templates.

The Enterprise Portal site definition files are stored in the AOT under Web\Web Files\Site Definitions. Custom templates are stored under Web\Web Files\Site Templates. The Enterprise Portal setup deploys these files from the AOT to the Web server file system and Windows SharePoint Services or Office SharePoint Server.

Enterprise Portal includes one default site definition, which has two configurations: one for authenticated users and another for public Internet users. Even though Enterprise Portal doesn't include any site templates, the AOT provides a mechanism for partners and customers to add custom templates and let the Enterprise Portal Deployment Wizard implement these files.

The site definition is deployed to the <*drive*>:\Program Files\Common Files\Microsoft Shared\Web Server Extensions\12\TEMPLATE\SiteTemplates\AXSITEDEF folder.

This folder contains the Enterprise Portal master page (defaultax.master) and the default.aspx and onet.xml files. The Web part page templates are deployed to the language-specific site definition folder: <*drive*>:\Program Files\Common Files\Microsoft Shared\Web Server Extensions\12\TEMPLATE\<*lcid*>\AXSITEDEF.

Enterprise Portal deployment is implemented as a set of four Windows SharePoint Services features. A Windows SharePoint Services site represents a modular server-side, file-system-level customization that contains items that can be installed and activated in a Windows SharePoint Services environment. The feature definitions are deployed to <*drive*>:\Program Files\Common Files\Microsoft Shared\Web Server Extensions\12\TEMPLATE\FEATURES.

These Enterprise Portal feature definitions are as follows:

- ***DynamicsSearch*** Enables Enterprise Portal search control on Enterprise Portal sites that enable searching across Dynamics AX and Windows SharePoint Services data.
- ***DynamicsAxEnterprisePortal*** Enables basic Enterprise Portal deployment steps such as deploying master and other files and components, setting navigation providers, and registering Dynamics AX. This feature is for the Windows SharePoint Services environment.
- ***DynamicsAxEnterprisePortalMOSS*** Includes environment-specific steps for deploying Office SharePoint Server.
- ***DynamicsAxDataConnection*** For deploying the Office Data Connection fields used by KPI lists and the Business Overview Web part in Role Centers.

Enterprise Portal feature-related files are stored in the AOT under Web\Web Files\Static Files. The *Static Files* node also has other infrastructure-related files, such as the aspx file used for importing and exporting page and list definitions, search control, document handling infrastructure files, the master page, common ASP.NET pages, images, style sheets, and configuration files.

EPSetupParams is an XML file used to define the default Enterprise Portal site attributes, such as title, description, and URL, when the site is autocreated through Enterprise Portal setup.

Proxies is a text file used during Enterprise Portal deployment to generate C# proxy files for the X++ class and table methods and *enums*.

The Enterprise Portal site definition contains the page templates embedded with the Web Menu Web part to display the global menu and the Dynamics Page Title Web part to display the page title using Dynamics AX labels. So when a page is created in Enterprise Portal, these two Web parts are already available on the Web page, creating consistency across all Web part pages in Enterprise Portal and supporting rapid application development. Figure 7-12 shows some of the key files that constitute the site definition and their locations on the Web server.

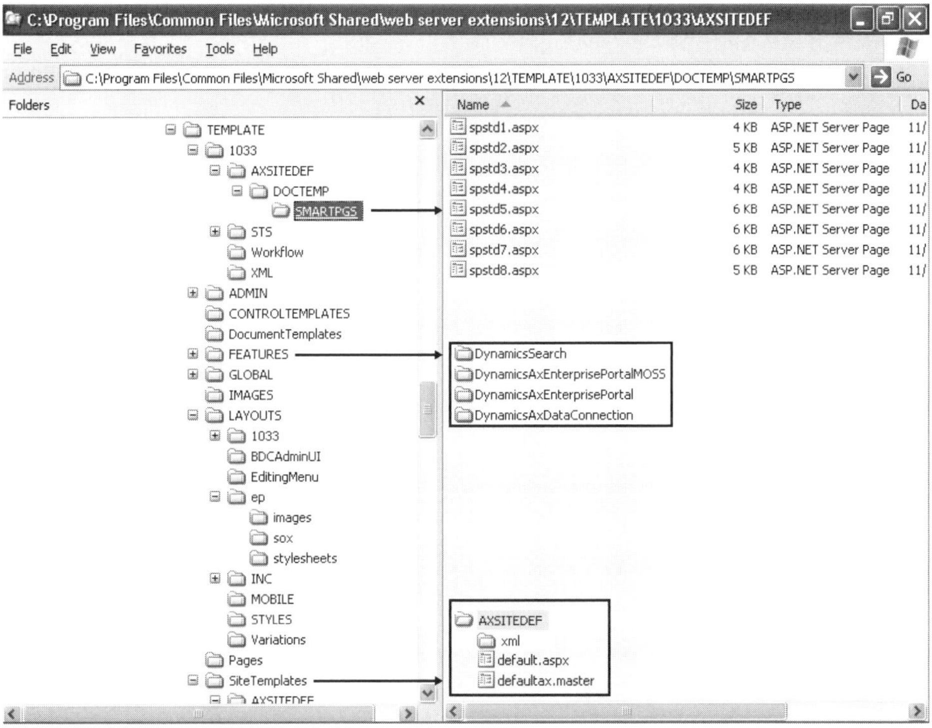

FIGURE 7-12 Enterprise Portal site definition on the Web server

Enterprise Portal Web parts are packed into one Web part package and kept in the AOT under Web\Web Files\Web Parts. If necessary, partners and customers can add their own Web part packages under this node, and Enterprise Portal will deploy these files to the global assembly cache on the Web server and add a safe control entry in the web.config file.

Web part pages display one or more Web parts. Web parts provide an easy way to build powerful Web pages that display a variety of information, ranging from a Dynamics AX data view of a list in the current site to external data presented in custom-built Web parts. You create Web part pages in Windows SharePoint Services by using Microsoft Internet Explorer. You simply drag Web parts onto Web part pages and set their properties with prepopulated lists. You can edit Web part pages in either SharePoint Designer or Internet Explorer. You can use Internet Explorer to edit a page and change its Web parts, arrange the order of the Web parts, and set the Web part properties. You can use SharePoint Designer to insert logos or other graphics, to customize document libraries or lists, to apply themes and styles, to customize the master page, and so on. Keep in mind, however, that you can't import pages edited with SharePoint Designer into the AOT.

All the Web parts on a Web page share the same Dynamics AX Web session. You can import Web part pages created in the Enterprise Portal site in Windows SharePoint Services into the AOT as page definitions by using the Import Page tool from the Web menu items of type URL. The page definitions are stored in the AOT under Web\Web Files\Page Definitions.

The page definitions imported into the AOT automatically create pages when a site is created with the Enterprise Portal site definition. The *PublicPage* property of the page definition node determines whether the page should be created on the public site. All the pages are created for the authenticated site. The page definition *Title* property, if used, must be set to a label so that the page displays the localized title when used with different language settings.

Style sheets and other necessary files, such as lookup files and images for Enterprise Portal, are kept under Web\Web Files\Static Files. Web parts refer to these style sheets. Each Web part applies the current theme and uses it to refer to the corresponding Enterprise Portal style sheets.

For example, if the folder name of the currently applied theme in the Enterprise Portal site is Afternoon, the Web part refers to the AXEP.css file from the Enterprise Portal Stylesheets folder. This folder is located on the Web server under <*drive*>:\Program Files\Common Files\Microsoft Shared\Web Server Extensions\12\TEMPLATE\LAYOUTS\ep\Stylesheets.

For each theme, Enterprise Portal has four style sheets. AXEP.css is the base style sheet. EP.AXEP_RTL.css is used for right-to-left languages, cascading on top of AXEP.css. AXEP_CRC.css and AXEP_CRC_RTL.css are used for Role Centers when rendered on *AxClient*.

If the Web part doesn't find a corresponding file, the default Enterprise Portal style sheet is applied. Dynamics AX includes four style sheets for Enterprise Portal that map to the default theme in Windows SharePoint Services. Partners and customers can also extend the built-in style sheets or create new ones that map to any Windows SharePoint Services theme. Windows SharePoint Services also allows you to create new themes.

Import and Deploy Page/List Tools

The Import and the Deploy Page/List tools provide a seamless integration between the AOT and Enterprise Portal sites based on Windows SharePoint Services or Office SharePoint Server.

The Import Page tool allows you to pull pages you create in Windows SharePoint Services into the *URL Web Menu* node in the AOT. The new page definitions are in XML format and are stored under Web\Web Files\Page Definitions. Importing pages into the AOT as page definitions allows the pages to be automatically re-created when a Windows SharePoint Services site is created with the Enterprise Portal site definition. The pages can then use the Dynamics AX labels for page titles so that the same page definitions can be used for sites in different languages.

The Import List tool allows you to import KPI lists you create in Office SharePoint Server into the AOT. The new list definitions are in XML format and are stored under Web\Web Files\List Definitions.

You can also deploy the page or list definitions at the individual page or list level, which means that you can import pages and lists created in Windows SharePoint Services (set as the AOT site in Administration\Setup\Internet\Enterprise Portal\Web Sites in the Dynamics AX client) into the AOT as page definitions by using the standard Dynamics AX Import and Export utilities. Then you can deploy the newly created or updated page or list definitions to the current Windows SharePoint Services site as Web part pages without having to delete and re-create the site, thereby avoiding problems with data migration from the old site to the new site.

The Import and Deploy Page/List tools use the AOT site setting specified in the Web Sites dialog box as the source or target Windows SharePoint Services site.

Record Context and Encryption

Record context is the interface for passing information through the query string to a Web part page to retrieve a record from Dynamics AX. Enterprise Portal uses record context to locate a record in the Dynamic AX database and display it in a Web form for viewing and editing.

Some of the parameters of the query string to the Enterprise Portal Web part page as record context are listed here:

- WTID = Table ID
- WREC = Rec ID
- WFID = Field ID
- WKEY = Unique Record KEY (the field identifier and the value of the field for the record to be retrieved)

These parameters are passed either in a query string or in post data on Web pages. If they are passed in clear text, an unauthorized user could view data or perform actions by guessing and manipulating their values. To help secure Enterprise Portal, Dynamics AX encrypts these parameters by default on the front-end Web server, making it impossible to extract or manipulate the parameters. For debugging and Web development, the administrator can turn off the encryption in the Enterprise Portal General tab of the Web Sites dialog box, which is located in Administration\Setup\Internet\Enterprise Portal\Web Sites. If the record-level security and other data-level security are already active and no security threats exist, turning off the encryption could result in better performance. However, we strongly recommend that you keep the encryption turned on.

Whether encryption is on or off, the functionality of the Web elements in Enterprise Portal must remain the same. A URL generated for one user can't be used by any other user. And if the encryption expiration interval is set, a user can't use the URL generated for him or her after the specified number of days has elapsed. The encryption key is stored in the database and protected by the AOS and .NET Business Connector proxy accounts.

Security

In Enterprise Portal, Dynamics AX security is layered on top of, and depends on, the security of the underlying products and technologies, such as Windows SharePoint Services and IIS. For externally facing sites, communication security and firewall configurations are also important for helping to secure Enterprise Portal.

Enterprise Portal has two configurations in its site definition. The first, referred to as Microsoft Dynamics Public, allows Internet customers or prospective customers to view product catalogs, request customer accounts, and so on. The second, referred to as the Microsoft Dynamics Enterprise Portal, is the complete portal for self-service scenarios involving intranet or extranet users for authenticated employees, vendors, and customers.

The Microsoft Dynamics Public configuration has anonymous authentication enabled in both IIS and Windows SharePoint Services so that anyone on the Web can access it. To connect to Dynamics AX, it uses a built-in Dynamics AX user account named Guest. The Guest account is part of the Enterprise Portal Guest user group, which has limited access to Dynamics AX components necessary for the public site to function. The Enterprise Portal configuration has Integrated Windows authentication or basic authentication over Secure Sockets Layer (SSL) enabled in IIS and Windows SharePoint Services.

This secured site restricts access to users with Active Directory accounts who are configured as Dynamics AX users with Web site access enabled for that particular site by the Dynamics AX administrator. You use the User Relations dialog box (accessed from Administration\Setup) to configure users with an employee, vendor, or business relation, or a customer account and contact. Then you can grant them access to Enterprise Portal sites through Site groups for that Windows SharePoint Services Enterprise Portal site.

Both types of Enterprise Portal site use the .NET Business Connector proxy account to establish connections to the AOS. The Windows SharePoint Services application pool must be configured with a Windows domain user account, and this account must be specified as the Dynamics AX .NET Business Connector proxy account for both sites to function. After the connection is established, Enterprise Portal uses either *LogonAsGuest* or *LogonAs*, depending on the type of Enterprise Portal site the current user has access to, to activate the Dynamics AX security mechanism. Dynamics AX provides various means and methods to limit user access, such as placing restrictions on individual tables and fields, limiting the availability of application features through configuration keys, and controlling user-level security with security keys.

Enterprise Portal security is role based. This means that you can easily group tasks associated with a business function into a role, such as Sales or Consultant, and assign users to this role to give them the necessary permissions on the Dynamics AX objects to perform those tasks in Enterprise Portal. To allow users access to more functionality, you can assign them to more than one role.

The Enterprise Portal Configuration Wizard imports the predefined user group rights from the *Resources* node in the AOT. You can easily extend this set of roles by importing the user group permissions into the AOT under the *Resources* node. You assign a user to a role simply by adding the user to the corresponding user groups.

In addition to the Dynamics AX elements, Enterprise Portal includes Windows SharePoint Services lists and document libraries, which are secured with Windows SharePoint Services site groups. The Dynamics AX user groups play no role in controlling access to the Windows SharePoint Services lists and documents. For consistency and simplicity of the Enterprise Portal roles concept, however, a standard set of Windows SharePoint Services site groups provides access to a specific set of document libraries and lists when the site is created. You can add new roles by modifying the XML file in the AOT under the *Web Files* node. Based on their Windows SharePoint Services site group membership, Dynamics AX users are granted various levels of permission on these Windows SharePoint Services objects.

Chapter 8

Role Centers

In this chapter:

The objectives of this chapter are to:

- Introduce the Role Center.
- Provide insight into the framework and components of Role Centers.
- Offer a detailed look at the development and customization of Role Centers.

Introduction

A tremendous amount of information and functionality are available to people who work with Microsoft Dynamics AX. Role Centers have been developed to help users manage that information, enabling them to prioritize their tasks and make quick business decisions.

Role Centers are available in Enterprise Portal and the Dynamics AX client. The Role Center is the home page the user sees when he or she starts Dynamics AX or Enterprise Portal. The Role Center displayed is based on the user profile that the user is assigned to.

Each Role Center is made up of different Web parts that display job-specific business information and the Dynamics AX functionality that the person regularly uses. For example, the Role Center for a sales manager, the Dynamics AX persona Kevin, includes a list of key performance indicators (KPIs) that Kevin needs to see every day; a business overview that shows him KPI trends over time; a chart that shows him his sales pipeline; a list of Quick Links that take him directly to the forms, reports, and Web sites he uses regularly; and a list of alerts and work tasks that he needs to act on. The Web parts in Kevin's Role Center are (optionally) interactive, enabling him to drill down into the overview information he sees to get to the underlying data with a few mouse clicks. Figure 8-1 shows Kevin's Role Center.

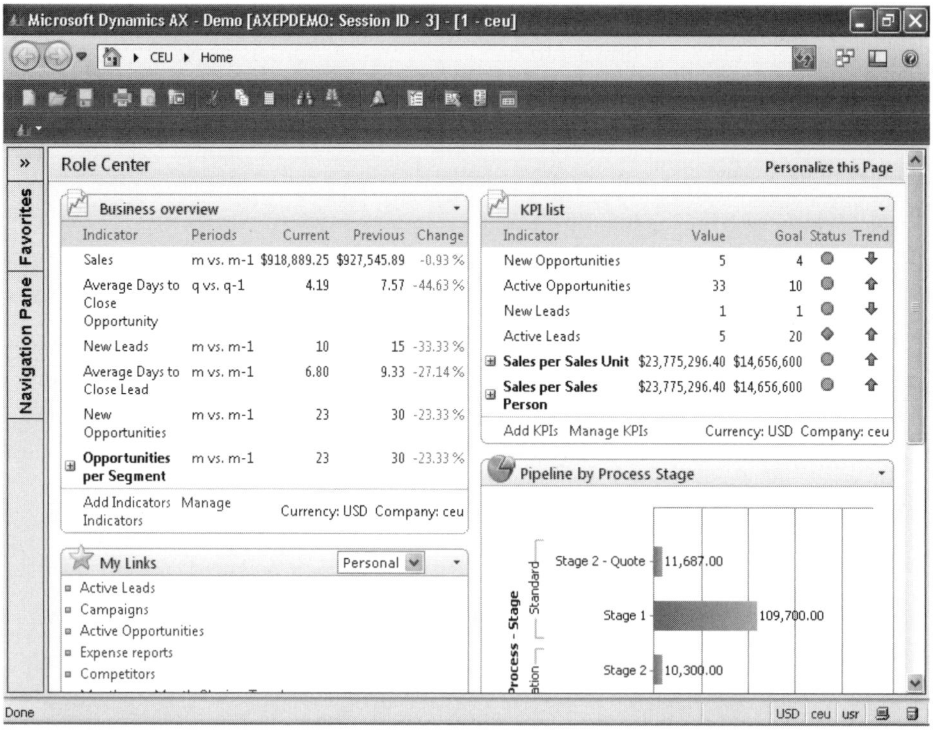

FIGURE 8-1 Example Role Center, for the Dynamics AX sales manager persona Kevin

Developers can create new Role Centers and customize the out-of-the-box content, predefined cubes, and analytical views that ship with Role Centers. Users can personalize the personal view of their Role Center to suit their day-to-day work.

This chapter describes Role Centers and the Role Center framework. It describes the process that a developer follows—and the building blocks that he or she has to work with—to customize an out-of-the box Role Center or to build a new one. The chapter concludes with a discussion of adding users to user profiles (Role Center authentication and authorization) and of security.

> **Note** This chapter assumes that you have installed Enterprise Portal and Role Centers. For more information on installing Enterprise Portal and Role Centers, see the Dynamics AX Implementation Guide. You can access that guide through the Using Dynamics AX site at *http://www.microsoft.com/Dynamics/AX/using/ax_installationinfo.mspx*.

Before we go into the details of Role Centers, let's take a look at some of the key benefits of using them. With Role Centers, users can do the following:

- **View business data at a glance.** Users can monitor and analyze business performance using actionable business intelligence, such as KPIs, charts, and reports directly in the Role Center. Having this information at their fingertips allows users to take action quickly and to drill down into details and transactions as necessary.

- **Boost productivity and improve effectiveness.** Role Centers provide a single, integrated view of the job-specific information and tasks employees need to make informed business decisions.
- **Prioritize their tasks.** Role Centers can help users keep critical tasks, projects, and orders on track with notifications and alerts initiated by automated workflows that are displayed in the Role Center.
- **Get up to speed quickly.** The familiar user interface offers intuitive navigation and makes it easy to find information, helping to minimize training time.
- **Personalize Role Centers.** Users can easily personalize Role Centers to fit their own unique work style and information needs.

Inside Role Centers

In this section, we take a brief tour of the underlying technology components that make up Role Centers. In subsequent sections, we discuss these components in detail.

Architecture

The Enterprise Portal framework forms the foundation for Role Centers; Role Center development takes place within this framework. (To read more about Enterprise Portal, see Chapter 7, "Enterprise Portal.") Windows SharePoint Services and Microsoft Office SharePoint Server form the Role Center front end, allowing developers and users to customize and personalize a Role Center. The Dynamics AX Reporting and Business Intelligence framework enables you to develop reports, KPIs, and other business intelligence that can appear in a Role Center. The Role Center framework itself consists of the following parts:

- User profiles
- Role Center Web parts, such as Cues, Quick Links, Business Overview, Dynamics Report Server Report, and Dynamics Unified Worklist
- Metadata store for Cues, Quick Links, and Business Overview Web parts, and user profiles in the AOT; and the import/export mechanism for Cues Quick Links, and user profiles
- Run-time style, navigation, and interaction adaptors for the client and Enterprise Portal, and run-time detection and rendering of Role Centers as the start page

Figure 7-2, in Chapter 7, shows the high-level architectural components of the Role Center.

The Enterprise Portal framework and the Reporting and Business Intelligence framework use .NET Business Connector to access the metadata stored in AOD files (represented by the Application Object Tree, or AOT) and the transactional data stored in the Dynamics AX database. The framework uses the ADOMD.NET data provider to get analytical data from OLAP.

Role Centers are built with Enterprise Portal and Reporting and Business Intelligence framework components in Windows SharePoint Services using ASP.NET. The same Role Center page is rendered with the appropriate themes and navigation based on the client platform (the Dynamics AX client or Enterprise Portal) on which it is hosted.

When a user accesses a Role Center through Enterprise Portal, the master page detects the user profile of the current users, retrieves the associated Role Center page for that user profile, and renders it in Enterprise Portal. A Role Center is just like any other Web part page in Windows SharePoint Services.

When a user accesses Dynamics AX through the client, a Web browser control that is hosted for the home tab displays the appropriate Role Center page from the Windows SharePoint Services site. The top and left navigation are stripped off the Web page, and a header with Role Center as the caption and a Personalize This Page link are added. The Dynamics AX client Role Center style sheets are applied so that the Role Center looks like other client user interface components. Any links in the Cue, Quick Links, and Dynamics Report Server Report Web parts point to client list pages or forms. The browser control detects the navigation event for these links and when clicked opens the respective client list page or form. If there are any hyperlinks that point to other Web pages, they open in a new browser window so that the client Role Center is never replaced with other pages in the Dynamics AX client.

Developing Role Centers

Developers can quickly customize Role Centers to add business-specific and industry-specific content, making Role Centers even more useful for businesses and the people who run them. In this section, we describe how to customize the Role Centers that ship with Dynamics AX 2009 and how to build a new one.

Customizing an Out-of-the-Box Role Center

Role Centers are based on the personas that represent the goals and behavior of a real group of Dynamics AX users. Each of the 33 persona-based Role Centers that ship with Dynamics AX 2009 can be deployed to customers with no additional changes as soon as setup tasks have been performed.

Tip You can see a full list of Role Centers, get an overview of the roles, and download details about the default information that is displayed for the role on the Using Microsoft Dynamics AX site at *http://www.microsoft.com/dynamics/ax/using/ax_rolecenterreference.mspx*.

As a developer or an administrator, you can also customize a Role Center for all users in a particular role. Users can further personalize their personal view of the Role Center. Other users associated with the Role Center don't see the customizations other users have made.

You can edit a Role Center page, just as you can any other page in Enterprise Portal. However, only the Role Center page associated with the current user's role is displayed. If you want to modify other Role Center pages, you must locate them directly in Windows SharePoint Services. You can see a list of Role Center pages at http://<server>/sites/DynamicsAx/Enterprise%20Portal/Forms/AllItems.aspx. You can also see the list of all available Role Centers under Administration\Setup\User Profiles. Just click the button View Role Center in the Dynamics AX client.

Role Center names begin with *RoleCenter*. The exception is the *EPDefaultRoleCenter* page, which is the Role Center displayed for users who are not assigned to a specific role. Click the page name to modify the page.

We explain how to customize the data underlying the Web parts in a Role Center in the upcoming "Role Center Web Parts" section.

Creating a New Role Center

In this section, we describe the high-level steps that developers and planners undertake when creating a new Role Center. For step-by-step instructions, see the Microsoft Dynamics AX 2009 SDK at *http://msdn.microsoft.com*.

The first step in creating a new Role Center is to identify the type of content you want to display in the Role Center, along with the layout of that content. If you need to display higher-level analytical information, you must create the KPIs and measures and dimensions in Microsoft SQL Server Analysis Services.

Note Measures and dimensions comprise the OLAP cubes that Analysis Services uses to contain the data you use to build KPIs and other analytical information. In Dynamics AX, *measures* are referred to as *indicators*. For a detailed description of OLAP cubes and Analysis Services, see MSDN.

The second step is to decide how the data is to be seen in the Role Center. For example, your team might decide that the data is to be displayed as a list of KPIs comparing current results with the target, and that it is displayed as a report. Or you might decide that the data should be displayed as a time comparison versus prior performance, in a chart.

The third step is developing the content. You can add a wealth of content to a Role Center, including Cues, Quick Links, Dynamics Report Server Report, Business Overview, and Dynamics Unified Worklist Web parts, KPIs, and other indicators. We discuss each content type in more depth later in this chapter.

The fourth step is to build the Role Center page in Enterprise Portal. You can create a Web part page in Enterprise Portal using any of the page templates available in Windows SharePoint Services. Just add the Role Center Web parts and set their properties to point to the right content, as described in the preceding steps.

Finally, you create the Web menu item pointing to the URL of the page you've just created. You mark the *HomePage* property of the Web menu item to *Yes* and assign this Web menu item as the Role Center in the user profile. You can read more about creating a user profile in the "User Profiles" section later in this chapter. Figure 8-2 shows the high-level flow of development activities for a Role Center.

Role Center Web Parts

Now that you have a high-level view of what Role Centers are, how they behave, and the basic development tasks that are involved in creating them, we'll tell you about the content—basically, the Role Center Web parts—that you can add to or customize in a Role Center.

Cues

A *cue* is a visual representation of invoices, purchase orders, accounts receivable, and so on. By providing greater visibility into the amount of work that needs to get done, a cue can help users prioritize their work. The Cues Web part mimics a pile of paper by visually representing each task as if it were lying on a desk. A Cue is not only a visual indicator; it acts as a shortcut that enables users to drill down into the list pages where they can take action.

Both developers and users can create Cues from any list page or form in the Dynamics AX client. To do so, define the filter that you want to apply, and save it as a Cue from the Advanced Filter folder (at Forms\List Pages) or directly from the list page. You can also perform more-complex tasks by defining the Cue so that it displays additional information. For example, you can add the sum of an invoice amount and a warning symbol to a Cue when a certain condition is met.

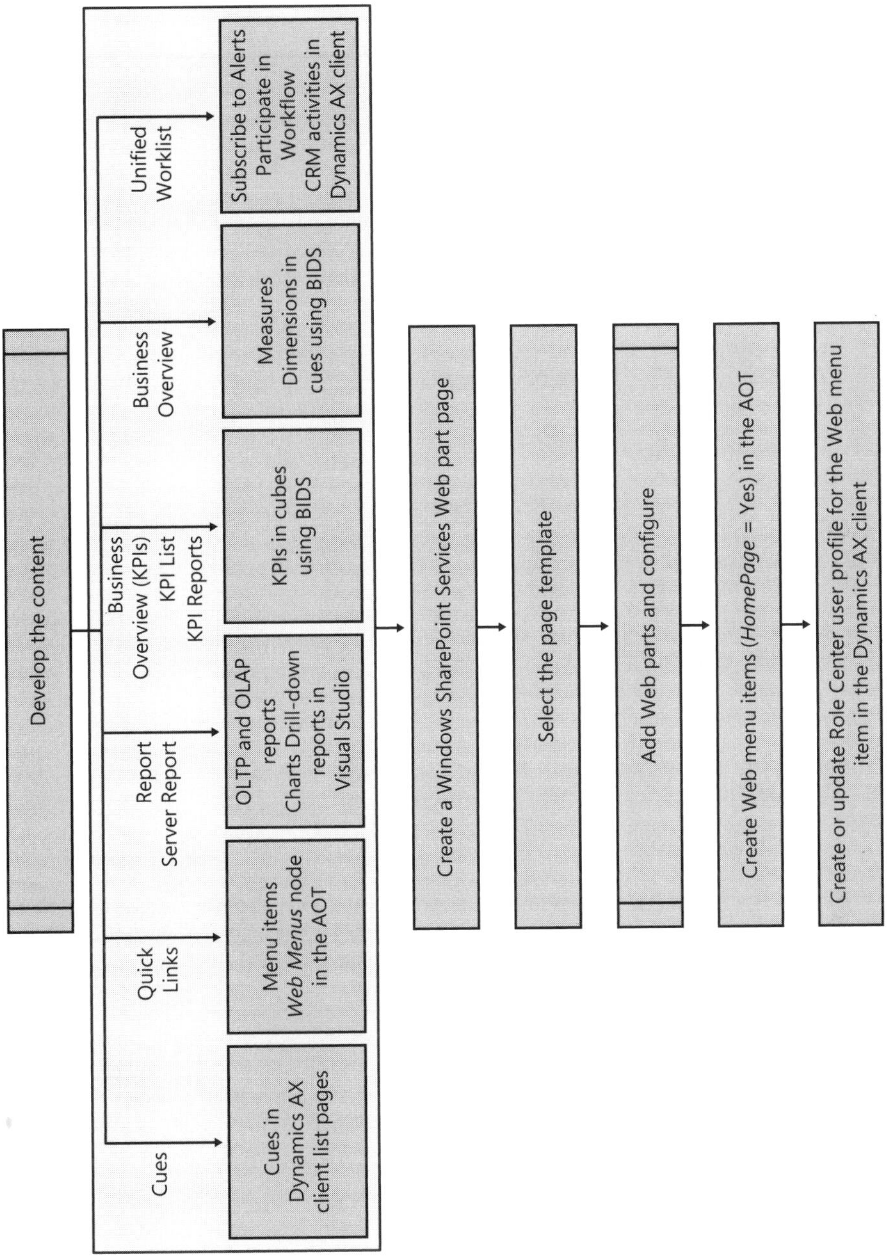

FIGURE 8-2 Role Center development flow

To define the filter, you can use the *SysQueryRangeUtil* class functions. Take, for example, the user persona Alicia. Imagine that you want to display all purchase orders where she is the order taker (this is a field on the Purchase Order form). In the filter, you set the order-taker field value equal to the user ID of the person currently logged on. The purchase orders are automatically filtered to display only those Alicia has taken.

Or imagine that the user persona April wants an indicator of how many vendor invoices are due for payment in the upcoming week because she pays invoices weekly. This indicator lets her know how many checks she needs to produce and allows her to plan her time accordingly. She can also drill down into the list of these vendors to initiate payment. The filter you use must allow April to define the date range so that whenever this filter is run, it displays the invoices for a particular week.

To meet these needs, the *SysQueryRangeUtil* class comes with a default set of filtering functions, such as *currentEmployeeId*, and many date functions. You can extend this class by creating your own methods and using them in the advanced filter. Here's an example.

```
Field - Order Taker , Criteria - (OrderTaker == currentEmployeeId())
Field - Date Opened, Criteria -(greaterThanDate(-8))
```

The information about Cues is stored in the *CuesQuery* and *CueQuerySecurity* tables.

A Cue stores the menu item from which it was created. So when the user clicks the Cue in the Dynamics AX client Role Center, the Cue returns to the list page or form that is linked to that menu item and then applies the filter.

When the Cue is displayed in Enterprise Portal, it gets the corresponding Enterprise Portal page from the *WebMenuItem* property of the menu item in the AOT and links to it; when the user clicks the Cue in Enterprise Portal, the Web page is displayed. If *WebMenuItem* is empty, the Cue is not linked to an Enterprise Portal page and just displays the Cue with information but without a link.

When creating a Cue, an administrator or developer can specify which user profiles can view it. Only users who belong to the profile and have access to the associated menu item (in the Dynamics AX client) or Web menu item (in Enterprise Portal) can view the Cue. Users who don't belong to the specified profiles or who don't have access to the menu item that the Cue is linked to can't view the Cue. Figure 8-3 shows the design-time and run-time rendering for Cues.

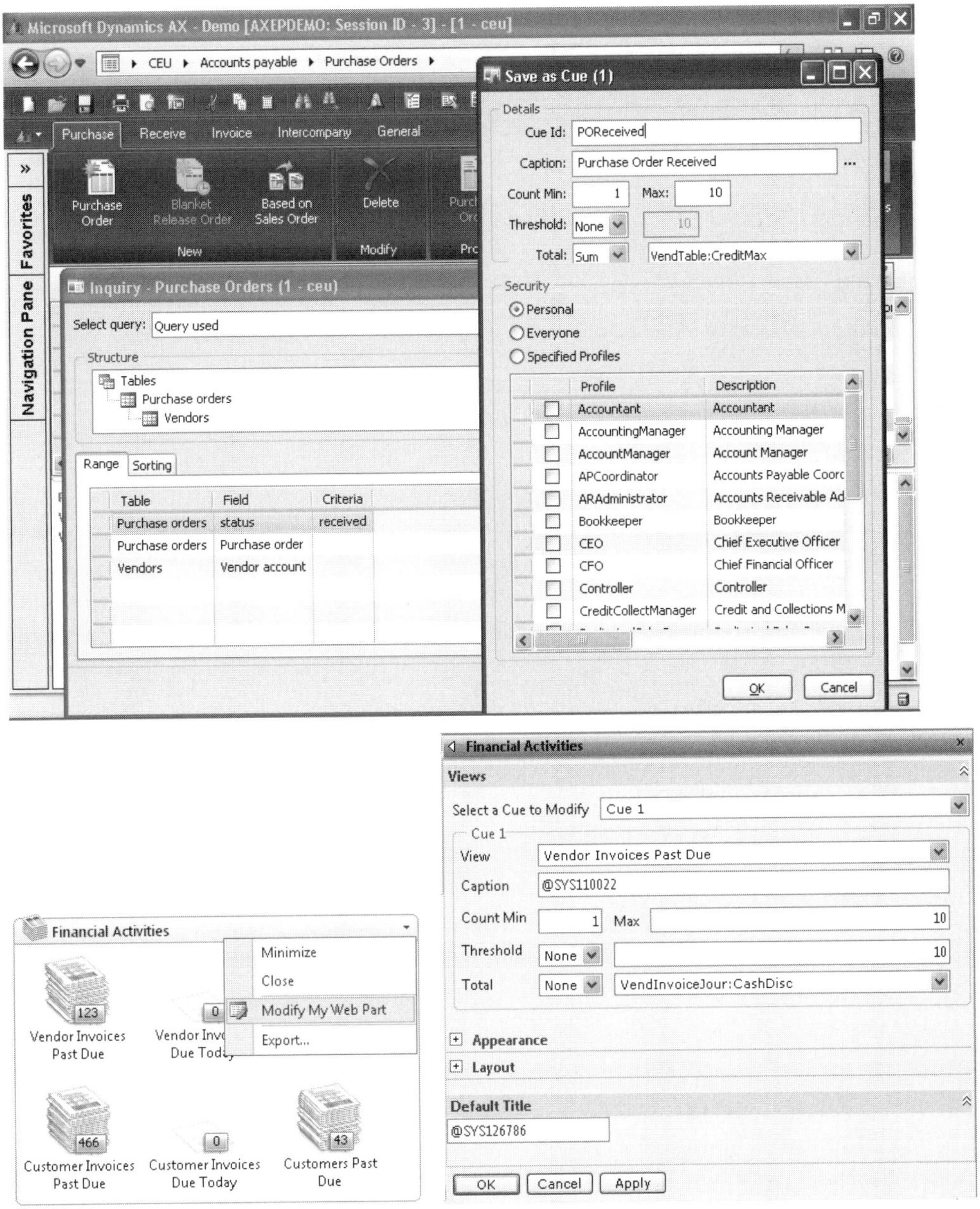

FIGURE 8-3 Creating and adding Cues to a Role Center

Quick Links

Quick Links is a Web part that displays a collection of links to Dynamics AX client list pages or forms, to Enterprise Portal Web pages, or to any Web URLs. Users can create shortcuts to their most frequently accessed forms, reports, pages and Web links, and organize them in one or more Quick Link Web parts in their Role Center.

Administrators or developers can create links that are common to all users in a profile. For developers and administrators, a drop-down menu to pick Shared or Personal mode is displayed. For users, only Personal mode is allowed, so this drop-down menu isn't displayed to them. Users can create only personal links, ones that are just for them.

Adding Quick Links The Add Links dialog box displays links from the main menu of the Dynamics AX client or from the Dynamics QuickLaunch Web part of Enterprise Portal. The desktop links are displayed in the Quick Links Web part only when the Role Center is rendered in the Dynamics AX client. These links are not displayed when the Role Center is displayed in Enterprise Portal. When you add a link to Enterprise Portal, you can specify whether or not it is displayed in the Dynamics AX client Role Center. If set to Yes, the Enterprise Portal link appears in both the Dynamics AX client and the Enterprise Portal Role Centers. If not set to Yes (checked), the link appears only when the Role Center is rendered in Enterprise Portal. The third type of link—that is, any Web URL—is displayed in both modes.

Maintaining Quick Links Quick Links are stored in the *SysQuickLinks* and *SysQuickLinksOrder* tables. A Quick Links Web Part stores the Quick Links group ID and default title label. The group ID is used to identify the links that need to be displayed from the *SysQuickLinks* table.

When a new Quick Links Web Part is added to the Role Center, it automatically adds a globally unique identifier (GUID) as the group ID. But you can rename the GUID to a readable string so that later you can manage these link groups (importing or exporting them, or deleting them) easily from the dialog box at Basic\Setup\Role Centers\Edit Cue Links. One or more Quick Links Web Parts can point to the same group ID and display the same set of links.

If a user removes the links or changes their order while in Personal mode, the links displayed to a different user in the same Web part are not affected. The links are security trimmed, so if a user doesn't have access to the links, they are not displayed in the Quick Links Web Part. The Manage Links dialog box displays all the links and their status, such as Hidden or No Access. Figure 8-4 shows the Quick Links design-time and run-time rendering.

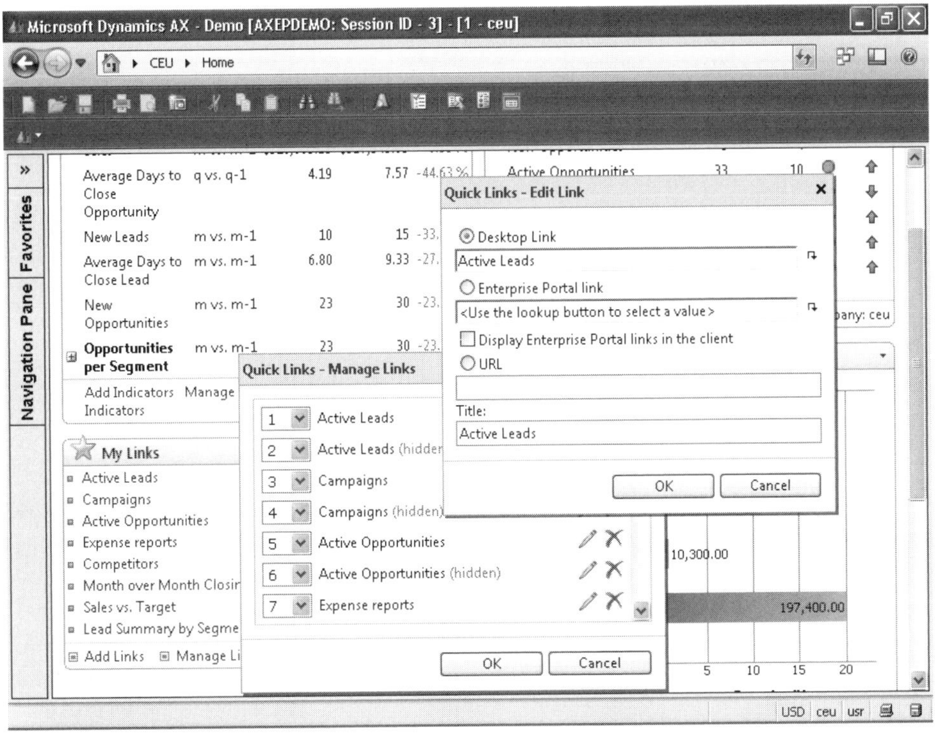

FIGURE 8-4 Quick Links

Business Overview

Key performance indicators (KPIs) are valuable to businesses, helping employees evaluate the progress made against measurable goals for key business metrics. Perhaps most useful is the ability for a business to compare a given KPI against a benchmark, helping managers assess the present state of the business compared with previous performance, say, during the preceding year. The Business Overview Web part shows the performance of one or more KPIs over an established time period, with the goal of helping users assess the present state of their business in comparison with a prior period.

The Business Overview Web part supports two modes of display: Business Overview and KPI List. In Business Overview mode, the Web part displays the indicator (e.g., Revenue), Time Periods (e.g., current quarter versus preceding quarter), and the Current and Previous values plus the changes in the values. The Business Overview mode is used for time comparison. In KPI List mode, the Web part displays the indicator (e.g., New Leads), Goal (e.g., 1), and Status and Trend; it is used for measuring progress toward a goal. In this section, we discuss the Business Overview Web part. We go into more depth about the KPI List Web Part later in this chapter.

You can customize and personalize the Business Overview Web part by using a predefined list of indicators and time periods for three roles: developers, administrators, and users. Developers can add more time periods and indicators to the Business Overview Web part. Users can further personalize this Web part and add or remove indicators according to their needs.

You can define each indicator to display the measure in detail in a given dimension and to be linked to a detailed report. In addition, you can configure the Business Overview Web part to display the indicators for the current company or for all companies in the organization, as well as the currency in which the amount indicators are displayed. Figure 8-5 shows the Business Overview Web part design-time and run-time rendering.

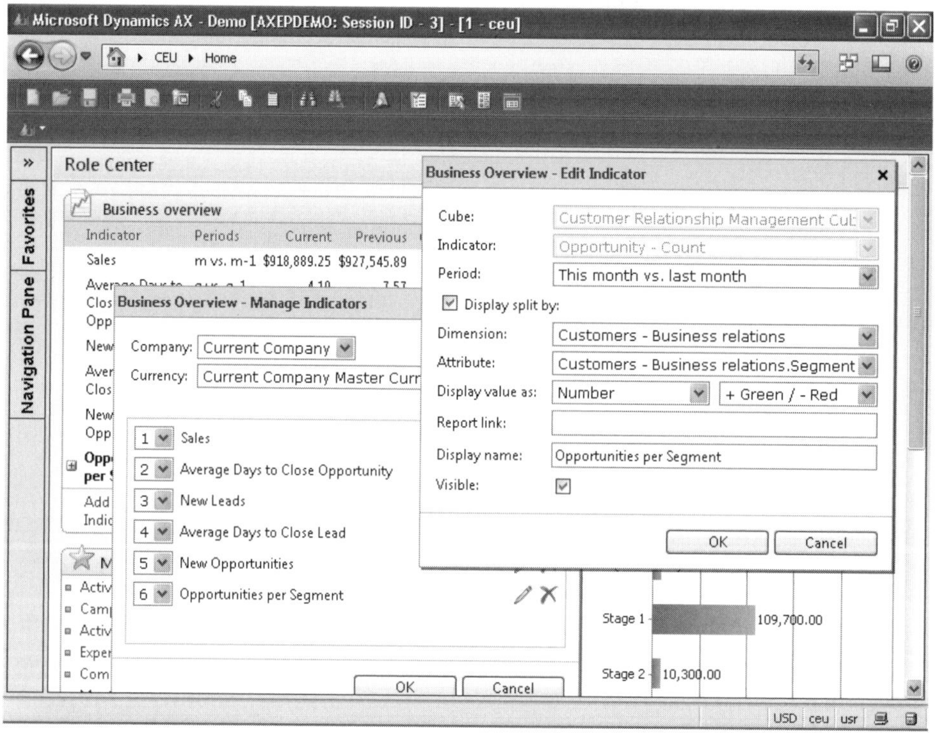

FIGURE 8-5 Business Overview Web part

Working with Measures Dynamics AX comes with a predefined list of indicators, including Goal, Status, and Trend expressions. As we mentioned earlier in the chapter, indicators are defined as *measures* in Analysis Services cubes. If you want to modify a measure or create a new one, you can use the Business Intelligence Development Studio (BIDS) tool that comes with Analysis Services. Details on modifying and creating measures are beyond the scope of this book. If you decide to modify or create a measure, please read the Microsoft Dynamics AX 2009 Business Intelligence Cube Reference Guide for guidance. The guide is available for download on the Using Microsoft Dynamics AX site at *www.http://microsoft.com/dynamics/ax/using.*

Working with Time Periods The Business Overview Web part comes with a list of predefined time periods—for example, This Month vs. Last Month, This Quarter vs. Last Quarter, and so on—that are used for comparison. Developers and administrators can extend this list through the Time Periods form: Administration/Setup/Business Analysis/OLAP/Time Periods. Figure 8-6 shows the Time Periods form.

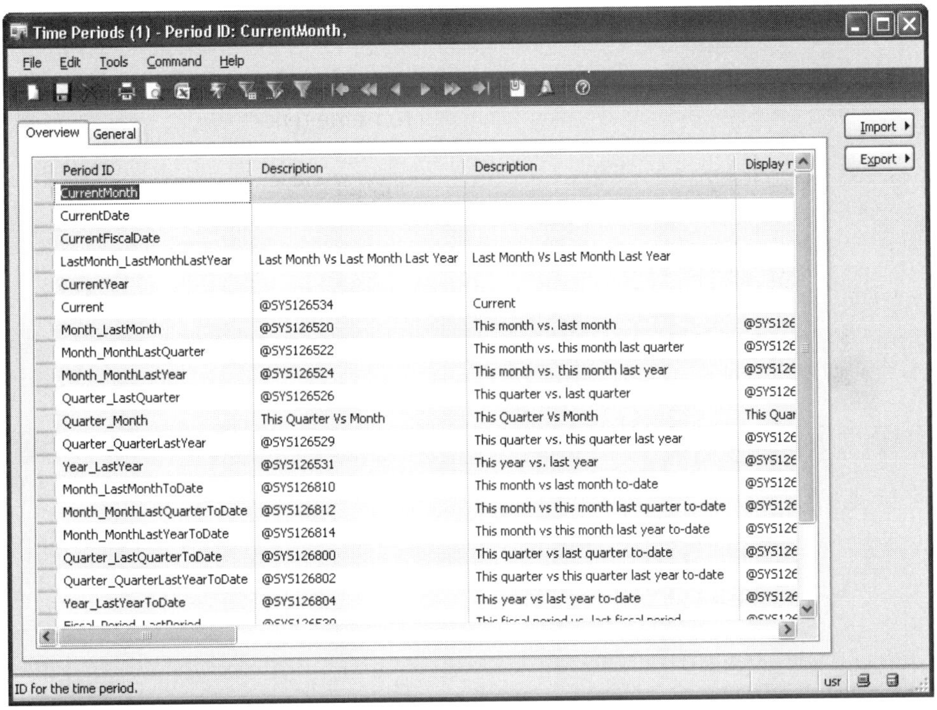

FIGURE 8-6 Time Periods Administration form

To add a new time period, add a new record to the Time Periods form and set the Period ID, Description, Display Name, Current Period MDX, and Previous Period MDX. You can also create an item as a template and use it in the Multidimensional Expressions (MDX) for the time period.

Note If you create template records, they won't be visible in the Business Overview Time Period drop-down menu. They are used only to enable the reuse of MDX across many time periods. For example, if you want to display an indicator comparing Last Month with Last Year Last Month, and if this time period setup isn't available out-of-the-box, you can add it. In the Time Periods form, create a new record and set the parameters as follows.

```
Period ID: LastMonth_LastMonthLastYear
Display Name: (m-1) vs (m-1)(y-1)
Current period MDX: (%CurrentMonth%).Lag(1)
Previous period MDX: (%CurrentMonth%).Lag(13)
Visible:Yes
```

The Current period and Previous period MDX in the preceding example use a template expression already created with the name *CurrentMonth*. Templates are a great way to simplify and reuse MDX. *%CurrentMonth%* refers to an entry on the General tab in the Time Periods form, where:

```
Period ID: CurrentMonth
Template MDX: STRTOMEMBER('[Time].[Years Quarters Months Weeks Days].[Months].&[' +
vba!format(vba![date](), 'yyyy-MM-01') + 'T00:00:00]')
Template:Yes
```

Business Overview Authentication The Business Overview Web part uses an Office Data Connection (.odc) file to connect to Analysis Services. By default, it uses /Sites/DynamicsAX/Data Connections/Dynamics AX.odc. You can change this to point to any .odc file using the Business Overview Web part Properties pane. By default, the Web part uses the current user authentication to connect to Analysis Services.

If you have Enterprise Portal and Role Centers installed on one machine and Analysis Services installed on another, you must enable Kerberos-constrained delegation to allow the authentication flow across machine boundaries for this multi-hop scenario. To learn more about Kerberos, refer to the "Kerberos Authentication" section later in this chapter. Alternatively, you can configure the .odc file to use the application pool's credential to connect to Analysis Services using NTLM, and use the user's alias for authorization.

The .odc file XML looks like this:

```
<xml id=docprops><o:DocumentProperties
  xmlns:o="urn:schemas-microsoft-com:office:office"
  xmlns="http://www.w3.org/TR/REC-html40">
  <o:Name>Data Connections/Dynamics AX.odc</o:Name>
</o:DocumentProperties>
</xml><xml id=msodc><odc:OfficeDataConnection
  xmlns:odc="urn:schemas-microsoft-com:office:odc"
  xmlns="http://www.w3.org/TR/REC-html40">
  <odc:Connection odc:Type="OLEDB">
   <odc:ConnectionString>Provider=MSOLAP.3;Integrated Security=SSPI;Persist Security
Info=True;Data Source=Server1;Initial Catalog=Dynamics AX</odc:ConnectionString>
   <odc:CommandType>Cube</odc:CommandType>
   <odc:CommandText></odc:CommandText>
  </odc:Connection>
</odc:OfficeDataConnection>
</xml>
```

If you're using Kerberos, you must modify this .odc file and append *;SSPI=Kerberos* to the *odc:ConnectionString* element. The result would look like this:

```
<odc:ConnectionString>Provider=MSOLAP.3;Integrated Security=SSPI;Persist Security
Info=True;Data Source=Server1;Initial Catalog=Dynamics AX;SSPI=Kerberos </odc:
ConnectionString>
```

To use the application's pool account for authentication and authorization to connect to Analysis Services, instead of the user's credentials, you must add the following element to the .odc file XML.

```
<odc:DynamicsConnectionAccount>AppPool</odc:DynamicsConnectionAccount>
```

Alternatively, if you want to connect to Analysis Services using the application's pool account instead of the user's credentials, but you still want to use the user's name for authorization, you must add the following element.

```
<odc:DynamicsConnectionAccount>AppPoolWithEffectiveUserName</odc:
DynamicsConnectionAccount>
```

Unified Worklist

The Dynamics Unified Worklist Web part in Role Centers keeps the work flowing between people by displaying all time-based information in one central place. The worklist allows users to take direct action on each item.

Dynamics AX has three different pieces of information—alerts, work items, and activities—that are time-based and assigned to a specific user. Combining and surfacing these pieces of information in a Unified Worklist reminds users of important information and tasks that await their action.

The Unified Worklist provides a flexible layout, allowing users to decide how to organize and display information. Users can configure the worklist to display at 100 percent or 50 percent width, depending on the layout. They can also decide whether to display, for example, all content or just Approvals and Tasks, Alerts, or Activities. The Unified Worklist also comes with a toolbar, which you can turn on or off, used to filter and group items. The Dynamics Unified Worklist Web part also comes into play when you are using the workflow infrastructure in Dynamics AX. Refer to Chapter 9, "Workflow in Dynamics AX," for further details. Figure 8-7 shows the Dynamics Unified Worklist Web part.

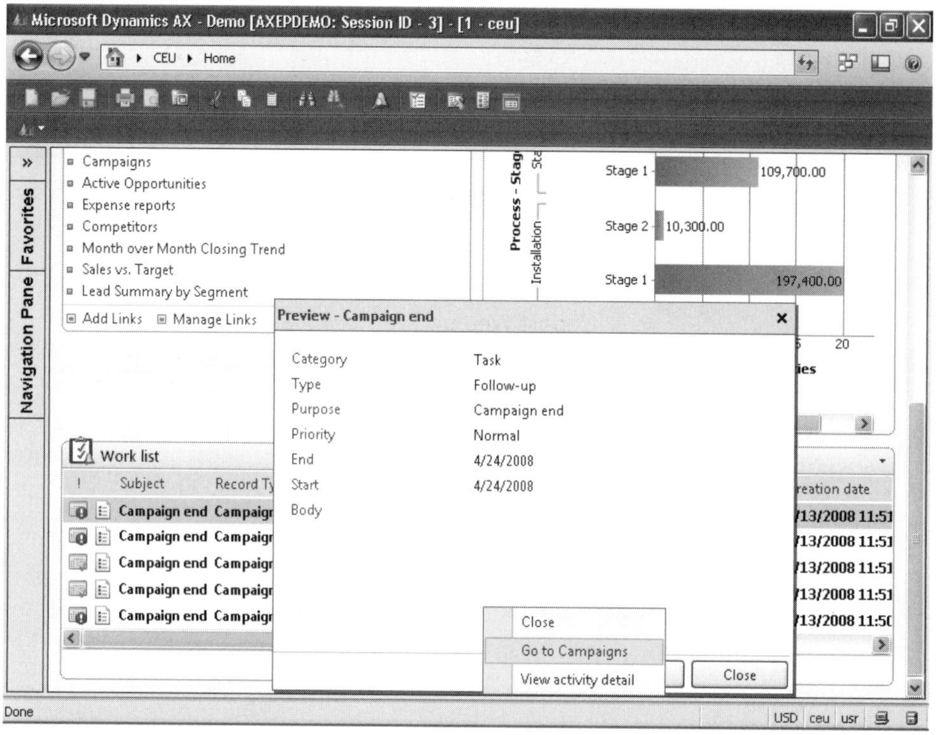

FIGURE 8-7 Dynamics Unified Worklist Web part

Reports

The Dynamics Report Server Report Web part is used to display Dynamics AX reports in Role Centers that are created in Microsoft SQL Server Reporting Services. Reporting Services reports provide rich designer tools and flexibility that allow you to create a variety of reports (summary reports, drill-down reports, charts, or details reports) and to get data from a transactional database or from Analysis Services cubes.

If you need to display or link to a report or chart in a Role Center, you must develop a Reporting Services report. The report has to connect to OLAP or OLTP to get the data.

To build the report, you use the Dynamics AX report development tools and then create a menu item in the AOT that is of *objecttype SQLReportLibraryReport* to refer to the report. Finally, you point the Dynamics Report Server Report Web part to the menu item you've created in the AOT, and the report renders in the Role Center.

The Dynamics Report Server Report Web part gets the report name and label from the menu item that it's pointing to. First, it verifies whether the user has access to the menu item. If so, the label of the menu item is set as the title for the Dynamics Report Server Report Web part. The Web part gets the company, the user's language setting in Dynamics AX, the Report Manager URL, and the root folder, and then it constructs the URL for rendering the report. It sets the constructed URL as the URL for an IFRAME (windowless inline floating frame) and then renders the IFRAME. The parameters that are set in the report Web part or passed through the query string are also set on the report.

The Dynamics Report Server Report Web part also supports the Microsoft Office SharePoint Server (MOSS) Filter consumer interface. So the report can be connected to a MOSS Filter, and parameters can then be passed from the Filter Web part to the Dynamics Report Server Report Web part.

If you need to pass parameters to the report through a query string, you can do so in the URL with this syntax:

```
<selector>.Parameters.<parameterName>=<parameterValue>
```

For example, in the Dynamics Report Server Report Web part, set the parameter selector value to *Report1*. And let's say the report has a parameter defined with the name *CashInflowvsCashOutflow_EndDate*. In that case, the query string is the one shown here.

```
http://axepdemo/sites/DynamicsAx/Enterprise%20Portal/RoleCenterCEO.
aspx?WCMP=CEU&Report1.Parameters.CashInflowvsCashOutflow_EndDate=01/01/2009
```

The underlying report can be opened in a new browser window by clicking Open in a New window link displayed in the Dynamics Report Server Report Web part menu. (The Web part menu is a drop-down menu located in the upper-right corner of the Web part.) Figure 8-8 shows the Dynamics Report Server Report Web part design-time and run-time rendering.

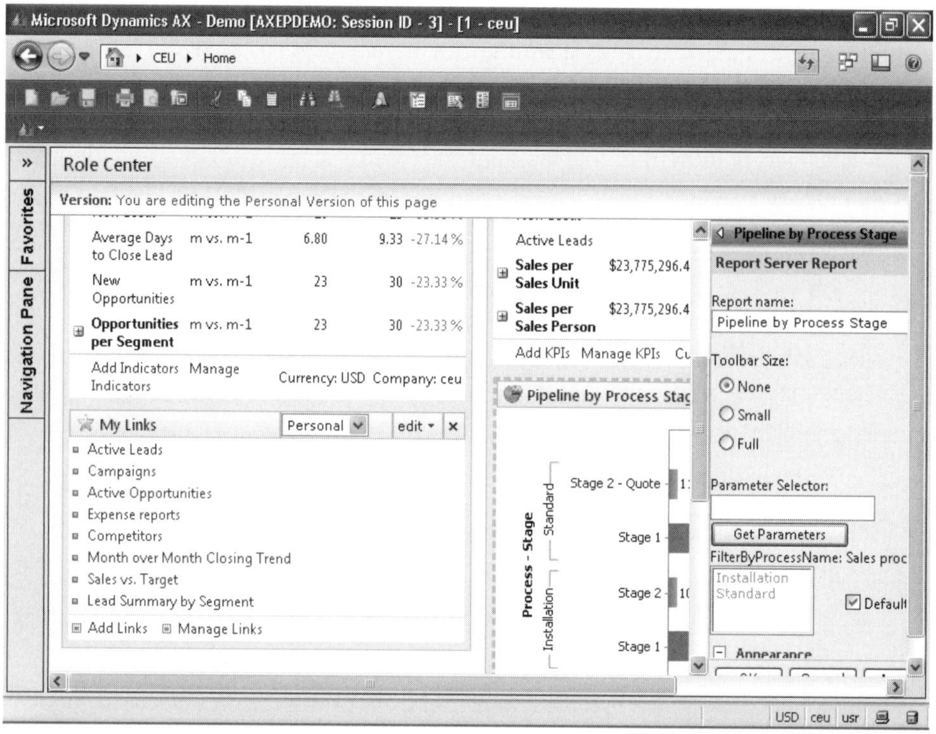

FIGURE 8-8 Dynamics Report Server Report Web part

Refer to the Chapter 11, "Reporting in Dynamics AX," for further details on creating and managing Dynamics AX reports.

Role Centers in MOSS

All the Role Centers work with Windows SharePoint Services, but two Role Centers light up with MOSS-specific components that come with the Microsoft Enterprise Client Access License (CAL): the CEO and the Sales and Marketing Executive Role Centers. If you have MOSS Enterprise, these Role Centers use the MOSS KPI list and filter instead of the equivalent functionality provided in the Windows SharePoint Services version of these Role Centers. (In the Windows SharePoint Services version of these Role Centers, that functionality is provided by Reporting Services.)

Using MOSS for these two Role Centers offers users some benefits:

- With MOSS, you can change the filter at a page level; in Windows SharePoint Services, you need to change the filter at the Web part level.
- MOSS uses a KPI list to display the KPIs, so the user can easily personalize the list to add or change KPIs. Windows SharePoint Services uses Reporting Services to display the same KPIs, so to change the KPIs you have to edit the report.

The other advantage of using MOSS is that you can use Excel Services or other business intelligence components; out-of-the-box Role Centers don't use Excel Services. Except for this one difference, all other built-in Role Centers behave the same way in Windows SharePoint Services and MOSS.

KPI Lists

MOSS has built-in features that allow you to manage and display KPI information in various ways. KPI indicators can be derived from a variety of sources: Windows SharePoint Services lists, Excel workbooks, data in Analysis Services, and manually entered information. For Role Centers, KPI information from Analysis Services can be used to quickly gauge the business access and compare the actual value to a target value. A KPI List Web Part is a navigation component that can be added to a Role Center, enabling the user to build an easy-to-use selection system for the KPIs needed most often. The KPI List Web Part provides a set of visual indicators to help the user be more aware of current performance status. The user can also build multiple lists, organizing KPIs based on personal criteria and requirements specific to a role-based view of the organization.

Filter Web Parts

Filters enable dashboards to be personalized by using shared parameters among Web parts on a dashboard. Adding a Dynamics Report Server Report Web part or KPI list to a Role Center renders a Reporting Services report or KPI. But what if you want to limit (or filter) the data displayed in the Web part based on a selection made at the page level? Filter Web parts that come with MOSS are handy for this situation.

For example, suppose you have two Dynamics Report Server Report Web parts on a page. Each displays a different view of company sales data. One displays a matrix report, and one shows a graph. It can be cumbersome to filter the date of each Web part separately, so a Date Filter Web part could be very helpful in assigning a date to each report at the same time.

Here's how to use a Filter Web part: after one or more Dynamics Report Server Report Web parts are added to the Web page, place a Date Filter Web part on the page and connect the Filter Web part to the Dynamics Report Server Report Web parts. This connection is necessary so that the Dynamics Report Server Report Web parts know when a date is entered into the Filter Web part. Once the Filter Web part is connected to the Dynamics Report Server Report Web parts, a date can be entered in the Filter Web part, and the reports are updated accordingly. You could connect the Filter Web part to Analysis Services cubes to get the possible values for the parameters. They could get the connection from the connected Web part or from an .odc file.

User Profiles

A user profile represents a persona in the customer model and a typical user of the system. It stores the default settings and configuration options of Role Centers for users of the same type.

Administrators create user profiles for each set of users who perform similar job functions. For example, Accounts Receivable Clerk is a job function or a typical user function—a persona—and in a given company, any number of users could perform this job function. The administrator can create one user profile for the Accounts Receivable Clerk persona, assign a Role Center to that user profile (a Web menu item of type URL with the *HomePage* property set to Yes) and add the users who perform the Accounts Receivable Clerk job to that user profile.

Associating Users with User Profiles

A system administrator assigns the user to a user profile in either the User form (Administration\Common Forms\Users) or in the User Profiles form (Administration\Setup\User Profiles). A user can be assigned to the same profile in all companies, to different user profiles in different companies, or to no profile.

When the user logs on to the system, the corresponding Role Center is displayed, based on the user's current company and user profile. If the user changes the company in the business application, the Role Center for that company for that user is displayed. If a user isn't associated with any user profile, the default Role Center is displayed. You can set which Role Center page should be used as the default Role Center in the User Profiles form in the Dynamics AX client.

You can also copy the user profiles from one system to another by exporting one or more of the user profiles to an XML file in the file system or to the AOT. When you export the user profile to the AOT, it creates a node under AOT\Resources with the name Profile_<ProfileID>. You can then export this as an .xpo file. On the other machine, you can import directly from the file system or from the AOT.

The user profiles that come with Dynamics AX are stored under AOT\Resources. Dynamics AX imports these user profiles from the AOT into your system during the Initialize Role Center Profiles step of the installation process. If you skipped this step, you can always initialize it from Basic\Role Center\Initialize Role Center Profiles.

Kerberos Authentication

Dynamics AX uses Integrated Windows authentication to authenticate users. When a user logs on to a Windows desktop and then uses the Dynamics AX client application or Enterprise Portal, that user's Windows authentication is used automatically to authenticate and authorize the user without prompting for the user's credential again.

Integrated Windows authentication can use either NTLM or Kerberos authentication methods. The authentication method could also be configured as Negotiate, which is a wrapper for Kerberos and NTLM that allows the client application to select the most appropriate security support provider for the situation.

When the user accesses a Web page, Internet Information Services (IIS) sends the *NTAuthenticationProvider* configuration (one or more of Negotiate, Kerberos, and NTLM) for that Web site from the *IISMetabase* as a *WWW-Authenticate* header. For example, if *Negotiate,NTLM* is configured as *NTAuthenticationProvider*, the client negotiates with the server to determine whether to use Kerberos or NTLM for authentication. If the client doesn't support the Negotiate method, the client uses NTLM.

With NTLM, the user name and password (credentials) are hashed before being sent across the network. When you enable NTLM, the client browser proves its knowledge of the password through a cryptographic exchange with your Web server that involves hashing. So although the Web server could use this information to authenticate the user and access the resources that are available on the Web server, it can't act on behalf of the user and access resources in other machines.

NTLM works fine for regular Enterprise Portal pages because the resources it accesses are all on the same Web server and it uses a trusted account to connect to the Application Object Server (AOS). The AOS doesn't use the user's credential to access the transactional database.

As mentioned earlier, Role Centers are powered by Enterprise Portal and use Analysis Services and Reporting Services components. If Analysis Services and Reporting Services are installed on the same box as the Web server, NTLM is enough. But if these components are installed on different machines than the Web server, NTLM doesn't work—because Analysis Services and Reporting Services require user credentials to authenticate and authorize them. When a user authenticates to a Web server and that Web server then needs to impersonate the user against another service on a different machine, the user's authentication ticket is "hopping" across two services. To establish a session with the second server (Analysis Services or Reporting Services), the primary server (Web) must be authenticated on behalf of the client's user account and authority level. In scenarios where there is a double hop, NTLM doesn't work. You have to use Kerberos authentication.

Kerberos authentication uses tickets that are encrypted and decrypted by secret keys and don't contain user passwords. These tickets are requested and delivered in Kerberos messages. Two types of tickets are used: ticket-granting tickets and service tickets. A ticket-granting ticket is issued for a specific client and can be reused by the client in requests for additional service tickets for the same service. Each service ticket issued by the ticket-granting service is for a specific service on a specific host computer.

The Kerberos protocol includes a mechanism called *delegation of authentication*. When this mechanism is used, the client (the requesting service) delegates authentication to a second service by informing the Key Distribution Center that the second service is authorized to act on behalf of a specified Kerberos security principal. The second service can then delegate authentication to a third service.

Administrators could also constrain this delegation to specify and enforce application trust boundaries by limiting the scope in which application services can act on a user's behalf. This flexibility to constrain a service's authorization rights helps improve application security design by reducing the opportunities for compromise by untrusted services.

For more information on setting up Kerberos delegation, see the white paper "Configuring Kerberos Authentication with Role Centers," available for download on the Using Microsoft Dynamics AX site at *www.http://microsoft.com/dynamics/ax/using*.

Security

Role Centers have four levels of security. Two are at the back end: transactional databases (OLTP) and cubes in Analysis Services (OLAP); two are at the front end (Windows SharePoint Services and Reporting Services).

Figure 8-9 shows the Role Center security configuration options you can set, depending on your usage and deployment topology.

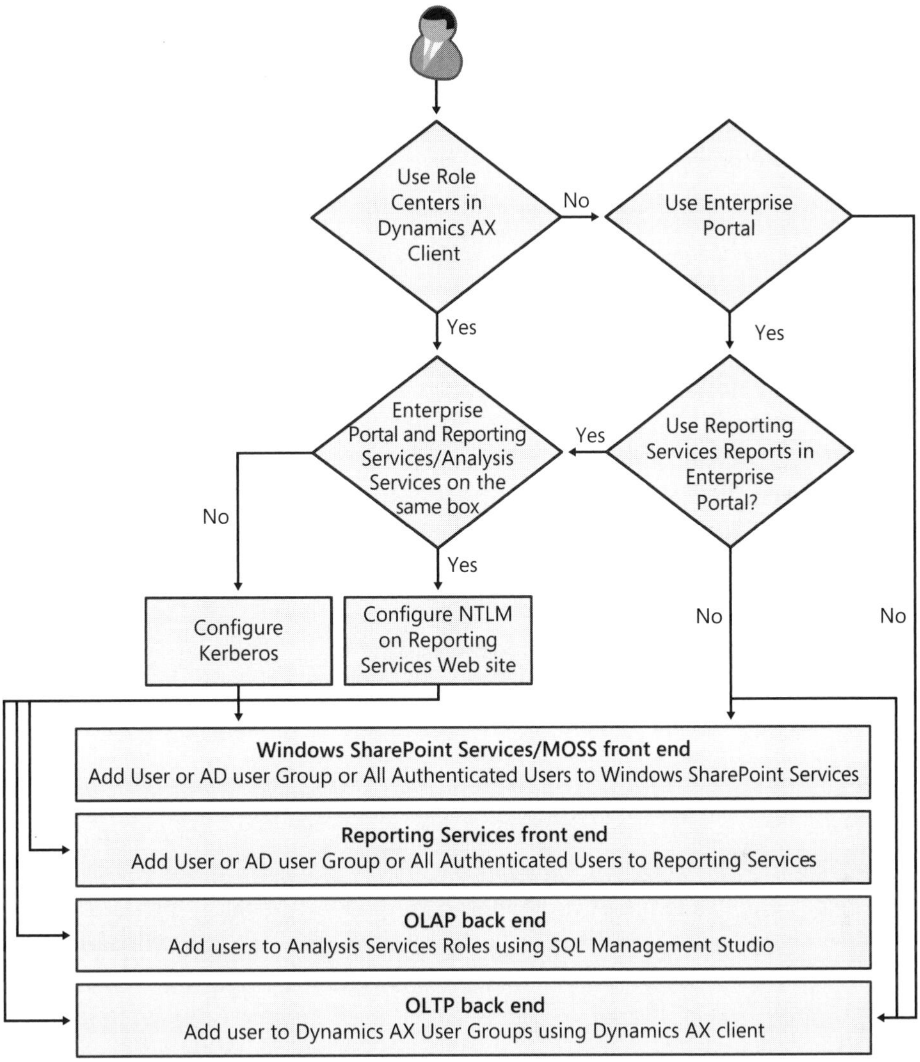

FIGURE 8-9 Role Center security configuration

For the OLTP system, the user must have access to Dynamics AX. The user's Active Directory account is added to the appropriate user groups in Dynamics AX. At a minimum, the user must be a member of EP_Int, an out-of-the-box Enterprise Portal user group, or have equivalent permission through other groups. EP_Int controls the user's access level to all Dynamics AX content, such as tables, rows, Web content, Web menu items, and Web modules, and it is secured through security keys, record level security (RLS), and the Trust Policy file (TPF).

If the Role Center displays content from Analysis Services cubes, the user must be granted permission in Analysis Services. A number of default Analysis Services roles are created in the Dynamics AX Analysis Database. You can use one of these roles or create your own, and add either the individual Analysis Database user account or user groups to these roles. Using Analysis Database user groups simplifies the user administration task in Analysis Services, and the groups can be reused for granting permission in Windows SharePoint Services and Reporting Services later. So essentially you use Dynamics AX user groups to secure Dynamics AX OLTP content, and Analysis Database groups for securing Windows SharePoint Services, Analysis Services, and Reporting Services.

The user must also have permission to view the Enterprise Portal site used for Role Centers. The permissions for this site control access to the Web site and its document libraries, lists, and pages. At a minimum, the user must have read permission. The Windows SharePoint Services site-level permission doesn't affect the user's access level to Dynamics AX content. A user who has only read permission on the Windows SharePoint Services site can create and edit records if he or she has write access to content through a Dynamics AX user group. So if you're planning to use Windows SharePoint Services document management and collaboration functionality, you need to grant specific permission to users. You can add an individual Analysis Database user account or user groups and grant specific Windows SharePoint Services permissions. If you're going to use the site just for Role Centers and will use Enterprise Portal for accessing Dynamics AX content, adding the All Authenticated Users group and giving the members read permission is good enough.

Finally, the user must have permission to view the reports in Reporting Services. The Reporting Services user groups control access to the Reporting Services Web sites and adding, modifying, and designing reports. At a minimum, the user must have browse permission. The permission level granted in Reporting Services doesn't affect the OLTP or OLAP access level. It only controls what reports the user can see and update in Reporting Services. If you plan to use other Reporting Services functionality, such as allowing users to publish reports, you need to grant specific permission to users. You can add an individual Analysis Database user account or user groups and grant specific Reporting Services permissions. If you're going to use the site just for Role Centers and Enterprise Portal for displaying reports, adding the All Authenticated Users group and giving the members browse permission is sufficient.

Chapter 9

Workflow in Dynamics AX

In this chapter:

The objectives of this chapter are to:

- Explain what workflow is and what it's designed to do, how it works, and why it's architected the way it is in Microsoft Dynamics AX 2009.
- Provide an overview of the most useful workflow concepts from a development perspective.
- Explain how to implement the artifacts that are required to build a workflow template.

Introduction

Very few of us would deny the importance or significance of the *processes* that drive the businesses and organizations that we work for and interact with on a daily basis. *Business processes* represent the key activities that, when carried out, are meant to achieve a specific goal of value to the business or organization:

- Think of a manufacturing operation in which business process activities include the initiation, design, development, quality assurance testing, and delivery of a saleable (and hopefully profitable) range of goods.
- Think of sales process activities for manufactured items, including marketing, locating prospects, providing quotes, converting quotes to orders and prospects to customers, shipping the product, invoicing, and obtaining payment.
- Finally, think about some of the supporting business processes that are concerned with hiring new employees and managing employee expenses, which contribute to the business or organization in tangible ways.

Viewing activities in terms of the business processes that encompass them affords businesses and organizations the opportunity to systematically define, design, execute, evaluate, and improve the way that these activities are performed. This systematic approach is extremely valuable, even critical, given that today's businesses and organizations have to react to the increasingly rapid rate of change we're witnessing in business and industry, and the ever-expanding influence of globalization.

Enterprise resource planning (ERP) suites, such as Dynamics AX, exist to automate business processes and to provide the capability to adapt these processes to the specific needs of businesses and organizations over time. Before Dynamics AX 2009, no standard workflow infrastructure existed, and each company had to write specific business logic to implement everyday activities, such as approvals. The Dynamics AX 2009 release includes a built-in workflow infrastructure precisely to make it easier for businesses and organizations to automate and manage business processes.

Dynamics AX 2009 Workflow Infrastructure

Fundamentally, workflows consist of one or more workflow activities that represent the items of work to be completed. Additionally, the concept of flows that connect the activities and govern the sequence of execution (referred to as the *structure* of a workflow) is key. The behavior of workflows is determined by their type. Figure 9-1 illustrates the major types of workflow and identifies where the emphasis of the workflow infrastructure is in Dynamics AX 2009.

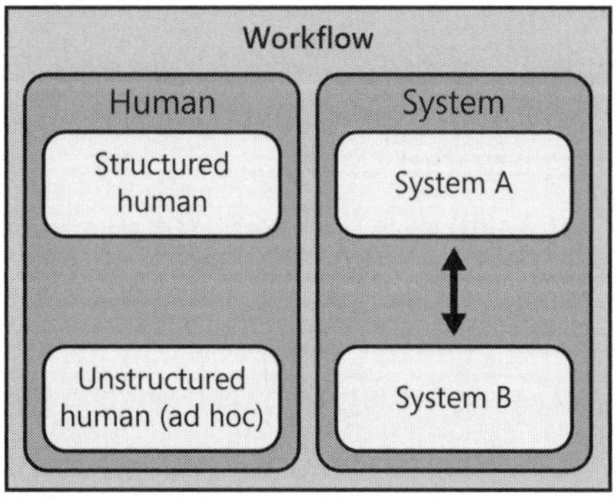

FIGURE 9-1 Major types of workflow

A major distinction exists between *human workflows* and *system workflows*. (For more information, see the following "Types of Workflow" sidebar.) Workflow in Dynamics AX 2009 is primarily designed to support structured human workflows. The structured human workflows that are shipped with the product include expense approval, requisition review and approval, and the approval of financial journals. Whereas the built-in workflows focus on structured human workflows that obtain *approvals*, you can also create workflows that contain tasks for humans to complete or a mixture of structured and unstructured tasks along with an approval. Customers, partners, and independent software vendors (ISVs) can create additional workflows to supplement those in the product. The workflows included in Dynamics AX 2009 will be augmented in future releases.

Types of Workflow

Two major types of workflow exist: human and system. In this sidebar, we look at some of the basic differences between the two types.

Human Workflows

A key attribute of human workflows is that *people* are involved in the workflow as it executes; in other words, human workflows are generally interactive (although a human workflow might contain activities that are noninteractive). Most often, the interaction takes the form of responding to and taking an action of some kind, such as approving or rejecting. Human workflows can be further subdivided into structured and unstructured types. Structured human workflows are used for processes in which execution needs to be repeatable and consistent over time. Structure is important, because to improve a business process, you must have a way to measure the performance of the workflows that are executed to automate that business process. If a workflow isn't structured for repeatability and consistency, you are going to have a difficult time identifying what to improve. Examples of structured human workflows include expense approval and purchase requisition processing.

Unstructured human workflows differ from structured ones in that the exact structure doesn't have to be defined up front—but it should be possible to easily establish and assign to the required people. An example of an unstructured human workflow is reviewing a document, where the participants and the type of approval required are decided just before the workflow is started. This variant of human workflow is therefore less useful when it comes to analysis for process improvement, because each unstructured workflow might behave differently, depending on how it is used, but it does help coordinate human activities.

System Workflows

System workflows are noninteractive workflows that automate a process that spans multiple systems, for example, transferring an order from one system to another. Generally, such workflows are structured because they need to be consistently repeatable.

In reality, you often need to combine human and system workflows to implement a given business process. For example, expense reports need to be approved, and the expense lines need to be posted after the approval.

> **Note** The main difference between *business processes* and *workflows* (as these terms are often used interchangeably) is their scope, level of abstraction, and purpose. Business processes represent the broad set of activities that a business or organization needs to carry out, and their interrelationships. Business processes are implementation independent and can combine manual as well as automated activities. Workflows are the automated parts of a business process that coordinate various human or system (or both) activities to achieve a particular outcome, and they are implementation specific. Therefore, workflows are used to implement parts of a business process.

Because existing Dynamics AX modules use approvals extensively, the workflow infrastructure in Dynamics AX 2009 is primarily intended to support structured human workflows. Focusing on this type of workflow lays the groundwork for enabling businesses and organization to more easily automate, analyze, and improve high-volume workflows across their ERP system.

Each structured human workflow in Dynamics AX 2009 acts on a single document type. The reason for this is that data is the key currency of ERP systems (think of the broad categories of data that exist in an ERP system: master data, transaction data, and reference data), and processes that operate within those systems are largely data-driven.

Here are some of the key tasks that you can do with structured human workflows in Dynamics AX 2009:

- Define the activities that need to take place based on the business process that is being automated.
- Sequence tasks, approvals, and subworkflows to reflect the order in which activities need to be completed in a business or an organization.
- Set up a condition that is used to determine which workflow to use in a given situation.
- Decide how to assign the activity to people.
- Specify the text that is displayed in the user interface for the various activities to help people understand what they need to do.
- Define a set of outcomes for an activity that someone can select from.
- Select which notifications to send, when to send the notifications, and who should receive the notifications.
- Establish how a workflow should be escalated if there is no timely response to an activity.

Four types of users interact with the workflow infrastructure in Dynamics AX 2009:

- Business users
- Developers
- Administrators
- End users (referred to as "users" in this book)

Business users and developers are primarily responsible for defining, designing, and developing workflows. Administrators and users interact with workflows that are executing.

- **Business users** understand the objectives of the business or organization within which they operate to the degree that they can envision how best to structure the various activities within their areas of responsibility. Business users therefore configure workflows that have already been implemented and work with developers to enable other modules or create new workflow templates in existing modules.
- **Developers** work with the business users to design and implement any underlying code that is required to support workflows that are being developed.
- **Administrators** are responsible for setting up and maintaining the development and production environments, for ensuring that the workflow infrastructure is configured correctly, for monitoring workflows as they execute, and for taking actions that are needed to resolve any issues with workflows.
- **Users** interact with workflows when needed, including taking a particular action (such as approving or rejecting), entering comments, viewing workflow history, and so on.

Windows Workflow Foundation

There is a relationship between the workflow infrastructure in Dynamics AX 2009 and Windows Workflow Foundation, which is part of the .NET Framework 3.5. Windows Workflow Foundation provides many fundamental capabilities that are used by the workflow infrastructure in Dynamics AX 2009. As a low-level infrastructure component, however, Windows Workflow Foundation has no direct awareness of or integration with Dynamics AX 2009. In Figure 9-2, the workflow infrastructure (labeled A) is an abstraction layer that sits above Windows Workflow Foundation (labeled B) and allows workflows that are specific to Dynamics AX to be designed, implemented, and configured in Dynamics AX 2009 and then executed by using Windows Workflow Foundation.

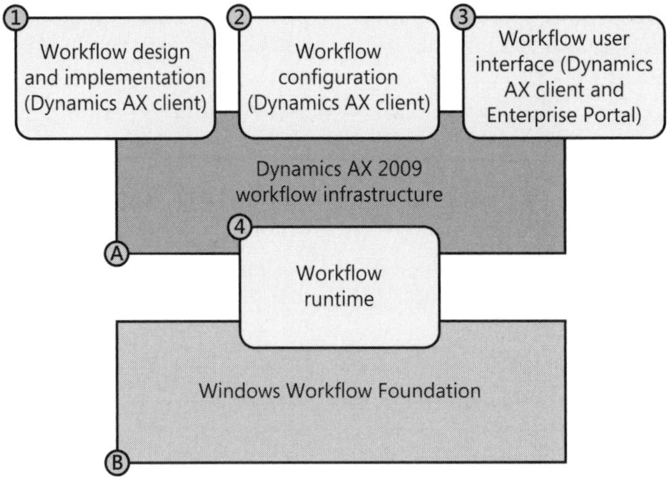

FIGURE 9-2 Relationship between the Dynamics AX 2009 workflow infrastructure and Windows Workflow Foundation

In the following list, each numbered item refers to the corresponding part of Figure 9-2.

1. The developer designs and implements workflow elements and business logic in the Application Object Tree (AOT).
2. The business user configures workflows in the Dynamics AX 2009 client.
3. The workflow runtime bridges both the Dynamics AX 2009 workflow infrastructure and Windows Workflow Foundation; it instantiates and then executes workflow configurations. (The administrator manages the runtime environments.)
4. Users interact with workflow user interface controls both in the Dynamics AX 2009 client and in Enterprise Portal.

Automating Business Processes

You can use the Dynamics AX 2009 workflow infrastructure to automate aspects of a business process that are part of a larger business process automation effort. There is no single, correct approach to this undertaking, but at a high level, you can follow the steps listed here to figure out and understand your existing business processes, then to determine how these business processes should function, and finally to automate them by using workflow.

1. Map out existing business processes. This effort is often referred to as developing the *as-is* model.
2. Analyze the as-is model to determine whether obvious improvements can be made to existing processes; these improvements are represented in another business process model, which is often referred to as the *to-be* model.

3. Design the way in which you're going to implement the to-be business process model—or the changes to the as-is model suggested by the to-be model. In this step, you might decide which parts of the to-be business process need to be automated with workflow and which parts should remain manual.
4. For the parts of the business process model in which workflow is going to be used—and for the parts you want to automate—define the workflow document and design one or more workflows. This step centers on the workflow document that the workflow will act over.
5. The developer implements the workflows.
6. The business user configures and enables the workflows, causing workflow instances to be created when a record for the workflow document is submitted.

The major advantage of the workflow infrastructure in Dynamics AX 2009 is that it provides a significant amount of functionality out of the box, meaning that custom workflows don't have to be written. Businesses and organizations will have more time to focus on *improving* their processes instead of writing and rewriting business logic. Additionally, the Dynamics AX 2009 workflow is continually being enhanced in response to feedback from customers, partners, and ISVs to provide even more value in subsequent releases, making the investment in workflow increasingly valuable over time.

Workflow from a Developer's Perspective

From your perspective as a Dynamics AX developer, workflow is something that you work with to help the users in your business or organization in their efforts to improve efficiency. The ultimate goal for workflow in Dynamics AX 2009 is to make it as easy as possible for business users to fully configure workflows themselves, freeing developers to work on other activities. Currently, developers and business users work together to create and customize workflows, which consumes time and resources for both parties.

Key Workflow Concepts

As a Dynamics AX developer, you need to understand a number of key concepts to successfully help business users implement workflows.

Workflow Document and Workflow Document Class

The workflow document, sometimes referred to as the Business Document, is the focal point for workflows in Dynamics AX 2009. Every workflow template and every workflow element must reference a workflow document because it provides the data context for the workflow. A workflow document is an AOT query supplemented by a class in the AOT (referred to as the *workflow document class*). The term *workflow document* is used instead of *query* because it more accurately portrays what the workflow is operating on. A query can reference multiple data sources and isn't constrained to a single table. In fact, a query can reference data sources hierarchically. However, if there are multiple data sources within a query, the first data source is considered the *primary* or *root* one.

> **Note** The workflow document and workflow document class are located in the AOT in the Dynamics AX 2009 client.

Workflow in Dynamics AX 2009 incorporates the use of an expression builder to enable conditions to be defined that control the behavior of an executing workflow. The expression builder uses the workflow document to enumerate all the fields that can be referenced in conditions. Calculated fields are not supported on queries in Dynamics AX 2009. Therefore, to make derived data available within conditions, you add *parm* methods to the workflow document class, into which X++ code can be introduced to produce the derived data. The workflow document then returns the fields from the underlying query plus the data generated by the *parm* methods.

> **Note** Referencing a workflow document from the workflow template and elements might be standardized in the future if it becomes possible to obtain derived data from the underlying query itself.

Workflow Categories

Workflow categories determine whether a workflow template is associated to a specific module. (Without these categories, you could see all workflows in the context of every module in Dynamics AX 2009.) For example, a workflow category named *ExpenseManagement*, which is mapped to the Expense Management module, comes with Dynamics AX 2009. All workflows associated to this module are visible in the Dynamics AX 2009 client within the Expense Management module. If you add a new module to Dynamics AX 2009, you must create a new module and then a new workflow category that references that module.

> **Note** The workflow categories are located in the AOT in the Dynamics AX 2009 client.

Workflow Templates

The workflow template is the primary building block used to create workflows. The developer defines the workflow template in AOT\Workflow\Workflow Templates. Defining the workflow template involves setting the various properties (including workflow document and workflow category). The business user later references this workflow template when creating a workflow configuration.

> **Note** The workflow templates are located in the AOT in the Dynamics AX 2009 client.

Event Handlers

Event handlers are well-defined integration points that enable you to execute application-specific business logic during workflow execution. Workflow events are exposed at the workflow level and the workflow element level. For more information about event handlers, including where they are used, see *http://msdn.microsoft.com/en-us/library/cc588240.aspx*.

> **Note** The event handlers are located in the AOT in the Dynamics AX 2009 client.

Menu Items

Workflow in Dynamics AX 2009 uses both display and action menu items. Display menu items are used to navigate to either a form in the Dynamics AX 2009 client or to a Web page in Enterprise Portal that displays the details of the record being processed by workflow. Action menu items are used for each possible action a user can take in relation to a workflow. They also provide another integration point for developers to integrate custom code. For more information about the menu items that are used in the workflow infrastructure, see *http://msdn.microsoft.com/en-us/library/cc602158.aspx* and *http://msdn.microsoft.com/en-us/library/cc604521.aspx*.

> **Note** The menu items are located in the AOT in the Dynamics AX 2009 client.

Workflow Elements

The elements of a workflow represent the activities that can be configured within a workflow. The business user configures these elements; the developer creates them. An element can be a task, an approval, or a subworkflow.

- Approvals are specialized tasks that allow sequencing of multiple steps and use a fixed set of outcomes.

- Tasks are generic workflow elements that represent a single unit of work. The developer defines the possible outcomes for each task.
- Subworkflows are workflows that are invoked from other workflows.

The workflow structure is made up of sequences of workflow elements.

> **Note** The workflow elements are located in the AOT in the Dynamics AX 2009 client.

Providers

Workflow in Dynamics AX 2009 uses the provider model as a flexible way of allowing application-specific code to be invoked for different purposes when a workflow is executing. There are three providers in workflow: due date, participant, and hierarchy. For more information about workflow providers, including where they are used, see *http://msdn.microsoft.com/en-us/library/cc519521.aspx*.

> **Note** The providers are located in the AOT in the Dynamics AX 2009 client.

Workflow Configurations

The business user creates the workflow configurations using the workflow configurations form in the Dynamics AX 2009 client. The business user first selects a workflow template and then configures the approvals and tasks that control the flow of activities through the workflow.

> **Note** The workflow configurations are located in the Dynamics AX 2009 client – workflow configurations form.

Workflow Instances

A workflow instance is an activated workflow created by combining the workflow configuration and the underlying AOT workflow elements on which the workflow configuration is based (the workflow template, tasks, and approvals).

> **Note** The workflow instances are located in the Dynamics AX 2009 workflow runtime.

Work Items

Work items are the actionable units of work that are created by the workflow instance at run time. When a user interacts with workflow, he or she is responding to a work item that has been generated from a task or approval element. Work items are surfaced in the Dynamics Unified Worklist Web part and in the Dynamics AX 2009 client.

> **Note** The workflow items are located in Dynamics AX 2009 workflow runtime, Enterprise Portal, and the Dynamics AX 2009 client.

Workflow Architecture

Microsoft designed the workflow infrastructure based on a set of assumptions and goals relating to the functionality it wanted to deliver. Two assumptions were the most significant:

- Business logic (X++) invoked by workflow would always be executed in the Application Object Server (AOS).
- Workflows would be managed by Windows Workflow Foundation in .NET Framework 3.5, which operates in a managed environment.

The first assumption reflects the fact that most business logic resides and is executed in the AOS. The second assumption was based on the opportunity to use existing Microsoft technology for executing workflows in Dynamics AX 2009 instead of designing and implementing this functionality from scratch. The choice, however, required finding a suitable host for Windows Workflow Foundation, because it wasn't possible to host by using the unmanaged AOS. In the end, Microsoft decided to host Windows Workflow Foundation by using Internet Information Services (IIS 6.0) and to establish a mechanism for communicating back and forth between AOS and IIS. Two workflow runtimes are the result of this decision: one in AOS, and another in IIS.

These primary goals influenced the architecture:

- To create an extensible/pluggable model for workflow integration (including events and providers), because the workflow *infrastructure* had to be flexible enough to address potentially unknown future requirements.
- To achieve reliable and durable communication between the AOS and IIS runtimes given that they would exist in separate processes.
- To secure communication between the runtimes given that they would be communicating across process boundaries.

- To minimize the performance impact on transactional X++ business logic to invoke workflow runtime services. For example, if workflow activation is triggered from saving a document, no adverse performance side-effects should result for doing this in the same physical transaction (*ttsbegin/ttscommit*) as the save operation.
- To build in scalability that accommodates the growth in use of workflow in Dynamics AX over time, and to provide options, such as multimachine deployments, to attain such scalability.

In the following section, we expand on the capabilities of each of the workflow runtimes.

AOS and IIS Workflow Runtimes

Figure 9-3 shows the parts of the AOS workflow runtime.

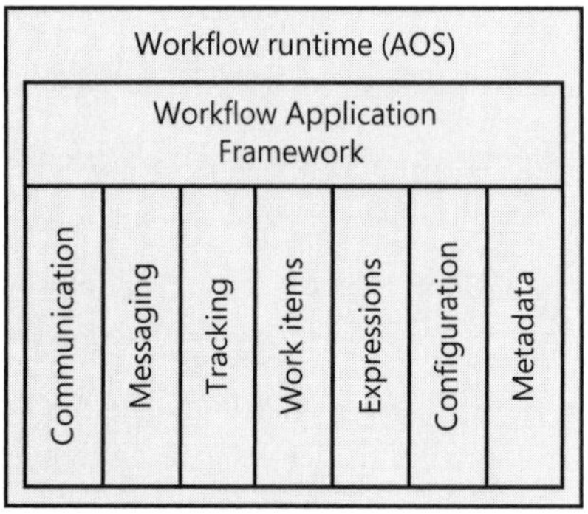

FIGURE 9-3 AOS workflow runtime

The AOS runtime includes the following parts:

- **Workflow Application Framework** A thin API that exposes the underlying workflow functionality to the rest of Dynamics AX 2009.
- **Communication** Manages the communication to IIS through CLR interop calls to the Web services that are exposed by the IIS workflow runtime. It then exposes the entry points for .NET Business Connector calls back into the AOS workflow runtime from IIS.
- **Messaging** Manages and processes workflow messages. Messages are processed on the AOS by a server-bound batch job.
- **Tracking** Manages the tracking information that is stored during workflow execution.
- **Work items** Manages the work items that are created when tasks and approvals get assigned to individual users.
- **Expressions** The condition evaluation engine that evaluates the Boolean expressions defined in a workflow configuration. Such Boolean expressions include workflow

activation conditions, approval/task autocomplete conditions, approval step preconditions, and hierarchy stop and filter conditions.

- **Configuration** Manages the workflow configurations that are created using the workflow configuration form or the workflow configuration API.
- **Metadata** Manages the metadata for the workflow artifacts in the AOT. These artifacts include workflow categories, tasks, approvals, and templates.

Figure 9-4 shows the IIS workflow runtime.

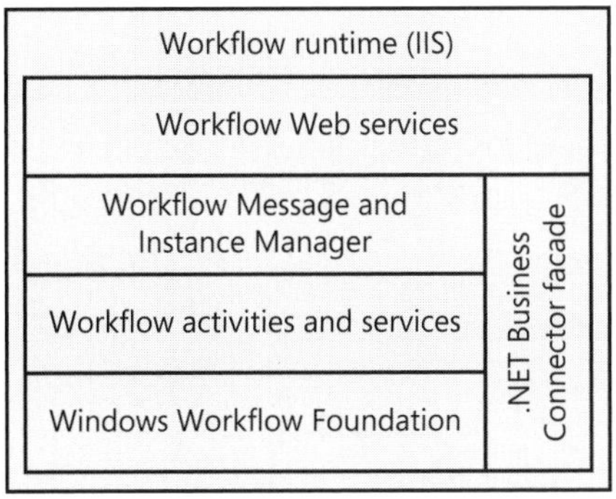

FIGURE 9-4 IIS workflow runtime

These are the parts of the IIS workflow runtime:

- **Workflow Web services** Entry point into the IIS workflow runtime for calls originating from the AOS through workflow message processing.
- **Workflow Message and Instance Manager** Manages the correlation of incoming messages to running workflow instances and the activation of new workflow instances.
- **Workflow activities and services** Dynamics AX 2009 extensions, called custom activities, to the activity model in Windows Workflow Foundation. These extensions provide logic tailored to Dynamics AX 2009 and provide the run-time semantics for the workflow elements that are exposed in the workflow configuration (approvals, tasks, subworkflows).
- **Windows Workflow Foundation** The workflow framework provided in .NET Framework 3.5.
- **.NET Business Connector facade** Abstracts the workflow runtime away from the AOS. This thin abstraction surfaces a set of services and proxy classes that enable communication from the IIS workflow runtime back into the AOS through .NET Business Connector.

Workflow Runtime Interaction

Figure 9-5 shows the logical interaction between the IIS and AOS workflow runtimes. Three main elements are involved: the client (which represents both the Dynamics AX 2009 client and Enterprise Portal), the AOS workflow runtime, and the IIS workflow runtime.

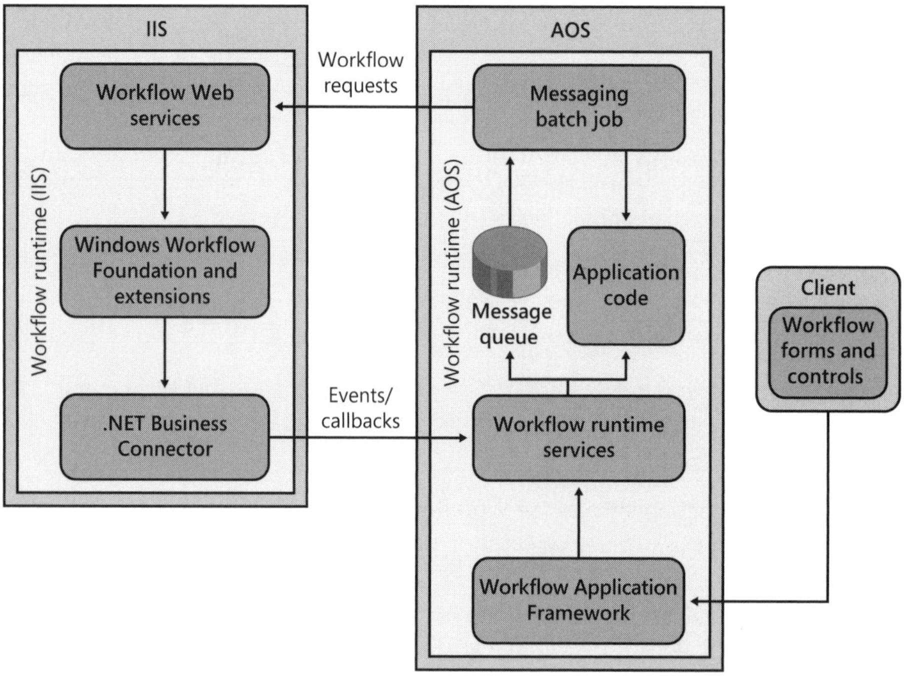

FIGURE 9-5 Interaction diagram of the workflow infrastructure in Dynamics AX 2009

The IIS workflow runtime consists of the following parts:

- **Workflow Web services** These act as the interface to the IIS workflow runtime. Web service calls are made from the messaging batch job to the IIS workflow runtime by using these services.
- **Windows Workflow Foundation and extensions** The core of the IIS runtime is Windows Workflow Foundation and the Dynamics AX 2009 extensions, or custom activities, of the framework.
- **.NET Business Connector** The Dynamics AX integration component, used in this case to complete the request round-trip back to the AOS runtime.

The AOS workflow runtime consists of the following parts:

- **Workflow Application Framework** A thin API that exposes the underlying workflow functionality to the rest of the application.
- **Workflow runtime services** The collective set of workflow subsystems hosted by the AOS to facilitate workflow processing.
- **Message queue** The workflow runtime in the AOS interacts with the IIS runtime by exchanging messages, and the message queue in the AOS is used to stage workflow messages before being processed by the messaging batch job.
- **Application code** The X++ code that is invoked by workflow, for example, in event handlers and providers.
- **Messaging batch job** A server-bound batch job that is dedicated to periodically processing messages in the message queue and sending requests to the IIS workflow runtime.

As an example of how these elements interact at run time, the following list explains what happens when a user clicks Submit to activate workflow processing on a record in Dynamics AX 2009:

1. The Submit action invokes the Workflow Application Framework to post an activation message for the selected workflow configuration. This causes a message to be inserted into the message queue, the purpose of which is to instantiate the workflow in the IIS workflow runtime.
2. The message is processed by the messaging batch job, and the request is dispatched to the Workflow Web services on the IIS workflow runtime.
3. The Workflow Web services process the request and invoke the Windows Workflow Foundation activation API.
4. After a workflow instance is activated, a workflow-started message is dispatched from the IIS workflow runtime to the AOS workflow runtime using a Dynamics AX 2009 custom activity, which calls through .NET Business Connector. The state of the workflow instance is persisted to the Dynamics AX database together with the posting of the workflow-started message. The activation message is also removed/dequeued at this time.
5. The workflow-started message is then processed by the workflow messaging batch job, which invokes the *WorkflowStarted* event handler for the corresponding workflow template.
6. After the *WorkflowStarted* event handler has been invoked, an acknowledgment message is posted to the message queue, to be sent back to the IIS workflow runtime to continue execution of the workflow instance. The workflow-started message is also removed/dequeued at this time.

This communication metaphor is repeated throughout the life cycle of a given workflow instance for all types of workflow messages.

Logical Approval and Task Workflows

One way to visualize how the key workflow concepts and architecture come together is to look at the interaction patterns of approval and task elements at run time. Four main types of interactions can occur: workflow events, acknowledgments (of events), provider callbacks, and infrastructure callbacks.

- **Workflow event** A callback to the AOS to post a message, save the workflow instance, and remove/dequeue the originating message. The workflow then waits for the corresponding message to be processed. The AOS processes the message by invoking the event handler on the corresponding workflow template, task, or approval. Then the AOS posts the acknowledgment message.
- **Acknowledgment** An acknowledgment message responds to every event processed by the AOS. Upon receiving the acknowledgment, the IIS workflow runtime loads the workflow instance from the Dynamics AX database and resumes the instance from where it left off.
- **Provider callback** A call from the IIS workflow runtime into the AOS workflow runtime to retrieve users or due dates. Workflow providers are integration points for developers to inject custom code for resolving users and due dates. A provider callback is a synchronous call from the IIS workflow runtime back into an X++ workflow provider hosted in the AOS.
- **Infrastructure callback** A call from the IIS workflow runtime back into the AOS workflow runtime to perform infrastructure-related activities. One example is to create work items for each user returned from a call to a participant provider.

Figure 9-6 shows the logical workflow interactions for approvals.

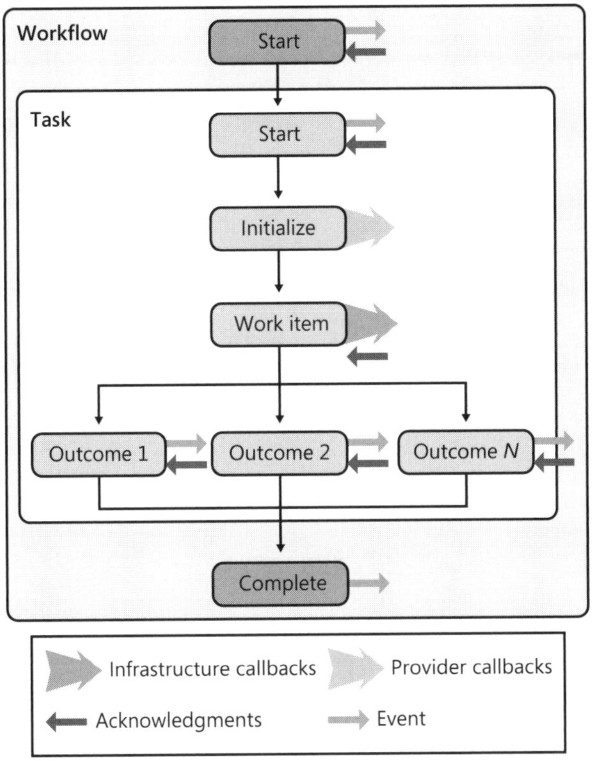

FIGURE 9-6 Logical approval workflow interactions

In Figure 9-6, the outermost box represents the workflow itself. Nested inside are the approval (element) and within that, a single step. (An approval can contain multiple steps.) The smaller rectangular boxes represent events or outcomes. The symbols in the legend represent the four interaction types, which are positioned in Figure 9-6 where that type of interaction occurs. When the workflow starts, an event and an acknowledgment occur. Acknowledgments confirm that the AOS workflow runtime received and processed a preceding event initiated in the IIS workflow runtime. The same event and acknowledgment occur for the start of the approval element. When a step starts, there are callbacks for the workflow providers, which are invoked at this point. (Typically, the participant provider is executed to obtain workflow participants, and the due date provider is executed to determine due dates for work items.) The work items are then created via an infrastructure callback, and the workflow waits for the corresponding acknowledgment for each work item that was created. Acknowledgments for work items are triggered when users take action on assigned work items. After the step (or steps) completes, the outcome is determined based on the completion policies of the step, and the corresponding event is raised for that outcome. The workflow then waits for acknowledgment that the AOS processed the outcome's event. Finally, the completion of the workflow itself raises an event.

The task interactions are similar to approvals, except no steps and outcomes can be unique per task. Figure 9-7 shows the logical workflow interactions for tasks.

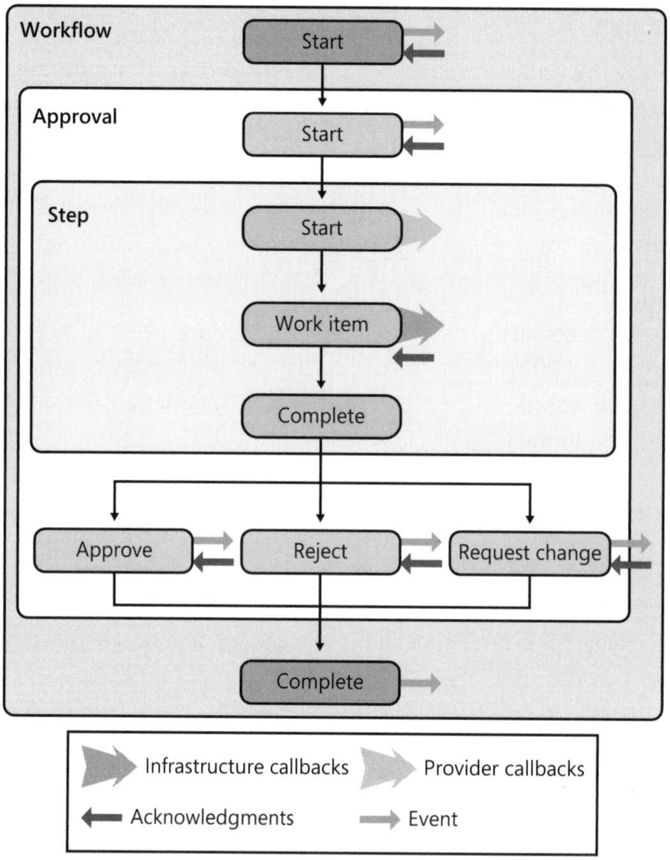

FIGURE 9-7 Logical task workflow interactions

In summary, the logical workflow interaction figures in this section clarify when event handlers fire during the life of a workflow and when a workflow needs to call out to providers.

Workflow Life Cycle

In this section, we describe the workflow life cycle, shown in Figure 9-8, and explain the design phase of the life cycle in detail.

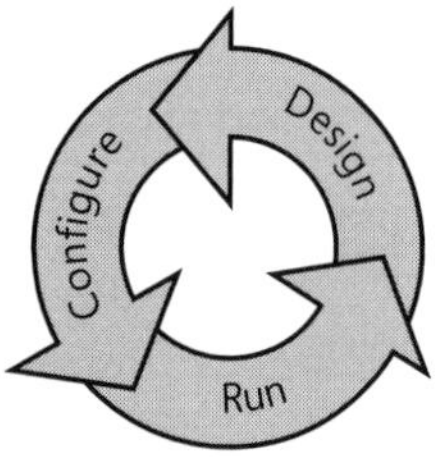

FIGURE 9-8 Workflow life cycle in Dynamics AX 2009

The workflow life cycle has three phases:

- **Design** Business users decide what parts of a business process that traverses Dynamics AX 2009 need to be automated and then design a workflow to achieve this automation, leveraging their understanding of the business processes and the organization. They can collaborate with developers in this phase, or they might just communicate the workflow requirements to the developers, who then create the necessary artifacts in Dynamics AX 2009. The artifacts enable the workflow that the business users will later configure.
- **Configure** After the necessary artifacts are in place, business users configure the workflow in Dynamics AX 2009. If this work is carried out on a test system, after successfully testing the workflow, the administrator deploys the related artifacts and workflow configuration to the live or production system.
- **Run** Users interact with Dynamics AX 2009 as part of their day-to-day work, and in the course of doing so, might submit workflow documents to the workflow for processing as well as interact with workflows that are already activated.

This cycle is repeated when the workflow that has been designed, configured, and deployed needs to change in some way, for example, because of a change in a business process or in the organization.

Designing Workflows

As a developer, once you understand the workflow requirements the business user has provided, you must create the corresponding workflow artifacts, dependent workflow artifacts, and business logic. You create all these in the AOT by using the Dynamics AX 2009 client. You write the business logic in X++.

Table 9-1 lists each workflow artifact and the steps you need to perform when creating it. The artifacts are explicitly listed in order of dependency.

TABLE 9-1 Workflow Artifacts

Artifact	Steps
Workflow category	Define the module within which the workflow template is enabled. For more information, see the "Key Workflow Concepts" section earlier in this chapter.
Approval	Define the approval workflow document. Define approval event handlers for *Started* and *Canceled*. Define approval workflow providers for *Participant*, *DueDate*, and *Hierarchy*. Define approval menu items for Document, DocumentWeb, Resubmit, ResubmitWeb, Delegate, and DelegateWeb. Enable or disable approval outcomes. Define approval outcome menu items for *Action* and *ActionWeb*. Define approval outcome event handler. Define the DocumentPreviewFieldGroup.
Task	Define the task workflow document. Define task event handlers for *Started* and *Canceled*. Define task workflow providers for *Participant*, *DueDate*, and *Hierarchy*. Define task menu items for Document, DocumentWeb, Resubmit, ResubmitWeb, Delegate, and DelegateWeb. Add/remove task outcomes. Define task outcome menu items for *Action* and *ActionWeb*. Define task outcome event handler. Define the DocumentPreviewFieldGroup.
Workflow template	Define the workflow document. Define event handlers for workflow *Started*, *Completed*, *ConfigDataChanged*, and *Canceled*. Define menu items for SubmitToWorkflow, SubmitToWorkflowWeb, Cancel, and CancelWeb. Define the workflow category. (Select from the existing categories.) Define required approvals and tasks, and sequencing of required approvals and tasks. Enable or disable activation conditions for workflow configurations based on the template. For information about creating workflow templates, see *http://msdn.microsoft.com/en-us/library/cc641259.aspx*.

Table 9-2 identifies the *dependent* workflow artifacts that are referenced in Table 9-1.

TABLE 9-2 Dependent Workflow Artifacts

Dependent Workflow Artifact	Description
Workflow document query	Defines the data in Dynamics AX 2009 that a workflow acts on, and exposes certain fields that the business user uses for constructing conditions in the workflow configuration form. The query is defined under the *AOT\Queries* node, and it is required for all workflows.
Workflow document class	References the workflow document query and any calculated fields to be made available when constructing conditions. This X++ class is created under the *AOT\Classes* node. It is required because workflow templates and elements must bind to a workflow document class. For information about derived data, see the "Key Workflow Concepts" section earlier in this chapter.
SubmitToWorkflow class	This X++ class is the menu item class for the *SubmitToWorkflow* menu item that displays the Submit To Workflow dialog box in the Dynamics AX 2009 user interface. The Submit To Workflow dialog box allows the user to enter comments associated with the submission. The *SubmitToWorkflow* class then activates the workflow. If state is being managed in the record that has been submitted to workflow, this class can be used to update the state of the record. This class is created under the *AOT\Classes* node.
State model	A defined set of states and state transitions (supported changes from one state to another) used to track the status of workflow document records during their life cycle. For example, a document can have the following states: *Not Submitted*, *Submitted*, *ChangeRequested*, or *Approved*. There is currently no state model infrastructure in Dynamics AX, so you have to implement any state model that is required. For more information, see the "State Model" section following this table.
Event handlers	Event handler code consists of business logic that is written in X++ and then referenced in the workflow template, the approval element, approval outcomes, the task element, and task outcomes. If a workflow document has an associated state model, you must write event handler code to transact workflow document records through the state model when being processed by using workflow. Event handler X++ code is created under the *AOT\Classes* node.

Dependent Workflow Artifact	Description
Action and display menu items	For information about menu items, see the "Key Workflow Concepts" section earlier in this chapter. Both types of menu item are created under the *AOT\Menu Items* or *AOT\Web\Web Menu Items* node. For more information about the menu items used in the workflow infrastructure, see: *http://msdn.microsoft.com/en-us/library/cc602158.aspx* *http://msdn.microsoft.com/en-us/library/cc604521.aspx*
Custom workflow providers	If the functionality of the workflow providers shipped with Dynamics AX 2009 isn't adequate for a given set of requirements, you can develop your own workflow provider. Custom workflow provider X++ classes are created under the *AOT\Classes* node and then referenced in one or more workflow elements. For more information about workflow providers, including where they are used, see *http://msdn.microsoft.com/en-us/library/cc519521.aspx*.
canSubmitToWorkflow method	This method is required on each Dynamics AX 2009 client form that is enabled for workflow, and it is used to inform the workflow common controls that the record in the form is ready to be submitted to the workflow.

State Model

A *state model* defines a set of states and the transitions that are permitted between the different states for a given record type, along with an initial state and a final state. The reason state models exist is to provide a very prescriptive life cycle for whatever data they are associated to. The current state value is often stored in a field on a record. For example, the *PurchReqTable* table (the header for a purchase requisition) has a *status* field that is used to track the approval state of a purchase requisition. The business logic for purchase requisitions has been coded to respect the meaning of each state and the supported state transitions so that a purchase requisition record can't be converted into a purchase order before the state is approved.

The simplest way to add and manage state on a record is to use a single field on the record to store the current state, but you have to determine what approach makes the most sense. You would then create a static X++ class that implements the state transition business logic. Conceptually, you can think of this class as the *StateManager* class. All the existing business logic that performs the state transitions should be refactored to use this single, central class to perform the state transitions, in effect isolating the state transition logic into a single class. From a workflow perspective, state transitions always occur at the beginning or conclusion of a workflow element. This is why all workflow tasks and workflow approvals have

*EventHandler*s that can be used to invoke the *StateManager* class. Figure 9-9 shows the dependency chain between an event handler and the workflow document state.

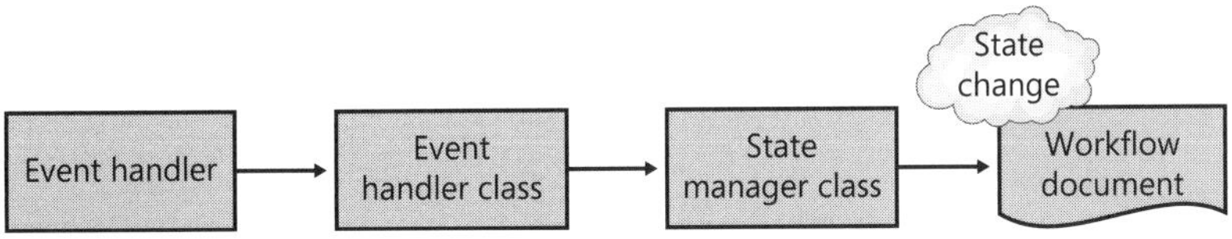

FIGURE 9-9 State management dependency chain

After you decide to enable a workflow for a table in Dynamics AX 2009, and that the table has state that must be managed, you *must* refactor all the business logic to respect the state model that you define to avoid getting unpredictable results. Create operations should always create a record with the *initial* state (for the state model). Update operations must respect the current state and fail if the state isn't as expected. For example, it shouldn't be possible to change the business justification of a purchase requisition after it has been submitted for approval. Managing the state of the record during each update so that the current state is verified and the next logical state is updated would typically be implemented in the update method on the table by calling the *StateManager* class; if it returns true, go ahead and do the update. If not, throw an exception and abort. Figure 9-10 shows a simple state model for a record.

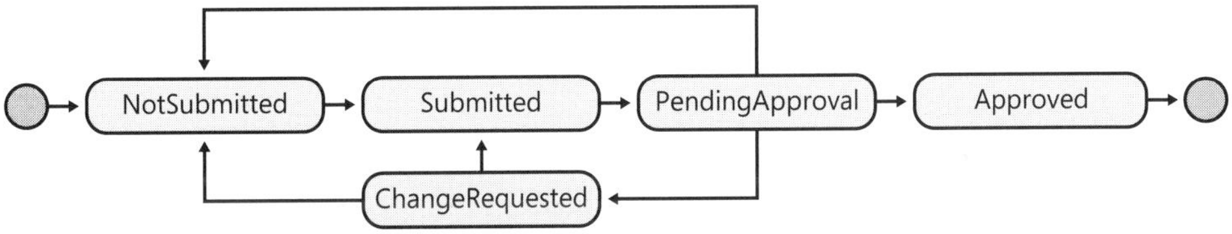

FIGURE 9-10 A simple state model for approvals

In Figure 9-10, the initial state is NotSubmitted. When a record is submitted to workflow, the state changes to Submitted. After the workflow is activated, the state becomes PendingApproval. If a workflow participant selects the Request Change action, the state changes to ChangeRequested. After all approvals are submitted, the final state is Approved.

Creating a Workflow Category

Workflow categories are used to associate a workflow template to a module. This association restricts the list of templates that are shown when you're configuring a workflow for a particular module. To avoid showing a long list of all the workflow templates in the system, you group the templates by module using workflow categories. For example, if a user is in the Accounts Payable module, the user sees only the workflow templates bound to Accounts Payable. The mechanism behind this grouping is a simple metadata property on the workflow template called *Workflow category*. This property allows you to select an element from the module *enum* (AOT\Data Dictionary\Base enums\ModuleAxapta).

With this mechanism, it is easy for ISVs and partners who create their own modules to extend the module enum and thus have workflow templates that can be associated to that module. Note that a workflow category can only be associated to one module.

Creating the Workflow Document Class

The purpose of a workflow is to automate all or part of a business process. To do this, it must be possible to define various rules over the document that is being processed by workflow. In Dynamics AX 2009, these rules are referred to as *conditions*. A business user creates conditions in workflow when configuring the workflow. Conditions can be used, for example, to decide whether a purchase requisition should be approved automatically (without any human intervention). Figure 9-11 shows a simple condition defined in the workflow configuration form.

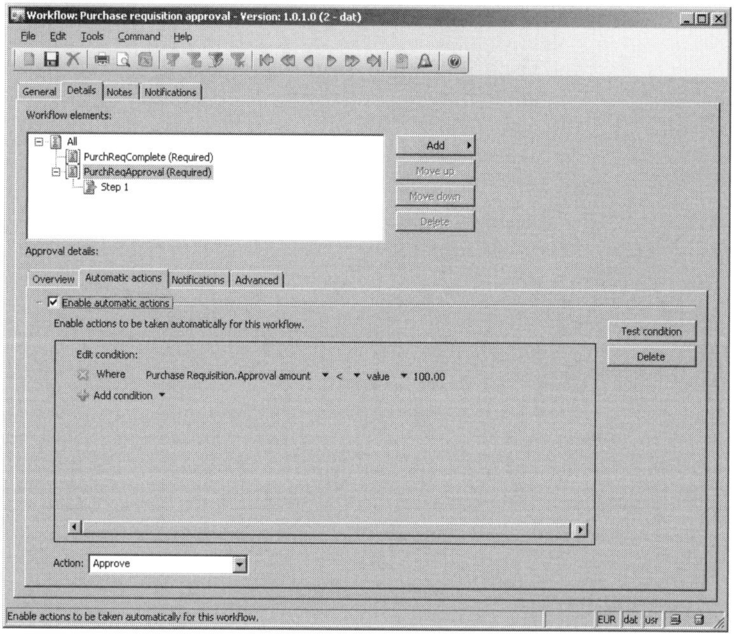

FIGURE 9-11 A simple condition defined in the workflow configuration form

When a business user is configuring a condition by using the workflow configuration form, he or she needs to make sure the users have a way to select the fields from the workflow documents they want to use. On the surface, this configuration seems simple, but two requirements complicate the task. First, the user must be able to filter the available fields because not all the fields in a table might make sense to the business user. Second, it must be possible to use calculated fields (also referred to as *derived data*). The workflow document class meets these two requirements by functioning as a thin wrapper around an AOT query that defines the available fields and by providing a mechanism for defining calculated fields.

The AOT query enables developers to define a subset of fields from one or more related tables. By adding nested data sources in a query, you can model quite complex data structures, but most commonly the nested query is used to model a header-line pattern. At design time, when the business user is configuring a workflow, the AOT query is simply used by the condition editor to figure out which fields to display to the business user.

The workflow infrastructure uses a prescriptive pattern to support calculated fields using *parm* methods that are defined within the workflow document class. These methods must be prefixed with *parm* and must implement a signature of *(CompanyId, TableId, RecId)*. The workflow infrastructure then, at run time, calls the *parm* method and uses the return value in the condition evaluation. This design enables developers to implement calculated fields in *parm* methods on the workflow document class.

> **Note** When the expression builder constructs the list of fields, it uses the labels of the table fields as the display name for the fields. The display name for calculated fields is defined by the extended data type label of the return types. For *enums*, this is defined by the *enum* element label.

Creating a workflow document class involves creating an X++ class that extends from *WorkflowDocument*. You must override *getQueryName* to return the name of the workflow document query. Figure 9-12 shows a sample X++ class that extends from the workflow document.

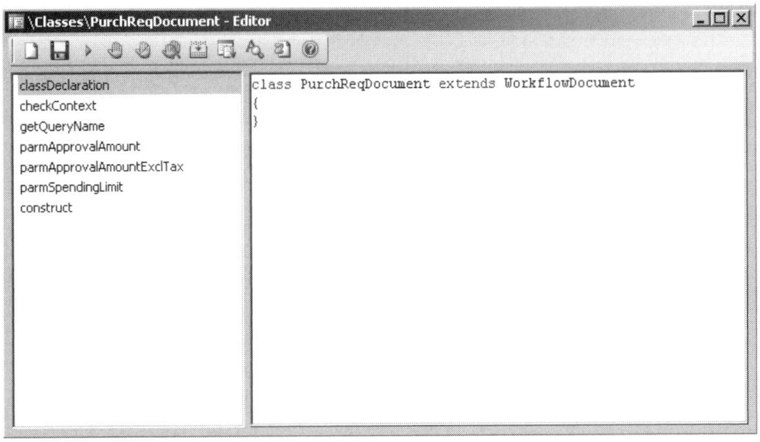

FIGURE 9-12 A sample X++ class that extends from the workflow document

Creating a *parm* method involves adding a method to the workflow document class and then adding X++ code to calculate or otherwise determine the value to be returned, as you can see in Figure 9-13.

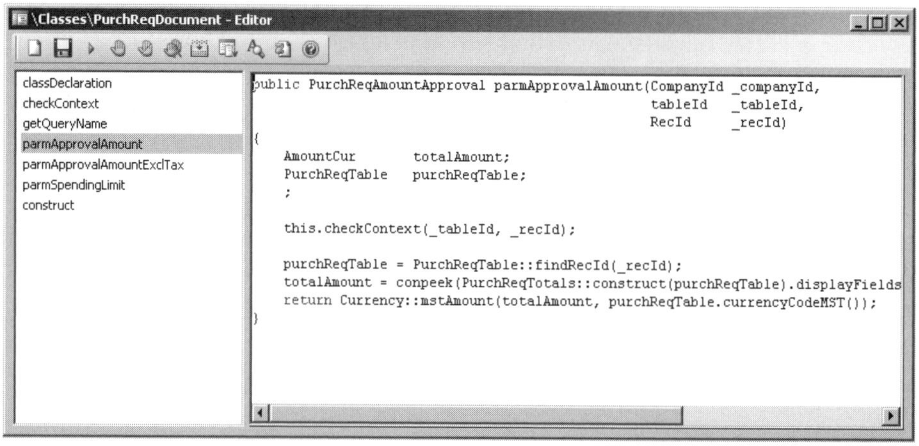
\Classes\PurchReqDocument - Editor
classDeclaration
checkContext
getQueryName
parmApprovalAmount
parmApprovalAmountExclTax
parmSpendingLimit
construct
public PurchReqAmountApproval parmApprovalAmount(CompanyId _companyId,
tableId _tableId,
RecId _recId)
{
AmountCur totalAmount;
PurchReqTable purchReqTable;
;
this.checkContext(_tableId, _recId);
purchReqTable = PurchReqTable::findRecId(_recId);
totalAmount = conpeek(PurchReqTotals::construct(purchReqTable).displayFields
return Currency::mstAmount(totalAmount, purchReqTable.currencyCodeMST());
}

FIGURE 9-13 A *parm* method within a workflow document class that returns the approval amount (which is calculated)

> **Note** All condition comparisons assume that any literal monetary value typed into a condition is in *AmountMST*, which is the default company currency. Thus, if a *parm* method returns a value that represents a monetary amount, it must always be returned in *AmountMST*.

Adding a Workflow Display Menu Item

The workflow display menu items enable users to navigate directly to the Dynamics AX 2009 client form (or Enterprise Portal Web page) upon which they can select one of the available workflow actions. A user is prompted to participate in a workflow when he or she receives a work item from the workflow at run time. When viewing the work item, the user can click Go To <Label>. This button is automatically mapped to the workflow display menu item, and the button text ("<Label>") is the label of the root table of the workflow document query.

This design enables developers to create task-based forms that are focused on the particular task at hand, rather than having to create monolithic forms that assume the user knows where in the process he or she is acting and which fields and buttons to use.

Activating the Workflow

Workflows in Dynamics AX 2009 are always explicitly activated; either a user does something in the Dynamics AX 2009 client or in Enterprise Portal that causes workflow processing to start, or the execution of business logic starts a workflow. (Once you understand how users activate a workflow, you can use this knowledge to activate workflows through business logic.)

For the first approach to activation to work, the workflow infrastructure must have a way to communicate information to the user about what to do. For example, it might be relevant to instruct the user to "Submit the purchase requisition for review and approval" at the appropriate time. The requirements to communicate with users throughout the workflow life cycle provided Microsoft an opportunity to standardize the way users interact with workflow in both the Dynamics AX 2009 client and Enterprise Portal, including activating a workflow, and this resulted in the development of *workflow common controls*. The workflow common controls include the yellow workflow message bar (highlighted in Figure 9-14) and the workflow action button, labeled Submit.

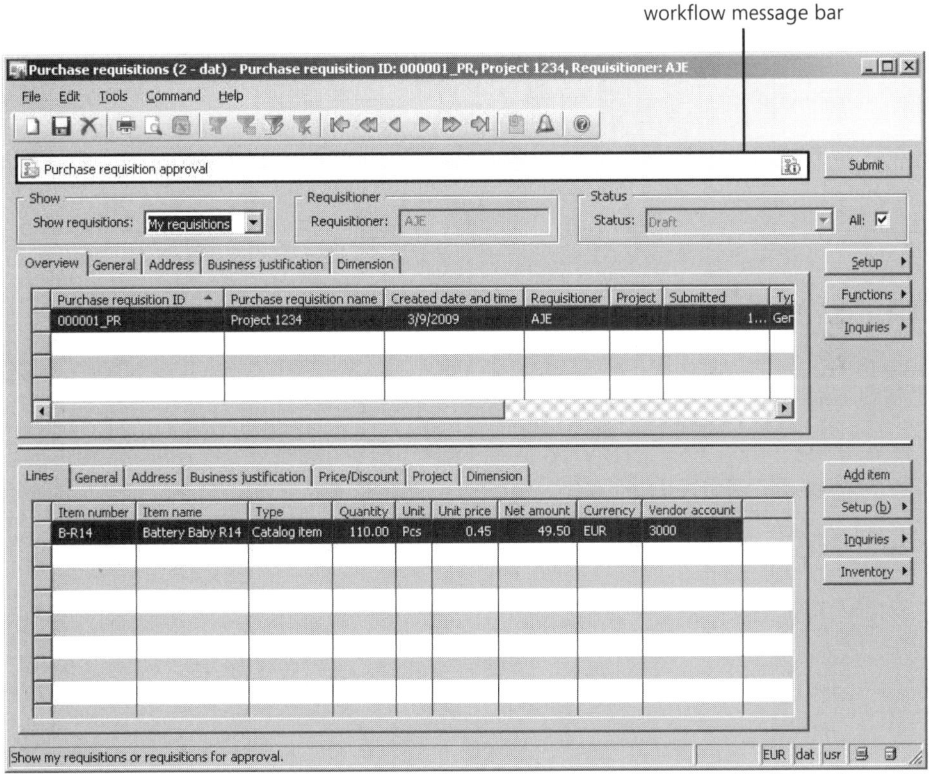

FIGURE 9-14 A purchase requisition ready to be submitted to workflow for processing

The workflow common controls appear on the purchase requisition form because it has been enabled for workflow. To enable workflow in a form, you must set the *WorkflowEnabled* property on the form to Yes in the Properties tab of the Design dialog box, which is shown in Figure 9-15. You must also set the *WorkflowDataSource* to one of the data sources on the form. The selected data source must be the same as the root data source that is used in the query referenced by the workflow document.

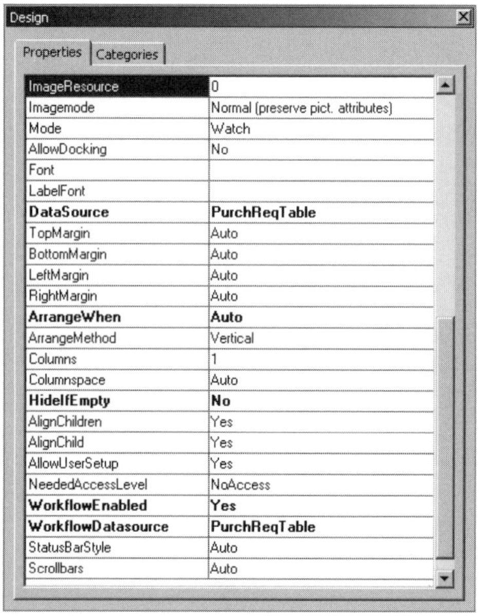

FIGURE 9-15 Design properties for a Dynamics AX 2009 form, including those for workflow

If workflow has been enabled in a form, the workflow common controls automatically appear in three cases:

- When the currently selected document can be submitted to workflow (the *canSubmitToWorkflow* form method returns true).
- When the current user is the originator of a workflow that has acted on the currently selected document.
- When the current user has been assigned to a work item on which he or she must take an action. The workflow common control uses the algorithm shown in Figure 9-16 to decide which workflow configuration to use.

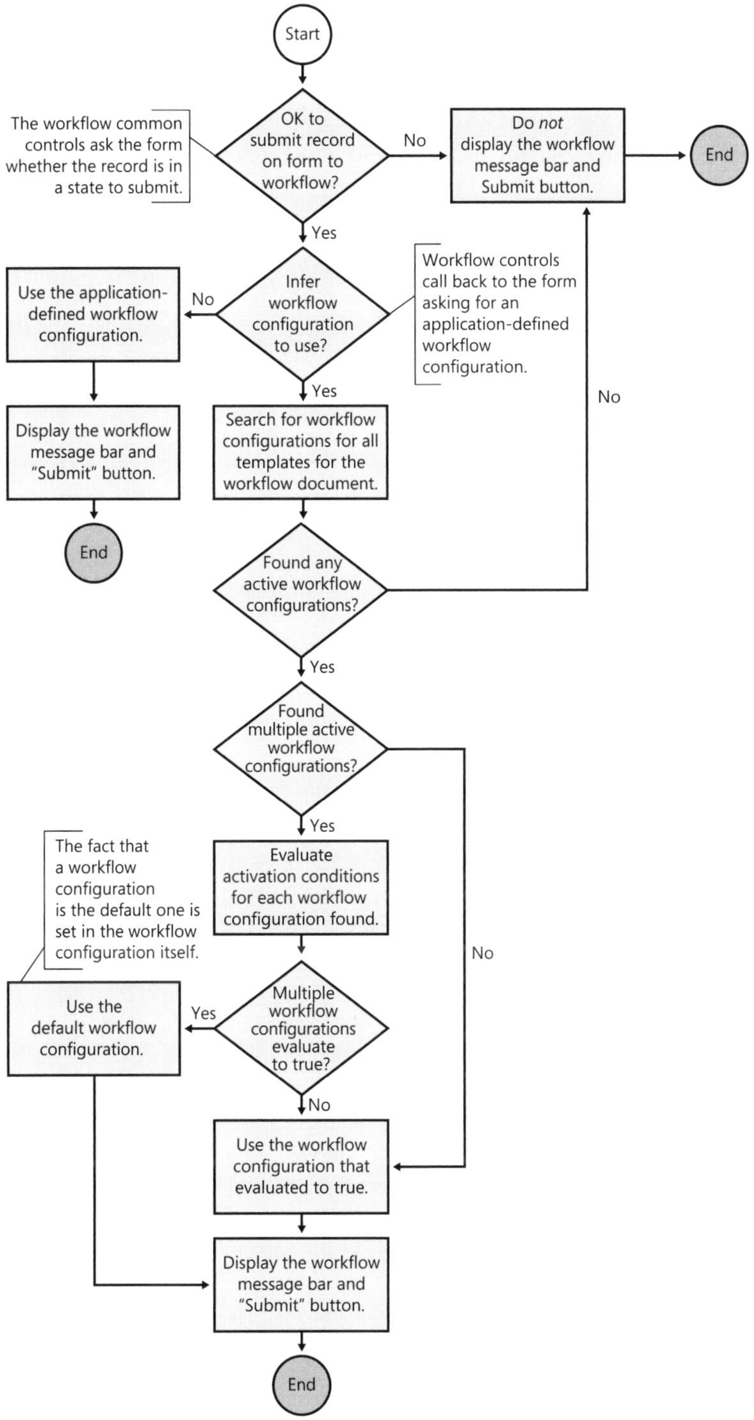

FIGURE 9-16 Workflow activation logic flow chart

After a workflow configuration has been identified, the workflow template is also known because there is a one-to-one relationship between a workflow configuration and a workflow template. When the workflow template is known, it's easy for the workflow common controls to obtain the *SubmitToWorkflow* action menu item. This action menu item is then dynamically added to the form, together with the yellow workflow message bar.

If you look at the *SubmitToWorkflow* action menu item for the *PurchReqApproval* workflow template, you notice that it is bound to the *PurchReqWorkflow* class. When you click the Submit button, the action menu items call the *main* method on the class it is bound to; thus the code that activates the workflow is called from the *main* method. In this case, the call to the workflow activation API has been isolated within the *submit* method.

In Figure 9-17, notice how the *Workflow::activatefromWorkflowTemplate* method is used. You can use two additional APIs to activate workflows: *Workflow::activatefromWorkflowConfiguration* and *Workflow::activateFromWorkflowSequenceNumber.*

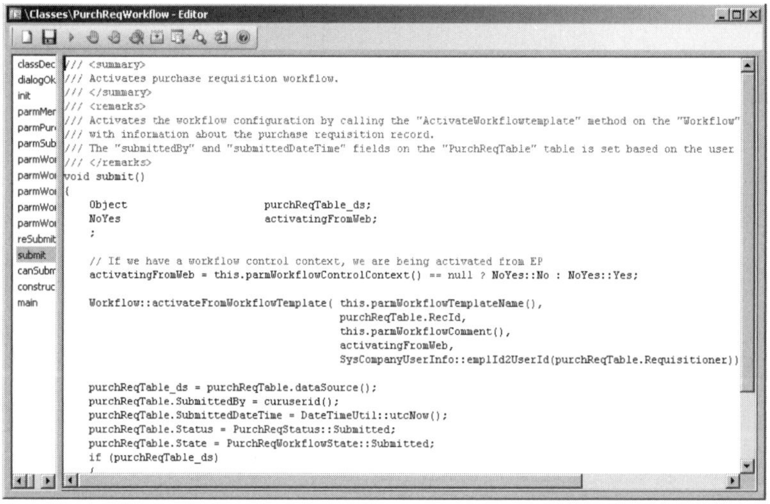

FIGURE 9-17 Submit method for the purchase requisition workflow

For information about how to use these APIs, see the Dynamics AX 2009 developer documentation on MSDN: *http://msdn.microsoft.com/en-us/library/cc642844.aspx*.

Understanding how to activate a workflow is important, but it is equally important to understand how to prevent a workflow from being activated. For example, you don't want a user to submit a record to workflow before it is in a state to be submitted. An override method on forms, *canSubmitToWorkflow*, addresses this requirement. The *canSubmitToWorkflow* method returns a Boolean. True indicates that the record can be submitted to workflow. When the workflow data source on the form is initialized or when the record changes, this method is called; if it returns true, the Submit button is enabled, and if it returns false, the Submit button is disabled. Typically, you should update the state of the document after invoking the workflow activation API so that you can correctly denote when a document has or has not been submitted to workflow. (In Figure 9-17, the purchase requisition is transitioned to the submitted state.)

Note If the *canSubmitToWorkflow* method hasn't been overridden, the workflow common controls won't appear on the form, leaving a reserved space at the top of the form where the controls would normally appear.

Chapter 10

.NET Business Connector

In this chapter:

The objectives of this chapter are to:

- Describe .NET Business Connector for Microsoft Dynamics AX, what it is intended to do, and how it relates to other integration components in Microsoft Dynamics AX 2009.
- Introduce the new features in .NET Business Connector for Dynamics AX 2009.
- Provide example scenarios that show how .NET Business Connector can be used.
- Explain how to use .NET Business Connector to build managed applications that integrate with Dynamics AX 2009.

Introduction

.NET Business Connector for Microsoft Dynamics AX is a versatile platform component that you can use to build software applications that interact deeply with both the data and the business logic residing in Dynamics AX 2009.

This chapter compares .NET Business Connector with other integration components included with Dynamics AX 2009. It also explains the architecture of .NET Business Connector to help you understand how it functions. Several example scenarios demonstrate the variety of potential uses for .NET Business Connector. The managed classes used to build applications are described, and code examples are provided to illustrate their usage. The following new features of .NET Business Connector in Dynamics AX 2009 are introduced, and changes to the existing functionality are explained:

- Support for cross-company queries
- Changes in the process hosting in .NET Business Connector

- Licensing changes that affect .NET Business Connector
- The ability to pass .NET objects to Dynamics AX via .NET Business Connector
- The capability to register managed callbacks through .NET Business Connector

Integration Technologies

Integrating enterprise resource planning (ERP) systems with other systems within and beyond an organization is a common requirement, and Dynamics AX provides a variety of ways to implement such integration. Figure 10-1 shows all the integration components in Dynamics AX 2009.

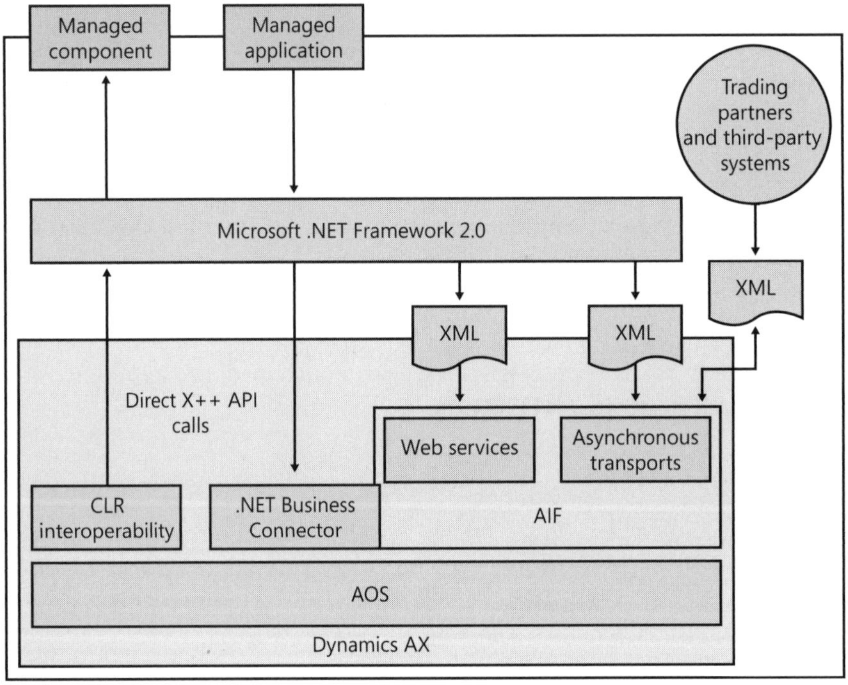

FIGURE 10-1 Integration components in Dynamics AX 2009

All the integration components interact with Dynamics AX through the Application Object Server (AOS). Dynamics AX 2009 supports a three-tier architecture (earlier versions supported both a two-tier and a three-tier architecture), which means that the integration components can interact with Dynamics AX only through the AOS. The majority of the integration components use the .NET Framework in some way, which is a reflection of Microsoft's goal to make it easier for developers to use the .NET platform to develop solutions.

.NET Business Connector enables you to develop managed applications by using the .NET Framework and a CLR-compatible language to integrate with Dynamics AX. In Figure 10-1, the arrow from the .NET Framework to .NET Business Connector shows that the managed applications interact with Dynamics AX through .NET Business Connector. The most general-purpose integration component in Dynamics AX, .NET Business Connector is particularly appropriate for developing custom applications that require a large degree of flexibility and control over implementation.

You can also use the Application Integration Framework (AIF) to integrate Dynamics AX with other applications through standards-based interfaces and XML-based message exchange. AIF is built on top of the Microsoft technology stack; it supports publishing Dynamics AX services through various transport technologies, such as synchronous Windows Communication Foundation (WCF) Web services and asynchronous technologies (Microsoft Message Queuing [MSMQ], Microsoft BizTalk Server, and direct XML file exchange), for external service clients to consume. You can jump-start your integration projects with any of the 56 Dynamics AX services that ship with Dynamics AX 2009 or the AIF wizards that help you create new services. You can also use the AIF to send business documents from Dynamics AX to external locations. Finally, AIF helps you integrate external Web services—whether they are deployed in your company's intranet or on the Internet—with your Dynamics AX application by consuming these Web services directly from X++. See Chapter 17, "The Application Integration Framework," for more information on the AIF.

Inside .NET Business Connector

As we stated earlier, .NET Business Connector is a versatile platform component. It contains the Dynamics AX kernel and provides a runtime environment for executing X++ code and interacting with other elements in the AOT. Nearly the entire Dynamics AX development and runtime environment is based on X++, and the kernel is responsible for interpreting and executing this code, part of the reason .NET Business Connector is so powerful.

Logical Component Stack

In .NET Business Connector, the following three logical components (illustrated in Figure 10-2) interoperate to deliver functionality:

- Managed classes
- Transition layer
- Interpreter

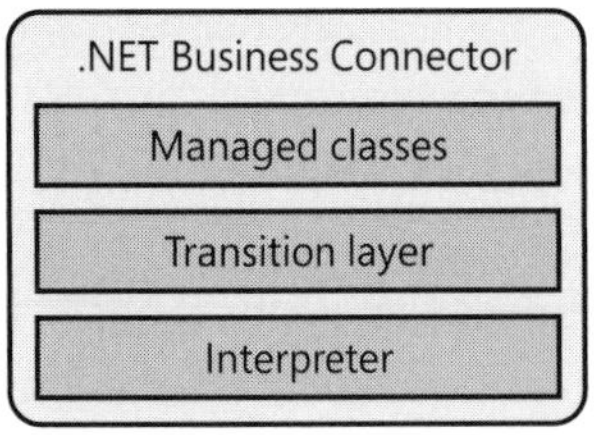

FIGURE 10-2 Logical component stack within .NET Business Connector

Managed Classes

The managed classes component is a set of .NET Framework–based classes that expose the functionality you can access through .NET Business Connector. It includes the following classes: *Axapta*, *AxaptaBuffer*, *AxaptaContainer*, *AxaptaObject*, and *AxaptaRecord*. (We describe each of these classes later in this chapter, in the section "Working with .NET Business Connector.") The functionality of the managed classes is mostly equivalent to the COM Business Connector, which will be discontinued in future versions of Dynamics AX. See the section "Migrating Applications" at the end of this chapter for more on the deprecation of the COM Business Connector.

Transition Layer

In the transition layer, .NET Framework objects and types are mapped to their Dynamics AX equivalents. This mapping occurs as part of both the request and the response processing in .NET Business Connector.

Interpreter

The interpreter is the part of the Dynamics AX kernel that is responsible for parsing and executing X++ code. Dynamics AX allows code to be executed locally in the kernel of .NET Business Connector or remotely in the kernel of the AOS. The interpreter manages local and remote code execution. It also manages connectivity to the AOS and other infrastructure, such as session management and security.

Run Time

At run time, .NET Business Connector interacts with the AOS. Figure 10-3 depicts the run-time interaction.

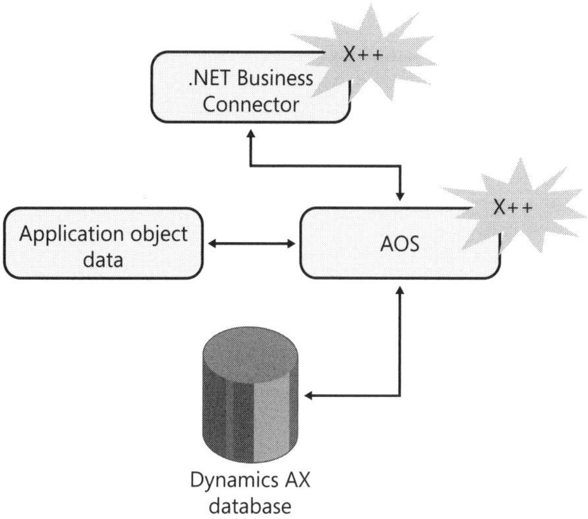

FIGURE 10-3 .NET Business Connector run-time interactions

The following list describes the important interactions among .NET Business Connector, the AOS, and the Dynamics AX database:

- .NET Business Connector authenticates against the AOS when the *Axapta.Logon* method is called. The credentials that .NET Business Connector passes to the AOS must correspond to an existing Dynamics AX user, who must be enabled and have the appropriate rights, granted through security keys, to use .NET Business Connector.
- The AOS completes the authentication and establishes a session for the Dynamics AX user.
- Other .NET Business Connector classes and methods are invoked as needed. Once the session is established, .NET Business Connector can be used to create, read, update, or delete (CRUD) Dynamics AX data. In addition, the X++ business logic that resides in the Dynamics AX metadata store, the application object data can be invoked and executed either on the AOS or in .NET Business Connector.

Web Interoperability

The Dynamics AX development environment includes a Web framework, the Enterprise Portal framework. (See Chapter 7, "Enterprise Portal," for more information about the Enterprise Portal framework.) This framework is used to develop the Web-based functionality in X++, which is then exposed in Enterprise Portal. Enterprise Portal uses .NET Business Connector to integrate with Dynamics AX, and .NET Business Connector can interoperate with Microsoft Internet Information Services (IIS) and Microsoft ASP.NET to provide access to the HTTP context information, including requests, responses, and view state, necessary to enable Web-based functionality.

Figure 10-4 illustrates how Web interoperability works.

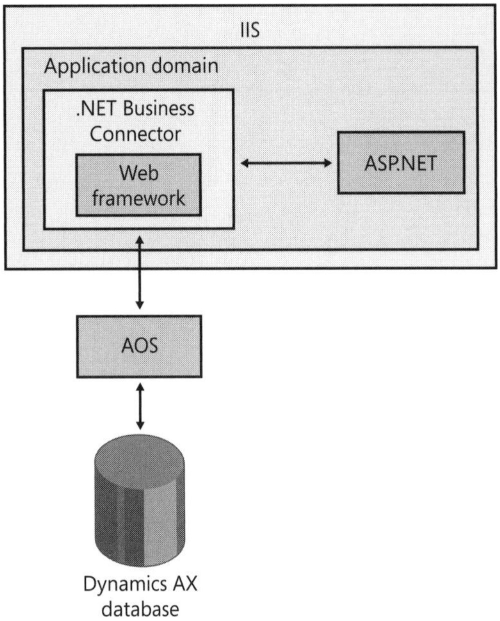

FIGURE 10-4 .NET Business Connector Web interoperability

Managed Web applications, including Enterprise Portal, execute in IIS within an application domain. Upon initialization, the application domain loads and instantiates .NET Business Connector. The managed application then uses .NET Business Connector to invoke Dynamics AX Web framework elements, such as Web menu items, Web forms, and Web reports. The X++ code stored in the application object data that defines these elements accesses the HTTP context as needed through the following classes (located in the AOT under System Documentation\Classes):

- *IISApplicationObject*
- *IISContextObject*
- *IISPostedFile*
- *IISReadCookie*
- *IISRequest*
- *IISRequestDictionary*
- *IISResponse*
- *IISServer*
- *IISSessionObject*

- *IISStringList*
- *IISVariantDictionary*
- *IISViewState*
- *IISWriteCookie*

For example, you could write an X++ class to retrieve a variable from the HTTP context, which you could then use in another X++ class. In the following code example, the method takes a parameter, which is the name of the HTTP context variable, the value of which is obtained using *IISRequest*.

```
str getIISServerVariable(str 80 var)
{
    IISRequest request;
    str res;
    ;
    request = new IISRequest();
    res = request.serverVariables().itemTxt(var);
    return res;
}
```

If you want to develop a new, custom Web-enabled application that integrates with Dynamics AX and can access managed HTTP context information, you can use both ASP.NET and .NET Business Connector. The interoperability among IIS, ASP.NET, and .NET Business Connector allows you to access HTTP context information from X++ code that is part of your application.

Note To successfully run with Dynamics AX 2009, existing applications developed with the previous version of the COM Business Connector and ASP that accessed the unmanaged HTTP context must be migrated to ASP.NET.

Security

This section highlights the security mechanisms in place for .NET Business Connector and covers authentication, authorization (including security keys), and code access security.

Authentication

Integrated Windows authentication is implemented throughout Dynamics AX 2009, including .NET Business Connector. The managed classes use parameters that are specific to Integrated Windows authentication.

Authorization

.NET Business Connector has an associated set of Dynamics AX security keys that control access to different parts of its functionality. Table 10-1 describes these security keys. You can find more information about these keys in the Data Dictionary under Security Keys.

TABLE 10-1 Dynamics AX Security Keys

Security Key	Description
SysCom	Enables or disables the use of COM Business Connector and .NET Business Connector
SysComData	Controls the user's level of access to data
SysComExecution	Controls access to execution rights of classes and jobs in .NET Business Connector
SysComIIS	Controls whether .NET Business Connector is accessible to users when it's running in the context of IIS

You can create sessions in .NET Business Connector either directly or indirectly. The direct approach uses the credentials of the current Dynamics AX user. The indirect approach uses the proxy impersonation mechanism whereby an AX user can be impersonated using the *LogonAs* API. You can control the use of .NET Business Connector in different user groups in Dynamics AX by configuring these security keys. If you do configure these security keys, they will apply only in sessions created directly.

Code Access Security

Code access security (CAS) was introduced in Dynamics AX 4.0. CAS is a mechanism intended to help Dynamics AX developers write code that invokes protected X++ APIs in a manner that minimizes the potential for them to be maliciously exploited. A protected API is an X++ API method that has been secured by using CAS. CAS also ensures that the protected APIs are executed only on the AOS, not on the Dynamics AX client or .NET Business Connector. CAS therefore restricts the X++ APIs that can be executed locally in .NET Business Connector. If an attempt to use a restricted API is made, a CAS exception is returned.

Usage Scenarios for .NET Business Connector

In this section, we provide several scenarios to demonstrate how you can use .NET Business Connector in real-world situations. The usage scenarios described fall into the following categories:

- Client
- Web
- Server

Client

In client-based scenarios, .NET Business Connector and the application that uses it are installed on a user's computer. To make client setup easier, Dynamics AX 2009 allows the installation of just .NET Business Connector on the development machine.

Business Data Lookup Snap for Microsoft Office

The business data lookup snap is an add-in for Microsoft Office that was written using .NET Business Connector. It allows information workers to access and use Dynamics AX data from within Office applications. For example, customer information stored in Dynamics AX can be retrieved using this snap and inserted into a letter being written in Microsoft Word.

This type of integration has some specific requirements:

- It must be possible to authenticate the current user as a valid, active Dynamics AX user.
- It must be possible to take a user-selected Dynamics AX record and search string, and retrieve any matching records from Dynamics AX.
- It must be possible to copy the retrieved data into the Office application being used.

The following actions are associated with the use of .NET Business Connector for the business data lookup snap:

1. The business data lookup snap is added to Office.
2. The snap authenticates the current user's credentials using .NET Business Connector and establishes a Dynamics AX session.
3. The selected Dynamics AX record and user-entered search criteria passed to the snap code are used to create a query that .NET Business Connector executes.
4. If any records are returned to .NET Business Connector from the query, they are passed back to the snap.

To find out more details about the business data lookup snap, go to the CodePlex site and search for "Snap-ins for Microsoft Dynamics AX." Note that you must register to see the snap-ins.

PDA Synchronization Example

A potential client-based use of .NET Business Connector is for PDA synchronization. For example, you could develop an application that allows a PDA to collect information that can be uploaded to Dynamics AX. PDAs generally rely on some kind of synchronization manager; if this synchronization program is customizable, you can extend it to integrate with Dynamics AX.

The specific requirements for this type of integration follow:

- It must be possible to verify that the current Windows user matches the identity of the device owner.
- It must be possible to retrieve the data to be uploaded from the PDA or from the local file system if downloaded from the PDA.
- It must be possible to validate and insert the downloaded data into the corresponding Dynamics AX tables.

The diagram in Figure 10-5 illustrates the topology of this integration.

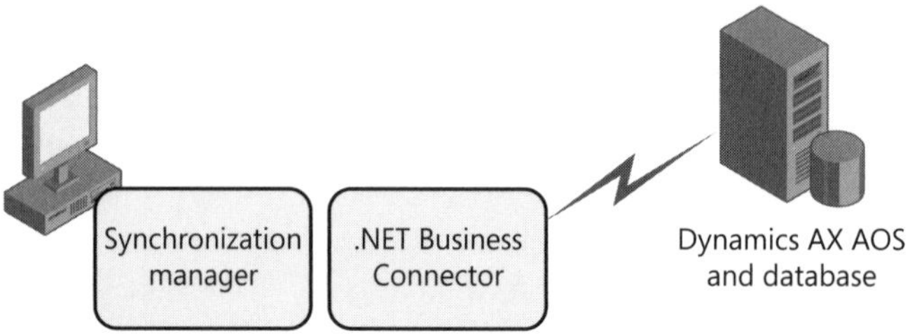

FIGURE 10-5 PDA synchronization using .NET Business Connector

The following actions are associated with the use of .NET Business Connector during PDA synchronization:

1. The synchronization manager downloads data from the PDA and recognizes that it needs to be uploaded to Dynamics AX.
2. The synchronization manager authenticates the current user's credentials with .NET Business Connector and establishes a Dynamics AX session.
3. Data read from the PDA is uploaded to Dynamics AX through .NET Business Connector. The data is validated using X++ business logic defined in Dynamics AX. Exceptions are reported as errors in the synchronization manager.
4. Validated data is persisted in the Dynamics AX database.

This usage scenario shows how you could incorporate .NET Business Connector into the synchronization mechanism for a PDA, and how data entered on the PDA can be transferred to Dynamics AX. For more information on this approach, look at the mobile solutions that have been developed for Dynamics AX (*http://www.microsoft.com/dynamics/ax/product/mobilesolutions.mspx*). They include development tools for building mobile applications.

Web

Earlier in this chapter, we explained how .NET Business Connector interacts with the managed HTTP context, thus enabling Web applications, including Enterprise Portal, to access and use this context information. One of the primary processes in Enterprise Portal is page processing, which is a good example of how you can use a .NET Business Connector to enable a Web application. Refer to Chapter 7 for a detailed description of Enterprise Portal page processing and the role of .NET Business Connector.

Server

A final usage scenario uses .NET Business Connector on the server that hosts the AOS and the Dynamics AX database, as shown in Figure 10-6.

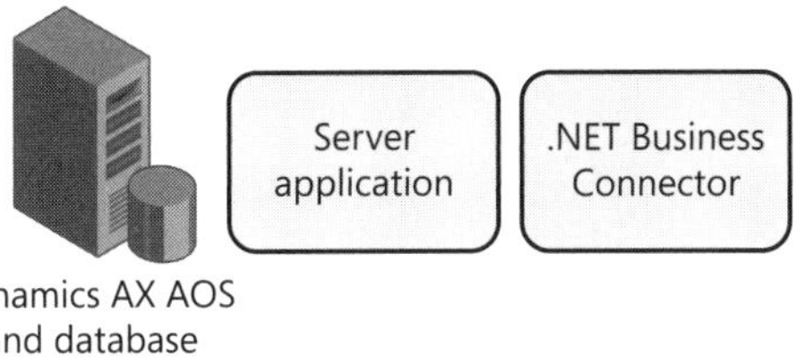

FIGURE 10-6 Server-based use of .NET Business Connector

In this scenario, a non-Web-based managed application uses .NET Business Connector to integrate with Dynamics AX. This approach can be used for a variety of purposes, but one example is offline processing. Typically, a Dynamics AX user must be logged on to a computer to authenticate in Dynamics AX. In some cases, this isn't possible. For example, the asynchronous integration offered by the AIF doesn't require the originating user to be logged on to the machine where data is processed and inserted into Dynamics AX. However, this task must be executed using the correct user identity.

The solution is to use .NET Business Connector to impersonate a Dynamics AX user, which you can do in one of three ways:

- Use the *Logon* API method and supply the original user's credentials, assuming they are known and maintained securely.
- Use the *LogonAs* API method and supply the credentials of the .NET Business Connector proxy user. The .NET Business Connector proxy user is a specifically created domain account used by the user impersonation mechanism in .NET Business Connector. For more details about this, review the online Help section "How to: Connect to Microsoft Dynamics AX Using the *LogonAs* Method."
- Execute .NET Business Connector in a Windows process owned by the .NET Business Connector proxy user, and then call the *LogonAs* API method.

If you use one of these methods to log on to .NET Business Connector, you can develop server-based applications that can process data using the correct Dynamics AX user identity.

Working with .NET Business Connector

In this section, we take a closer look at building applications with .NET Business Connector, including the following topics:

- Data types and mappings
- Managed classes
- Request and response processing
- Exception handling

Data Types and Mappings

.NET Business Connector makes it easier to develop managed applications that integrate with Dynamics AX by bridging two programming environments: the managed .NET Framework environment and the Dynamics AX X++ environment. Inevitably, some form of translation is required when passing objects and data between these two environments. Table 10-2 maps equivalent data types between the .NET Framework and Dynamics AX.

TABLE 10-2 Data Type Mappings

Dynamics AX Data Type	.NET Framework Data Type
String	*System.String*
Int	*System.Int32*
Real	*System.Double*
Enums	*System.Enum* .NET Business Connector uses integers for enumerations.
Time	*System.Int* You must convert this value to Dynamics AX time format. The value is the number of seconds since midnight.
Date	*System.Date* You need to use only the date portion because time is stored separately in Dynamic AX.
Container	*AxaptaContainer*
Boolean (enumeration)	*System.Boolean* Dynamics AX uses integers to represent Boolean values of *true* and *false*.
GUID	*System.GUID*
Int64	*System.Int64*

The managed class methods in .NET Business Connector explicitly support specific data types for parameters and return values. Refer to the Microsoft Dynamics AX 2009 software development kit (SDK) for more information.

Managed Classes

This section provides an overview of the managed classes in .NET Business Connector. You develop applications with .NET Business Connector by instantiating and using the public managed classes described in Table 10-3.

TABLE 10-3 .NET Business Connector Managed Classes

Class Name	Description
Axapta	Provides methods for connecting to a Dynamics AX system, creating Dynamics AX objects (class objects, record objects, container objects, and buffer objects), and executing transactions.
AxaptaBuffer	Represents an array of bytes and provides methods for manipulating the buffer contents. *AxaptaBuffer* objects can be added to *AxaptaContainer* objects.
AxaptaContainer	Provides methods for reading and modifying containers.
AxaptaObject	The managed representation of an X++ class. Instance methods can be called through it.
AxaptaRecord	Provides methods for reading and manipulating common objects (tables in the Dynamics AX database).

Examples of how these classes are used in an application are provided in the following section.

Processing Requests and Responses

Much like any integration component, .NET Business Connector processes requests and returns responses associated with the use of the managed classes by applications across all the established .NET Business Connector user sessions. The steps described in the following section traverse the logical component stack presented in Figure 10-2.

Request Processing

Figure 10-7 depicts the processing steps associated with a request made through the managed classes.

1. A request is initiated by invoking a managed class.
2. The request is received and marshaled across the transition layer (where .NET objects and data are converted from .NET to X++).
3. The transition layer dispatches the request to the interpreter in .NET Business Connector.
4. If the request involves executing X++ code, this code is run either locally or remotely on the AOS, depending on the directive associated with the code.

5. After the request is processed, a response is generated.

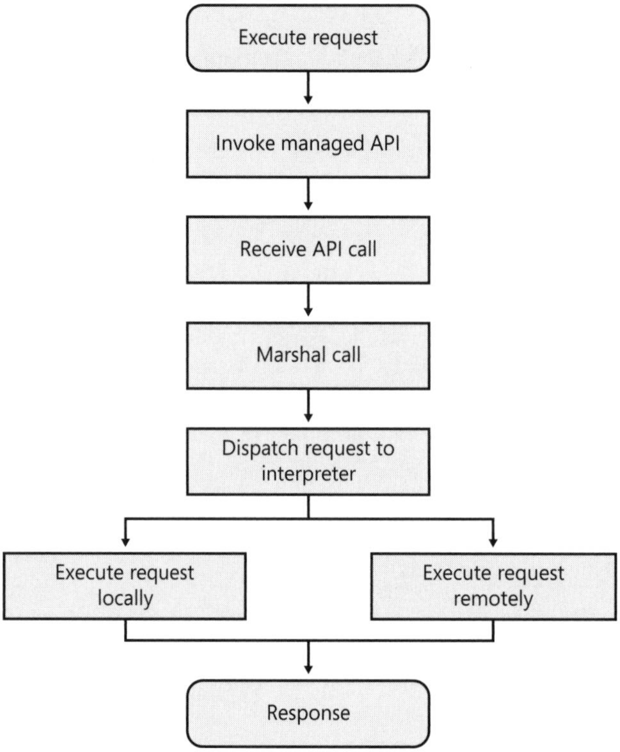

FIGURE 10-7 Request processing in .NET Business Connector

Response Processing

Figure 10-8 depicts the processing steps associated with generating a response.

1. The active request processed by .NET Business Connector completes, successfully or unsuccessfully.
2. The interpreter instantiates and dispatches the response to the transition layer.
3. The transition layer marshals the response to the managed classes (converting objects and data from X++ to .NET).
4. The response is returned to the caller, which is the application that initially invoked .NET Business Connector.

The main variation in the request and response cycle is the location where the X++ code being invoked is executed. The declaration associated with the X++ code controls this location. By default, the X++ code runs where called—that is, from the interpreter where it is invoked. If the *client* keyword is used, execution is forced on either .NET Business Connector or the Dynamics AX client. If the *server* keyword is used, the AOS executes the code.

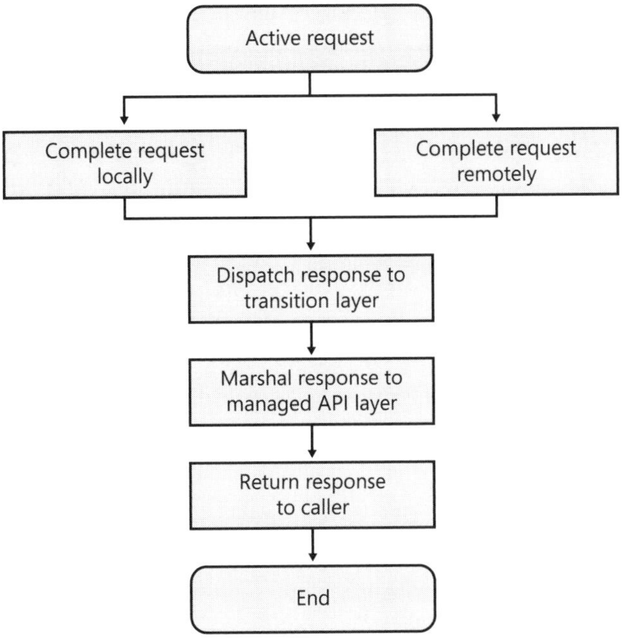

FIGURE 10-8 Response processing in .NET Business Connector

Exception Handling

.NET Business Connector has a large set of managed exceptions that can be raised at run time. This set of managed exceptions provides improved granularity, and therefore more flexibility, in handling those exceptions. Most notable are several remote procedure call (RPC)–related exceptions, which you can use to control error handling associated with the connectivity between .NET Business Connector and the AOS. As a general rule, .NET Business Connector does not catch unhandled exceptions (such as *OutOfMemoryException*). This type of exception is simply propagated to the calling application and prevents .NET Business Connector from masking or hiding such unhandled exceptions.

Refer to the Microsoft Dynamics AX 2009 SDK for more information on the data types, managed classes, and managed exceptions referenced in this section.

HelloWorld Example

How do you write C# code that uses .NET Business Connector? The simple example that follows (the .NET Business Connector equivalent of "Hello World") demonstrates logging on to Dynamics AX. To use the following code, you must be able to log on successfully using the Dynamics AX client. Also, .NET Business Connector must be installed from wherever you execute the code. Create a new project in Microsoft Visual Studio. In the New Project dialog box, select Console Application under Visual C#. This creates the project file structure and files, and presents you with a program named Program.cs. Paste the code in the following example between the curly brackets associated with the *Main* method. In Solution Explorer, right-click References and choose Add Reference. In the Add Reference dialog box, click the Browse tab. Use the file controls to navigate to the Dynamics AX Client\Bin folder. Select Microsoft.Dynamics.BusinessConnectorNet.dll, and then click OK. This makes .NET Business Connector accessible to the C# application. Now you can build and run the solution.

```
using System;
using Microsoft.Dynamics.BusinessConnectorNet;
namespace Demo
{
    class HelloWorldFromBC
    {
        public static void Main(string[] args)
        {
            using (Axapta ax = new Axapta())
            {
                try
                {
                    ax.Logon(null, null, null, null);

                    Console.WriteLine("Hello World from Business Connector!");
                     Console.ReadKey();
                    // Logoff
                    ax.Logoff();
                }
                catch (Exception e)
                {
                    Console.WriteLine("Exception occurred: " + e.Message);
                }
            }
        }
    }
}
```

First, you must instantiate the *Axapta* class to authenticate, using one of the methods within *Axapta*. You use *Logon* method to provide authentication. If you don't provide non-null parameter values, the following values, which you can override as needed, are used:

- Current Windows user
- Default Dynamics AX company for the user
- Default language for the user
- Default active configuration

A message appears on the console, and the Dynamics AX session is terminated using the *Logoff* method.

Accessing Data

To access data in Dynamics AX, you must use the *AxaptaRecord* class. The following example shows how to retrieve a list of inventory items that are classified as "raw material."

```
using System;
using Microsoft.Dynamics.BusinessConnectorNet;

namespace Demo
{
    // ListInvItemRecords
    // Shows how to retrieve and iterate through a list of Dynamics AX records
    class ListInvItemRecords
    {
        public static void Main(string[] args)
        {
            String invItemNameField = "ItemName";
            Object invItemName;
            String invItemIdField = "ItemId";
            Object invItemId;

            using (Axapta ax = new Axapta())
            {
                try
                {
                    // Logon
                    ax.Logon(null, null, null, null);

                    Console.WriteLine("*** List inventory item records");

                    // Instantiate the Dynamics AX record.
                    AxaptaRecord axRecord = ax.CreateAxaptaRecord("InventTable");

                    // Execute a query.
                    axRecord.ExecuteStmt(
                        "select * from %1 where %1.ItemGroupId == 'RawMat'");

                    // Loop through matching Dynamics AX records.
                    while (axRecord.Found)
                    {
                        invItemName = axRecord.get_Field(invItemNameField);
                        invItemId = axRecord.get_Field(invItemIdField);

                        Console.WriteLine(invItemId + "\t" + invItemName);

                        axRecord.Next();
                    }
                    Console.ReadKey();
                    // Logoff
                    ax.Logoff();
                }
```

```
                catch (Exception e)
                {
                    Console.WriteLine("Exception occurred: " + e.Message);
                }
            }
        }
    }
}
```

Here are the important aspects of the code example:

- Variables are declared to store the Dynamics AX record data that is retrieved and to hold the field names used.
- Authentication is the same as in the HelloWorld example.
- To begin working with a specific type of Dynamics AX record, you must first instantiate an *AxaptaRecord* object, and you must provide the name or ID of the record as an argument.
- A query is executed against the Dynamics AX record using *ExecuteStmt*, which parses the query syntax and replaces the substitution variable (%1) with the name of the record. The query syntax is generic. Dynamics AX executes the query with the exact syntax appropriate for the database being used, whether Microsoft SQL Server or Oracle.
- A *while* loop cycles through the records returned from Dynamics AX, which uses another method, *Found*, on *AxaptaRecord* to determine that matching records exist.
- For each record, *get_Field* retrieves each field value and assigns a value to the appropriate variable declared earlier.
- To proceed to the next record, the *Next* method is called.
- *Logoff* is called to terminate the session.

This code sample shows one way of accessing data in Dynamics AX. Another approach uses the *Query* object, which is described in the upcoming section "Method 2: Using the *Query* Object." In addition to accessing data, you can also invoke X++ business logic directly from .NET Business Connector, as shown in the following section.

Querying Data Across Companies

When you log on to Dynamics AX with .NET Business Connector, you establish a session that is dedicated to one specific company that the Dynamics AX user has access to. (This is similar to selecting a company in the Dynamics AX client.) At times, however, an application you're developing might need to access data that resides in a number of companies. For example, you might want to query vendors across all the companies in Dynamics AX. To address this need, Dynamics AX 2009 supports defining and executing cross-company queries from .NET Business Connector.

Cross-company queries can be executed in two ways. The first is to use the *ExecuteStmt* API. The second is to use the *Query* object. In the following subsections, we explain each approach, using code samples to demonstrate.

Method 1: Using *ExecuteStmt*

When using *ExecuteStmt* to query Dynamics AX, you can extend the scope of the query to cover more than one company. (Querying against just one company is the default behavior.) The following code sample shows how to do this.

```
using System;
using Microsoft.Dynamics.BusinessConnectorNet;

namespace Demo
{
    // ListVendors - shows how to retrieve and iterate through a list of Dynamics AX records
    // (assumes you have two companies: DMO and DMO2 - replace with your own
    // companies)

    class CrossCompanyQuery
    {
        public static void Main(string[] args)
        {
            String vendAccountNumField = "AccountNum";
            Object vendAccNum;
            String vendNameField = "Name";
            Object vendName;

            using (Axapta ax = new Axapta())
            {
                try
                {
                    // Logon
                    ax.Logon("DMO", null, null, null);

                    Console.WriteLine("*** List vendor records");

                    // Instantiate record
                    AxaptaRecord axRecord = ax.CreateAxaptaRecord("VendTable");

                    // Execute a query against VendTable

                    axRecord.ExecuteStmt(
                        "container c=['DMO','DMO2']; select crosscompany:c %1");

                    // Loop through found records
                    while (axRecord.Found)
                    {
                        vendAccNum = axRecord.get_Field(vendAccountNumField);
                        vendName = axRecord.get_Field(vendNameField);

                        Console.WriteLine(vendName + "\t" + vendAccNum);
```

```
                    axRecord.Next();
                }
                Console.ReadKey();
                // Logoff
                ax.Logoff();
            }
            catch (Exception e)
            {
                Console.WriteLine("Exception occurred: " + e.Message);
            }
        }
    }
  }
}
```

The key here is the special syntax within *ExecuteStmt* that permits multiple company IDs to be specified.

Method 2: Using the *Query* Object

The second method uses the Dynamics AX *Query* object, which provides a lot of flexibility for constructing and executing queries. The following code sample shows how a cross-company query is enabled by using this approach.

```
using System;
using Microsoft.Dynamics.BusinessConnectorNet;

namespace Demo
{
    // ListVendors - shows how to retrieve Dynamics AX records from multiple companies
    // using the Query object (assumes you have two companies: DMO, and DMO2
    // - replace with your own companies)
    class CrossCompanyQueryUsingQueryObject
    {
        public static void Main(string[] args)
        {
            String vendAccountNumField = "AccountNum";
            String vendNameField = "Name";
            AxaptaObject axQuery;
            AxaptaObject axQueryRun;
            AxaptaObject axQueryDataSource;

            using (Axapta ax = new Axapta())
            {
                try
                {
                    // Logon
                    ax.Logon("DMO", null, null, null);
```

```
                Console.WriteLine(
                 "*** List vendor records from DAT and DMO using Query object");

                // Get the table ID of the table to query
                int vendTableId = (int)ax.CallStaticClassMethod("global",
                   "tablename2id", "VendTable");

                // Instantiate the Query object
                axQuery = ax.CreateAxaptaObject("Query");

                // Add a data source
                axQueryDataSource = (AxaptaObject)axQuery.Call(
                   "AddDataSource", vendTableId);

                // Enable cross company query
                axQuery.Call("AllowCrossCompany", true);

                // Add two companies for the cross company query
                axQuery.Call("AddCompanyRange", "DMO2");
                axQuery.Call("AddCompanyRange", "DMO");

                // Run the query!
                axQueryRun = ax.CreateAxaptaObject("QueryRun", axQuery);

                while ((bool)axQueryRun.Call("next"))
                {
                    using (AxaptaRecord axRecord =
                       (AxaptaRecord)axQueryRun.Call("get", vendTableId))
                    {
                        Object vendAccNum = axRecord.get_Field(
                            vendAccountNumField);
                        Object vendName = axRecord.get_Field(vendNameField);
                        Console.WriteLine(vendName + "\t" + vendAccNum);
                    }
                }
                Console.ReadKey();
                // Logoff
                ax.Logoff();
            }
            catch (Exception e)
            {
                Console.WriteLine("Exception occurred: " + e.Message);
            }
        }
    }
  }
}
```

Notice that *AllowCrossCompany* has to be invoked to enable a cross-company query. The call to *AddCompanyRange* allows an arbitrary number of companies to be added to the query.

Invoking Business Logic

In addition to accessing data, you can also invoke business logic defined in Dynamics AX directly from .NET Business Connector. In this example, you call a method in an X++ class to update inventory item details in Dynamics AX based on data from a separate inventory management system. To do this, you use the *CallStaticClassMethod* method in the *Axapta* managed class, as shown in the following code.

```
using System;
using Microsoft.Dynamics.BusinessConnectorNet;

namespace Demo
{
    // UpdateInventoryQuantity - shows how to call a static X++ class method
    class UpdateInventoryQuantity
    {
        public static void Main(string[] args)
        {
            object returnValue;

            using (Axapta ax = new Axapta())
            {
                try
                {
                    // Logon
                    ax.Logon(null, null, null, null);

                    // InventoryManager is the class, updateInventoryQty
                    // is the method to be invoked
                    returnValue = ax.CallStaticClassMethod("InventoryManager",
                       "updateInventoryQty");

                    // Write a message according to the result of the
                    // class/method call
                    if ((Boolean)returnValue)
                        Console.WriteLine(
                            "Inventory quantity updated successfully");
                    else
                        Console.WriteLine("Inventory quantity update failed");
                }
                catch (Exception e)
                {
                    Console.WriteLine("Exception occurred: " + e.Message);
                }
            }
        }
    }
}
```

The X++ class returns a Boolean result in this case, which is then used to determine the next action in the application.

As you can see from these examples, developing applications that integrate with Dynamics AX using .NET Business Connector is relatively straightforward. Although real applications would use the managed classes more extensively, the approach to accessing data and invoking business logic would remain the same.

Enhanced CLR Interoperability with the Dynamics AX Interpreter and X++

As we stated earlier in the chapter, the reason Microsoft developed .NET Business Connector was to simplify the creation of applications that integrate with Dynamics AX by using the .NET Framework. Although the managed classes delivered with .NET Business Connector are a good first step to achieving this integration, CLR interoperability takes this integration one step further. In Dynamics AX 4.0, CLR interoperability represented the ability to access classes in assemblies managed by the .NET Framework CLR from X++. (For more information on CLR interop in Dynamics AX 4.0, go to *http://msdn.microsoft.com/en-us/library/bb986586(AX.10).aspx*.) Because CLR interoperability was built into the Dynamics AX 4.0 kernel, it was available to use from .NET Business Connector in that release. In Dynamics AX 2009, CLR interoperability from .NET Business Connector has been augmented with two capabilities: the ability to pass managed objects to Dynamics AX, and the ability to register managed callbacks. (For more on CLR interop in Dynamics AX 2009, refer to *http://msdn.microsoft.com/en-us/library/cc598160.aspx*.)

Passing Managed Objects to Dynamics AX

Building on the idea of accessing classes in .NET assemblies from X++, it is possible in Dynamics AX 2009 to pass managed objects into X++, and then act on them from there. This capability existed in Dynamics AX 4.0; however, it was limited to a specific set of managed types. Any attempt to pass a managed object anything other than one of the supported managed types generated an exception. In Dynamics AX 2009, the type mappings are the same; however, the managed types not explicitly supported are marshaled as *CLRObjects*. Table 10-4 summarizes the marshaling behavior by .NET type.

TABLE 10-4 .NET Type Marshaling Behavior

.NET Type	X++ Type
Base types (see Table 10-2, Data Type Mappings)	X++ equivalent
.NET Business Connector event delegate	*ManagedEventDelegate*
Other	*CLRObject*

The following code samples illustrate this functionality by showing how a *strBuilder* managed object is passed to an X++ method, the contents of which are then appended and returned to the calling C# application.

The first code sample is a static X++ method in Dynamics AX within a class called *Class1*.

```
public static str method1(System.Text.StringBuilder strBuilder)
{
    str s = "";

    if(strBuilder)
    {
        strBuilder.Append(" of passing arbitrary .net objects to X++");

        s = strBuilder.ToString();
    }
    return s;
}
```

The next code sample is the corresponding C# code.

```
using System;
using Microsoft.Dynamics.BusinessConnectorNet;

namespace Demo
{
    class PassingDynamicObjectsToDynamicsAX
    {
        public static void Main(string[] args)
        {
            using (Axapta ax = new Axapta())
            {
                try
                {
                    // Logon
                    ax.Logon(null, null, null, null);

                    string str = (string)ax.CallStaticClassMethod(
                       "Class1", "method1",
                       new System.Text.StringBuilder("This is a test"));

                    Console.WriteLine(str);
                    Console.ReadKey();

                    // Logoff
                    ax.Logoff();

                }
                catch (Exception e)
                {
                    Console.WriteLine("Exception occurred: " + e.Message);
                }
            }
        }
    }
}
```

Figure 10-9 displays the output, showing the combined string.

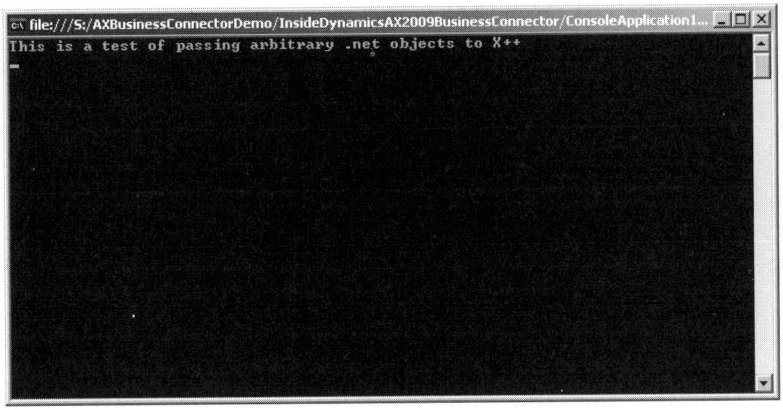

FIGURE 10-9 The output from running the sample code, which demonstrates passing managed objects to Dynamics AX by using .NET Business Connector

Registering Managed Callbacks

Another aspect of CLR interoperability is the ability to communicate events from X++ to managed code by using the new delegate functionality in .NET Business Connector. Enterprise Portal uses delegate functionality to enable ASP.NET user interface controls (such as data grids) to respond synchronously to changes in the underlying Dynamics AX data. In this case, managed callbacks ensure that the data displayed in the grid corresponds to the actual stored data. To implement a managed callback, follow these steps:

1. Define an X++ event *args* class. (This is optional; you can also use the default one.)
2. Create a managed event handler that expects the event *args* defined in step 1.
3. Register the event handler by passing it to an X++ class that maintains it.
4. When the condition is triggered, invoke the managed handler that you registered in step 3.

The following two code samples illustrate the use of managed callbacks. The first is a segment of X++ code that triggers the event and also extends the *ManagedEventArgs* to include some data that represents the payload from the managed callback.

```
// This X++ method triggers the event
public void method2(ManagedEventDelegate delegate)
{
    // Based on some condition, trigger the managed event handler

    delegate.invoke(this, new MyEventArgs("This is a test of managed event handler"));
}
```

```
// Define my own event args if the standard one is not good enough
class MyEventArgs extends ManagedEventArgs
{
    str strSpecificToMyEvent;
}
public void new(str data)
{
    strSpecificToMyEvent = data;
}
str eventData()
{
    return strSpecificToMyEvent;
}
```

The second sample is the C# managed event handler code triggered from the preceding X++ code.

```
using System;
using Microsoft.Dynamics.BusinessConnectorNet;
namespace Demo
{
    class RegisteringManagedCallbacks
    {
        // This is the managed event handler that will be triggered from X++
        static void ManagedEventHandler(AxaptaObject sender, AxaptaObject eventArgs)
        {
            Console.WriteLine(eventArgs.Call("eventData"));

            Console.ReadKey();
        }
        public static void Main(string[] args)
        {
            using (Axapta ax = new Axapta())
            {
                try
                {
                    ax.Logon(null, null, null, null);
                    AxaptaObject axObj = ax.CreateAxaptaObject("Class1");
                    axObj.Call("method2", new
                        AxEventHandlerDelegate(
                        RegisteringManagedCallbacks.ManagedEventHandler));
                }
                catch (Exception e)
                {
                    Console.WriteLine("Exception occurred: " + e.Message);
                }
            }
        }
    }
}
```

Figure 10-10 shows the output from running the sample code, where the managed callback payload is displayed.

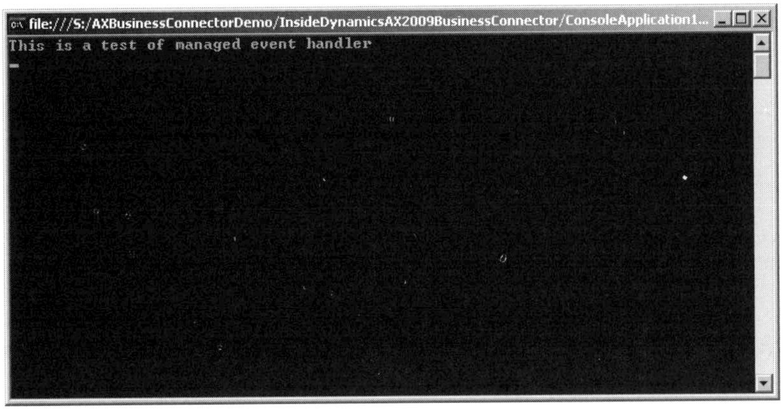

FIGURE 10-10 The output from running the sample code, which demonstrates registering managed callbacks using .NET Business Connector

Migrating Applications

The COM Business Connector has been deprecated in Dynamics AX 2009. It ships in Dynamics AX 2009, but it is being minimally supported and will be entirely removed in the next release of Dynamics AX. If you own or maintain existing applications that use the COM Business Connector, and they need to work with the next release of Dynamics AX, you should plan to migrate the applications to use .NET Business Connector. Refer to the guidelines for migrating applications that are provided in *Inside Microsoft Dynamics AX 4.0*.

Chapter 11

Reporting in Dynamics AX 2009

In this chapter:

The objectives of this chapter are to:

- Describe reporting in Microsoft Dynamics AX 2009.
- Provide an architectural overview of reporting with Microsoft SQL Server Reporting Services.
- Describe how to build and customize production reports using the Dynamics AX reporting tools.
- Explain how to integrate Reporting Services reports into Dynamics AX applications and Enterprise Portal.
- Describe how to use Reporting Services to enable users to build ad hoc reports.

Introduction

In the context of business intelligence (BI) in Dynamics AX 2009, reporting is the mechanism through which users extract and use data from the Dynamics AX system. Reporting is a critical component for any business because it is a primary way for users to have visibility into their business. This visibility helps users understand how to proceed in their day-to-day work, make more-informed decisions, support critical thinking and analysis, and finally, take action.

This chapter provides a high-level overview of how the reporting components work together in Dynamics AX 2009. It describes how, through Dynamics AX, customers can leverage SQL Server Reporting Services and integrate it into the Dynamics AX enterprise resource planning (ERP) framework. This chapter also highlights the new features in the Dynamics AX 2009 reporting development tools, describes how the ad hoc reporting system works, and gives guidance to developers and administrators about how to configure ad hoc reporting.

Reporting Overview

Before delving into the details of building Reporting Services reports and creating ad hoc reporting models, you should know the primary reporting concepts in Dynamics AX and have a high-level understanding of how the Dynamics AX Reporting Framework is designed. We discuss these topics in the following subsections.

What Is a Report?

For the purposes of this chapter, a report is simply data from Dynamics AX that has been rendered into human-readable form. For example, at its simplest, a report could be a list of customers shown on the screen. A report could also be a printed piece of paper containing details about a specific customer. A Web page listing inventory is a report. A Microsoft Office Excel worksheet showing all the statistics of on-time deliveries is also a kind of report. This definition of a report is broad, but it reflects the varied, real-world usage of reporting in Dynamics AX.

Reporting and Users

You can categorize reporting on two axes: data depth and business activity. As shown in Figure 11-1, the role users play in an organization and the reports they use fall at one point (or perhaps several points) on these axes.

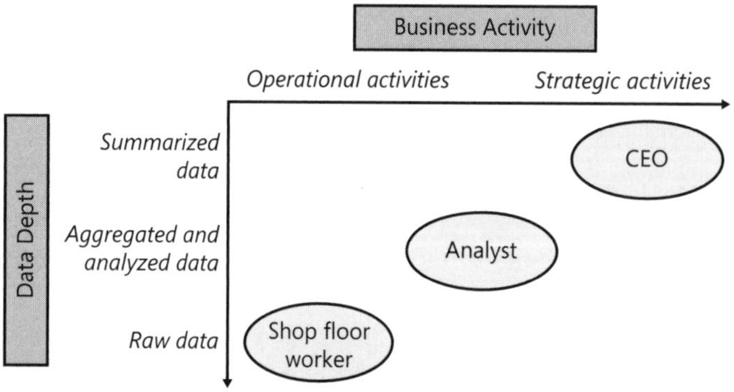

FIGURE 11-1 Depiction of how users in different business roles work with different kinds of data, requiring different kinds of reports

Here are some details about the reporting needs of the roles shown in Figure 11-1:

- A CEO who is interested in monitoring the business periodically uses strategic reports that provide summarized data across time periods.
- An analyst examines the business looking for patterns that might lead to changing business plans and priorities and uses reports that allow the data to be interactively

sliced by region or time period. This makes it easier to detect trends and patterns, and the results of this analysis feed into the CEO's decisions.

- A shop floor worker is concerned with the day-to-day activities of the business and uses reports that reflect the immediate needs of the shop floor. For example, a shop floor worker would use a simple report that lists all the items in the inventory.

Dynamics AX reports help satisfy the needs of these users so that relative to an individual's role in the business, he or she has the data necessary to be effective.

Providing Reports in Dynamics AX 2009

Dynamics AX 2009 supports both production reports and ad hoc reports. Production reports, which can range from simple to complex, are designed and created by developers. Ad hoc reports are generally simpler and created directly by users, without help from developers.

> **Note** In Latin, *ad hoc* means "for this," and the term indicates something done, often impromptu, for a specific purpose. In the context of Dynamics AX reporting, an ad hoc report is very specific to the needs of the user who created it.

Report Categories

Dynamics AX 2009 reports fall within three general categories:

- Production reports that use one of the two reporting platforms—MorphX or Reporting Services—supported by Dynamics AX 2009. Developers create these reports because of their complexity.
- Ad hoc reports built on MorphX or Reporting Services. Once developers and administrators have put ad hoc reporting models in place, users can create their own ad hoc reports.
- Ad hoc reports that access Dynamics AX data directly.

> **Note** Read more about the MorphX and Reporting Services platforms used for Dynamics AX 2009 reporting later in this section.

Kinds of Reports in Dynamics AX 2009

Table 11-1 lists the different kinds of reports available in Dynamics AX 2009 and some characteristics of each.

TABLE 11-1 Kinds of Reports Available in Dynamics AX 2009

Type of Report	Production Reporting?	Ad Hoc Reporting?	Reporting Platform	Report Creation Tool
MorphX production reports	Yes	No	MorphX	MorphX tools
Reporting Services production reports	Yes	N/A	Reporting Services	Visual Studio 2008
Auto reports	No	Yes	MorphX	Dynamics AX client
Reporting Services ad hoc reports	N/A	Yes	Reporting Services	SQL Report Builder
Export list page to Excel	No	Yes	N/A—direct access to Dynamics AX	Dynamics AX client and Excel
Connect Excel to Dynamics AX cube	No	Yes	N/A—direct access to Dynamics AX	Excel

Note For more information about Dynamics AX list pages, see Chapter 5, "Customizing Dynamics AX." To learn more about Dynamics AX cubes, read the white paper "Microsoft Dynamics AX 2009 Business Intelligence Cube Reference Guide," available from the Using Microsoft Dynamics AX 2009 Web site at *http://microsoft.com/dynamics/ax/using/ax_installorupgrade*, or directly from the Microsoft Download Center at *http://www.microsoft.com/downloads*.

Reporting Platforms in Dynamics AX 2009

Dynamics AX 2009 integrates with two reporting platforms: MorphX, the Dynamics AX–specific reporting platform, and Reporting Services (SQL Server Reporting Services), which is the Microsoft standard reporting platform.

MorphX has been the traditional Dynamics AX reporting platform since the first version of the product and has been supporting customer needs for a long time. Starting with Dynamics AX 2009, Reporting Services is considered the primary reporting platform for the product.

Microsoft decided to shift to Reporting Services as the standard reporting platform for Dynamics AX rather than standardizing on MorphX, which is a proprietary reporting platform, for several reasons, including these:

- Advantages from the availability of a much larger pool of resources, including developers, partners, and training partners who are already familiar with Reporting Services and Visual Studio.
- It aligns with the overall direction in Microsoft to standardize on Reporting Services.

Here are some of the features that Reporting Services offers that are unavailable in MorphX:

- Charting
- Reports using non–Dynamics AX data sources
- Reports using OLAP cube data
- Interactivity
- Ad hoc reporting

Transitioning from MorphX to Reporting Services

Dynamics AX 2009 is the first release that features integration with Reporting Services. Here are some suggestions for gently introducing Reporting Services reports to your business:

- Start experimenting with the Reporting Services technology and features.
- Pick some simple existing MorphX-based reports and create Reporting Services versions of them.
- When a new production report has to be written, create it using Reporting Services if possible.
- Replace an existing production report with one of the several ad hoc reporting features available.

Report Entry Points

Users can view reports in Dynamics AX 2009 from several locations. When working in the Dynamics AX client, users can view reports in the following ways:

- Export data from a Dynamics AX list page into an Excel worksheet.
- View and print an auto report, which Dynamics AX can automatically build from any list page or form the user sees.
- Launch MorphX production reports or Reporting Services production reports from menu items.

Even when users are not working in the Dynamics AX client, they can view reports in these ways:

- Go to the Reporting Services Report Manager Web site to locate and launch production reports or ad hoc reports directly.
- Start Excel and connect it to a Dynamics AX cube to analyze Dynamics AX OLAP data via Excel pivot tables.

Figure 11-2 is a conceptual depiction of how users can access the different kinds of reports available in Dynamics AX.

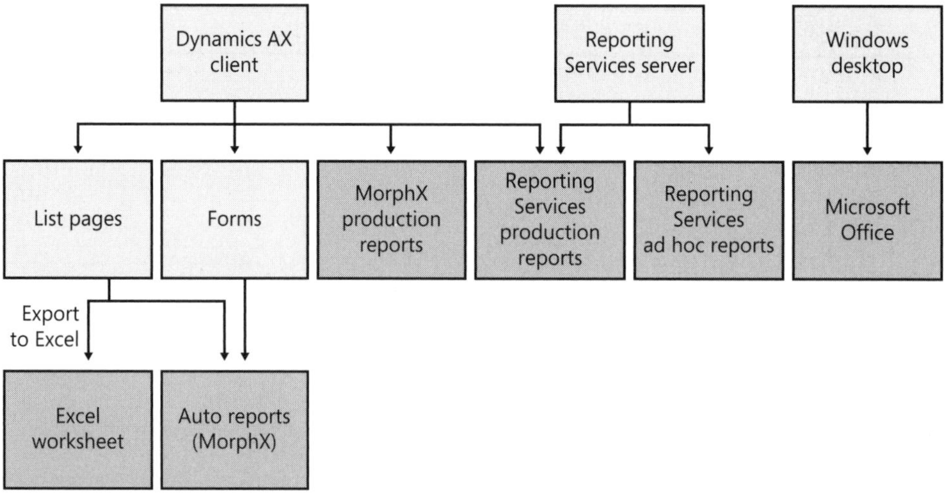

FIGURE 11-2 Kinds of reports in Dynamics AX and how users can access them for viewing

Inside the Dynamics AX 2009 Reporting Framework

In this section, we identify the key components of the Reporting Services reporting framework and describe their functions. We also show how data flows through those components to provide production reports and ad hoc reports, and to allow Excel to access Dynamics AX OLAP data.

Data Flow Overview

Figure 11-3 shows the components of and the data flow in the Reporting Services reporting framework.

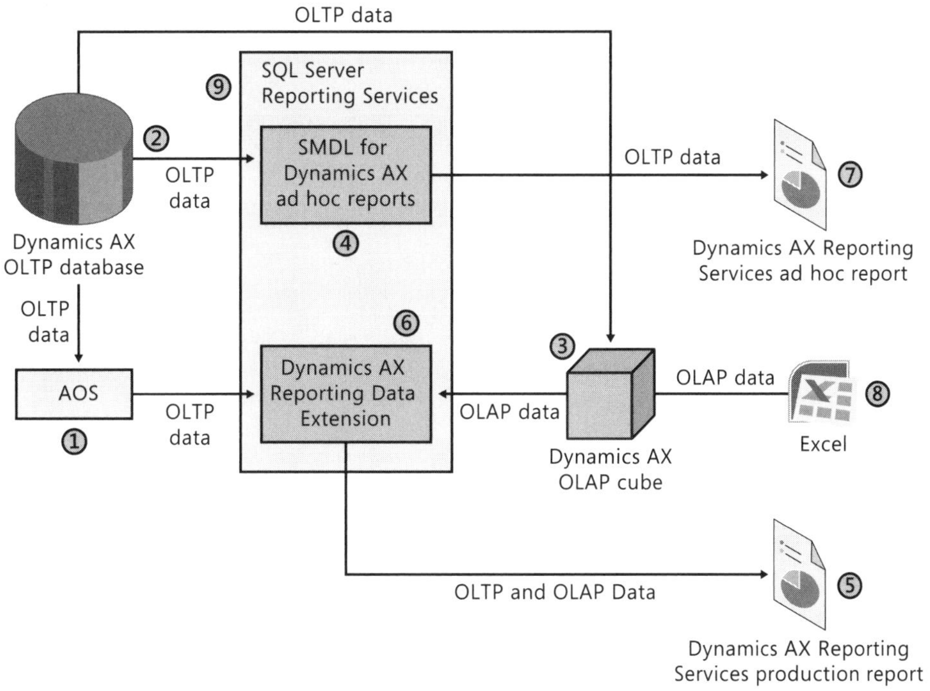

FIGURE 11-3 How Reporting Services reports and Excel retrieve data from Dynamics AX 2009

Each of the key components shown in Figure 11-3 is described in the following list. Every number in the figure corresponds to an item in the list.

1. **Application Object Server (AOS)** The AOS is the core of the Dynamics AX server platform. Dynamics AX production reports retrieve Dynamics AX OLTP data via the AOS. You can read more about the AOS in Chapter 1, "Architectural Overview," and Chapter 14, "The Database Layer."
2. **Dynamics AX OLTP database** This database stores the raw transactional data in the Dynamics AX system. In general, users shouldn't access this database directly but must instead go through the AOS to maintain security. (Reporting Services ad hoc reports are an exception because security is maintained using SQL views ["secure views"] instead of the AOS.)
3. **Dynamics AX OLAP cube** This OLAP cube contains the aggregated and sliced analysis of the OLTP data.
4. **Semantic Model Definition Language (SMDL)** SMDL models are published to the Reporting Services server; they enable users to create and use ad hoc reports that retrieve Dynamics AX OLTP data.

5. **Dynamics AX Reporting Services production reports**
   - These reports always communicate via the Dynamics AX Reporting Data Extension on the Reporting Services server.
   - The Dynamics AX Reporting Data Extension allows the production reports to access Dynamics AX OLTP and OLAP data.
   - When accessing Dynamics AX OLTP data, the Dynamics AX Reporting Data Extension always goes through the AOS.
6. **Dynamics AX Reporting Data Extension**
   - For Dynamics AX Reporting Services production reports, all data access is provided through the Dynamics AX Reporting Data Extension.
7. **Dynamics AX Reporting Services ad hoc reports**
   - Ad hoc reports (7) don't fetch OLTP data (2) via the AOS (1). Instead, they connect to the OLTP database (2) directly.
   - When the IT staff initially configures ad hoc reporting, SQL views ("secure views") are created in the OLTP database that maintain Dynamics AX security when the views are accessed directly from a Reporting Services ad hoc report. Again, OLAP data is fetched directly from the OLAP cubes.
8. **Excel**
   - Excel can directly bind to the Dynamics AX OLAP cubes, allowing users to create pivot tables or pivot charts in Excel to interactively analyze Dynamics AX data.

Reporting Services Production Reporting Technical Scenario

Once Dynamics AX 2009 has been deployed and configured to use Reporting Services, a developer can create a report and have it show data. In the following list, we walk you through the steps for creating a production report in more detail. The numbers in brackets refer to Figure 11-3.

1. A user clicks a menu item attached to a report in the Dynamics AX client.
2. Microsoft Internet Explorer is launched with the URL to the report.
3. Internet Explorer requests the report from the Reporting Services server [9].
4. The Reporting Services server [9] asks the Dynamics AX Reporting Data Extension [6] for any data the report uses.
5. Depending on the report, the Dynamics AX Reporting Data Extension can fetch data from the following sources:
   - The Dynamics AX OLTP database [2] via the AOS [1] (The AOS enforces the security.)

- Directly from a Dynamics AX OLAP cube [3] (Developers should have previously secured the cubes as needed.)
- Some custom source of data

6. The Dynamics AX Reporting Data Extension [6] sends the data back to Reporting Services [9].
7. Reporting Services [9] renders the report as HTML.
8. Reporting Services sends the HTML to Internet Explorer.
9. Internet Explorer displays the report.
10. The user views the report [5].

Reporting Services Ad Hoc Reporting Technical Scenario

Once Dynamics AX 2009 has been deployed and configured to use Reporting Services ad hoc reporting, a users can create a report. The following steps describe how to create an ad hoc report. The numbers in brackets refer to Figure 11-3.

1. A user downloads and installs SQL Server Report Builder 2.0.
2. The user creates a new report.
3. The user can have the report fetch Dynamics AX OLAP or OLTP data.
4. The user publishes the report to the Reporting Services server.
5. The user then launches Internet Explorer and goes to the report.
6. Internet Explorer requests the report from the Reporting Services server [9].
7. The Reporting Services server fetches Dynamics AX data.
   - OLTP data comes directly from the Dynamics AX OLTP database [2].
   - OLAP data comes directly from a Dynamics AX OLAP cube [3].
8. Reporting Services renders the report as HTML.
9. Reporting Services returns the HTML to Internet Explorer.
10. Internet Explorer displays the report.
11. The user views the report [7].

Building Dynamics AX Reporting Services Reports Using Visual Studio

Developers can use the Visual Studio integrated development environment (IDE) to create Dynamics AX Reporting Services reports. In this section, we cover the tools and processes that developers and administrators can use to develop Reporting Services production reports.

Dynamics AX Reporting Development Tools

Dynamics AX 2009 includes development tools that enable developers to create Dynamics AX Reporting Services production reports in Visual Studio 2008. The new development tools have been created from the ground up to be fully integrated with Dynamics AX. These tools provide report designers the benefit of working within the familiar Visual Studio 2008 IDE and the ability to leverage rich reporting features from Reporting Services.

The Dynamics AX reporting development tools comprise a modeling tool that allows report designers to visualize the report elements as they are developing a report. The report is fully customizable within Visual Studio. The reports created are in the Report Definition Language (RDL) format specified by Reporting Services. By utilizing this widely adopted format, report designers can leverage the many features (e.g., charting, interactivity, and access to multiple data sources, as mentioned earlier) that make Reporting Services a popular choice for production reports. These reports can then be deployed, stored, managed, and processed on the report server using the Reporting Services technology.

Integration with Dynamics AX

The Dynamics AX reporting tools include a new Visual Studio project type called "Dynamics AX Reporting Project." This project type allows developers to create Reporting Services reports that bind to data in Dynamics AX.

A Dynamics AX Reporting Project has the following features:

- Allows a report to retrieve from AOS via .NET Business Connector
- Defines report parameters
- Uses localized strings for report elements
- Edits and saves reports in the AOT
- Deploys reports to the report server

Report Development Life Cycle

Figure 11-4 is a high-level view of the report development process.

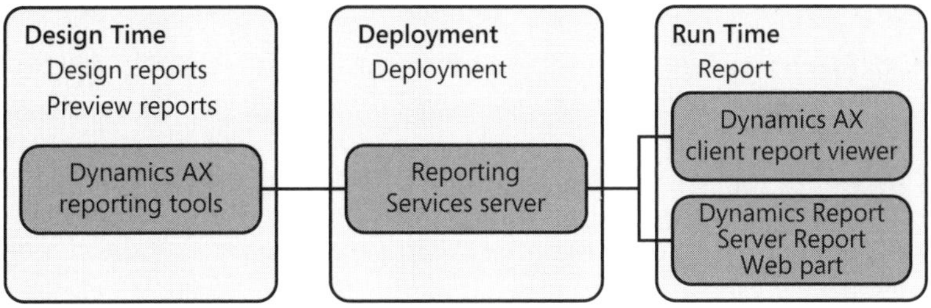

FIGURE 11-4 Report life cycle

Figure 11-4 illustrates the primary tasks performed during the two major stages of the report life cycle. At design time, the report developer designs the report with the Dynamics AX reporting tools in Visual Studio 2008, performs the desired customization, and previews the report design. When the report is ready, the developer deploys the report by using the built-in report deployment feature in Visual Studio or the Dynamics AX 2009 Reports Deployment tool. After the reports are deployed, they are ready to be viewed in the Dynamics AX client and Enterprise Portal. Administrators can configure menu items, and Web parts open the deployed reports.

To learn how to create a report for Dynamics AX in Visual Studio 2008, refer to the useful step-by-step guide on MSDN. These pages have comprehensive descriptions for all the major scenarios report developers would encounter: *http://msdn.microsoft.com/en-us/library/cc653472.aspx*.

Reporting Tools Model Elements

In the following sections, we introduce several important model elements of reporting tools. If you understand these model elements and the way they work, you can develop reports quickly and easily. Figure 11-5 shows a typical Report Model Editor as it appears when you first create a report project.

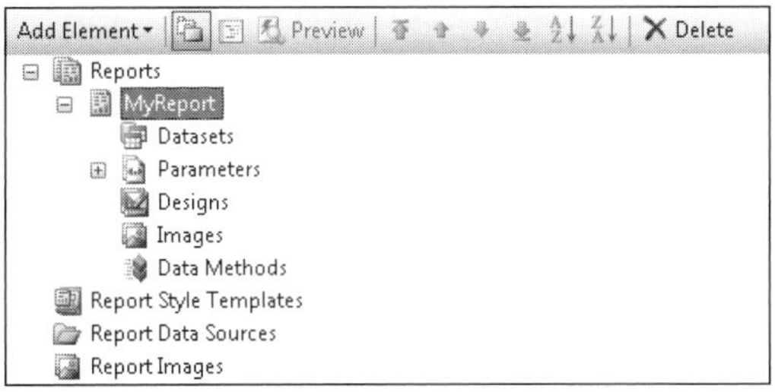

FIGURE 11-5 Report Model Editor

A few collection objects, such Reports and Report Style Templates, are at the root level. Each collection object has zero or more child objects.

Reports

Each Dynamics AX Reporting Project contains one or more report models. Each model has exactly one root Reports element. This element contains all the reports in the current model.

Every model corresponds to a .moxl file displayed in Solution Explorer. Figure 11-6 shows a report project in Visual Studio 2008 Solution Explorer.

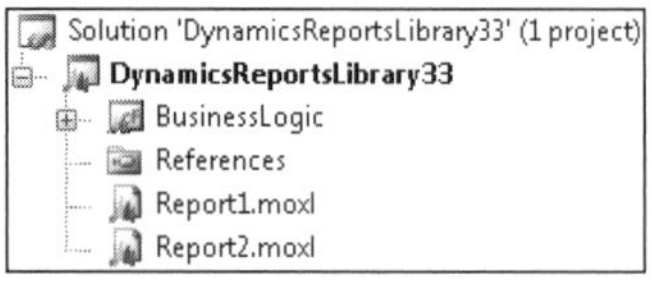

FIGURE 11-6 Dynamics AX report project in Visual Studio 2008 Solution Explorer

Report Designs

A report design is a particular layout for a report. A single report can have multiple designs that form the basic blueprints for the rendered reports. Report developers have the option of creating auto designs or precision designs.

- **Auto designs** An auto design is automatically generated based on the information specified in the report model. You create auto designs in Model Editor. The auto design functionality provides an efficient way to create the most common types of reports, such as a customer list or a list of inventory items.
- **Precision designs** Precision designs are typically used when a report requires a precise layout, such as invoices or bank checks. When creating a precision design, you can manually drag fields onto a report, placing them exactly where you want them.

Auto design layout An auto design follows a particular layout. It has a header, a body containing one or more data regions, and a footer, as shown in Figure 11-7.

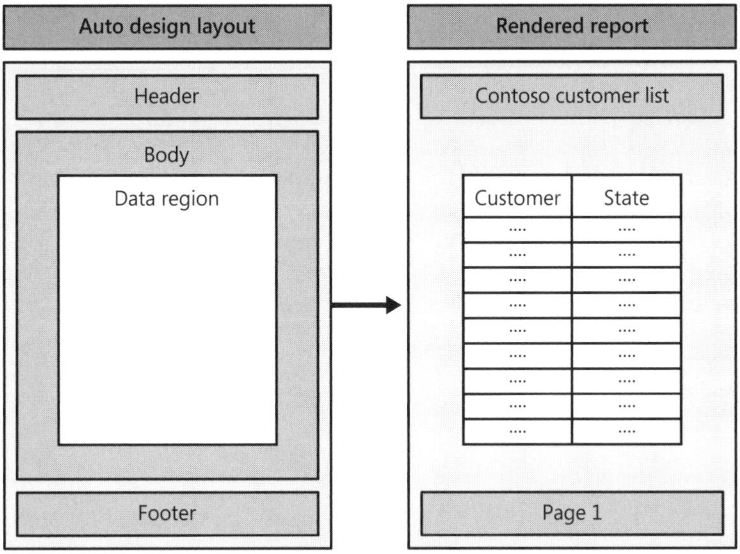

FIGURE 11-7 Auto design layout and the resulting rendered report

You can control the content that is displayed in each area within an auto design. For example, you can include a report title and the date in the header and display the page number in the footer, or you can leave the header and footer blank.

The data regions that display in an auto design depend on the data sets you create when you define the data for the report in Model Editor. When you define a data set, you can specify the type of data region that is used to render the data whenever that data set is used in an auto design. Data can be displayed in table, list, matrix, or chart format. One way to create an auto design is simply to drag a data set onto the *Designs* node for the auto design in the model.

Precision design layout A precision design is free-form, and its format can vary depending on the layout required for particular reports.

Structure of a Dynamics AX Reporting Project

Figure 11-8 shows the hierarchical relationship among project, model, reports, and designs.

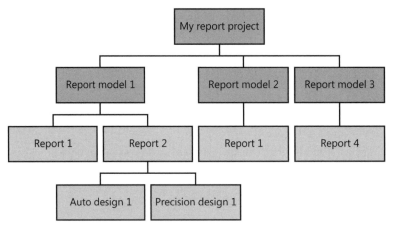

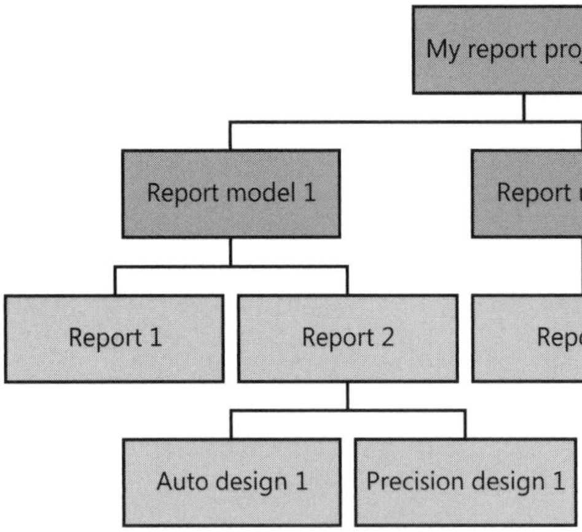

FIGURE 11-8 Report design relationship

Report projects are Microsoft Visual C# or Microsoft Visual Basic container projects in which one or more report models can be stored as .moxl files. Each report model, visualized in Model Editor, can include multiple reports, and each report can contain multiple designs, regardless of whether they are auto designs or precision designs.

Report Data Sources

Data sources are crucial to the development of useful production reports. The very purpose of a production report is to retrieve data from its source and to display the data in a fashion that is easy for users to consume. A major benefit of the Dynamics AX Visual Studio reporting tools is the ability to connect to a variety of different types of report data sources. Even better, a report can display data from multiple data sources. Table 11-2 lists the data source types supported by the Dynamics AX Visual Studio reporting tools.

TABLE 11-2 Data Source Types Supported by Visual Studio Reporting Tools

Data Source Type	Data Content
Dynamics AX	Queries that are defined in the AOT Data methods that are defined within a reporting project in Visual Studio 2008
SQL	T-SQL query Stored procedure
OLAP	MDX query

Dynamics AX is a predefined data source that allows you to connect to OLTP data stored in Dynamics AX. It supports both SQL Server and Oracle databases. It also allows you to bind data sets to data methods that contain your custom business logic that returns a *DataTable*.

The report developer needs to define the *SQL* or *OLAP* data source type. You need to create a new data source under the *Report DataSources* node, specify the *Connection String* property, and select the desired data provider type (SQL or OLAP). By doing so, you give your reports the ability to connect directly to the data source instead of having to go through the AOS, which is the process with the *Dynamics AX* data source type.

Data Methods

You use a data method to write the code for your report's business logic. You can add a data method by creating a new subnode under Data Methods in the Report Model. After you have done so, you can bring up the code editing window by double-clicking the new data method node. What you see is the standard C# or Visual Basic code editing environment that every .NET developer should be familiar with.

You can find all the Visual Studio features you're familiar with, such as IntelliSense and syntax highlighting. You can also reference any of the .NET libraries to increase your productivity and get creative with your business logic. By adding references in the project, you also have access to a wider variety of helper classes and libraries that you've created.

Ad Hoc Reporting

Reporting Services ad hoc reporting, the second major category of Dynamics AX reports, enables users to create and view Dynamics AX reports without needing assistance from developers or IT staff. Users can simply use SQL Server Report Builder to create their own ad hoc reports.

Deployment: Perspectives and SMDL Models

Before users can create and view ad hoc reports, developers and administrators must configure the ad hoc reporting functionality in Dynamics AX by deploying ad hoc reporting models to the Reporting Services server. Once these models are deployed and secured, users can start creating ad hoc reports without further assistance from developers or IT staff.

Developers build the ad hoc models from Dynamics AX perspectives, which is nothing but a collection of references to tables in Dynamics AX. Developers create the Dynamics AX perspectives, and the IT staff deploys the ad hoc models in the Reporting Services server. These models are stored as SMDL files, which Reporting Services understands.

The section "Creating Ad Hoc Reports" later in this chapter provides an overview of the process involved in enabling and creating an ad hoc report. You can also find more details about the ad hoc reporting process in the Microsoft Dynamics AX 2009 software development kit (SDK) on MSDN.

Performance and Platform Considerations

The performance of ad hoc reports doesn't match the performance of production reports. Ad hoc reports work best for simple, small reports that don't involve large data sets. If the performance of an ad hoc report is insufficient, you should consider whether creating a production report instead is worth the time and effort.

Ad hoc reports are implemented in SMDL. Because SMDL is a concept specific to SQL Server, ad hoc reports work only with SQL Server. Dynamics AX 2009 doesn't support ad hoc reporting with Oracle databases.

Security

Unlike production reporting, which depends on the AOS to implement security, the ad hoc reporting framework is based on secure views. A secure view is a normal SQL database view that enforces security on tables when they are accessed from outside Dynamics AX. When the IT staff generates or updates a report model, the Dynamics AX application creates secure views in the OLTP database for every table referenced in a report model. When a user accesses report data using Report Builder, security is automatically enforced via these secure views, so users see only the data they are supposed to see (according to their user group membership).

You can also generate secure views using the Create All Secure Views form in Dynamics AX, which is at Administration\Periodic\Business Analysis.

Creating Ad Hoc Reports

To create an ad hoc report, go through the following steps in order. The steps shown here are meant to give you an overview of the end-to-end scenario involved in deploying SMDL models and creating ad hoc reports. Dynamics AX has published detailed procedures for each of these steps in the Microsoft Dynamics AX 2009 SDK.

1. Configure the Reporting Server in Dynamics AX for report models. (Find the Reporting Servers form, shown in Figure 11-9, at Tools\Business Intelligence Tools\Reporting Servers.) Enter the Server Name, Description, Report Manager, and Web Service URLs.

> **Note** This form is automatically populated when you install the Dynamics AX reporting extensions component on your report server. Make sure you enter the correct port number for the Report Manager and Web Service URLs. If you are using SSL, make sure the URLs are preceded by https.

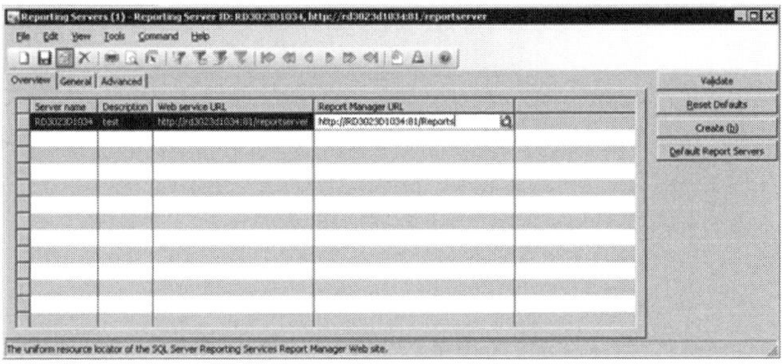

FIGURE 11-9 Reporting Servers form, in which you configure the report servers in Dynamics AX

2. Define perspectives in the AOT.
3. Configure BI properties on the tables and fields that are included in the perspectives. Make sure to set the *Usage* property to ad hoc reporting for the perspective in question. Figure 11-10 shows the AOT Perspectives form.

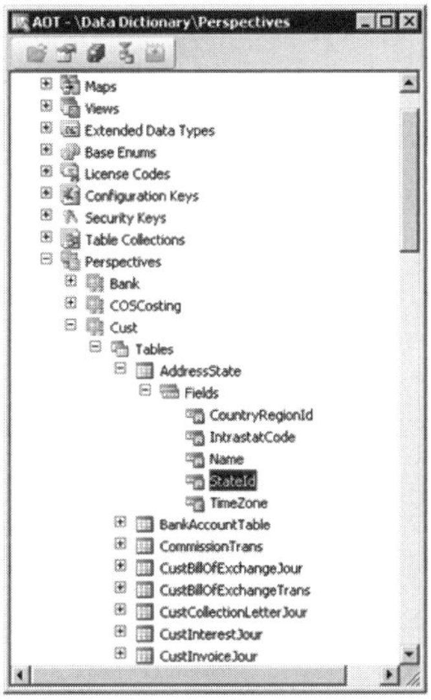

FIGURE 11-10 AOT perspectives

4. Configure the model generation options in the Model Generation Options form (shown in Figure 11-11), found at Tools\Business Intelligence Tools\Report Model Generation Options. Choose the languages that are needed, and set the corresponding report servers.

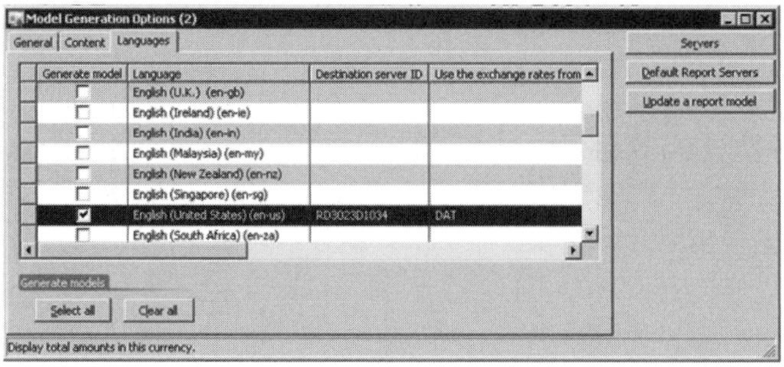

FIGURE 11-11 Model Generation Options form

5. Set the default report server to be used for report models in the Default Report Servers form, found at Tools\Business Intelligence Tools\Default Report Servers.

> **Note** At any given time, you can use only a single report server instance for report models.

6. Publish the SMDL models on the report server by clicking the Update A Report Model button in the Model Generation Options form.
7. Launch the Report Builder Options form (shown in Figure 11-12) from Tools\Business Intelligence Tools\Report Builder Options. In this form, you can specify the report model you want to use and the required language. Choose the report data (Perspective label) and the language, and click OK.

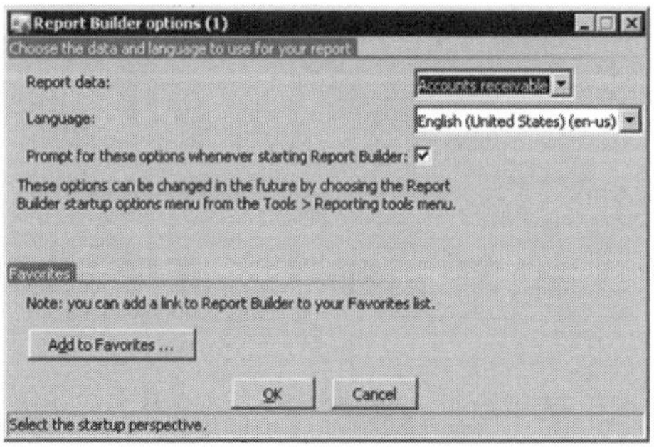

FIGURE 11-12 Report Builder Options form

8. Launch the Report Builder from Tools\Business Intelligence Tools\Report Builder, and design the report by dragging the required fields from the left side onto the report design.
9. Generate the report.

Troubleshooting

This section contains some of the most common ad hoc reporting framework issues and possible solutions that testers identified during the Dynamics AX 2009 release cycle. You can find related information posted on the following closely monitored online community: *https://community.dynamics.com/forums/33.aspx*.

Unable to Validate the Report Server

- Click the Create button in the Reporting Servers form, found at Tools\Business Intelligence Tools\Reporting Servers, and make sure that a report folder and data source have been created on the report server. Click the Validate button.
- Configure the firewall settings appropriately on the report server box.
- Make sure the report manager and report server URLs are correct.
- Make sure the Dynamics AX user has permissions on the report server box.

Unable to Generate a Report

- Make sure the report server account configured in the report data source on the report server has read permissions on the Dynamics AX SQL database.
- Configure the firewall settings on the database box appropriately.
- Check that the user name and password provided for the report server account in the data source on the report server are correct.

SMDL Model Is Not Seen on the Report Server After Successful Model Generation

- Check that the correct report server is configured in the Default Report Servers form for report models.
- Make sure the Publish To Report Server option is selected in the Report Generation Options form.

Unable to Generate an SMDL Model Because One or More Languages Are Missing Some Information

- Make sure the Default Currency for the Default Exchange Rate Company has been specified correctly in the Company Information form, found at Basic\Setup\Company Information.
- Make sure the Destination Server is specified for the selected language.

Chapter 12
Performance

In this chapter:

The objectives of this chapter are to:

- Describe how to control the execution of logic in a three-tier environment and what issues to consider when designing and implementing high-performance X++ code.
- Explain how to optimize database performance and minimize database interaction by using set-based operators and caching, limiting locking, and optimized *sql* statements.
- Explain the usage of tools available in the Microsoft Dynamics AX 2009 development environment for monitoring client/server calls, database calls, and X++ calls.

Introduction

Performance is often an afterthought. Many development teams rarely pay attention to performance until late in the development process or, more critically, after a customer reports severe performance problems in a production environment. After a feature is implemented, making more than minor performance improvements is often too difficult. But if you know how to use the performance-optimization features in Dynamics AX, you can create designs that allow for optimal performance within the boundaries of the Dynamics AX development and runtime environments.

This chapter describes what to consider when developing features to be executed in a three-tier environment in which X++ code can be executed on either the client tier or the server tier. It also introduces the performance-enhancing features available within the Dynamics AX development environment, such as set-based operators for database interaction; caching, which can be set up in metadata or directly in code; and optimistic concurrency control for limiting database locking. The chapter concludes by describing some of the performance-monitoring tools available within the Dynamics AX development environment that provide a reliable foundation for monitoring client/server calls, database activity, and X++ code execution.

Client/Server Performance

Client/server communication is one of the key areas of optimization for Dynamics AX. In this section, we detail the best practices, patterns, and programming techniques that yield optimal communication between the client and the server.

Reducing Round-Trips Between the Client and the Server

The following three techniques can cover between 50 and 80 percent of round-trips in most scenarios:

- Use *CacheAddMethod* for all display and edit methods on a form.
- Refactor *RunBase* classes to support marshaling of the dialog between client and server.
- Properly index tables.

CacheAddMethod

Display and edit fields are used on forms to display data that must be derived or calculated based on other information in the table. They can be written on either the table or the form. By default, these fields are calculated one by one, and if there is any need to go to the server during one of these methods, as there usually is, each of these functions goes to the server individually. These fields are recalculated every time a refresh is triggered on the form, which can originate from editing fields, using menu items, or the user requesting a form refresh. Such a technique is expensive both from a round-tripping perspective as well as in the number of calls it places to the database from the Application Object Server (AOS).

For display and edit fields declared in the form's Data Source, no caching can be performed because the fields need access to the form metadata. If possible, you should move these methods to the table. For display and edit fields declared on a table, you have to use *FormDataSource.CacheAddMethod* to enable caching. (See *http://msdn.microsoft.com/en-us/library/aa893273.aspx* for a detailed definition of display methods.) This method allows the form's engine to calculate all the necessary fields in one round-trip to the server and then to cache the results from this call. To use *cacheAddMethod*, in the *init* method of a Data Source that uses display or edit methods, call *cacheAddMethod* on that Data Source, passing in the method string for the display or edit method. For an example of this, look at the *SalesTable* form's *SalesLine* Data Source. In the *init* method, you find the following code.

```
public void init()
{
    super();
    salesLine_ds.cacheAddMethod(tablemethodstr(SalesLine, invoicedInTotal));
    salesLine_ds.cacheAddMethod(tablemethodstr(SalesLine, deliveredInTotal));
    salesLine_ds.cacheAddMethod(tablemethodstr(SalesLine, reservedPhysicalInSalesUnit));
    salesLine_ds.cacheAddMethod(tablemethodstr(SalesLine, reservedOnOrderInSalesUnit));
    salesLine_ds.cacheAddMethod(tablemethodstr(SalesLine, onOrderInSalesUnit));
    salesLine_ds.cacheAddMethod(tablemethodstr(SalesLine, qualityOrderStatusDisplay));
}
```

If this code is commented out, each of these display methods is computed for every operation on the form Data Source, thus increasing the number of round-trips to the server as well as the number of calls to the database server.

For Dynamics AX 2009, Microsoft made a significant investment in the *CacheAddMethod* infrastructure. In previous releases, this worked only for display fields, and only on form load. In Dynamics AX 2009, the cache is used for both display and edit fields, and is used throughout the lifetime of the form, including reread, write, refresh, and any other method that reloads the data behind the form. On all these methods, the fields are refreshed, but the kernel now refreshes them all at once rather than individually, as it did in previous versions of Dynamics AX.

RunBase Technique

RunBase classes form the basis for most business logic inside of Dynamics AX. *RunBase* provides much of the basic functionality needed to perform a business process, such as displaying a dialog, running the business logic, and running the business logic in batches. When business logic executes through *RunBase*, the logic flows as shown in Figure 12-1.

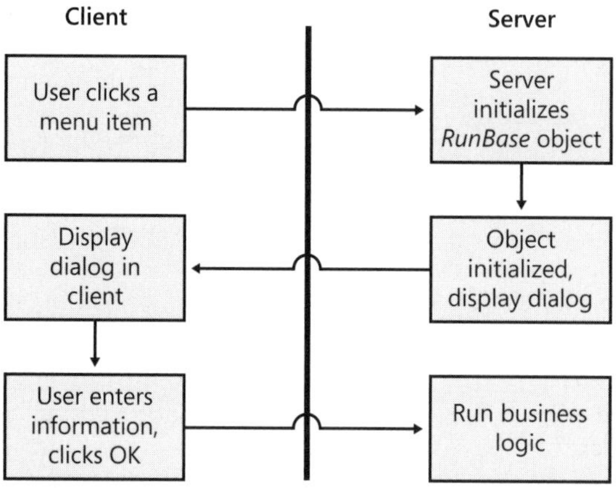

FIGURE 12-1 *RunBase* communication pattern

Most of the round-trip problems of *RunBase* originate with the dialog. The *RunBase* class should be running on the server for security reasons as well as for the fact that it is accessing lots of data from the database and writing it back. A problem occurs when the *RunBase* class itself is marked to run on the server. When the *RunBase* class is running on the server, the dialog is created and driven from the server, causing an immense number of round-trips between the client and the server.

To avoid excessive round-trips, mark the *RunBase* class to run on *Called From*, meaning that it will run on either tier, and then mark either the *construct* method for the *RunBase* class or the menu item to run on the server. *Called From* enables the *RunBase* framework to marshal the class back and forth between the client and the server without having to drive the dialog from the server, significantly reducing the round-trips needed across the application. Keep in mind that you must implement the *pack* and *unpack* methods in a way that allows this serialization to happen.

For an example of the *RunBase* class, examine the *SalesFormLetter* class in the base application. For an in-depth guide to implementing *RunBase* to optimally handle round-trips between the client and the server, refer to the Microsoft Dynamics AX 2009 White Paper, "*RunBase* Patterns," which you can find at the Microsoft Download Center.

Caching and Indexing

Dynamics AX has a data caching framework on the client that can help you greatly reduce the number of times the client goes to the server. In previous releases of Dynamics AX, this cache operated only on primary keys. In Dynamics AX 2009, this cache has been moved and now operates across all the unique keys in a table. Therefore, if a piece of code is accessing data from the client, the code should use a unique key if possible. Also, you need to ensure that all keys that are unique are marked as such in the Application Object Tree (AOT). You can use the Best Practices tool to ensure that all your tables have a primary key.

Properly setting the *CacheLookup* property is a prerequisite for using the cache on the client. Table 12-1 shows the values that *CacheLookup* can have.

TABLE 12-1 Table Cache Definitions

Cache Setting	Description
Found	If a table is accessed by a primary key or a unique index, the value is cached for the duration of the session or until the record is updated. If another AOS updates this record, all AOSs will flush their cache. This cache setting is appropriate for master data.
NotInTTS	Same as *Found* except every time a transaction is started, the cache is flushed and the query goes to the database. This cache setting is appropriate for transactional tables.
FoundAndEmpty	Same as *Found* except if the query fails to find a record, the absence of the record is stored. This cache setting is appropriate for region-specific master data or master data that isn't always present.
EntireTable	The entire table is cached in memory on the AOS, and the client treats this cache as "Found." This cache setting is appropriate for tables with a known number of limited records, such as parameter tables.
None	No caching occurs. This setting is appropriate in only a few cases, such as when optimistic concurrency control has to be disabled.

When caching is set, the client stores up to 100 records per table, and the AOS stores up to 2000 records per table.

Index caching works only if the *where* clause has column names that are unique. In other words, caching won't work if a *join* is present, if the query is a cross-company query, or if any range operations are in the query. Therefore, if you're checking whether a query record that has a particular primary key and some other attribute exists, search the database only by primary key. For an example of this, refer to *xDataArea.isVirtualCompany*.

```
static boolean isVirtualCompany(DataAreaId dataAreaId)
{
    DataArea dataArea1;

    boolean fRetVal;
    ;
    fRetVal=FALSE;
    select Id,isVirtual from dataArea1 where dataArea1.Id == dataAreaId;
        if(dataArea1.Id && dataArea1.isVirtual==1)
    {
        fRetVal=TRUE;
    }
    return fRetVal;

}
```

Notice that this code queries the database by ID and then the primary key, and then it checks the virtual company in memory. This operates at around the same speed but allows the query to hit the cache and the result of the query to be cached on both the client and server tiers.

EntireTable caches store the entire contents of a table on the server, but the cache is treated as a "Found" cache on the client. For tables that have only one row per company, such as parameter tables, you should add a key column that always has a known value, such as 0. This allows the client to use the cache when accessing these tables. An example of the use of a key column in the base application (i.e., Dynamics AX 2009 without any customizations) is *CustParameters* table.

Writing Tier-Aware Code

When you're writing code, you should be aware of what tier the code is going to run on and what tier the objects you're accessing are on. Objects that have their *RunOn* property set to Server/Client/Called From are always instantiated on the server. Objects that are marked to *RunOn Client* are always instantiated on the client, and *Called From* is instantiated wherever the class is created. One caveat: if you mark classes to *RunOn* either the client or the server, you can't serialize them to another tier via *pack* and *unpack*. If you attempt to serialize a server class to the client, all you get is a new object on the server with the same values. Static methods run on whatever tier they are specified to run on via the *Client*, *Server*, or *Client Server* keyword in the declaration.

Working with Temp Tables

Temp tables can be a common source of both client callbacks and calls to the server. Unlike regular table buffers, temp tables reside on the tier on which the first record was inserted. For example, if a temp table is declared on the server, the first record is inserted on the client, and the rest of the records are inserted on the server, all access to that table from the server happens on the client. It's best to populate a temp table on the server because the data you need is probably coming from the database; still, you must be careful when your intent is to iterate over the data to populate a form. The easiest way to achieve this efficiently is to populate the temp table on the server, serialize the entire table down to a container, and then read all the records from the container back into a temp table on the client.

Removing Client Callbacks

Client callbacks occur when the client places a call to a server-bound method, and then the server places a call to a client-bound method. These calls can happen for two reasons. First, they occur when the client doesn't send enough information to the server during its call, or sends the server a client object that encapsulates the information. Second, client callbacks occur when the server is either updating or accessing a form.

To remove the first kind of call, ensure that you send all the information the server needs in a serializable format, such as a packed container, record buffers, or value types (e.g., *int*, *str*, *real*, *boolean*). When the server accesses these types, it doesn't need to go back to the client, as it does if you use an object type.

To remove the form's logic, just send any necessary information about the form into the method, and manipulate the form only when the call returns instead of directly from inside the server. One of the best ways to defer operations on the client is with *pack* and *unpack*. By utilizing *pack* and *unpack*, you can serialize a class down to a container and then deserialize it on the other side.

Chunking Calls

To ensure the minimum number of round-trips between the client and the server, chunk them into one, static server method and pass in all the state needed to perform the operation.

One static server method you can use is *NumberSeq::getNextNumForRefParmId*. This method call is a static server call that contains the following line of code.

```
return NumberSeq::newGetNum(CompanyInfo::numRefParmId()).num();
```

Had this code run on the client, it would have caused four remote procedure call (RPC) round-trips (one for *newGetNum*, one for *numRefParmId*, one for *num*, and one to clean up the *NumberSeq* object that was created). By using a static server method, you can complete this operation in one RPC round-trip.

Another common example of chunking occurs when the client is doing Transaction Tracking System (TTS) operations. Frequently, a developer writes code similar to the following.

```
Ttsbegin;
Record.update();
TTSCommit
```

You can save two round-trips if you chunk this code into one static server call. All TTS operations are initiated only on the server. To take advantage of this fact, do not invoke the *ttsbegin* and *ttscommit* call from the client to start the database transaction when the *ttslevel* is 0.

Transaction Performance

In the preceding section, we focused on limiting traffic between the client and server tiers. When a Dynamics AX application is executed, however, these tiers are just two of the three tiers involved. The third tier is the database tier. You need to optimize the exchange of packages between the server tier and the database tier, just as you do between the client and server tiers. In this section, we explain how you can optimize the transactional part of the execution of application logic. The Dynamics AX application runtime helps you minimize calls made from the server tier to the database tier by supporting set-based operators and data caching. However, you should also do your part by reducing the amount of data you send from the database tier to the server tier. The less data you send, the faster that data is fetched from the database. Fewer packages are sent back as well. These reductions result in less memory consumed. All these efforts promote faster execution of application logic, which results in smaller transaction scope, less locking and blocking, and improved concurrency and throughput.

Set-Based Data Manipulation Operators

As mentioned in Chapter 14, "The Database Layer," in the section "Database-Triggering Methods," the X++ language contains specific operators and classes to enable set-based manipulation in the database. The set-based constructs have an advantage over record-set constructs—they make fewer round-trips to the database. The following X++ code example, which shows the selection of several *custTable* records, each updated with a new value in the *creditMax* field, illustrates that a round-trip is required for the execution of the *select* statement and for each execution of *update*.

```
static void UpdateCustomers(Args _args)
{
    CustTable custTable;
    ;
    ttsbegin;

    while select forupdate custTable
        where custTable.CustGroup == '20' // Round trip to database
    {
        custTable.CreditMax = 1000;
        custTable.update(); // Round trip to database
    }

    ttscommit;
}
```

In a scenario in which 100 *custTable* records qualify for the *update* because the *custGroup* field equals 20, the number of round-trips would be 1 *select* + 100 *updates* = 101 round-trips.

The number of round-trips for the *select* statement might be slightly higher, depending on the number of *custTable* records that can be retrieved simultaneously from the database and sent to the AOS.

Theoretically, you could rewrite the preceding scenario to result in only one round-trip to the database by changing the X++ code as indicated in the following example. The example shows how to use the *update_recordset* operator, resulting in a single *SQL UPDATE* statement being parsed to the database.

```
static void UpdateCustomers(Args _args)
{
    CustTable custTable;
    ;
    ttsbegin;

    update_recordset custTable setting creditMax = 1000
        where custTable.CustGroup == '20'; // Single round trip to database

    ttscommit;
}
```

For several reasons, however, using a *custTable* record buffer doesn't result in only one round-trip. We explain why in the following subsections on the set-based constructs supported by the Dynamics AX application runtime. In these sections, we also describe features available that allow you to modify the preceding scenario to ensure a single round-trip to the database, even when you're using a *custTable* record buffer.

> **Important** None of the following set-based operations improves performance when used on temporary tables. The Dynamics AX application runtime always downgrades set-based operations on temporary tables to record-based operations. This downgrading happens regardless of how the table became a temporary table (whether specified in metadata in the table's properties, disabled because of the configuration of the Dynamics AX application, or explicitly stated in the X++ code using the table). Also, the downgrade by the application runtime always invokes the *doInsert*, *doUpdate*, and *doDelete* methods on the record buffer, so no application logic in the overridden methods is executed.

The *insert_recordset* Operator

The *insert_recordset* operator enables the insertion of multiple records into a table in one round-trip to the database. The following X++ code illustrates the use of *insert_recordset* as the code copies sizes from one item to another item. The item to which the sizes are copied is selected from *inventTable*.

```
static void CopySizes(Args _args)
{
    InventSize  inventSizeTo;
    InventSize  inventSizeFrom;
    InventTable inventTable;
    ;
    ttsbegin;
    insert_recordset inventSizeTo (ItemId, InventSizeId, Description, Name)
        select itemId from inventTable
            where inventTable.ItemId == '1000'
        join inventSizeId, description, name from inventSizeFrom
            where inventSizeFrom.ItemId == '1002';
    ttscommit;
}
```

The round-trip to the database involves the execution of three statements in the database:

- The *select* part of the *insert_recordset* statement is executed where the selected rows are inserted into a temporarily created new table in the database. The syntax of the *select* statement when executed in Microsoft SQL Server is similar to *SELECT <field list> INTO <temporary table> FROM <source tables> WHERE <predicates>*.
- The records from the temporary table are inserted directly into the target table using syntax such as *INSERT INTO <target table> (<field list>) SELECT <field list> FROM <temporary table>*.
- The temporary table is dropped with the execution of *DROP TABLE <temporary table>*.

This approach has a tremendous performance advantage over inserting the records one by one, as shown in the following X++ code, which addresses the same scenario as the preceding X++ code.

```
static void CopySizes(Args _args)
{
    InventSize  inventSizeTo;
    InventSize  inventSizeFrom;
    InventTable inventTable;
    ;
    ttsbegin;
    while select itemId from inventTable
            where inventTable.ItemId == '1000'
        join inventSizeId, description, name from inventSizeFrom
            where inventSizeFrom.ItemId == '1002'
    {
        inventSizeTo.ItemId          = inventTable.ItemId;
        inventSizeTo.InventSizeId    = inventSizeFrom.InventSizeId;
        inventSizeTo.Description     = inventSizeFrom.Description;
        inventSizeTo.Name            = inventSizeFrom.Name;
        inventSizeTo.insert();
    }
    ttscommit;
}
```

If 10 sizes were copied, this scenario would result in 1 round-trip caused by the *select* statement and an additional 10 round-trips caused by the inserts, totaling 11 round-trips.

The *insert_recordset* operation could be downgraded, however, from a set-based operation to a record-based operation. The operation is downgraded if any of the following conditions is true:

- The table is entire-table cached.
- The *insert* method or the *aosValidateInsert* method is overridden on the target table.
- Alerts have been set to be triggered by inserts into the target table.
- The database log has been configured to log inserts into the target table.
- Record level security (RLS) is enabled on the target table. If RLS is enabled only on the source table or tables, *insert_recordset* isn't downgraded to row-by-row operation.

The Dynamics AX application runtime automatically handles the downgrade and internally executes a scenario similar to the *while select* scenario shown in the preceding example.

Important When the Dynamics AX application runtime checks for overridden methods, it determines only whether the methods are implemented. It doesn't determine whether the overridden methods contain only the default X++ code. A method is therefore considered to be overridden by the application runtime even though it contains the following X++ code.

```
public void insert()
{
    super;
}
```

Any set-based insert is then downgraded. You need to remember to delete such a method to avoid the downgrade, with its performance ramifications.

If a table is not entire-table cached, however, you can avoid any downgrade caused by the previously mentioned functionality. The record buffer contains methods that turn off the checks that the application runtime performs when determining whether to downgrade the *insert_recordset* operation.

- Calling *skipDataMethods(true)* prevents the check that determines whether the *insert* method is overridden.
- Calling *skipAosValidation(true)* prevents the check on the *aosValidateInsert* method.
- Calling *skipDatabaseLog(true)* prevents the check that determines whether the database log is configured to log inserts into the table.
- Calling *skipEvents(true)* prevents the check that determines whether any alerts have been set to be triggered by the *insert* event on the table.

The following X++ code, which includes the call to *skipDataMethods(true)*, ensures that the *insert_recordset* operation is not downgraded because the *insert* method is overridden on the *InventSize* table.

```
static void CopySizes(Args _args)
{
    InventSize  inventSizeTo;
    InventSize  inventSizeFrom;
    InventTable inventTable;
    ;
    ttsbegin;
    inventSizeTo.skipDataMethods(true); // Skip override check on insert.
    insert_recordset inventSizeTo (ItemId, InventSizeId, Description, Name)
        select itemId from inventTable
            where inventTable.ItemId == '1000'
        join inventSizeId, description, name from inventSizeFrom
            where inventSizeFrom.ItemId == '1002';
    ttscommit;
}
```

You must use skip methods with extreme caution because they can lead to the logic in the *insert* method not being executed, events not being raised, and potentially, the database log not being written to. If you override the *insert* method, you should use the cross-reference system to determine whether any X++ code calls *skipDataMethods(true)*. If you don't, the X++ code could fail to execute the *insert* method. Moreover, when you implement calls to *skipDataMethods(true)*, make sure that not executing the X++ code in the overridden *insert* method won't lead to data inconsistency.

Skip methods can be used only to influence whether the *insert_recordset* operation is downgraded. If a call to *skipDataMethods(true)* is implemented to prevent downgrading because the *insert* method is overridden, the overridden version of the *insert* method will eventually be executed if the operation is still downgraded. The operation would be downgraded, if, for example, the database log had been configured to log inserts into the table. In the previous example, the overridden *insert* method on the *InventSize* table would be executed if the database log were configured to log inserts into the *InventSize* table because the *insert_recordset* operation would then revert to a *while select* scenario in which the overridden *insert* method would get called.

Dynamics AX 2009 introduces support for literals in *insert_recordset*. The literal support for *insert_recordset* was introduced primarily to support upgrade scenarios in which the target table is populated with records from one or more source tables (using joins) and one or more columns in the target table need to be populated with a literal value that doesn't exist in the source. The following code example illustrates the usage of literals in *insert_recordset*.

```
static void InsertRecordSetLiteralExample(Args _args)
{
    CusttTable customer;
    CustTable custTable;
    boolean flag =  boolean::false;
    ;

    ttsbegin;
    insert_recordset
        customer
            (
                Name,
                Active
            )
    select
        Name,
        flag
    from
        custTable;
    ttscommit;
}
```

The *update_recordset* Operator

The behavior of the *update_recordset* operator is very similar to that of the *insert_recordset* operator. This similarity is illustrated by the following piece of X++ code, in which all sizes for an item are updated with a new description.

```
static void UpdateSizes(Args _args)
{
    InventSize  inventSize;
    ;
    ttsbegin;
    update_recordset inventSize
        setting Description = 'This size is for item 1000'
        where inventSize.itemId == '1000';
    ttscommit;
}
```

The execution of *update_recordset* results in one statement being parsed to the database, which in SQL Server uses a syntax similar to *UPDATE <table> <SET> <field and expression list> WHERE <predicates>*. As with *insert_recordset*, *update_recordset* provides a tremendous improvement in performance over the record-based version, in which each record is updated individually. This improvement is shown in the following X++ code, which serves the same purpose as the preceding example. The code selects all the records qualified for update, sets the new description value, and updates the record.

```
static void UpdateSizes(Args _args)
{
    InventSize  inventSize;
    ;
    ttsbegin;
    while select forupdate inventSize
        where inventSize.itemId == '1000'
    {
        inventSize.Description = 'This size is for item 1000';
        inventSize.update();
    }
    ttscommit;
}
```

If 10 records qualified, 1 *select* statement and 10 *update* statements would be parsed to the database rather than the single *update* statement that would be parsed if you used *update_recordset*.

The *update_recordset* operation can be downgraded if specific methods have been overridden or the the Dynamics AX application is configured. The *update_recordset* operation is downgraded if any of the following conditions is true:

- The table is entire-table cached.
- The *update* method, the *aosValidateUpdate* method, or the *aosValidateRead* method is overridden on the target table.
- Alerts have been set up to be triggered by *update* queries into the target table.
- The database log has been configured to log *update* queries into the target table.
- RLS is enabled on the target table.

The Dynamics AX application runtime automatically handles the downgrade and internally executes a scenario similar to the *while select* scenario shown in the preceding example.

You can avoid any downgrade caused by the previously mentioned functionality unless the table is entire-table cached. The record buffer contains methods that turn off the checks that the application runtime performs when determining whether to downgrade the *update_recordset* operation.

- Calling *skipDataMethods(true)* prevents the check that determines whether the *update* method is overridden.
- Calling *skipAosValidation(true)* prevents the checks on the *aosValidateUpdate* and *aosValidateRead* methods.
- Calling *skipDatabaseLog(true)* prevents the check that determines whether the database log is configured to log updates to records in the table.

- Calling *skipEvents(true)* prevents the check to determine whether any alerts have been set to be triggered by the *update* event on the table.

As we explained earlier, you should use the skip methods with great caution, and you should take the same precautions before using the skip methods in combination with the *update_recordset* operation. Again, using the skip methods only influences whether the *update_recordset* operation is downgraded to a *while select* scenario. If the operation is downgraded, database logging, alerting, and execution of overridden methods occurs even though the respective skip methods have been called.

Tip If an *update_recordset* operation is downgraded to a *while select* scenario, the *select* statement uses the concurrency model specified at the table level. You can apply the *optimisticlock* and *pessimisticlock* keywords to the *update_recordset* statements and enforce a specific concurrency model to be used in case of downgrade.

Dynamics AX 2009 supports inner and outer joins in *update_recordset*. Previous versions of Dynamics AX supported only *exists* and *not exists* joins. The support for joins in *update_recordset* enables an application to perform set-based operations when the source data is fetched from more than one related Data Source.

The following example illustrates the usage of joins with *update_recordset*.

```
static void UpdateRecordsetJoinsExample(Args _args)
{
    NewTaxes taxTable;
    Orders ordersTable;
    ;
    ttsbegin;
    UPDATE_RECORDSET
        ordersTable
    SETTING
        Total = ordersTable.Total + ( ordersTable.Total * ( taxTable.TaxPercent / 100 ) )
    JOIN
        taxTable
    WHERE
        ordersTable.CountryId == taxTable.CountryId
    ;
    ttscommit;
}
```

The *delete_from* Operator

The *delete_from* operator is similar to the *insert_recordset* and *update_recordset* operators in that it parses a single statement to the database to delete multiple rows. The following X++ code shows the deletion of all sizes for an item.

```
static void DeleteSizes(Args _args)
{
    InventSize  inventSize;
    ;
    ttsbegin;
    delete_from inventSize
        where inventSize.itemId == '1000';
    ttscommit;
}
```

This code parses a statement to SQL Server in a similar syntax to *DELETE <table> WHERE <predicates>* and executes the same scenario as the following X++ code, which uses record-by-record deletes.

```
static void DeleteSizes(Args _args)
{
    InventSize  inventSize;
    ;
    ttsbegin;
    while select forupdate inventSize
        where inventSize.itemId == '1000'
    {
        inventSize.delete();
    }
    ttscommit;
}
```

Again, the use of *delete_from* is preferred with respect to performance because a single statement is parsed to the database, rather than the multiple statements that the record-by-record version parses.

Like the downgrading *insert_recordset* and *update_recordset* operations, the *delete_from* operation could also be downgraded, and for similar reasons. Downgrade occurs if any of the following is true:

- The table is entire-table cached.
- The *delete* method, the *aosValidateDelete* method, or the *aosValidateRead* method is overridden on the target table.
- Alerts have been set up to be triggered by deletes into the target table.
- The database log has been configured to log deletes into the target table.

Downgrade also occurs if delete actions are defined on the table. The Dynamics AX application runtime automatically handles the downgrade and internally executes a scenario similar to the *while select* scenario shown in the preceding example.

You can avoid downgrades caused by the previously mentioned functionality, unless the table is entire-table cached. The record buffer contains methods that turn off the checks that the application runtime performs when determining whether to downgrade the *delete_from* operation. Here are the skip descriptions:

- Calling *skipDataMethods(true)* prevents the check that determines whether the delete method is overridden.
- Calling *skipAosValidation(true)* prevents the checks on the *aosValidateDelete* and *aosValidateRead* methods.
- Calling *skipDatabaseLog(true)* prevents the check that determines whether the database log is configured to log deletion of records in the table.
- Calling *skipEvents(true)* prevents the check that determines whether any alerts have been set to be triggered by the *delete* event on the table.

The preceding descriptions about the use of the skip methods, the no-skipping behavior in the event of downgrade, and the concurrency model for the *update_recordset* operator are equally valid for the use of the *delete_from* operator.

> **Note** The record buffer also contains a *skipDeleteMethod* method. Calling the methods as *skipDeleteMethod(true)* has the same effect as calling *skipDataMethods(true)*. It invokes the same Dynamics AX application runtime logic, so you can use *skipDeleteMethod* in combination with *insert_recordset* and *update_recordset*, although it might not improve the readability of the X++ code.

The *RecordInsertList* and *RecordSortedList* Classes

In addition to the set-based operators, Dynamics AX also allows you to use the *RecordInsertList* and *RecordSortedList* classes when inserting multiple records into a table. When the records are ready to be inserted, the Dynamics AX application runtime packs multiple records into a single package and sends it to the database. The database executes individual inserts for each record in the package. This process is illustrated in the following example, in which a *RecordInsertList* object is instantiated, and each record to be inserted into the database is added to the *RecordInsertList* object. When all records are inserted into the object, the *insertDatabase* method is called to ensure that all records are inserted into the database.

```
static void CopySizes(Args _args)
{
    InventSize          inventSizeTo;
    InventSize          inventSizeFrom;
    InventTable         inventTable;
    RecordInsertList    recordInsertList;
    ;
    ttsbegin;
    recordInsertList = new RecordInsertList(tableNum(InventSize));
```

```
    while select itemId from inventTable
            where inventTable.ItemId == '1000'
        join inventSizeId, description, name from inventSizeFrom
            where inventSizeFrom.ItemId == '1002'
    {
        inventSizeTo.ItemId          = inventTable.ItemId;
        inventSizeTo.InventSizeId    = inventSizeFrom.InventSizeId;
        inventSizeTo.Description     = inventSizeFrom.Description;
        inventSizeTo.Name            = inventSizeFrom.Name;
        recordInsertList.add(inventSizeTo); // Insert records
                                            // if package is full.
    }
    recordInsertList.insertDatabase();      // Insert remaining records
                                            // into database.
    ttscommit;
}
```

Based on the Server Configuration buffer size, the Dynamics AX application runtime determines the number of records in a buffer as a function of the size of the records and buffer size. If the buffer is filled up, the records in the RecordInsertList object are packed, parsed to the database, and inserted individually on the database tier. This check is made when the *add* method is called. When the *insertDatabase* method is called from the application logic, the remaining records are inserted with the same mechanism.

Using these classes has an advantage over using *while select*: fewer round-trips are made from the AOS to the database because multiple records are sent simultaneously. However, the number of *INSERT* statements in the database remains the same.

Note Because the timing of insertion into the database depends on the size of the record buffer and the package, you shouldn't expect a record to be selectable from the database until the *insertDatabase* method has been called.

You can rewrite the preceding example using the *RecordSortedList* class instead of *RecordInsertList*, as shown in the following X++ code.

```
static void CopySizes(Args _args)
{
    InventSize          inventSizeTo;
    InventSize          inventSizeFrom;
    InventTable         inventTable;
    RecordSortedList    recordSortedList;
    ;
    ttsbegin;
    recordSortedList = new RecordSortedList(tableNum(InventSize));
    recordSortedList.sortOrder(fieldNum(InventSize, ItemId),
                               fieldNum(InventSize, InventSizeId));
```

```
    while select itemId from inventTable
            where inventTable.ItemId == '1000'
        join inventSizeId, description, name from inventSizeFrom
            where inventSizeFrom.ItemId == '1002'
    {
        inventSizeTo.ItemId          = inventTable.ItemId;
        inventSizeTo.InventSizeId    = inventSizeFrom.InventSizeId;
        inventSizeTo.Description     = inventSizeFrom.Description;
        inventSizeTo.Name            = inventSizeFrom.Name;
        recordSortedList.ins(inventSizeTo); //No records will be inserted.
    }
    recordSortedList.insertDatabase();//All records are inserted in database.
    ttscommit;
}
```

When the application logic uses a *RecordSortedList* object, the records aren't parsed and inserted in the database until the *insertDatabase* method is called. The number of round-trips and *INSERT* statements executed is the same as for the *RecordInsertList* object.

Both *RecordInsertList* objects and *RecordSortedList* objects can be downgraded in application logic to record-by-record inserts, in which each record is sent in a separate round-trip to the database and the *INSERT* statement is subsequently executed. Downgrading occurs if the *insert* method or the *aosValidateInsert* method is overridden, or if the table contains fields of type *container* or *memo*. Downgrading doesn't occur if the database log is configured to log inserts or alerts that have been set to be triggered by the *insert* event on the table. One exception is if logging or alerts have been configured and the table contains *CreatedDateTime* or *ModifiedDateTime* columns—in this case, record-by-record inserts are performed. The database logging and eventing occurs on a record-by-record basis after the records have been sent and inserted into the database.

When instantiating the *RecordInsertList* object, you can specify that the *insert* and *aosValidateInsert* methods be skipped. You can also specify that the database logging and eventing be skipped if the operation isn't downgraded.

Restartable Jobs and Optimistic Concurrency

In multiple scenarios in the Dynamics AX application, the execution of some application logic involves manipulating multiple rows from the same table. Some scenarios require that all rows be manipulated within a single transaction scope; if something fails and the transaction is aborted, all modifications are rolled back, and the job can be restarted manually or automatically. Other scenarios commit the changes on a record-by-record basis; in case of failure, only the changes to the current record are rolled back, and all previously manipulated records are already committed. When a job is restarted in this scenario, it starts where it left off by skipping all the records already changed.

An example of the first scenario is shown in the following code, in which all *update* queries to the *custTable* records are wrapped into a single transaction scope.

```
static void UpdateCreditMax(Args _args)
{
    CustTable   custTable;
    ;
    ttsbegin;
    while select forupdate custTable where custTable.creditMax == 0
    {
        if (custTable.balanceMST() < 10000)
        {
            custTable.creditMax = 50000;
            custTable.update();
        }
    }
    ttscommit;
}
```

An example of the second scenario, executing the same logic, is shown in the following code, in which the transaction scope is handled record by record. You must reselect each individual *custTable* record inside the transaction for the Dynamics AX application runtime to allow the update of the record.

```
static void UpdateCreditMax(Args _args)
{
    CustTable   custTable;
    CustTable   updateableCustTable;
    ;
    while select custTable where custTable.creditMax == 0
    {
        if (custTable.balanceMST() < 10000)
        {
            ttsbegin;
            select forupdate updateableCustTable
                where updateableCustTable.AccountNum == custTable.AccountNum;

            updateableCustTable.creditMax = 50000;
            updateableCustTable.update();
            ttscommit;
        }
    }
}
```

In a scenario in which 100 *custTable* records qualify for the update, the first example would involve 1 *select* and 100 *update* statements being parsed to the database, and the second example would involve 1 large *select* query and 100 single ones, plus the 100 *update* statements. So the first scenario would execute faster than the second, but the first scenario would also hold the locks on the updated *custTable* records longer because it wouldn't commit for each record. The second example demonstrates superior concurrency over the first example because locks are held for less time.

The optimistic concurrency model in Dynamics AX lets you take advantage of the benefits offered by both of the preceding examples. You can select records outside a transaction scope and update records inside a transaction scope—but only if the records are selected optimistically. In the following example, the *optimisticlock* keyword is applied to the *select* statement while maintaining a per-record transaction scope. Because the records are selected with the *optimisticlock* keyword, it isn't necessary to reselect each record individually within the transaction scope. (For a detailed description of the optimistic concurrency model, see Chapter 14.)

```
static void UpdateCreditMax(Args _args)
{
    CustTable   custTable;
    ;
    while select optimisticlock custTable where custTable.creditMax == 0
    {
        if (custTable.balanceMST() < 10000)
        {
            ttsbegin;
            custTable.creditMax = 50000;
            custTable.update();
            ttscommit;
        }
    }
}
```

This approach provides the same number of statements parsed to the database as in the first example, with the improved concurrency from the second example because commits execute record by record. The code in this example still doesn't perform as fast as the code in first example because it has the extra burden of the per-record transaction management. You could optimize the example even further by committing on a scale somewhere between all records and the single record, without decreasing the concurrency considerably. However, the appropriate choice of commit frequency always depends on the circumstances of the job.

Best Practices You can use the *forupdate* keyword when selecting records outside the transaction if the table has been enabled for optimistic concurrency at the table level. The best practice, however, is to explicitly use the *optimisticlock* keyword because the scenario won't fail if the table-level setting is changed. Using the *optimisticlock* keyword also improves the readability of the X++ code because the explicit intention of the developer is stated in the code.

Caching

The Dynamics AX application runtime supports the enabling of single-record and set-based record caching. You can enable set-based caching in metadata by switching a property on a table definition or writing explicit X++ code, which instantiates a cache. Regardless of how you set up caching, you don't need to know which caching method is used because the application runtime handles the cache transparently. To optimize the use of the cache, however, you must understand how each caching mechanism works.

The Microsoft Dynamics AX 2009 software development kit (SDK) contains a good description of the individual caching options and how they are set up (*http://msdn.microsoft.com/en-us/library/bb278240.aspx*). In this section, we focus on how the caches are implemented in the Dynamics AX application runtime and what you should expect when using the individual caching mechanisms.

Record Caches

You can set up three types of record caching on a table by setting the *CacheLookup* property on the table definition:

- *Found*
- *FoundAndEmpty*
- *NotInTTS*

One additional value (besides *None*) is *EntireTable*, which is a set-based caching option we describe later in this section.

The three record-caching possibilities are fundamentally the same. The differences lie in what is cached and when cached values are flushed. For example, the *Found* and *FoundAndEmpty* caches are preserved across transaction boundaries, but a table that uses the *NotInTTS* cache doesn't use the cache when first accessed inside a transaction scope—it uses it in consecutive *select* statements, unless a *forupdate* keyword is applied to the *select* statement. The following X++ code example describes when the cache is used inside and outside a transaction scope, when a table uses the *NotInTTS* caching mechanism, and when the *AccountNum* field is the primary key. The code comments indicate when the cache is or isn't used. In the example, it appears that the first two *select* statements after the *ttsbegin* command don't use the cache. The first doesn't use the cache because it's the first statement inside the transaction scope; the second doesn't use the cache because the *forupdate* keyword is applied to the statement. The use of the *forupdate* keyword forces the application runtime to look up the record in the database because the previously cached record wasn't selected with the *forupdate* keyword applied.

```
static void NotInTTSCache(Args _args)
{
    CustTable custTable;
    ;
    select custTable                            // Look up in cache. If record
        where custTable.AccountNum == '1101'; // does not exist, look up
                                                // in database.
```

```
    ttsbegin;                                   // Start transaction.

    select custTable                            // Cache is invalid. Look up in
        where custTable.AccountNum == '1101'; // database and place in cache.

    select forupdate custTable                  // Look up in database because
        where custTable.AccountNum == '1101'; // forupdate keyword is applied.

    select custTable                            // Cache will be used.
        where custTable.AccountNum == '1101'; // No lookup in database.

    select forupdate custTable                  // Cache will be used because
        where custTable.AccountNum == '1101'; // forupdate keyword was used
                                                // previously.

    ttscommit;                                  // End transaction.

    select custTable                            // Cache will be used.
        where custTable.AccountNum == '1101';
}
```

If the table had been set up with *Found* or *FoundAndEmpty* caching in the preceding example, the cache would have been used when executing the first *select* statement inside the transaction, but not when the first *select forupdate* statement was executed.

Note By default, all Dynamics AX system tables are set up using a *Found* cache. This cannot be changed.

For all three caching mechanisms, the cache is used only if the *select* statement contains equal-to (==) predicates in the *where* clause that exactly match all the fields in the primary index of the table or any one of the unique indexes defined for the table. The *PrimaryIndex* property on the table must therefore be set correctly on one of the unique indexes used when accessing the cache from application logic. For all other unique indexes, without any additional settings in metadata, the kernel automatically uses the cache, if it is already present. Support for unique-index-based caching is a new feature in Dynamics AX 2009.

The following X++ code examples show when the Dynamics AX application runtime will try to use the cache and when it won't. The cache is used only in the first *select* statement; the remaining three statements don't match the fields in the primary index, so they will all perform lookups in the database.

```
static void UtilizeCache(Args _args)
{
    CustTable custTable;
    ;
    select custTable                            // Will use cache because only
```

```
        where custTable.AccountNum == '1101';   // the primary key is used as
                                                // predicate.

    select custTable;                           // Cannot use cache because no
                                                // "where" clause exists.

    select custTable                            // Cannot use cache because
        where custTable.AccountNum > '1101';    // equal to (==) is not used.

    select custTable                            // Will not use cache because
        where custTable.AccountNum == '1101'    // where clause contains more
        &&    custTable.CustGroup  == '20';     // predicates than the primary
                                                // key.
}
```

Note The *RecId* index, which is always unique on a table, can be set as the *PrimaryIndex* in the table's properties. You can therefore set up caching using the *RecId* field.

The following X++ code examples show how unique-index caching works in the Dynamics AX application runtime. *InventDim* in the base application has *InventDimId* as the primary key and a combination of keys (*inventBatchId*, *wmsLocationId*, wmsPalletId, *inventSerialId*, *inventLocationId*, *configId*, *inventSizeId*, *inventColorId*, and *inventSiteId*) as the unique index on the table.

```
static void UtilizeUniqueIndexCache(Args _args)
{
    InventDim InventDim;
    ;
    select inventDim                                // Will use cache because only
    where inventDim.inventDimId == '00000001_082';  // the primary key is used as
                                                    // predicate.

    select inventDim                                // Will use cache
     where inventDim.inventBatchId == ''            // because the column list in
     && inventDim.wmsLocationId    == ''            // the "where" clause
     && inventDim.wmsPalletId      == ''            // match that of a unique
     && inventDim.inventSerialId   == ''            // index for table inventdim
     && inventDim.inventLocationId == '400'         // and the key values point to
     && inventDim.ConfigId         == '01'          // same record as the primary
     && inventDim.inventSizeId     == ''            // key fetch (inventDimId ==
     && inventDim.inventColorId    == ''            // '00000001_082').
     && inventDim.inventSiteId     == '4';          //


    select inventDim                                // Cannot use cache because
    where inventDim.inventLocationId== '400'        // where clause does not
     && inventDim.ConfigId          == '01'         // match the unique key list
     && inventDim.inventSiteId      == '4';         // or primary key.
}
```

The Dynamics AX application runtime ensures that all fields on a record are selected before they are cached. The application runtime therefore always changes a field list to include all fields on the table before submitting the *SELECT* statement to the database when it can't find the record in the cache. The following X++ code illustrates this behavior.

```
static void expandingFieldList(Args _args)
{
    CustTable custTable;
    ;
    select creditRating  // The field list will be expanded to all fields.
        from custTable
        where custTable.AccountNum == '1101';
}
```

If the preceding *select* statement doesn't find a record in the cache, it expands the field to contain all fields, not just the *creditRating* field. This ensures that the fetched record from the database contains values for all fields before it is inserted into the cache. Even though performance when fetching all fields is inferior compared to performance when fetching a few fields, this approach is acceptable because in subsequent use of the cache, the performance gain outweighs the performance loss from populating it.

Tip You can disregard the use of the cache by calling the *disableCache* method on the record buffer with a Boolean *true* parameter. This method forces the application runtime to look up the record in the database, and it also prevents the application runtime from expanding the field list.

The Dynamics AX application runtime creates and uses caches on both the client tier and the server tier. The client-side cache is local to the rich client, and the server-side cache is shared among all connections to the server, including connections coming from rich clients, Web clients, .NET Business Connector, and any another connection.

The cache used depends on which tier the lookup is made from. If the lookup is made on the server tier, the server-side cache is used. If the lookup is executed from the client tier, the client first looks in the client-side cache; if it doesn't find anything, it makes a lookup in the server-side cache. If there is still no record, a lookup is made in the database. When the database returns the record to the server and on to the client, the record is inserted into both the server-side cache and the client-side cache.

The caches are implemented using AVL trees (which are balanced binary trees), but the trees aren't allowed to grow indefinitely. The client-side cache can contain a maximum of 100 records for a given table in a given company, and the shared server-side cache can contain a maximum of 2000 records. When a new record is inserted into the cache and the maximum is reached, the application runtime removes approximately 5 to 7 percent of the oldest records by scanning the entire tree.

Note You can't change the maximum number of records to be cached in metadata or from the X++ code.

Scenarios that repeat lookups on the same records and expect to find the records in the cache can suffer performance degradation if the cache is continuously full—not only because records won't be found in the cache because they were removed based on the aging scheme, forcing a lookup in the database, but also because of the constant scanning of the tree to remove the oldest records. The following X++ code shows an example in which all *SalesTable* records are looped twice, and each loop looks up the associated *CustTable* record. If this X++ code were executed on the server and the number of *CustTable* record lookups was more than 2000, the oldest records would be removed from the cache, and the cache wouldn't contain all *CustTable* records when the first loop ended. When the code loops through the *SalesTable* records again, the records might not be in the cache, and the selection of the *CustTable* record would continue to go to the database to look up the record. The scenario would therefore perform much better with fewer than 2000 records in the database.

```
static void AgingScheme(Args _args)
{
    SalesTable salesTable;
    CustTable custTable;
    ;
    while select SalesTable order by custAccount
    {
        select custTable        // Fill up cache.
            where custTable.AccountNum == salesTable.CustAccount;
        // More code here.
    }

    while select SalesTable order by custAccount
    {
        select custTable        // Record might not be in cache.
            where custTable.AccountNum == salesTable.CustAccount;
        // More code here.
    }

}
```

Important If you test code on small databases, you can't track repeat lookups only by tracing the number of statements parsed to the database. When you execute such code in a production environment, you can encounter severe performance issues because this scenario doesn't scale very well.

Before the Dynamics AX application runtime searches for, inserts, updates, or deletes records in the cache, it places a mutually exclusive lock that isn't released until the operation is complete. This lock means that two processes running on the same server can't perform insert, update, or delete operations in the cache at the same time; only one process can hold the lock at any given time, and the remaining processes are blocked. Blocking occurs only when the application runtime accesses the server-side cache. So although the caching possibilities the application runtime supports are useful features, you shouldn't abuse them. If you can reuse a record buffer that is already fetched, you should do so. The following X++ code shows the same record fetched twice. The second fetch uses the cache even though it could have used the first fetched record buffer. When you execute the following X++ code on the server tier, the process might get blocked when the application runtime searches the cache.

```
static void ReuseRecordBuffer(Args _args)
{
    CustTable custTable;
    ;
    select custTable
        where custTable.AccountNum == '1101';

    // Some more code, which does not change the custTable record.

    select custTable                          // The cache will be used, but
        where custTable.AccountNum == '1101'; // blocking might occur.
                                              // Reuse the record buffer
                                              // instead.
}
```

The *EntireTable* Cache

In addition to using the three caching methods described so far—*Found*, *FoundAndEmpty*, and *NotInTTS*—you can set a fourth caching option, *EntireTable*, on a table. *EntireTable* enables a set-based cache. It causes the AOS to mirror the table in the database by selecting all records in the table and inserting them into a temporary table when any record from the table is selected for the first time. The first process to read from the table could therefore experience a longer response time because the application runtime reads all records from the database. Subsequent *select* queries then read from the entire-table cache instead of from the database.

A temporary table is usually local to the process that uses it, but the entire-table cache is shared among all processes that access the same AOS. Each company (as defined by the *DataAreaId* field) has an entire-table cache, so two processes requesting records from the same table but from different companies use different caches, and both could experience a longer response time to instantiate the entire-table cache.

The entire-table cache is a server-side cache only. When requesting records from the client tier on a table that is entire-table cached, the table behaves as a *Found* cached table. If a request for a record is made on the client tier that qualifies for searching the record cache, the client first searches the local *Found* cache. If the record isn't found, the client calls the

AOS to search the entire-table cache. When the application runtime returns the record to the client tier, it inserts the record into the client-side *Found* cache.

The entire-table cache isn't used when executing a *select* statement by which an entire-table-cached table is joined to a table that isn't entire-table cached. In this situation, the entire *select* statement is parsed to the database. However, when *select* statements are made that access only the single entire-table cached table, or when joining other entire-table cached tables, the entire-table cache is used.

The Dynamics AX application runtime flushes the entire-table cache when records are inserted, updated, or deleted in the table. The next process, which selects records from the table, suffers a degradation in performance because it must reread the entire table into the cache. In addition to flushing its own cache, the AOS that executes the insert, update, or delete also informs other AOSs in the same installation that they must flush their caches on the same table. This prevents old and invalid data from being cached for too long in the entire Dynamics AX application environment. In addition to this flushing mechanism, the AOS flushes all the entire-table caches every 24 hours.

Because of the flushing that results when modifying records in a table that has been entire-table cached, you should avoid setting up entire-table caches on frequently updated tables. Rereading all records into the cache results in a performance loss, which could outweigh the performance gain achieved by caching records on the server tier and avoiding round-trips to the database tier. You can overwrite the entire-table cache setting on a specific table at run time when you configure the Dynamics AX application.

Even if the records in a table are fairly static, you might achieve better performance by not using the entire-table cache if the table has a large number of records. Because the entire-table cache uses temporary tables, it changes from an in-memory structure to a file-based structure when the table uses more than 128 kilobytes (KB) of memory. This results in performance degradation during record searches. The database search engines have also evolved over time and are faster than the ones implemented in the Dynamics AX application runtime. It might be faster to let the database search for the records than to set up and use an entire-table cache, even though a database search involves round-trips to the database tier.

The *RecordViewCache* Class

The *RecordViewCache* class allows you to establish a set-based cache from the X++ code. You initiate the cache by writing the following X++ code.

```
select nofetch custTrans where custTrans.accountNum == '1101';
recordViewCache = new RecordViewCache(custTrans);
```

The records to cache are described in the *select* statement, which must include the *nofetch* keyword to prevent the selection of the records from the database. The records are selected when the *RecordViewCache* object is instantiated with the record buffer parsed as a parameter. Until the *RecordViewCache* object is destroyed, *select* statements will execute on the cache if they match the *where* clause defined when it was instantiated. The following X++ code shows how the cache is instantiated and used.

```
static void RecordViewCache(Args _args)
{
    CustTrans       custTrans;
    RecordViewCache recordViewCache;
    ;
    select nofetch custTrans                          // Define records to cache.
        where custTrans.AccountNum == '1101';

    recordViewCache = new RecordViewCache(custTrans); // Cache the records.

    select firstonly custTrans                        // Use cache.
        where custTrans.AccountNum == '1101' &&
              custTrans.CurrencyCode == 'USD';
}
```

The cache can be instantiated only on the server tier. The defined *select* statement can contain only equal-to (==) predicates in the *where* clause and is accessible only by the process instantiating the cache object. If the table buffer used for instantiating the cache object is a temporary table or it uses *EntireTable* caching, the *RecordViewCache* object isn't instantiated.

The records are stored in the cache as a linked list of records. Searching therefore involves a sequential search of the cache for the records that match the search criteria. When defining *select* statements to use the cache, you can specify a sort order. When a sort order is specified, the Dynamics AX application runtime creates a temporary index on the cache, which contains the requested records sorted as specified in the *select* statement. The application runtime iterates the temporary index when it returns the individual rows. If no sorting is specified, the application runtime merely iterates the linked list.

If the table cached in the *RecordViewCache* is also record-cached, the application runtime can use both caches. If a *select* statement is executed on a *Found* cached table and the *select* statement qualifies for lookup in the *Found* cache, the application runtime performs a lookup in this cache first. If nothing is found and the *select* statement also qualifies for lookup in the *RecordViewCache*, the runtime uses the *RecordViewCache* and updates the *Found* cache after retrieving the record.

Inserts, updates, and deletes of records that meet the cache criteria are reflected in the cache at the same time that the data manipulation language (DML) statements are sent to the database. Records in the cache are always inserted at the end of the linked list. A hazard associated with this behavior is that an infinite loop can occur when application logic is iterating the records in the cache and at the same time inserting new records that meet the cache criteria. An infinite loop is shown in the following X++ code example, in which a *RecordViewCache* object is created containing all *custTable* records associated with *CustGroup '20'*. The code iterates each record in the cache when executing the *select* statement, but because each cached record is duplicated and still inserted with *CustGroup '20'*, the records are inserted at the end of the cache. Eventually, the loop fetches these newly inserted records as well.

```
static void InfiniteLoop(Args _args)
{
    CustTable       custTable;
    RecordViewCache recordViewCache;
    custTable       custTableInsert;
    ;
    select nofetch custTable                         // Define records to cache.
        where custTable.CustGroup == '20';
    recordViewCache = new RecordViewCache(custTable); // Instantiate cache.

    ttsbegin;
    while select custTable                           // Loop over cache.
        where custTable.CustGroup == '20'
    {
        custTableInsert.data(custTable);
        custTableInsert.AccountNum = 'dup'+custTable.AccountNum;
        custTableInsert.insert();      // Will insert at end of cache.
                                       // Records will eventually be selected.
    }
    ttscommit;
}
```

To avoid the infinite loop, simply sort the records when selecting them from the cache, which creates a temporary index that contains only the records in the cache from where the records were first retrieved. Any inserted records are therefore not retrieved. This is shown in the following example, in which the *order by* operator is applied to the *select* statement.

```
static void FiniteLoop(Args _args)
{
    CustTable       custTable;
    RecordViewCache recordViewCache;
    custTable       custTableInsert;
    ;
    select nofetch custTable                         // Define records to cache.
        where custTable.CustGroup == '20';
    recordViewCache = new RecordViewCache(custTable); // Instantiate cache.

    ttsbegin;
    while select custTable                           // Loop over a sorted cache.
        order by CustGroup                           // Create temporary index.
        where custTable.CustGroup == '20'
    {
        custTableInsert.data(custTable);
```

```
        custTableInsert.AccountNum = 'dup'+custTable.AccountNum;
        custTableInsert.insert();       // Will insert at end of cache.
                                        // Records are not inserted in index.
    }
    ttscommit;
}
```

Changes made to records in a *RecordViewCache* object can't be rolled back. If one or more *RecordViewCache* objects exist, if the *ttsabort* operation executes, or if an error is thrown that results in a rollback of the database, the *RecordViewCache* objects still contain the same information. Any instantiated *RecordViewCache* object that is subject to modification by the application logic should therefore not have a lifetime longer than the transaction scope in which it is modified. The *RecordViewCache* object must be declared in a method that isn't executed until after the transaction has begun. In the event of a rollback, the object and the cache are both destroyed.

As described earlier, the *RecordViewCache* object is implemented as a linked list that allows only a sequential search for records. When you use the cache to store a large number of records, a performance degradation in search occurs because of this linked-list format. You should weigh the use of the cache against the extra time spent fetching the records from the database where the database uses a more optimal search algorithm. Consider the time hit especially when you search only for a subset of the records; the application runtime must continuously match each record in the cache against the more granular *where* clause in the *select* statement because no indexing is available for the records in the cache.

However, for small sets of records, or for situations in which the same records are looped multiple times, *RecordViewCache* offers a substantial performance advantage compared to fetching the same records multiple times from the database.

Limiting Field Lists

Most of the X++ *select* statements in Dynamics AX retrieve all fields on a record, although the values in only a few of the fields are actually used. The main reason for this coding style is that the Dynamics AX application runtime doesn't report compile-time or run-time errors if a field on a record buffer is accessed and it hasn't been retrieved from the database. The following X++ code, which selects only the *AccountNum* field from the *CustTable* table but evaluates the value of the *CreditRating* field and sets the *CreditMax* field, won't fail because the application runtime doesn't detect that the fields haven't been selected.

```
static void UpdateCreditMax(Args _args)
{
    CustTable custTable;
    ;
```

```
    ttsbegin;
    while select forupdate accountNum from custTable
    {
        if (custTable.CreditRating == '')
        {
            custTable.CreditMax = custTable.CreditMax + 1000;
            custTable.update();
        }
    }
    ttscommit;
}
```

This code updates all *CustTable* records to a *CreditMax* value of 1000, regardless of the previous value in the database for the *CreditRating* and *CreditMax* fields. Adding the *CreditRating* and *CreditMax* fields to the field list of the *select* statement might not solve the problem because the application logic could still update other fields incorrectly because the *update* method on the table could be evaluating and setting other fields on the same record.

> **Important** You could, of course, examine the *update* method for other fields accessed in the method and then select these fields as well, but new problems would soon surface. For example, if you customize the *update* method to include application logic that uses additional fields, you might not be aware that the X++ code in the preceding example also needs to be customized.

Limiting the field list when selecting records does result in a performance gain, however, because less data is retrieved from the database and sent to the AOS. The gain is even bigger if you can retrieve the fields by using the indexes without lookup of the values on the table. This performance gain can be experienced and the *select* statements written safely when you use the retrieved data within a controlled scope, such as a single method. The record buffer must be declared locally and not parsed to other methods as a parameter. Any developer customizing the X++ code can easily see that only a few fields are selected and act accordingly.

To truly benefit from a limited field list, you must understand that the Dynamics AX application runtime sometimes automatically adds extra fields to the field list before parsing a statement to the database. We explained one example earlier in this chapter, in the "Caching" section. In this example, the application runtime expands the field list to include all fields if the *select* statement qualifies for storing the retrieved record in the cache. In an example in Chapter 14, in the "Transaction Semantics" section, you see that the application runtime ensures that the fields contained in the unique index, used by the application runtime to update and delete the record, are always retrieved from the database.

In the following X++ code, you can see how the application runtime adds additional fields and how to optimize some *select* statements. The code calculates the total balance for all customers in customer group *'20'* and converts it into the company's currency unit. The *amountCur2MST* method converts the value in the currency specified by the *currencyCode* field to the company's monetary unit.

```
static void BalanceMST(Args _args)
{
    CustTable   custTable;
    CustTrans   custTrans;
    AmountMST   balanceAmountMST = 0;
    ;
    while select custTable
            where custTable.CustGroup == '20'
          join custTrans
            where custTrans.AccountNum == custTable.AccountNum
    {
        balanceAmountMST += Currency::amountCur2MST(custTrans.AmountCur,
                                                    custTrans.CurrencyCode);
    }
}
```

When the *select* statement is parsed to the database, it retrieves all *CustTable* and *CustTrans* record fields, even though only the *AmountCur* and *CurrencyCode* fields on the *CustTrans* table are used. The result is the retrieval of more than 100 fields from the database.

You can optimize the field list simply by selecting the *AmountCur* and *CurrencyCode* fields from *CustTrans* and, for example, only the *AccountNum* field from *CustTable*, as shown in the following code.

```
static void BalanceMST(Args _args)
{
    CustTable   custTable;
    CustTrans   custTrans;
    AmountMST   balanceAmountMST = 0;
    ;
    while select AccountNum from custTable
            where custTable.CustGroup == '20'
          join AmountCur, CurrencyCode from custTrans
            where custTrans.AccountNum == custTable.AccountNum
    {
        balanceAmountMST += Currency::amountCur2MST(custTrans.AmountCur,
                                                    custTrans.CurrencyCode);
    }
}
```

As explained earlier, the application runtime expands the field list from the three fields shown in the preceding X++ code example to five fields because it adds the fields used when updating the records. These fields are added even though neither the *forupdate* keyword nor any of the specific concurrency model keywords are applied to the statement. The statement parsed to the database starts as shown in the following example, in which the RECID column is added for both tables.

```
SELECT A.ACCOUNTNUM,A.RECID,B.AMOUNTCUR,B.CURRENCYCODE,B.RECID
FROM CUSTTABLE A,CUSTTRANS B
```

To prevent retrieval of any *CustTable* fields, you can rewrite the *select* statement to use the *exists join* operator, as shown here.

```
static void BalanceMST(Args _args)
{
    CustTable   custTable;
    CustTrans   custTrans;
    AmountMST   balanceAmountMST = 0;
    ;
    while select AmountCur, CurrencyCode from custTrans
        exists join custTable
            where custTable.CustGroup  == '20' &&
                  custTable.AccountNum == custTrans.AccountNum
    {
        balanceAmountMST += Currency::amountCur2MST(custTrans.AmountCur,
                                                    custTrans.CurrencyCode);
    }
}
```

This code retrieves only three fields (*AmountCur*, *CurrencyCode*, and *RecId*) from the *CustTrans* table and none from the *CustTable* table.

In some situations, however, it might not be possible to rewrite the statement to use *exists join*. In such cases, including only *TableId* as a field in the field list prevents the retrieval of any fields from the table. The original example is modified as follows to include the *TableId* field.

```
static void BalanceMST(Args _args)
{
    CustTable   custTable;
    CustTrans   custTrans;
    AmountMST   balanceAmountMST = 0;
    ;
    while select tableid from custTable
            where custTable.CustGroup == '20'
          join AmountCur, CurrencyCode from custTrans
            where custTrans.AccountNum == custTable.AccountNum
    {
        balanceAmountMST += Currency::amountCur2MST(custTrans.AmountCur,
                                                    custTrans.CurrencyCode);
    }
}
```

This code causes the application runtime to parse a *select* statement to the database with the following field list.

```
SELECT B.AMOUNTCUR,B.CURRENCYCODE,B.RECID
FROM CUSTTABLE A,CUSTTRANS B
```

If you rewrite the *select* statement to use *exists join* or include only *TableId* as a field, the *select* statement sent to the database retrieves just three fields instead of more than 100. As you can see, you can substantially improve your application's performance just by rewriting queries to retrieve only the necessary fields.

Best Practices A best practice warning is implemented in Dynamics AX 2009 to analyze X++ code for the use of *select* statements and recommend whether to implement field lists based on the number of fields accessed in the method. The best practice check is made if (in the Best Practice Parameters dialog box) the AOS Performance Check under General Checks is enabled and the Warning Level is set to Errors And Warnings.

Field Justification

Dynamics AX supports left and right justification of extended data types. With our current releases, nearly all extended data types are left justified to reduce the impact of space consumption because of double and triple byte storage as a result of Unicode enablement. Left justifying also helps performance by increasing the speed of access through indexes.

Where sorting is critical, you can use right justification. This has to be an exception as is clearly evident in our usage within the application layers we ship.

Other Performance Considerations

You can further improve transactional performance by giving more thought to the design of your application logic. For example, ensuring that various tables and records are always modified in the same order helps prevent deadlocks and ensuing retries. Spending time preparing the transactions before starting a transaction scope to make it as brief as possible can reduce the locking scope and resulting blocking, and ultimately improve the concurrency of the transactions. Database design factors, such as index design and use, are also important. These topics are beyond the scope of this book.

Dynamics AX Monitoring Tools

Without a way to monitor the execution of the implemented application logic, you would implement features almost blindly with regard to performance. Fortunately, the Dynamics AX development environment contains a set of easy-to-use tools to help you monitor client/server calls, database activity, and application logic. These tools provide good feedback on the feature being monitored. The feedback is integrated directly with the development environment, making it possible for you to jump directly to the relevant X++ code.

Dynamics AX Trace Parser

The Dynamics AX Trace Parser is a user interface and data analyzer added to Dynamics AX 2009 and built on top of SQL Server 2005 and SQL Server 2008 and the Event Tracing for Windows (ETW) framework enabled in the core Dynamics AX kernel. The Event Tracing for Windows framework allows an administrator to conduct tracing with system overhead of approximately 4 percent. This low overhead allows administrators to diagnose performance problems in live environments as opposed to just development environments.

The Trace Parser enables rapid analysis of traces to find the longest-running code, longest-running SQL query, highest call count, and other metrics useful in debugging a performance problem. In addition, it provides a call tree of the code that was executed, allowing you to quickly gain insight into unfamiliar code. It also provides the ability to jump from the search feature to the call tree so that the person analyzing the trace can determine how the problematic code was called.

The Dynamics AX Trace Parser is available as a free download from Partner Source and Customer Source.

Setting Tracing Options

Dynamics AX Tracing provides multiple locations where you can set tracing options for server and client activity:

- In the Microsoft Dynamics AX Server Configuration Utility, on the computer running the AOS instance.
- In the Microsoft Dynamics AX Configuration Utility, on a client.
- Within Dynamics AX, in the Tools\Options dialog box, on the Development and SQL tabs.

The following procedures describe how to set tracing options in the AOS and the Dynamics AX client.

> **Note** SQL Trace isn't available unless you also select Allow Client Tracing On Application Object Server Instance using the following instructions:
>
> 1. Open the Microsoft Dynamics AX Server Configuration Utility.
> 2. If you're using the original (installed) configuration, you need to create a new configuration via Manage\Create Configuration.
> 3. Under the Tracing tab, select Allow Client Tracing On Application Object Server Instance.

Setting Tracing Options on the AOS

1. Open the Microsoft Dynamics AX Server Configuration Utility (Start\Administrative Tools\Microsoft Dynamics AX 2009 Server Configuration Utility).
2. Verify that the currently selected AOS instance and configuration are the ones you want to modify.
3. On the Tracing tab, choose Options, and click Start Trace. If the AOS service is running, the trace starts within 15 seconds. If the service is stopped, the trace starts the next time the service is started.

Setting Tracing Options on the Client

1. Open the Microsoft Dynamics AX Server Configuration Utility (Start\Control Panel\Administrative Tools\Microsoft Dynamics AX Configuration Utility).
2. Verify that the currently selected configuration is the one you want to modify.
3. On the Tracing tab, evaluate the type of tracing you need to do, and choose Settings.
4. To start tracing once you've set the options you want, close the utility and restart your Dynamics AX client.

Tracing Options and Other Tracing Activities

The tracing options in the configuration utilities are described in Table 12-2. Later in this section, we cover additional tracing information you need to know, such as troubleshooting common tracing problems and importing and analyzing traces.

TABLE 12-2 Tracing Options in the Configuration Utilities

Tracing Option	Description
RPC round-trips to server	Traces all RPC round-trips from any client to the server
X++ method calls	Traces all X++ methods that are invoked on the server
Number of nested calls	Limits tracing to the specified number of nested method calls
Function calls	Traces all function calls that are invoked on the server
SQL statements	Traces all SQL Server statements that are invoked on the server

Tracing Option	Description
Bind variables	Traces all columns that are used as input bind variables
Row fetch	Traces all rows that are fetched using SQL Server
Row fetch summary (count and time)	Counts all rows that are fetched, and records the time spent fetching
Connect and disconnect	Traces each time the AOS connects and disconnects from the database
Transactions: *ttsBegin*, *ttsCommit*, *ttsAbort*	Traces all transactions that use the *TTSBegin*, *TTSCommit*, and *TTSAbort* statements

Files from traces are saved to the locations described in Table 12-3.

TABLE 12-3 Trace Locations

Type of Trace	Location
AOS trace files	**AOS computer** log*<servername>*_*<timestamp>*.trc
AOS settings and SQL Settings triggered from the client (Allow Client Tracing On Application Object Server Instance is selected.)	**AOS computer** log*<username>*_*<clientIP>*_*<sessionID>*_*<server>*.trc
Client method trace triggered from the client (Enable Method Tracing To Client Desktop is selected.)	**Client computer** log*<username>*_*<clientIP>*_*<sessionID>*_*<client>*.trc

A new file is created each time tracing is started or at the start of each new day. If you're running frequent traces, be sure to remove or archive unneeded trace files often.

The default trace buffer settings in Dynamics AX 2009 are not optimal for collecting traces and can lead to dropped events. Dropping events leaves much of the trace file unusable. We recommend that you set values for the following registry settings for the AOS: (HKEY_LOCAL_MACHINE\SYSTEM\CurrentControlSet\Services\Dynamics Server\5.0\01\ *Configurationname*):

- *tracebuffersize* = 512
- *traceminbuffers* = 30
- *tracemaxbuffers* = 120

Troubleshooting Tracing

In this section, we provide information on how to troubleshoot the two most common issues you encounter while tracing.

Sometimes a trace that appears to be running in the configuration utility doesn't look like it's running in Windows. Here's why: When a trace file reaches its size limit, Windows stops the trace. The configuration utility interface doesn't synchronize with Windows until Stop Trace is clicked. Additionally, the Event Tracing for Windows framework drops the trace and the trace events when the disk has insufficient space. So make sure that there is more free space than the value set in *tracemaxfilesize* in the registry.

If you run more than one client-tracing session simultaneously, don't be surprised when your system slows down. Tracing is processing intensive and space intensive. We recommend that you don't turn on tracing for more than one client at a time.

Importing Traces

You can import traces collected on either the client or the server by downloading the Dynamics AX Trace Parser. Detailed documentation for importing traces is available with the tool.

Analyzing Traces

Once you load the trace files into the Trace Parser, they are available with ready-made analysis views. Figure 12-2 shows the Open Trace Database view.

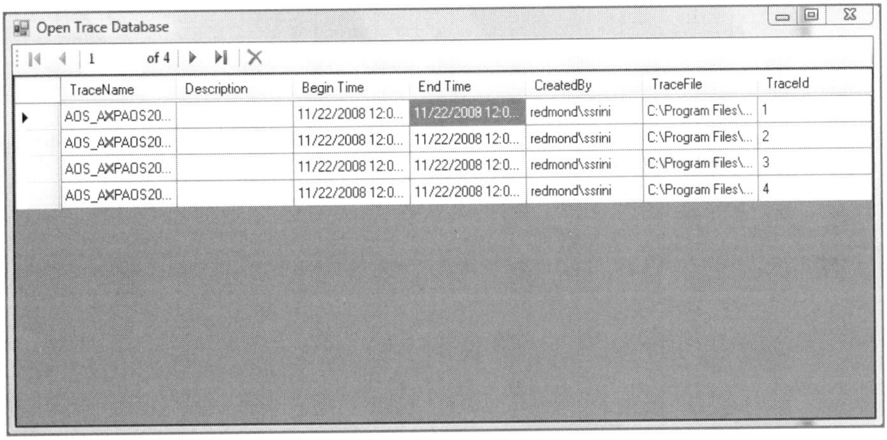

FIGURE 12-2 Trace listings view

When you open a trace from the trace listings view, you see a summary view with many search capabilities and an integrated view of the code as the call tree is analyzed.

Figure 12-3 shows a sample trace summary view.

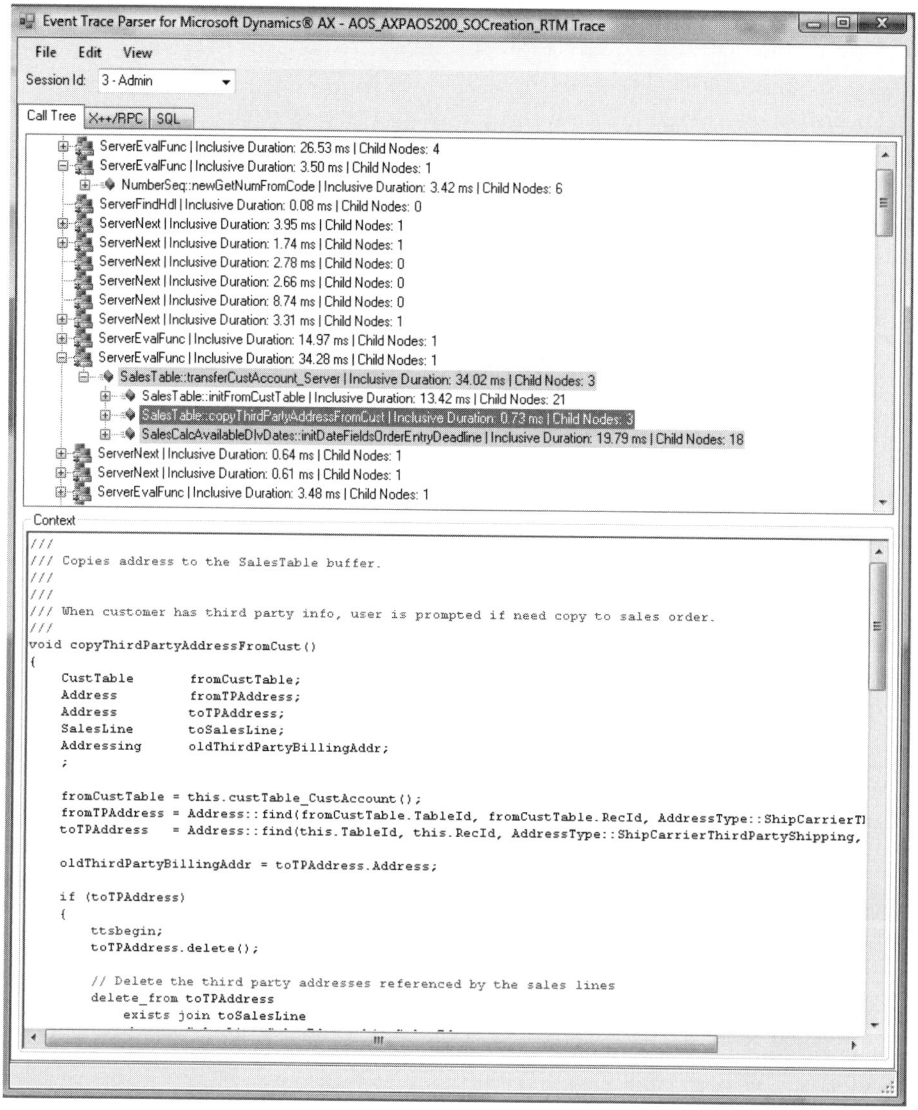

FIGURE 12-3 Sample trace summary view

Monitoring Client/Server Calls

When you develop and test a Dynamics AX application, you can monitor the client and server calls by turning on the Client/Server Trace option, found on the Development tab in the Options dialog box, which can be accessed from the Tools menu. The Development tab shows the calls made that force the application runtime to parse from one tier to the other. Figure 12-4 shows an example of the client/server trace for one of the previous X++ examples.

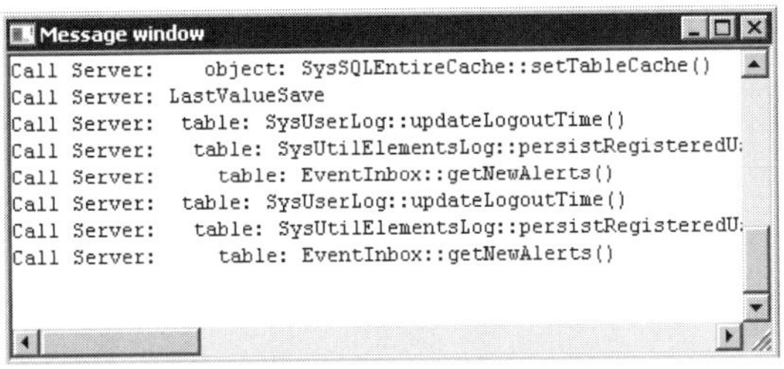

FIGURE 12-4 Client/server trace message window

Monitoring Database Activity

You can also trace database activity when you're developing and testing the Dynamics AX application logic. You can enable tracing on the SQL tab in the Options dialog box. You can trace all SQL statements or just the long queries, warnings, and deadlocks. SQL statements can be traced to the Infolog, a message window, a database table, or a file. If statements are traced to the Infolog, you can use the context menu to open the statement in the SQL Trace dialog box, in which you can view the entire statement as well as the path to the method that executed the statement. The SQL Trace dialog box is shown in Figure 12-5.

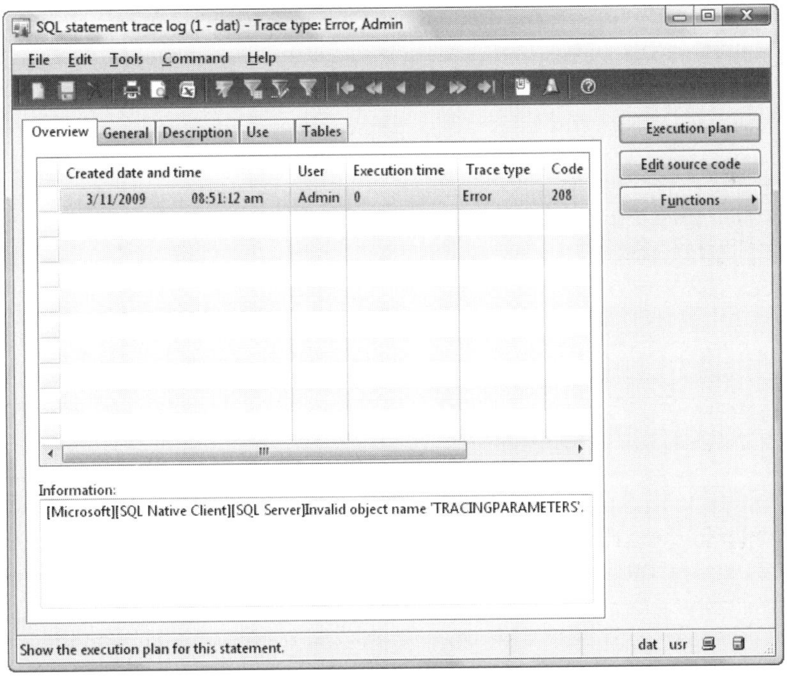

FIGURE 12-5 SQL Trace dialog box

You can open the Statement Execution Plan dialog box from the SQL Trace dialog box, as shown in Figure 12-6. This dialog box shows a simple view of the execution plan to help you understand how the the underlying database will execute the statement.

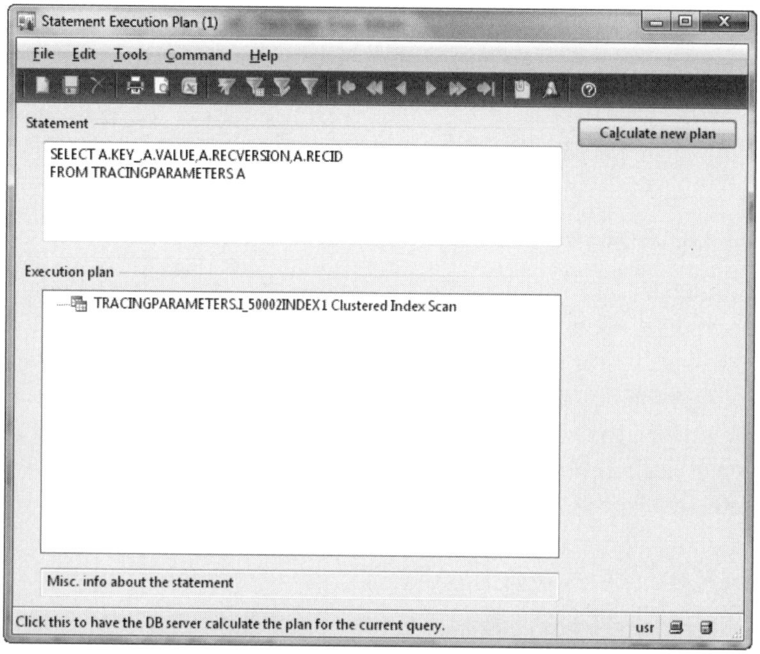

FIGURE 12-6 Statement Execution Plan dialog box

Important To trace SQL statements, you must select the Allow Client Tracing On Application Object Server Instance option on the Tracing tab in the Microsoft Dynamics AX Server Configuration Utility.

From either the SQL Trace or the Statement Execution Plan dialog box, you can copy the statement and, if you're using SQL Server 2005, paste it into SQL Server Query Analyzer to get a more detailed view of the execution plan. In SQL Server 2008, open a new Query window in SQL Server Management Studio and paste in the query. If the Dynamics AX application runtime uses placeholders to execute the statement, the placeholders are shown as question marks in the statement. These must be replaced by variables or constants before they can be executed in the SQL Server Query Analyzer. If the application runtime uses literals, the statement can be pasted directly into the SQL Server Query Analyzer and executed.

When you trace SQL statements in Dynamics AX, the application runtime displays only the DML statement. It doesn't display other commands sent to the database, such as transaction commits or isolation level changes. With SQL Server 2008, you can use the SQL Server Profiler to trace these statements using the event classes *RPC:Completed* and *SP:StmtCompleted* in the Stored Procedures collection, and the *SQL:BatchCompleted* event in the TSQL collection, as shown in Figure 12-7.

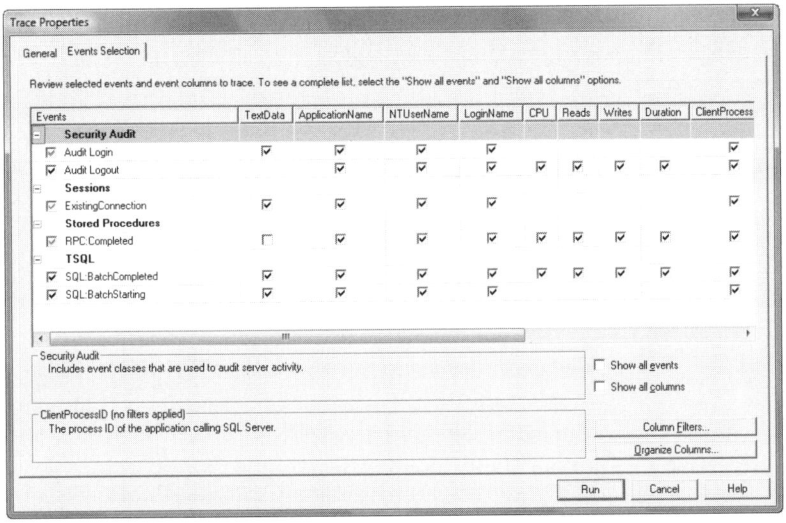

FIGURE 12-7 SQL Server Profiler trace events

Code Profiler Tool

The Code Profiler tool in Dynamics AX 2009 calculates the profile much faster, and it includes a new view of the code profile, providing a better user experience. Figure 12-8 shows the traverse view, in which each of the called methods in the profiled scenario appears in the top grid. The view also displays a duration count that shows the number of ticks that it took to execute the method and a method count that shows the number of times the methods have been called. The grid for parent calls and children calls shows the methods that called the specific method and the other methods calling the specific method, respectively.

If you use the Code Profiler as a performance optimization tool, you can focus on the methods with the longest duration to optimize the internal structure of the method, or you can focus on the methods called the most and try to limit the number of calls to those methods. You can inspect the internal operation of the methods by clicking the Profile Lines button, which opens the view shown in Figure 12-9. This view shows the duration of every line in the method.

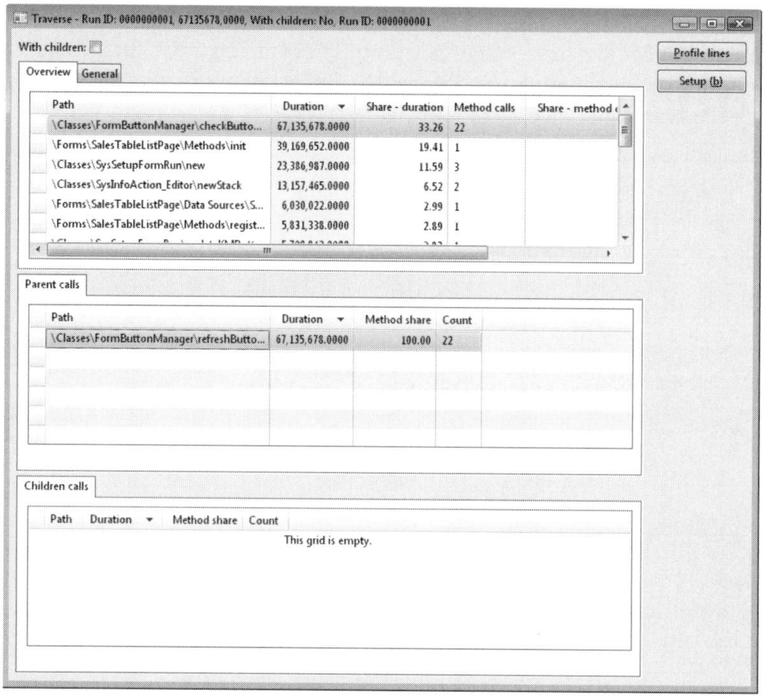

FIGURE 12-8 Traverse view in the Code Profiler

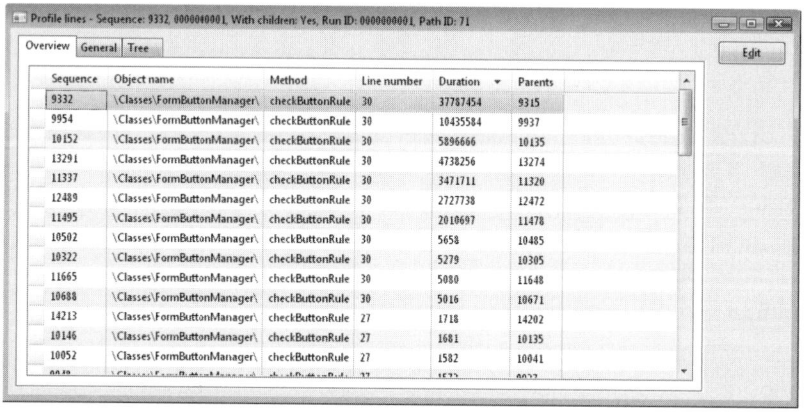

FIGURE 12-9 Profile Lines view in the Code Profiler

The Code Profiler is a powerful tool for finding issues such as problem areas in the X++ code, code that doesn't have to be executed in certain scenarios, and code that makes multiple calls to the same methods.

Chapter 13

Configuration and Security

In this chapter:

The objectives of this chapter are to:

- Introduce the IntelliMorph layout technology.
- Explain how the license and configuration systems in Microsoft Dynamics AX 2009 affect application functionality throughout the system.
- Describe the security framework and discuss data security.

Introduction

Dynamics AX 2009 is targeted at companies and organizations whose size, geography, language, complexity, and lines of business vary widely. Securing and configuring the Dynamics AX system correctly has a significant impact on how the system can be implemented and used and on how it performs.

This chapter describes how the Dynamics AX application runtime implements configuration and security and how these concepts determine the interface that the user sees. IntelliMorph is the unique technology used to design and develop Dynamics AX application forms, reports, menus, and menu items. It includes essential framework elements that influence the rendering of the user interface by enforcing licensing, configuration, and security restrictions. The licensing and configuration frameworks give you the option to license application modules, thus providing access to various application areas. You can also enable and disable functionality independently of the licensing.

This chapter discusses security in the context of the application runtime, and it also offers details about important security aspects to consider when developing your application. Near the end of this chapter, we cover data security, which makes it possible to differentiate business data access across user profiles. This feature enables you to construct queries to extend the table permission options available in Microsoft SQL Server. The feature that differentiates business data access is the record level security framework.

IntelliMorph

Although Dynamics AX is an international product with support for multiple countries, languages, company sizes, and industries within the same deployment, it is also a productive development platform that ensures a uniform yet very configurable and automatically arranged layout of application functionality. The unique presentation technology is based on model element properties, licensing, configuration and security settings, and personalization, which together lay out the presentation controls on forms, reports, menus, menu items, and corresponding Web elements for each individual user. The technology is called IntelliMorph, and it works with both the rich client and the Web client types in Dynamics AX.

A primary driver of the IntelliMorph technology design is support for international distribution, but with a different approach than other enterprise resource planning (ERP) products; IntelliMorph needs to be ready for multiple countries in multiple languages within the same deployment, and it has to offer the same user experience, regardless of the user interface language. These requirements necessitate the design of a metadata-driven and property-driven user interface in which forms, reports, menus, and menu items react to both global and local configuration and security settings. A positive side-effect of this design is that users can personalize the interface in multiple ways. The personalization capability has been extended even further in Dynamics AX 2009, in which individual users can choose from the following options:

- Reference all rich client forms as individual favorites to which they can attach any query.
- Show or hide controls.
- Change the size of forms and controls.

IntelliMorph automatically arranges functionality based on licensing, configuration and security, and personalization—without programmable changes. Figure 13-1 illustrates the filtering structure for the layout of elements such as forms, reports, menus, and Web pages.

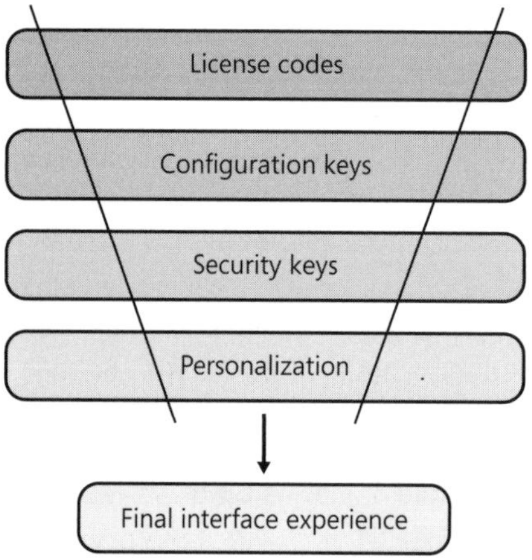

FIGURE 13-1 IntelliMorph presentation structure

The layout includes the license code that opens the parent configuration key, which holds either the security key references or the configuration key children to the security keys. Security keys determine access to the menu items that reference available functionality for user groups and individual users. The final factor in the interface experience is personalization, which allows the user to modify the user interface by hiding, showing, and configuring the presentation controls.

We describe the elements and their interactions and dependencies in greater detail in the following sections, and we also drill down on personalization options.

> **Note** The presentation and layout of the user interface are not limited to support for IntelliMorph technology; they also provide a rich set of design options for developing Windows forms with many different control types, such as ActiveX and list view controls. You can also customize Dynamics AX reports with the Visual Report Designer, which allows you to visually design a report while using both the X++ syntax and the properties window for arranging and formatting.

Best Practices

Understanding how IntelliMorph works can help you develop the run-time presentation for application extensions. If you follow the best practice design rules and patterns, you can optimize your use of the IntelliMorph technology and ensure a uniform application run-time interface. The best practice principles focus on using the default property settings for the presentation controls that determine how to present elements and functionality. They also cover the general use of labels, field groups, extended data types, auto groups, security and configuration keys, and menu items. The standard Dynamics AX application is developed using all the best practice rules and patterns, which provide a uniform way of interacting with the application and the underlying business logic. Chapter 3, "The MorphX Tools," describes the Best Practices tool in depth. You can find details on best practice rules and patterns in the Microsoft Dynamics AX 2009 SDK, on MSDN.

Principles for Forms

Designing application forms can be a very time-consuming task if you always design from scratch, especially if your application must run in a multiple-language deployment. To avoid this time and effort, you should follow the best practice of creating forms and reports by dragging as often as possible and setting very few properties manually. If the system's default property values don't suit your needs, you can customize almost any property to fit your application.

When you design the layout of a form for which a table or view is used as the underlying data source, you find that the same field groups and field structures in the original *Tables* and *Views* nodes are in the Application Object Tree (AOT). This allows you to drag these field groups and field structures from the form's *Data Sources* node directly to the form's *Design* node. You should configure the Data Sources to use the Dynamics AX *AutoJoin* system to ensure that data is synchronized when two forms are linked. When you work with the layout and property settings, you must keep the Auto or Default settings. These settings optimize the use of the auto-arrange technology and limit the need to move pixels to unify and align the form presentation with the rest of the application.

When designing forms, you should adhere to the recommendations in the following list whenever possible to optimize the use of the auto-arrange technology. Most patterns are property settings on the form design.

- Use default settings, especially for the attributes *Left*, *Top*, *Width*, *Height*, *Frame*, *WindowResize*, *WindowType*, and *HideToolbar*.
- Use the *DataGroup* attribute when using tables or views as Data Sources.
- When using the *DataGroup* attribute, change the *AutoDataGroup* property to *Yes*. This setting adjusts the overall behavior based on the data source behavior.
- Use labels instead of hardcoded strings.
- Add Help text (status bar Help) as labels instead of hardcoded strings.
- Use the *TitleDatasource* property to provide a better and more visible data experience for the user.
- Set the *AutoDeclaration* property to *Yes* if the control features must be accessible from X++ code.
- Use the *AutoJoin* system where possible.

If your customers require a unique user experience, you could completely remodel the user interface—no design restrictions prevent you from taking that step. One disadvantage of such an overhaul is that training, flexibility, and upgrading become more complex.

Principles for Reports

IntelliMorph is even more important for reports than for forms. The best practices for reports primarily involve retaining the default settings for properties. When you design a report, however, you often don't know much about the environment in which the report will execute. The following examples illustrate the types of information you won't have at design time:

- The size of the paper in the user's printer
- The length or content of the labels according to the user's installation profile and language
- The names of the fields disabled by security and configuration key settings

- The length of the fields (extended data types) in the user's installation
- The sort order of the data sent to the report
- Whether the user wants to print using the *subtotals* setting or just the *totals* setting
- The default settings for font and font size
- The number of records in the tables from which the report gets its data

Reports can be broadly classified into internal or external reports. *Internal reports* are circulated and viewed only inside the organization. In such reports, the report presentation and format aren't critical. Some examples of internal reports are Ledger Transaction List, Project Profitability Statement, bank transactions, and so on. *External reports* are circulated external to the organization, so their format and layout are important. Such reports include Purchase Orders, Sales Invoices, Vendor Check Payments, and so on. Such reports are usually printed on preprinted stationery and require precision design. Both internal and external reports can be created using the Auto design or Generated design reporting features of Dynamics AX. You can use Auto design for all internal reports and Generated design for external reports that can't be implemented with Auto designs because they require precise design and layout capabilities such as the following:

- Reports that are forms with externally determined layouts and where the information is expected to display in specific positions.
- Reports that are forms for which the design is likely to be adjusted to the customer needs at deployment time. Invoices are one example. Most controls should have their positions fixed (not set to Auto) to simplify moving them by using the Visual Report Designer.

You should follow these design patterns whenever possible:

- Use default property settings, especially for orientation, width, label, width of label, and other formatting information because fixed settings cause the report controls to disregard the IntelliMorph auto-arrange technology available from the property window.
- Use the Auto design report type when possible.

Working with IntelliMorph

IntelliMorph provides numerous options for personalizing Dynamics AX forms. These options allow you to move controls, set properties on controls, and add extra fields to forms. Forms are customized at application run time, and settings are saved on a per-user basis. You can invoke the personalization options from multiple places, depending on the type of personalization desired. The personalization options use the same framework whether a column is hidden via the Command entry on the menu bar, moved within the form runtime by using the mouse, or renamed by using the advanced personalization form.

The advanced personalization form, shown in Figure 13-2, provides the user with customization options.

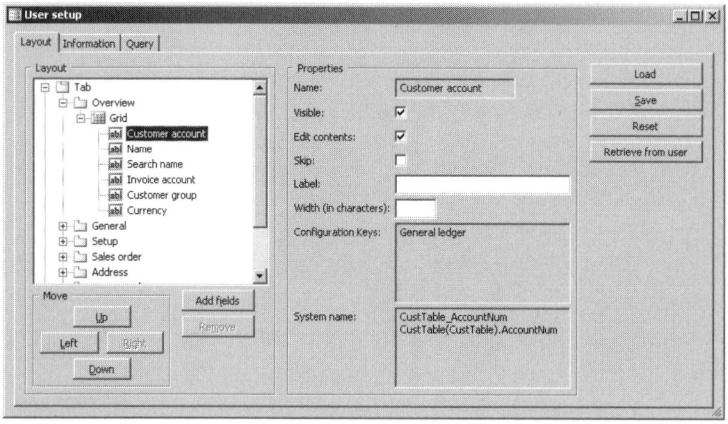

FIGURE 13-2 Advanced personalization form

By using this form, the user can change the tab page order, move elements around, remove fields, add additional fields from existing form Data Sources, rename the field, prevent the field content from being edited, change the default field length, and even choose among multiple versions of the form presentation. The personalization settings can also be shared. For example, a department that wants a common presentation that differs from the standard company presentation but doesn't want to modify the global form layout could have all users personalize their form settings in the same way.

To make user personalization work, you must define different levels of personalization by using the form design properties *AllowUserSetup* and *AllowAdd*. Four levels of personalization are presented in Table 13-1.

TABLE 13-1 Personalization Levels

Personalization Level	Description	*AllowUserSetup*	*AllowAdd*
Limit user personalization of forms	User can change only the size and position of the form, not the properties of individual controls. Position and size of the form are saved (the size is saved if *SaveSize* is set to *Yes*), so an entry for this form is in the *SysLastValue* table even though no personalization is allowed.	*No*	*No*
Enable customization of controls	User can change the behavior of individual controls but can't move them or add new controls. Personal values can be defined for *Enabled*, *Visible*, *Skip*, *Width*, and *Label*.	*Restricted*	*No*

Personalization Level	Description	*AllowUserSetup*	*AllowAdd*
Enable customization of layout	User can adjust properties on controls and move controls between containers, move controls from within the Setup form by dragging or by using the navigation buttons, and move grid columns within the grid by dragging them directly onto the form. This feature lets the user create a tab page that encompasses all the information normally entered for a given record or grid, so most forms you create should support this level of personalization.	*Yes*	*Restricted*
Enable customization of layout and content	User can customize layout and add new fields from the Setup form. To support this level of personalization, all code must be moved to the data source fields. Added controls don't have any code. The properties are the default values for this type of control and data. Only data fields can be added, not any unbound controls or controls bound to display methods.	*Yes*	*Yes*

The personalization levels also depend on how the form's X++ code is written. For example, if you override the methods that take the position of the control into account, the kernel can automatically restrict the user setup level.

Licensing and Configuration

Dynamics AX allows licensing of application modules, multiple user types, languages, server technology, the Web framework, database logging, record level security, development tools, run-time execution, and integration frameworks. The system elements and application modules are locked by license codes that must be unlocked by license keys.

Unlocking a license code is the initial step in configuring the Dynamics AX system because the license codes reference the configuration key that links to the physical functionality. You unlock the license code by using the License Information form, shown in Figure 13-3, which you access from Administration\Setup\System\License Information.

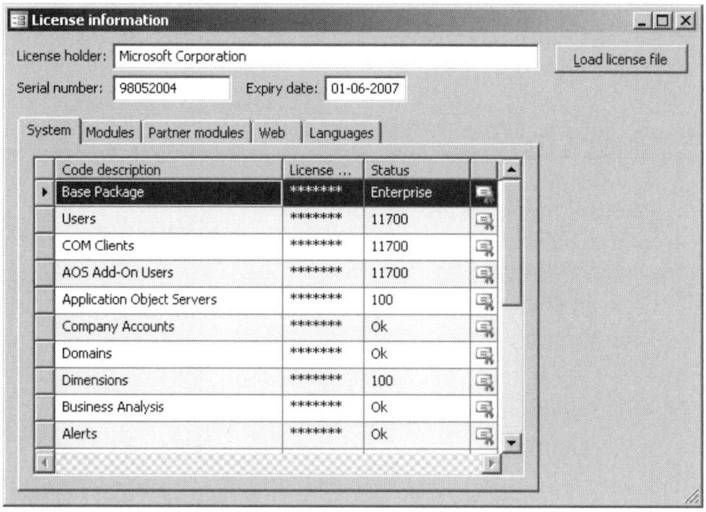

FIGURE 13-3 License Information form

You enter the license codes manually or import them by clicking the Load License File button. All the license codes and license files available for import are supplied by Microsoft through the Microsoft Partner Program.

The license codes are validated individually based on the license holder name, the serial number, the expiration date, and the license key being entered or imported. The validation process either accepts the license key and updates the status field with *counts*, *names*, or *OK* or returns a negative result in the Infolog form.

> **Note** Standard customer licenses don't contain an expiration date. Licenses for other uses, such as evaluation, independent software vendor projects, education, and training, do include an expiration date. When a license reaches its expiration date, the system changes execution mode and becomes a restricted demo product for a limited amount of time.

The license code elements are created in the AOT and divided into five tab pages—System, Modules, Partner Modules, Web, and Languages—based on type of functionality, as shown in Figure 13-3. The grouping is determined by a license code property, and the *SysLicenseCodeSort* table and its *createSortIdx* method handle sorting inside the groups. The Partner Modules tab allows you to include licensed partner modules. Partners can sign an agreement with Microsoft that gives other partners and customers the opportunity to purchase and request partner-developed functionality. Contact your local Microsoft subsidiary for more information about this program.

The licensing framework can also track dependencies among various licenses. A license can have up to five different prerequisites. Adding a prerequisite for a license ensures that the Application Object Server (AOS) tracks the license dependencies. So if your application depends on multiple licenses, you don't need to check whether a particular license exists in your code.

Configuration Hierarchy

The license codes reside at the top of the configuration hierarchy, which is the entry point for working with the configuration system that surrounds all the application modules and system elements available within Dynamics AX. The configuration system is based on approximately 200 multiple configuration keys that enable and disable functionality in the application for the entire deployment. Each license key controls access to a specific set of functions; when a key is disabled, its functionality is automatically removed from the database and the user interface. The application runtime renders presentation controls only for menu items that are associated with the active configuration key or where no configuration key is available.

The relationship between license codes and configuration keys is very comprehensive. An individual license key not only enables a variety of configuration keys but also removes the visibility of configuration keys and their functions throughout the entire system if the license key is not valid. Removing configuration keys with invalid license keys reduces the configuration complexity. For example, if a license key is not entered or not valid in the license information form (accessed from Administration/Setup/System), the Configuration form hides it and displays only the valid license keys and the configuration and security keys that depend on them. This functionality reduces the number of security keys you need to configure when you create user groups. (We talk more about user groups, which are essential to the security subsystem, later in this chapter.) Figure 13-4 shows the system-wide configuration hierarchy followed by most functionalities within an implementation—except those that don't comply with best practices for developing Dynamics AX application modules.

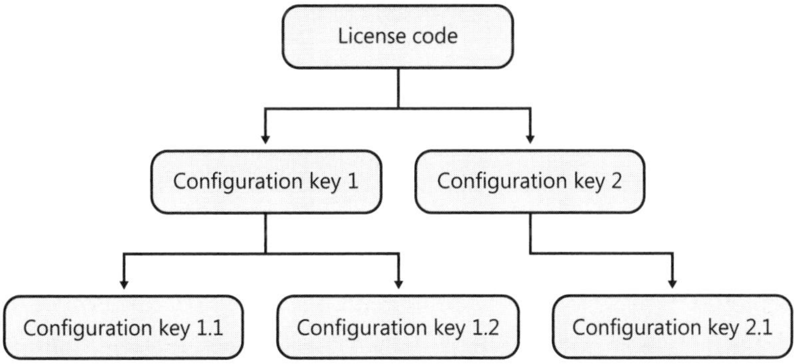

FIGURE 13-4 Configuration hierarchy

The configuration hierarchy might seem complex. However, easy-to-use administrator checklists and forms, such as the License Information, Configuration, and Permission forms, reduce the initial complexity.

Configuration Keys

The application modules and the underlying business logic that license codes and configuration keys enable are available when Dynamics AX is deployed. Everything from forms, reports, and menus to data elements and the Data Dictionary, as well as the entire development environment, is already present in the product, existing in a temporary state in which the elements don't affect the enabled functionality.

Using the configuration hierarchy shown in Figure 13-4, you can enable parent configuration keys with valid license keys to appear in the global configuration form by navigating to Administration\Setup\System\Configuration. The parent configuration keys controlled by the license codes appear with a red padlock overlay and can't be disabled; any configuration key children displayed below the parent can be changed. Parent configuration keys with no children are not available from the configuration form.

> **Note** Parent configuration keys can exist without an attached license key. These are available for the administrator to enable or disable at all times from within the Configuration form.

The Dynamics AX configuration philosophy is to enable functionality as needed. The consequence of this philosophy is that the system starts minimized by default, with all child configuration keys disabled. An example of the Configuration form and the minimized approach is shown in Figure 13-5.

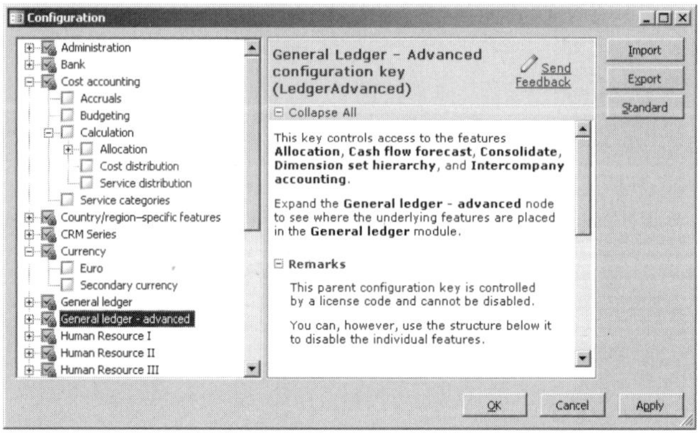

FIGURE 13-5 Configuration form

As a more detailed example, consider a company buying the Trade module license code. The company wants most of the functionality in the module, but it doesn't do business with other countries. The company therefore chooses to disable the Foreign Trade configuration key.

By using the configuration key flow chart shown in Figure 13-6, an administrator can determine whether a configuration key is enabled, and if not, what it would take to enable it, which depends the configuration key's parent.

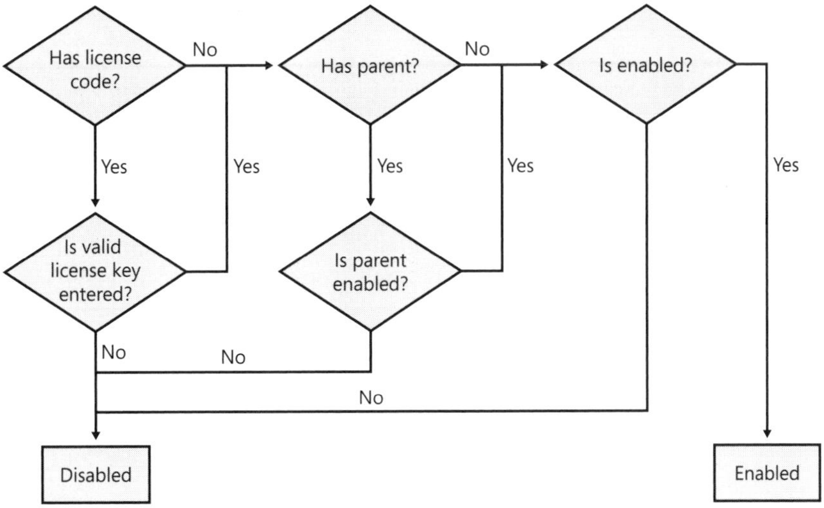

FIGURE 13-6 Configuration key flow chart

Using Configuration Keys

An important part of the application development process is mapping extensions to the configuration-based security frameworks that integrate the extensions into the complete solution. Correctly using the configuration keys throughout the system can make enterprise-wide deployment flexible and economical, with divisions, regions, or sites all using the same deployment platform and customizing local deployment by using configuration keys rather than by developing specific customizations in each installation. You can't entirely avoid individualized development, however, because of the nature of businesses and their development needs.

Configuration keys affect the Data Dictionary, the presentation, and the navigation infrastructure directly, meaning that you can reference a configuration key property on all relevant elements. Table 13-2 lists the elements that can be directly affected by configuration keys.

TABLE 13-2 Configuration Key References

Grouping	Element Types
Data Dictionary	Tables, including fields and indexes
	Maps
	Views
	Extended data types
	Base enumerations
	License codes
	Configuration keys
	Security keys
	Perspectives

Grouping	Element Types
Windows presentation and navigation	Menus Display: Menu items Output: Menu items Action: Menu items
Web presentation and navigation	URL: Web menu items Action: Web menu items Display: Web content Output: Web content Web menus Weblets
Documentation references	System documentation Application developer documentation Application documentation HTML Help files

When a configuration key is enabled, the functionality associated with that configuration key is enabled. This means that appropriate menu items, submenu items, tables, buttons, and fields are enabled when the configuration key is turned on. A user has access only to those areas that the administrator has granted access to and that have been enabled by the configuration key.

Figure 13-7 illustrates a frequently used security hierarchy in which the configuration key is the gatekeeper for interaction with the functionality underneath.

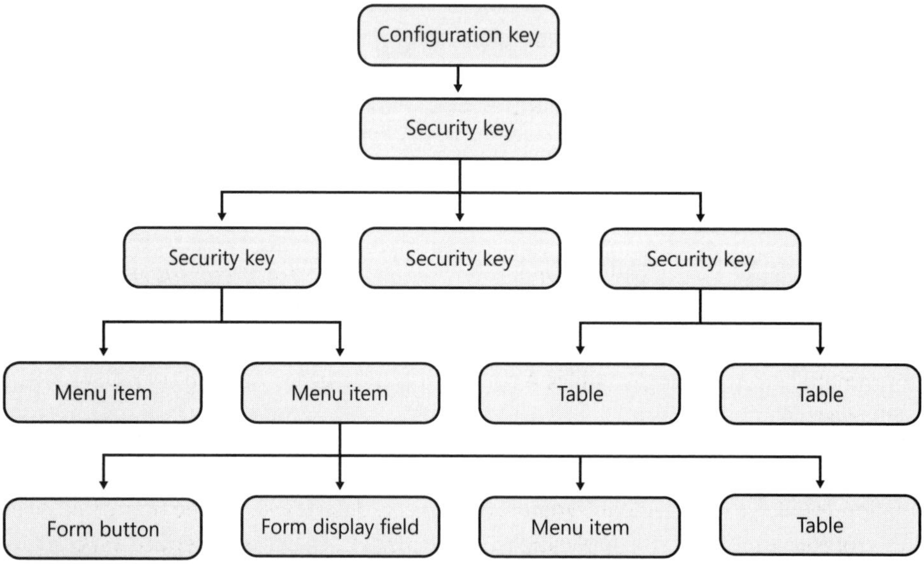

FIGURE 13-7 Security keys as permission gates

The hierarchy is based on security keys that, working together with user groups, act as permission gates that allow users to see, invoke, and work with the user interface, business logic, and rules represented by menu items, submenu items, tables, buttons, and fields.

This introduction to the security hierarchy provides a high-level overview of the concept. The particular hierarchy shown in Figure 13-8 demonstrates how the *LedgerBasic* configuration key opens for a subset of the vendor functionality that is managed by a subhierarchy of security keys. The subhierarchy is the link to functionality such as the Purchase Order form and the Vendor form that are referenced via display menu items. These display menu items explicitly reference specific tables to decrease the complexity of configuring security.

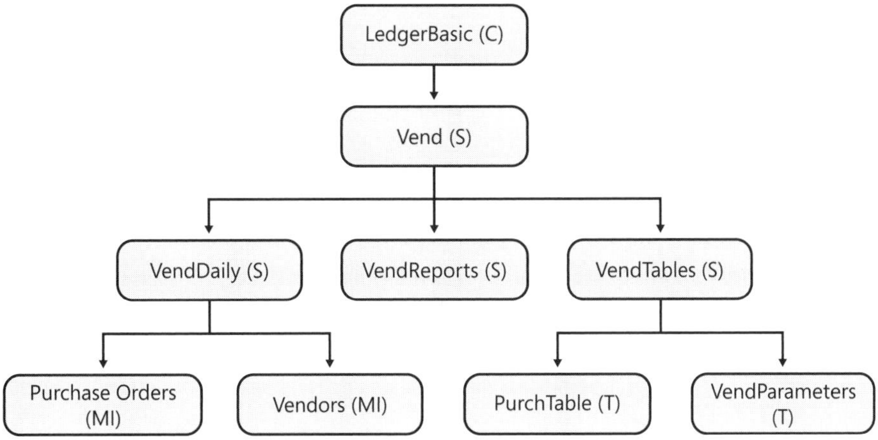

FIGURE 13-8 Security hierarchy example

This illustration doesn't depict all possible elements and combinations within the security hierarchy, which would include such things as reports, classes, Web elements, or an explanation of how to invoke country-specific functionality for an individual user.

Security Framework

The security framework within Dynamics AX uses Integrated Windows authentication and Active Directory to authenticate user and system interactions before they are authorized by the Dynamics AX security framework. Using Integrated Windows authentication allows automatic logon to the Dynamics AX application without collecting user name and password information.

A Windows-authenticated user can be associated with only one Dynamics AX user. The application role for the individual Dynamics AX user is determined by the user groups with which the role is associated. The application role also defines the user interface actions that a user is authorized to perform and the data that the user is authorized to view and modify. You can create an application role by adding all the necessary functionality to one user group, or you can create a collection of user groups that define the entire application role. A user group can contain multiple Dynamics AX users, and each Dynamics AX user can be part of multiple user groups, as shown in Figure 13-9.

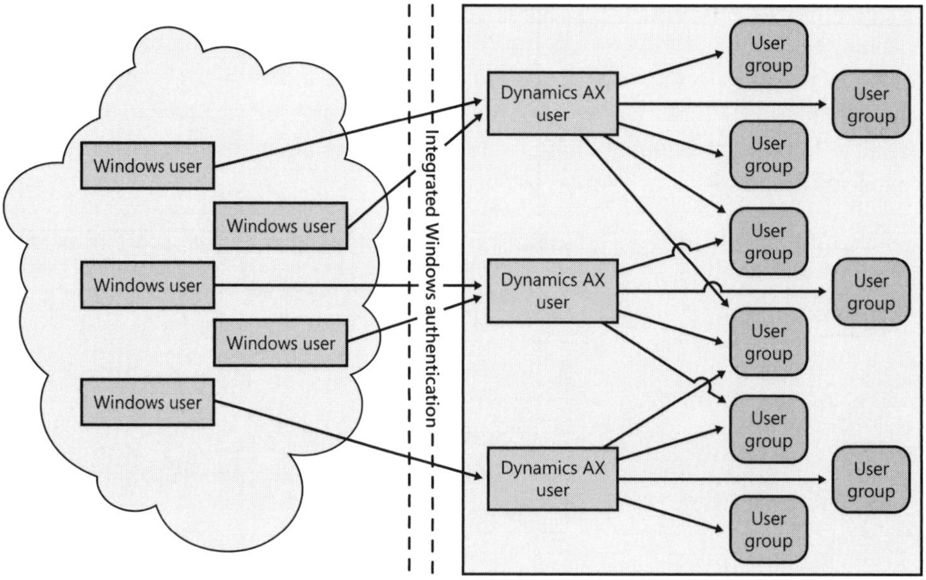

FIGURE 13-9 Authentication overview

> **Note** Integrated Windows authentication is the only authentication scheme available in Dynamics AX 4.0. The option to work with the SQL Server authentication, available in versions earlier than 4.0, no longer exists.

Organizing Security

The Dynamics AX security framework is composed of users, company accounts, domains, user groups, table and field permissions, and record level security. The organization of application security in Dynamics AX is associated with security keys and their relationships with menu items, form controls, tables, and fields, which together operate as the connection layer between the application logic and the application role configuration. The security keys reduce the complexity of setting up the overall security of individual user groups per domain because the references to configuration keys can remove unused functionality. Parent security keys can enable or disable entire application modules for user groups. Subcategories of application modules are structured by using the method that matches the main menu structure.

The flow chart in Figure 13-10 illustrates how authorization is validated for an individual user group and how configuration keys and parent security keys affect the final security access.

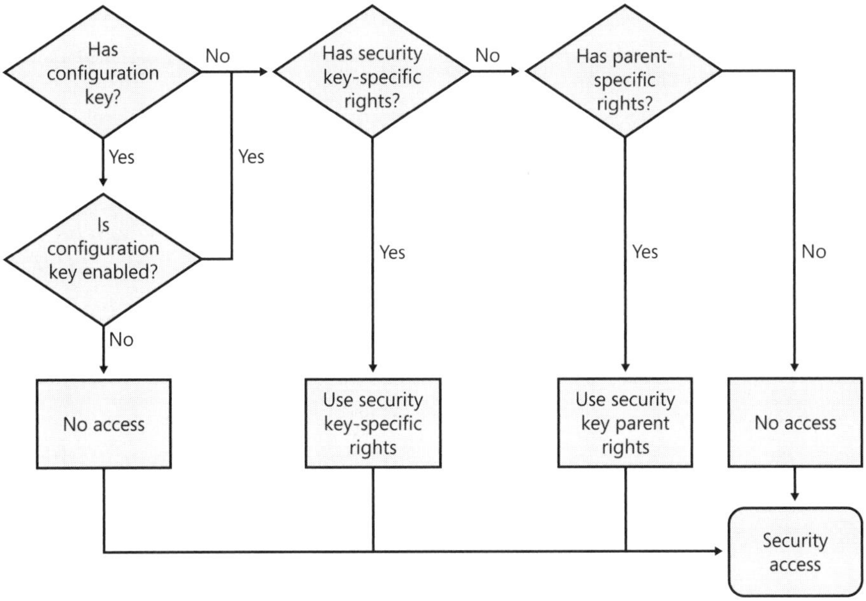

FIGURE 13-10 Validation of authorization

Note Configuration keys and parent security keys are element properties that are added to the individual security key. When adding the properties, you can use only one of the two properties at a time because a configuration key indicates that the security key is the parent, and the parent property indicates that the security key is a subcategory.

When you create security keys, the parent security keys function as the application module keepers for the underlying child security key categories: Daily, Setup, Journals, Inquiries, Reports, Periodic, Miscellaneous, and Tables. These categories define the user interface for the substructure of the application module within the Dynamics AX main menu. This arrangement makes it easy to relate the main menu items with the security elements when you're configuring user group permissions.

Tip To simplify the navigation experience, use category naming for all application modules.

The security keys control the initial permission levels to functionality within the application, but they depend on the menu items and the table permissions framework for detailed security configuration. The permissions are assigned to user groups within their corresponding domains using the following five permission levels:

- **No access** Members of the user group can't access the item or any subitems that the item controls.

- **View access** Members of the user group are allowed to view the item, but they can't use it.
- **Edit access** Members of the user group are allowed to view and use the item.
- **Create access** Members of the user group are allowed to view and use the item, and they can also add new items.
- **Full control** Members of the user group are allowed to view the item, but they can't create, delete, or edit. Members can also provide additional rights in special cases if full access is given to the administration items.

If you set the access level for a menu item or security key to full control, all children of the selected node are automatically set to full control. If you set the access level to anything other than full control, the children do not inherit the permissions automatically. In such cases, you can use the cascade functionality by clicking the Cascade button. Clicking the Cascade button automatically grants the same access level to all the nodes in the subtree under the node.

> **Note** The security framework presents only the user interface elements that the user has access to, and it handles the appropriate access level for individual users. Security is applied on the user interface, which is the user's entry to the application through menus, menu items, reports, and forms.

Permission levels are assigned and accessible from the user group permission form, which facilitates the entire permission assignment process beyond simple node creation.

Applying Security

The process for applying the security framework to the Dynamics AX application includes the following seven steps, which must be performed after the licensing and generic configuration is completed:

1. Create company accounts.
2. Create domains.
3. Create user groups.
4. Create users.
5. Set permissions for user groups and domain combinations.
6. Set table and field access.
7. Set record level security.

Domains

Configuring the security of a Dynamics AX application involves the use of domains. A domain is a collection of one or more company accounts that allow you to define user groups with the same permissions in a company with several subsidiary businesses, while allowing the same user groups to have other permissions within other companies. Domains make it easier to maintain user group security when several companies use the same security profile.

> **Note** A single company account can belong to more than one domain.

Domains allow great flexibility in the configuration of user group permissions. A domain can generate a strict security policy, in which each user group in each domain is a distinct entity with absolutely no access between groups or domains, or it can allow one user group company account access to similar group data, forms, and modules across multiple domains. The latter option simplifies the access configuration of corporate services such as controllers, multisite planners, human resource functions, and other functions that centralize or share assignments and tasks. Figure 13-11 illustrates how domains and user groups can work together in multiple ways within the same security framework.

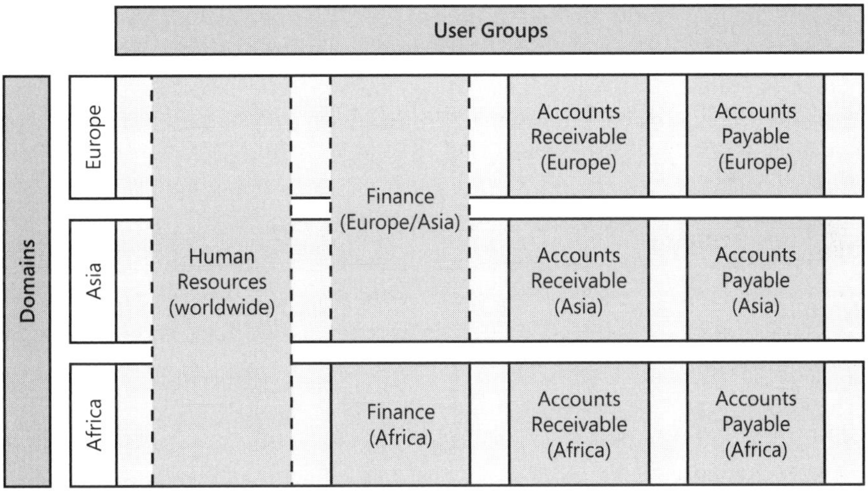

FIGURE 13-11 Example of the relationship between domains and user groups

The domain security key *SysOpenDomain* controls access to information about users, user groups, company accounts, and domains. Using the domain security key in user groups provides access to records in all domains.

> **Note** Dynamics AX includes only one domain by default: Admin. The Admin domain always includes all companies. It can't be removed, and no companies can be deleted. Use the Admin domain for any user groups that need access to all companies. When the license key domain isn't purchased, domains are still visible and functioning, but access is limited to the Admin domain.

User Group Permissions

Permissions and user rights are granted to groups, allowing the system administrator to define a set of users that share common security privileges. When you add a user to a group, you give the user all the permissions and user rights assigned to that group. By default, user groups can't access any menus, reports, forms, tables, or fields in Dynamics AX unless the administrator grants them access. User groups can be shared among all Dynamics AX users.

> **Note** A user who is a member of more than one group inherits the higher permission level of the two groups. A user can't access the application without being added to at least one user group.

When configuring group permissions, the system administrator works with a hierarchical security tree that represents all the available security keys and includes application module access, individual permission levels, and Help text that explains the security element. The User Group Permissions form allows you to configure high-level permissions and very detailed permission levels for individual user groups. Figure 13-12 shows the configuration interface that system administrators work with to assign permissions.

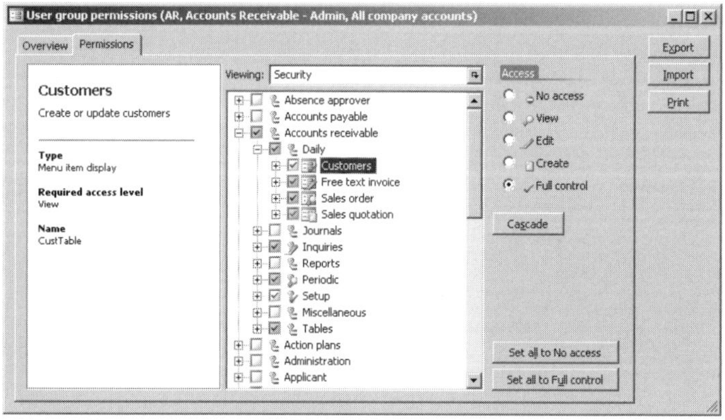

FIGURE 13-12 User Group Permissions form

You can use the User Group Permissions form to display the security elements by selecting one of the following Viewing filters, which are available near the top of the form:

- **Security** Windows-relevant security elements, sorted alphabetically

- **Security (including Web)** All security elements, including Web-specific elements (such as activity centers, deployment options, and cross functions), sorted alphabetically
- **Country/Region-Specific** Legacy functions relevant for individual countries and regions, sorted alphabetically
- **Main Menu** Functions structured according to the main menu within the Dynamics AX application runtime

These elements are the main overview elements, but additional filters are available if the menu node doesn't have a parent, such as Task Panes or Tools. If the preceding criteria are met, you can present customized menus automatically in the filter.

If you set the permission level to Full Control on the parent node key, security key children, menu items, and tables inherit the same permissions. However, if you set any other permission level, permissions are not inherited below the parent menu item. If a permission level is required for the entire subtree, the Cascade button grants the current permission level when clicked.

> **Important** If you change permissions for a user group, especially if you demote permissions, you should instruct all group members to restart the Dynamics AX client so that the permission changes take effect. If a group member doesn't restart his or her instance of the client, you should use the Online Users form, found in the Administration module, to kill the user's session. Keep in mind that killing a session through the Online Users form immediately terminates the session, so if the user has open transactions, they are rolled back.

Record Level Security

Within any enterprise, some users are restricted from working with certain sensitive data because of confidentiality, legal obligations, or company policy. In Dynamics AX, authorization for access to sensitive data is managed via the table-based record level security (RLS) framework that builds on the restrictions enforced by user group permissions. With user group permissions, you restrict access to menus, forms, and reports for group members. The RLS framework allows you to add additional restrictions to the information displayed in reports and on forms. The Dynamics AX application runtime automatically applies these restrictions when the application requests data from the database table included in the RLS framework. You include the restrictions by extending the *WHERE* clause within the SQL statement with the defined RLS query details.

Common uses of record level security include the following situations:

- Allowing members of a sales user group to see only the accounts they manage
- Prohibiting financial data from appearing on forms or reports for a specific user group

- Prohibiting account details or account IDs from appearing on forms or reports for a specific user group
- Restricting form and report data according to location, country, or region

When you enable record level security, you select user groups and the appropriate database table by using the Record Level Security Wizard, and then you execute a query that specifies the fields and criteria to be applied. The query criteria are specified using the generic Query form and are added to the individual database table that you chose with the wizard. Record level security is configured per company, so the wizard and criteria definitions must be executed for each company.

> **Important** If an application role that uses multiple user groups has record level security applied on a certain table within a company account, maximum access is given to the role. For example, if one user group has no record level security for the Customer table and another user group allows users to see only a subset of the Customer table, the user has access to all customers.

Use the following process for enabling record level security for a user group for a particular database table:

1. Start the Record Level Security Wizard.
2. Select a user group.
3. Select tables.
4. Complete the wizard.
5. Mark an available table, and then click Query.
6. Add the query criteria.

By default, the tables in the wizard are presented based on the *TableGroup* property with the value set to *Main*, and they are grouped according to the parent security key matching the main menu structures. Setting the value to *Main* results in a subset of the tables. However, you can expand the selection by clicking Show All Tables.

The kernel automatically invokes the RLS framework when criteria have been applied to database tables. In certain situations, such as those in the following list, you might need to do additional work to invoke the RLS framework:

- When using display and edit methods
- When using a *FormListControl*, *FormTreeControl*, or *TableListControl* control to show data
- When using a temporary table as a data source

Whenever you use a display or edit method to return a value from another row, you must evaluate the business impact of displaying the data. To avoid displaying particular information, you need to perform an explicit authorization in X++ code to check permissions before calling these methods. The following code shows an explicit authorization.

```
if (hasSecurityKeyAccess(securitykeyNum(mySecurityKey), AccessType::View))
{
    myMethod();
}
if (hasMenuItemAccess(menuItemDisplayStr(myMenuItem), MenuItemType::Display)))
{
    myMethod();
}
DictTable dictTable = new DictTable(tablenum(myTable));
if (dictTable.rights >= AccessType::Insert))
{
    myMethod();
}
if (isConfigurationkeyEnabled(configurationkeyNum(myConfigurationKey))
{
    myMethod();
}
```

Note For more security-related information on using display and edit methods, refer to the Microsoft Dynamics AX 2009 SDK.

If you don't want to display certain query data that populates a *FormListControl*, *FormTreeControl*, or *TableListControl* control, you must manually activate record level security, as shown here.

```
public void run
{
    CustTable custTable;
    super();
    // Ensure that record-level security is used.
    custTable.recordLevelSecurity(true);
    while select custTable
    {
        listView.add(custTable.name);
    }
}
```

When the form cache is filled with data from a temporary table, you must ensure that the data conforms to the record level security you've set. This includes tables declared as temporary in the code, as illustrated in the following code example, and tables in the AOT whose *Temporary* property is set to *Yes*.

```
public void run
{
    CustTable custTable, tmpDatasource;
    ;
    // Ensure that record-level security is used.
    custTable.recordLevelSecurity(true);
    while select custTable
    {
        tmpDataSource.data(custTable);
        tmpDataSource.insert();
    }
    formDataSource.setTmp();
    formDataSource.checkRecord(false);
    formDataSource.setTmpData(tmpDatasource);
    super();
}
```

Record level security is not required in the following situations:

- When the value is calculated
- When the value is based only on fields in the current record

Security Coding

In this section we cover the Trustworthy Computing features of Dynamics AX, focusing on how they affect security coding. We describe table permissions, code access security, impersonation in batch execution, and the best practice rules for ensuring deployment-wide compliance. Find out more about this subject in the white paper "Writing Secure X++ Code" from the Microsoft Download Center: *http://www.microsoft.com/downloads/details.aspx?displaylang=en&FamilyID=5e050494-1613-4b3a-9363-d69d60c56877*.

Table Permissions

The table permissions framework provides security for tables that reside in the database and are available through the AOT. Annotating specific create, read, update, and delete operations on tables, combined with assigning user group permissions on tables, enables the AOS to authorize individual user permissions on tables.

The *AOSAuthorization* property specifies the operations that can be performed on a table when combined with user permissions set on the User Group Permissions form. Figure 13-13 shows the table property form and values for *AOSAuthorization*.

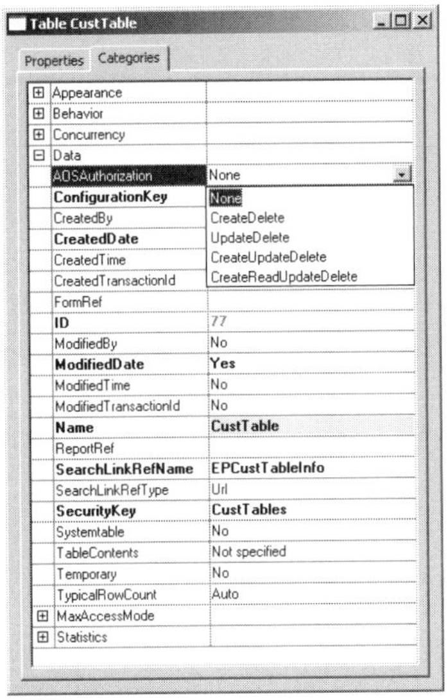

FIGURE 13-13 Table property form

The *AOSAuthorization* property is an enumeration with the possible values described in Table 13-3.

TABLE 13-3 *AOSAuthorization* Values

Value	Description
None	No AOS authorization validation is performed (default value).
CreateDelete	Create and delete authorization validation is performed on the AOS.
UpdateDelete	Update and delete authorization validation is performed on the AOS.
CreateUpdateDelete	Create, update, and delete authorization validation is performed on the AOS.
CreateReadUpdateDelete	All operations are validated on the AOS.

To secure the database tables even further, you must have a set of data manipulation language (DML) validation routines at the AOS server location when inserting, reading, updating, or deleting records from the database tables. The following four system-defined methods are included in the *Override Method* group to support the routine validation, located in the AOT under Data Dictionary\Table\Methods:

- *AOSValidateDelete*
- *AOSValidateInsert*
- *AOSValidateRead*
- *AOSValidateUpdate*

Table 13-4 describes the behavior of the AOS when authorizing an authenticated user on a table, including the user group permissions setting and the *AOSAuthorization* property value.

TABLE 13-4 *AOSAuthorization* Property Values

		Property Value				
		None	Create	Read	Update	Delete
User Group Access Value	No access	Success	Failure	Failure	Failure	Failure
	View	Success	Failure	Success	Failure	Failure
	Edit	Success	Failure	Success	Success	Failure
	Create	Success	Success	Success	Success	Failure
	Full control	Success	Success	Success	Success	Success

Code Access Security

The code access security (CAS) framework provides methods that can make dangerous APIs more secure against invocation attempts by nontrusted code (code that doesn't originate in the AOT). If you extend the *CodeAccessPermission* class, a derived class can determine whether code accessing the API is trusted by checking for the appropriate permission.

If the API executes on the server tier, the impact of malicious code that could exploit the API is more severe in a shared environment, so you must secure the API. To secure a class that executes on the server tier, follow these steps:

1. Derive a class that can't be extended from the *CodeAccessPermission* class.
2. Create a method that returns the class parameters.
3. Create a constructor for all the class parameters that store permission data.
4. Override the *CodeAccessPermission::isSubsetOf* method to compare the derived permission class with *CodeAccessPermission* to determine the existence of the required permissions for invoking the API you want to secure.
5. Override the *CodeAccessPermission::copy* method to return a copy of an instance of the class created in the first step. This step helps prevent the class object from being modified and passed to the API that is being secured.
6. Call the *CodeAccessPermission::demand* method before executing the API functionality that you're securing. The method checks the call stack to determine whether the permission required to invoke the API has been granted to the calling code.

Additional information about code access security and securing APIs is available in the Microsoft Dynamics AX 2009 SDK.

Batch Jobs

Dynamics AX 2009 introduces a new and more secure type of batch framework that is completely server bound. Rather than having to start a client and open the Batch Processing form, you can now schedule a batch job so that the server automatically picks up and executes it at a given time.

A batch job can be composed of multiple batch tasks that can be executed in sequence or in parallel. For a batch task to run on the server using the new batch framework, the job must use the *runAs* function. When this type of batch processing is used, the user who initiates the batch processing can't interact with the batch task or view its output. In addition, the task must not access any client-side resources while executing.

Dynamics AX 2009 also continues to support batch processing that doesn't use the *runAs* function and requires the client to execute. And if you need to, you can easily update old batch-enabled classes to use the *runAs* function.

> **Note** When you move batch tasks to the *runAs* function, you must ensure that there are no additional Dynamics AX application runtime interactions.

To identify possible runtime interactions, use any of the following approaches:

- Perform a manual code review.
- Identify transition exceptions in the Infolog by converting the X++ class to a server-bound batch job (as in the following syntax example), submitting the X++ class for batch processing, and checking the Infolog for transition exceptions.
- Identify client/server interactions using the client/server trace by submitting the unmodified X++ class for batch processing and checking the client/server trace for client/server interactions.

If you discover any runtime interactions, you should eliminate them by refactoring the application logic involved. When the class is ready to use the *runAs* function, you must override a method shown to return *true*, as shown here.

```
public boolean runsImpersonated()
{
    return true;
}
```

> **Note** Batch jobs in Dynamics AX 2009 can contain a mixture of legacy and new batch tasks. The tasks that use the new framework automatically execute on the server, whereas the legacy tasks require the batch processing form on the client to be running.

Best Practice Rules

The Best Practice tool can help you validate your application logic and ensure that it complies with the Trustworthy Computing initiatives. The rules that apply to Trustworthy Computing are grouped under General Checks\Trustworthy Computing in the Best Practice Parameters dialog box, as shown in Figure 13-14. The Best Practice Parameters dialog box is accessible from Tools\Options.

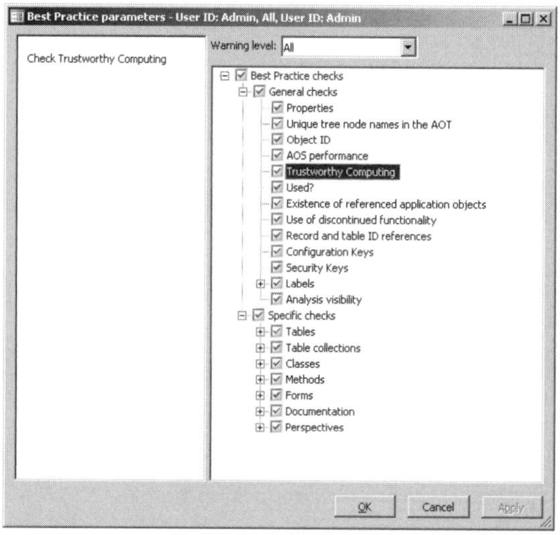

FIGURE 13-14 Best Practice Parameters dialog box with Trustworthy Computing rules

Part III

Under the Hood

Chapter 14

The Database Layer

In this chapter:

The objectives of this chapter are to:

- Describe the transaction semantics of the X++ language and explain how the Microsoft Dynamics AX 2009 application runtime supports database transactions.
- Introduce record and company identification.
- Provide an overview of the Unicode support available in Dynamics AX 2009.
- Introduce the database access layer in the application runtime.
- Discuss the database-triggering methods that are available on record buffer instances.
- Explain the concept of temporary tables and describe when and how they are used.
- Introduce Query framework enhancements and describe modeling and the reuse of complex query models in Dynamics AX.

Introduction

The Dynamics AX 2009 application runtime provides a set of strong features that can help you quickly design international functionality. These runtime features store data in a database without requiring you to consider user locales or the databases that Dynamics AX supports.

This chapter describes how the application runtime supports atomicity, consistency, isolation, durability (ACID) transactions in a multiple-user environment and explains the intricacies of the two supported concurrency models: optimistic concurrency and pessimistic concurrency. When committing transactions, identification is important at both the individual record level and the company level. This chapter also explains how identifiers work across application areas. Dynamics AX supports concurrent handling of multiple languages through its application runtime, which fully supports Unicode.

Two sections in this chapter focus on how Dynamics AX implements a database abstraction layer. Queries executed using specialized X++ methods provide operations support that is independent of the supported databases. Combined with the ability to write X++ code tied to specific database triggers, this independence makes it easy to write code that is reused throughout an application, whether specific data is accessed through a rich client or a Web client, or through X++.

We also explain the concept of temporary tables. Temporary tables make it possible to have local database data that is isolated from other users but that can be accessed as if it were stored directly in the database with other shared data. The concept of temporary tables is also important when you're designing an application that allows the licensing of multiple modules; when designing the modules, you don't need to consider whether they are enabled or disabled.

The query model enhancement sections explain the core concepts behind the reusability and complex query modeling techniques. The composite Query framework enables application developers to reuse a named query and apply additional filters and to embed a query in another query definition.

Paging extensions to the query runtime enable batch retrieval of a query result set using two modes: position-based paging and value-based paging. Position-based paging is useful for applications that need to retrieve a batch of records from a starting position in the result set. Value-based paging is useful for applications that need to retrieve a batch of records relative to a record.

The Query modeling framework enhancements allow Dynamics AX developers to model advanced query patterns. The new modeling framework introduces Query as a central data metamodel construct that can be reused across various constructs such as forms, views, and reports and within query definitions. The framework introduces functional predicates, which can be used in range filters in a query definition.

Transaction Semantics

X++ includes the statements *ttsbegin*, *ttscommit*, and *ttsabort* for marking the beginning and ending of database transactions. To write effective business logic for Dynamics AX, you need to understand how the transaction scope affects exception handling. This section describes *tts*-prefixed statements and exception handling, as well as the optimistic and pessimistic concurrency models.

In this section, we include code examples of how the *ttsbegin*, *ttscommit*, and *ttsabort* statements affect interaction with SQL Server 2005. The X++ statements executed in the application are written in lowercase letters (*select*, for example), and SQL statements passed to and executed in the database are written in uppercase letters (*SELECT*, for example).

Note An instance of a Dynamics AX table type is both a record object and a cursor object. In the remainder of this chapter, we refer to this combined object as a *record buffer*.

Transaction Statements

A transaction in X++ starts with *ttsbegin* and ends with either *ttscommit* or *ttsabort*. When these statements are used to start or end a transaction, the following equivalent statements are being sent to SQL Server 2005: *BEGIN TRANSACTION*, *COMMIT TRANSACTION*, and *ROLLBACK TRANSACTION*. In Dynamics AX 2009, transactions behave differently when they begin and end differently than they did in Dynamics AX 4.0. Whereas Dynamics AX 4.0 runs on SQL Server 2000 using implicit transaction mode, Dynamics AX 2009 runs on SQL Server 2005 using explicit transaction mode, so a transaction in the database is always initiated when a *ttsbegin* statement is executed. When *ttsabort* is executed, the equivalent statement *ROLLBACK TRANSACTION* is executed in the database. The execution of *ttscommit* results in the execution of *COMMIT TRANSACTION* if a SQL data manipulation language (DML) statement has been executed after the transaction has started. Otherwise, the *ttscommit* results in the execution of *ROLLBACK TRANSACTION*. *COMMIT TRANSACTION* is executed only if a *SELECT*, an *UPDATE*, an *INSERT*, or a *DELETE* is executed after *BEGIN TRANSACTION*. The execution of the different *TRANSACTION* statements is illustrated in the following X++ code, in which the comments show the SQL statements that are sent to the database and executed. The remaining code samples in this chapter contain the same notation, with the SQL statement shown in comments.

```
boolean b = true;
;
ttsbegin; // BEGIN TRANSACTION
update_recordset custTable // First DML statement within transaction
    setting creditMax = 0;
```

```
if ( b == true )
    ttscommit; // COMMIT TRANSACTION
else
    ttsabort; // ROLLBACK TRANSACTION
```

You can, however, have nested levels of transaction blocks to accommodate encapsulation and allow for the reuse of business logic. Setting up these accommodations involves the notion of transaction level, also known as *ttslevel*, and nested transaction scopes involving inner and outer transaction scopes.

> **Note** Consider a class developed to update a single customer record within a transaction. This class contains a *ttsbegin/ttscommit* block, which states the transaction scope for the update of the single instance of the customer. This class can be consumed by another class, which selects multiple customer records and updates them individually by calling the first class. If the entire update of all the customers is executed as a single transaction, the consuming class also contains a *ttsbegin/ttscommit* block, stating the outer transaction scope.

When X++ code is executed outside a transaction scope, the transaction level is 0. When a *ttsbegin* statement is executed, the transaction level is increased by one, and when a *ttscommit* statement is executed, the transaction level is decreased by one. Only when the transaction level is decreased from 1 to 0 is the *COMMIT TRANSACTION* statement sent. The execution of *ttsabort* causes a *ROLLBACK TRANSACTION* statement to be sent to the database and the transaction level to be reset to 0.

The following example illustrates the use of nested transactions and *TRANSACTION* statements sent to the database, as well as the changes in the transaction level.

```
static void UpdateCustomers(Args _args)
{
    CustTable custTable;
    ;
    ttsbegin; // BEGIN TRANSACTION - Transaction level changes from 0 to 1.

    while select forupdate custTable
        where custTable.CustGroup == '40'
    {
        ttsbegin;   // Transaction level changes from 1 to 2.

        custTable.CreditMax = 1000;
        custTable.update();

        ttscommit;  // Transaction level changes from 2 to 1.
    }

    ttscommit;// COMMIT TRANSACTION - Transaction level changes from 1 to 0.
}
```

Tip You can always query the current transaction level by calling *appl.ttslevel*. The returned value is the current transaction level.

The number of *ttsbegin* statements must balance the number of *ttscommit* statements. If the Dynamics AX application runtime discovers that the *ttsbegin* and *ttscommit* statements are not balanced, an error dialog box (shown in Figure 14-1) is presented to the user, or an error with the following text is written to the Infolog: "Error executing code: Call to TTSCOMMIT without first calling TTSBEGIN."

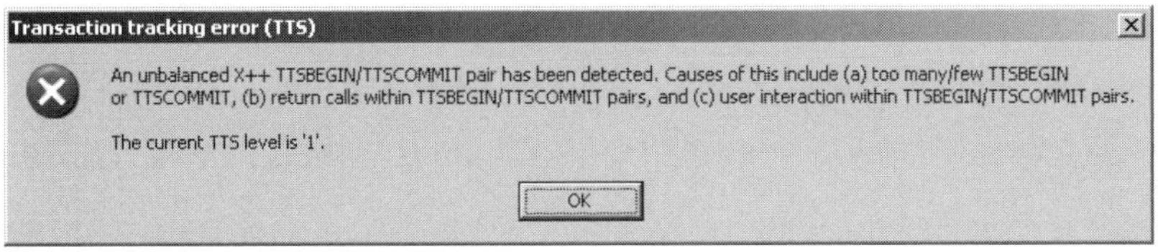

FIGURE 14-1 Unbalanced transaction-level error

Note In the event of an unbalanced TTS error, you might need to log out of the Dynamics AX client to reset the transaction level. When you log out, the started transaction in the database is rolled back.

Isolation Levels

Prior versions of Dynamics AX supported installations running on a SQL Server 2000 database. Dynamics AX 2009, however, supports only installations running on the SQL Server 2005 and SQL Server 2008 versions of the SQL Server database. With this change, Dynamics AX no longer supports the *READ UNCOMMITTED* isolation level and no longer provides the ability to read uncommitted data. Installations running on a SQL Server 2005 database must have Read Committed Snapshot Isolation (RCSI) enabled on the database.

RCSI prevents readers from being blocked behind writers—the reader simply reads the prior version of the record. In earlier versions of Dynamics AX, when installations were running on a SQL Server 2000 database, readers could be blocked behind writers. The *READ UNCOMMITTED* isolation level partly mitigated this issue when executing select statements outside a transaction scope. Now that SQL Server 2000 databases are not supported, the isolation level is READ COMMITTED both outside and inside a transaction scope in Dynamics AX.

The *selectLocked* record buffer method is essentially obsolete because executing *selectLocked(false)* on a record buffer before selecting any rows with it has no effect. Records are no longer read as *uncommitted.pass*.

Autocommit

As explained earlier, explicit transaction mode is used inside a transaction scope in Dynamics AX 2009 when it is running on SQL Server 2005. Outside the transaction scope, the autocommit transaction mode is used. Any insert, update, or delete statement sent to the database in autocommit mode is automatically committed. Although it's still possible to execute these statements outside a transaction scope, we advise you not to because insert, update, or delete statements are committed instantly to the database. In the event of an error, you wouldn't be able to roll back the database.

Transaction IDs

The Application Object Server (AOS) gives each transaction in Dynamics AX a unique transaction ID only if one of the following circumstances is true:

- A record is inserted into a table in which the *CreatedTransactionId* property is set to *Yes*.
- A record is updated on a table in which the *ModifiedTransactionId* property is set to *Yes*.
- The X++ code explicitly requests a transaction by calling *appl.curTransactionsId(true)*.

We explain allocation and types of transaction IDs in the "Record Identifiers" section later in this chapter.

AOS Process Pool

The AOS doesn't open a new process in the database every time it needs a process. Any open process that is no longer needed is placed in a pool of processes, and the AOS selects a process from this pool when it needs one.

Concurrency Models

The Dynamics AX application runtime has built-in support both in metadata and in X++ for the two concurrency models used when updating data in the database: optimistic concurrency and pessimistic concurrency. The optimistic model is also referred to as *optimistic concurrency control* (OCC), which is the term used in properties and in the application runtime.

The differences between the two models are the methods they use to avoid "last writer wins" scenarios and, consequently, to control the timing of locks requested in the database. In a "last writer wins" scenario, two or more processes select and update the same record with different data, each believing that it is the only process updating that record. All processes commit their data assuming that their version has been stored in the database. In reality, only the data from the last writing process is stored in the database. The data from the other processes is stored only for a moment, but there is no indication that their data has been overwritten and lost.

Caution In Dynamics AX, you can develop "last writer wins" X++ code both intentionally and unintentionally. If you don't select records for update before actually updating them, and you simply skip the transaction check by calling *skipTTSCheck(true)* on the record buffer, you're likely to overwrite a different version of the record than the one you selected.

The Dynamics AX runtime manages the two concurrency models generically, and you don't need to decide whether to use pessimistic or optimistic concurrency when you are writing transactional X++ code. You can switch from optimistic to pessimistic concurrency merely by changing a property on a table.

The following example illustrates what happens from a locking perspective when executing X++ code using pessimistic concurrency and running SQL Server 2005. The *select* statement contains the *forupdate* keyword that instructs the application runtime to execute a *SELECT* statement in the database with an *UPDLOCK* hint added. The database is instructed to acquire an update lock on all the selected records and to hold it until the end of the transaction, thereby ensuring that no other process can modify the rows. Other readers aren't prevented from reading the rows, assuming that they don't require an update lock. Later, when the *update* method is called, an *UPDATE* statement is executed in the database, knowing that no other process has been able to modify the record since it was selected. At the same time, the update lock is transformed into an exclusive lock, which is held until the transaction is committed to the database. The exclusive lock blocks readers requiring an update lock, as well as other writers.

```
static void UpdateCreditRating(Args _args)
{
    CustTable custTable;
    ;
    ttsbegin;
    while select forupdate custTable // SELECT … WITH (UPDLOCK)
                                     // Acquire an update lock.
    {
        if (custTable.CreditMax < custTable.balanceMST())
        {
            if (custTable.CreditMax < 1000)
                custTable.CreditRating = 'Good customer';
            else
                custTable.CreditRating = 'Solid customer';

            custTable.update();      // UPDATE … WHERE ACCOUNTNUM = <Id>
                                     // Acquire an exclusive lock.
        }
    }
    ttscommit;
}
```

The following X++ code illustrates the same scenario as in the preceding code, but it uses optimistic concurrency and SQL Server 2005. The *select* statement contains the *forupdate* keyword, which instructs the application runtime to execute a *SELECT* statement without acquiring any locks. Because the process doesn't hold any locks, other processes can potentially modify the same rows. When the *update* method is called, an *UPDATE* statement is executed in the database, at which time a predicate is added to determine whether the *RecVersion* field still contains the value that it contained when the record was originally selected.

Note The *RecVersion* field is a 32-bit integer with a default value of 1, which is changed to a random value when the record is updated.

If the *RecVersion* check fails when executing the *UPDATE* statement, another process has modified the same record. If the check doesn't fail, an exclusive lock is acquired for the record and the record is updated. In the event of a failure, the Dynamics AX application runtime throws an update conflict exception.

```
static void UpdateCreditRating(Args _args)
{
    CustTable custTable;
    ;
    ttsbegin;
    while select forupdate custTable // SELECT
    {
        if (custTable.CreditMax < custTable.balanceMST())
        {
            if (custTable.CreditMax < 1000)
                custTable.CreditRating = 'Good customer';
            else
                custTable.CreditRating = 'Solid customer';

            custTable.update();      // UPDATE ... WHERE ACCOUNTNUM = <Id>
                                     // AND RECVERSION = <RecVersion>
                                     // Acquire an exclusive lock.
        }
    }
    ttscommit;
}
```

The two models differ in concurrency and throughput. The concurrency difference lies in the number of locks held at the time of the commit. Whether the preceding scenario is executed using the optimistic or pessimistic model doesn't affect the number of exclusive locks the process holds because the number of *custTable* records that need to be updated is the same.

When you use the pessimistic model, the update locks are held for the remainder of the *custTable* records that were not updated. When you use the optimistic model, no locks are held on rows that are not updated. The optimistic model allows other processes to update these rows, and the pessimistic model prevents other processes from updating the rows, which results in lower concurrency. The optimistic model involves a risk, however: the update could fail because other processes can update the same rows.

The optimistic model is better than the pessimistic model for throughput. Fewer database resources are used because fewer locks are acquired. When an update fails, however, the optimistic model must retry, which leads to inferior throughput.

To illustrate the difference in the models, assume that the preceding X++ code example selected 100 *custTable* rows but updated only 35 of them; the updated rows are distributed evenly among the 100 selected rows. Using the pessimistic concurrency model, a graphical representation would appear as shown in Figure 14-2.

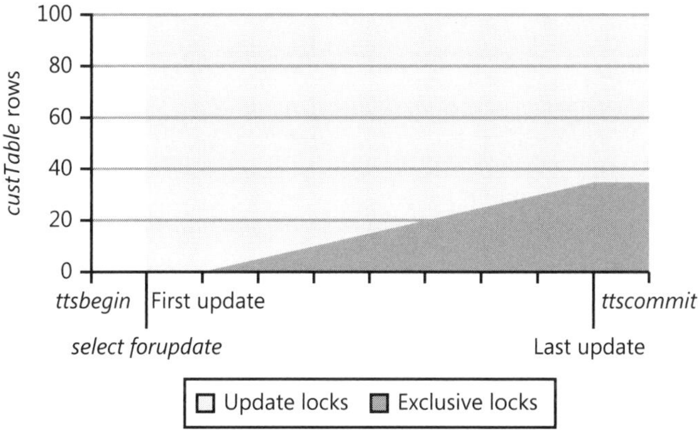

FIGURE 14-2 Update and exclusive locks using the pessimistic concurrency model

If the optimistic concurrency model were used, the picture would look slightly different, as shown in Figure 14-3. The number of exclusive locks would be the same, but there would be no update locks. Also notice that no locks would be held from the time of the selection of the rows until the first record was updated.

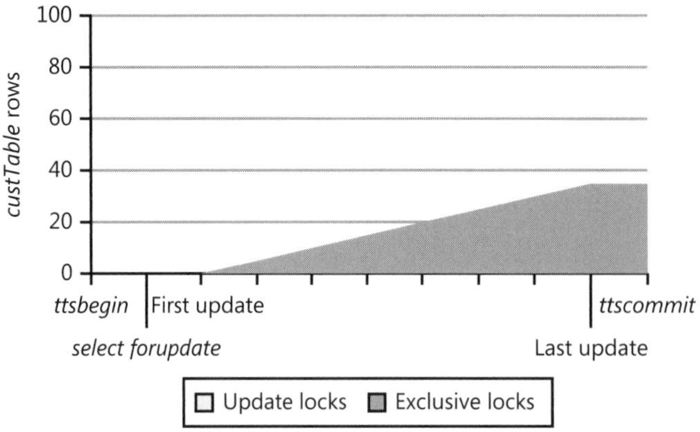

FIGURE 14-3 Update lock and exclusive locks using the optimistic concurrency model

When choosing between the two models, you must consider the potential risk or likelihood of an update conflict. If the risk is minimal, the optimistic concurrency model most likely fits the scenario; if the risk is significant, the pessimistic concurrency model is probably your best choice. But the estimated cost of handling an update conflict and retrying can also influence your decision.

> **Note** Although all the preceding examples mention updates only, the same *RecVersion* check is made when deleting records and is therefore also applicable in those scenarios.

Concurrent Scenarios

When two processes attempt to update the same record at the same time, locking, blocking, or potential failure can occur, depending on the concurrency model. The following scenario illustrates the behavior differences when two processes using SQL Server 2005 attempt to update two fields on the same records using pessimistic and optimistic concurrency.

Figure 14-4 illustrates pessimistic concurrency, in which Process 1 selects the *CustTable* record with a *forupdate* keyword and holds an update lock on the records. When Process 2 attempts to read the same record, also with a *forupdate* keyword, it is blocked behind the lock acquired by Process 1. Process 1 continues to set the new customer group and updates the record, and it converts the update lock into an exclusive lock. But Process 1 must commit before the locks can be released, and Process 2 can continue by acquiring the update lock and reading the record. Process 2 can then set the new credit maximum, update the record, and commit the transaction.

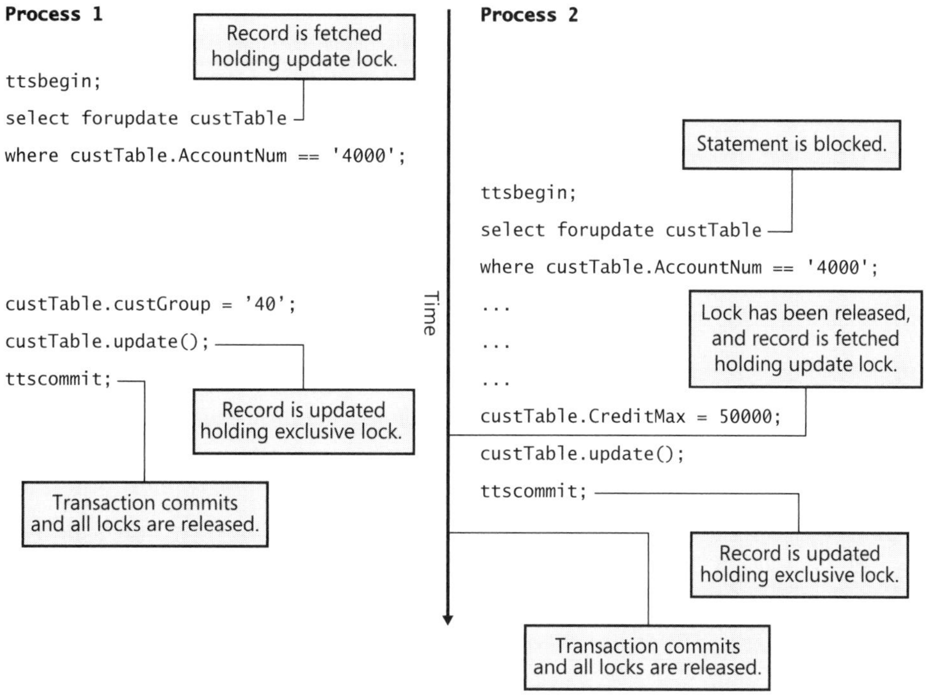
Process 1
Record is fetched holding update lock.
ttsbegin;
select forupdate custTable
where custTable.AccountNum == '4000';
custTable.custGroup = '40';
custTable.update();
ttscommit;
Record is updated holding exclusive lock.
Transaction commits and all locks are released.
Time
Process 2
Statement is blocked.
ttsbegin;
select forupdate custTable
where custTable.AccountNum == '4000';
...
...
...
Lock has been released, and record is fetched holding update lock.
custTable.CreditMax = 50000;
custTable.update();
ttscommit;
Record is updated holding exclusive lock.
Transaction commits and all locks are released.

FIGURE 14-4 Simultaneous update of the same record using pessimistic concurrency

Figure 14-5 illustrates one possible outcome of the same two processes executing, using optimistic concurrency. Process 1 selects the same *CustTable* record with the *forupdate* keyword, but no locks are acquired or held for the remainder of the transaction. Process 2 can therefore select the same record in the same way, and both processes hold a record with a *RecVersion* value of 789. Process 1 again sets the customer group field to a new value, updates the record, and acquires an exclusive lock. At the same time, the selected *RecVersion* is compared to the value in the database to ensure that no other processes have updated the same record, and then the *RecVersion* field is assigned a new value of 543. Process 2 takes over and assigns a new credit maximum value and executes an update. As the database first attempts to acquire an exclusive lock on the record, Process 2 gets blocked behind the lock of Process 1 on the same record until Process 1 commits and releases its locks. Process 2 can then acquire the lock, but because the selected *RecVersion* of 789 is not equal to the value of 543 in the database, the update fails and an update conflict is thrown.

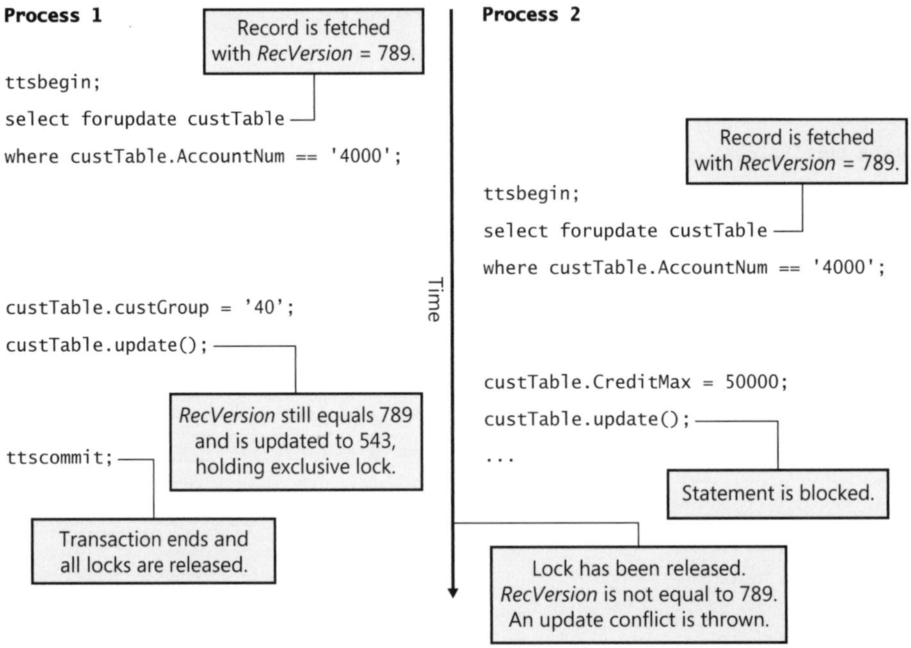
Process 1
Record is fetched with RecVersion = 789.
ttsbegin;
select forupdate custTable
where custTable.AccountNum == '4000';
custTable.custGroup = '40';
custTable.update();
RecVersion still equals 789 and is updated to 543, holding exclusive lock.
ttscommit;
Transaction ends and all locks are released.
Time
Process 2
Record is fetched with RecVersion = 789.
ttsbegin;
select forupdate custTable
where custTable.AccountNum == '4000';
custTable.CreditMax = 50000;
custTable.update();
...
Statement is blocked.
Lock has been released. RecVersion is not equal to 789. An update conflict is thrown.

FIGURE 14-5 Failing simultaneous update of the same record using optimistic concurrency

If, however, Process 1 updates its changes before Process 2 selects the record, the two processes complete successfully. This scenario is shown in Figure 14-6, in which Process 2 reads the updated version where the *RecVersion* value is 543. Although Process 2 is blocked behind Process 1 when it tries to update the record, the *RecVersion* check does not fail when Process 1 commits and releases its locks because Process 2 has read the uncommitted version from Process 1.

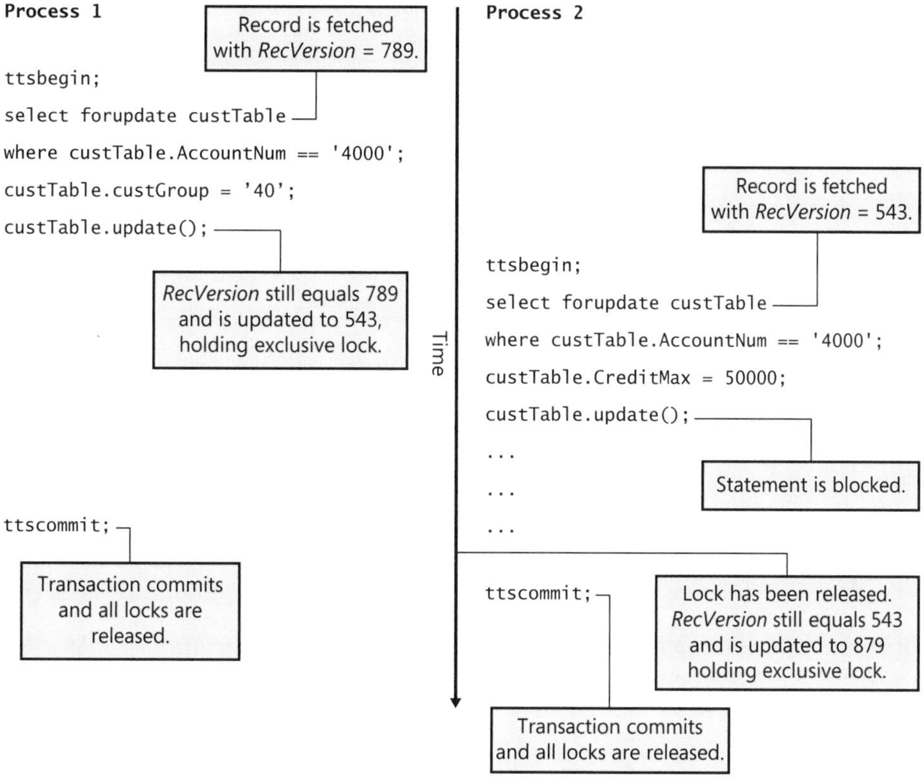

Process 1
Record is fetched with RecVersion = 789.
ttsbegin;
select forupdate custTable
where custTable.AccountNum == '4000';
custTable.custGroup = '40';
custTable.update();
RecVersion still equals 789 and is updated to 543, holding exclusive lock.
ttscommit;
Transaction commits and all locks are released.
Time
Process 2
Record is fetched with RecVersion = 543.
ttsbegin;
select forupdate custTable
where custTable.AccountNum == '4000';
custTable.CreditMax = 50000;
custTable.update();
...
...
...
Statement is blocked.
ttscommit;
Lock has been released. RecVersion still equals 543 and is updated to 879 holding exclusive lock.
Transaction commits and all locks are released.

FIGURE 14-6 Successful simultaneous update of the same record using optimistic concurrency

The examples shown in Figures 14-5 and 14-6 illustrate how the application runtime behaves when the same record is updated by two processes. In the following section, we describe how the runtime behaves when the same record is updated more than once within the same process.

Disconnected Updates of the Same Record

Consider a scenario in which two separate pieces of application logic in the same process have copied the same record into two separate buffers, both with the intent of updating different fields on each buffer. Both records would have been selected with the *forupdate* keyword added to the *select* statement. In a pessimistic concurrency scenario, both *select* statements would request an update lock, but because the *select* statements are both executed with the same database process, they wouldn't lock or block each other. In an optimistic concurrency scenario, both select statements would retrieve the same value for the *RecVersion* field but wouldn't, of course, acquire any locks.

When the two pieces of application logic consequently change and update their records, the Dynamics AX application runtime doesn't encounter a problem when using pessimistic concurrency because each *update* statement updates its changed fields by using the primary key to locate the record in the database. When the application logic uses optimistic concurrency, however, the first *update* statement determines whether the selected *RecVersion* value is equal to the value in the database and also updates the *RecVersion* to a new value. But when the second *update* statement executes, it ought to fail because the selected *RecVersion* value no longer matches the value in the database. Fortunately, the Dynamics AX application runtime manages this situation. When the *update* statement is executed, the application runtime locates all other buffers holding the same record that have been retrieved with the *forupdate* keyword and changes the *RecVersion* value on these buffers to the value in the database. The second update, therefore, doesn't fail.

The following X++ code illustrates the behavior of the Dynamics AX application runtime when the same record is copied into three different buffers. Two of the *select* statements also include the *forupdate* keyword and copy the record into the *custTableSelectedForUpdate* and *custTableUpdated* buffers. When the *creditMax* field on the *custTableUpdated* buffer changes and is later updated in the database, the *RecVersion* field in the *custTableUpdated* buffer changes to the new value in the database—but now the *RecVersion* field in the *custTableSelectedForUpdate* buffer also changes to the same value. The *RecVersion* field in the *custTableSelected* buffer doesn't change, however, because the record was retrieved without the *forupdate* keyword. The X++ code is shown here.

```
static void RecVersionChange(Args _args)
{
    CustTable custTableSelected;
    CustTable custTableSelectedForUpdate;
    CustTable custTableUpdated;
    ;
    ttsbegin;

    select custTableSelected
        where custTableSelected.AccountNum == '1101';

    select forupdate custTableSelectedForUpdate
        where custTableSelectedForUpdate.AccountNum == '1101';

    select forupdate custTableUpdated
        where custTableUpdated.AccountNum == '1101';

    // At this point, instances of RecVersion in all three buffers are equal.

    custTableUpdated.CreditMax = custTableUpdated.CreditMax;
    custTableUpdated.update();

    // At this point, RecVersion is changed in the custTableUpdated
    // and custTableSelectedForUpdate buffers. CustTableSelected still
    // has its original value in RecVersion.

    ttscommit;
}
```

> **Caution** When multiple processes want to simultaneously update the same record, the application runtime prevents the "last writer wins" scenario by acquiring update locks when using pessimistic concurrency and by performing the *RecVersion* check when using optimistic concurrency. However, nothing in the database or the application runtime prevents the "last writer wins" scenario if disconnected application logic within the same scenario and database process changes the same field by using two different buffers.

Using Relative Updates to Prevent Update Conflicts

Dynamics AX has always included built-in support for relative updates. But it is in combination with optimistic concurrency that this support is truly useful. Relative updates can be applied only to fields of type *integer* and *real*. You apply them by changing the *FieldUpdate* property from the default value of *Absolute* to *Relative*, as shown in Figure 14-7.

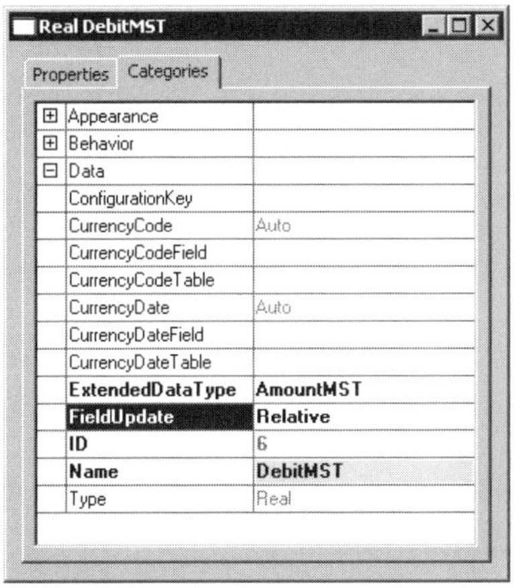

FIGURE 14-7 *FieldUpdate* table field property

The difference between an absolute update and a relative update is that an absolute update submits *FIELD = <new value>* in the *UPDATE* statement sent to the database, and a relative update submits *FIELD = FIELD + <delta value>*. The delta value is the difference between the originally selected value and the newly applied value. So if you change the *SalesQty* field on the *SalesLine* table from 2 to 5, the update statement contains either *SALESQTY = 5* or *SALESQTY = SALESQTY + 3*, depending on whether you set the *FieldUpdate* property on the *SalesQty* field to *Absolute* or *Relative*.

When you use relative updates, neither the previous value in the database nor the value it becomes is important to the updating of the application logic. The only important thing is that the difference is added to the value in the database. If all fields being updated in an *update* statement use relative updates and the record is selected using optimistic concurrency, the *RecVersion* check isn't added to the *update* statement. The previous value isn't added because it isn't important, regardless of whether any other process changes the value between the select and the update.

Using relative updates on tables combined with pessimistic concurrency has no benefit because an update lock is acquired when the application logic selects the record, so no other processes can update the same record between the select and the update.

> **Warning** You shouldn't use relative updates for fields on which the application logic is making decisions if the select is made using optimistic concurrency. You can't guarantee that any decision made is based on the actual value of the field. For example, a Boolean field shouldn't be set to true or false based on whether a relative updated field is equal to zero because another process could update the relative field at the same time. The Boolean field would be set based on the value in memory, which might not be the value that is eventually written to the database.

Choosing a Concurrency Model During Development

When developing applications in Dynamics AX, you can control the use of a concurrency model on two levels. The first is at a table level, by setting a property on the table definition in the Application Object Tree (AOT), and the second is by enforcing a specific model in X++ code.

Figure 14-8 shows the table-level setting, in which the *OccEnabled* property can be set to either *Yes* (the default value) or *No*.

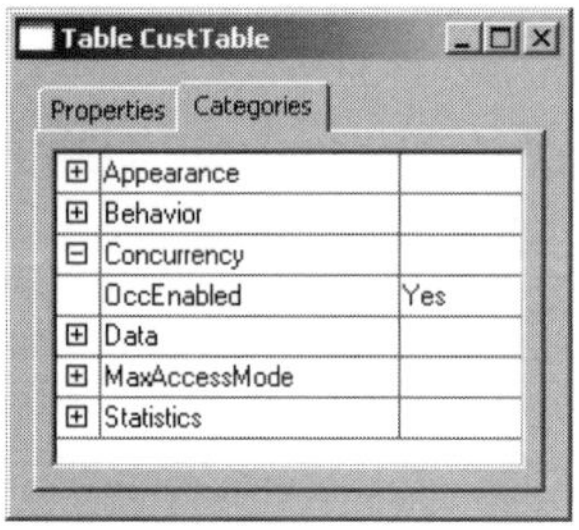

FIGURE 14-8 Optimistic concurrency control table property

When the runtime has to execute a statement such as *select forupdate custTable where custTable.AccountNum == '4000'*, it consults the *OccEnabled* property on the table and translates the statement into an SQL statement with either no hint or an *UPDLOCK* hint added to the *SELECT* statement.

The concurrency model setting on the tables in Dynamics AX is based on an assessment of whether the risk of update conflict is minimal for the majority of the daily business scenarios in the application in which the specific table is updated or deleted. The scenarios can be found by using the cross-reference system in Dynamics AX or by searching for places in the X++ code where the table is either updated or deleted. If a table is never updated or deleted in the X++ code, the execution of the code isn't influenced by whether the table is

OCC enabled because the table is manipulated only from a rich client form or a Web client form. Because the form application runtime doesn't use the table-level setting when updating records, the *OccEnabled* property is set to Yes by default on these tables.

> **Note** Only about 40 of the approximately 2100 tables in the SYS layer don't use optimistic concurrency.

If you encounter business scenarios that require the use of a different concurrency model, you should handle them individually by applying statement-level concurrency code.

You can apply statement-level concurrency control by exchanging the *forupdate* keyword with either *optimisticlock* or *pessimisticlock*. This enforces the use of either optimistic or pessimistic concurrency in a scenario in which the keyword is used and overrules the table-level setting. In case of enforced pessimistic concurrency, the *select* statement would be written as follows: *select pessimisticlock custTable where custTable.AccountNum == '4000'*.

> **Note** You can also control the concurrency model with the use of a variable by calling the *concurrencyModel(ConcurrencyModel concurrencyModel)* method on a cursor and passing the concurrency model as the parameter. The *ConcurrencyModel* type is an enumeration type. A similar method is available on the *QueryBuildDataSource* class, and you can even specify the concurrency model in metadata when defining a query element in the AOT.

You should enforce pessimistic concurrency when serialization is necessary; serialization is implemented by requiring an update lock on a record in the database. The lock prevents two processes from entering the same scenario because entering requires an update lock. Only the process holding the update lock can enter the scenario, and the other process is blocked until the lock is released. The serializing *select* statement should therefore include the *pessimisticlock* keyword.

> **Best Practices** Enforcing pessimistic concurrency by using the *pessimisticlock* keyword is a best practice for developing serialization logic, although you can implement the same pessimistic concurrency behavior by using the *forupdate* keyword on a table where pessimistic concurrency is chosen at the table level. The X++ code explicitly states that an update lock is required; more important, the scenario doesn't fail if the table property is changed. You can change the *OccEnabled* property through customization in higher layers.

You should enforce optimistic concurrency in situations in which it is apparent that the optimistic model would improve concurrency and throughput compared to the pessimistic model, especially when use of the pessimistic model would cause major blocking because of update locks that are never converted into exclusive locks. For example, optimistic concurrency is enforced in the Dynamics AX consistency check classes, where you can assume that only a few records are in an inconsistent state and therefore need to be corrected and updated.

Best Practices You should explicitly state the use of optimistic concurrency in the X++ code if the scenario always qualifies for the use of this model.

Setting a Concurrency Model Globally

You can disable the table-level concurrency settings at run time. Disabling these settings has a global impact on the business logic, however. You can override the table-level setting and enforce either optimistic or pessimistic concurrency for all tables by using the Concurrency Model Configuration form from the Administration menu. The property on the tables doesn't change, but when the Dynamics AX application runtime interprets the *forupdate* keyword, it uses the global setting rather than the table-level setting. The global setting honors the interpretation of the *optistimiclock* or *pessimisticlock* keyword, so optimistic and pessimistic concurrency are still enforced in scenarios in which these keywords are used.

Warning You should disable the table-level settings with great care and only after considerable testing in a nonproduction environment—and only if you completely understand and accept all the consequences of the change.

Optimistic Concurrency and Exception Handling

Although exception handling is described in Chapter 4, "The X++ Programming Language," it deserves special attention in a discussion of optimistic concurrency because an *UpdateConflict* exception is thrown when the application runtime discovers an update conflict. The *UpdateConflict* exception is one of only two exceptions that can be caught both inside and outside a transaction scope. All other exceptions in X++ can be caught only outside a transaction scope. When the update conflict exception is caught inside a transaction scope, the database isn't rolled back, as it is when caught outside a transaction scope.

Update conflict exceptions can be caught inside a transaction scope so that you can catch the exception, execute compensating logic, and then retry the update. The compensating logic must insert, update, or delete records in the database to get to a state in which you can retry the application logic.

There are two types of update conflicts exceptions, structured and unstructured. With structured exception handling, the *catch* block signature that is specific to this exception type contains an instance of the table variable. This *catch* block is executed only when the update conflict happens on the table instance specified in that signature. A structured exception handling framework can be particularly useful when a block of code issues multiple updates and the application intends to catch and recover from an *updateconflict* exception in a table buffer. The following example demonstrates the use of a structured *updateconflict* exception.

```
static void Occ2StructuredMultipleUpdateConflictMgmt(Args _args)
{
    CustTable cust1;
    CustTable cust2;
    ;
    ttsbegin;
    try
    {
        select forupdate cust1 where cust1.AccountNum == '1101' &&
cust1.CustGroup == '10';
        select forupdate cust2 where cust2.AccountNum == '1102' &&
cust2.CustGroup == '10';
        cust1.CreditRating = strfmt("%1",str2int(cust1.CreditRating)+1);
        cust2.CreditRating = strfmt("%1",str2int(cust2.CreditRating)+1);

        cust2.update();
        cust1.update();
    }
    catch(Exception::UpdateConflict, cust1)
{
        ttsabort;
        throw Exception::UpdateConflictNotRecovered;
    }
    catch(Exception::UpdateConflict, cust2)
    {
         cust2.reread();
         cust2.CreditRating = strfmt("%1",str2int(cust2.CreditRating)+1);
         cust2.update();
    }
    ttscommit;
}
```

You might find it very difficult, however, to write compensation logic that reverts all changes within a given scenario and makes it possible to retry the application logic from a consistent state, especially because update methods can be customized to manipulate records in other tables. These changed records are then not compensated for by the compensation logic, which might be located in a completely different element. Because of these difficulties, the standard Dynamics AX application doesn't attempt to compensate for changes to database records and retry within a transaction scope. The implemented X++ code to catch the update conflict exception and retry outside transaction scopes uses the X++ code pattern shown in the following example. The validation on the returned value from *appl.ttsLevel* determines whether the exception is caught inside or outside the transaction. If the exception is caught inside a transaction scope, the exception is simply thrown again. If the exception is caught outside a transaction scope, the transaction is retried unless the scenario has already been retried a certain number of times, in which case the application logic stops trying and throws an *UpdateConflictNotRecovered* exception. In Dynamics AX, the maximum number of retries, which is set in the *OCCRetryCount* macro element in the AOT, is 5.

```
#OCCRetryCount
catch (Exception::UpdateConflict)
{
    if (appl.ttsLevel() == 0)
    {
        if (xSession::currentRetryCount() >= #RetryNum)
        {
            // Don't retry anymore.
            throw Exception::UpdateConflictNotRecovered;
        }
        else
        {
            // Transaction is rolled back, so retry.
            // Possible additional code here.
            retry;
        }
    }
    else
    {
        // Rethrow exception because execution is within transaction.
        throw Exception::UpdateConflict;
    }
}
```

Concurrency Models in Forms

The execution of the rich client and Web client form application runtime always uses optimistic concurrency when updating and deleting records in forms. This means that the form application runtime doesn't use the *OccEnabled* property on the tables.

In a Dynamics AX installation that uses SQL Server 2005, records are always read into the form by using an uncommitted isolation level, and when records are updated or deleted, the *RecVersion* check is performed. This check prevents an extra round-trip to the database to reselect the record and requires an update lock. This was not the case in earlier versions of Dynamics AX (Microsoft Axapta 3.x and earlier), in which optimistic concurrency wasn't not implemented.

Repeatable Read

If you don't need to modify any data and merely want to ensure that the same data can be read numerous times within a transaction scope without changes, you can use the *repeatable read* option supported in Dynamics AX. You ensure repeatable read by issuing the following *select* statement, which includes the *repeatableread* keyword.

```
select repeatableread custTable where custTable.CustGroup == '40';
```

When Dynamics AX running with SQL Server 2005 executes the preceding statement, it adds a *REPEATABLEREAD* hint to the SQL *SELECT* statement, which is passed to the database. This hint ensures that a shared lock is held until the end of the transaction on all records the statement selects. Because the *repeatableread* keyword prevents any other process from modifying the same records, it guarantees that the same record can be reselected and that the field values remain the same.

> **Caution** The *repeatableread* option only prevents the records from being updated or deleted. It doesn't prevent the insertion of new records that match the criteria applied when the shared locks were acquired. The same *SELECT* statement can therefore return more rows the second time it is executed.

Record Identifiers

When a transaction scope is committed and a record set is inserted in the database table, the AOS assigns the inserted record a unique record identifier. Record identifiers are also referred to as record IDs, and *RecID* is the column name. Record IDs are 64-bit integers that are used throughout the application to ensure data integrity. MorphX automatically creates *RecID* fields in all Dynamics AX application tables and system tables. Unlike the IDs in normal fields, record IDs can't be removed from the tables because they are defined by the MorphX environment.

> **Note** The transaction ID framework uses the same numbering scheme to identify unique transactions across the application and within the company accounts. It is also modified to use a 64-bit integer as the transaction identifier. The approach in Dynamics AX 2009 is the same one used in earlier versions of the application.

The record ID allocation method uses a sequential numbering scheme to allocate record identifiers to all rows inserted in the Dynamics AX database. Sequential numbering isn't strictly required (numbers can be used out of sequence, manually modified, or skipped), but duplicates aren't allowed.

Allocation

The AOS allocates record IDs as needed when a record is about to be inserted in the database. Each AOS allocates blocks of 250 record IDs, which are allocated per table. So each AOS holds an in-memory pool of up to 249 record IDs per table. When the entire pool for a table is used, the AOS allocates 250 new record IDs for that table.

There is no guarantee that records inserted in the same table will have sequential record IDs if they are inserted by different instances of the AOS. There is also no guarantee that the sequence of record IDs will not be fragmented. Used record IDs are not reclaimed when transactions are aborted. Unused record IDs are lost when an AOS is stopped. Because of the 64-bit integer scheme, the available number of record IDs is inexhaustible, and the fragmentation has no practical impact.

The *SystemSequences* database table holds the next available record ID block for each table. A specific record for a table isn't created in *SystemSequences* until Dynamics AX inserts the first record into the specific table. Keep in mind that the allocation of record IDs is not per company (as it was in versions prior to Dynamics AX 4.0), but per table.

Inserted records always have a record ID, but they can also have a company account identifier (*DataAreaID*) for grouping all data that belongs to a legal business entity. If data in a table must be saved per company (meaning that the developer has set the *SaveDataPerCompany* table property to Yes), the Dynamics AX application runtime always applies the *DataAreaID* column as part of every index and every database access command.

In Dynamics AX 2009, multiple instances of a record ID within the same company are allowed as long as they don't occur within the same table. The coexistence of identical record IDs is possible because the generator that creates the individual identifier exists on a per-table basis, and the uniqueness of the record includes the table ID in the reference. All companies share the same record ID allocator per table, which ensures that only one instance of each record ID exists across all companies within a particular table.

Figure 14-9 shows the differences in generation and allocation between Dynamics AX 2009 and versions prior to Dynamics AX 4.0.

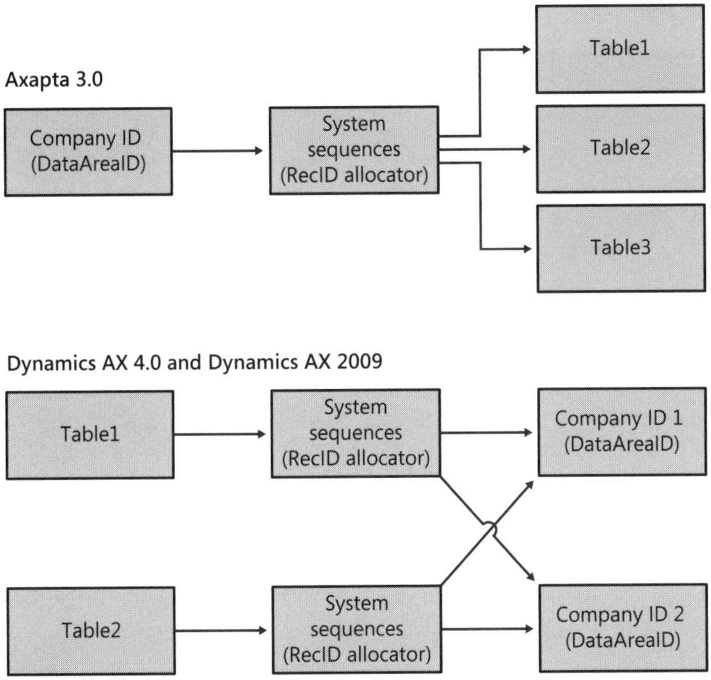

FIGURE 14-9 Record ID allocation comparison

In Dynamics AX 4.0, the record ID type changed from 32-bit to 64-bit integer to prevent particularly high-volume customers from running out of available record IDs. Another reason for the change was to balance the requirements for maximum performance, minimum impact on customer and partner extensions, database upgrade time, and code upgrade time. The 64-bit integer enhancement allows for a total of 18,446,744,073,709,551,615 (0xFFFF FFFF FFFF FFFF) record IDs and provides more flexibility in allocating certain ranges for specific purposes.

From Dynamics AX 4.0, the record ID range, equivalent to the entire 32-bit range used in earlier versions, is reserved to support existing customers when they upgrade. This approach is the safest and most efficient model and can be implemented without modifying any record IDs, including foreign key references to record IDs. Only the content of the sequence number allocation table is modified during upgrade. The range from 0x0000 0001 0000 0000 through 0x7FFF FFFF FFFF FFFF is used for new records after Dynamics 4.0 to prevent possible conflict with data from previous versions.

Figure 14-10 illustrates the new allocation range for record IDs using the 64-bit integer, and it also shows where the *SystemSequences* database table operates. The complete identifier range is essentially divided into three groups (Upgrade Range Only, All New Record IDs, and Reserved—Do Not Use), thus extending the existing record ID range of use from 2^{32} to $2^{63} - 1$ numbers.

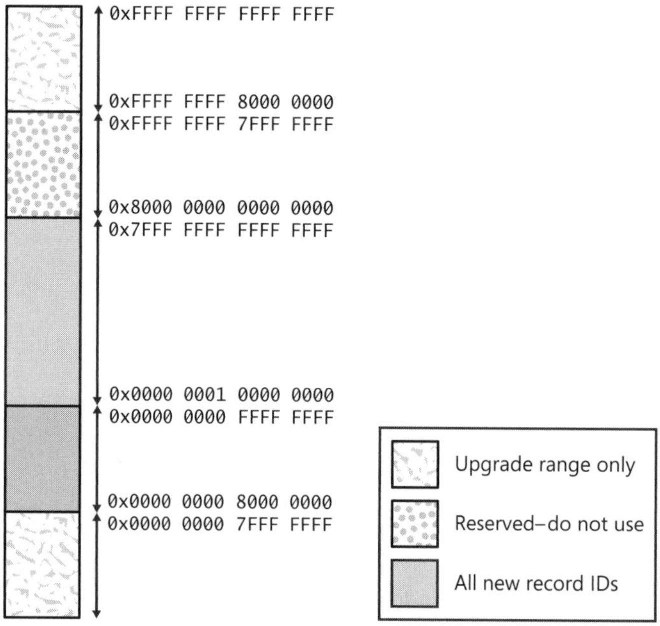

FIGURE 14-10 Record identifier allocation ranges

Programming Model

The kernel generates the record ID that the AOS allocates and assigns. In two prominent scenarios, you might want the application code to overwrite this behavior:

- **Upgrade** The DB Upgrade Preparation tool uses the direct SQL statement to insert data into the destination table from one or more source tables. In this scenario, the record ID can be allocated up front for optimization. You can also refactor the *direct* SQL statement by using *INSERT_RECORDSET.*
- **Performance optimization using constructs such as *RecordInsertList* and *RecordSortedList*** The application can use these two constructs to perform a bulk insert operation. In addition, the application might want to maintain referential integrity between the parent and the child table. For example, assume that the application inserts more than one customer record and the related customer transaction records. In such cases, the related record ID (foreign key) of the customer transaction record is the record ID of the customer record. To maintain this referential integrity, your application code can preallocate record IDs and assign them to the record buffers when using *RecordInsertList/RecordSortedList* to bulk insert records.

Dynamics AX offers a programming model to preallocate record IDs in your application. The programming model has been enhanced in Dynamics AX 2009 to have stricter control over allocation and assignment.

The *SystemSequence* class exposes this programming model. This class has three methods you need to know and understand:

- ***SuspendRecId*** Suspends the record ID allocation for the table passed as a parameter. The kernel no longer allocates a record ID automatically for this table for the current session.
- ***RemoveRecIdSuspension*** Releases the record ID allocation suspension for the table passed as a parameter for the current session.
- ***ReserveValues*** Reserves (preallocates) record IDs and returns the starting sequence number for the application to use. The number of record IDs to allocate is passed in as a parameter.

The following example shows how an application would use the *SystemSequence* class to preallocate record IDs.

```
static void RecidAllocationExample(Args _args)
{
    CustTable customer;
    SystemSequence sequence = new SystemSequence();
    int64 sequenceStart;
    int i = 0;
    ;
    sequence.suspendRecIds(tablenum(CustTable));
    sequenceStart = sequence.reserveValues(10, tablenum(CustTable));
    sequence.removeRecIdSuspension(tablenum(CustTable));
    ttsbegin;
    while ( i < 10 )
    {
        customer.RecId = sequenceStart+i;
        customer.accountNum = int2str(i);
        customer.partyId = int2str(i);
        customer.doInsert();
        i++;
    }
    ttscommit;
}
```

If the application assigns a record ID without suspending the record ID allocator, the system throws an exception. Once the record ID allocation is suspended, the system raises an exception if the application assigns a record ID that wasn't reserved by that session.

Administration

The Dynamics AX application runtime administers the numbering scheme automatically, according to individual record IDs and record ID blocks. The record IDs are managed in memory at the AOS cache level, whereas the block allocation uses the *SystemSequences* database to get information about the next record ID block value (*NextVAL*), native Dynamics AX table IDs (*TabID*), and the corresponding *DataAreaID*. By default, the administration toolset provides very limited manipulation possibilities for the database administrator, who can set the next block value but can't manipulate the next individually assigned record ID. You can, however, use the *SystemSequence* system class to manually alter the automatic record ID assignment behavior, but only for local block assignment.

> **Caution** To avoid destruction of data integrity and to maintain the inter-table referencing, use the *SystemSequence* class with the utmost caution.

The entities in the *SystemSequences* table are not created when synchronizing the table definition from the MorphX Data Dictionary, nor does the record ID block of 250 numbers get allocated when starting the AOS. The entity is created the first time a record is inserted into the table.

Upgrade

The enhanced record ID is based on a 64-bit integer and requires existing 3.0 installations to upgrade. The upgrade process for the record ID requires changes to the 3.0 application that must be made before starting the application and data upgrade. The Dynamics AX DB Upgrade Preparation tool handles the record ID data pre-upgrade. However, some prerequisites must be met before you can use the tool. Additionally, the existing application logic must be upgraded to support the 64-bit integer. For detailed information on upgrading from Axapta 3.0 to Dynamics AX 2009, see Chapter 18, "Code Upgrade," and the Upgrade Guide on the *http://www.microsoft.com/dynamics/ax/default.mspx*.

Company Accounts

The business and system information in Dynamics AX is associated with company accounts and their interactions with the database tables. Several company accounts can share the same database infrastructure and use the same application logic. However, each company account must have its own set of data that other company accounts can't directly access. Tables can contain information that can be reused by several company accounts. The design of company accounts involves the following elements:

- **Companies** A company account can be based on one or more virtual company accounts. When you add data to a table that isn't in a virtual company account, the data is stored directly in the company account.
- **Virtual companies** A virtual company account is a collection of data from several company accounts that is common to all the companies and uses a list of one or more

table collections to define the tables that it contains. The data in the tables included in the table collections is stored in the virtual company account. The user can't work directly in a virtual company account, but the contents of the shared tables can be changed through the company account.

- **Table collections** A table collection is a specification of a list of table names. Table collections define a graph of tables that have no foreign key relationships with tables outside the table collection. Developers define table collections. Each table and view in the system can occur only once in any one table collection, but tables and views can be added to more than one table collection. A table collection stores no table data; only companies and virtual companies store data.

The Dynamics AX application runtime uses these components to provide a powerful framework for integrating and optimizing the available and required business data across the enterprise, allowing chosen processes and structures to be centralized. The virtual company feature also improves data integrity because identical information is administrated only once and doesn't have to be saved in multiple companies. Another significant benefit is that users don't perceive the virtual company as a separate company account because it is completely transparent to users who are using the current company account.

Figure 14-11 illustrates how three virtual company accounts interact with company accounts and how a virtual company account can have multiple table collections associated with the individual virtual company account. Company AAA and Company BBB share the maintenance of currencies, whereas Company CCC and Company DDD share the chart of accounts. All companies share the maintenance of zip codes and countries. The last virtual company account also shows how company accounts can use multiple virtual company accounts.

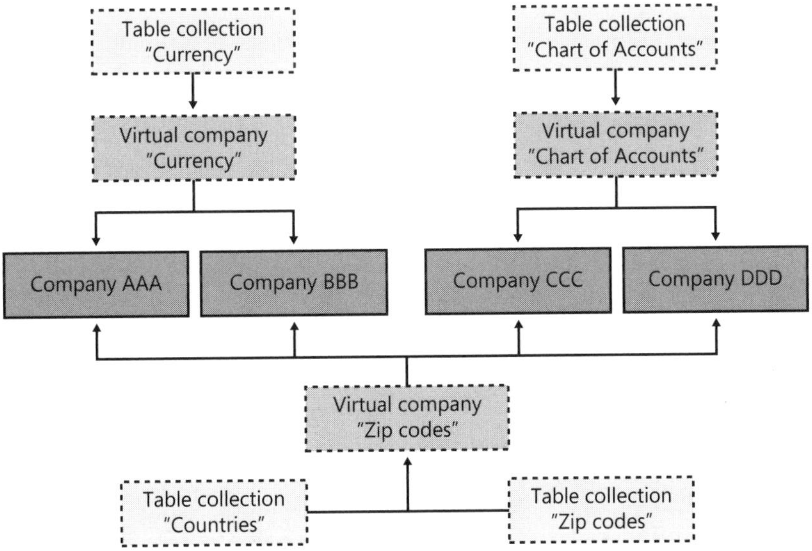

FIGURE 14-11 Company account overview

Company accounts translate the organizational structures of the enterprise into elements that can be configured using Dynamics AX applications. Building the company structures by using company accounts involves the following straightforward steps:

1. Create company accounts.
2. Create table collections.
3. Create virtual company accounts and associate the company accounts.

When you create a table collection, the foreign keys must not be part of the table in a virtual company where the key is in the (nonvirtual) company. When developing the table collection, you might have to adjust the data model to get the full benefit of the collection. Figure 14-12 shows the location of the table collection within the AOT and the tables included in the particular table collection.

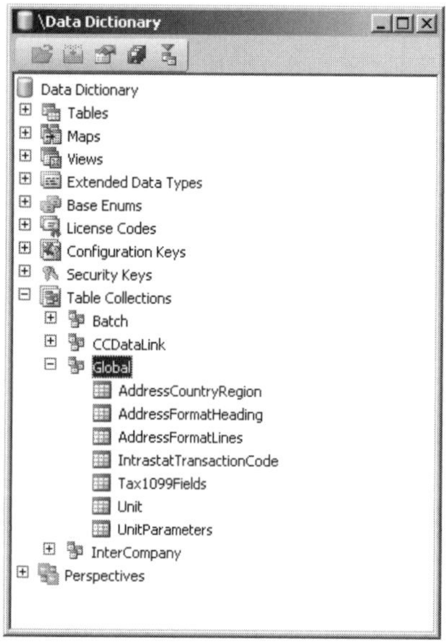

FIGURE 14-12 Table collections in the AOT

Identification

Company accounts are identified by any four characters within the Unicode-supported character set in arbitrary combination, covering both real company accounts and virtual company accounts. So the Dynamics AX application can host thousands of companies within the same database using the same application logic. When choosing identification characters, be aware of characters that can affect the generated SQL statement (such as reserved words, !, '' and "") because the company identifier is an important part of the statement.

The *DataArea* table the application runtime uses when saving data stores information about company accounts. The *SaveDataPerCompany* table property determines, on a table level, whether data should be saved per company or exist as general available data without company account affiliation. If the property is set to Yes, the *DataAreaID* column is applied automatically for storing the company account reference.

The data flow diagram in Figure 14-13 illustrates how records are evaluated before they are inserted into tables. The process for inserting records into non-company-specific tables is important to recognize because data is related across companies, installation, database, AOT, tracing, or OLAP and is therefore accessible from all company accounts.

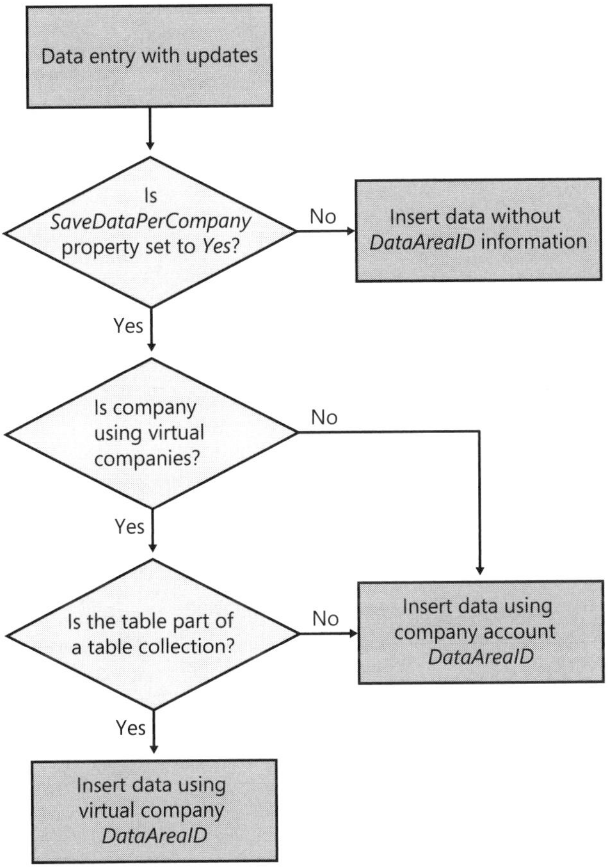

FIGURE 14-13 Data flow diagram for inserting data

Changing the Company Account

You can change the company account context at run time by using multiple methods, but you can also change the context at startup by using the configuration utility or by adding a company parameter directly in the application shortcut. Within the application runtime, users can launch the selection form to change the context by double-clicking the company name in the system's status bar or by clicking File\Open\Company on the menu bar.

Changing the company account from within the code is even more interesting when working across company accounts, such as with consolidations, sales between operations, or multisite planning. MorphX supports changing of the company account by using the *changeCompany* function in X++, which also exists as a reserved keyword. The *changeCompany* statement alters the database settings to another (separate) company account. Here is the syntax of the statement.

```
changeCompany ( expression ) { statement }
```

In this statement, *expression* is a string that defines the company to be used. The statement is executed on the new company. The following code example shows how to use the *changeCompany* statement.

```
static void main()
{
    CustTable custTable;
    ;

    // Assume that we are running in company 'dat'.
    changeCompany('dmo') // Default company is now 'dmo'.
    {
        custTable = null;
        while select custTable
        {
            // custTable is now selected in company 'dmo'.
        }
    }
    // Default company is now set back to 'dat'.

    changeCompany('int') // Default company is now 'int'.
    {

    // Clear custTable to let the select work on the new default company.
        custTable = null;

        while select custTable
        {
            // custTable is now selected in company 'int'.
        }
    }
    // Default company is now 'dat' again.
}
```

The *changeCompany* function is heavily used by the classes tagged *InterCompany**, but you can also find it elsewhere.

External Accessibility

You can access the company-specific data in Dynamics AX from external sources by using COM Business Connector or .NET Business Connector and the X++ application logic for extracting or modeling the required data sets, or by using the Application Integration Framework (AIF). You can also access the data by interacting directly with the database.

Consultants often prefer to work directly with the database because they usually know the database tools well but sometimes don't have experience with Dynamics AX. This approach can be challenging, however, if virtual company accounts are part of the company account data set. The database doesn't include any information about references between company accounts and virtual company accounts.

You can use business views to expose a collection of data as self-contained database views that provide an accurate picture of a company's status translated into human-readable format. Using business views can also provide valuable details about natively calculated fields (based on either edit or display methods), numeric field values, grouping of data, and company accounts, thereby increasing the data visibility for external parties. The Dynamics AX administrator defines and populates the business view to the database for further external processing. Creating business views doesn't necessarily require changes to the application logic or Data Dictionary because the views are created from the application side and are data driven. Business views use existing tables and views from the AOT, but they create new database views within the same transactional database that the application runtime uses.

Here is the process for creating business views:

1. Create database view prefixes.
2. Manage the virtual company accounts from within the business views.
3. Define the company accounts collection.
4. Define groups of particular values, such as colors, numbers, and text.
5. Define calculated fields by company accounts.
6. Manage the numeric field values.
7. Create and define the business view.
8. Synchronize the created business view with the database.

Unicode Support

In Dynamics AX 2009, the application runtime completely supports Unicode and multiple-locale input and output without the risk of data loss. The version prior to Dynamics AX 4.0 provided support for data storage in the database as Unicode data and handled Asian characters in double-byte character sets, but the application runtime didn't support multiple codepage characters or Unicode. In any given installation, only one character set was supported because data from one character set written to the database might not get correctly converted into another character set. Data could be lost when incorrectly converted data was eventually written back to the database.

This problem was eliminated from Dynamics AX 4.0, but developers and users of Dynamics AX 2009 should still be aware that Unicode support doesn't imply multiple-locale sorting and comparison or other features such as multiple time zone functionality or multiple country-specific functionality.

Databases

The Dynamics AX application runtime supports only Unicode data types in the database, so all data persists in the *N*-prefixed versions of the data types in SQL Server and Oracle. These are the *NVARCHAR* and *NTEXT* data types in SQL Server and the *NVARCHAR2* and *NCLOB* data types in Oracle. When you upgrade to Dynamics AX 2009 from versions prior to Dynamics AX 4.0, the conversion from non-Unicode to Unicode is handled as part of the upgrade process.

> **Note** Although the upgrade process handles the conversion of text stored in *VARCHAR*, *TEXT*, and the equivalent Oracle data types, text could still be stored in fields of type *container*, which persists in columns in the database of type *IMAGE* in SQL Server and *BLOB* in Oracle. These values are not converted during the upgrade process, but the Dynamics AX application runtime converts non-Unicode data to Unicode data when the values are read from the database and extracted from the *container* field.

SQL Server 2005 and SQL Server 2008 store Unicode data using the UCS-2 encoding scheme, and Oracle Database 10*g* stores Unicode data using the UTF-16 encoding scheme. Every Unicode character generally uses 2 bytes, but in special cases, 4 bytes, to store the single character. The required disk space to store the database is therefore higher for a Dynamics AX 2009 installation than it is for installations of versions prior to Dynamics AX 4.0, given the same amount of tables and data. The required disk space isn't doubled, however, because only string data is affected by the conversion to Unicode; the *int*, *real*, *date*, and *container* data types don't consume additional space in the database.

As the amount of space needed to store the data increases, so does the time required to read and write data because more bytes have to be read and written. Obviously, the size of packages sent between the client tier and the server tier, and on to the database tier, is affected as well.

When you create the database to be used for the Dynamics AX installation, you can specify a collation. Collation determines the sorting order for data retrieved from the database and the comparison rules used when searching for the data.

Note Although SQL Server 2005, SQL Server 2008, and Oracle Database 10*g* support the specification of collations at lower levels than the database instance (such as at the column level), the Dynamics AX application runtime does not.

Because the collation is specified at the database instance level, the Dynamics AX application runtime supports sorting using the collation setting only; it doesn't support sorting using a different locale. Dynamics AX supports input and output according to multiple locales, but not sorting and comparison according to multiple locales.

Application Runtime

The Dynamics AX application runtime supports Unicode through the use of UTF-16 encoding, which is also the primary encoding scheme used by Windows 2000, Windows XP, Windows Vista, Windows Server 2003, and Windows Server 2008. The use of UTF-16 encoding makes the Dynamics AX application surrogate-aware; it can handle more than 65,536 Unicode characters, which is the maximum number of Unicode characters supported by the UCS-2 encoding scheme. Dynamics AX generally uses only 2 bytes to store the Unicode character, but it uses 4 bytes when it needs to store supplementary Unicode characters. Supplementary characters are stored as surrogate pairs of 2 bytes each. An example of a supplementary character is the treble clef music symbol shown in Figure 14-14. The treble clef symbol has the Unicode code point 01D120 expressed as a hexadecimal number.

FIGURE 14-14 Example of a supplementary character

Although the application runtime uses UTF-16 encoding and the SQL Server back-end database uses UCS-2 encoding, you won't experience loss of data because the SQL Server database is surrogate safe; it stores a Unicode character occupying 4 bytes of data as two unknown 2-byte Unicode characters. It retrieves the character in this manner as well, and returns it intact to the application runtime.

The maximum string length of a table field is, however, passed directly as the string length to use when creating the *NVARCHAR* type column in the database. A string field with a maximum length of 10 characters results in a new column in the SQL Server database with a maximum length of 10 double bytes. A maximum length of 10, therefore, doesn't necessarily mean that the field can contain 10 Unicode characters. For example, a string field can store a maximum of 5 treble clef symbols, with each occupying 4 bytes, totaling 20 bytes, which is equivalent to the maximum length of 10 double bytes declared for the column in the database. No problems result, though, because the expected use of supplementary characters is minimal, especially in an application such as Dynamics AX 2009. Supplementary characters are currently used, for example, for mathematical symbols, music symbols, and rare Han characters.

The Dynamics AX application runtime also supports the use of temporary tables that are stored either in memory or in files. The temporary tables use an indexed sequential access method (ISAM)–based architecture, which doesn't support the specific setting of collations, so data stored in temporary tables is sorted locale invariant and case insensitive. The indexes on the temporary tables have a similar behavior, so searching for data in the temporary table is also locale invariant and case insensitive.

The application runtime also performs string comparisons in a locale-invariant and case-insensitive manner. However, some string functions, such as *strlwr* and *strupr*, use the user's locale.

Important String comparison was changed slightly in Dynamics AX 4.0. Dynamics AX 2009 ignores case when comparing strings, but it doesn't ignore diacritics, meaning that the letter A is different from the letter Ä. The versions prior to Dynamics AX 4.0 ignored most, but not all, diacritics. For example, the letter A was equal to Ä, but not equal to Å.

MorphX Development Environment

The MorphX development environment also supports Unicode. You can write X++ code and define metadata that contains Unicode characters. However, you can define elements only in the Data Dictionary, which conforms to the ASCII character set, and you can declare variables only in X++, which also conforms to the ASCII character set. The remaining metadata and language elements allow the use of all Unicode characters. So you can write comments in X++ using Unicode characters as well as string constants in X++ and in metadata.

All strings and string functions in X++ support Unicode characters, so the *strlen* function returns the number of Unicode characters in a string, not the number of bytes or double bytes used to store the Unicode characters. Therefore, a string that contains only the treble clef symbol, as shown earlier, has a string length of 1 rather than 2, even though it uses 2 double bytes to store the single Unicode character.

> **Important** Because SQL Server stores Unicode characters using UCS-2 encoding, it could return a different value when using the *LEN* function in Transact-SQL (T-SQL). A column that contains a single treble clef symbol stored by the Dynamics AX application would return a length of 2 when using the *LEN* function because the treble clef symbol is stored as two unknown Unicode characters in the database. The Dynamics AX application runtime doesn't use or expose the *LEN* function, so this behavior isn't an issue for users of the Dynamics AX application; an issue arises only if the database is accessed directly from other programs or if direct SQL statements are written from within X++, thereby circumventing the database access layer.

Files

Dynamics AX 2009 supports reading, creation, and writing of Unicode files. All text files written by the Dynamics AX application runtime are created as Unicode files, and all text files that are part of the Dynamics AX installation are Unicode files. The application runtime also supports reading of non-Unicode files.

Two file I/O classes exist that allow you to implement X++ code that reads and writes Unicode text files: *TextIO* and *CommaTextIO*. These classes are equivalent to the *AsciiIO* and *CommaIO* ASCII character set classes. You should use these classes instead of the ASCII file I/O classes to avoid losing data when writing to files. However, you might encounter scenarios in which market, legal, or proprietary requirements demand the use of the ASCII file I/O classes.

DLLs and COM Components

All areas of Dynamics AX 2009 that use DLLs and COM components use the Unicode-enabled versions of the DLLs. The *createFile* method in the *WinApi* class has been replaced with the *CreateFileW* implementation, rather than the *CreateFileA* implementation of the *createFile* function, because *CreateFileW* supports Unicode and *CreateFileA* supports ANSI. When passing parameters to the functions in X++ code, the parameters are defined as *ExtTypes::WString* when passing in Unicode characters, whereas the *ExtTypes::String* expects non-Unicode characters to be passed.

The *Binary* helper class used for COM interoperability and DLL function calls has also been changed. A *wString* function is available to support Unicode characters to complement the existing *string* function.

Database Access

The Dynamics AX application runtime supports the following three database platforms:

- SQL Server 2005
- SQL Server 2008
- Oracle Database 10*g*

However, as mentioned earlier, you don't usually need to focus on the underlying database because most of the differences in the databases are abstracted away by the application runtime. Unless an individual database offers very specific features, you can be almost certain that application logic developed using one database platform will execute without problems on the other platforms.

The Dynamics AX application runtime also supports the concurrent use of temporary tables where data is stored in files. You use these tables for temporary storage of records, and the application runtime uses them to mirror database records. Temporary tables are described near the end of this chapter.

Figure 14-15 shows how the execution of an update method on a record buffer in the application logic results in subsequent execution of application runtime logic. The database layer decides how to issue the correct statement through the appropriate API based on the installed database, the table itself, and how the table is mapped to the underlying database.

As shown in the diagram, database statements to the SQL Server 2005 and SQL Server 2008 database platforms are invoked through the Open Database Connectivity (ODBC) interface, and statements to Oracle database 10*g* are invoked through the Oracle Call Interface (OCI).

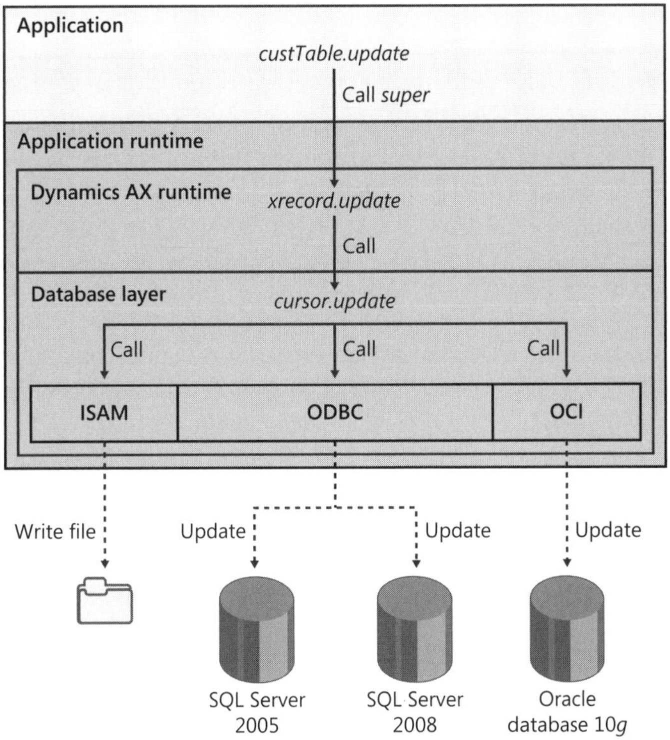

FIGURE 14-15 Database abstraction layer and platform support

Database Synchronization

When tables with fields and indexes are defined in the AOT, they eventually become tables in a database. Through its database layer, the Dynamics AX application runtime synchronizes the tables defined in the application with the tables in the database. Synchronization is invoked when any of the following actions occurs:

- A Dynamics AX application is installed or upgraded.
- Newly licensed modules and configurations are enabled.
- A table is created, changed, or deleted.
- An extended data type is changed.

The Dynamics AX application runtime uses one-way synchronization in which the table definitions in the Dynamics AX application are the master, and the database schemas in the database reflect the definitions inside Dynamics AX. If the database schemas don't match the table definitions in Dynamics AX, the schemas are modified to match the table definitions in Dynamics AX when the application is synchronized against the database.

Not all tables, fields, and indexes defined in Dynamics AX are reflected in the database. A table is synchronized to the database if it isn't defined in metadata as a temporary table (its *Temporary* property is set to Yes) and the associated configuration key isn't disabled. The configuration key could be explicitly disabled, or it could be implicitly disabled if the associated license key isn't enabled. A field is synchronized to the database if the content should be stored in the database (its *SaveContents* property is set to Yes) and the associated configuration key isn't disabled. An index is synchronized to the database if it is enabled (its *Enabled* property is set to Yes) and the associated configuration key isn't disabled.

When you compare a table defined in Dynamics AX to the corresponding table in the database, the database table could contain fewer columns than defined fields in Dynamics AX and fewer indexes than defined in Dynamics AX. The indexes in the database could also contain fewer columns than defined because a defined field might not be enabled, preventing it from appearing in the database index.

Important There is no guarantee that the application runtime can synchronize the database if a configuration key is disabled while there is data in the database because re-creating the indexes could result in duplicate values in the index.

The Dynamics AX runtime applies several system fields to each table, which are synchronized to the database. The system fields are real columns in the database tables even though they aren't visible as columns in the AOT. The database table could therefore contain more columns than you see when you view the table definition in the AOT. Also, in certain circumstances, the Dynamics AX runtime includes an extra column in a database index to make it unique.

The Dynamics AX application runtime applies the columns shown in Table 14-1 to the tables in the database based on whether the following system fields are enabled on the table.

TABLE 14-1 Dynamics AX System Fields

Dynamics AX System Field	Database Column	Table Property
RecID	RECID	*Always*
recVersion	RECVERSION	*Always*
dataAreaId	DATAAREAID	*SaveDataPerCompany* = Yes
createdBy	CREATEDBY	*CreatedBy* = Yes
createdDateTime	CREATEDDATETIME	*CreatedDateTime* = Yes
createdTransactionId	CREATEDTRANSACTIONID	*CreatedTransactionId* = Yes
modifiedBy	MODIFIEDBY	*ModifiedBy* = Yes
modifiedDateTime	MODIFIEDDATETIME	*ModifiedDateTime* = Yes
modifiedTransactionId	MODIFIEDTRANSACTIONID	*ModifiedTransactionId* = Yes

The Dynamics AX application runtime requires a unique index on each table in the database to ensure that it can specifically identify each record in the database through the use of an index. The application runtime always ensures that at least one unique index exists on each table in the database; if no indexes are defined on the table or they are all disabled, the application runtime creates a *RecID* index as if the *CreateRecIdIndex* property had been set to Yes on the table. If indexes exist but none are unique, the application runtime estimates the average key length of each index, chooses the index with the lowest key length, and makes this index unique by appending the *RECID* column.

If you want data in the tables to be saved per company (you set the *SaveDataPerCompany* property to Yes), the application runtime always applies the *DATAAREAID* column as the first column on every index.

> **Note** Because a table definition inside the Dynamics AX application is the master definition and the database schemas are always changed to reflect the Dynamics AX table definitions, it is difficult—if not impossible—to attach a Dynamics AX application to an existing legacy database.

Table, Column, and Index Naming

The tables and columns in the database generally have the same name as defined in Dynamics AX. Indexes, however, are prefixed with I_<*table id*>. Any index on the *SALESTABLE* table in the database is therefore prefixed with I_366 because the ID for the *SalesTable* table in Dynamics AX is 366. The Dynamics AX application runtime allows a maximum of 30 characters for names in the database, so if names of tables, fields, or indexes exceed this number, they are truncated to 30 characters, including the appended ID of the table, field, or index. For example, a table named *LedgerPostingJournalVoucherSeries* with an ID of 1014 becomes *LEDGERPOSTINGJOURNALVOUCHE1014*.

> **Tip** If the *name* method is called on a *dictTable*, *dictField*, or *dictIndex* object with *DbBackend::Sql* as a parameter, as in *dictTable.name(DbBackend::Sql)*, the method returns the exact name in the database.

Left and Right Justification

The Dynamics AX application runtime provides support for left and right justification of fields of type *string*. By default, *string* fields are left-justified, and values are stored without modification in the database. If a *string* field is right-justified, however, the value is prefixed with enough blanks when inserted into the database that all available space in the field is used. When values from a right-justified field are selected from the database, the application runtime removes the blanks. The application logic doesn't know whether a field is right-justified or left-justified because both left-justified and right-justified fields appear the same when used in the X++ application code.

When the application runtime formulates *WHERE* clauses in DML statements, it must determine whether fields are left-justified or right-justified because it adds extra blanks to a search value when searching for values equal to, lower than, higher than, and not equal to a field in the database. The application runtime adds extra blanks to the variable in a statement like the following when passing the statement to the database. In the following statement, assume that the *accountNum* field is right-justified.

```
select custTable where custTable.accountNum == '4000'
```

The statement passed to the database looks like this.

```
SELECT … FROM CUSTTABLE A WHERE A.ACCOUNTNUM = '                    4000'
```

But if the search condition contains wildcard characters, as in the following X++ *select* statement, the application runtime must remove the blanks from the field being searched by applying *LTRIM* to the statement.

```
select custTable where custTable.accountNum like '4%';
```

This code produces the expected result of selecting all *custTable* records where the *accountNum* field starts with '4', and the preceding X++ statement produces a statement like the following.

```
SELECT … FROM CUSTTABLE A WHERE LTRIM(A.ACCOUNTNUM) LIKE '4%'
```

The introduction of the *LTRIM* function in the *WHERE* clause prevents both of the supported databases from searching in an index for the value in *accountNum*, which could have a severe effect on the performance of the statement.

Note None of the preceding SQL statements is a clear match to the statement passed to either of the databases; they are intended to serve as examples only. The application runtime applies some additional functions when the *LIKE* operator is used.

The application runtime also applies *LTRIM* if a right-justified field is compared with a left-justified field. In the following *select* statement written in X++, assume that *accountNum* is right-justified and *accountRelation* is left-justified.

```
select priceDiscTable
notexists join custTable
where priceDiscTable.accountRelation == custTable.accountNum
```

The statement passed to the database wraps the right-justified column in an *LTRIM* function, and it looks like this.

```
SELECT … FROM PRICEDISCTABLE A
WHERE NOT EXISTS (SELECT 'x' FROM CUSTTABLE B
WHERE A.ACCOUNTRELATION=LTRIM(B.ACCOUNTNUM))
```

As mentioned earlier, this behavior could have a severe effect on performance, so you should decide whether this possible degradation of performance is acceptable before you change a field from left to right justification.

Placeholders and Literals

The database layer in the Dynamics AX application runtime formulates SQL statements containing either placeholders or literals—that is, variables or constants. Whether the application runtime chooses to use placeholders instead of literals has nothing to do with using variables or constants when the statements are formulated in either X++ or the application runtime. The following X++ select statement, which selects the minimum price for a given customer, contains constants and a variable.

```
select minof(amount) from priceDiscTable
where priceDiscTable.Relation        == PriceType::PriceSales &&
      priceDiscTable.AccountCode     == TableGroupAll::Table  &&
      priceDiscTable.AccountRelation == custAccount
```

The statement is passed to the SQL Server 2005 database when placeholders are used, as shown here.

```
SELECT MIN(A.AMOUNT) FROM PRICEDISCTABLE A
WHERE DATAAREAID=@P1 AND RELATION=@P2
AND ACCOUNTCODE=@P3 AND ACCOUNTRELATION=@P4
```

The statement is passed as follows when literals are used. Assume that the statement is executed in the *'dat'* company and that you are searching for the lowest price for customer *'4000'*.

```
SELECT MIN(A.AMOUNT) FROM PRICEDISCTABLE A
WHERE DATAAREAID=N'dat' AND RELATION=4
AND ACCOUNTCODE=0 AND ACCOUNTRELATION=N'4000'
```

As you can see, the use of constants or variables in the formulation of the statement in X++ has no effect on the use of placeholders or literals when the SQL statement is formulated. However, using *join* or specific keywords in the statement when formulating the statement in X++ does have an effect.

The default behavior of Dynamics AX is to use placeholders, but if the Microsoft Dynamics AX Server Configuration Utility option Use Literals In Complex Joins From X++ is selected, statements containing joins use literals if the application runtime considers the statement to be a complex join. The application runtime determines that a join is complex if the statement contains two or more tables associated with the following table groups: Main, WorksheetHeader, WorksheetLine, Transaction, and Miscellaneous. Tables associated with the Group and Parameter table groups are not included when determining whether the join is complex.

> **Note** The SYS layer in Dynamics AX contains approximately 2100 ordinary tables, and about 700 of these are associated with the Group and Parameter table groups.

Figure 14-16 shows an example of the *TableGroup* property in the list of metadata properties for a table.

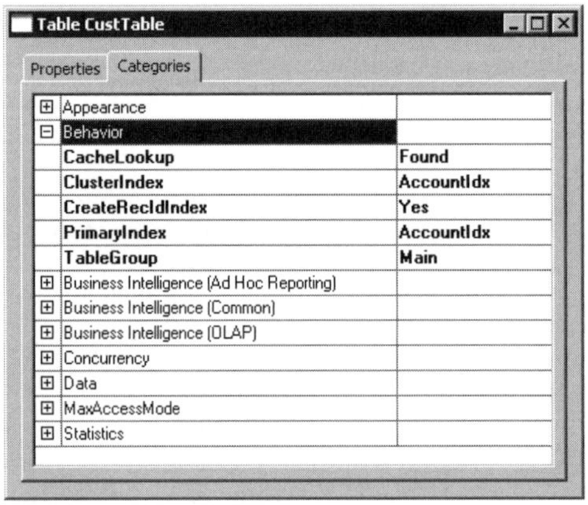

FIGURE 14-16 *TableGroup* property defined for *CustTable*

Note The Server Configuration Utility option Use Literals In Complex Joins From X++ is selected by default when you install Axapta 3.0 and cleared when you install or upgrade to Dynamics AX 2009.

The difference between using placeholders and literals lies mainly in the ability of the database to reuse execution plans and the accuracy of the calculated execution plan. When literals are used in a statement, the query optimizer in the database knows the exact values being searched for and can therefore use its statistics more accurately; when placeholders are used, the optimizer doesn't know the values. But because the execution plan is based on the exact values when literals are used, it can't be reused when the same statement is passed again with different search values. Placeholders do allow reuse of the execution plan. Whether placeholders or literals result in the best performance depends on three factors:

- How often the same statement is executed with different values
- How much better the query optimizer is at calculating the optimal execution plan when the exact values are known
- The total time required to execute the actual statement

Usually, both approaches result in similar execution plans; placeholders are generally preferred because execution plans can be reused, which results in better performance overall.

You can explicitly state that a *join* statement should always use placeholders when the SQL statement is formulated by the application runtime, regardless of the table group settings on the tables in the statement and the Server Configuration Utility options. You do this by adding the *forceplaceholders* keyword to the statement in X++, as shown in the following *select* statement (which would use literals if the previously mentioned Server Configuration Utility option were selected).

```
select forceplaceholders priceDiscTable
notexists join custTable
where priceDiscTable.accountRelation == custTable.accountNum
```

The alternate keyword *forceliterals* is also available in X++. This keyword explicitly causes literals to be used when the application runtime formulates the SQL statements.

Tip The Query framework also allows you to explicitly state whether placeholders or literals should be used for a given query by calling *query.literals(1)* to enforce literals, *query.literals(2)* to enforce placeholders, and *query.literals(0)* to let the application runtime decide which to use. Unfortunately, no enumeration is available from the Dynamics AX application runtime to use in place of these integer constants, but the macros *#QueryLiteralsDefault*, *#QueryForceLiterals*, and *#QueryForcePlaceholders* are available from the Query macro library.

Dynamics AX Type System vs. Database Type System

Because Dynamics AX application table definitions are the master for the table definitions in the database, the Dynamics AX application runtime also explicitly controls the mapping between the Dynamics AX data types and types in the supported databases. Table 14-2 describes the mapping between the Dynamics AX type system and the database type system. The Dynamics AX application runtime doesn't support database types not shown in this table.

TABLE 14-2 Dynamics AX and Database Type Systems

Dynamics AX	SQL Server 2005	SQL Server 2008	Oracle Database 10*g*
int	*INT*	*INT*	*NUMBER*(10,0)
real	*NUMERIC*(28,12)	*NUMERIC*(28,12)	*NUMBER*(32,16)
string (fixed length)	*NVARCHAR*(length)	*NVARCHAR*(length)	*NVARCHAR2*(length)
string (memo)	*NTEXT*	*NTEXT*	*NCLOB*
date	*DATETIME*	*DATETIME*	*DATE*
time	*INT*	*INT*	*NUMBER*(10,0)
utcdatetime	*DATETIME*	*DATETIME*	*DATE*
enum	*INT*	*INT*	*NUMBER*(10,0)
container	*IMAGE*	*IMAGE*	*BLOB*
guid	*UNIQUEIDENTIFIER*	*UNIQUEIDENTIFIER*	*RAW*(16)
int64	*BIGINT*	*BIGINT*	*NUMBER*(20,0)

Database Log and Alerts

Dynamics AX includes two features that base their functionality on the fact that data has been manipulated in tables: the database log and alerts. Both features use information the Dynamics AX application runtime exposes when specific data is manipulated and when the application runtime uses configuration data entered into a Dynamics AX framework table from the application. The configuration that identifies which statements to trace and log is stored in the *Databaselog* table provided by the application runtime. When a statement that should be traced and logged is executed, the application is notified by executing a callback method on the *Application* class.

Figure 14-17 illustrates a scenario in which Dynamics AX is configured to log updates to *custTable* records. When the *custTable.update* method is called, it invokes the base version of the *update* method on the *xrecord* object by calling *super*. The base version method determines whether database logging has been configured for the given table and the update statement by querying the *Databaselog* table. If logging is enabled, a call is made to the *logUpdate* method on the *Application* object, and the X++ application logic inserts a record into the *SysDataBaseLog* table.

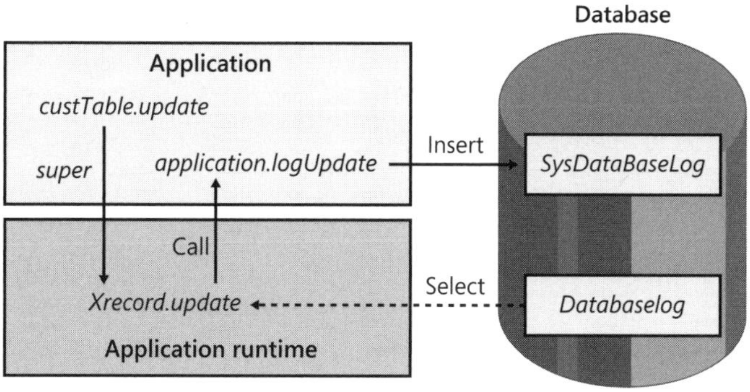

FIGURE 14-17 Logging database updates

The scenario is the same for inserts, deletes, and renaming of the primary key as well as for raising events that triggers alerts.

You can use the application runtime table *Databaselog* to configure all the logging and events because it contains a *logType* field of type *DatabaseLogType*, which is an enumeration that contains the following four values for the database log feature: *Insert*, *Delete*, *Update*, and *RenameKey*. It also contains the following four values for alerts: *EventInsert*, *EventDelete*, *EventUpdate*, and *EventRenameKey*. When the application runtime queries the *Databaselog* table, it therefore queries for the configuration of a specific type of logging on a given table.

Table 14-3 shows the correlation between the database log and alert configuration. It shows what triggers the log or event, which method on *Application* the callback is made to, and to which table the log or event is logged.

TABLE 14-3 Database Log and Alert Implementation Details

Logged Event	Triggering Method on *Xrecord* Class	Callback Method on *Application* Class	Where Logged
Database insert	*insert*	*logInsert*	*SysDataBaseLog*
Database update	*update*	*logUpdate*	*SysDataBaseLog*
Database delete	*delete*	*logDelete*	*SysDataBaseLog*
Database rename primary key	*renamePrimaryKey*	*logRenameKey*	*SysDataBaseLog*
Insert event	*insert*	*eventInsert*	*EventCUD*
Update event	*update*	*eventUpdate*	*EventCUD*
Delete event	*delete*	*eventDelete*	*EventCUD*
Rename primary key event	*renamePrimaryKey*	*eventRenameKey*	*EventCUD*

Note The application runtime doesn't query the *Databaselog* table in the database every time a trigger method is executed because the AOS caches all records in memory when first needed. When records are changed in the *Databaselog* table, the cached version must be flushed. To flush the cache, call *SysFlushDatabaseLogSetup::main* from X++, which not only flushes the cached memory on the current AOS but also informs other AOSs that they should flush their caches as well. The other AOSs read the flushed information from the database at predefined intervals, so they are flushed with minor delays.

Database-Triggering Methods

A record buffer contains a variety of instance methods, and when called directly or indirectly, it results in statements or affects the number of statements sent to the database. Some of the methods can be called explicitly, and some are called implicitly by the Dynamics AX application runtime. Some of the methods are final, and others can be overridden. All the base versions of these methods are implemented on the *xRecord* system class. In this section, we provide an overview of these methods and describe how the Dynamics AX application runtime interprets the execution of these methods and other built-in constructs in X++. We also explain how this interpretation results in different SQL statements being passed to the database for execution.

insert, *update*, and *delete* Methods

The three main methods used on the record buffer to manipulate data in the database are *insert*, *update*, and *delete*. When called, each method results in an *INSERT*, an *UPDATE*, or a *DELETE* statement being passed from the AOS to the database where each statement manipulates a single row.

Note If a *RecID* index exists on the table when the Dynamics AX application runtime formulates an *UPDATE* or a *DELETE* statement, *RECID* is used as a predicate in the *WHERE* clause to find the record. Otherwise, the shortest unique index is used as the predicate.

You can override all three methods on each table individually, as shown for the *insert* method in the following code. You follow the same pattern for *update* and *delete*. The *super* call to the base class method makes the application runtime formulate the SQL DML statement and passes it to the database. Consequently, when you override one of these methods, the application can execute additional X++ code before or after the statement is passed to the database.

```
public void insert()
{
    // Additional code before insertion record
    super(); // The SQL statement is formulated when executing super();
    // Additional code after insertion of record
}
```

Although none of the three methods explicitly contains the *server* or *client* method modifier, they all are always executed on the tier where the data source is located. The methods are executed on the server tier, but the methods on a temporary table can be executed on either the client tier or the server tier. Applying the *server* or *client* method modifier to these methods doesn't change this behavior.

There are also three equivalent methods for inserting, updating, and deleting: *doInsert*, *doUpdate*, and *doDelete*. Each method executes the same run-time logic as the base class version of the *insert*, *update*, and *delete* methods; using these methods circumvents any X++ logic in the overridden versions of *insert*, *update*, and *delete*, so use them with caution. The *doInsert*, *doUpdate*, and *doDelete* methods can't be overridden.

> **Caution** If you override the *insert*, *update*, and *delete* methods, you should honor the application runtime logic in the base class methods. If you move the logic in the methods to a class hierarchy, make sure that the X++ code there executes the equivalent *doInsert*, *doUpdate*, and *doDelete* methods on the record buffer. If this isn't possible because of an error, an exception should be thrown.

The record buffer also contains a *write* method that can be overridden. The execution of this methods leads to the execution of either the *update* method or the *insert* method, depending on whether the record has already been inserted.

> **Caution** Any X++ application logic written in an overridden version of the *write* method is executed only if the method is explicitly called from other X++ code or when records are inserted or updated from rich client forms or Web client forms. If you've written X++ code using the *write* method, you should consider migrating the code to the *insert* or *update* method.

As with the *insert*, *update*, and *delete* methods, *write* is forced by the application runtime to execute on the tier where the data source is located, no matter what is stated in the definition of the method.

Selecting Rows

The record buffer also contains the overridable method *postLoad*. You don't need to execute *postLoad* from X++ because the application runtime executes it when the AOS retrieves records from the database. When you override *postLoad*, the *super* call copies the retrieved buffer to the original record buffer that is accessible through the *orig* method. Before an overridden *postLoad* method calls the base class method, the state of the original buffer is undefined.

> **Caution** Any application logic written in the *postLoad* method should be lightweight code because it executes every time a record of this type is retrieved from the database. You should always consider whether the X++ code could be written elsewhere, such as in a display method.

The application runtime also forces *postLoad* to execute on the tier where the data source is located. Assuming that the table isn't temporary and a client retrieves multiple records, *postLoad* executes on all the retrieved records sent from the database to the AOS before the AOS sends them individually to the client.

Validating Rows

The record buffer contains two sets of validation methods that can be overridden: the *validateField*, *validateWrite*, and *validateDelete* methods and the *aosValidateRead*, *aosValidateInsert*, *aosValidateUpdate*, and *aosValidateDelete* methods, which were introduced in Dynamics AX 4.0.

The difference between the two sets of methods is that *validateField*, *validateWrite*, and *validateDelete* are invoked only from rich client and Web client forms or if called directly from X++ code, whereas *aosValidateInsert*, *aosValidateUpdate*, and *aosValidateDelete* are invoked implicitly from the *insert*, *update*, and *delete* base version methods, respectively. The *aosValidateRead* method is invoked when the application retrieves records from the database.

The *aosValidate* methods prevent reading, writing, or deleting, so they should return a Boolean value of false if the user isn't allowed to perform the operation that the method is validating. If the method returns false, an error is written to the Infolog, and the Dynamics AX application runtime throws an *Exception::Error*. The form application runtime also writes an error to the Infolog if any of the validate methods return false. When a validate method is called from X++ code, the calling method determines how to handle a validate method that returns false.

Changing the Default Behavior

The record buffer contains a dozen methods used to change the default behavior of DML statements issued in X++ code. You can call all the methods except one, *concurrencyModel*, with a Boolean parameter to change the default behavior, and you can call all of them without a parameter to query the current status. None of the methods can be overridden.

The following methods on the record buffer influence how the application runtime interprets *select* statements that use the record buffer.

SelectForUpdate

Calling *selectForUpdate(true)* on a record buffer replaces the use of the *forupdate* keyword in a *select* statement. The X++ code

```
custTable.selectForUpdate(true);
select custTable where custTable.AccountNum == '4000';
```

is equal in behavior to this code

```
select forupdate custTable where custTable.AccountNum == '4000';
```

Depending on the concurrency model settings on the table, no hint or *UPDLOCK* hint is added to the *SELECT* statement passed to SQL Server 2005.

> **Tip** If you use the Query framework instead of *select* statements to retrieve records, you can also retrieve these records as if a *forupdate* keyword had been used, by calling *update(true)* on the *QueryBuildDataSource* object.

concurrencyModel

Calling *concurrencyModel(ConcurrencyModel::OptimisticLock)* on a record buffer replaces the use of the *optimisticlock* keyword, and calling *concurrencyModel(ConcurrencyModel::PessimisticLock)* replaces the use of the *pessimisticlock* keyword. The X++ code

```
custTable.concurrencyModel(ConcurrencyModel::OptimisticLock);
select custTable where custTable.AccountNum == '4000';
```

is equal in behavior to this code

```
select optimisticlock custTable where custTable.AccountNum == '4000';
```

This method overrules any concurrency model setting on the table and causes either no hint or a *UPDLOCK* hint to the *SELECT* statement passed to SQL Server 2005. The type of hint depends on whether the *OptimisticLock* or *PessimisticLock* enumeration value was passed as a parameter when the application logic called the *concurrencyModel* method.

> **Tip** If you use the Query framework instead of *select* statements to retrieve records, you can retrieve these records with a specific concurrency model by calling *concurrencyModel (ConcurrencyModel::OptimisticLock)* or *concurrencyModel(ConcurrencyModel::PessimisticLock)* on the *QueryBuildDataSource* object.

selectWithRepeatableRead

Calling *selectWithRepeatableRead(true)* on a record buffer replaces the use of the *repeatableread* keyword in a *select* statement. The X++ code

```
custTable.selectWithRepeatableRead(true);
select custTable where custTable.AccountNum == '4000';
```

is equal in behavior to this code

```
select repeatableread custTable where custTable.AccountNum == '4000';
```

Using this keyword results in the addition of a *REPEATABLEREAD* hint to the *SELECT* statement passed to SQL Server 2005.

> **Tip** If you use the Query framework instead of *select* statements to retrieve records, you can retrieve these records with a *REPEATABLEREAD* hint as well, by calling *selectWithRepeatableRead (true)* on the *QueryBuildDataSource* object.

readPast

When *readPast(true)* is called on a record buffer, a *READPAST ROWLOCK* hint is added to the *SELECT* statement passed to SQL Server 2005. This hint instructs the database to skip rows on which an exclusive lock is held. But because RCSI is enabled, SQL Server 2005 doesn't skip records on which an exclusive lock is held; it only returns the previous committed version.

skipTTSCheck

The record buffer also contains a method that affects the behavior of updates and deletes. Calling *skipTTSCheck(true)* on a record buffer makes it possible to later call *update* or *delete* on the record buffer without first selecting the record for update. The following code, in which a *custTable* record is selected without a *forupdate* keyword and is later updated with *skipTTSCheck* set to true, doesn't fail.

```
static void skipTTSCheck(Args _args)
{
    CustTable custTable;

    ttsbegin;

    select custTable where custTable.AccountNum == '1101';
    custTable.CreditMax = 1000;

    custTable.skipTTSCheck(true);
    custTable.update();

    ttscommit;
}
```

The execution of *update* method doesn't throw an error in this example because the Dynamics AX application runtime doesn't verify that the buffer was selected with *forupdate* or an equivalent keyword. In a pessimistic concurrency scenario, no update lock would be acquired before the update, and in an optimistic concurrency scenario, the *RecVersion* check wouldn't be made. Using *skipTTSCheck(true)* could lead to the "last writer wins" scenarios described earlier in this chapter.

If *skipTTSCheck* hadn't been called in the preceding scenario, the application runtime would have thrown an error and presented the following in the Infolog: "The operation cannot be completed, since the record was not selected for update. Remember TTSBEGIN/TTSCOMMIT as well as the *FORUPDATE* clause."

selectLocked

As mentioned earlier in this chapter, the *selectLocked* record buffer method is essentially obsolete because executing *selectLocked(false)* on a record buffer before selecting any rows with it has no effect. Records will not be read uncommitted.

Set-Based DML Statements

As explained in the preceding sections, *insert*, *update*, and *delete* methods are available on the buffer to manipulate data in the database. The buffer also offers the less frequently used *write*, *doInsert*, *doUpdate*, and *doDelete* methods for use when writing application logic in X++ code. All these methods are record-based methods; when they are executed, at least one statement is sent to the database, representing the *INSERT*, *UPDATE*, or *DELETE* statement being executed in the database. Each execution of these statements therefore results in a call from the AOS to the database server in addition to previous calls to select and retrieve the records.

X++ contains set-based *insert*, *update*, and *delete* operators as well as set-based classes that can reduce the number of round-trips made from the AOS to the database tier. The Dynamics AX application runtime can downgrade these set-based operations to row-based statements because of metadata setup, overriding of methods, or configuration of the Dynamics AX application. The record buffer, however, offers methods to change this behavior and prevent downgrading. The set-based statements and the remaining methods on the record buffer are covered in Chapter 12, "Performance."

Temporary Tables

By default, any table defined in the AOT is mapped in a one-to-one relationship to a table in the underlying relational database. Any table can also, however, be mapped to an ISAM file–based table that is available only during the runtime scope of the AOS or a client. This mapping can take place as follows:

- At design time by setting metadata properties
- At configuration time by enabling licensed modules or configurations
- At application run time by writing explicit X++ code

The ISAM file contains data and all the indexes defined on the table that maps to the temporary table that the file represents. Because working on smaller data sets is generally faster than working on larger data sets, the Dynamics AX application runtime monitors the space each data set needs. If the number exceeds 128 kilobytes (KB), the data set is written to the ISAM file; everything is kept in memory if the consumed space is less than 128 KB. Switching from memory to file has a significant effect on performance. A file with the *syntax $tmp<8 digits>.$$$* is created when data is switched from memory to file. You can monitor the threshold limit by noting when this file is created.

> **Note** A small test run by the product development team using the Dynamics AX demo data showed that 220 *CustTable* records could be stored in the temporary table before data was written to the file. However, this number varies depending on the amount of data in each record.

Although the temporary tables don't map to a relational database, all the DML statements in X++ are valid for tables operating as temporary tables. The application runtime executes some of the statements in a downgraded fashion because the ISAM file functionality doesn't offer the same amount of functionality as a relational database. Therefore, set-based operators always execute as record-by-record operations.

Using Temporary Tables

Any table that acts as a temporary table is, indeed, temporary. When you declare a record buffer of a temporary table type, the table doesn't contain any records, so you must insert records to work with the temporary table. The temporary table and all the records are lost when no more declared record buffers point to the temporary data set.

Memory and file space aren't allocated to the temporary table before the first record is inserted, and the table resides on the tier where the first record was inserted. For example, if the first insert occurs on the server tier, the memory is allocated on this tier, and eventually a file is created on the server tier. The tier on which the record buffer is declared or subsequent inserts, updates, or deletes are executed is insignificant.

> **Important** A careless temporary table design could lead to a substantial number of round-trips between the client and the server and result in degraded performance.

A declared temporary record buffer contains a pointer to the data set. If two temporary record buffers are used, they point to different data sets by default, even though the table type is the same. To illustrate this, the X++ code in the following example uses the *TmpLedgerTable* temporary table defined in Dynamics AX 2009. The table contains three fields: *AccountName*, *AccountNum*, and *CompanyId*. The *AccountNum* and *CompanyId* fields are both part of a unique index, *AccountNumIdx*, as shown in Figure 14-18.

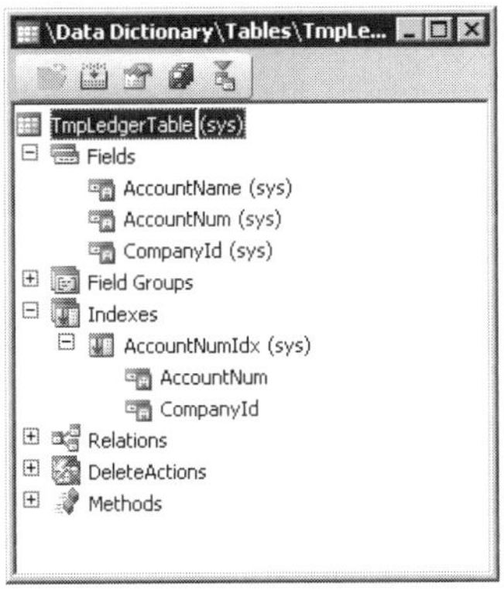

FIGURE 14-18 *TmpLedgerTable* temporary table

The following X++ code shows how the same record can be inserted in two record buffers of the same type. Because the record buffers point to two different data sets, a "duplicate value in index" failure doesn't result, as it would if both record buffers had pointed to the same temporary data set or if the record buffers had been mapped to a database table.

```
static void TmpLedgerTable(Args _args)
{
    TmpLedgerTable tmpLedgerTable1;
    TmpLedgerTable tmpLedgerTable2;
    ;
    tmpLedgerTable1.CompanyId = 'dat';
    tmpledgerTable1.AccountNum = '1000';
    tmpLedgerTable1.AccountName = 'Name';
    tmpLedgerTable1.insert(); // Insert into tmpLedgerTable1's dataset.

    tmpLedgerTable2.CompanyId = 'dat';
    tmpledgerTable2.AccountNum = '1000';
    tmpLedgerTable2.AccountName = 'Name';
    tmpLedgerTable2.insert(); // Insert into tmpLedgerTable2's dataset.
}
```

To share the same data set, you must call the *setTmpData* method on the record buffer, as illustrated in the following similar X++ code in which the *setTmpData* method is called on the second record buffer and passed in the first record buffer as a parameter.

```
static void TmpLedgerTable(Args _args)
{
    TmpLedgerTable tmpLedgerTable1;
    TmpLedgerTable tmpLedgerTable2;
    ;
    tmpLedgerTable2.setTmpData(tmpLedgerTable1);

    tmpLedgerTable1.CompanyId = 'dat';
    tmpledgerTable1.AccountNum = '1000';
    tmpLedgerTable1.AccountName = 'Name';
    tmpLedgerTable1.insert(); // Insert into shared dataset.

    tmpLedgerTable2.CompanyId = 'dat';
    tmpledgerTable2.AccountNum = '1000';
    tmpLedgerTable2.AccountName = 'Name';
    tmpLedgerTable2.insert(); // Insert will fail with duplicate value.
}
```

The preceding X++ code fails on the second insert with a "duplicate value in index" error because both record buffers point to the same data set. You would notice similar behavior if, instead of calling *setTmpData*, you simply assigned the second record buffer to the first record buffer, as illustrated here.

```
tmpLedgerTable2 = tmpLedgerTable1;
```

However, the variables would point to the same object, which means that they use the same data set.

When you want to use the *data* method to copy data from one temporary record buffer to another, where both buffers point to the same data set, you should write the copy like this.

```
tmpLedgerTable2.data(tmpLedgerTable1);
```

Warning The connection from the two record buffers to the same data set would be lost if the code were written as *tmpLedgerTable2 = tmpLedgerTable1.data*. The temporary record buffer would be assigned to a new record buffer in which only the data part is filled in, but with a connection to a new data set.

As mentioned earlier, when no record buffer points to the data set, the records in the temporary table are lost, the allocated memory is freed, and the file is deleted. The following X++ code example illustrates this situation, in which the same record is inserted twice using the same record buffer. But because the record buffer is set to null between the two inserts, the first data set is lost, so the second insert doesn't result in a duplicate value in the index because the new record is inserted into a new data set.

```
static void TmpLedgerTable(Args _args)
{
    TmpLedgerTable tmpLedgerTable;
    ;
    tmpLedgerTable.CompanyId = 'dat';
    tmpledgerTable.AccountNum = '1000';
    tmpLedgerTable.AccountName = 'Name';
    tmpLedgerTable.insert(); // Insert into first dataset.

    tmpLedgerTable = null; // Allocated memory is freed
                           // and file is deleted.
    tmpLedgerTable.CompanyId = 'dat';
    tmpledgerTable.AccountNum = '1000';
    tmpLedgerTable.AccountName = 'Name';
    tmpLedgerTable.insert(); // Insert into new dataset.
}
```

These temporary table examples don't use *ttsbegin* and *ttscommit* statements because you must call the *ttsbegin*, *ttscommit*, and *ttsabort* methods on the temporary record buffer to work with transaction scopes on temporary tables. The *ttsbegin*, *ttscommit*, and *ttsabort* statements affect only manipulation of data related to ordinary tables that are mapped to relational database tables, as illustrated in the following X++ code, where the value of the *accountNum* field is printed to the Infolog even though the *ttsabort* statement was executed.

```
static void TmpLedgerTableAbort(Args _args)
{
    TmpLedgerTable tmpLedgerTable;

    ttsbegin;
    tmpLedgerTable.CompanyId = 'dat';
    tmpledgerTable.AccountNum = '1000';
    tmpLedgerTable.AccountName = 'Name';
    tmpLedgerTable.insert(); // Insert into table.
    ttsabort;

    while select tmpLedgerTable
    {
        info(tmpLedgerTable.AccountNum);
    }
}
```

To successfully abort the inserts of the table in the preceding scenario, you must instead call the *ttsbegin* and *ttsabort* methods on the temporary record buffer, as shown here.

```
static void TmpLedgerTableAbort(Args _args)
{
    TmpLedgerTable tmpLedgerTable;

    tmpLedgerTable.ttsbegin();
    tmpLedgerTable.CompanyId = 'dat';
    tmpledgerTable.AccountNum = '1000';
    tmpLedgerTable.AccountName = 'Name';
    tmpLedgerTable.insert(); // Insert into table.
    tmpLedgerTable.ttsabort();

    while select tmpLedgerTable
    {
        info(tmpLedgerTable.AccountNum);
    }
}
```

When you work with multiple temporary record buffers, you must call the *ttsbegin*, *ttscommit*, and *ttsabort* methods on each record buffer because there is no correlation between the individual temporary data sets.

Important When exceptions are thrown and caught outside the transaction scope, where the Dynamics AX application runtime has already called the *ttsabort* statement, temporary data isn't rolled back.

When you work with temporary data sets, make sure that you're aware of how the data sets are used inside and outside transaction scopes.

Important It is generally not a problem that the *ttsbegin*, *ttscommit*, and *ttsabort* statements have no impact on temporary data if the temporary record buffer isn't declared until after the first *ttsbegin* statement is executed. This only means that the record buffer will be out of scope and the data set destroyed if an exception is thrown and caught outside the transaction scope.

The database-triggering methods on temporary tables behave in almost the same manner as they do with ordinary tables, with a few exceptions. When *insert*, *update*, and *delete* are called on the temporary record buffer, they don't call any of the database-logging or event-raising methods on the application class if database logging or alerts have been set up for the table.

Note In general, you can't set up logging or events on defined temporary tables. However, because ordinary tables can be changed to temporary tables, logging or events could already be set up. We describe how to change the behavior of an ordinary table later in this chapter.

Delete actions are also not executed on temporary tables. Although you can set up delete actions, the Dynamics AX application runtime doesn't try to execute them.

Tip You can query a record buffer for acting on a temporary data set by calling the *isTmp* record buffer method, which returns true or false depending on whether the table is temporary.

Dynamics AX allows you to trace SQL statements, either from within the rich client or from the Dynamics AX Configuration Utility or the Server Configuration Utility. However, SQL statements can be traced only if they are sent to the relational database. You can't trace data manipulation in temporary tables with these tools.

Design-Time Setting

As explained earlier, you can make a table temporary during various phases of a Dynamics AX implementation. To define a table as temporary, you change the *Temporary* property on the table from the default value of No to Yes. This prevents a matching table from being created in the underlying relational database when the table is synchronized against the database. Instead, memory or a file is allocated for the table when needed. Figure 14-19 shows the *Temporary* property on a table where the value is set to Yes, thereby marking the table as temporary at design time.

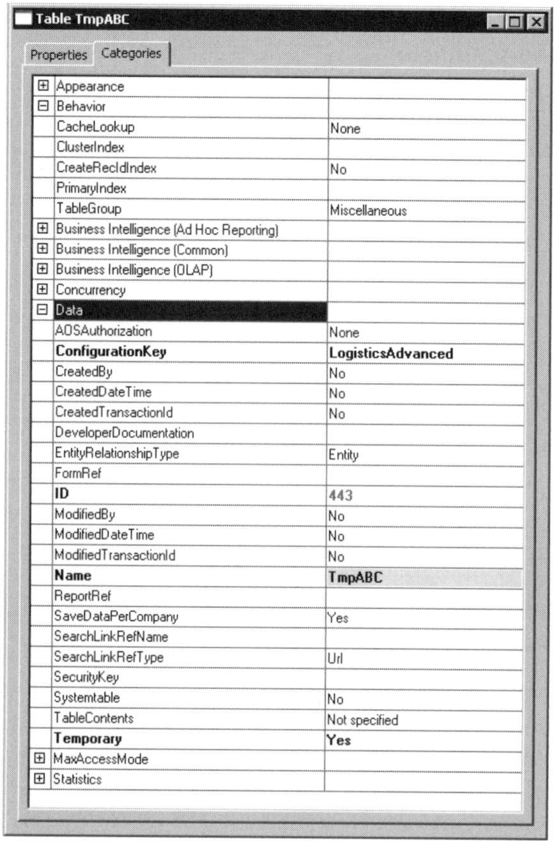

FIGURE 14-19 Marking a table as temporary at design time

> **Best Practices** Tables that are defined as temporary at design time should have *Tmp* inserted as part of the table name rather than at the beginning or end (e.g., *InventCostTmpTransBreakdown*). This improves readability of the X++ code when temporary tables are explicitly used. In previous versions of Dynamics AX, the best practice was to prefix temporary tables with *Tmp*, which is why a number of temporary tables are still using this syntax.

Configuration-Time Setting

When you define a table by using the AOT, you can attach a configuration key to the table by setting the *ConfigurationKey* property on the table. The property belongs to the Data section of the table properties, as illustrated in Figure 14-19.

When the Dynamics AX application runtime synchronizes the tables to the database, it synchronizes tables for licensed modules and enabled configurations only. Whether a table belongs to a licensed module or an enabled configuration depends on the settings in the

ConfigurationKey property. If the configuration key is enabled, the table is synchronized to the database; if the configuration key isn't enabled, the table is disabled and behaves like a temporary table. Therefore, a run-time error doesn't occur when the application runtime interprets X++ code that accesses tables that aren't enabled.

> **Note** Whether or not a configuration key is enabled isn't important to a table that is already set as temporary. The table remains temporary even though its configuration key is disabled, and you can expect the same behavior regardless of the configuration key setting.

Application Runtime Setting

You can use X++ code to turn an ordinary table into a temporary table and use it as such by calling the *setTmp* method on the record buffer. From then on, the record buffer is treated as though the *Temporary* property on the table were set to Yes.

> **Note** You can't define a record buffer of a temporary table type and turn it into an ordinary table, partly because there is no underlying table in the relational database.

The following X++ code illustrates the use of the *setTmp* method, in which two record buffers of the same type are defined; one is made temporary, and all records from the database are inserted into the temporary version of the table. The temporary record buffer therefore points to a data set containing a complete copy of all the records from the database belonging to the current company.

```
static void TmpCustTable(Args _args)
{
    CustTable custTable;
    CustTable custTableTmp;
    ;
    custTableTmp.setTmp();
    ttsbegin;
    while select custTable
    {
        custTableTmp.data(custTable);
        custTableTmp.doInsert();
    }
    ttscommit;
}
```

Notice that the preceding X++ code uses the *doInsert* method to insert records into the temporary record buffer. It does this to prevent execution of the overridden *insert* method.

This method inserts and updates records in other tables that aren't switched automatically to temporary mode just because the *custTable* record buffer is temporary.

> **Caution** You should use great care when changing an ordinary record buffer to a temporary record buffer because application logic in overridden methods that manipulates data in ordinary tables could be inadvertently executed. This could happen if the temporary record buffer is used in a form and the form application runtime makes the call to the database-triggering methods.

Composite Queries

The composite query framework builds on the extensible query framework in Dynamics AX. A composite query allows you to embed one query into another query to provide database subquery equivalent functionality. Composite queries are very useful for personalization. For example, if a query *'Cust'* retrieves all the data from *CustTable*, you can bind this query to one or more primary list pages. The secondary list pages are personalized for the user. In this example, the secondary list page displays only the customers belonging to a particular customer group or all the customers who live or operate in a particular state. The fundamental idea here is that the secondary list page provides additional filters on the data displayed in the primary list page. To facilitate this framework, composite queries build additional filters on top of existing queries.

Follow these steps to create a composite query:

1. Create a new query.
2. Change the name to **CustomersInWA**.
3. Drag the existing Cust query to the Composite Query node of the query CustomersInWA.
4. Expand the Cust query under the Composite Query node.
5. Expand the Data Sources node under the Cust query.
6. Expand the Customers data source under the Data Sources node.
7. Right-click Ranges and add a new range.
8. Select properties for the range.
9. Change the field to **State**.
10. Change the value to **WA**.

This composite query is now ready to use. When this composite query is bound to the secondary list page, the list page displays only customers who live and or operate in Washington State.

Note The composite query doesn't guarantee to return more data than the primary query it is built on.

The list pages framework in Dynamics AX 2009 is built using composite queries.

Paging Framework for Queries

The paging framework for queries is new in Dynamics AX 2009. It supports primarily the Enterprise Portal framework and the list pages framework.

There are two types of paging: position-based paging and value-based paging.

Position-Based Paging

Position-based paging is used primarily in Enterprise Portal. In position-based paging, a Web page displays a specified number of records. The user has to click Next or Previous to navigate to additional records.

Position-based paging uses the *ROW_NUMBER* function provided by the database and has the same limitations as the *ROW_NUMBER* function. Performance degrades when the table has huge amounts of data and the page appears toward the end of the result set. The database is then forced to use table scans. Though this is not a common usage pattern for Web-based scenarios, we discourage using position-based paging for such scenarios.

Two APIs, both available on the *QueryRun* object, are important to understand when you're using position-based paging:

- *QueryRun.EnablePositionPaging(true/false)* enables or disables position-based paging and is false by default.
- *QueryRun.AddPageRange(startingPosition, numberOfRecordsToFetch)* indicates the starting position and the number of records to fetch.

The following example illustrates the usage of position-based paging APIs.

```
static void PositionBasedPagingExample(Args _args)
{
    QueryRun queryRun;
    Query query;
    CustTable cust;
    ;

    query = new Query(querystr(Cust));
    queryRun = new QueryRun(query);
    queryRun.enablePositionPaging(true);
```

```
    queryRun.addPageRange(1, 10);
    info('First 10 records of Cust Query');
    while(queryRun.next())
    {
        cust = queryRun.get(tablenum(CustTable));
        info(cust.Name);
    }

    queryRun = new QueryRun(query);
    queryRun.enablePositionPaging(true);
    queryRun.addPageRange(11, 10);

    info('Next 10 records of Cust Query');
    while(queryRun.next())
    {
        cust = queryRun.get(tablenum(CustTable));
        info(cust.Name);
    }
}
```

Note A query should have at least one valid data source with at least one valid *'ORDER BY'* field. Position-based paging doesn't support temporary tables.

Value-Based Paging

Value-based paging is primarily used by the list pages framework. In value-based paging, records that are greater or lesser than the specific value for a field in the *'ORDER BY'* clause are returned.

Note The query should have at least one valid data source with at least one valid *'ORDER BY'* field. The *'ORDER BY'* field indicates the location of the records to be fetched. Like position-based paging, value-based paging doesn't support temporary tables. Also, value-based paging can't be used on queries that contain outer joins.

Two APIs, both available on the *QueryRun* object, are used in value-based paging:

- *QueryRun.EnableValueBasedPaging(true/false)* enables or disables value-based paging and is false by default.
- *QueryRun.ApplyValueBasedPaging(Common,ForwardDirection)* indicates the starting position and direction in which to fetch. The first parameter takes the table as a parameter. The assumption is that this table has the value for all the *'ORDER BY'* fields that can be used as a starting position. The first parameter should match the exact structure of the query.

The following example illustrates the usage of value-based paging in queries.

```
static void ValueBasedPagingExample(Args _args)
{
    QueryRun queryRun;
    Query query;
    CustTable cust;
    ;
    cust.Name = 'Light and Design';
    query = new Query(querystr(Cust));
    queryRun = new QueryRun(query);
    queryRun.enableValueBasedPaging(true);
    queryRun.applyValueBasedPaging( cust, true);

    info('Customers with name >= Light and Design');
    while(queryRun.next())
    {
        cust = queryRun.get(tablenum(CustTable));
        info(cust.Name);
    }

    cust.Name = 'Light and Design';
    queryRun = new QueryRun(query);
    queryRun.enableValueBasedPaging(true);
    queryRun.applyValueBasedPaging( cust, false);
    info('Customers with name <= Light and Design');
    while(queryRun.next())
    {
        cust = queryRun.get(tablenum(CustTable));
        info(cust.Name);
    }
}
```

Query Framework Enhancement

The Query framework in Dynamics AX 2009 has some noticeable enhancements. You can now write complex queries, such as nested joins, and design union queries. You can also create a query once and use it in multiple places; in earlier versions, you had to remodel the same query to achieve this functionality.

Complex Queries

Using the X++ *select* statement and the AOT Query object model are two ways to retrieve data from the database. AOT Query provides a set of object models and APIs that allow the query to be constructed and modified dynamically at run time. For example, based on run-time requirements, such as user input, you can add or modify query data sources, range filters, order by fields, and group by fields. AOT Query is more flexible than the X++ *select* statement, which can't be modified at run time.

Prior to Dynamics AX 2009, AOT Query had some limitations when compared with the X++ statement. The most noticeable was the lack of support for complex query structures. Certain query structures would lead to dropped data sources and thus an incorrect SQL statement.

In Dynamics AX 2009, Exist Join statements are nested only when joined nodes are nested on the AOT.

To join a query data source to another query data source that isn't its direct parent inside MorphX, you can choose the name of any data source from the drop-down list of the *JoinDataSource* property, as shown in Figure 14-20.

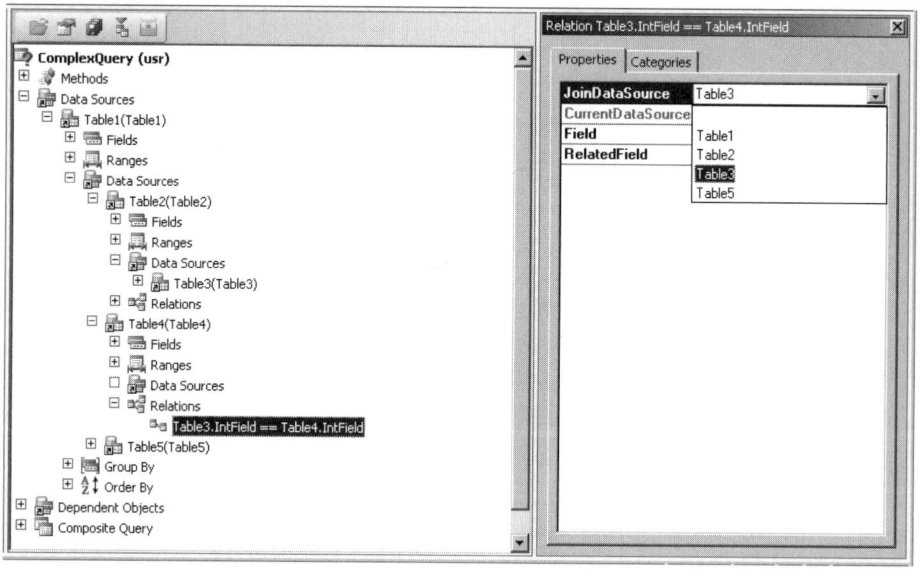

FIGURE 14-20 Choosing a name from the list given in the *JoinDataSource* on the Properties tab

The drop-down list is prepopulated with a list of query data sources that the current query data source can join to. Query data sources inside an Exist Join, for example, can't be joined to another query data source outside of the Exist Join because the Exist Join query data source doesn't return any data. To join data sources in X++, add the name of the query data source to the current data source.

```
Query q = new Query();
    QueryRun qr;
    QueryBuildDataSource dsTable1,dsTable2,dsTable3,dsTable4,dsTable5;

    dsTable1 = q.addDataSource(tablenum(Table1),'Table1');
    dsTable1.fetchMode(0);
    dsTable2 = dsTable1.addDataSource(tablenum(Table2), 'Table2');
    dsTable2.fetchMode(0);
    dsTable3 = dsTable2.addDataSource(tablenum(Table3), 'Table3');
    dsTAble3.fetchMode(0);
    dsTable4 = dsTable1.addDataSource(tablenum(Table4), 'Table4');
    dsTable4.fetchMode(0);
    dsTable5 = dsTable1.addDataSource(tablenum(Table5), 'Table5');
    dsTable5.fetchMode(0);

    // Add join and range conditions
    //...

    // Add a join condition from Table4 to Table3 which is not the direct parent.
    dsTable4.addLink(fieldnum(Table3,IntField),fieldnum(Table4,IntField), 'Table3');

    //...
```

Union Queries

In SQL, when you want to merge the results of two or more *select* statements and work on them as one, you use a union query. Dynamics AX 2009 supports union queries through the AOT Query object. When designing a union query, you must pick the first query data source and its fields carefully because all the data retrieved is stored inside the table buffer of the first data source.

You also need to be sure that the configuration key associated with the table of the first data source is a super key of the configuration keys of the rest of the query data sources. Using this super key ensures that the first query data source isn't disabled while some of the secondary data sources are enabled.

To create a union query on the AOT, follow these steps:

1. Create a query and specify the *QueryType* to be *Union*, as shown in Figure 14-21.

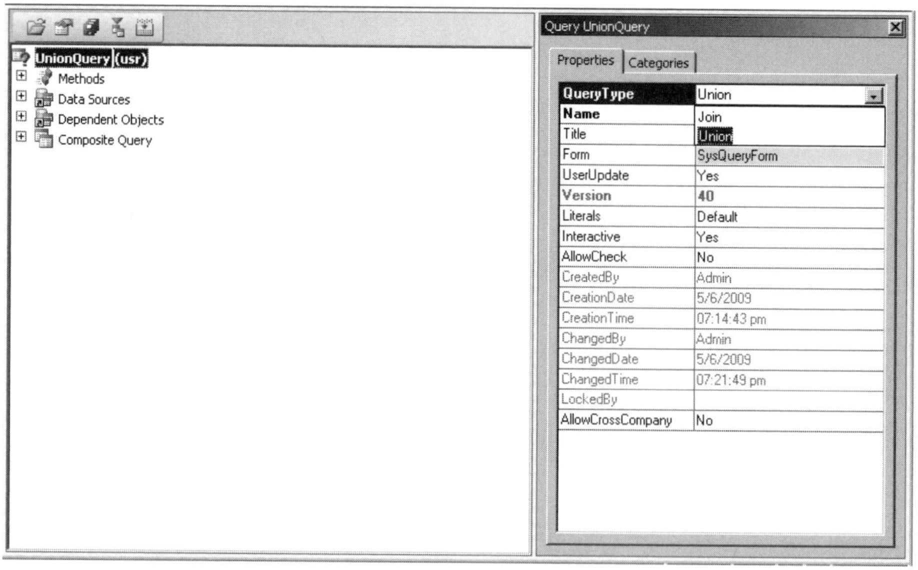

FIGURE 14-21 Creating and specifying *QueryType* for a union query

2. Add the first query data source. Optionally add Exist Joins and NotExist Joins.
3. Add the secondary query data sources and specify the union type, as shown in Figure 14-22. You can add Exist Joins and NotExist Joins as an option.

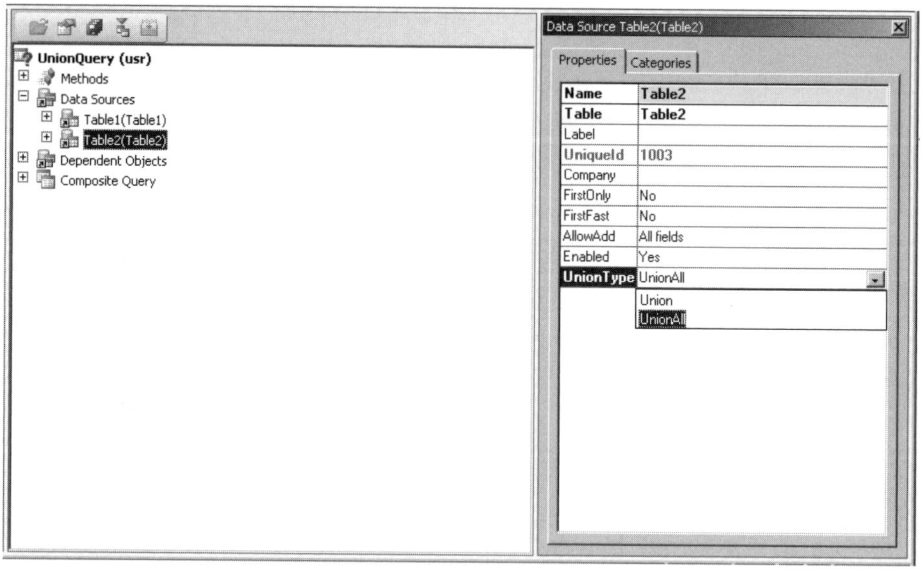

FIGURE 14-22 Adding secondary query data sources and specifying union types

Be sure to align the fields of the query data sources properly. The data types of the fields need to be compatible—both type compatible and size compatible—with those of the first query data source. The size of the field of the first query data source can't be smaller than that of the corresponding field in other query data sources. Figure 14-23 shows the Align field in a union query.

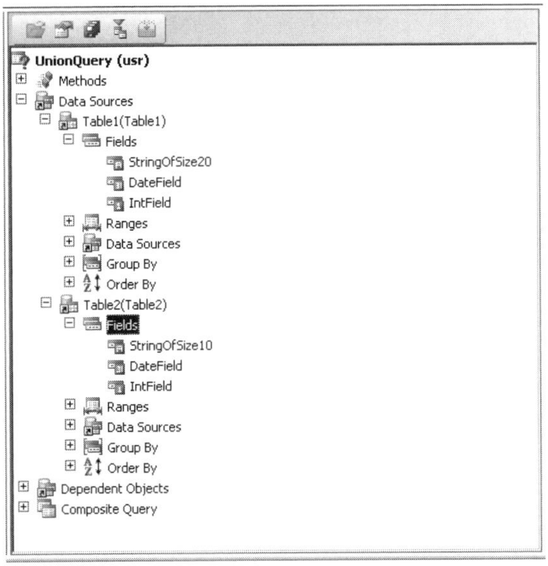

FIGURE 14-23 Align field in a union query

When aligning fields, you also need to consider that the field size could change during customization. For a union query, if the size of an extended data type associated with a field in the secondary query data source is increased, incompatibility could result. In Figure 14-23, the first field of the first data source has a string size of 20, and the first field of the second data source has a string size of 10. So they are compatible in size.

Note A couple other issues can come up when you're using union queries. First, when a secondary query data source is disabled through the configuration key, the union ignores that branch. Second, the configuration key has another implication for field alignment. If a field in the first query data source of a union query is disabled, the corresponding fields in the secondary query data sources must also be disabled.

When you use union queries, two code elements are important: the *UnionBranchID* field and the *Forupdate* flag.

UnionBranchID Field

All the data retrieved is stored in the records in the table buffer of the first query data source. When you want to know where the data on the current record came from, check the *UnionBranchId* field on the table buffer. This field returns the 1-based branch number of the data source. The reason a branch number is used instead of a table ID value is because a table might appear multiple times in a union. Also, if future versions of Dynamics AX support inner/outer joins, fields might need to come from multiple tables. Keep in mind that when *UnionBranchId* is calculated, all branches are taken into account, including those disabled through configuration keys. So you can write code without having to worry about configuration keys at run time.

forupdate Flag

When you set the *forupdate* flag on the data sources of a union query, the union query can be used to update the data in the underlying tables. *UnionBranchId* and the alignment mapping information on the Query object help in this effort. Dynamics AX 2009 maps the data on the table buffer of the first query data source to the table buffer of the corresponding query data source and performs an update.

The following code example shows how to create and use a union query in X++.

```
Query q = new Query();
    QueryRun qr;
    QueryBuildDataSource dsTable1,dsTable2;
    Table1 t1;
    ;


    // Mark query as union query.
    q.queryType(QueryType::Union);

    // Add two data sources
    dsTable1 = q.addDataSource(tablenum(Table1),'Table1');
    dsTable2 = q.addDataSource(tablenum(Table2),'Table2');

    // Set the union type
    dsTable2.unionType(UnionType::UnionAll);

    // Flag that I want to update through the union query.
    dsTable1.update(TRUE);
    dsTable2.update(TRUE);

    // Add fields and make sure that they are aligned
    // for type and size
    dsTable1.addSelectionField(fieldnum(Table1,StringOfSize20));
    dsTable2.addSelectionField(fieldnum(Table2,StringOfSize10));

    dsTable1.addSelectionField(fieldnum(Table1,DateField));
    dsTable2.addSelectionField(fieldnum(Table2,DateField));

    dsTable1.addSelectionField(fieldnum(Table1,IntField));
    dsTable2.addSelectionField(fieldnum(Table2,IntField));
```

```
qr = new QueryRun(q);

ttsbegin;
while(qr.next())
{
    // All data is stored on the table buffer of the first data source
    t1 = qr.getNo(1);
    t1.IntField++;
    t1.update();
}
ttscommit;
```

> **Note** Although the Exist Join and the NotExist Join are supported in union queries, inner and outer joins are not, which means that you can have unions only between single tables. Neither join is a constant supported when specifying a union field.

Query as a Central Data Modeling Tool

People often work with data specific to their domain. This data comes from different tables. The same data may be created, displayed, and modified on forms and Web forms. The forms are then processed in business logic and analyzed in reports.

Before Dynamics AX 2009, the shape of the data had to be defined in multiple places: on forms and Web forms, and forms and data set data sources; in X++ code, the X++ *select* statement, or the AOT Query object; and view uses view data source, and report uses report query. In other words, view data source is the building block for view. View data sources, which represent tables, are added to view to form the definition of view. The report query construct under each report in the AOT defines the table joins for the report. Shaping data for so many different places is not only redundant but also error-prone and not maintainable. The design of the AOT imposes some extra limitations. For example, when you design a form using a form data source, you can't explicitly choose a join relationship between two form data sources. The first relationship between the two is automatically picked up, which in some cases might be incorrect. Another example is view, in which you can construct only a single parent/child lineage. Also, any enhancement made to AOT Query, like the union support just added, needs to be duplicated in all the other places.

Dynamics AX 2009 lets you deal with all these data reuse issues by using a single tool: AOT Query. In AOT Query, you can define the collection of tables and the relationship between the tables once and then reuse the data in many different venues. As we mentioned earlier, AOT Query now supports complex joins and union queries. In most cases, reusing a query is as easy as dragging and dropping an AOT Query. You can do this in AOT *Reports* and AOT *View* nodes, as shown in Figure 14-24 (for reports) and Figure 14-25 (for views).

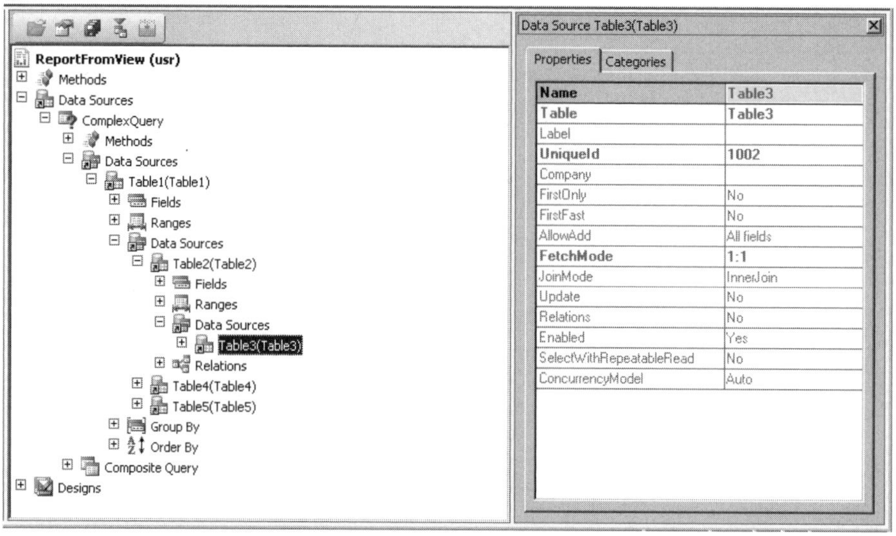

FIGURE 14-24 Report using a modeled query

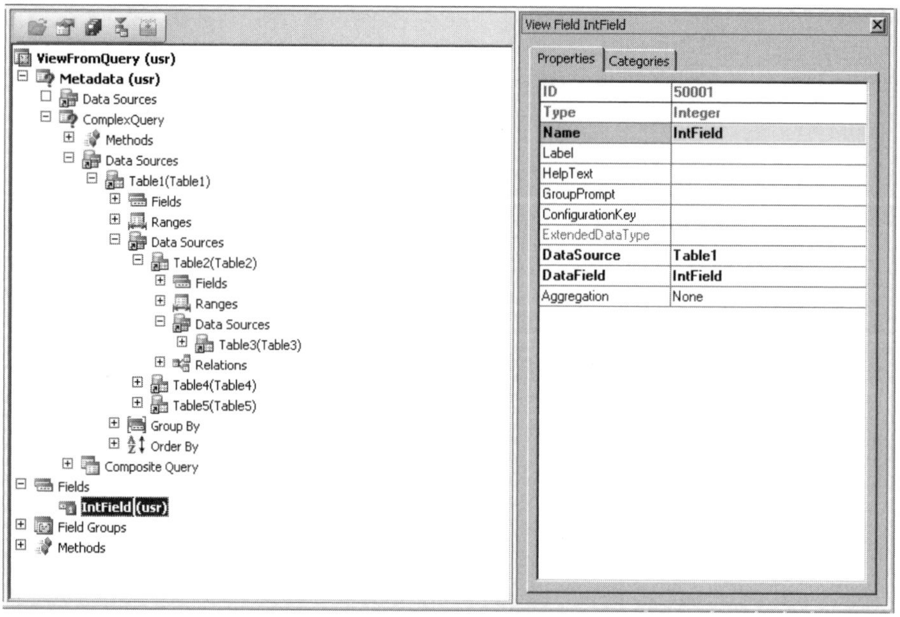

FIGURE 14-25 View using a modeled query

When you drag a modeled query onto a form or a Web form, a number of form data sources are automatically generated. These form data sources match the visible query data sources of the modeled query. Just as on conventional forms, these places are where you specify form-specific behavior and add form-specific code.

When using a modeled query on forms and Web forms, users need to specify how the data is to be retrieved to match the behavior of the user interface. For example, when you define the shape of your data to include a sales header with sales lines, your query is simply an outer join between *SalesTable* and *SalesLine*. But when you design a form that has a sales header shown in one grid and a sales line shown in another grid, where the sales line grid shows only the sale lines of the sales order that is currently selected, you don't issue a single outer join to retrieve data for both sales orders and sales lines in one query. Instead, you need to issue two queries, one for the sales header grid to retrieve all sales headers and one for the sales line to retrieve sales lines only for the sales header that is currently selected.

To reuse the same query on forms, you have to annotate the data-fetching behavior of the form data sources through *LinkType*, on the join between *SalesTable* and *SalesLine*. The *LinkType* concept is on par with the existing form data source design experience. *LinkType* has six values for designing the form data source: *active*, *delayed*, *inner*, *outer*, *exist*, and *NotExist*. When you use a modeled query on a form, the modeled query has already captured inner, outer, exist, and NotExist joins. The only relevant *LinkType* is active and delayed. For a single join relationship, you can specify the *LinkType* on either end of the joined data source. To decide where to put an active or delayed *LinkType*, ask the question, which data needs to be retrieved first on the user interface? Depending on the answer to that question, put the *LinkType* on the other data source.

Figure 14-26 shows a form using a modeled query and the setting of the *LinkType* property between the Table3 and Table4 data sources.

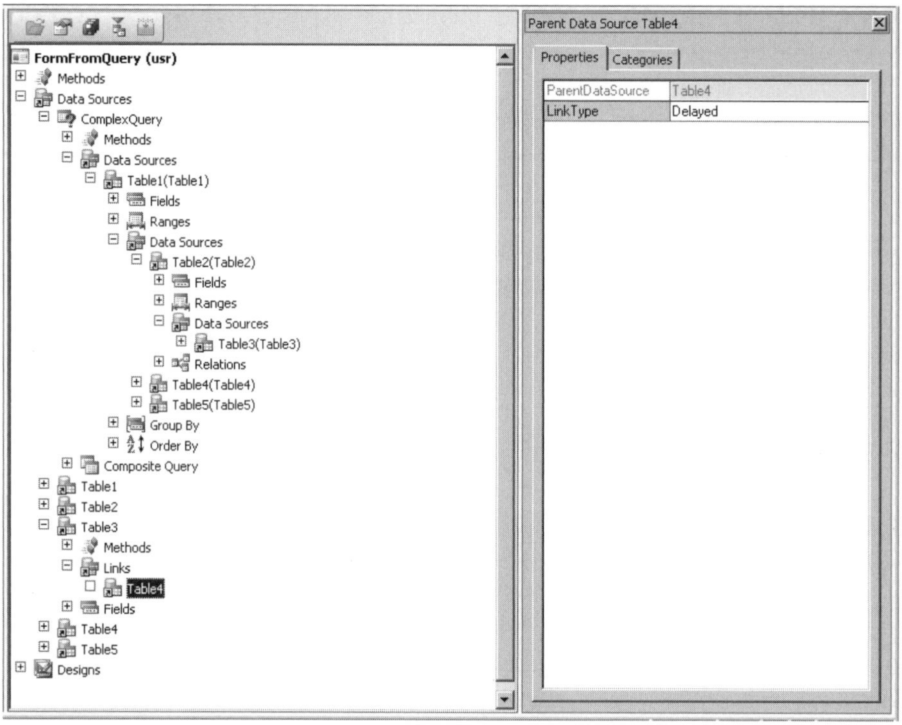

FIGURE 14-26 Form using a modeled query

The collection of active or delayed link types specified effectively break a single query into multiple queries. These subqueries have to be executed in a specific order in response to user interface events. Some of these subqueries are linked through dynalinks to other subqueries.

When a modeled query is used on a form or a Web form, the form engine does the following:

- It generates corresponding form data sources from query data sources. If some form data sources already exist, it checks the compatibility of the form data sources and keeps all the compatible form data sources. This means that no work is lost on those form data sources. For data sources that are not compatible, it issues a dialog box asking the user to confirm that the form data source should be deleted.
- When the form is opened, the form engine takes the *LinkType* annotation on the form, analyzes the query structure, checks for any error conditions, and computes the subqueries that are associated with a form data source.

Compare this behavior to how the form engine works on a conventional form that doesn't use a modeled query. Both create queries and associate them to form data sources. One computes that from a query, using query structure and *LinkType* information. The other uses *JoinSource* and *LinkType* information.

Specifying Query Ranges Using the *SysQueryRangeUtil* Class

Dynamics AX 2009 allows you to specify range values for queries using a restricted set of function calls. This mechanism is in addition to the existing ways to specify range values, which use either literal values or specify expressions by enclosing them in "( )" symbols. To use the new syntax, you need to follow these rules:

- The function should be a static function in the *SysQueryRangeUtil* class.
- The function should return a value that is of the same syntax as regular range values.

The *SysQueryRangeUtil* class in Dynamics AX 2009 includes a number of functions that list pages used to dynamically control the data that is shown based on the value that is returned by the function. For example, the *currentUserId* function returns the user ID of the current logged-on user. Some other functions and their usage are shown here.

```
  (currentUserId())
(greaterThanDate(0))
(OwnerId == currentEmployeeId())
```

The function call has to use the same syntax as passing expressions in a range value. The whole value needs to be surrounded by an opening "(" and closing ")" parenthesis. You can see the *SysQueryRangeUtil* class for a number of examples of the functions that ship with Dynamics AX 2009, and you can see their usage in some of the queries in the AOT for example, *EmplTableListPage*. In this class, all the functions return string values. You can write functions that return any of the primitive data types supported by Dynamics AX 2009. For example, if you have a function named *orders* that returns the count of orders that might be an *int64*, you can use it in the query in a number of ways, such as (*orders()*) or (*orders() + 1*). The following code shows how to specify range values using this syntax.

```
     Query q;
QueryRun qr;
QueryBuildDataSource qbds;
QueryBuildRange qbr;
MyTable myTable;

q = new Query();
qbds = q.addDataSource(tablenum(MyTable));
qbr = qbds.addRange(fieldnum(MyTable, StrField));
qbr.value("(currentUserId())");
qr = new QueryRun(q);
qr.next();
myTable = qr.get(tablenum(MyTable));
print myTable.StrField;
pause;
```

Chapter 15

Reflection

In this chapter:

The objectives of this chapter are to:

- Introduce the concept of reflection.
- Demonstrate the capabilities and limitations of the available reflection system functions and APIs.

Introduction

Reflection is a programmatic discoverability mechanism of the Microsoft Dynamics AX application model. In other words, reflection provides APIs for reading and traversing element definitions. By using the reflection APIs in the MorphX development environment, you can query metadata as though it were a table, an object model, or a tree structure.

You can do interesting analyses with the reflection information. The Reverse Engineering tool is an excellent example of the power of reflection. Based on element definitions in MorphX, the tool generates Unified Modeling Language (UML) models and Entity Relationship Diagrams (ERDs) that you can browse in Microsoft Office Visio.

Reflection also allows you to invoke methods on objects. This capability is of little value to business application developers who construct class hierarchies properly. For framework developers, however, the power to invoke methods on objects can be valuable. Suppose, for example, you want to programmatically write any record to an XML file that includes all of the fields and display methods. Reflection allows you to determine the fields and their values and also to invoke the display methods to capture their return values.

X++ features a set of system functions that you can use for reflection, as well as three reflection APIs. The reflection system functions follow:

- **Intrinsic functions** A set of functions that allow you to refer to an element's name or ID safely at compile time
- **TypeOf system function** A function that returns the primitive type for a variable

- **ClassIdGet system function** A function that returns the ID of the class for an instance of an object

These are the reflection APIs:

- **Table data** A set of tables that contains all element definitions. The tables give you direct access to the contents of the .aod files. You can query for the existence of elements and certain properties, such as *created by* and *created datetime*. You can't retrieve information about the contents or structure of each element.
- **Dictionary** A set of classes that provide a type-safe mechanism for reading metadata from an object model. *Dictionary* classes provide basic and more abstract information about elements in a type-safe manner. With few exceptions, this API is read-only.
- **Treenodes** A class hierarchy that provides the Application Object Tree (AOT) with an API that can be used to create, read, update, and delete any piece of metadata or source code. This API can tell you everything about anything in the AOT. You navigate the tree-nodes in the AOT through the API and query for metadata in a non-type-safe manner.

We spend the rest of this chapter delving into the details of these system functions and APIs.

Reflection System Functions

The X++ language features a set of system functions that can be used to reflect on elements. They are described in the following sections.

Intrinsic Functions

You should use *intrinsic functions* whenever you need to reference an element from within X++ code. Intrinsic functions provide a way to make a type-safe reference. The compiler recognizes the reference and verifies that the element being referenced exists. If the element doesn't exist, the code doesn't compile. Because elements have their own life cycles, a reference doesn't remain valid forever; an element can be renamed or deleted. Using intrinsic functions ensures that you are notified of any broken references at compile time. A compiler error early in the development cycle is always better than a run-time error.

All references you make using intrinsic functions are captured by the Cross-reference tool. So you can determine where any element is referenced, regardless of whether the reference is in metadata or code. The Cross-reference tool is described in Chapter 3, "The MorphX Tools."

Consider these two implementations.

```
print "MyClass";           //Prints MyClass
print classStr(MyClass);   //Prints MyClass
```

They have exactly the same result: the string "MyClass" is printed. As a reference, the first implementation is weak. It will eventually break when the class is renamed or deleted, meaning that you'll need to spend time debugging. The second implementation is strong and unlikely to break. If you were to rename or delete *MyClass*, you could use the Cross-reference tool to do an impact analysis of your changes and correct any broken references.

Using the intrinsic functions *<Concept>Str*, you can reference all the elements in the AOT by their names. You can also reference elements that have an ID with the intrinsic function *<Concept>Num*. Intrinsic functions are not limited to parent objects; they also exist for class methods, table fields, indexes, and methods. More than 50 intrinsic functions are available. Here are a few examples of intrinsic functions.

```
print fieldNum(MyTable, MyField);   //Prints 50001
print fieldStr(MyTable, MyField);   //Prints MyField
print methodStr(MyClass, MyMethod); //Prints MyMethod
print formStr(MyForm);              //Prints MyForm
```

An element's ID is assigned when the element is created. The ID is a sequential ID dependant on an application model layer. In the preceding example, *50001* is the ID assigned to the first element created in the USR layer. Element IDs are explained in Chapter 1, "Architectural Overview."

Two other intrinsic functions are worth noting: *identifierStr* and *literalStr*. *IdentifierStr* allows you to refer to elements when a more feature-rich intrinsic function isn't available. *IdentifierStr* provides no compile-time checking and no cross-reference information. Using the *identifierStr* function is much better than using a literal, because the intention of referring to an element is captured. If a literal is used, the intention is lost—the reference could be to user interface text, a file name, or something completely different. The Best Practices tool detects the use of *identifierStr* and issues a best practice warning.

The Dynamics AX runtime automatically converts any reference to a label identifier to the label text for the label identifier. In most cases, this behavior is what you want; however, you can avoid the conversion by using *literalStr*. *LiteralStr* allows you to refer to a label identifier without converting the label ID to the label text, as shown here.

```
print "@SYS1";              //Prints Time transactions
print literalStr("@SYS1"); //Prints @SYS1
```

In the first line of the example, the label identifier (*@SYS1*) is automatically converted to the label text (*Time transactions*). In the second line, the reference to the label identifier isn't converted.

TypeOf System Function

The *TypeOf* system function takes a variable instance as a parameter and returns the primitive type of the parameter. Here is an example.

```
int i = 123;
str s = "Hello world";
MyClass c;
Guid g = newGuid();

print typeOf(i);  //Prints Integer
print typeOf(s);  //Prints String
print typeOf(c);  //Prints Class
print typeOf(g);  //Prints Guid
pause;
```

The return value is an instance of the *Types* system enumeration. It contains an enumeration for each primitive type in X++.

ClassIdGet System Function

The *ClassIdGet* system function takes an object as a parameter and returns the class ID for the class element of which the object is an instance. If the parameter passed is Null, the function returns the class ID for the declared type, as shown here.

```
MyBaseClass c;
print classIdGet(c);  //Prints 50001

c = new MyDerivedClass();
print classIdGet(c);  //Prints 50002
pause;
```

This function is particularly useful for determining the type of an object instance. Suppose you need to determine whether a class instance is a particular class. The following example shows how you can use *ClassIdGet* to determine the class ID of the *_anyClass* variable instance. If the *_anyClass* variable really is an instance of *MyClass*, it's safe to assign it to the variable *myClass*.

```
void myMethod(object _anyClass)
{
    MyClass myClass;
    if (classIdGet(_anyClass) == classNum(MyClass))
    {
        myClass = _anyClass;
        ...
    }
}
```

Notice the use of the intrinsic function, which evaluates at compile time, and the use of *classIdGet*, which evaluates at run time.

Because inheritance isn't taken into account, this sort of implementation is likely to break the object model. In most cases, any instance of a derived *MyClass* class should be treated as an actual *MyClass* instance. The simplest way to handle inheritance is to use the *is* and *as* static methods on the *SysDictClass* class. You'll recognize these methods if you're familiar with C#. The *is* method returns true if the object passed in is of a certain type, and the *as* method can be used to cast an instance to a particular type. The *as* method returns *null* if the cast is invalid.

These two methods also take interface implementations into account. So with the *as* method, you can cast your object to an interface. Here is a revision of the preceding example using the *as* method.

```
void myMethod(object _anyClass)
{
    MyClass myClass = SysDictClass::as(_anyClass, classNum(MyClass));
    if (myClass)
    {
        ...
    }
}
```

Here is an example of an interface cast.

```
void myMethod2(object _anyClass)
{
    SysPackable packableClass =
        SysDictClass::as(_anyClass, classNum(SysPackable));
    if (packableClass)
    {
        packableClass.pack();
    }
}
```

Note This book promotes customization through inheritance using the Liskov substitution principle. Read more about Dynamics AX Smart Customization techniques in Chapter 18, "Code Upgrade."

Reflection APIs

The X++ system library includes three APIs that can be used to reflect on elements. They are described in the following sections.

Table Data API

Suppose that you want to find all classes whose names begin with *Invent* and that have been modified within the last month. The following example shows one way to conduct your search.

```
static void findInventoryClasses(Args _args)
{
    UtilElements utilElements;

    while select name from utilElements
        where utilElements.RecordType == UtilElementType::Class
           && utilElements.Name like 'Invent*'
           && utilElements.ModifiedDateTime >
              DateTimeUtil::addDays(DateTimeUtil::getSystemDateTime(), -30)
    {
        info(strfmt("%1", utilElements.Name));
    }
}
```

The *UtilElements* table provides access to all elements. The *RecordType* field holds the concept. Other fields in the *UtilElements* table that can be reflected on are *Name*, *CreatedBy*, *CreatedDateTime*, *ModifiedBy*, and *ModifiedDateTime*.

Because of the nature of the table data API, the *UtilElements* table can also be used as a data source in a form or a report. A form showing the table data is available from Tools\Development Tools\Application Objects\Application Objects. In the form, you can use the standard query capabilities to filter and search the data.

Some elements have sub-elements associated with them. For example, a table has fields and methods. This parent/child association is captured in the *ParentId* field of the sub-element. The following job finds all static method elements on the *CustTable* table element by selecting only table static method elements whose *ParentId* equals the *CustTable* table ID.

```
static void findStaticMethodsOnCustTable(Args _args)
{
    UtilElements utilElements;

    while select name from utilElements
        where utilElements.recordType == UtilElementType::TableStaticMethod
           && utilElements.ParentId == tableNum(CustTable)
```

```
    {
        info(strfmt("%1", utilElements.name));
    }
}
```

Notice the use of field lists in the *select* statements in the examples in this section. Each record in the table also has a *binary large object* (*BLOB*) field that contains all the metadata, source code, and bytecode. This *BLOB* field can't be interpreted from X++ code, so you don't need to fetch it. When you specify a file list to the *select* statement with fields from the primary index, fetching the actual record is avoided, and the *select* statement returns the result much faster. The primary index contains these fields: *RecordType*, *ParentId*, *Name*, and *UtilLevel*.

The *UtilLevel* field contains the layer of the element. The following job finds all parent elements in the USR layer.

```
static void findParentElementsInUSRLayer(Args _args)
{
    UtilElements utilElements;

    while select recordType, name from utilElements
        where utilElements.ParentId == 0
           && utilElements.utilLevel == UtilEntryLevel::usr
    {
        info(strfmt("%1 %2", utilElements.recordType, utilElements.name));
    }
}
```

As you learned in Chapter 1, elements can have IDs. The *UtilElements* table can't provide ID information. To get ID information, you must use the *UtilIdElements* table. The two tables are both views on the elements in the .aod files; the only difference is the inclusion of the *ID* field in the *UtilIdElements* table. The following code is a revision of the previous job that also reports IDs.

```
static void findParentElementsInUSRLayer(Args _args)
{
    UtilIdElements utilIdElements;

    while select RecordType, Id, Name from utilIdElements
        where utilIdElements.ParentId == 0
           && utilIdElements.UtilLevel == UtilEntryLevel::usr
    {
        info(strfmt("%1 %2 %3",
            utilIdElements.RecordType,
            utilIdElements.Name,
            utilIdElements.Id));
    }
}
```

Although we have discussed two tables that contain the .aod files in this section, all the application data files have a table reflection API similar to the ones we have mentioned. Table 15-1 lists some additional reflection tables.

TABLE 15-1 Reflection Tables

Table Name	Description
UtilElements, *UtilIdElements*	Tables containing the .aod files, which contain elements.
UtilElementsOld *UtilIdElementsOld*	Tables containing the .aod files in the Old application folder. This information is useful during code upgrades.
UtilApplHelp	Table containing the .ahd files, which contain online Help information for users.
UtilApplCodeDoc	Table containing the .add files, which contain developer documentation information for elements.
UtilCodeDoc	Table containing the .khd files, which contain developer documentation information for Dynamics AX system APIs.

All the tables listed in Table 15-1 have an associated class. These classes contain a set of static methods that are generally helpful. All the classes have the same name as the table, prefixed with an *x*.

Suppose you want to report the AOT path for *MyForm* from the table *utilIdElements*. You could use the *xUtilIdElements* function to return this information, as in the following code.

```
static void findAOTPathForMyForm(Args _args)
{
    UtilIdElements utilIdElements = xUtilIdElements::find(
        UtilElementType::Form, FormStr(MyForm));

    if (utilIdElements)
        info(xUtilIdElements::getNodePath(utilIdElements));
}
```

Note When you use the table data API in an environment with version control enabled, the values of some of the fields are reset during the build process. For file-based version control systems, the build process imports .xpo files into empty layers in Dynamics AX. The values of the *CreatedBy*, *CreatedDateTime*, *ModifiedBy*, and *ModifiedDateTime* fields are set during this import process and therefore don't survive from build to build.

Dictionary API

The dictionary API is a type-safe reflection API that can reflect on many elements. The following code sample is a revision of the preceding example that finds inventory classes by using the dictionary API. You can't use this API to get information about when an element was modified. Instead, this example reflects a bit more on the class information and lists only abstract classes.

```
static void findAbstractInventoryClasses(Args _args)
{
    Dictionary dictionary = new Dictionary();
    int i;
    DictClass dictClass;

    for(i=1; i<=dictionary.classCnt(); i++)
    {
        dictClass = new DictClass(dictionary.classCnt2Id(i));

        if (dictClass.isAbstract() &&
            strStartsWith(dictClass.name(), 'Invent'))
        {
            info(strfmt("%1", dictClass.name()));
        }
    }
}
```

The *Dictionary* class provides information about which elements exist. With this information, you can instantiate a *DictClass* object that provides specific information about the class, such as whether the class is abstract, final, or an interface; which class it extends; whether it implements any interfaces; and what methods it includes. Notice that the *DictClass* class can also reflect on interfaces. Also notice how the class counter is converted into a class ID; this conversion is required because the IDs aren't listed consecutively.

When you run this job, you'll notice that it's much slower than the implementation that uses the table data API—at least the first time you run it! The job performs better after the information is cached.

Figure 15-1 shows the object model for the dictionary API. As you can see, some elements can't be reflected upon by using this API.

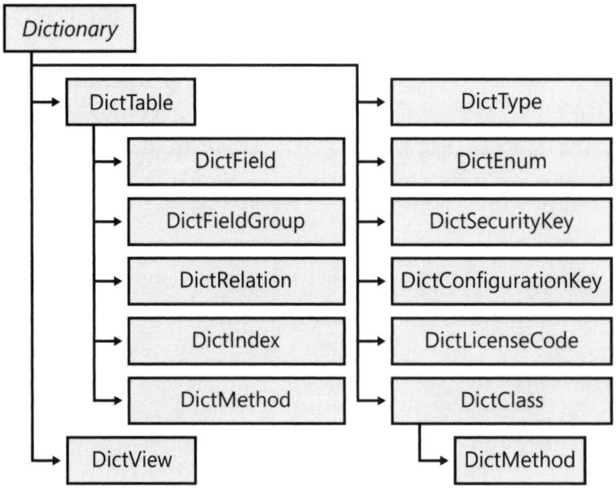

FIGURE 15-1 The object model for the dictionary reflection API

The following example revises the *FindStaticMethodsOnCustTable* from the preceding code by using the dictionary API. It also reports the method parameters of the methods.

```
static void findStaticMethodsOnCustTable(Args _args)
{
    DictTable dictTable = new DictTable(tableNum(CustTable));
    DictMethod dictMethod;
    int i;
    int j;
    str parameters;

    for (i=1; i<=dictTable.staticMethodCnt(); i++)
    {
        dictMethod = new DictMethod(
            UtilElementType::TableStaticMethod,
            dictTable.id(),
            dictTable.staticMethod(i));

        parameters = '';
        for (j=1; j<=dictMethod.parameterCnt(); j++)
        {
            parameters += strfmt("%1 %2",
                extendedTypeId2name(dictMethod.parameterId(j)),
                dictMethod.parameterName(j));

            if (j<dictMethod.parameterCnt())
                parameters += ', ';
        }
        info(strfmt("%1(%2)", dictMethod.name(), parameters));
    }
}
```

As mentioned earlier, reflection can also be used to invoke methods on objects. This example invokes the static *Find* method on the table *CustTable*.

```
static void invokeFindOnCustTable(Args _args)
{
    DictTable dictTable = new DictTable(tableNum(CustTable));
    CustTable customer;
;
    customer = dictTable.callStatic(
        tableStaticMethodStr(CustTable, Find), '1201');

    print customer.Name;    //Prints Sparrow Wholesales
    pause;
}
```

Notice the use of the intrinsic function *tableStaticMethodStr* to make a reference to the *Find* method.

You can also use this API to instantiate class and table objects. Suppose you want to select all records in a table with a given table ID. The following example shows you how.

```
void findRecords(TableId _tableId)
{
    DictTable dictTable = new DictTable(_tableId);
    Common common = dictTable.makeRecord();
    FieldId primaryKeyField = DictTable.primaryKeyField();

    while select common
    {
        info(strfmt("%1", common.(primaryKeyField)));
    }
}
```

First, notice the call to the *makeRecord* method that instantiates a table cursor object that points to the correct table. You can use the *select* statement to select records from the table. If you wanted to, you could also insert records by using the table cursor. Notice the syntax used to get a field value out of the cursor object; this syntax allows any field to be accessed by its field ID. This example simply prints the content of the primary key field. You can use the *makeObject* method on the class *DictClass* to create an object instance of a class.

All the classes in the dictionary API discussed so far are defined as system APIs. On top of each of these is an application-defined class that provides even more reflection capabilities. These classes are named *SysDict<Concept>*, and each class extends its counterpart in the system API. For example, *SysDictClass* extends *DictClass*.

Consider the following example. Table fields have a property that specifies whether the field is mandatory. The *DictField* class returns the value of the mandatory property as a bit set in the return value of its *flag* method. Testing of a bit set is somewhat cumbersome, and if the implementation of the flag changes, the consuming applications breaks. The *SysDictField* class encapsulates the bit-testing logic in a *mandatory* method. Here is how the method is used.

```
static void mandatoryFieldsOnCustTable(Args _args)
{
    DictTable dictTable = new DictTable(tableNum(CustTable));
    SysDictField sysDictField;
    int i;

    for (i=1; i<=dictTable.fieldCnt(); i++)
    {
        sysDictField = new SysDictField(
            dictTable.id(), dictTable.fieldCnt2Id(i));

        if (sysDictField.mandatory())
            info(sysDictField.name());
    }
}
```

You might also want to browse the *SysDict* classes for static methods. Many of these provide additional reflection information and better interfaces. For example, the *SysDictionary* class provides a *classes* method that has a collection of *SysDictClass* instances. You could use this method to simplify the earlier *findAbstractInventoryClasses* example.

Notice how all the examples instantiate the dictionary classes by using their *new* constructor. Some developers use an alternative way to instantiate the dictionary classes, but you should avoid it. Recall the hierarchy of the objects shown in Figure 15-1. A parent object can return an instance of a child object, as shown here.

```
DictTable dictTable = new DictTable(tableId);
DictField firstField, nextField;
firstField = dictTable.fieldObject(dictTable.fieldNext(0));
nextField = dictTable.fieldObject(dictTable.fieldNext(dictField.id()));
```

The primary reason to avoid this construct is that you can't substitute *Dict* classes with *SysDict* classes. If you ever need reflection methods available only on the *SysDict* classes, you must refactor the code. Writing the code so that it is easy to substitute the class makes refactoring easier and lowers the risk of introducing bugs in the refactoring process. Another reason to avoid this construct is the lack of API consistency. The examples used in this section that instantiate dictionary classes all follow the same structure, which is consistent for all the classes in the dictionary API.

Treenodes API

The two reflection APIs discussed so far both have limitations. The table data API can reflect only on the existence of elements and a small subset of element metadata. The dictionary API can reflect in a type-safe manner but only on the element types that are exposed through this API.

The treenodes API can reflect on everything, but as always, power comes at a cost. The treenodes API is harder to use than the other reflection APIs discussed. It can cause memory and performance problems, and it isn't type-safe.

The following example revises the example from the "Table Data API" section, now using the treenodes API to find inventory classes.

```
static void findInventoryClasses(Args _args)
{
    TreeNode classesNode = TreeNode::findNode(@'\Classes');
    TreeNodeIterator iterator = ClassesNode.AOTiterator();
    TreeNode classNode = iterator.next();
    ClassName className;

    while (classNode)
    {
        className = classNode.treeNodeName();
        if (strStartsWith(className, 'Invent'))
            info(strfmt("%1", className));

        classNode = iterator.next();
    }
}
```

First, notice how you find a node in the AOT based on the path as a literal. The *AOT* macro contains definitions for the primary AOT paths. For readability reasons, the examples in this chapter don't use the macro. Also notice the use of a *TreeNodeIterator* class to loop over the classes.

If you stay at the class level in the AOT, you don't encounter problems—but be careful if you go any deeper. Tree nodes in MorphX contain data that the Dynamics AX runtime doesn't manage, and nodes' memory isn't automatically deallocated. For each parent node that is expanded, you should call the *TreenodeRelease* method to free the memory. For an example of this, see the *doTreeNode* method on the *SysBpCheck* class.

The following small job prints the source code for the *doTreeNode* method by calling the *AOTgetSource* method on the *treenode* object for the *doTreeNode* method.

```
static void printSourceCode(Args _args)
{
    TreeNode treeNode =
        TreeNode::findNode(@'\Classes\SysBpCheck\doTreeNode');
;
    info(treeNode.AOTgetSource());
}
```

The treenodes API provides access to the source code of nodes in the AOT. You can use the class *ScannerClass* to turn the string that contains the source code into a sequence of compilable tokens.

The following code revises the preceding example to find mandatory fields on the table *CustTable*.

```
static void mandatoryFieldsOnCustTable(Args _args)
{
    TreeNode fieldsNode = TreeNode::findNode(
        @'\Data Dictionary\Tables\CustTable\Fields');

    TreeNode field = fieldsNode.AOTfirstChild();

    while (field)
    {
        if (field.AOTgetProperty('Mandatory') == 'Yes')
            info(field.treeNodeName());

        field = field.AOTnextSibling();
    }
}
```

Notice the alternate way of looping over subnodes. Both this and the iterator approach work equally well. The only way to determine whether a field is mandatory with this API is to know that your node models a field and that field nodes have a property named *Mandatory*, which is set to Yes (not to True) for mandatory fields.

Use the *Properties* macro when referring to property names. It contains text definitions for all property names. By using this macro, you avoid using literal names, as in the reference to *Mandatory* in the preceding example.

Unlike the dictionary API, which can't reflect all elements, the treenodes API reflects everything. The *SysDictMenu* class exploits this fact, providing a type-safe way to reflect on menus and menu items by wrapping information provided by the treenodes API in a type-safe API. The following job prints the structure of the *MainMenu* menu, which typically is shown in the navigation pane.

```
static void printMainMenu(Args _args)
{
    void reportLevel(SysDictMenu _sysDictMenu)
    {
        SysMenuEnumerator enumerator;

        if (_sysDictMenu.isMenuReference() ||
            _sysDictMenu.isMenu())
        {
            setPrefix(_sysDictMenu.label());
            enumerator = _sysDictMenu.getEnumerator();
            while (enumerator.moveNext())
                reportLevel(enumerator.current());
        }
        else
            info(_sysDictMenu.label());
    }

    reportLevel(SysDictMenu::newMainMenu());
}
```

Notice how the *setPrefix* function is used to capture the hierarchy and how the *reportLevel* function is called recursively.

The treenodes API also allows you to reflect on forms and reports, as well as their structure, properties, and methods. The Compare tool in MorphX uses this API to compare any node with any other node. The *SysTreeNode* class contains a *TreeNode* class and implements a cascade of interfaces, which makes *TreeNode* classes consumable for the Compare tool and the Version Control tool. The *SysTreeNode* class also contains a powerful set of static methods.

The *TreeNode* class is actually the base class of a larger hierarchy. You can cast instances to specialized *TreeNode* classes that provide more specific functionality. The hierarchy isn't fully consistent for all nodes. You can browse the hierarchy in the AOT by clicking System Documentation, clicking Classes, right-clicking TreeNode, pointing to Add-Ins, and then clicking Application Hierarchy.

The *xUtil* classes shown in the table data API examples contain methods for transitioning between the class paradigm of *TreeNode* classes and the table paradigm of *UtilElements* tables. Here is an example.

```
TreeNode node1 = TreeNode::findNode(@'\Data Dictionary\Tables\CustTable');
UtilElements utilElements = xUtilElements::findTreeNode(custTableNode);
TreeNode node2 = xUtilElements::getNodeInTree(utilElements);
```

Although we've covered only the reflection functionality of the treenodes API, you can use the API just as you would use the AOT designer. You can create new elements and modify properties and source code. The Wizard Wizard uses the treenodes API to generate the project, form, and class implementing the wizard functionality. You can also compile and get layered nodes and nodes from the Old application folder (located in Program Files\Microsoft Dynamics AX\5.0\Application\Appl\DynamicsAx1\Old). The capabilities that go beyond reflection are very powerful, but proceed with great care. Obtaining information in a non-type-safe manner requires caution, but writing in a non-type-safe manner can lead to cataclysmic situations.

Chapter 16
The Batch Framework

In this chapter:

The objectives of this chapter are to:

- Introduce the batch processing framework in Microsoft Dynamics AX 2009.
- Describe typical scenarios for using the Batch framework.
- Provide instructions for how to create batch tasks and batch jobs.
- Explain how to use Dynamics AX tools to manage and control the batch server exection process.
- Provide an overview of the X++ Batch API and examples of its usage.

Introduction

Microsoft extensively updated the framework used to process batch jobs—the Batch framework—for the Dynamics AX 2009 release. Among other enhancements, the Dynamics AX Batch framework is now server based; it gives system administrators and developers increased control over batch jobs and enables greater performance and reliability when those jobs are processed.

To support the new Batch framework, Dynamics AX has some new tools. The Batch Job designer form gives system administrators increased flexibility in the design, setup, and execution of complex batch jobs as well as the ability to add many batch tasks to a single batch job and to define the dependencies among those tasks. An enhanced Batch API gives X++ application developers more control over complex batch jobs along with the ability to process batch jobs directly from business logic.

This chapter introduces the Dynamics AX 2009 Batch framework, first explaining the main concepts behind it and then showing how businesses can use it to support key business scenarios. Next, the chapter walks through the process of creating and executing a batch job in the context of the Batch framework tools, and describes functionality that helps you manage batch jobs after they are scheduled. The process for configuring a batch server is also briefly described, and the chapter concludes with some tips for debugging a batch task.

> **Note** The intention of this chapter is to give you a solid overview of the concepts, tools, and processes in the new Batch framework. For in-depth procedures and more information, refer to the Microsoft Dynamics AX Server and Database Administration Guide available from *http://www.microsoft.com/downloads/en/default.aspx*. You can also find a wealth of batch-specific information in the Microsoft Dynamics 2009 software development kit (SDK).

Batch Processing in Dynamics AX

In batch processing, you create *batch jobs* to organize "batchable" tasks for processing, schedule and define the conditions under which the batch tasks are executed, add the tasks to a queue, and set them to run automatically on a batch server. After the execution is completed, the batch server logs the errors and sends alerts. For example, a batch job might involve printing reports, closing inventory, performing maintenance, or sending electronic documents using the Application Integration Framework (AIF)—at a specified time on a specified computer. When you use a batch job to process these types of resource-intensive tasks, you avoid slowing down the user's computer or the server during working hours.

In the following sections, we explain how each of these batch processing concepts are put into action in Dynamics AX.

Dynamics AX Batch Concepts

Table 16-1 describes how standard batch processing concepts are represented in Dynamics AX. We provide more information about each of these concepts later in this chapter.

TABLE 16-1 Batch Processing Concepts in Dynamics 2009

Batch Concept	In Dynamics AX 2009
Batch framework	An asynchronous server-based batch execution environment. The environment is capable of executing multiple batch tasks within a batch job, in parallel, across multiple instances of the Application Object Server (AOS). The Batch framework gives developers and administrators the flexibility to control the schedule and the order in which tasks are executed. For example, an administrator can set up a job to process invoices automatically at the end of every month on a specific AOS, and set up a different sequence of tasks depending on whether an earlier task succeeds or fails. The Batch framework also provides transaction control, logging, and alerting mechanisms.

Batch Concept	In Dynamics AX 2009
Batch task	A batch-enabled class. A class must be enabled for batch processing before it can run as a batch task, and any class that is batch-enabled can execute as a batch task. The section "Batch-Enabling a Class" later in this chapter provides more information on this topic. The Dynamics AX classes that are used for batch tasks are designated to run on either the client or the server. Tasks that run on the server can run automatically as part of a batch job, regardless of whether a client is open. However, tasks that run on the client must be run manually by using the Batch processing form.
Batch job	A complete process that achieves a goal, such as printing a report or performing the inventory closing process. A batch job is made up of one or more tasks.
Batch group	An attribute of a batch task that allows the administrator to determine which AOS runs the job. Batch groups are used to direct batch tasks to specific servers. If a new task is created, by default it is assigned to an "empty" batch group, which is a valid batch group.
Batch server	An instance of the AOS that processes batch jobs. Read more about the AOS in Chapter 1, "Architectural Overview," and about configuring an AOS to be a batch server later in this chapter.

Batch Framework Capabilities

As a system administrator or developer, you can use the new server-based Batch framework to create larger, more complex batch jobs than before. You can also monitor the status of batch jobs and control which AOS runs the batch job and at what time. The following list includes specific tasks you can do with the new Batch framework capabilities in Dynamics AX 2009:

- Run server-based batch jobs using the security credentials of the user who created the job. Running the batch job under the credentials of the user who created the job provides the benefits of security isolation.
- Create dependencies between batch tasks, and control the order in which the tasks are executed. The tasks in a batch job can run sequentially or simultaneously. You can set up a different sequence of tasks, depending on whether an earlier task succeeds or fails.
- Set the time at which the batch job is executed, and specify which AOS executes the batch job. The servers in your environment might have different software installed or might be available at different times of the day. You can select the most appropriate server on which to run a batch job using the Batch Group attribute.
- Create recurrence patterns for batch jobs. Some batch jobs need to be run on a recurring basis. For example, your company might need to process invoices automatically at the end of every month.

- Monitor the batch job. You can ask for an alert to be sent when a batch job succeeds or fails, or just when it finishes.
- Check the status, cancel, or review the history of the batch job. After a batch job has been processed, you can view its history, including any messages encountered while running the job.

We cover these capabilities in more detail throughout the rest of this chapter.

Performance

Along with more complex and larger batch jobs comes the need for performance enhancements to the Batch framework. The Dynamics AX 2009 Batch framework provides parallel execution to improve performance for long-running processes.

Microsoft developers use the Batch framework as a foundation for many performance-critical processes, such as maximizing hardware scalability during data upgrade and maximizing posting throughput during journal posting. The white paper "Journal Batch Posting," available at *http://www.microsoft.com/downloads/en/default.aspx*, describes many of the ways in which Microsoft uses the Batch framework.

Because it is a server-based component, the Batch framework enables you to design multithreading server processes in a controlled manner. By configuring the number of parallel execution threads, defining the set and order of tasks for processing, and setting the execution schedule, you can achieve greater scalability across your hardware. In addition, your batch tasks are running securely on a server, so you can process them without having a client open.

Common Uses of Batch Processing

Businesses typically want to create batch jobs to address the following kinds of needs:

- **To enable scheduling flexibility** The Batch framework can perform periodic data clean-up jobs or run invoice processing on a regular schedule. To run invoice processing at the end of every month, for example, you could set up a recurring batch job that runs at midnight on the last working day of each month and selects the invoice processing job from the list of available jobs. You could then save the schedule (along with its batch job), and the system automatically picks up the job at the specified time and executes it without having to open the client.
- **To control task execution order** With the Batch framework, you can develop a workflow or perform a complex data upgrade in an order you choose. When creating a new batch job and adding tasks to the job, you can set up dependencies between the jobs and create a dependency tree that ensures that certain tasks run in sequence while others run in parallel.

- **To enable different processing if a particular task succeeds or fails** Task processing based on decision trees can help you implement a reliable way of processing data. The Batch framework allows developers or system administrators to set up dependencies between tasks such that different tasks are executed depending on whether a particular task succeeds or fails. (Figure 16-4, later in the chapter, shows an example of a dependency tree.) The system administrator or developer can also set up alerts to be notified if a job fails for any reason.
- **To improve performance using multithreading** Multithreading ensures that your processor's capabilities are fully utilized, which is particularly important for long-running processes like inventory closing. You can gain additional performance enhancements by breaking a process into separate subjobs and executing them against different AOS instances, increasing throughput and reducing overall execution time.
- **To gain advanced logging capabilities** The Batch framework lets you see errors or exceptions thrown during the last run of the batch and to see how long a process takes to execute. Advanced logging capabilities are also useful for performance benchmarking and security auditing.

Batch-Enabling a Class

As mentioned earlier in the chapter, each batch task is a batch-enabled class, and a class must be enabled for batch processing before it can be scheduled for execution as a batch task. The classes used for batch tasks are designated to run on either the client or the server. Tasks that run on the server can run automatically as part of a batch job, regardless of whether a client is open. Tasks that run on the client, however, must be run manually via the Batch processing form, which is in the Dynamics AX basic module, at Periodic\Batch\Processing.

Many classes included with Dynamics AX 2009 are already enabled for batch processing. You can also design a class that you create for execution within the Batch framework, as shown in the following example.

To allow your class to run as a batch task, you have to extend it from the *RunBaseBatch* class.

```
public class ExampleBatchTask extends RunBaseBatch
```

The *RunBaseBatch* class itself is an extension of the *RunBase* framework, so your batch class must adhere to the patterns and guidelines of the *RunBase*-extended classes. (For more information, refer to the "*RunBase* Framework Extension" section in Chapter 6, "Extending Dynamics AX.")

To convert a class so that it's batchable, you need to use the pack-unpack pattern and implement the methods *pack* and *unpack* to allow a class to be serialized. When a batch task gets created, its member variables are saved in a container using the *pack* method and stored in the *Batch* table. Later, when the batch server picks up the task for execution, it restores class member variables from the container using the *unpack* method, so it's important to provide a correct list of variables necessary for class execution. If any member variable isn't packable, the class can't be packed and reinstantiated to the same state.

Following is an example of the *pack* and *unpack* methods.

```
public container pack()
{
    return [#CurrentVersion,#CurrentList];
}

public boolean unpack(container packedClass)
{
    Version version     = RunBase::getVersion(packedClass);
    switch (version)
    {
        case #CurrentVersion:
            [version,#CurrentList] = packedClass;
            break;
        default:
            return false;
    }
    return true;
}
```

The macros *#CurrentList* and *#CurrentVersion* referenced in the preceding code must be defined in the class declaration. *#CurrentList* is a macro holding a list of the class member variables to pack, as shown here.

```
    #define.CurrentVersion(1)
    #localmacro.CurrentList
         methodVariable1,
     methodVariable2
    #endmacro
```

You must implement the core logic of your batch class in the *run* method. If your batch class is designed to be executed on the server, there are some limitations on the operations you can use in the *run* method. For example, you can't call any client logic or dialogs. However, you can still use Infolog classes—all Infolog and exception error messages are captured during batch class execution and stored in the *Batch* table.

You can also implement some *RunBaseBatch*-specific methods in your class to control its behavior as a batch task:

- ***runsImpersonated*** Determines whether the batch task is run on the server or on a client. The base method always returns true, which means that the batch must run under the authority of the person who scheduled the batch and that no client session is involved.

> **Note** You can also verify whether a batch task runs on an AOS or client by selecting the Run Location field in the Batch Tasks form. It's a good idea to write your batch job to be executed on a server to take advantage of the Dynamics AX 2009 batch features for servers.

- ***canGoBatchJournal*** Determines whether the batch task class appears in the list of available classes when you create a new batch task using the Batch task form. See the "Add a Task to a Batch Job" section later in this chapter for an example using *canGoBatchJournal*.

Creating a Batch Job

You can create a batch job in three different ways in Dynamics AX: from the dialog box of a batch-enabled class, using the Batch Job designer form, or using the Batch Developer API.

The technique you use depends on the size and complexity of your batch job. A simple batch job consisting of a single task with no dependencies on other tasks would typically be created from the dialog box of a batch-enabled class; a more complex batch job composed of several batch tasks that might have dependencies is created using the Batch Job form; and highly complex and very large batch jobs, or those that need to be integrated with other business logic, are created from the Batch Developer API. In the following subsections, we provide an example in each category.

From the Dialog Box of a Class

The simplest way to execute a class as a batch job is to select the Batch Processing check box on the Batch tab of your class's dialog box, as shown for the Calendar Cleanup class dialog box in Figure 16-1. If you enable that option and click OK, the class is saved as a new batch job with one task. The batch job doesn't run immediately; instead, it runs at the date and time you set, and with the frequency you indicate, in the Recurrence form.

> **Tip** You can remove recurrence from a batch job by clicking Functions and then Remove Recurrence on the Batch Job form.

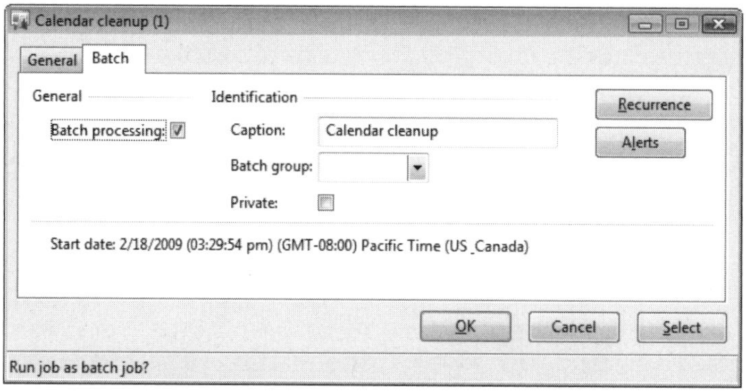

FIGURE 16-1 Example of the batch processing tab on a class

Two other controls in the dialog box are of particular interest: the Batch Group attribute and the Alerts button.

- **Batch Group** This batch-task attribute allows an administrator to determine which AOS runs the task, how many tasks an AOS can run in parallel, and on which servers a task can be executed.
- **Alerts** This functionality sends an alert when a batch job ends successfully, fails, or is canceled. Alerts are particularly helpful for monitoring jobs that run on the server outside of business hours. You can set up alerts for the job by clicking the Alerts button, choosing the conditions for the alert, and saving your choices. The system stores the alert rule and triggers it when the conditions are met.

From the Batch Job Form

You use the Batch Job form for jobs that include many tasks that might have a complex set of dependencies. You can use this form to create a batch job, add tasks to it, and set up dependencies between tasks. The Batch Job form is accessed through the Dynamics AX basic module: Inquiries\Batch Job.

Create a Batch Job

Creating a batch job from the Batch Job form is straightforward. Press Ctrl+N to create a new batch job, and then enter the details for the job: a description and the date and time at which you want the job to start.

> **Note** If you don't enter a date and time, the current date and time are entered automatically.

You can also set up Recurrence for the batch job by clicking the Recurrence button and entering a range and pattern for the recurrence. Make sure to save the batch job by pressing Ctrl+S.

After you create the batch job, you add tasks to it and any dependencies the tasks have.

Figure 16-2 shows the Batch Job form.

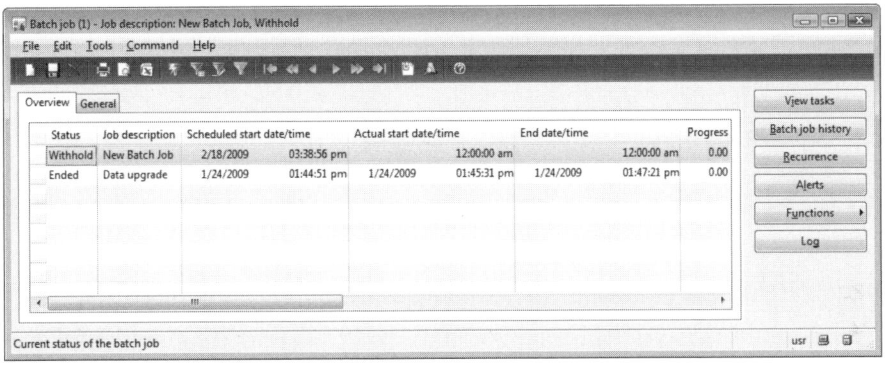

FIGURE 16-2 Batch Job form

Add a Task to a Batch Job

After you create a batch job, you can start adding tasks to it and creating dependencies between them by using the Batch Tasks form. The Batch Tasks form opens when you click the View Tasks button on the Batch Job form.

> **Note** You can open the Batch Tasks form from several places. For example, you can open it by clicking Batch Jobs in the main menu or by choosing Batch Job List—User. Both menu items open the same form, but information presented to the user in the Batch Tasks form differs depending on which menu item you use to open it.

Depending on how you open the Batch Tasks form and your level of access, you can view either the batch jobs that you have created or all batch jobs that have been scheduled in the system.

From the Batch Tasks form, you can also change the status of batch tasks or delete tasks that are no longer needed. Press Ctrl+N to create a new task, and then specify the data associated with that task: enter a description for the task in the Task Description field, select the company in which the task runs in the Company Accounts field, and in the Class Name field, select the process you want the task to run—classes appear in the list (a look-up list that appears, containing all available classes) only if the property *CanGoBatchJournal* is enabled.

If necessary, select a batch group for the task, and then make sure you save the task by pressing Ctrl+S.

> **Note** Some classes are designated to run on the client. You can add client tasks to a batch job. However, you must run client tasks manually by using the Set Up Batch Processing form, available in the Dynamics AX basic module: Periodic\Batch\Processing. In addition, client tasks must belong to a batch group.

Figure 16-3 shows the Batch Tasks designer form.

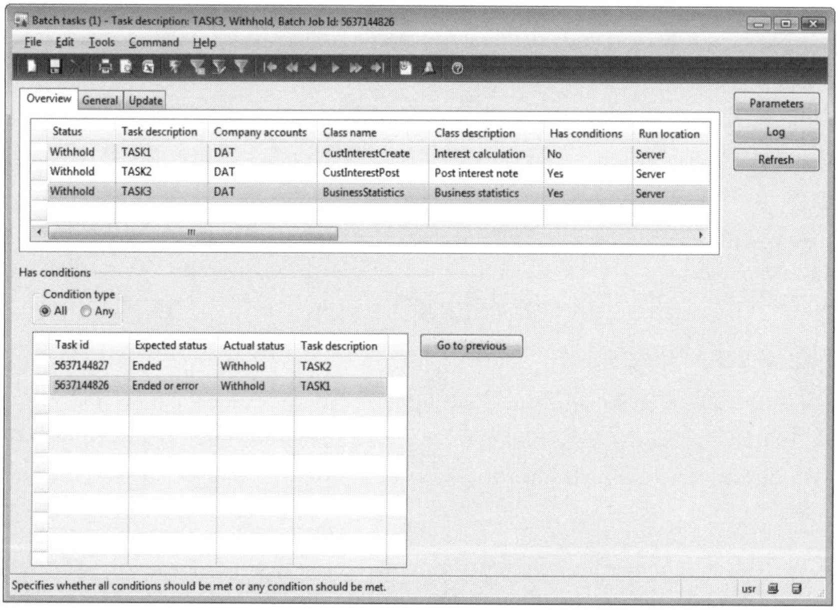

FIGURE 16-3 Batch Tasks designer form

Class parameters As we've said, each batch task represents a batch-enabled class. Sometimes you need to set up parameters for that class. For example, you might need to specify posting parameters for invoice posting. To do that, click the Parameters button in the Batch Tasks form. A dialog box specific to the selected class is displayed. After you specify the necessary parameters and click OK, the class parameters are packed and saved in the *Batch* table and are restored during class execution.

Define dependencies between tasks After you've created the batch job and added tasks to it, you can use the Batch Tasks designer form to define dependencies between the tasks. If no dependencies or conditions are defined within a job, the batch server schedules all tasks in parallel, up to a maximum you configure with the parameter Maximum Batch Threads in the Server Configuration form.

If you need to use advanced sequencing for batch tasks to accommodate your business process flow requirements, you can use the Batch Task designer or Batch Developer API, both of which are included in the Batch framework. You can use these tools to construct complex dependency trees, which allow you to schedule batch jobs tasks in parallel, add multiple dependencies between jobs tasks, choose different execution paths based on the results of the previous job task, and so on.

To control execution order, you can make a task dependent on another task in the same job, and set up conditions for the execution of both tasks.

For example, consider the job JOB1, with seven tasks: TASK1, TASK2, TASK3, TASK4, TASK5, TASK6, and TASK7:

- TASK1 is the first task.
- TASK2 runs ON COMPLETION ("Ended or Error") of TASK1 (regardless of the success or failure of TASK1).
- TASK3 runs ON SUCCESS ("Ended") of TASK2.
- TASK4 runs ON SUCCESS ("Ended") of TASK2.
- TASK5 runs ON FAILURE ("Error") of TASK2.
- TASK6 runs ON FAILURE ("Error") of TASK3.
- TASK7 runs ON SUCCESS ("Ended") of both TASK3 and TASK4.

Figure 16-4 shows the dependency tree for JOB1.

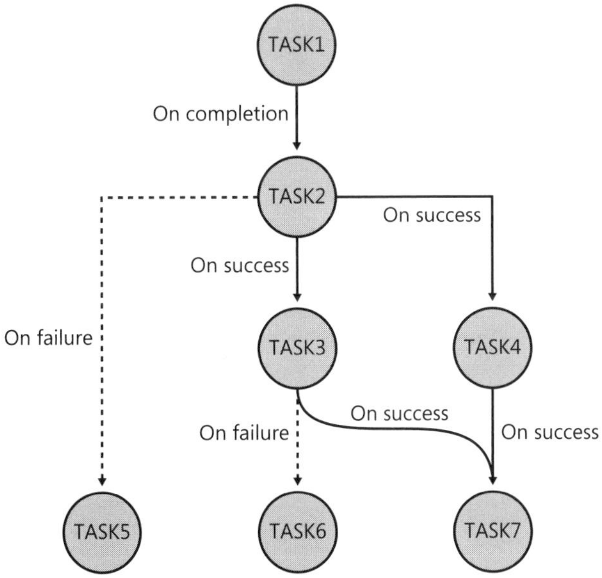

FIGURE 16-4 Batch task dependency tree

To define these task dependencies and to tell the system how to handle them, select a child task (for example, TASK2 from the preceding list), click the Has Conditions grid in the Batch Tasks form, and follow these steps:

1. Press Ctrl+N to create a new condition.
2. Select the task ID of the parent task, such as TASK1.
3. Select the expected status that the parent task must reach before the dependent task can run. For example, TASK2 starts when TASK1 becomes "Ended or Error."
4. Press Ctrl+S to save the condition.
5. If you've entered more than one condition and if all conditions must be met before the dependent task can run, select a condition type of All.
6. Select a condition type of Any if the dependent task can run after any of the conditions are met.

You can also choose how the system handles task failures in the Batch Tasks designer form. To ignore the failure of a specific task, select Ignore Task Failure for that task. If this option is selected, the failure of the task doesn't cause the job to fail. You can also use the Maximum Retries field to specify the number of times a task should be retried before it is considered to have failed.

Using the Batch API

For advanced scenarios requiring complex or large batch jobs, such as inventory closing or data upgrades, the batch server framework provides an X++ API that enables developers to create or modify batch jobs, tasks, and their dependencies as needed as well as to dynamically create run-time batch tasks on the fly. This flexible API helps automate task creation and integrate batch processing into other business processes. It can also be useful when your batch job or task requires some additional logic.

Create a Batch Job

First, you have to create a Batch Job instance class named *BatchHeader*.

```
batchHeader = BatchHeader::construct();
```

Note When you construct an instance of the *BatchHeader* class, no batch jobs are physically created in the system yet. All operations are performed in memory until you call the *batchHeader.save* function, which saves your changes in the database.

You can also construct a *BatchHeader* object for an existing *BatchJob* by providing an optional *batchJobId* parameter to the *construct* method, as shown here.

```
batchHeader = BatchHeader::construct(this.parmCurrentBatch().BatchJobId);
```

The *BatchHeader* class allows you to access and modify most *BatchJob* parameters using *parm* methods. For example, you can set up recurrence and alerts for your batch job as shown in the following example.

```
// Set the batch recurrence
sysRecurrenceData = SysRecurrence::defaultRecurrence();
sysRecurrenceData = SysRecurrence::setRecurrenceStartDateTime(sysRecurrenceData,
DateTimeUtil::utcNow());
sysRecurrenceData = SysRecurrence::setRecurrenceNoEnd(sysRecurrenceData);
sysRecurrenceData = SysRecurrence::setRecurrenceUnit(sysRecurrenceData,
SysRecurrenceUnit::Hour, 1);
batchHeader.parmRecurrenceData(sysRecurrenceData);
// Set the batch alert configurations
batchHeader.parmAlerts(NoYes::No, NoYes::Yes, NoYes::No, NoYes::No, NoYes::No);
```

Add a Task to the Batch Job

After you create a batch job using the Batch API, you can add tasks to it by calling the *addTask* method. The first parameter for this method is an instance of a batch-enabled class that will be scheduled for execution as a batch task.

```
void addTask(Batchable batchTask,
 [BatchConstraintType constraintType])
```

Another way to create a task is to use the method *addRuntimeTask*, which creates a dynamic batch task. It exists only for the current run, and it gets copied into the history tables and deleted at the end of the run. It copies settings such as batch group and child dependencies from the *inheritFromTaskId* task.

```
void addRuntimeTask(Batchable batchTask,
RecId inheritFromTaskId,
[BatchConstraintType constraintType])
```

Define Dependencies Between Tasks

After you add tasks, you can use the Batch API to specify any dependencies between them. The *BatchHeader* class provides the method *addDependency*, which you can use to define a dependency between the tasks *batchTaskToRun* and *dependsOnBatchTask*.

The optional parameter *batchStatus* allows you to specify the type of the dependency. By default a dependency of type *BatchDependencyStatus::Finished* is created, which means that the task starts execution only if the task which it depends on finishes successfully. Other allowed options are *BatchDependencyStatus::Error* (the task will start execution if the preceding task finished with an error) and *BatchDependencyStatus::FinishedOrError* (the preceding task finished processing with any status result).

```
public BatchDependency addDependency(
    Batchable batchTaskToRun,
    Batchable dependsOnBatchTask,
   [BatchDependencyStatus batchStatus])
```

Save a Batch Job

After you have finished defining the batch job, it's important to call the *batchHeader.save* method. Under the hood, the *save* method inserts records into the *BatchJob*, *Batch*, and *BatchConstraints* tables where the batch server can automatically pick them up for execution. However, you must run client tasks manually by using the Set Up Batch Processing form (from the Dynamics AX basic module, click Periodic\Batch\Processing).

Example of a Batch Job

The following example shows how you can create a batch job and two batch tasks using the Batch API.

```
static void ExampleSchedulingJob (Args _args)
{
    BatchHeader       batchHeader;
    RunBaseBatch batchTask;
    ;
    // create batch header
    batchHeader = BatchHeader::construct();
       // create and add batch tasks
    batchTask1 = new ExampleBatchTask();
    batchTask1.parmCaption("Example batch job 1");
    batchHeader.addTask(batchTask1);

    batchTask2 = new ExampleBatchTask();
    batchTask2.parmCaption("Example batch job 2");
```

```
    batchHeader.addTask(batchTask2);
    // add dependencies between batch tasks
        batchHeader.addDependency(batchTask1, batchTask2);
      // save batch job in the database
    batchHeader.save();
}
```

For more examples on programmatic batch job creation, you can refer to the Microsoft Dynamics AX 2009 SDK section "Walkthrough: Extending *RunBaseBatch* Class to Create and Run a Batch" at *http://msdn.microsoft.com/en-us/library/cc636647.aspx*.

Managing the Batch Server Execution Process

Before a batch job can be executed on an AOS, you must configure the AOS as a batch server and set up the batch groups that tell the system which AOS needs to execute the job. In addition to these initial configuration duties, you'll likely need to manage the batch tasks and jobs: checking status, reviewing history, and sometimes canceling a batch job. You'll probably need to debug a batch task at some point as well. In the following section, we describe how to configure an AOS as a batch server, set up batch groups, manage batch jobs, and debug a batch task.

Set Up Server Configuration

You can configure an AOS to be a batch server, including specifying when the batch server is available for processing and how many tasks it can run, using the Server Configuration form. The Server Configuration form is in Administration\Setup\Server Configuration. Note that the first AOS is automatically designated as a batch server. Figure 16-5 shows the Server Configuration form.

> **Tip** Use multiple batch servers to increase throughput and reduce the amount of time it takes to run batches.

1. On the Overview tab, select a server.
2. Select Is Batch Server to enable batch processing on the server, as shown in Figure 16-5.

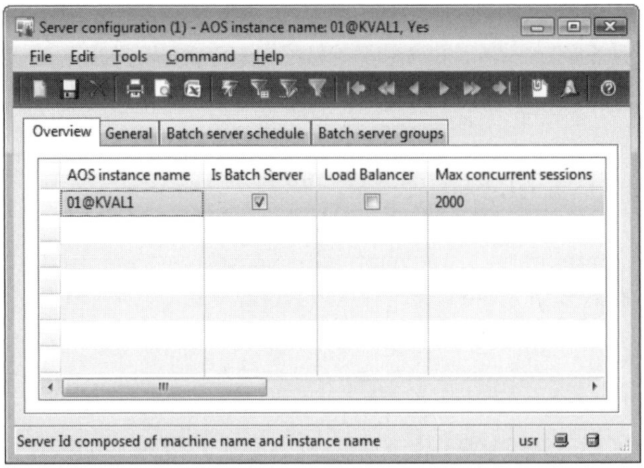

FIGURE 16-5 Server Configuration form

3. On the Batch Server Schedule tab, enter the maximum number of batch tasks that can be run on the AOS instance at one time. The server continues to pick up tasks from the queue until it reaches its maximum.
4. Enter a starting time in the Start Time field and an ending time in the End Time field to schedule the batch processing. Press Ctrl+N to enter an additional time period.

> **Tip** It's a good idea to exclude a server from batch processing when it is busy with regular transaction processing. You can set server schedules so that each AOS is available for user traffic during the day and for batch traffic overnight. Keep in mind that if the server is running a task when its batch processing availability ends, the task continues running to completion. However, the server doesn't pick up any more tasks from the queue.

5. On the Batch Server Groups tab, use the arrow buttons to specify the batch groups that can run on the selected server.

Create a Batch Group

A batch group is an attribute of a batch task that allows a user (typically a system administrator) to determine which AOS runs the batch job. In this section, we show you how to create a batch group so that it can be selected from the Batch Server Groups tab in the Server Configuration form. You create batch groups on the Batch Group form, which is in Administration\Setup\Batch Group.

> **Note** For client tasks to be run manually from the Set Up Batch Processing form, they must be assigned to batch groups.

To create a batch group, press Ctrl+N in the Batch Group form, and then type a name and description for the batch group. The Batch Group form is shown in Figure 16-6.

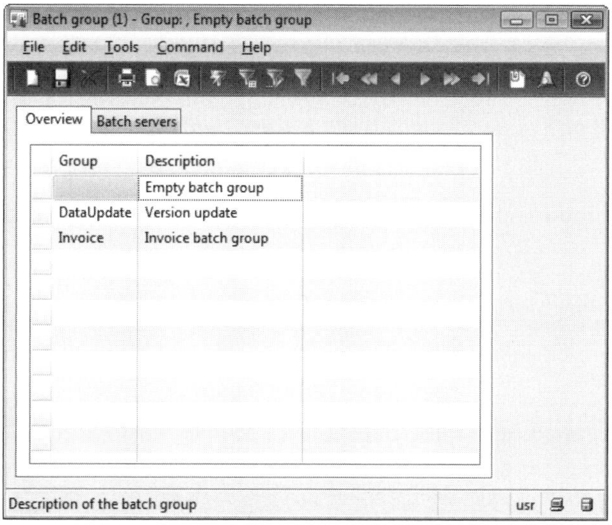

FIGURE 16-6 Batch Group form

Note An empty Batch Group exists in the system by default and can't be removed.

After you create a batch group, you have to set it up to run server batch tasks on a specific server. Select the appropriate batch group in the Batch Groups form, and then follow these steps:

1. Click the Batch Servers tab. The Selected Servers list displays the AOS instances that the selected group is specified to run on. The Remaining Servers list displays the remaining AOS instances that are available as batch servers.
2. Click the arrow buttons to select additional servers or remove servers from the Selected Servers list.

Manage Batch Jobs

Once you've created and scheduled a batch job, you might want to check its status, review its history, or even cancel it. To verify the status of batch jobs or to cancel them, use the Batch Job form, which is at Basic\Inquiries\Batch Job.

Batch Job Status

If jobs are in progress, you can view their percentage complete. You can also see whether any jobs are scheduled to start soon.

You can view the status of all batch jobs in the system or only the jobs that you ordered. You can change the status of batch jobs by selecting the batch job from the list and then following these steps:

1. Click Functions, and then click Change Status.
2. In the Select New Status dialog box, select the new status for the job. For example, if the batch job status is Waiting, temporarily remove the batch job from the waiting list by changing the status to Withhold.

> **Tip** If an error occurs, restart the job by changing the status to Waiting. If you want to rerun a job that has ended, change the status from Ended to Waiting.

Control Maximum Retries

When an AOS restarts and is configured to run batch jobs, it immediately attempts to recover from previous runs if it finds batch tasks in the Executing state. These tasks go back to the status Ready, and their Actual Retries field, in the Update tab in the Batch Tasks form, increases by one.

You use Maximum Retries to configure how many times an AOS can rerun a batch task that has failed because of infrastructure problems, such as a power outage or a server crash. By default, this value is set to 1; you can change it in the General tab of the Batch Tasks form. When the Actual Retries field in the Update tab exceeds the maximum number of retries, the AOS fails the batch task instead of attempting to run it again. If this happens, the recurrence of the batch job is not honored, and the status of the batch job is set to either Success or Error.

Cancel a Batch Job

You can cancel a batch job by changing its status to Canceling in the Batch Job form. If the job is currently executing, the tasks in the Waiting or Ready state are changed to Not Run, and currently executing tasks are interrupted and their status changed to Canceled.

Review the Batch Job History

After a batch job has finished running, you can view its history, including any messages encountered while running the batch job, in the Batch Job History form, which is in the Dynamics AX basic module: Inquiries\Batch Job History.

You can also view the logs for each batch job in the Batch Job History form.

- To view log information for the whole batch, select a batch job and then click Log.
- To view log information for individual tasks, select a batch job and then click View Tasks. In the Batch History List form, select a task and click Log.

> **Tip** You can change the batch job settings to log onto the history tables Always (default), On Error, or Never. Use On Error or Never to save disk space for batch jobs that are constantly running. This option is in the General tab of the Batch Job form.

Debug a Batch Task

Because server batch tasks run in noninteractive mode, to debug a server batch task, you have to perform additional steps to configure your Dynamics AX server and client as well as set up the usual debug breakpoint steps.

> **Note** Running in *noninteractive* mode means that a user can't interact directly with a batch task while it's running. So you can't, for example, present a dialog box to gather user input once a batch task has started executing on a server.

You first configure the AOS for batch debugging, and then you configure the Dynamics AX client for batch debugging. For both tasks, you use the Server Configuration Utility, which you access through All Programs\Administrative Tools\Microsoft Dynamics AX Server Configuration. For configuration specifics, consult the Microsoft Dynamics AX 2009 SDK, available on MSDN.

Configure the AOS for Batch Debugging

You can use the Dynamics AX Server Configuration Utility to configure the AOS for batch debugging. The utility is available on the machine where you installed your AOS, from All Programs\Administrative Tools\Microsoft Dynamics AX 2009 Server Configuration.

1. In the Server Configuration Utility, select the check boxes for the following:
    - Enable Breakpoints To Debug X++ Code Running On This Server
    - Enable Global Breakpoints To Debug X++ Code Running In Batch Jobs
2. Click OK to close the utility, and then restart the AOS.

Figure 16-7 shows the Dynamics AX 2009 Server Configuration Utility.

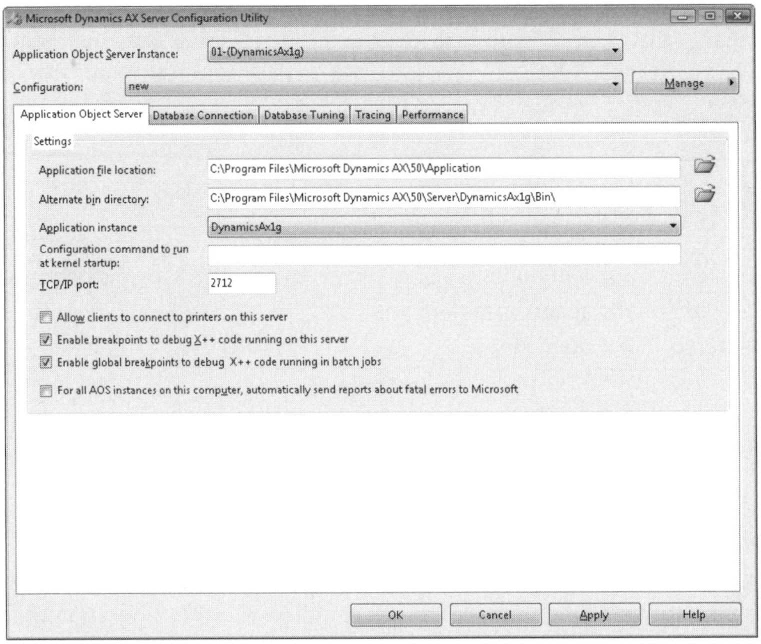

FIGURE 16-7 Microsoft Dynamics AX 2009 Server Configuration Utility

Configure the Client for Batch Debugging

To configure the client for batch debugging, you use the Microsoft Dynamics AX 2009 Configuration Utility. (This utility is different than the Server Configuration Utility.) Figure 16-8 shows the Microsoft Dynamics AX Configuration Utility.

The Configuration Utility is available from All Programs\Administrative Tools\Microsoft Dynamics AX 2009\Configuration. (The line might not specify server versus client.)

1. In the Configuration Utility, select the check box for Enable Global Breakpoints To Debug Code Running In The Business Connector Or Client.
2. Click OK to close the utility.

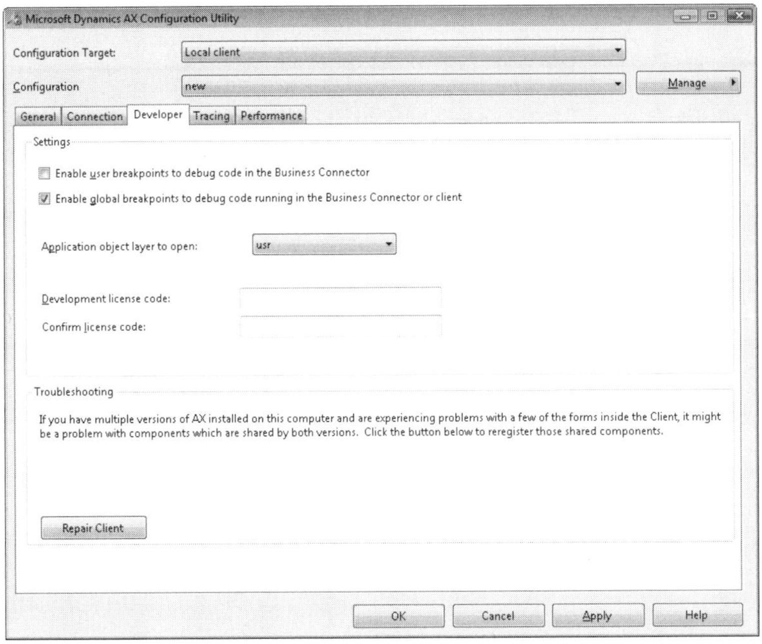

FIGURE 16-8 Microsoft Dynamics AX 2009 Configuration Utility

Run AxDebug.exe on the Client Computer

In Windows Explorer, locate the Client\Bin\Directory of your Dynamics AX installation. Double-click the AxDebug.exe program to run it. Now you're ready to debug batch jobs running on the server.

> **Note** For more information about debugging server-side batch jobs, refer to the Microsoft Dynamics AX 2009 SDK section "Walkthrough: Debugging a Batch that Runs on the AOS" at *http://msdn.microsoft.com/en-us/library/cc588679.aspx.*

Chapter 17

The Application Integration Framework

In this chapter:

The objectives of this chapter are to:

- Introduce common software integration scenarios.
- Show how the Microsoft Dynamics AX 2009 Application Integration Framework (AIF) can be applied to integration scenarios.
- Introduce the Dynamics AX 2009 services and service references.
- Explain how to exchange XML messages with other applications and trading partners.
- Discuss the security considerations when integrating other software with Dynamics AX.

Introduction

Once you implement Dynamics AX in a production environment, you immediately benefit from using it to manage your business. To help you realize the full potential of Dynamics AX, you can use the Application Integration Framework (AIF) to integrate your company's other software systems and those of your trading partners with Dynamics AX.

This chapter describes the AIF and the integration scenarios it enables. The chapter starts with a description of the AIF and the services that comprise it. It then explores the Dynamics AX services in greater depth—explaining what they are and how they're created, published, and configured. The final section of the chapter discusses how to consume Dynamics AX services, Dynamics AX Web services, and external Web services. Troubleshooting tips, guidance on security, and pointers to other documentation sources that have detailed procedures for implementing AIF appear throughout the chapter.

> **Note** In this chapter, we discuss configuration and administration tasks only where necessary to help you better understand the development scenarios. For additional details, refer to the Microsoft Dynamics AX 2009 documentation on TechNet.

Overview of the Application Integration Framework

The AIF provides a programming model, tools, and infrastructure support for services-based integration of application functionality and data with Dynamics AX.

The published AIF interfaces to Dynamics AX are compliant with industry standards and based on core Microsoft technologies including the Windows software development kit (SDK) for Windows Server 2008, Microsoft .NET Framework 3.5, Windows Communication Foundation (WCF), Microsoft Message Queuing (MSMQ), and Microsoft BizTalk Server.

In addition to the built-in programming model and tools for implementing integration scenarios, Dynamics AX also has the following functionality:

- Provides a set of bindings to transport technologies that can be used to exchange data with Dynamics AX, such as MSMQ, BizTalk Server, and synchronous (WCF) Web services.
- Supports the exchange of XML files through configurable file locations.
- Through *service references*, provides an abstraction and related tools for integrating Dynamics AX with external applications (services) through X++ code (software), allowing partners to reap the benefits of Software-plus-Services, popularly known as S+S.

Overview Scenarios

Once your company has deployed Dynamics AX 2009, you can benefit from automating your business processes. To realize the full potential of Dynamics AX 2009 and maximum return on investment (ROI) of your Dynamics AX 2009 deployment, however, you should consider automating interactions between Dynamics AX 2009 and the other software in your company and in the companies of your trading partners.

Many business scenarios require reading or manipulating information that is stored in Dynamics AX or in external applications. Figure 17-1 shows several of the scenarios in which people access information managed in Dynamics AX to accomplish a business task. It also shows sample scenarios in which Dynamics AX accesses information that external applications manage. The large arrows show who accesses information.

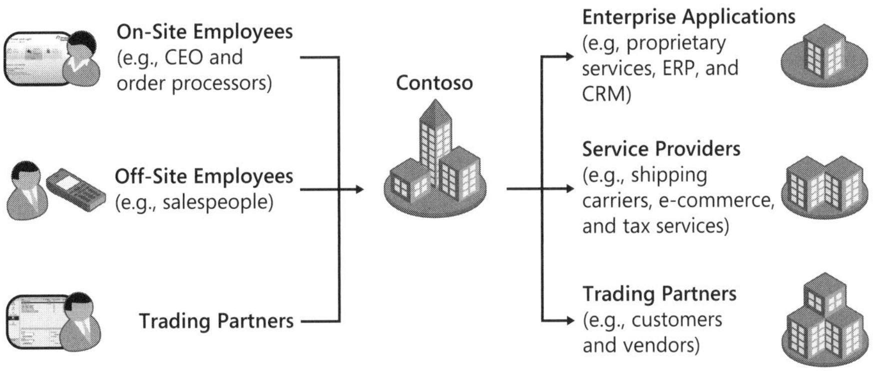

FIGURE 17-1 Common integration scenarios

Here are the sample scenarios with a few more details:

- The company's CEO analyzes sales data in Microsoft Office Excel.
- A salesperson who is visiting a prospect's site uses a Microsoft Office InfoPath form to create a new customer account and the first sales order. The salesperson is required to run both background and credit checks on the new customer before entering the data.
- A sales processor enters a sales order and uses customer records that are stored in a CRM application to populate the customer section of the order.
- An operations worker needs to find the most economical shipping rate for a certain shipment given the delivery requirements specified by the customer.
- A trading partner manages its sales orders and inquires about the status of its orders using its own custom application.
- An order processor needs to send an invoice to a trading partner.

These tasks are often done manually—without integrating Dynamics AX with other applications and business processes—but manual processes don't scale well. Manual processing can also adversely affect the quality of the data managed in Dynamics AX, such as when data is entered incorrectly. In the following section, we show you how the AIF can help you automate these interactions and further streamline your business processes.

Overview of Dynamics AX Services

If you look at Figure 17-1 again, you can see that the people on the left side of the figure use applications that interact with the Dynamics AX data store. They send requests (e.g., to read a sales order) into Dynamics AX and in most cases expect a response from Dynamics AX (e.g., the requested sales order instance). For these applications to be able to submit requests into Dynamics AX, Dynamics AX must expose service interfaces that can receive requests. These service interfaces are part of Dynamics AX services, which can be created, managed, and published through the AIF.

Dynamics AX services are a service-oriented abstraction used to encapsulate Dynamics AX business logic—such as functionality to create a sales order in Dynamics AX—in a reusable way. These services can be used to participate in *service-oriented architecture* (SOA).

> **Note** Service-oriented architecture (SOA) is a significant area of software development. A complete discussion of SOA is outside the scope of this book, and in this chapter we assume you have a fundamental understanding of SOA concepts. Good information on SOA abounds, including the Organization for the Advancement of Structured Information Standards (OASIS) specification "Reference Model for Service Oriented Architecture 1.0" and the book *Service-Oriented Architecture: Concepts, Technology, and Design* by Thomas Erl.

Dynamics AX services can be exposed to external applications, called service clients, through a variety of interfaces, such as MSMQ or WCF Web services. Publishing Dynamics AX services is a simple task that a Dynamics AX administrator can do at run time. (See the section "Publishing Dynamics AX Services" later in this chapter for more details.) Once a Dynamics AX service has been published, client applications can consume it.

Components of Dynamics AX Services

Dynamics AX services come in two flavors: document services and custom services. The following artifacts are part of the implementation of both types of services:

- **Service implementation class** An X++ class that implements the business logic encapsulated by a service. For example, the X++ class *SalesSalesOrderService* that comes with Dynamics AX 2009 is a service implementation class.
- **Service interface** A child node of the *Services* node in the Dynamics AX Application Object Tree (AOT). A service interface includes properties, such as Namespace, Class, and SecurityKey. For example, the AOT node *SalesSalesOrderService* (underneath the AOT node *Services*) is a service interface. A valid service interface references a service implementation class and exposes a subset of the methods of the service implementation class as service operations.
- **Data object** An X++ class, such as *SalesSalesOrder*, that can be used as a parameter for service operations.

Overview of Document Services

The term *document services* stems from the reality that businesses need to exchange documents, such as sales orders and invoices, with their partners. Document services provide an external application interface. These services are built on top of a query and provide a subset of create, read, update, delete, find (CRUDF) service operations for a particular *Axd*<Document> type. The *Axd*<Document> represents a business entity.

> **Note** Document services are a subset of custom services.

Document services provide document-centric APIs—that is, APIs that operate on electronic documents. In Dynamics AX, these documents are referred to as *Axd*<Documents> and are derived from Dynamics AX queries.

Examples of document-oriented APIs for a sales order service include *create sales order, read sales order, update sales order, delete sales order,* and *find sales order.*

Each of these APIs operates on an instance of a sales order document. *Create sales order,* for example, takes a sales order document, persists it in the Dynamics AX data store, and returns the sales order identifier for the persisted instance.

Document Services Artifacts

All document services that come with Dynamics AX 2009, as well as the ones you generate from Dynamics AX queries using the Create New Document Service Wizard, include the following artifacts:

- **Service contract** Service-related metadata (no code) that is stored in AOT nodes, underneath the AOT node *Services*, such as *SalesSalesOrderService*. Service contracts are not specific to document services and are also used for custom services. The metadata includes the following information:
  - Service operations that are available to external service clients
  - A reference to the X++ service implementation class that implements these service operations
- **Service implementation** The code that exposes business logic. It mainly consists of the following elements:
  - Service implementation class An X++ class that derives from *AifDocumentService* and implements the service operations that are published through the service contract. There is one service implementation class for each Dynamics AX service. For example, *SalesSalesOrderService* is the service implementation class for *SalesSalesOrderService.*
  - *Axd*<Document> class An X++ class that derives from *AxdBase*. It primarily implements code for XML serialization, but it also coordinates cross-table validation and cross-table defaulting. There is one *Axd*<Document> class for each document service. For example, *AxdSalesOrder* is the *Axd*<Document> class for *SalesSalesOrderService.*
  - One or more *Ax*<Table> classes An *Ax*<Table> class is an X++ class that derives from *AxInternalBase* and implements validation, defaulting, and substitution logic for table fields. There is one *Ax*<Table> class for each table that is used in the

query that is used to generate the Dynamics AX document service. For example, *AxSalesTable* and *AxSalesLine* are two *Ax*<Table> classes that have been generated for the *SalesSalesOrderService*.

- **Data object** An X++ class that represents a parameter type. The parameter types that the Create New Document Service Wizard generates derive from *AifDocument* represent business documents. For example, *SalesSalesOrder* is the data object that is created for the *SalesSalesOrderService*.

You can find a complete list of document services artifacts in the AIF documentation in the Microsoft Dynamics AX 2009 SDK on MSDN.

Axd<Document> Classes

Axd<Document> classes (e.g., *AxdSalesOrder*) derive from the X++ class *AxdBase* and are generated from Dynamics AX queries. *Axd*<Document> classes provide default implementations for the XML serialization of used data objects as well as hooks for validation code. *Axd*<Document> classes also call *Ax*<Table> classes to perform value mapping and can filter data.

Axd<Document> classes derive XML schema definitions used for XML serialization directly from the structure of the underlying query; all generated schema definitions comply with principles described in the Reference Model for Service Oriented Architecture 1.0 mentioned earlier in the chapter. The generated XML serialization code leverages Dynamics AX concepts such as *extended data types* (EDTs) to further restrict valid XML schemas and improve XML schema validation. During serialization, *Axd*<Document> classes use *Ax*<Table> classes to persist data to tables and to read from tables. Because *Ax*<Table> classes implement business logic such as defaulting and value mapping, *Axd*<Document> classes never bypass *Ax*<Table> classes to access tables directly.

Figure 17-2 illustrates the mapping between a Dynamics AX query used for the *Axd*<Document> class *Axd*<Document> and the generated XML schema definition.

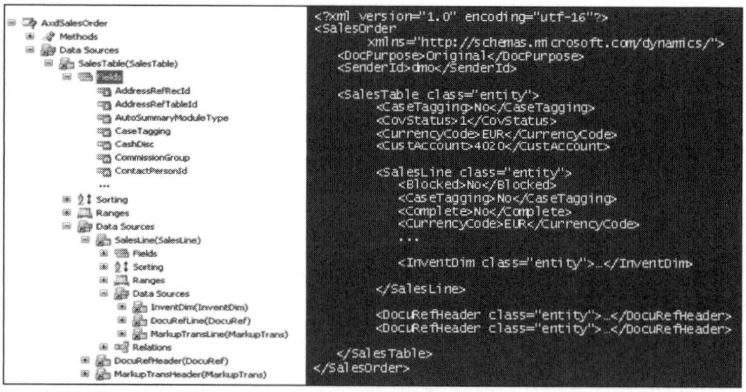

FIGURE 17-2 Correlation between the AOT query and the XML document structure

Axd<Document> classes also provide an API for orchestrating cross-table validation and defaulting. Validation and defaulting logic that is relevant only for a specific document service can also be implemented in *Axd*<Document> classes, such as by using the methods *prepareForSave*, *prepareForUpdate*, and *prepareForDelete*.

The *AifEntityKey* class is used for all service operations that require one or more specific records. It is also used for the return values for service operations of type *create*. An *AifEntityKey* instance uniquely identifies an entity. It consists of a table identifier (ID), the field IDs for a unique index of that table, and the values of the respective fields. In addition, it holds the record ID of the retrieved records. The following code shows a partial implementation from the *AxdBaseCreate* class.

```
protected void setEntityKey()
{
    Map     keyData;
    ;
    keyData = SysDictTable::getKeyData(axBcStack.top().currentRecord());

    entityKey = AifEntityKey::construct();
    entityKey.parmTableId(axBcStack.top().currentRecord().TableId);
    entityKey.parmRecId(axBcStack.top().currentRecord().RecId);
    entityKey.parmKeyDataMap(keyData);

    // More code lines go here.

}
```

The section "Customizing Document Services" later in the chapter offers additional information on using *Axd*<Document> classes.

> **Note** An in-depth discussion of *Axd*<Document> and *Ax*<Table> classes is beyond the scope of this book. Refer to the Document Services section in the Microsoft Dynamics AX 2009 SDK for complete information.

Ax<Table> Classes

Ax<Table> classes (e.g., *AxSalesTable* and *AxSalesLine*) derive from the X++ class *AxInternalBase*. There is one *Ax*<Table> class for each table that is used in a document service. More specifically, the same *Ax*<Table> class is used by *Axd*<Document> classes that are based on queries referencing the same table. Here are some uses of *Ax*<Table> classes:

- Help implement defaulting scenarios, such as automatically changing a table field when a related table field is changed. For example, an *Ax*<Table> class can automatically update or reset the table field *Delivery Address* when the related Sales Order *table field, Customer Account,* is changed.

- Keep track of the defaulting state of table fields. For example, when a Dynamics AX user sets a specific table field explicitly, the defaulting logic must not overwrite the explicitly set value.
- Implement validation logic for table fields, value substitution, and logic for fetching numbers or identifiers from number sequences.
- Implement *parm* methods for fields on the underlying table.

Note *Ax*<Table> classes are frequently referred to as *AxBC* classes, both in code and in documentation.

Document Services Use Cases

The standard create, read, update, delete (CRUD) service operations for document services are particularly useful and efficient in business-to-business (B2B) scenarios or in offline integration scenarios in which communication between systems is unreliable and slow and changes to documents occur infrequently.

Document services are also useful for integrating Dynamics AX with systems through the exchange of coarse-grained business documents, such as sales orders and leads. This type of data exchange is commonly used in the following scenarios:

- Exchanged data is transacted. For example, if a request to create a sales order fails, the state of the Dynamics AX database must remain unchanged. No side-effects must occur: artifacts such as address or customer records that were created as part of the processing of the failed request must not be left; instead, the entire transaction must be rolled back.
- Data exchanges are expensive because, for example, the request and response messages are exchanged through the Internet. Coarse-grained data exchange in the form of business documents can help reduce the number of exchanged messages.
- The response time—that is, the time between sending the request (e.g., to create a sales order) to Dynamics AX and receiving a response—isn't critical.

In addition to their use in B2B integration scenarios, coarse-grained document services are helpful in application-to-application (A2A) integration scenarios, such as when you're integrating Dynamics AX with certain document-centric Microsoft Office products.

Document Service Development Tools

Although you can create document services manually, we don't recommend it. Instead, you should use the Create New Document Service Wizard to quickly generate new document services from AOT queries and the Update Document Service form to update existing document services. You can find this wizard and form at Tools\Development Tools\

Application Integration Framework. (To read more about the AOT, see Chapter 2, "The MorphX Development Environment.")

Dynamics AX 2009 also includes more than 50 ready-to-use document services. These include services such as *SalesOrderService* and *CustomerService*. You can find a complete list of these built-in services in the AOT *Services* node at design time or through the AIF Services Administration form at run time.

You can also extend out-of-the-box services with more fine-grained custom service operations, such as updating the delivery address for a specific sales order.

Overview of Custom Services

Custom services can provide any kind of API. Even so, you should never use custom services to replace document services, and you should not use them to implement CRUD functionality for query-based entities. Instead, you should be use custom services to implement functionality that can't be directly tied to a Dynamics AX query, such as when you want to stop payment on a check or start an invoice approval process.

Custom Service Use Cases

Custom services are indispensible in A2A scenarios in which systems are tightly integrated and small chunks of data need to be exchanged efficiently between external applications and Dynamics AX. Examples of such applications are interactive applications that manipulate data managed in Dynamics AX, such as Microsoft Office Business Applications (OBAs).

Custom Services Development

Dynamics AX 2009 doesn't provide wizards or other tools for implementing custom services. Instead, custom services must follow certain rules, which we cover in the following section.

> **Note** Although the design-time experience for document and custom services differs, both service types are configured and published in the same way.

Working with Custom Services

Because document services are a subset of custom services, the concepts described in this section apply to both custom services and document services.

To implement a custom service, follow these steps:

1. Create a service implementation class.
2. Create a service contract.

3. Implement data objects—if necessary.
4. Discover services.

Creating a Service Implementation Class

Service implementation classes contain the business logic that can be published through service contracts for consumption by external service clients.

You can use any X++ class as a service implementation class; service implementation classes don't need to implement any interfaces or extend any super classes. A class definition for a service implementation class *MyDataObjectService* could look like this.

```
public class MyDataObjectService
{
}
```

The following code sample illustrates how one of the service operations of *MyDataObjectService* could look. All input and return parameters of service operations must be either of primitive X++ types or of X++ classes that implement the X++ interface *AifXmlSerializable*.

```
public MyDataObject CreateMyDataObject(str _s)
{
  MyDataObject mdo; // see below for a definition of class MyDataObject
  ;

  mdo = new MyDataObject();
  mdo.parmMyString(_s);

  // do something with 'mdo', for instance persist it ...

  return mdo;
}
```

Creating a Service Contract

Service contracts define the subset of functionality implemented by a service that can be published for consumption by external service clients.

To create a new service contract, you need to create a new AOT node under the AOT node *Services*. In this example, the service contract is named *MyDataObjectService*, just like the service implementation class.

The newly created AOT node *MyDataObjectService* has a few properties that need to be initialized before external clients can consume the service:

- **(Service implementation) class** This property links the service interface to the service implementation; in the preceding example, the value would be *MyDataObjectService*.
- **Security key** Each service needs its own security key. The security key should have the same name as the service it protects; for example, *MyDataObjectService* should have the parent key *Services* in a functional area like Accounts Receivable. For this example, it makes sense to create a new security key, *MyDataObjectService*, without a parent key because the new service really doesn't fit into a functional area.
- **Namespace** Optionally, you can specify the XML namespace that should be used in the Web Services Description Language (WSDL). If the XML namespace isn't specified, *http://tempuri.org* is used by default. This example uses the namespace *http://schemas.contoso.com/axbook/2009/services*.
- **External name** Optionally, you can assign an external name for each service. In this example, the external name is left blank.

Finally, you need to add service operations to the service contract. You do this by right-clicking the new AOT node and selecting Add Operations. The service exposes only service operations that have been explicitly added to the service interface.

Implementing Data Objects

Service operations can automatically use primitive X++ types (e.g., *int* and *str*) as types for input and return parameters. X++ classes that are to be used as data objects—that is, as input or return parameters for service operations—must implement the interface *AifXmlSerializable*. Here's an example.

```
public class MyDataObject implements AifXmlSerializable
{
  str myString;
  // more fields ...

  #define.MyDataObjectNS ('http://schemas.contoso.com/samples/MyDataObject')
  #define.MyDataObjectRoot ('MyDataObject')
}
```

> **Note** *Axd*<Document> classes implement the *AifXmlSerializable* interface and thus can be used as parameter types.

You need to use *AifXmlSerializable* mainly to define the serialization to and the deserialization from XML for that class. Note that the methods *serialize* and *deserialize* must be inverse functions because they use the same XML schema definition. In other words, it must be possible to deserialize an XML document that was created by serializing a data object, and vice versa.

The following code examples show what such implementations can look like. For additional information about any of the implemented methods, see the AIF information in the Microsoft Dynamics AX 2009 SDK.

The method *serialize* defines the serialization of the data object to XML. The code for serializing the previously defined class to XML could look like this.

```
AifXml serialize()
{
  str xml;
  XmlTextWriter xmlTextWriter;
  ;

#Aif

  xmlTextWriter = XmlTextWriter::newXml();

  // turn off indentation to reduce file size
  xmlTextWriter.formatting(XmlFormatting::None);

  // initialize XML document
  xmlTextWriter.writeStartDocument();

  // write root element
  xmlTextWriter.writeStartElement2(#MyDataObjectRoot, #MyDataObjectNS);

  // write custom data
  xmlTextWriter.writeElementString('MyString', myString);
  // more fields ...

  // serialize XML document into XML string
  xmlTextWriter.writeEndDocument();
  xml = xmlTextWriter.writeToString();
  xmlTextWriter.close();

  return xml;
}
```

The method *deserialize* defines the deserialization of a data object from XML. The code for deserializing an instance of the class defined from XML could look like this.

```
void deserialize(AifXml xml)
{
  XmlTextReader xmlReader;
  ;
```

```
    xmlReader = XmlTextReader::newXml(xml);

    // turn off whitespace handling to avoid extra reads
    xmlReader.whitespaceHandling(XmlWhitespaceHandling::None);

    xmlReader.moveToContent();
    while ((xmlReader.nodeType() != XmlNodeType::Element) && !xmlReader.eof())
    xmlReader.read();

    xmlReader.readStartElement3(#MyDataObjectRoot, #MyDataObjectNS);
    if (!xmlReader.eof() && xmlReader.isStartElement())
    {
      myString = xmlReader.readElementString3('MyString', #MyDataObjectNS);
      // more fields ...
    }

    xmlReader.readEndElement();
    xmlReader.close();
}
```

In X++, *parm* methods are used to define properties. In data objects, all fields that are used for serialization or deserialization must be accessible through *parm* methods; they must also be optional and thus have a default value. Here's an example.

```
public str parmMyString(str _myString = '')
{
  if (!prmisdefault(_myString))
  {
    myString = _myString;
  }
  return myString;
}
```

The method *getRootName* returns the root name used for deriving names for service artifacts, as shown here.

```
public AifDocumentName getRootName()
{
  return #MyDataObjectRoot;
}
```

The method *getSchema* returns the XML schema definition (XSD) that is used for serializing and deserializing the data object.

```
public AifXml getSchema()
{
  str schema =
    @'<?xml version="1.0"?>
    <xsd:schema xmlns="http://schemas.contoso.com/samples/MyDataObject"
    targetNamespace="http://schemas.contoso.com/samples/MyDataObject"
    xmlns:xsd="http://www.w3.org/2001/XMLSchema"
    elementFormDefault="qualified">
      <xsd:complexType name="MyDataObjectType">
        <xsd:sequence>
          <xsd:element name="MyString" type="xsd:string" />
          <!-- more fields ... -->
        </xsd:sequence>
      </xsd:complexType>
      <xsd:element name="MyDataObject" type="MyDataObjectType"/>
    </xsd:schema>'
  ;

  return schema;
}
```

Tip XML schemas are used for validation, to avoid processing request messages with invalid content, for example. To ensure that your XML schema definition is valid, you should always use a data modeling tool or an XML editor to generate the XSD rather than typing it manually.

Discovering Custom Services

Once you've created a custom service, you need to register it with AIF. To register the custom service (in this example, *MyDataObjectService*) with AIF, expand the *Services* node in the AOT, select *MyDataObjectService* and open its context menu, point to Add-Ins, and then click Register Actions. Alternatively, you can register the service with AIF through the AIF administration form Services, which is located in Basic\Setup\Application Integration Framework. Click the Refresh button; this refreshes all service entries and thus takes longer than using the AOT *Services* node.

As a result of the registration, *MyDataObjectService* shows up along with all other services and is now ready for use. It can be published for external service clients to consume. The section "Publishing Dynamics AX Services" later in this chapter explains how to publish these services.

Working with Document Services

In this section, we go into greater detail about how to create, generate, customize, publish, configure, and consume Dynamics AX document services. Before getting into those details, we're going to remind you of the best way to create document services and look at an overview of the life cycle of Dynamics AX document services.

As we mentioned earlier in the chapter, even though you could create document services manually, we don't recommend that you do it. Creating them in either of the following ways is more efficient and less prone to error:

- Use the Create New Document Service Wizard to generate new document services from queries.
- Use the Update Document Service form to update existing document services.

Again, you can find this wizard and form at Tools\Development Tools\Application Integration Framework.

In this section, we assume that this AIF wizard and form manage both the document services and the document services artifacts.

Figure 17-3 shows the typical life cycle of a document service.

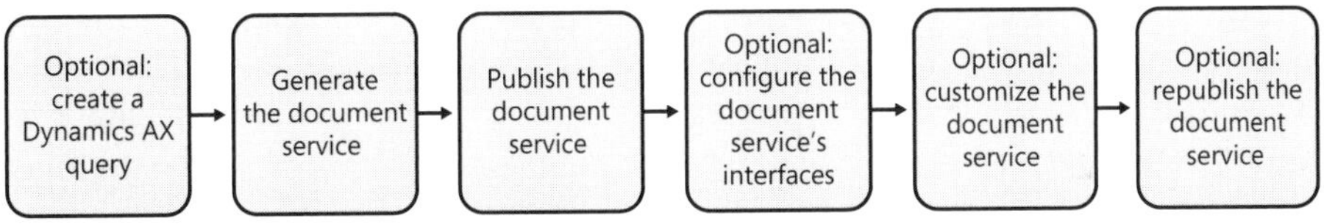

FIGURE 17-3 Typical life cycle of a Dynamics AX document service

You can find out more about publishing and republishing document services in the "Publishing Dynamics AX Services" section and more about configuring the interface of a document service in the "Configuring Dynamics AX Services" section, both later in this chapter.

Creating Dynamics AX Queries

Document services are generated from queries. (See the Database Queries section of the Microsoft Dynamics AX 2009 SDK for details on creating Dynamics AX queries.) Although general guidelines for working with Dynamics AX queries apply to document services queries, some constraints and additional guidelines apply:

- As a best practice, always name Dynamics AX queries that are used for document services with the prefix *Axd* and then the document name. For example, the document service query for the document *SalesOrder* should be *AxdSalesOrder*.

- Only one root table per query is allowed. You can associate the unique entity key that is used to identify document instances with this root table. For example, the entity key *SalesId* is defined on the *AxdSalesOrder* root table *SalesTable*.
- When your query's data sources are joined by an inner join, you should use fetch mode 1:1; when they are joined by an outer join, you should use fetch mode 1:*n*. If you don't use these settings, your query and thus the service operations that use this query could yield unexpected results.
- If you want to use a Dynamics AX document service to write data back to the database—that is, if you need to support the service operation *update*—you need to set the AOT property Update to *Yes* for all data sources the query used to generate the service.

> **Note** For security reasons, checks in X++ code by default prevent system tables from being used in queries that are used for document services.

Dynamics AX queries that are used to generate Dynamics AX document services and thus comply with the preceding rules are also referred to as *Axd* queries.

Generating Document Services

As mentioned earlier, you should always use the Create New Document Service Wizard to generate document services from existing *Axd*<Document> queries. Find this wizard from the Dynamics AX drop-down menu. In this section, we provide a high-level description of the Create New Document Service Wizard and some important notes that govern its use.

In the wizard, you can select the service operations you want to generate: *create*, *read*, *update*, *delete*, *find*, and *findKeys*. If you select *Generate AxBC classes* when running the wizard, the wizard generates new *Ax*<Table> classes with *parm* methods for the fields of the underlying table when necessary. It then adds missing *parm* methods to existing *Ax*<Table> classes. The wizard never removes any *parm* methods from existing *Ax*<Table> classes—even if the corresponding table fields have been removed from the underlying table.

The Create New Document Service Wizard uses the document name—which you enter on the first screen of the wizard—to derive names for the generated artifacts. You can change the document name (and thus the derived names for the artifacts) in the wizard before the artifacts are generated. Names of AOT objects are limited to 40 characters. If you choose a document name that yields names that are too long for one or more artifacts, you could get an error message.

Once the wizard finishes, it displays a report of all generated artifacts and any errors encountered. You need to fix any before you start customizing the generated code with additional validation or defaulting logic, which we talk about next.

> **Tip** The wizard creates a new project for each generated service. It then adds the generated artifacts automatically to the created project.

For a more comprehensive discussion of the Create New Document Service Wizard and generating *Axd*<Document> and *AX*<Table> classes and related APIs, refer to the Microsoft Dynamics AX 2009 SDK.

Customizing Document Services

In many cases, you need to customize the document services that have been generated from a query or that come with Dynamics AX 2009 to better fit business needs. In this section, we touch on some of the most common scenarios for customizing document services, including customizing the application, service operations, validation, defaulting, queries, and security.

Customizing Tables

When you customize a table (e.g., by adding a column) that a document service uses, you need to update the service implementation—that is, the *Axd*<Document> and *Ax*<Table> classes and the data objects—to reflect these changes. You should always enable best practice checks with the Best Practices tool to detect potential discrepancies between the table structure and the service implementation.

If the best practice checks on any of your customized tables fail, you can use the Update Document Service form to update the *Axd*<Document> class, *Ax*<Table> classes, and data objects to reflect the changes.

> **Caution** When you modify the structure of tables or queries (e.g., by adding a column to a table), you must also change your service contract—for example, the XSD for the corresponding data objects. This change in turn potentially breaks integrations that were built using the original service contract.

Adding Custom Service Operations

You can change the behavior of any service operation simply by modifying its X++ implementation. In addition, you can add custom service operations to any document service by following the same steps used for adding service operations to custom services.

Customizing Validation Logic

You can customize the validation logic that is used when the service operations *create, update,* and *delete* are executed. Validation logic is crucial to enforce data hygiene. Ideally, invalid data must never be persisted in the Dynamics AX database. You must add validation logic to any services—custom services or document services—that you create or customize. Well-designed validation logic has the following characteristics:

- **Reusable** Ideally, the same (generic) validation logic can be used from the Dynamics AX client as well as from Dynamics AX services. Keep in mind that nongeneric validation code, code that applies only to the Dynamics AX client or Dynamics AX services, is also possible.
- **Well performing** Validation code runs whenever the respective Dynamics AX entity is modified. As a consequence, one of your key goals for writing validation logic must be adequate performance.
- **Sufficient** Validation logic must guarantee a sufficient level of data hygiene. You might have to trade off sufficiency versus performance in a way that satisfies your application's requirements.

Validation code consists mainly of the following elements:

- Code that orchestrates cross-table validation by invoking validation code that is implemented on the respective tables; this code is implemented in the respective *Axd*<Document> class methods *prepareForSave*, *prepareForUpdate*, and *prepareForDelete*. These *prepareForXxx* methods are called once for each *Ax*<Table> class that the *Axd*<Document> class uses.
- Code that enforces table-level validation logic is implemented by the table methods *validateField* and *validateWrite* for maximum code reusability. These methods call into specific validation methods, such as *checkCreditLimit* on *SalesTable*.
- Code that performs document-level validation, which is implemented by the *Axd*<Document> class method *validateDocument*. This method is called immediately before changes are persisted to tables, and after the *prepareForXxx* methods have been called for each *Ax*<Table> class.
- Code that performs validation once data has been persisted to the table, which is implemented by the *Axd*<Document> class method *updateNow*.

The following code, the *prepareForSave* method for *AxdSalesOrder*, is an example of cross-table validation. It calls validation methods for the *Ax*<Table> classes *AxSalesTable* and *AxSalesLine* (as well as other *Ax*<Table> classes, which have been removed from this sample).

```
public boolean prepareForSave(AxdStack _axdStack, str _dataSourceName)
{

    // ...
    // code removed

    switch (classidget(_axdStack.top()))
    {
        case classnum(AxSalesTable) :
            axSalesTable = _axdStack.top();
            this.checkSalesTable(axSalesTable);
            this.prepareSalesTable(axSalesTable);
            return true;

        case classnum(AxSalesLine) :
            axSalesLine = _axdStack.top();
            this.checkSalesLine(axSalesLine);
            this.prepareSalesLine(axSalesLine);
            return true;

        // ...
        // code removed
}
```

Customizing Defaulting Logic

You can customize the defaulting logic for table fields that is executed as part of creating or updating table rows. Defaulting logic helps increase the usability of both interactive Dynamics AX client applications and Dynamics AX service interfaces. It derives initial values for table fields from other data—such as values of other table fields—and thus doesn't require explicit value assignments for the defaulted table fields. It also helps reduce the amount of data required to manipulate more-complex entities, such as sales orders, while lowering the probability of erroneous data entry.

Well-designed defaulting logic has the following characteristics:

- **Reusable** You should implement defaulting logic so that it is reusable—that is, so the same logic can be used regardless of which Dynamics AX client (e.g., a user interface or a service client) creates or updates the entity. In certain scenarios, the defaulting of table fields might require different logic, depending on whether the Dynamics AX client is interactive (e.g., a user interface) or noninteractive (e.g., a request from a service client).
- **Well performing** Because the defaulting logic for a table field is invoked every time the field is set, its execution time directly impacts the processing time for manipulating

the entity (e.g., a sales order). In particular, you should try to avoid redundant defaulting steps—that is, setting a field value that is overwritten again as part of the same defaulting logic.

- **Sufficient** To reduce the number of required fields for manipulating entities, as many fields as possible should be defaulted—while still meeting the performance goals.

The defaulting logic consists mainly of the following elements:

- **Defaulting rules** *Ax*<Table> classes provide methods for setting fields, which the framework uses for assigning values to table fields. This method, *set<Fieldname>*, implements the defaulting logic for the table field *Fieldname* of the table that is associated with the *Ax*<Table> class.
- **State tracking of the defaulting state of table fields**
  - The method *isMethodExecuted*, which is implemented by *Ax*<Table> classes, is used to check whether the respective *set<Fieldname>* method has already been invoked (see the following code). This check is necessary to detect and avoid loops in the defaulting logic.
  - The method *isFieldSet*, which is implemented by *Ax*<Table> classes, checks whether a table field has been set.

The following code shows the *set<Fieldname>* method for the table field *DeliveryCounty*, that is, *setDeliveryCounty*, as implemented by the *Ax*<Table> class *AxSalesTable*. You should add defaulting logic similar to that shown in this example to new *set<Field>* methods of newly generated or updated *Ax*<Table> classes, if applicable.

```
protected void setDeliveryCounty()
{
    if (this.isMethodExecuted(funcname(), fieldnum(SalesTable, DeliveryCounty)))
    {
        return;
    }

    this.setZipCodeRecordFields();

    if (this.isZipCodeRecordFieldsSet())
    {
        this.parmDeliveryCounty(this.zipCodeRecord().County);
        return;
    }

    this.setCustAccount();

    if (this.isFieldSet(fieldnum(SalesTable, CustAccount)))
    {
        if (this.axAddress().addressTable())
```

```
        {
            this.parmDeliveryCounty(this.axAddress().parmCounty());
        }
        else
        {
            this.parmDeliveryCounty(this.custAccount_CustTableRecord().County);
        }
    }
}
```

Customizing *Axd*<Document> Queries

You can customize the *Axd*<Document> queries that come with Dynamics AX to generate document services for new or existing AOT elements. For example, assume that you've created a new table containing several illustrations per inventory item. Now you want to include those illustrations with purchase orders and to update the document service associated with the purchase orders. To do that, you would modify the query *AxdPurchaseRequisition* to include the new table and then use the Update Document Service form to update the document service associated with *AxdPurchaseRequisition*.

Your process would look like this:

1. Modify the query *AxdPurchaseRequisition* to include the new *ItemIllustration* table. Figure 17-4 shows what the query looks like after the new table has been added. The boxed area must be added to the original query that came with Dynamics AX 2009.

2. Open the Update Document Service form and enter *AxdPurchaseRequisition* for the query name. The remaining fields are indifferent to the processing because no modifications are made to existing *Axd*<Document> classes. If you carefully created the relationships in the query, the form can construct all required code in the *prepareForSave* method.

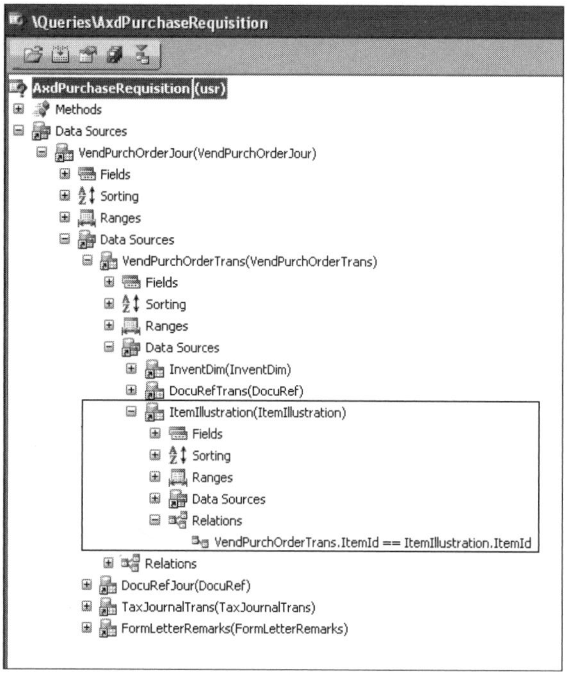

FIGURE 17-4 Query after adding the *ItemIllustration* table

3. You need to generate new *Ax*<Table> classes, but you shouldn't need to update existing *Ax*<Table> classes.

After you close the Update Document Service form, you must fix potential compilation errors and all the to-do comments that the Create New Document Wizard produces in the generated code. First, you remove the caching if it isn't needed. You do this by removing the methods *CacheObject* and *CacheRecordRecord*. When removing these classes, you must also remove the two static variables from the class declarations *cacheRecordIdx* and *cacheObjectIdx*. Assume that *InventDim* isn't influencing the illustration; then you simply remove the optional parameter so that the *parmItemId* method looks like the code shown here.

```
public str parmItemId(str _itemId = '')
{
    DictField   dictField;
    ;
    if (!prmisdefault(_itemId))
    {
```

```
        dictField = new DictField(tablenum(ItemIllustration),fieldnum(ItemIllustration,ItemId));
        this.validateInboundItemIdString(_itemId,dictField);
        if(this.valueMappingInbound())
        {
            item = _itemId;
        }

        this.setField(fieldNum(ItemIllustration, ItemId), _itemId);
    }

    if (this.valueMappingOutbound())
    {
        return conpeek(this.axSalesItemId('', itemIllustration.ItemId),1);
    }
    else
    {
        return itemIllustration.ItemId;
    }
}
```

To use the updated service, you have to open and refresh the Services form. If you published *PurchaseRequisitionService* as a Web service, you also need to regenerate the Web service on the Services form.

Customizing Security

By default, record-level and column-level security are applied to all data retrieval. In certain scenarios, however, you need to ignore record-level and column-level security—for example, when invoices need to be sent. In those scenarios, the user must be able to see the same data that is posted, regardless of the security settings. The following code sample shows how to override the default behavior.

```
protected void unpackPropertyBag(AifPropertyBag _aifPropertyBag)
{
    AxdSendContext  axdSendContext = AxdSendContext::create(_aifPropertyBag);
    ;
    // Get send context properties.
    ...
    this.security(axdSendContext.parmSecurity());
    ...
}
```

Caution Be very diligent when customizing security mechanisms, and make sure you understand the implications of your modifications.

Publishing Dynamics AX Services

You have now created and customized your service; however, external applications can't yet consume it. To allow external applications to consume your service, you need to publish it. Figure 17-5 gives an overview of the transport technologies that AIF supports out of the box.

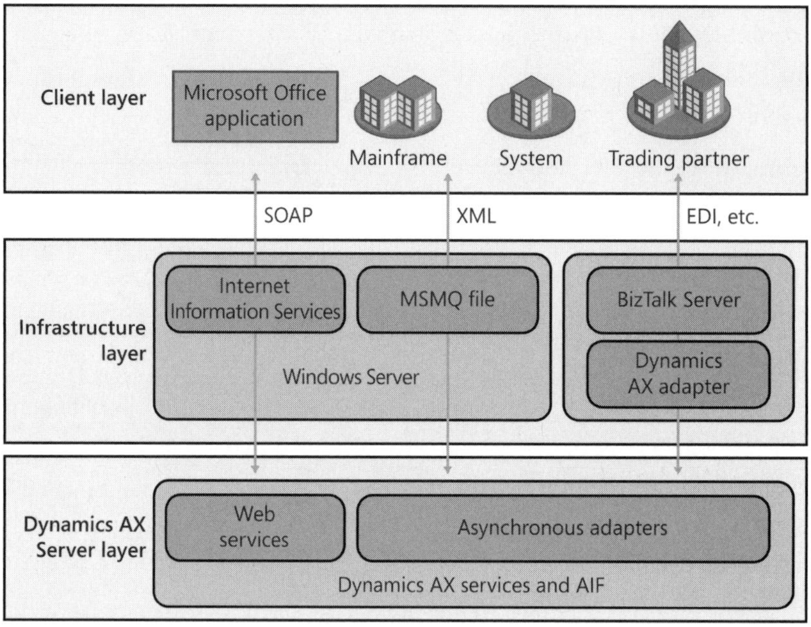

FIGURE 17-5 Overview of transport interfaces

Consult the Microsoft Dynamics AX 2009 documentation on TechNet for detailed instructions on how to publish Dynamics AX services using AIF administration forms through synchronous WCF Web services or asynchronous transports such as MSMQ, BizTalk Server, or XML file exchange. The guide is available for download at *http://www.microsoft.com/dynamics/ax/using/default.mspx.*

Configuring Dynamics AX Services

In this section, we briefly cover some key concepts related to configuring Dynamics AX services. A complete discussion of configuring Dynamics AX services is well beyond the scope of this book. Refer to the "Configuring and Managing AIF" topic on TechNet for more information.

Configuring WCF Parameters

When Dynamics AX services are published as synchronous WCF Web services, a WCF configuration file (web.config) is generated. This file is not generated when Dynamics AX services are published through any of the asynchronous AIF adapters. Note that a single web.config file contains the WCF configuration for all published Dynamics AX services.

Be sure to install Windows SDK for Windows Server 2008 before you modify any WCF configuration settings. Always use *SvcConfigEditor* instead of Notepad or an XML editor. Dynamics AX services published through WCF Web services support three bindings:

- *basicHttpBinding* (used as the default binding when Dynamics AX services are published as WCF Web services)
- *customBinding* (with WS-Addressing)
- *wsHttpBinding* (with WS-Addressing)

> **Caution** Publishing Dynamics AX services as WCF Web services introduces additional dependencies on .NET Framework 3.5, Internet Information Server (IIS) 6.0 or later, and Windows Server 2008. Improper or incomplete installation of these external dependencies or default configurations that are inadequate for Dynamics AX services can prevent Dynamics AX services that have been published through WCF from working properly.

Configuring AIF Parameters

AIF provides a variety of configuration options for administrators of Dynamics AX services, including action policies, data policies, pipeline components, value mappings, and constraints.

Refer to the *Microsoft Dynamics AX 2009 Server* and *Database Administration Guide* for more details about service administration and related concepts, such as setting up and using AIF endpoints, action policies, and data policies.

Configuring Access to Services

Security keys protect access to each Dynamics AX service from external service clients. These security keys represent an additional security gate that helps guard Dynamics AX from unauthorized access by external users over the network; these security keys do not protect data. The existing Dynamics AX data access control applies in addition to these service security keys. Just as is recommended for general security in Dynamics AX, you should grant administrators access to services only when necessary and try to configure minimal access.

Refer to the Microsoft Dynamics AX 2009 documentation on TechNet for details on how to create and manage security keys and for detailed instructions on how to protect services with security keys.

Troubleshooting Tips for Services

When troubleshooting integrations, you can generally start with these two steps:

- The forms *Queue Manager*, *Document History*, and *Exception Log*—all located under Basic\Periodic\Application Integration Framework—provide additional information about errors that have occurred during request processing in Microsoft Dynamics AX.
- The *Event Log* provides additional information about errors that occurred in external components such as IIS or BizTalk Server.

The Microsoft Dynamics AX AIF blog at *http://blogs.msdn.com/aif/.* also offers a good set of troubleshooting tips for AIF. Here's a sample of some of the troubleshooting guidance you can find on the AIF blog:

- If the AIF administration Services form is empty, click Refresh and wait until the form has been populated.
- If a service contract or data object doesn't reflect *changes* you've applied to the service (e.g., added service operations or modified data objects), open the Services form in the Dynamics AX client, click Refresh, and then click Generate.
- If a service returns error messages related to validation logic, first verify that your requests messages are well-formed XML and comply with the expected XML schema definitions. If your request messages don't use message headers to override the default settings for message identifier, target company, source endpoint, or source endpoint user, check the default values (e.g., the submitting user's default company, which is used for the target company).

Consuming Dynamics AX Services

Now that you've published your Dynamics AX services through one of the supported transport technologies, external service clients can consume them. By consuming published Dynamics AX services, service clients can leverage business functionality that is implemented in Dynamics AX. For instance, they can consume the *SalesOrderService* to manage sales orders in Dynamics AX—to *create*, *read*, *update*, *delete*, and *find* them.

How the published Dynamics AX services are consumed depends on what transport technology you use to publish your services. We don't go into the details of configuring asynchronous adapters for message exchanges in this book; instead, we use WCF Web service clients to illustrate the overall process and highlight a few features.

For a more complete description of the available functionality and of asynchronous adapters, refer to the *Dynamics AX 2009 Server* and *Database Administration Guide*.

Sample WCF Client for Dynamics AX Services

For the following discussions, we use a .NET service client. If you want to consume a Dynamics AX service that has been published as a WCF Web service, you need to do the following:

- Instantiate and initialize parameters for the call.
- Instantiate the service proxy.
- Set (optional) SOAP headers if necessary.
- Consume the service.
- Evaluate the response and handle exceptions.

The following samples show C# code for each of these steps to consume the *find* service operation of the Dynamics AX document service *CustomerService* as it ships with Dynamics AX 2009, with its default configuration. We assume a service reference with the name *CustomerService* has been added to the project.

To consume the service operation *find* of the *CustomerService* document service, you need to instantiate and populate an object of the class *QueryCriteria*. The following code formulates a query for all *Customer* entities with an account number that is greater than or equal to 4000.

```
CustomerService.CriteriaElement[] qe = { new CustomerService.CriteriaElement() };
qe[0].DataSourceName = "CustTable";
qe[0].FieldName = "AccountNum";
qe[0].Operator = CustomerService.Operator.GreaterOrEqual;
qe[0].Value1 = "4000";
CustomerService.QueryCriteria qc = new CustomerService.QueryCriteria();
qc.CriteriaElement = qe;
```

The following code shows how to instantiate a service proxy and consume the service operation *find*, which executes a query and returns matching entities.

```
// instantiate proxy
CustomerService.CustomerServiceClient customerService =
    new CustomerService.CustomerServiceClient();

CustomerService.AxdCustomer customer;

// see [4] for details about this using directive
using (new OperationContextScope(customerService.InnerChannel))
{
    // set optional SOAP headers (see "Overriding Default Values in SOAP Headers")
    ...
```

```
    // consume the service operation find()
    customer = customerService.find(qc);
}

// error handling - additionally, exceptions should be handled properly
if (null == customer || 0 == ekList.Length)
{
    // error handling
}
CustomerService.AxdEntity_CustTable[] custTables = customer.CustTable;
if (null == custTables || 0 == custTables.Length)
{
    // error handling
}

// evaluate response
foreach (AxdEntity_CustTable custTable in custTables)
{
    custTable.AccountNum = ...
}
```

When you instantiate the proxy, you should always specify the name of a WCF client configuration. In addition, if you expect large amounts of data as a result of the consumption of the service operation *find*, you might want to use *findKeys*, which returns only entity keys for the matching entities instead of the entire record. You can then, for example, implement pagination logic that retrieves the matching entities in sizeable chunks.

The other service operations that are supported for document services are consumed in similar ways.

Updating Business Documents

In many scenarios, you need to update data that already exists in the Dynamics AX data store, for example, to add a line to a sales order or to update a customer address. Dynamics AX offers several ways to update your business documents, from full and partial updates to a document hash.

Full updates The framework for Dynamics AX services supports document-centric update operations, that is, updating business documents (e.g., sales orders). The default behavior for updating documents is *full updates*, which includes the following:

- Read the document.
- Apply changes to the document.
- Send the updated document with the update request.
- Handle errors, if any.

The following C# code sample shows the programmatic process of updating a sales order conceptually, using full updates.

```
// instantiate and populate entityKeys
EntityKey[] entityKeys;
...

// read sales order(s) (including document hash(es)) using entityKeys
AxdSalesOrder salesOrder = service.read(entityKeys);

// process sales order, update data
...

// consume the service to update the record (exception handling not shown)
service.update(entityKeys, salesOrder);
```

In many scenarios, using full updates is inefficient. Imagine a large sales order with many sales lines—more than 1000 sales lines are not uncommon. According to the full updates process, you would have to retrieve the entire sales order with all sales lines, apply your changes to the one sales line you want to update, and then send the entire sales order with all sales lines—including all unchanged sales lines—back. This operation can be costly when you consider the validation and defaulting logic invoked for each sales line.

Partial updates Instead of performing full updates, you can apply *partial updates*. Partial updates use the same service operation as full updates do, that is, *update*. Partial updates allow you to send partial documents instead of full documents. Partial documents contain only changed (added, modified, or deleted) records and processing instructions for AIF that specify how to handle each (child) record included in the partial document; the processing instructions are necessary to avoid ambiguity. Consequently, the process for updating documents using partial updates contains one more step in addition to the steps for full updates:

- Read the document (e.g., a sales order).
- Apply changes to the document.
- Explicitly request the mode partial update and add processing instructions.
- Send the updated document with the update request.
- Handle errors, if any.

The following code shows the programmatic process of updating a sales order conceptually, using partial updates.

```
// instantiate and populate entityKeys
EntityKey[] entityKeys;
...
```

```
// read sales order(s) (including document hash(es)) using entityKeys
AxdSalesOrder salesOrder = service.read(entityKeys);

// process sales order, pick data to be updated
...

// update the first sales order and mark it for partial update
AxdEntity_SalesTable[] salesTables = salesOrder.SalesTable;
salesOrder.SalesTable = new AxdEntity_SalesTable[] { salesTables[0] };
salesOrder.SalesTable[0].action = AxdEnum_AxdEntityAction.update;

// delete the first sales line; send only the modified data as part of update()
AxdEntity_SalesLine[] salesLines = salesOrder.SalesTable[0].salesLine;
salesOrder.SalesTable[0].SalesLine = new AxdEntity_SalesLine[] { salesLines[0] };
salesOrder.SalesTable[0].SalesLine[0].action = AxdEnum_AxdEntityAction.delete;

// remove other child data sources (DocuRefHeader, etc.) from salesTable
...

// consume the service to update the record (exception handling not shown)
service.update(entityKeys, salesOrder);
```

In request messages, these processing instructions present themselves in the form of XML *action* attributes; this is true for both XML messages sent to asynchronous adapters as well as for SOAP messages sent to synchronous WCF Web services. For more details, refer to the Document Services classes documentation in the Microsoft Dynamics AX 2009 SDK.

Document hashes Document hashes are hashes that are computed for a specific document. They include data not only from the root level data source (e.g., the sales header) but also from all the joined data sources (e.g., a sales line). In other words, if a table field included in the business document changes, the document hash changes too.

AIF uses the document hash to implement optimistic concurrency control (OCC) to compare versions of business documents. Your code must always read the document before updating it using the service operation *update*.

> **Tip** Caching a document for a long time on a service client without refreshing it increases the probability of update requests being rejected because of colliding updates from other client applications.

Overriding Default Values in SOAP Headers

To streamline both AIF setup and configuration, AIF doesn't require values to be specified in requests for context information, such as destination endpoint, source endpoint, source endpoint user, and message identifier. To override the default values for each of those parameters, you can use code similar to samples in this section. All the code examples use standard WCF APIs to set the respective SOAP headers. For these SOAP headers to take effect in the current message, you must wrap the code in a *using* directive (for *OperationContextScope*) as outlined in the section "Sample WCF Client for Dynamics AX Services" earlier in this chapter.

Message identifier By default, WCF generates and uses a message identifier. Alternatively, you can explicitly specify the message identifier to be used for sending a request message by explicitly setting the value for the SOAP header used to exchange message identifiers. The client application can then use this message identifier to correlate received response messages with the original requests, for example.

```
// generate guid
Guid guid = new Guid();

// use guid as message identifier
OperationContext.Current.OutgoingMessageHeaders.MessageId =
  new System.Xml.UniqueId(guid);

// store guid for later use ...
```

Destination endpoint (target company) By default, AIF uses the default company that the admninistrator has configured for the user sending the request. If the request needs to be executed in the context of another company, you can can specify that company explicitly.

```
// This assumes that a local endpoint with the name "Contoso" has been configured
// in Dynamics AX and is associated with a company that exists in Dynamics AX
String targetCompany = "Contoso";

// Execute the request in the context of "targetCompany"
OperationContext.Current.OutgoingMessageHeaders.Add(
  MessageHeader.CreateHeader(
    "DestinationEndpoint",
    "http://schemas.microsoft.com/dynamics/2008/01/services",
    targetCompany
  )
);
```

Source endpoint and source endpoint user By default, AIF uses the default endpoint as the default value for the source endpoint and the submitting user as the default value for the source endpoint user. If the request needs to be executed in the context of another source endpoint and source endpoint user, both can be specified explicitly using a standard SOAP header.

```
// We assume that a source endpoint user "submittingUser" exists in the domain
// "ContosoDomain"; we also assume that the user credentials used to authenticate
// a user from "NorthwindTraders" have been mapped onto an identity within the
// domain "Contoso".
Uri sourceEndpoint = new Uri("urn:NorthwindTraders");
String sourceEndpointUser = "submittingUser\ContosoDomain";

// Create a WCF endpoint address builder.
EndpointAddressBuilder eab = new EndpointAddressBuilder(
  new EndpointAddress(
    sourceEndpoint
    AddressHeader.CreateAddressHeader(
      "User",
      "http://schemas.microsoft.com/dynamics/2008/01/services",
      endpointUser
    )
  )
);

// Initialize standard SOAP header "From" (see WS Addressing).
OperationContext.Current.OutgoingMessageHeaders.From =
  endpointAddress.ToEndpointAddress();

// Execute the request in the context of the given source endpoint and source
// endpoint user ...
```

Sample SOAP message The following SOAP message represents a request to create a sales order. This SOAP message overrides the default values for all the optional headers as described earlier. The overriding XML elements are shown in bold.

```
<s:Envelope xmlns:a="http://www.w3.org/2005/08/addressing"
    xmlns:s="http://www.w3.org/2003/05/soap-envelope">
  <s:Header>
    <a:Action s:mustUnderstand="1">http://schemas.microsoft.com/dynamics/2008/01/
services/SalesOrderService/create
    </a:Action>
    <a:From>
      <a:Address>urn:RemoteEP</a:Address>
      <a:ReferenceParameters>
        <SourceEndpointUser xmlns="http://schemas.microsoft.com/dynamics/2008/01/
services">redmond\apurvag</SourceEndpointUser>
      </a:ReferenceParameters>
    </a:From>
    <DestinationEndpoint xmlns="http://schemas.microsoft.com/dynamics/2008/01/
services">LocalEP</DestinationEndpoint>
    <a:MessageID>urn:uuid:670bf145-5be2-4c9f-920c-468a4199aa75</a:MessageID>
    <a:ReplyTo>
      <a:Address>http://www.w3.org/2005/08/addressing/anonymous</a:Address>
    </a:ReplyTo>
  </s:Header>
```

```
  <s:Body xmlns:xsi="http://www.w3.org/2001/XMLSchema-instance"
      xmlns:xsd="http://www.w3.org/2001/XMLSchema">
    <SalesOrderServiceCreateRequest
        xmlns="http://schemas.microsoft.com/dynamics/2008/01/services">
      <!-- sales order document -->
    </SalesOrderServiceCreateRequest>
  </s:Body>
</s:Envelope>
```

Sending One-Way Requests from Dynamics AX

In many scenarios, receiving a response or an error message from the consuming application isn't required. An acknowledgment that the message has successfully been delivered to the next hop in a chain of reliable transport links (e.g., MSMQ) can be sufficient. Messages that are transmitted without a synchronous end-to-end feedback channel for response or error messages are referred to as *one-way messages*.

When you think about exchanging business documents electronically with your trading partners, you need to accept that it might not be realistic to assume that your trading partners' applications will always be online and ready to receive your messages. With some partners, building more robust, loosely coupled integrations using one-way messages might be a better solution.

AIF provides APIs to send unsolicited one-way messages by using Dynamics AX services and the AIF infrastructure (e.g., channels and endpoints). The Dynamics AX client features Send Electronically buttons on several forms that allow you to transmit business documents (such as invoices) as unsolicited one-way messages through AIF channels to AIF endpoints. Dynamics AX is aware of only the AIF channel it needs to send the message to (i.e., the next hop); it doesn't know the final destination of the message. Moreover, Dynamics AX doesn't rely on any external document schema definitions to be provided by the remote receiving application; it uses its own format instead—the same *Axd*<Document> class-based XSDs that are also used as data contracts for published Dynamics AX services.

Implementing unsolicited messages exchanges requires the following two steps:

- Implementing a trigger for transmission (design time)
- Configuring transmission mechanisms (admin time)

Implementing a Trigger for Transmission

You can implement a trigger for transmission by using either the AIF *Send* API or the *AxdSend* API.

AIF *Send* API

The *Send* API in AIF features a set of methods that can be used to send unsolicited one-way messages from Dynamics AX to AIF channels, through which the consumers can pick up the messages. This API sends a single message; the body of the message is the XML that is generated by invoking the service operation *read* of the AIF document service referenced by *serviceClassId* (it must reference a class that derives from *AifDocumentService*) with the parameter *entityKey*.

To see a working example of how you can use this API, look at the code behind the method *clicked* for the button *SendXmlOriginal* on the form *CustInvoiceJournal*. The API methods are defined on the class *AifSendService* and include the method *submitDefault*.

```
public static void submitDefault(
    AifServiceClassId serviceClassId,
    AifEntityKey entityKey,
    AifConstraintList constraintList,
    AifSendMode sendMode,
    AifPropertyBag propertyBag = connull(),
    AifProcessingMode processingMode = AifProcessingMode::Sequential,
    AifConversationId conversationId = #NoConversationId
)
```

The two optional parameters in the preceding signature, *processingMode* and *conversationId*, are new in Dynamics AX 2009. They allow you to leverage the newly introduced parallel message processing feature for asynchronous adapters:

- ***processingMode*** Specifies whether messages can be moved from the AIF outbound processing queue to the AIF gateway queue in parallel (*AifProcessingMode::Parallel*) or whether first in first out (FIFO) order must be enforced for all messages (*AifProcessingMode::Sequential*).
- ***conversationId*** If specified, moves from the AIF outbound processing queue to the AIF gateway queue in FIFO order, relative to all other messages with the same *conversationId*. The order relative to all other messages with other *conversationIds* isn't guaranteed.

AxdSend API

The *AxdSend* API provides functionality to send unsolicited one-way messages for which the user needs to select AIF endpoints dynamically at run time or in which the message body contains more than a single entity. The user dynamically selects the exact range of entities, such as a range of ledger accounts, at run time. This feature has been implemented for several Dynamics AX document services, including *AxdChartOfAccounts* and *AxdPricelist*.

The *AxdSend* framework provides default dialog boxes for selecting endpoints and entity ranges and allows the generation of XML documents with multiple records. The framework allows you to provide specific dialog boxes for documents that need more user input than the default dialog box provides.

The default dialog box includes an endpoint drop-down list and, optionally, a Select button to open the standard query form. The query is retrieved from the *Axd*<Document> class the caller specifies. Many endpoints can be configured in the AIF, but only a few are allowed to receive the current document. The lookup shows only the endpoints that are valid for the document, complying with the constraint set up for the service operation *read* for the current document.

The framework requires minimal coding to support a new document. If a document requires you to simply select an endpoint and fill out a query range, most of the functionality is provided by the framework, without requiring additional code.

The standard dialog box for the *AxdSend* framework is shown in Figure 17-6.

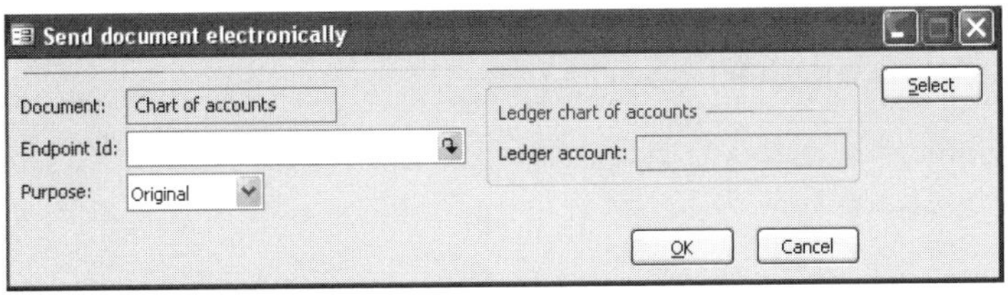

FIGURE 17-6 Send Document Electronically dialog box for Chart of accounts

If a document requires a more specific dialog box, you simply inherit the *AxdSend* class and provide the necessary user interface interaction to the dialog box method. In the following code example, an extra field has been added to the dialog box. You simply add one line of code (shown in bold in the following code from the *AxdSendChartOfAccounts* class) to implement *parmShowDocPurpose* from the *AxdSend* class and to make this field appear on the dialog box.

```
static public void main(Args args)
{
    AxdSendChartofAccounts          axdSendChartofAccounts ;
    AifConstraintList               aifConstraintList;
    AifConstraint                   aifConstraint;
    ;
    axdSendChartofAccounts          = new  AxdSendChartofAccounts();
    aifConstraintList               = new AifConstraintList();
    aifConstraint                   = new AifConstraint();

    aifConstraint.parmType(AifConstraintType::NoConstraint);
    aifConstraintList.addConstraint(aifConstraint);
```

```
    axdSendChartofAccounts.parmShowDocPurpose(true) ;

     axdSendChartofAccounts.sendMultipleDocuments(classnum(AxdChartOfAccounts),A
ifSendMode::Async,aifConstraintList) ;

}
```

Sorting isn't supported in the *AxdSend* framework, and the query structure is locked to ensure that the resulting query matches the query defined by the XML document framework. This need for matching is why the *AxdSend* class enforces these sorting and structure limitations. The query dialog box shows only the fields on the top-level tables because of the mechanics of queries with an outer join predicate. The result set will likely be different from what would be expected from a user perspective. For example, restrictions on inner data sources filter only these data sources, not the data sources that contain them. The restrictions are imposed on the user interface to match the restrictions on the query when using the document service's operation *find*.

Configuring Transmission Mechanisms

For details on configuring AIF channels and information on AIF channels and AIF endpoints in general, refer to the *Dynamics AX 2009 Server* and *Database Administration Guide*.

Consuming Web Services from Dynamics AX

Web services are a popular and well-understood way of integrating applications that are deployed within an enterprise's perimeter, or intranet. Examples of such applications include enterprise resource planning (ERP) applications, CRM applications, productivity applications such as Microsoft Office, and so on.

Integrating applications with third-party Web services over the Internet has also become viable and in many cases is the preferred approach to quickly adding new functionality to complex applications. Web services can range from simple address validation or credit card checks to more-complex tax calculations or treasury services. Integrating applications such as Dynamics AX with external Web services is often referred to as Software-plus-Services (S+S).

Note To find out more about S+S, see the article "Microsoft Software + Services—Bring It All Together" at *http://www.microsoft.com/softwareplusservices*.

The power of S+S lies in the opportunity to leverage the functionality of (almost) any Web service that is available as needed and thus in being able to outsource certain parts of business processes to trusted, specialized service providers in a cost-efficient way.

If you look at Figure 17-1 again, you can see the S+S scenarios in which Dynamics AX consumes external Web services on the right side.

Dynamics AX Service References

Dynamics AX service references can help you quickly integrate Dynamics AX with external Web services. Dynamics AX service references are conceptually similar to the service references in Microsoft Visual Studio 2008: each service reference represents a local interface to a remote Web service. A local API, that is, a *proxy*, can be used to communicate with the Web service. The proxy that is generated with Dynamics AX service references consists of .NET artifacts that can be discovered and used from X++ through CLR interop. Figure 17-7 illustrates how an external Web service can be integrated with Dynamics AX.

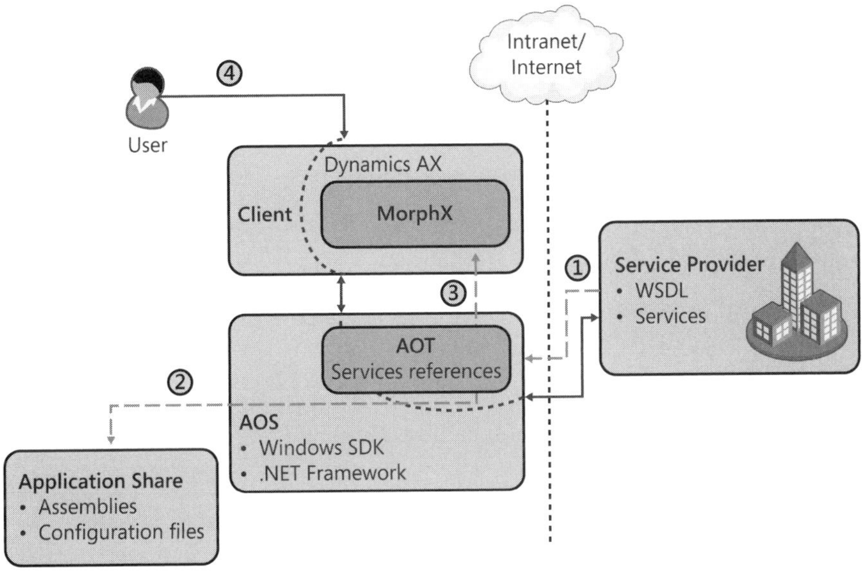

FIGURE 17-7 Integrating an external Web service with Dynamics AX

You generate Dynamics AX service references by using standard Microsoft tools that are part of .NET Framework 3.5 and Windows SDK for Windows Server 2008.

Consuming an External Web Service

In Dynamics AX, you can write code that consumes external Web services fairly easily. You need to take these simple steps at design time:

1. Get the WSDL file for the external Web service.
2. Create a Dynamics AX service reference.

3. Write integration code.
4. Then at run time, consume just the Web service as part of a business task and configure the service references as needed. We go over these steps in more detail in the following subsections.

> **Tip** Once you make sure Dynamics AX can connect to the external Web service, it is ready to go.

Getting the WSDL and Creating a Service Reference

First, you need to get access to the WSDL file for the service you want to consume. You can generate service references from WSDL files that are available online (addressed through http or https URLs) or offline in the file system (addressed through Universal Naming Convention [UNC] file paths).

> **Tip** Make sure the service contract (WSDL file) hasn't changed since the integration was implemented.

To create a service reference, right-click the AOT node References, select Add Service Reference, and enter four pieces of information:

- **WSDL URL** The (http or https) URL or UNC file path pointing to the WSDL file for the target Web service.
- **.NET code namespace** Lets you discover the generated .NET artifacts with IntelliSense.
- **Reference name** A unique name by which the service reference can be identified in the Dynamics AX client.
- **Description (optional)** A short text description of the service reference.

> **Tip** If you get the error "Cannot load CLR Object" while creating a service reference at run time, restart the AOS.

Once you fill in the information required for creating the service reference and click OK, an AOT node representing the new service reference is added.

Writing Integration Code

When the service reference is created, a .NET proxy for the external Web service is generated. You can use this .NET proxy from X++ code, through CLR interop, to communicate with the external Web service. You must grant CLR interop permissions to the code that accesses

.NET assemblies to instantiate parameters used for invoking an operation of an external Web service or for consuming the service itself.

Use the .NET namespace you provided when you created the service reference and IntelliSense to discover the generated .NET artifacts from X++.

When you write code to consume external Web services from X++, you need to make sure it has the following characteristics:

- It is marked to run on the server (AOS).
- It grants and revokes interop permissions.
- It explicitly passes a WCF endpoint name into the proxy constructor. The names of the available WCF endpoints are in the proxy's WCF configuration file (in the AIF administration form Service References, click Configure).
- It uses a valid license code for the external Web service (if applicable).

The following code sample uses the .NET proxy to consume the external Web service.

```
public static server boolean CheckCustomer (str customerName)
{
    DynamicsOfac.OfacSoapClient c;
    boolean b;

    // grant interop permissions
    new InteropPermission(InteropKind::ClrInterop).assert();

    // instantiate proxy using WCF endpoint name
    c = new DynamicsOfac.OfacSoapClient("OfacSoap");

    // consume Dynamics OFAC Web service
    b = c.LookupSdnByName(customerName);

    // revoke interop permissions
    CodeAccessPermission::revertAssert();

    // return results
    return b;
}
```

You need to write or modify code to use the results returned by the external Web service: for example, validation code that invokes a method similar to the one above that consumes an external Web service and returns the results.

Configuring Service References

You can view a list of available service references in the form Service References. To configure the WCF parameters for the new service reference, click Configure. Keep in mind that any changes you apply to the WCF configuration of the service proxy must be compatible with the WCF configuration of the service.

For more details on available WCF configuration parameters, see the Microsoft Dynamics AX 2009 SDK.

Note To configure Dynamics AX Services, we strongly recommend that you install Windows SDK for Windows Server 2008 so you can leverage the WCF configuration tools that are part of that SDK.

Guidelines for Consuming External Web Services

The main driver for programmatically consuming external Web services is improved efficiency—both technically and economically.

Integration Guidelines

Web services are a means for machine-to-machine integration. To streamline business processes, you should minimize the user's interaction with the external Web service. The consumption of external Web services should always be in the background whenever possible and involve the user only when additional input is needed. The fact that the implementation of the business task consumes an external Web service is an internal implementation detail that isn't relevant to the user.

When integrating external Web services, you should try to avoid duplicate data entry, which is time-consuming and error-prone. For example, assume that a sales order form has been filled out and a Web service needs to be invoked to calculate the best shipping option for delivering the goods to the recipient. It wouldn't make sense to launch a form that prompts for details such as delivery address, weight, and so on. Instead, that information can be retrieved from the sales order form, transparent to the user; other data, such as weight, might be easily read from the database. Automatic data correlation helps reduce the risks inherent in data entry.

You should integrate external Web services in a way that allows you to switch service providers without affecting the rest of your Dynamics AX application code. One way of achieving this is through defining X++ interfaces for (relevant) functionality the external Web service exposes. This switching capability also shields your application logic from changes in the service contract (WSDL) published by the service provider.

Security Guidelines

You need to be very careful in choosing your service providers whenever you plan on exchanging confidential or business-critical data. Service-level agreements with your service providers should clearly define the provided security precautions as well as other parameters that are necessary for your scenario, such as guaranteed system uptime, response times, and so on. Be sure to conduct a proper security review before you go live with integrations with external Web services.

Refer to other literature or expert advice for more-complete information on securing integrations.

Privacy When you exchange data with an external system—especially when that external system is outside the perimeter of your enterprise—you should always make sure that both data integrity and privacy are guaranteed. Because it is the external service that dictates the communication protocol and its configuration (including security), you should consider the supported security mechanisms when making a decision on what service provider to use for a particular integration.

Authentication Because the code that consumes the external Web service is executed on the Dynamics AX server (AOS), AOS's identity—not the user's identity—is used for authenticating requests to external Web services. In most scenarios in which a third-party service provides the external Web service, using AOS's identity isn't a restriction. Authentication (and billing) would typically be per Web service call per company instead of per user.

To prevent spoofing, we strongly recommend that you request server certificates for server authentication.

Authorization When consuming external Web services that are published by a third-party service provider, users who are authorized to perform a business task should automatically be authorized to consume all Web services needed to accomplish that task. For example, a user who is authorized to create a new customer record should automatically be authorized to use an external Web service for running a background check. The user shouldn't have to be explicitly authorized to consume the Web service that performs the background check.

Custom SOAP Headers

If configured, WCF automatically inserts standard SOAP headers (such as used for WS-Addressing) into messages. Custom SOAP headers—that is, SOAP headers that are not understood by the WCF stack—are not supported in Dynamics AX 2009. In other words, the service proxies generated for service references don't have an API for setting SOAP headers programmatically.

Keep in mind that the use of custom SOAP headers isn't yet widely spread. Most commercial Web services don't rely on them to increase interoperability.

Performance Considerations

In scenarios with more stringent performance requirements, the topology that supports the Dynamics AX deployment becomes even more critical. Consult the Dynamics AX Implementation Guide for details on properly sizing your deployment. It's available for download from *http://www.microsoft.com/dynamics/ax/using/default.mspx*.

By default, messages received in AIF channel adapters process all request messages in sequence; this is true for incoming request messages as well as outgoing ones. To increase the number of request messages that can be processed, you can leverage additional instances of the AOS. Refer to the Microsoft Dynamics AX 2009 SDK on MSDN for more information on how to configure inbound channels for parallelism and how to use extensions to the AIF *Send* API.

Note that because synchronous WCF Web services are deployed to IIS, request processing is inherently parallel.

Chapter 18

Code Upgrade

In this chapter:

The objectives of this chapter are to:

- Provide a high-level overview of the Microsoft Dynamics AX 2009 code upgrade process.
- Explain the significance of code upgrade in Dynamics AX.
- Define different types of conflicts and describe how to resolve them.
- Introduce the code upgrade toolset.
- Discuss the Smart Customization techniques that can help reduce the cost of upgrade.

Introduction

In Dynamics AX, code upgrade involves finding and resolving conflicts that result from customizations so that an upgraded version of Dynamics AX can successfully use those customizations. The code upgrade process is initialized from the Dynamics AX Upgrade checklist. Code upgrade can take place during a major version upgrade or when you're applying a service pack or hotfix. You can also run the code upgrade tools separately to detect Trustworthy Computing violations or issues with record ID and table ID references, topics that are covered in more depth later in this chapter.

This chapter begins with a discussion of the terminology used in code upgrade and the reasons code upgrade is necessary and then describes conflicts and explains how they're introduced. Next, the chapter describes the tools used to find and organize conflicts, and it provides some tips that can help you resolve them. Finally, the chapter describes how to avoid conflicts and the related workload by using Smart Customization techniques when you're customizing Dynamics AX.

Terminology

Before delving into the details about code upgrade, you need to understand the terms used to describe the process.

- **Element** A type definition in the Application Object Tree (AOT). For example, tables, classes, forms, and reports are elements. Elements are sometimes called application objects.
- **Original** Version of the element before it was customized. Original is usually the version delivered by Microsoft—or the independent software vendor (ISV) or Value Added Reseller (VAR).
- **Yours** Original installation including customization you introduce (i.e., customization you introduce on behalf of the business you work for).
- **Theirs** Original version including updates that Microsoft or the ISV or VAR has made.
- **Current** Version created by merging the Original version, the Yours version, and the Theirs version.
- **Layer** A file that contains all the Dynamics AX business logic (elements such as forms, tables, reports, and so on).
- **Customization** In the context of code upgrade, one or more changes that have been made to an element in the AOT, such as adding a field to a table.
- **Overlayering** A method of customization in which an Original element is copied into a current layer and modified; overlayering can lead to conflicts during the upgrade process, and you should use it carefully. See the section "Smart Customizations" at the end of this chapter for more information about ways to avoid overlayering.
- **Conflict** A mismatch that occurs when the customized definition of an element clashes with the new definition. Conflicts are typically identified during the system upgrade process; they can occur between layers, because of Trustworthy Computing errors, and from errors in record ID and table ID references.

Why Code Upgrade Is Necessary

One of the strengths of Dynamics AX is that it can be extensively customized to suit the needs of an individual business. In fact, because of the layered architecture in Dynamics AX, licensed parties can tailor the entire code base to fit their organization's requirements. When a business upgrades to a newer version of Dynamics AX or installs a service pack, however, it can encounter conflicts that occur because both Microsoft and the business have made changes to the same element (e.g., the metadata of a form or a report). Conflicts require manual intervention to ensure that both the business customizations (the Yours version) and the new version (the Theirs version) work properly when the business rolls out an upgraded version of Dynamics AX (the Current version).

> **Note** If you're working with the Microsoft .NET Framework, you don't encounter such conflicts because applications can't change the implementation of the .NET Framework. They are limited to using the APIs the framework provides, so a similar code upgrade process isn't necessary.

You must develop Dynamics AX customizations carefully, to avoid potential conflicts when possible or to make them easier to manage during the upgrade process. You can find out more about best practices for developing customization in the section "Smart Customizations" at the end of this chapter.

Role of Customization

Imagine that your business has implemented a customized version of Dynamics AX 4.0 (the circle Yours and the box Customized Dynamics AX 4.0 in Figure 18-1). Your business decides to upgrade to Dynamics AX 2009 (Theirs and Dynamics AX 2009 in Figure 18-1) while keeping the customizations it has developed intact. During the upgrade, you have to merge the customizations made in Yours with the changes made in Theirs to be able to continue to use the functionality from both versions (Current, Customized Dynamics AX 2009 in Figure 18-1).

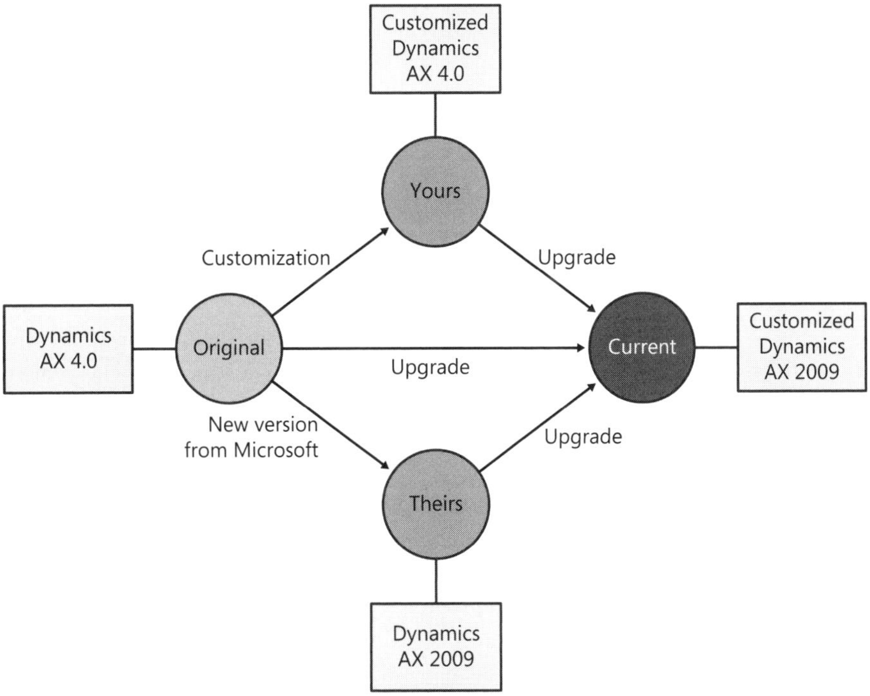

FIGURE 18-1 Top-level view of code upgrade

Obviously, Dynamics AX 2009 includes changes, some of which might clash with the customization in Yours, resulting in one or more conflicts. You must resolve the conflicts before you can continue with the version upgrade.

Note Keep in mind that from the system life cycle perspective, even releases of service packs and hotfixes require code upgrade.

Role of Layers

Layers contain the definition of the product, including the database schema and business logic, and are part of what enables developers to customize Dynamics AX so extensively. The changes to the contents of the layers (that is, AOT elements) during customization can cause conflicts, and these conflicts must be resolved during the code upgrade process. (To find out more about the application model layering system in Dynamics AX, refer to Chapter 1, "Architectural Overview.")

Figure 18-2 can help you visualize a layer and the elements it contains.

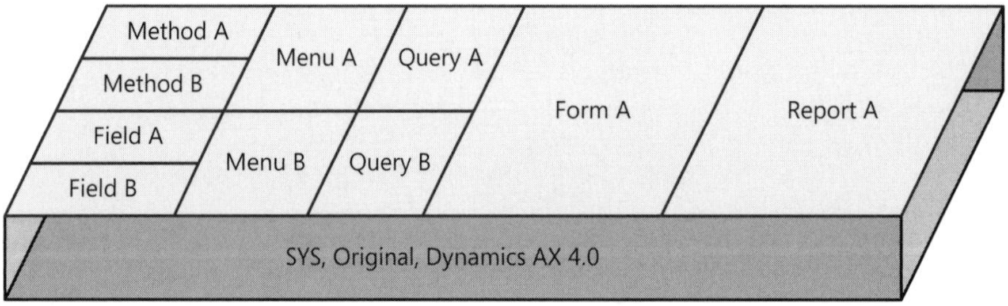

FIGURE 18-2 Representation of the SYS layer and the elements it contains

All Dynamics AX elements that Microsoft delivers are stored in layers that only Microsoft can access. These layers include SYS, SYP, GLS, GLP, HFX, SL1, SL2, and SL3. The most important thing for you to understand when customizing Dynamics AX is that when you customize an element, you are creating a modified copy of that element in another layer. This method of customization, called *overlayering*, frequently results in conflicts. Depending on the type of element that is modified, the scope and potential impact of the overlaying differs.

The effect of the overlaying varies by element type because different AOT elements have different sizes. For example, class methods, table methods, and table fields are smaller than menus and queries, which in turn are smaller than forms and reports. If you customize a form or a report, the entire form or report is copied into your current layer. When you modify the code of a single class method, only this single class method is copied into your current layer (creating Yours).

Tip Look at the status bar to see which layer you're working on.

To get a sense of the size of an AOT element, enable the AOT layer indicator: from the Microsoft Dynamics AX drop-down menu, point to Tools and then Options. On the Development tab, select Show All Layers from the Application Object Layer drop-down menu. Each element has a layer indicator in parentheses—for example, (SYS). A node without a layer indicator is contained within its parent. An element containing many child nodes is more likely to cause conflicts when customized than an element without any child nodes.

Overlayering and Conflicts

Consider a situation in which you customize Field A, Menu A, and Form A to create the Yours version of Dynamics AX 4.0. When you customize these elements, they are copied into the layer you're currently working in (USR in this case). The resulting overlayering is shown in Figure 18-3. As you can see in Figure 18-3, the customized versions of Field A, Menu A, and Form A have been automatically copied into the upper layer (USR), overshadowing their definition in the lower layer (SYS).

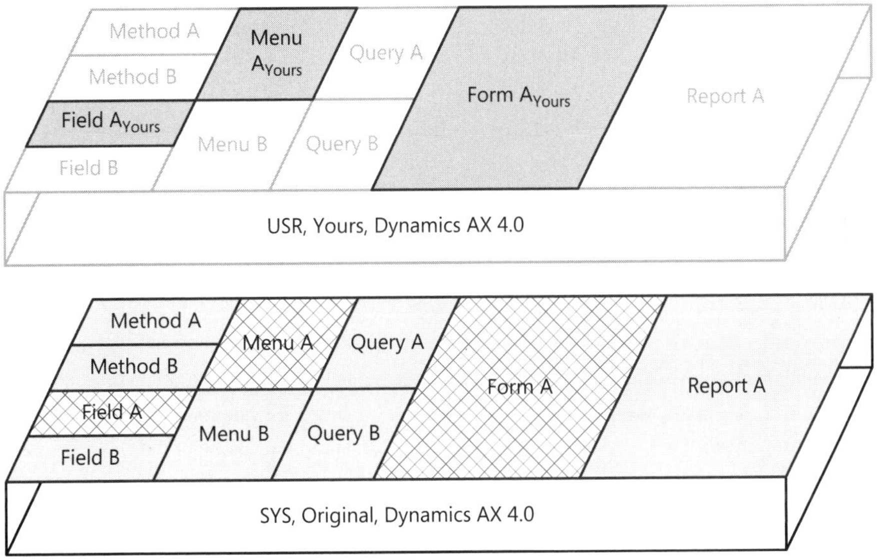

FIGURE 18-3 Overlayering conflicts

Assume that during the development of a new version of Dynamics AX, Microsoft changes Field A, Method B, Menu B, Query B, and Form A, as indicated in Figure 18-4.

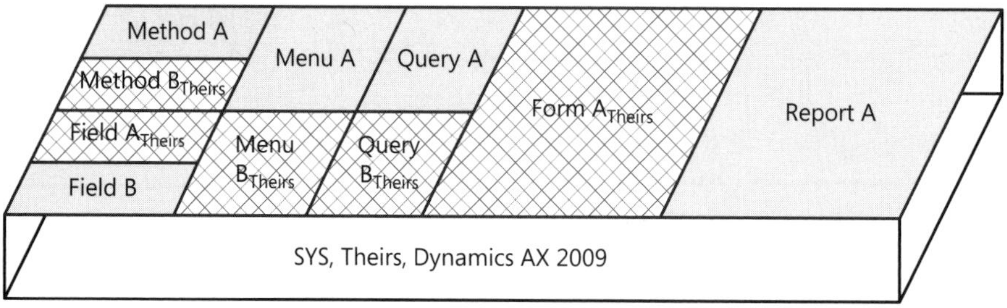

FIGURE 18-4 Hypothetical changes made by Microsoft in a new version of Dynamics AX

When your business upgrades to the new version, you have to merge the customizations you made (Figure 18-3) with the changes Microsoft introduced (Figure 18-4). Figure 18-5 shows the conflicts created by the differences between your customization and Microsoft's new version of Field A and Form A.

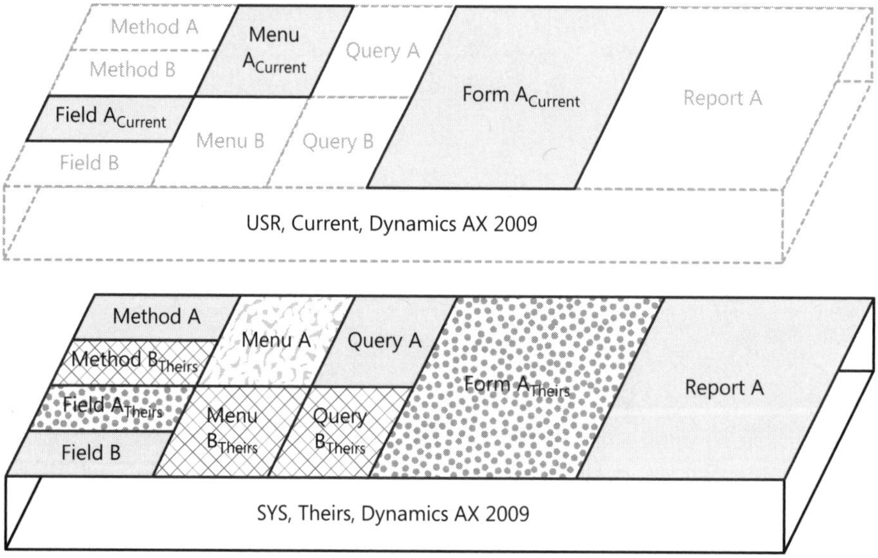

FIGURE 18-5 Conflicts in Field A and Form A resulting from customer changes in the USR layer and Microsoft changes in the SYS layer

As you can see in the figures, conflicts have occurred where you have made changes (Yours in Figure 18-3) and where Microsoft has (Theirs in Figure 18-4): Field A and Form A. You must find and resolve the conflicts so you can successfully merge the different versions. After a successful merge, Field A and Form A become Field $A_{Current}$ and Form $A_{Current}$ (Figure 18-5). You must then test the merged changes.

As long as the overlayered elements haven't been changed in the Theirs version—Menu A in this example—no additional work is required: Menu $A_{Current}$ is the same as Menu A_{Yours}. The same concept applies to elements that have been changed in the Theirs version but not in the Yours version—Menu B and Query B in this example.

The cost of merging—in both time and money—can be substantial when many conflicts occur. That is one of the reasons you should apply the Smart Customization techniques described later in this chapter when you're customizing Dynamics AX.

Starting a Code Upgrade

After the upgrade preparation work has been completed, the next major step in the upgrade process is code upgrade. Assume that you are upgrading a customized version of Dynamics AX 4.0 to Dynamics AX 2009. Here's how you proceed. Starting from the Dynamics AX Upgrade checklist tool, you use the conflict detection tool (formally known as the Detect Code Upgrade Conflicts tool) to find the conflicts between layers and (optionally) to identify Trustworthy Computing violations and record ID and table ID reference errors. Any conflicts found are collected into specific upgrade projects. You also use the Element Usage Log report to find elements that are no longer used and can be deleted. Based on the list of conflicts, you can use the Upgrade Estimate report to estimate how much time it will take to complete the upgrade. Armed with this information, you can resolve conflicts using the Compare tool, the AOT property sheet, and the X++ code editor. The AOT continuously mirrors the progress of the upgrade.

> **Note** You can read more about upgrade preparation, data upgrade, and data migration in the Microsoft Dynamics AX 2009 Upgrade Guide, found on the Using Microsoft Dynamics AX site: *http://microsoft.com/dynamics/ax/using.*

In this section, we describe the types of conflicts, the conflict detection tool and the conflicts it finds, and the algorithm the tool uses. Then in the next section, "Upgrade Projects," we describe how conflicts are grouped and, where possible, how conflicts are resolved. The Element Usage Log report, Upgrade Estimate report, Compare tool, property sheet, and X++ code editor are described in the "Code Upgrade Tools" section.

Conflict Types

As mentioned earlier, conflicts can occur between elements in layers and can also result from Trustworthy Computing violations and from issues with record ID and table ID references. There are three categories of conflicts:

- Layer conflicts, including overlayering, code, property, ordering, and deletion conflicts
- Trustworthy Computing conflicts, including record level security, parameter validation, and dangerous API use
- Record ID and table ID reference conflicts, including inconsistencies among record ID and table ID relationships

Conflict Detection Tool

The first step of the code upgrade process is to detect all the conflicts between the Theirs and Yours versions. The conflict detection tool (or officially, the Detect Code Upgrade Conflicts tool) finds any conflicts and then generates one or more upgrade projects that collect the conflicts into manageable categories.

The conflict detection tool can find any type of conflict from the three categories of conflicts. You can also have the tool automatically resolve any autoresolvable property conflicts it finds.

The conflict detection tool is available from the Dynamics AX 2009 drop-down menu: Tools\Development Tools\Code Upgrade\Detect Code Upgrade Conflicts. Figure 18-6 shows a screen shot of the tool.

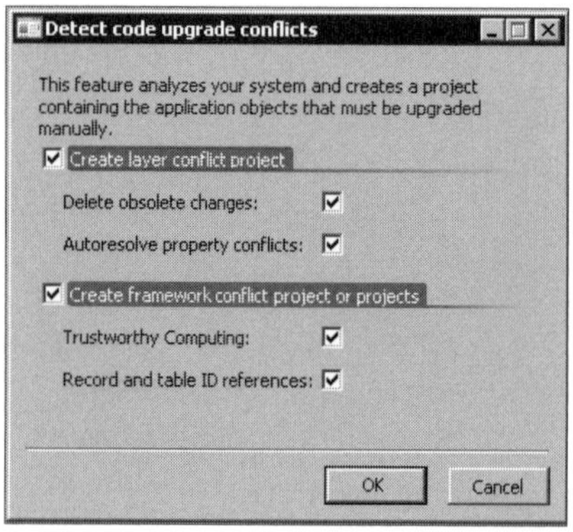

FIGURE 18-6 Conflict detection tool (also known as the Detect Code Upgrade Conflicts tool)

Conflict Detection Algorithm

The algorithm used to detect conflicts is straightforward. It searches for elements that exist in both the current layer and the underlying layer. It then compares both versions of the elements. If they differ, the algorithm puts the element (the Current version) into an upgrade project to be resolved. The algorithm can be illustrated as shown in Figure 18-7.

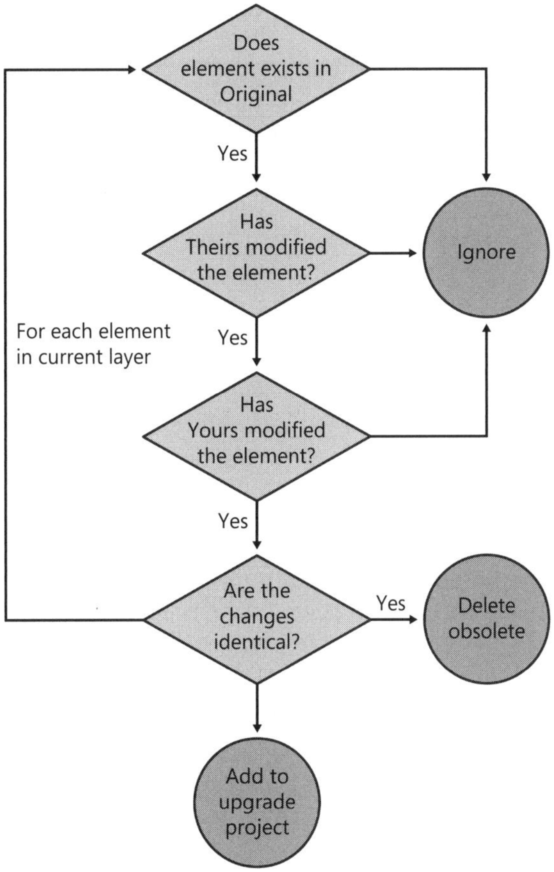

FIGURE 18-7 Algorithm that detects conflicts between a customized and a new version of Dynamics AX

Best Practices Do your initial code upgrade against an empty database. If you encounter problems, export the customizations, delete them from Dynamics AX, and run the code upgrade again. Then import the customizations and resolve the conflicts manually. Also do your code upgrade one layer at a time.

Upgrade Projects

The conflict detection tool creates upgrade projects. The purpose of an upgrade project is to collect the elements that have conflicts. This categorization, along with special visual indicators, enables you to easily find the elements with conflicts and to resolve them—either manually or by using the autoresolve property conflicts feature in the conflict detection tool. Upgrade projects also help you track the progress of the code upgrade. By default, upgrade projects are located under Private Projects in the AOT projects window.

Depending on the options you select in the conflict detection tool, one or more of the following kinds of upgrade projects are created:

- Layered upgrade project
- Framework conflict projects, which are Trustworthy Computing upgrade projects and/or record ID and table ID references upgrade projects

IIn the following sections, we describe some typical conflicts you could find in an upgrade project and suggest ways to resolve them.

Conflicts in Layered Upgrade Projects

The layered upgrade project collects contents conflicts, overlayering conflicts, and delete conflicts. In turn, each type of layered upgrade project contains additional kinds of conflicts.

> **Note** To be able to find conflicts between layers, your system must be properly configured for upgrade. If your system isn't configured properly, you get the following message in the Infolog window: "No elements are found in AOD files in the *Old* directory. The layer conflict project will not be created." For detailed procedures about how to configure your system for upgrade, please refer to the Microsoft Dynamics AX 2009 Upgrade Guide, available for download at *http://microsoft.com/dynamics/ax/using*.

Contents Conflicts

A contents conflict is a generic type of conflict that categorizes the conflicts that can happen among the contents of a node. A node can contain X++ code, properties, and subnodes. Contents conflicts include property conflicts, code conflicts, and ordering conflicts.

Property conflicts Generally speaking, a property conflict is a mismatch between property values in the Yours version and the Theirs version as compared to the Original version. There are three types of property conflicts:

- **Autoresolved** Property conflict that has been automatically resolved
- **Autoresolvable** Property conflict that can be resolved but hasn't been automatically resolved
- **Manually resolvable** Property conflict that must be resolved manually

Resolution Tip

You can automatically resolve many property conflicts by selecting Autoresolve Property Conflicts in the conflict resolution tool. You can usually resolve property conflicts that must be manually resolved by using the property sheet or the Compare tool. Following is a description of how the tool determines whether a property conflict can be automatically resolved and an example that shows the result of an automatically resolved property conflict.

If you enable the Autoresolve Property Conflicts option in the conflict detection tool, eligible property conflicts are automatically resolved and reported in the upgrade project with a yellow visual indicator. (The section "Visual Indicators" later in this chapter includes more information about the various visual indicators.)

The algorithm used to automatically resolve property conflicts is uncomplicated. Property conflicts can be automatically resolved when the property has been changed in either the Yours version or the Theirs version. If the same property has been changed in both the Yours and the Theirs versions and the property values are different, the conflict on the node can't be automatically resolved. The algorithm is shown in Figure 18-8.

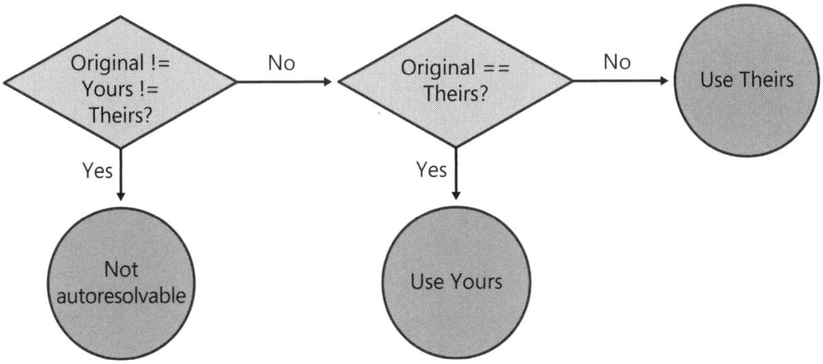

FIGURE 18-8 Algorithm used to automatically resolve property conflicts

Table 18-1 shows how some example property conflicts would be resolved.

TABLE 18-1 Results of Applying Autoresolve Property Conflicts Algorithm to Example Property Conflicts

Property	Original	Yours	Theirs	Autoresolved As
Font size	8	9	8	9
Font color	Blue	Blue	Red	Red
Text	Original	Yours	Theirs	Not autoresolvable (must resolve manually)

If even one property conflict that must be resolved manually occurs on a node, none of the autoresolvable conflicts are resolved.

Code conflict A code conflict occurs if the same method has been changed in different ways in the Yours and Theirs versions as compared to the Original version.

Resolution Tip
Given the variety of possible code conflicts, the resolutions depend on the source of the conflict. In a simple case in which the Yours version matches the Theirs version, you would simply delete the Yours copy in the upper layer.

A more complicated code conflict would arise if the business has adjusted the Dynamics AX business logic. In this case, the organization must investigate whether to preserve or to update that logic, depending on the changes that Microsoft has made in the new version.

Ordering conflict An ordering conflict occurs when the order of subnodes has been changed in both the Yours version and the Theirs version as compared to the Original version. The reasons for changing the subnode order are unique to each business, so there is no single way to resolve ordering conflicts. Your development team must investigate and decide whether it wants to preserve the Yours order of the subnodes or to update it to reflect the order in the Theirs version.

Overlayering Conflicts

In an overlayering conflict, a node is changed in the Theirs version, but the Yours version redefines the element containing the node but not the node itself.

Resolution Tip
Resolving this type of conflict is a matter of copying the Theirs version of the node into the Current version.

Delete Conflicts

In a delete conflict, one party has deleted the node and the other has changed it.

Resolution Tip
Depending on the element type, Microsoft either deletes the element or adds the prefix *DEL_* to the element name. Elements prefixed with *DEL_* are typically tables and fields, and they are required for the data upgrade portion of the version upgrade to succeed. Elements with the *DEL_* prefix are deleted in the next release, so if you encounter a delete conflict, you should rework your solution so that it doesn't depend on any deleted elements.

Conflicts in Framework Conflict Projects

The framework conflict projects collect Trustworthy Computing violations and record ID and table ID reference errors.

Framework conflict projects don't require the version update configuration to run. These projects are created on top of the Best Practices framework, so you do not need any infrastructure preparation before you run them. (For more information on the Best Practices framework, see Chapter 3, "The MorphX Tools.")

Trustworthy Computing Conflicts

The Trustworthy Computing upgrade project collects the following types of conflicts: record level security, parameter validation, use of a dangerous API, reference to an unsigned .NET assembly, and validation of display or edit values. Where possible, we provide tips for resolving these conflicts. As always, you should follow secure coding best practices. For more information about secure coding practices for X++, refer to the Microsoft Dynamics AX X++ Security white paper, which is available from the Microsoft Download Center at *http://microsoft.com/Downloads*.

Record level security Record level security builds on the restrictions enforced by user-group permissions. With user-group permissions, you restrict which menus, forms, and reports members of a group can access. Record level security also enables you to restrict the information shown in reports and on forms. However, record level security is bypassed in several situations in which the data binding to a control is performed manually—for example, when you use *ListView*, *TreeView*, or a table control to show data. These situations are detected automatically and reported as conflicts, enabling you to pay attention to the potential security issues.

Resolution Tip

Depending on the conflicts, you can resolve record level security violations in several ways. One possible resolution is to manually enable record level security. When a list view, tree view, or table control is populated with data from a query, you must manually enable record level security. In this example, record level security isn't enabled.

```
public void run()
{
    CustTable custTable;

    super();

    while select custTable
    {
        listView.add(custTable.name);
    }
}
```

To resolve this conflict, you have to enable the record level security from code, as shown here.

```
public void run()
{
    CustTable custTable;

    super();

    // Ensure that RLS is used.
    custTable.recordLevelSecurity(true);

    while select custTable
    {
        listView.add(custTable.name);
    }
}
```

Parameter validation One example of a parameter validation conflict is when the user can call the managed code directly with a parameter that isn't validated.

```
public void testMethodConflict( str name )
{
    CLRObject clrObj;
    ;
    clrObj = new CLRObject( name );
}
```

Resolution Tip

To mitigate threats associated with calls to unmanaged code, follow this guideline: always validate the (string) input parameters that are used to create instances of these objects. If an adversary can control which DLL/COM object to use, the adversary can compromise parts of the system through Dynamics AX APIs that would normally be inaccessible. The following example shows how to make the parameter constant, which helps prevent attacks using an injection technique.

```
public void testMethodResolution()
{
    CLRObject newClrObj;
    #define.Name('test')
    ;
    newClrObj = new CLRObject( #Name );
}
```

Use of dangerous API A dangerous API is an API that when used inappropriately can become a threat to the system. When you surface a dangerous API conflict, you should substitute an API that is not classified as dangerous. If a feature must access a dangerous API, you should perform an authorization check to make sure that only trusted code from that feature can use the API in question.

A good example of a dangerous API conflict follows. The method here is using direct access to the database by executing SQL statements through the *Statement* class API.

```
void MyFunction( str _value)
{
    DictTable  dictTable  = new DictTable(tableNum(custTable));
    Connection connection = new Connection();
    Statement  statement  = connection.createStatement();
    str sql = strfmt("SELECT * FROM %1 WHERE %2 == %3",
                dictTable.name(DbBackend::Sql),
                fieldStr(Custtable, accountNum),
                _value);
    ;
    statement.executeUpdate(sql);
}
```

Resolution Tip
To resolve this conflict you should use a proper data access mechanism. For example, use the X++ *select* statement.

```
void MyFunctionMitigated( str 20 _value )
{
    CustTable table;
    select table where table.AccountNum == _value;
}
```

Reference to unsigned .NET assembly This conflict occurs when you have added a reference to a managed assembly, and that assembly is unsigned.

Resolution Tip
Use the following rules when you add a reference to the .NET assembly in the AOT:

- The reference must use a fully qualified name.
- The assembly referenced must be strongly signed.

Validation of display or edit values If a user has access to a table, the user also has access to all the display methods (from ad hoc reports), as you can see in this example.

```
display ForecastHasSales hasSalesBudget()
{
    return (select forecastSales
                where forecastSales.itemGroupId == this.itemGroupId).recId != 0;
}
```

In theory, a display method can expose any data from any table. If a display method returns data from another table (or another row in the same table), it poses a threat—this threat is surfaced as a Trustworthy Computing conflict.

Resolution Tip
To resolve conflicts associated with the use of display and edit methods, follow these steps:

- Evaluate each display method that returns data from another row, either in the same table or in a different table.
- Determine whether this data poses an information-disclosure threat.
- If the data does pose a threat, perform explicit authorization checks and throw an exception if access is unauthorized.

Record ID and Table ID Reference Conflicts

The record ID and table ID reference project collects the following types of conflicts: *RecId* relation missing, *TableId* relation missing, field uses *RecId*, field uses *TableId*, type extends *RecId*, and type extends *TableId*.

Similar to the Trustworthy Computing upgrade project, the record ID and table ID reference upgrade project is created on the top of the best practice check framework and doesn't require version update to run. For more information about the Best Practices tool, see Chapter 3.

***RecId* relation missing** This conflict occurs when a table contains a field that uses the *RefRecId* extended data type (or derived type) but no relation is defined for that field.

Resolution Tip
To resolve a *RecId* relation missing conflict, either define the missing relation or don't use *RefRecId* as an extended data type on the field.

***TableId* relation missing** This conflict occurs when a table contains a field that uses the *RefTableId* extended data type (or derived type) but no relation is defined for that field.

Resolution Tip
To resolve a *TableId* relation missing conflict, either define the missing relation or don't use *RefTableId* as an extended data type on the field.

Field uses *RecId* This conflict occurs when a table field uses the *RecId* extended data type.

Resolution Tip
To resolve a field uses *RecId* conflict, you must use *RefRecId* or a derived extended data type and define the relation that actually uses this field.

Field uses *TableId* This conflict occurs when a table field uses the *TableId* extended data type.

Resolution Tip
To resolve a field uses *TableId* conflict, you must use *TableRecId* or a derived extended data type.

Type extends *RecId* This conflict occurs when you create a new extended data type that extends the *RecId* type.

Resolution Tip
To resolve a type extends *RecId* conflict, you have to change the extending type to *RefRecId*.

Type extends *TableId* This type of conflict is similar to the type extends *RecId* conflict. It occurs when an extended data type extends the *TableId* type.

Resolution Tip
To resolve a type extends *TableId* conflict, you have to change the extending type to *RefTableId*.

Upgrade Project Tools

The tools described in this section can help you manage your upgrade projects.

Visual Indicators

To help you find the exact place where a conflict is located and to show you the status of the conflict, Dynamics AX 2009 has added visual indicators to the upgrade project. There are two kinds of visual indicators. The first type reflects the status of the conflict and has three subtypes:

Resolved A green box with a check mark

Auto resolved A yellow box with a check mark

Manually resolvable A red circle with an X

The second type of visual indicator, also three subtypes, can help you navigate the upgrade project and easily find the nodes where conflicts have occurred:

Resolved conflict below A green arrow

Auto resolved conflict below A yellow arrow

Manually resolvable conflict below A red arrow

If there is more than one conflict on a node, the visual indicator points out the most severe one. Conflicts that must be manually resolved are the most severe, followed by conflicts that have been automatically resolved.

Tip When you hover over the node with a conflict, you see a tooltip that describes the type of conflict on the node.

Mark As Resolved, Unresolved This option is dedicated to helping you keep track of the progress you're making in resolving conflicts. After you review and resolve a conflict, use this option to update the status of the conflict. Select the node in the Upgrade project, open the context menu, point to Add-Ins, and select the appropriate option.

Note The conflict status shows up in the Upgrade Estimate report and enables easy tracking of the progress of the code upgrade process.

The Mark As Unresolved option can help you when you have to revisit a place in the code, reevaluate the property value, or inspect the order of controls.

Remove Resolved Elements To create a clear workspace, you can remove elements with resolved conflicts from an upgrade project. Open the context menu from the root of the appropriate upgrade project, and click Remove Resolved Elements.

Rerun Conflict Detection You might occasionally need to rerun the conflict detection functionality—for example, if you accidentally mark the conflict on a node as resolved. Select the node in the upgrade project, open the context menu, point to Add-Ins, and select the appropriate option.

Caution Use the Rerun Conflict Detection option carefully. It overwrites the status of conflicts, which is then reflected in the Upgrade Estimate report.

Code Upgrade Tools

Dynamics AX ships several tools that you can use to plan your code upgrade and resolve the conflicts you find. In this section, we describe the tools you can use to find and resolve these conflicts so that you can successfully merge your customizations with a newer version of Dynamics AX.

Element Usage Log Report

If you have conflicts on forms or reports and you're not sure anyone uses those elements, you can use the Element Usage Log report to see how often certain elements are used.

The purpose of this tool is to collect information about the usage of forms and reports, elements that can be expensive to upgrade. The log can help you to decide whether you want to invest in upgrading these elements.

The algorithm used to collect usage information is simple. Every time a form or report is opened, the usage is logged in memory.

You can find the Element Usage Log report in the Administration module: Reports\System\Element Usage Log or in the AOT under Reports\SysUtilElementsLog.

Upgrade Estimate Report

More conflicts in the system mean more development work during upgrade. The Upgrade Estimate report can help you plan the development team's code upgrade work. As soon as you know the number and type of conflicts you have in your system, you can use the Upgrade Estimate report to give you a good estimate of how much time is needed to resolve the conflicts.

Tip The Upgrade Estimate report provides time estimations in fractions of an hour, not in minutes.

You can invoke the Upgrade Estimate report from two places: from the context menu of a root node of an upgrade project and from the Microsoft Dynamics AX drop-down menu under Tools\Development Tools\Code Upgrade\Estimation Report. There is an essential difference between these two reports: the estimation report created from the root of the upgrade project considers only those conflicts that are in the particular upgrade project. The estimation report from the Dynamics AX drop-down menu considers conflicts from all upgrade projects you've created—that is, the total number of conflicts in your system—which can help you estimate the time required for the entire (layered upgrade, Trustworthy Computing upgrade, and record and table ID references upgrade) code upgrade process.

Dynamics AX has defined default time estimates for each type of conflict. Depending on your level of experience with Dynamics AX, you might want to adapt the predefined values so they better reflect your real world. To change the predefined values, from the root of the upgrade project, open the Upgrade Parameters form. You can edit any of the six default settings to specify custom default values for specific conflict types and object types.

Compare Tool

The Compare tool is the primary tool that can help you resolve the conflicts in your system. To open the Compare tool, select an element in the AOT, open the element's context menu, and point to Compare (or use the Ctrl+G shortcut after selecting an element in the AOT). Similar to the conflict detection tool, the Compare tool can be used to inspect and resolve conflicts. The Compare tool can compare two different elements, the same element in two different layers, two versions of the same element (if you're using version control), and two versions of the same element with the original version of the element.

You can also use the Compare tool to resolve conflicts by inserting, deleting, or moving code. For more information about the Compare tool, including procedures, see the Microsoft Dynamics AX 2009 Upgrade Guide, which is available for download from *http://microsoft.com/dynamics/ax*.

Property Sheet

Sometimes the Compare tool can't help you resolve conflicts—for example, if one of the parties (Yours or Theirs) has normalized a table that resulted in splitting data sources and caused the removal of the old data sources. In this case, you can use the property sheet to resolve property conflicts and the X++ code editor to resolve code conflicts. For more information about the property sheet, see Chapter 3.

X++ Code Editor

When code changes between the Yours version and the Theirs version are significant and complex, you can't use the Compare tool to resolve conflicts. Instead, you need to use the X++ code editor to make the code changes that resolve the conflict. For more information about the X++ code editor, see Chapter 3.

Finishing a Code Upgrade

After you have found and resolved all conflicts, test the system to make sure that the code upgrade has succeeded. Testing involves performing unit tests to ensure that users can still execute their most common and vital tasks, that administrators can run system maintenance tasks, and that permission settings are working properly. For more information on unit tests, see Chapter 3 or the Microsoft Dynamics AX 2009 software development kit (SDK) on MSDN. For more information about performing post–code upgrade tests, see the Microsoft Dynamics AX 2009 Upgrade Guide.

Smart Customizations

The goal of Smart Customizations is to provide guidelines that help you customize an application so that you can avoid overlayering and thus minimize conflicts during the upgrade process. Generally, you should try to add new elements instead of changing existing ones. If you must customize the application in a way that causes overlayering, try to change a small element—a class method, for example—instead of a big element, like a form. If you customize a class method, only that class method is affected, and future code upgrades will be smoother. On the other hand, if you update one property on a grid that is placed on a form, the entire form is copied into the layer you're working on. The large "size" of the copied form means that future upgrades will be more time-consuming.

Following are some specific techniques you can use to avoid overlayering conflicts.

> **Note** You can see a recording about Smart Customizations on the Channel 9 site, accessible through MSDN.

Using IntelliMorph Technology

Instead of customizing forms and reports, you should use field groups and extended data types, and take advantage of the dynamic rendering functionalities of the IntelliMorph technology. Let's assume that you add a new field on a table and you want to display it on a form. Instead of customizing the form by adding a new control for the new data field, you can add the field to an existing field group on the table and let IntelliMorph do the work for you. By doing this, you have customized only the field group, not the form or the table. A conflict on a field group has a much lower impact than adding a new control to the form. For more information about using IntelliMorph technology, see the Microsoft Dynamics AX 2009 SDK.

Creating New Elements or Using Class Substitution

As mentioned earlier, you can also avoid overlayering by creating a new element instead of modifying an existing element; new elements don't overlayer any existing element.

For classes, you should consider using the class substitution technique. Think about this as an implementation of the Liskov Substitution Principle (LSP). When you follow the LSP, you substitute one implementation of a class with another implementation by using inheritance. The class being substituted must have its constructor encapsulated, so the developer has to modify the construction of the original class in only one place. This is why you find static *construct* methods on most classes in Dynamics AX.

The static *construct* method is responsible for creating a new instance of a given class. You use this *construct* method across the application whenever a new instance of a given class is required. You can easily change the behavior of a given class by modifying the *construct* method and creating an instance of derived type instead of creating an instance of base type. (A similar technique, the extract and override factory method, is commonly used to remove dependencies. You can read more about that technique in the book *Working Effectively with Legacy Code* by Robert Martin.) In the derived type, you specialize original behavior with the required behavior. This customizes the application by adding new code, resulting in minimum overlayering.

Modifying Stable Application Elements

Finally, you should consider how likely it is that Microsoft, the ISVs, or the VARs you work with (the creators for Theirs) will change a given application element in the future. For example, complicated logic or large elements such as forms are more likely to change than factory methods. Generally speaking, the more complicated the logic, the more likely it is that it could change in the future and cause hard-to-resolve upgrade conflicts.

Part IV

Appendices

In this part:

Appendix A
Application Files

All application model elements are stored in application files in an application folder on a file system that is usually located on an Application Object Server (AOS). Deploying application extensions, customizations, and patches requires changes to the application files. Application files have the file extensions listed in the following table.

Application File Extensions

First Letter	Second Letter	Third Letter
A (for *application*) The file is an application file.	**O** (for *object*) The file contains application model elements.	**D** (for *data*) The file is a data file. The *data* designation is historical, not factual. The file can contain model elements, X++ source code, and corresponding bytecode.
K (for *kernel*) The file is a kernel (system) file and should not be modified.	**L** (for *label*) The file contains label resources.	**I** (for *index*) The file is an index file to a data file. If the index file is not found, the application server re-creates it.
	H (for *Help*) The file contains links to the online documentation.	**T** (for *temporary*) The file contains data that will be written to a data file.
	D (for *developer Help*) The file contains online documentation for application developers.	**C** (for *cache*) The file contains cached data. It can be deleted without compromising integrity—only performance is compromised.
	T (for *text*) The file contains system text. This letter is used only in .ktd files.	

In light of the preceding table, the following file extensions, which are drawn from the file types that typically make up a Microsoft Dynamics AX application, are readily comprehensible:

- The .aod files contain the application object data, or more precisely, the model element, X++ source code, and bytecode data for a specific model element layer.
- The .aoi file contains the index to the .aod file.

- The .khd files contain kernel Help data (system documentation in the Application Object Tree).
- The .ald files contain the application label data.
- The .alc files contain the application label cache.

> **Note** In Dynamics AX 4.0 and Dynamics AX 2009, the application object cache file is named .auc (application Unicode object cache). In earlier versions, it was named .aoc, which strictly followed the naming conventions outlined in the table. The new name reflects the fact that the objects are now stored in Unicode format.

The file name itself can also contain comprehensible information:

- All the object, label, Help, and developer Help files contain model elements from specific model element layers. One file is created for each layer, and the layer name is part of the file name.
- All label, Help, and developer Help files are localizable. There is one file for each locale, and the locale is a part of the file name. Here are a few examples:
  - AxSys.aod
  - AxSysEn-us.ald
  - AxSysEn-us.ahd

> **Note** The actual Help contents is stored in stand-alone Help files (.chm files); the application Help files contain only the links between elements and their documentation. For details about the documentation, refer to the Microsoft Dynamics AX 2009 SDK.

Appendix B

SQL Server 2005, SQL Server 2008, and Oracle Database 10*g* Comparison

The following table shows the statements that are sent to the supported databases when database transactions are handled.

Dynamics AX 2009	SQL Server 2005	SQL Server 2008	Oracle Database 10*g*
First *ttsbegin* statement	BEGIN TRANSACTION	BEGIN TRANSACTION	No statement sent
Final *ttscommit* statement	COMMIT TRANSACTION	COMMIT TRANSACTION	COMMIT
ttsabort statement	ROLLBACK TRANSACTION	ROLLBACK TRANSACTION	ROLLBACK
selectLocked(false)	Not supported, so no hint added	Not supported, so no hint added	Not supported, so no hint added
Select *optimisticlock concurrencyModel (ConcurrencyModel:: OptimisticLock)*	No hint	No hint	No hint
Select *pessimisticlock concurrencyModel (ConcurrencyModel:: PessimisticLock)*	WITH (UPDLOCK) hint added to SELECT statement	WITH (UPDLOCK) hint added to SELECT statement	FOR UPDATE OF clause added to SELECT statement
readPast(true)	WITH (READPAST) added to SELECT statement	WITH (READPAST) added to SELECT statement	Not supported, so no hint added
Select *repeatableread selectWithRepeatableRead (true)*	WITH (REPEATABLEREAD) added to SELECT statement	WITH (REPEATABLEREAD) added to SELECT statement	FOR UPDATE OF clause added to SELECT statement

Appendix C

Source Code Changes Required for Upgrade

When you upgrade to Microsoft Dynamics AX 2009 from an earlier version, you must make changes to the source code to ensure that the internal references comply with the new best practices. These changes include code changes, metadata changes, and table modifications, as described in the following sections.

Code Changes

For fields of the *int64* data type assigned to a 32-bit integer value, the assigned-to variable must be rewritten as a variable of the same type, or explicitly cast to an *int* value. For example,

```
int RecId = table.RecId;
```

must be rewritten like this:

```
RecId RecId = table.RecId;
```

When a variable that derives from *int64* is used as an index to an array, the code must be refactored to use a map. For example,

```
int array[,1];
array[table.RecId] = 123;
```

must be written either as a map (in memory, used for few records), as shown here,

```
Map map = new Map(TypeId2Type(TypeId(RecId)),Types::Integer);
map.insert(table.RecId, 123);
```

or as a temporary table (on disk, used for many records), as shown here,

```
TmpTable tmp;
tmp.RecIdRef = table.RecId;
tmp.value    = 123;
tmp.insert();
```

For fields of the type *int64* that are placed into a collection class, as shown here,

```
Set set = new Set(Types::integer);
Set.insert(myTable.RecId);
```

the code must be updated to use the appropriate data type, as shown here:

```
Set set = new Set (TypeId2Type(TypeId(RecId)));
Set.insert(myTable.RecId);
```

When a record ID is used inside a *pack* method, the code should be refactored to persist that record ID to a table field.

Metadata Changes

You should notice that the extended data type *RefRecId* derives from the *RecId* system data type and is automatically increased to 64 bit. The following are the extended data type requirements:

- Extended data types used by fields that contain *RecIds* must derive from the *RecId* data type or one of its derived extended data types to automatically increase the extended data type to 64 bits.
- Extended data types used by fields that contain *RecIds* must derive from the *RefRecId* extended data type or one of its derived types.
- Extended data types must define a relation to the *RecId* column of a table if:
    - The extended data type has *RefRecId* as an ancestor type.
    - The extended data type has a deterministic relationship to exactly one other table.
- Extended data types must not define a relation to the *RecId* column of a table if:
    - It doesn't have *RefRecId* as an ancestor type.
    - The extended data type, or one of its derived types, can be used to refer to *RecIds* in more than one table.

- Extended data types used by fields that contain table IDs must derive from the *tableID* data type.
- Extended data types used by fields that contain table IDs should derive from the *RefTableId* extended data type.

Table Modifications

The following are the required table modifications for upgrade:

- Table fields that contain a *RecId* (other than the system-defined *RecId* field itself) must be associated with an extended data type of *RefRecId* or one of its derived types.

> **Note** The *RecId* extended data type should be used only by the system *RecId* fields.

- Table fields that contain a *RecId* (other than the system-defined *RecId* field) should be associated with an extended data type that is strictly derived from the *RefRecId* data type (not including the *RefRecId* data type itself).
- Existing table fields that have *RecId* or *RefRecId* as an ancestor and define their own deterministic single-field relation should have that relation removed.
- Relations must be defined for every table field associated with a *RecId*-derived extended data type (hereafter called *RecId-derived field*) that doesn't define its own single fixed-field relations. Fixed-field relations (defined with the Related Field Fixed option when adding a relation on an extended data type) are those in which the related table depends on the value of another field.
- If the table to which a *RecId*-derived field is related depends on the value of another field, and that other field contains an enumeration (or other value) to indicate the table to relate to for each row, one relation in the table must be defined for each value in the enumeration using a combination of a Related Field Fixed relation and a Normal relation.
- If the table to which a *RecId*-derived field is related depends on the value of another field, and that other field contains table IDs, one of the following approaches must be adopted:
    - A relation must be defined for each legal value of the field containing the table ID. (From inspecting the Application Object Tree, you see that this is a very common approach.)
    - A single relation must be defined in the table to express that relationship in terms of the Common table.

- All fields that are used to refer to a table ID must be associated with the *RefTableId* extended data type or a derived type.

> **Note** The *tableID* system type should be used only by the system-created *tableID* fields.

- All fields that are used to refer to a table ID should be associated with a type strictly derived from *RefTableId*.

Multiple Time Zones

To support multiple time zones, a new type, *UtcDateTime*, has been introduced in Dynamics AX 2009.

Language Enhancements

A new primitive data type *UtcDateTime* is available in X++. This data type supports all operations that are supported by other existing primitive types, such as *Int* and *Date*. Here is an example of the new data type.

```
void CheckNewType()
{
    UtcDateTime utcDt;
    ;
    utcDt = 2000-03-14T22:10:10;
    print utcDt;
}
```

API Enhancements

New functions have been added that can be used when working with the new type. These functions have been added to the *DateTimeUtil* system class. All the functions in this class are static.

Metadata Enhancements

Metadata enhancements are provided at three levels. These changes allow you to create *DateTime* type nodes for extended data types, table fields, and form controls.

You can create extended data types of type *DateTime* as you do any other extended data type.

System Field Changes

The system fields have also changed. The *CREATEDDATE* and *CREATEDTIME* columns that store the date and time data separately have been merged to a single *CREATEDDATETIME* column. The existing *CREATEDTIME* column has been renamed to *DEL_CREATEDTIME*. Similarly, *MODIFIEDDATE* and *MODIFIEDTIME* have merged to *MODIFIEDATETIME*, and *MODIFIEDTIME* has been renamed to *DEL_MODIFIEDTIME*. A side-effect of this change is that the kernel-defined user types on which these columns are based have been renamed accordingly. The field IDs for these fields haven't changed.

These columns always store the UTC date time value unless the application developer explicitly overrides it. For tables stored in the database, the UTC date time value is generated at the database. For tables using the native database, the UTC date time value is generated based on the machine's clock setting.

The upgrade framework handles upgrades automatically. You don't have to write upgrade scripts.

Upgraded System Fields

Existing tables that have the preceding system fields have been updated to the new system fields. When reading the metadata information from the AOD, we checked whether existing tables had either *CreatedDate* or *CreatedTime*. If either of those fields is set to *Yes*, the new *CreatedDateTime* property is set to *Yes*. Similarly, if an existing .xpo file for a table contains either *CreatedDate* or *CreatedTime*, the new property is set. When the table is saved or if it is exported, only the new property is saved.

Best Practice Don't explicitly overwrite system fields unless your application requires you to. And don't overload *system* fields and use them for unrelated purposes in your application. It's better to create a separate *datetime* field.

DateTime Control and Form Changes

You can use the new *DateTime* control in forms and map to *DateTime* database fields or any *DateTime* value.

Use the *DisplayOption* property to configure the control to show only date, only time, or both date and time values. The default auto option shows both the date and time values.

Use the *TimeZonePreference* property to enable time zone conversions at the control level. For example, if you currently have an extended type configured to return *UTC* date time, you can instead convert to the user's time zone by setting the *TimeZonePreference* property for the control.

Best Practice The *DateTime* control should show the data in the user's time zone.

Glossary

The following list contains terms and abbreviations used throughout the book. For an in-depth terminology list, refer to the product documentation.

Term	Definition
.add	The file extension for application developer documentation data. For details on application files, refer to Appendix A, "Application Files."
.ahd	The file extension for application Help data. For details on application files, refer to Appendix A, "Application Files."
.ald	The file extension for application label data. For details on application files, refer to Appendix A, "Application Files."
.aod	The file extension for Application Object Data (AOD). Files with the extension .aod contain application objects—more precisely, the model element, X++ source code, and byte code data for a specific model element layer. An .aod file contains all the code for a layer and is used to distribute solutions.
.khd	The file extension for kernel Help data. For details, refer to Appendix A, "Application Files."
.xpo	The file extension for the export of Dynamics AX elements.
A2A	Application-to-application communication between a business and its external trading partners.
accessor method	A method that can get, set, or both get and set member variable values. In X++, typically referred to as a *parm* method.
ACID	Abbreviation for Atomicity, Consistency, Isolation, Durability. *Atomicity:* Every operation in the transaction is either committed or rolled back. *Consistency:* When committed, the transaction should leave the database in a consistent state. *Isolation:* Any uncommitted changes are not visible to other transactions. *Durability:* After a transaction is committed, the changes are permanent, even in the event of system failure.
ad hoc report	Report that an end user creates.
adapter	A software component that enables message exchange using a specific transport.
AIF	Abbreviation for Application Integration Framework. The AIF provides a programming model, tools, and infrastructure support for services-based integration of application functionality and data with Dynamics AX.
AOC	Abbreviation for Application Object Cache.
AOI	Abbreviation for Application Object Index (index to the AOD).
AOS	Abbreviation for Application Object Server.

Term	Definition
AOT	Abbreviation for Application Object Tree. The AOT is a development tool whose nodes are populated with the metadata model and X++ source code. Some model elements in the tree are class and interface definitions that specify the structure and behavior of application logic and framework types. The top-level nodes in the AOT, such as Forms and Reports, are model concepts that organize the model elements of the dictionary.
application model element	The building blocks used to model a Dynamics AX application. Application model elements contain metadata, structure, properties (key and value pairs), and X++ code. For example, a table element includes the name of a table, the properties set for a table, the fields, the indexes, the relations, the methods, and so on.
AUC	Abbreviation for Application Unicode Object Cache.
AutoDataGroup	A control property that, if set to *Yes*, inherits the field group design dynamically from the specific table. This removes the option to further customize the group layout at the control level in the AOT, but you may do so from the code when the form is executed.
AVL	A data structure of self-balanced binary search trees. The term is named after its two inventors, G. M. Adelson-Velskii and E. M. Landis, who described it in their 1962 paper "An Algorithm for the Organization of Information."
***Axd* classes**	Dynamics AX document classes.
B2B	Short for business-to-business.
base enumeration element	Defines a name for a group of symbolic constants that are used in X++ code statements. For example, an enumeration with the name WeekDay can be defined to name the group of symbolic constants that includes Monday, Tuesday, Wednesday, Thursday, Friday, Saturday, and Sunday. Also known as enum.
batch group	An attribute of a batch task that allows the administrator to determine which AOS runs the job. Batch groups are used to direct batch tasks to specific servers.
batch server	A batch server is an Application Object Server (AOS) instance that processes batch jobs.
batch task	A work item that makes up a batch job. Each task completes a portion of the batch job, and the tasks may have complex dependencies between them. In Dynamics AX, each task is a batch-enabled class.
batch-enabled class	A class that can be queued as a batch task and run as a batch job.
CLR	Abbreviation for the Microsoft .NET Common Language Runtime.
conflict	A mismatch that occurs when the customized definition of an element clashes with the new definition. Conflicts are typically identified during the system upgrade process; they can occur between layers, because of Trustworthy Computing errors, and from errors in record ID and table ID references.

Term	Definition
Cue	An icon depicting a stack of papers that represent filtered lists. The Cue appears in the Activities home part on the Role Center. The height of each Cue roughly represents the number of entities in the underlying list; thus the more entities, the taller the Cue. A number value on each Cue gives the precise count. Each Cue has a label to indicate the type of document it represents.
custom services	Any non-AXD service that the customer implements and publishes. Custom services can be used to implement functionality that goes beyond management of business entities.
customization	In the context of code upgrade, one or more changes that have been made to an element in the AOT, such as adding a field to a table.
data object	An X++ class that can be used as parameter for service operations.
DataGroup	A form and report control property that references a field group on a table.
DDE	Abbreviation for Dynamic Data Exchange.
DML	Abbreviation for data manipulation language.
document class	An X++ class (prefixed with Axd) with methods that perform actions on documents.
document services	Document services provide an external application interface. These services are built on top of a query and provide a subset of CRUDF service operations for a particular Axd<*Document*> type. The Axd<*Document*> represents a business entity.
EAI	Abbreviation for enterprise application integration.
Enterprise Portal	The Web platform for Dynamics AX 2009. Developers can use the Enterprise Portal framework to create new Web applications for Dynamics AX or to customize existing ones.
enum	Short for enumeration element.
ERP	Abbreviation for enterprise resource planning.
extended data type element	Extends a base enumeration by providing a new name for a group of symbolic constants that includes the base enumeration elements and any additional symbolic constants or symbolic constraints defined in the extension.
field group	A grouping of fields for a table with similar characteristics or purposes, used to optimize the design of forms and reports.
GUID	Abbreviation for globally unique identifier.
IDE	Abbreviation for integrated development environment.
IIS	Abbreviation for Microsoft Internet Information Services.
information worker	An individual who creates, uses, transforms, consumes, or manages information in the course of his or her work. Also referred to as IWorker or IW.

Term	Definition
IntelliMorph	A control layout technology. The Dynamics AX runtime uses IntelliMorph to lay out controls on both rich client and Web client forms and reports.
ISAM	Abbreviation for indexed sequential access method. ISAM is a method for storing data for fast retrieval.
ISV	Independent software vendor. ISVs develop customized vertical or horizontal solutions or modules in the BUS layer.
layer	A file that contains all the Dynamics AX business logic (elements such as forms, tables, reports, and so on).
Liskov Substitution Principle	A particular definition of subtype in object-oriented programming that was introduced by Barbara Liskov and Jeannette Wing in a 1993 paper titled "Family Values: A Behavioral Notion of Subtyping."
LTRIM	An SQL function that returns a character expression after removing leading blanks.
model concepts	The types of building blocks available to model a Dynamics AX application. Also known as "element categories." For example, the support for reports in the AOT. An instance of a model concept is a Model Element. An instance of a Model Element is an object.
MorphX	The Microsoft Dynamics AX integrated development environment (IDE).
MSMQ	Abbreviation for Microsoft Message Queuing. MSMQ is a Microsoft technology that enables applications running at different times to communicate across heterogeneous networks and systems that may be temporarily offline.
node	The term used in the AOT for leaves and folders.
Number Sequence framework	The Number Sequence application framework creates a new sequential number for uniquely identifying business transaction records in database tables. You can specify whether the numbers are sequential or allow gaps in the generated sequences. You can also specify the number format by using a specification string.
OCC	Abbreviation for optimistic concurrency control.
OCI	Abbreviation for Oracle Call Interface.
ODBC	Abbreviation for Open Database Connectivity.
Old directory	A directory under *Standard* that contains the previous version of the application.
overlayering	A method of customization in which an Original element is copied into a new layer and modified.
parallel batch processing	The ability of a framework to run several tasks at the same time on the same AOS.
***parm* method**	X++ term for accessor method. Accessor methods are called *parm* methods in X++ because most of the methods start with *parm*.
production report	Reports that are created by developers using either the MorphX or Reporting Services reporting platform.

Term	Definition
rich client	The Dynamics AX client built using the Microsoft Windows Graphics Device Interface (GDI) API. The rich client is opened by executing Ax32.exe.
Role Center	A page that provides quick access to information that is regularly viewed, such as a list of activities and links to forms and reports that are used frequently.
RPC	Abbreviation for remote procedure call.
runtime	The Dynamics AX runtime. The runtime comprises the virtual machine in which Dynamics AX objects and the Dynamics AX system API operate.
service implementation class	An X++ class that implements the business logic encapsulated by a service.
service interface	A child node of the *services* node in the Dynamics AX Application Object Tree (AOT). A service interface includes properties, such as Namespace, Class, and SecurityKey.
service reference	A service reference enables a project to consume an external Web service from X++ code in Dynamics AX.
Standard directory	A directory containing the working copy of the application object files.
System API	The Dynamics AX System API. The System API is the system programming interface that X++ objects use to interact with Dynamics AX system objects.
System Dictionary	The host for all metadata and X++ source code that comprise a Dynamics AX application. The dictionary has a programmable Dynamics AX System API that can be used from X++ code. Elements of the dictionary are either composite, such as Form, Report, and Class; or primitive, such as method or class header. Elements are stored in Application Object Files and are loaded into the *UtilElement* table by the Dynamics AX runtime. Elements are copied between layers when there are modifications to lower-layered elements. Elements are also versioned with the version control system.
table	1. *Overloaded table semantics:* Table reference objects have overloaded semantics. For example, the *MyTable myTable*; variable can be interpreted both as a database record (*myTable.Field*) and as a cursor (*next myTable*). The base type for tables is *common*, and the methods for *common* are defined on the *XRecord* Dynamics AX system type. 2. *Temporary tables:* Temporary tables and database tables have different behaviors. Temporary tables are managed as ISAM database tables. Joining temporary tables and database tables requires that the temporary table be defined on the AOS, for example.
Web client	The Dynamics AX client built on Web and Windows SharePoint Services technologies.

Term	Definition
workflow document	An AOT query supplemented by a workflow document class in the AOT. Workflow documents are the focal point for workflows in Dynamics AX.
workflow work item	The units of work created by the workflow instance at runtime. Work items appear in the unified work list and in the Dynamics AX 2009 client.
X++	The built-in Dynamics AX object-oriented programming language.
XAL	Abbreviation for Extended Application Language.

Index

Symbols and Numbers

A

B

C

D

N

Q

R

S

T

U

V

W

X

About the Authors

Principal Authors

Lars Dragheim Olsen is a software architect on the Dynamics AX team at the Microsoft Development Center in Copenhagen, Denmark. He joined Damgaard Data in 1998 as a software design engineer, shortly after the first version of Dynamics AX was released. His work has focused mainly on the Supply Chain Management modules within Dynamics AX and the integration of these modules with other modules, such as Financials and Project. During the development of Dynamics AX 2009, he worked as a software architect, concentrating primarily on the multisite features within the Supply Chain Management modules. Before working for Damgaard Data, Navision, and Microsoft, he worked for seven years as a system consultant on another ERP product. He lives in Denmark with his four children, Daniel, Christian, Isabella, and Maja, and his girlfriend, Camilla.

Michael Fruergaard Pontoppidan joined Damgaard Data in 1996 as a software design engineer on the MorphX team, delivering the developer experience for the first release of Dynamics AX after graduating from DTU (Technical University of Denmark). In 1999, he became the program manager and lead developer for the Application Integration and Deployment team that delivered on the Load 'n Go vision. For Dynamics AX 4.0, he worked as a software architect on version control, unit testing, and Microsoft's Trustworthy Computing initiative, while advocating code quality improvements through Engineering Excellence, tools, processes, and training. For Dynamics AX 2009, Michael joined the Developer and Partner Tools team and continued driving high-quality productivity features into the toolsets delivered with Dynamics AX. Michael lives in Denmark with his wife, Katrine, and their two children, Laura and Malte. His blog is at *http://blogs.msdn.com/mfp*.

Hans Jørgen Skovgaard joined Microsoft in 2003 as product unit manager for the Dynamics AX product line. As part of Microsoft's Navision acquisition process, Hans facilitated and managed the introduction of Engineering Excellence initiatives, aligned developer competence, created new teams, and organized training for new developers. Hans joined Microsoft with more than 20 years of professional software development and management experience. Before his engagement with Dynamics AX, Hans was vice president of engineering at Mondosoft, a search engine company, for three years. Before that, he was vice president of CRM development in the ERP company Baan for 10 years, during which time he architected a product configuration technology and associated tools. Hans has an MSc in AI (artificial intelligence) and an MBA from IMD, one of the world's leading business schools. Hans lives in Denmark with his wife, Nomi, and his three lovely daughters, Ristil, Simone, and Mikala. He holds a black belt in karate and is an avid mountain biker.

Tomasz Kaminski joined Microsoft in 2007 as a software design engineer in test on the Developers and Partner Tools team at the Microsoft Development Center in Copenhagen. Before Microsoft, he worked in Poland as software design engineer on data acquisition systems at WINUEL SA and embedded systems at Siemens Sp. z o.o. For Dynamics AX 2009, Tomasz worked on Code Upgrade, the MorphX IDE, and the Rapid Configuration tool. Professionally, he is passionate about software design, architecture, and test-driven development. He holds an MSc in computer science from the Wroclaw University of Technology in Poland. In his free time, he enjoys bird watching and biking. Tomasz lives in Denmark with his wife, Anna.

Deepak Kumar is a program manager at Microsoft working on Dynamics AX Server and Data Upgrade features. He has more than 13 years of industry experience, spending the last eight of those years at Microsoft. Deepak's experience is primarily within the large enterprise, working on ERP, database administration (SQL Server and Oracle), development, performance tuning, and management. He has a master's degree in information management, a bachelor's degree in computer science, and Microsoft (MCP) and Oracle DBA (OCP) certifications. Deepak has been a technical columnist and technology reviewer for national newspapers in India and ran his own small business focusing on consultancy, ERP implementation, and corporate training. Deepak lives in Seattle with his wife, Nupur, and his two young children, Ayan and Arisha. In his spare time, he likes reading research articles, playing tennis, taking short hikes, and doing outdoor activities with his family.

Mey Meenakshisundaram is a principal program manager lead in the Dynamics AX product group who focuses on Enterprise Portal, Role Centers, and search. He has 16 years of experience in software engineering, consulting, and management, the last eight years of which have been spent at Microsoft. Prior to his current role, he led the engineering team that developed and implemented the portal, content management, and Web services for the customer relationship system used by the internal Microsoft Sales team. Before Microsoft, he led software product development teams in Singapore and India for the manufacturing, service, and banking sectors in the Asia Pacific.

Mey is a coauthor of the book *Inside Microsoft Dynamics AX 4.0* and is a highly rated speaker at Microsoft conferences. His self-made mission is to get Enterprise Portal onto every desktop of every Dynamics AX customer. He lives in Sammamish, Washington, with his wife, Amutha, and his children, Meena and Shammu. Mey regularly blogs at *http://blogs.msdn.com/solutions*.

Michael Merz is a program manager focusing on tools for integrating Dynamics AX with other systems. Although his passions include applying innovative patterns and technologies to integrating heterogeneous systems in general, he is currently focused on Software-plus-Services (S+S). Before joining Microsoft, Michael worked in various engineering roles for companies including Amazon.com and BEA Systems as well as for early-stage startup companies; he has also worked as a researcher for the European Union and holds an MSc in computer science from Ulm University, Germany. Michael blogs at *http://blogs.msdn.com/aif*.

Karl Tolgu is a senior program manager for Microsoft Dynamics AX. He is responsible for the delivery of the workflow infrastructure in Dynamics AX. Previously, Karl worked on Project Accounting modules in Dynamics SL and Dynamics GP. He has worked in the software industry in both the United Kingdom and the United States since graduating. He has held various software development management positions at Oracle Corporation and Niku Corporation. Karl resides in Seattle, Washington, with his wife, Karin, and three sons, Karl Christian, Sten Alexander, and Thomas Sebastian.

Kirill Val joined Microsoft in 2005 and has worked as a software design engineer for various Dynamics AX teams, such as Finance, Application Implementation, Server, and Upgrade. He has eight years of experience developing ERP, Web, Financials, and Supply Chain Management applications; before joining Microsoft, he worked for several Microsoft Dynamics partners as a software development lead and program manager.

Kirill's work on Dynamics AX 2009 included contributions to the architecture, design, and development of the data upgrade framework; the batch server processing framework and the electronic signature feature; and integration solutions for enterprise-level businesses. He has an MSc degree in applied mathematics and computer science, and he enjoys playing volleyball, hiking, and traveling in his free time.

Contributing Authors

Srikanth Avadhanam is a development manager for the Dynamics AX product line. He is responsible for overseeing the development of the Dynamics AX application server platform. Before his engagement with Dynamics AX, Srikanth spent a few years designing and implementing various subsystems of the Microsoft SQL Server relational engine; he holds several patents in areas related to SQL query optimization.

Srikanth's technical interests include engineering scalable and performant metadata-driven application servers and database technologies. Srikanth lives in Redmond, Washington, with his wife and two children. Srikanth's team blogs at *http://blogs.msdn.com/daxis*.

Chris Garty is a senior program manager on the Dynamics AX Client team in Fargo, North Dakota. During the Dynamics AX 2009 cycle, Chris was an integral part of the list-page creation effort and continues to work on user experience improvements to the Dynamics AX client. Before his current role, he was a program manager on the Microsoft Business Framework and Dynamics Tools projects focused on business logic and Web services. He has 10 years of experience in software development and consulting, with the last five years spent at Microsoft.

Chris was born and raised in New Zealand, near Hobbiton, and he is lucky enough to visit there almost yearly to see his family. He moved to Fargo to work for the best company in the world and lives there, five winters and one big flood later, with his wife, Jolene. He spends time away from Microsoft slowly working toward an MBA, traveling occasionally, playing soccer and tennis frequently, and relaxing with friends as much as possible. Chris occasionally blogs at *http://blogs.msdn.com/chrisgarty*.

Raghavendran Gururajan is a program manager with the Dynamics AX Server platform team, with direct responsibility for the Data Access stack for the past two releases. Before this role, his experience as a Microsoft consultant in the field included building business applications for the high-tech manufacturing, auto industry, telecom, and financial sectors. He has a total of 17 years, experience in software development. He is a frequent speaker at customer and partner-focused events such as Convergence. He lives in Redmond, Washington, with his wife, Bhuvaneshwari, and son, Nanda.

Thejas Haridev Durgam joined Microsoft in 2005 as a software engineer on the Business Intelligence and Reporting team. During this time, he has worked on X++ reporting, SQL Server Reporting Services ad hoc reporting and SQL Reporting Services report integration with Enterprise Portal, and the Dynamics AX client. Before joining Microsoft, he worked for a year as a software development intern at Websense Inc. in San Diego, California.

Thejas has his master's degree in computer science from the State University of New York at Binghamton and has a bachelor's degree in computer science from R.V. College of Engineering, Bangalore, India. His hobbies include cricket, tennis, Xbox, and the stock market. He currently resides in downtown Bellevue, Washington.

Josh Honeyman is a senior development lead in Microsoft Business Solutions. He joined Microsoft as part of the acquisition of Great Plains Software, Inc., in 2001, after which he continued to work on Microsoft Dynamics GP. He is now responsible for the development of the workflow and business process infrastructure for Dynamics AX.

Wayne Kuo is a software design engineer in test who joined Microsoft in 2006 as a college graduate from the University of Waterloo in Ontario, Canada. He has been with the Business Intelligence and Reporting team in Dynamics AX for three years and has been primarily responsible for building the testing framework for the Microsoft Visual Studio report design experience in Dynamics AX 2009. He also worked on the SQL Server Reporting Services team to help deliver the Report Customization Definition Extension project that was part of the SQL Server 2008 release. During his school years, he held software development internships at a variety of organizations, including Environment Canada, Toronto Star Media, and Embarcadero Technologies. He now lives in Seattle and enjoys outdoor activities, motor racing, and music production at his local church.

Vijay Kurup is a senior program manager on the Dynamics AX product team working on the Dynamics AX Application Object Server (AOS) and in security areas. He is responsible for features such as memory management, session management, licensing and configuration, and security. For Dynamics AX 2009, he worked on designing the new server-bound Batch framework and adding multiple time-zone support and various other features to improve the performance and reliability of the AOS. Vijay has worked in the software industry both in India and the United States. He joined Microsoft in 2005 and has been a program manager on the Dynamics AX server team in Redmond since then. Vijay resides in Sammamish, Washington, with his wife, Anuradha, and two-year-old son, Nikhil.

Tete Mensa-Annan is a senior program manager lead on the Dynamics AX team. He is an 11-year Microsoft veteran focusing on workflow and business process management.

Amar Nalla is a senior software design engineer who has been working on Dynamics AX since version 4.0. He works on the platform team, primarily in the data access layer and other Dynamics AX server-related areas. He has been with Microsoft for the past eight years; before working on Dynamics AX, he worked on SQLXML and other XML technologies on the SQL Server team.

He blogs actively at *http://blogs.msdn.com/daxis*, where he covers a variety of topics related to the Dynamics AX platform.

Saveen Reddy has worked for Microsoft for 13 years on projects including Exchange Server, PhotoDraw, Windows Server, and Forefront Client Security. Currently he manages the Program Management team that builds business intelligence platform components and features into Dynamics AX. He regularly posts to his MSDN blog (*http://blogs.msdn.com/saveenr*) on topics such as program management, graphics and visualization, business intelligence, and software development.

Sri Srinivasan works as PM Architect for Dynamics AX, with responsibilities for driving performance initiatives, architecture changes, and scalability for the solution. Sri has been working with Microsoft Dynamics for four years and has been instrumental in the release of the benchmarks for Dynamics AX 4.0 and Dynamics AX 2009. Sri comes with an extensive ERP product development background, working on performance for other ERP solutions, such as PeopleSoft, JD Edwards, and Oracle before joining Microsoft. He blogs on the Performance team blog at *http://blogs.msdn.com/axperf*.

Satish Thomas is a software design engineer in the Dynamics AX product group with a focus on everything upgrade-related in Dynamics AX. He joined Microsoft in 2006 after graduating from Illinois Institute of Technology in Chicago, Illinois. Satish grew up in Africa (Nigeria, Botswana) before moving to the United States for college, and he currently lives in Sammamish, Washington.

This book substantially builds on content written for the *Inside Microsoft Dynamics AX 4.0* book. That content was written by Arthur Greef, Michael Fruergaard Pontoppidan, Lars Dragheim Olsen, Mey Meenaskshisundaram, Karl Tolgu, Hans Jørgen Skovgaard, Palle Agermark, Per Baarsoe Jorgensen, and Thomas Due Kay.